NOLO Products & Services

"In Nolo you can trust." —THE NEW YORK TIMES

Books & Software

Nolo publishes hundreds of great books and software programs on the topics consumers and business owners want to know about. And every one of them is available in print or as a download at Nolo.com.

Plain-English Legal Dictionary

Free at Nolo.com. Stumped by jargon? Look it up in America's most up-to-date source for definitions of cutting edge legal terminology. Emphatically not your grandmother's law dictionary!

Legal Encyclopedia

Free at Nolo.com. Here are more than 1,200 free articles and answers to frequently asked questions about everyday consumer legal issues including wills, bankruptcy, small business formation, divorce, patents, employment and much more. As *The Washington Post* says, "Nobody does a better job than Nolo."

Online Legal Forms

Make a will or living trust, form an LLC or corporation or obtain a trademark or provisional patent at Nolo.com, all for a remarkably affordable price. In addition, our site provides hundreds of high-quality, low-cost downloadable legal forms including bills of sale, promissory notes, nondisclosure agreements and many more.

Lawyer Directory

Find an attorney at Nolo.com. Nolo's unique lawyer directory provides in-depth profiles of lawyers all over America. From fees and experience to legal philosophy, education and special expertise, you'll find all the information you need to pick a lawyer who's a good fit.

Nolo's Aim: to make the law...

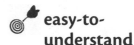 **easy-to-understand**

 **affordable**

 **hassle free**

Keep Up to Date!

*Old law is often bad law. That's why Nolo.com has free updates for this and every Nolo book. And if you want to be notified when a revised edition of any Nolo title comes out, sign up for this free service at **nolo.com/ legalupdater.***

"Nolo is always there in a jam." —NEWSWEEK

13th edition

Fight Your Ticket
& Win
in California

By Attorney David W. Brown

THIRTEENTH EDITION	JUNE 2009
Editor	CATHERINE CAPUTO
Cover Design	SUSAN PUTNEY
Production	MARGARET LIVINGSTON
Proofreading	JIM BRUCE
Index	ELLEN SHERRON
Printing	DELTA PRINTING SOLUTIONS, INC.

Brown, David Wayne, 1949-
    Fight your ticket & win in California / by David W. Brown. -- 13th ed.
        p. cm.
    Includes bibliographical references and index.
    ISBN-13: 978-1-4133-1030-6 (pbk. : alk.paper)
    ISBN-10: 1-4133-1030-3 (pbk. : alk.paper)
    1. Traffic violations--California--Popular works. 2. Traffic courts--California--Popular
works. I. Title.
    KFC477.B76 2009
    345.794'0247--dc22

                            2009011093

Acknowledgments

This book could not have been published without the generous assistance of many people. I'd especially like to gratefully acknowledge the major contributions of Ralph ("Jake") Warner and Peter Jan Honigsberg, whose incisive editing and folksy phraseology have added readability, clarity, and brevity to this book.

Also, a big smile and an even bigger chuckle for Linda Allison, whose characteristically wonderful illustrations have actually succeeded in bringing a smile to the law.

Thanks also to Nolo editors Spencer Sherman, Janet Portman, Patti Gima, Lisa Guerin, Rich Stim, Albin Renauer, and Steve Elias.

Special thanks to Attorney David Olenczuk, who has been putting this book to practical use while developing even more elaborate strategies to contest unjust traffic tickets. David incorporated these strategies into the sixth edition and essentially made it a new book.

Finally, many thanks to the webmaster of www.highwayrobbery.net, for his thorough critique (on the site) of the 11th and 12th editions. He has helped to make this 13th edition a more up-to-date resource.

Table of Contents

16 Appealing a Conviction

17 Staying Out of Trouble

18 Where Do We Go From Here?

Appendix

Informal Discovery Request

Proof of Service by Mail

Request for Trial by Written Declaration

Request for New Trial (Trial de Novo)

Demand for Court Report or Electronic Recording of Proceedings

Peremptory Challenge

Civil Subpoena

Civil Subpoena Duces Tecum

Notice of Appeal (Infraction)

Proposed Statement on Appeal (Infraction)

Index

Your Legal Companion for Fighting Your Ticket

Your first thoughts after getting a ticket might be:

- I wonder if my insurance will go up.
- Should I just pay the ticket? (After all, didn't I break the law?)
- Will the state revoke my license?

Police officers know that very few people—perhaps one out of 50—ever contest their tickets. Those who do fight are often so unprepared and nervous that they have a tough time winning. Occasionally police officers cite motorists in borderline situations where the ticket may or may not stand up in court even if the motorist bothered to contest. In some situations, the police officer may be convinced that the ticket was merited and—with all due respect to the officer—you may feel quite differently.

It all comes down to whether or not you want to take on the system and fight your ticket.

The message of this book is a simple one. If you want to fight your ticket—whether for parking or for a moving violation—you can only do so effectively if you're well prepared and know your rights.

To help you fight your ticket, we:

- instruct you on how to look up, read, and understand the specific law you allegedly violated so you might discover a few technicalities of your own (Chapter 2)
- explain the various traffic laws that are most commonly violated (Chapters 4–8)

- tell you which violations go on your record and which ones are likely to raise your insurance rates (Chapter 3)
- explore the most common grounds for defending against a ticket issued under these laws (Chapters 4–8), and
- provide instructions on how to use these defenses to get your ticket dismissed (Chapters 4–8).

We also:

- help you decide whether to fight the ticket (Chapter 9)
- give you step-by-step guidance on the necessary procedures for fighting your ticket, suggest effective shortcuts and tactics where appropriate, and explain how the sentencing process works in case you lose (Chapters 10–14), and
- show you when and how to appeal a conviction, and how to fight a license suspension by the DMV, should the worst happen (Chapters 15–16).

Finally, in Chapter 17, you'll find tips on what to do the next time a police officer pulls you over. You'll learn how to be a good observer and look for things that will help you fight your ticket more effectively later on. And in Chapter 18 we have a few suggestions for how the traffic enforcement system can be improved.

In summary, if you have a reason and a motivation to fight your ticket, this book is your how-to manual, guiding you through the process and explaining the traffic laws in a down-to-earth, easy-to-understand manner.

First Things

A Typical Case

You're driving home from your friend's place after a beautiful, romantic Friday evening. It's 2:30 in the morning. As you're reflecting on this, you suddenly realize you took a wrong turn someplace. You're now in the middle of a quiet residential district and realize you should turn around. You look for traffic coming from either direction and all you see is a car parked about three blocks away with its headlights on, so you make a U-turn.

Suddenly, in your rear view mirror you see a flashing red and blue light that seemingly grows out of the parked car. You begin to pull over to the right to let it pass. Instead, the car follows you to the curb. You realize you've just been pulled over by the police. As soon as your car stops, the officer has his high-intensity spotlight pointed at you. Then, you hear his door slam, the sound of gravel under his boots, and finally you see a big, grim face just behind the flashlight pointed into your eyes.

Before you get a chance to ask him what's the problem, he says, *"May I see your driver's license, please?"* You fumble through your wallet, slowly and carefully, since he has his hand uncomfortably close to the butt of what looks to be a very big gun. Finally, hands shaking slightly, you hand him your license. (Don't you feel like a common criminal?)

The police officer returns to his car and uses the radio. A minute later he returns, hands you your license, and unemotionally says, *"You made an unlawful U-turn in a residential district. Sign here, please,"* and he thrusts a three-part form in your face. You meekly sign the ticket (which he tells you is not an admission of guilt, but merely a promise to appear), and he hands you a copy. You gaze at the ticket, wondering how this could be happening to you. The officer spins out, off to catch another "criminal."

If you don't fight the ticket, you may very well end up:

- paying a fine you can barely afford
- paying a higher insurance premium for the next three to five years, and
- starting or adding to a bad driving record with the DMV.

Should You Fight Your Ticket?

Does it make sense for you to fight your ticket? The answer is that it depends. There are some people who almost always answer this question with a proud and forceful *"Yes!"* unless they have done something incredibly stupid or dangerous (such as driving through a busy school zone at 50 mph). But there are others who don't believe in spending large amounts of time fighting cases where there is but a small chance of winning. It might be wise to try to separate the hopeless cases from those with a reasonable chance of success. (On the other hand, thousands of seemingly hopeless cases are won when police officers fail to show up in court to testify.) A determined person can achieve great success in traffic court if he or she knows what to do.

In deciding whether or not to fight, you should first consider the consequences of giving up and paying the ticket. Will your insurance rates increase? Will you increase your chances of losing your license? Can you get your case dismissed by attending traffic school? Do you want to spend the time and effort it will take to fight your ticket effectively? This book will help you answer all these questions.

Once you understand the consequences of not fighting your ticket, you should try to determine your chances of winning, taking into account these tips:

- The main way to beat traffic tickets is to request a trial with the officer present and then get the ticket dismissed when the officer doesn't show up. There's a chance this might happen to you. You may want to try your luck. You've got nothing to lose but your time.

- Even if the officer does show up, "guilt" (and "innocence") is often a matter of subjective interpretation. For example, under California law it's not illegal to drive 45 mph in a 35 mph zone if it is possible to show that your 45 mph speed was safe under the circumstances. (See Chapter 4 on speed violations.)

- You might not be guilty of a particular violation, even if you think you are. When you read the Vehicle Code section, you will find that the offense you are accused of committing is more complex than you might have thought. It may be that you didn't do all the things that the prosecution must prove in order to convict you. We tell you in the next chapter how to read a Vehicle Code section with this in mind.

There are indeed the situations in which you were in fact scrupulously obeying the law and the police officer just plain got it wrong. The radar gun was used improperly, the police officer's visual perspective resulted in a mistake, you were accused of rolling through a stop sign when in fact you did come to a complete stop. When you get a ticket under these circumstances, and realize that you will have to undergo what can be a considerable hassle to fight it, you will most likely be torn between giving it a good fight and cutting your losses by paying your fine and getting on with your life.

What about the times when you were doing something wrong, but not wrong enough, in your opinion, to warrant intervention by a police officer? While most people manage to obey every traffic rule when they take their driving test, there are few—if any—drivers who continue to be the model of good driving once they get their license. Rather, the average driver tends to find an individual compromise between fanatical adherence to the law and unsafe behavior. Most people will commonly technically violate one or more traffic rules virtually every time they get in their car—but usually not, if ever, under circumstances that pose any danger to themselves or others. In fact, traveling a few miles over the speed limit on a clear and dry road will tend to put you among the snails rather than the greyhounds.

When people are behaving badly or stupidly in their cars, they are inclined to welcome a ticket (after some initial grumbling) as a warning to get their act in order. The problem is, many tickets are given not for bad or stupid behavior but rather for insignificant violations of obscure rules in a book—things that are, in the classic sense, "mere technicalities." How many times have you seen cars run red lights with impunity, only to find the blue light flashing when you have rolled through a stop sign—however cautiously—at four o'clock in the morning at a deserted intersection? The problem is, when mere technical violations end up costing $150 in fines, adding points to your driving record and dollars to your insurance rates, they have a way of getting under your skin. You don't think you deserved the ticket. Why do the police waste time on you, when they could be doing serious work?

In this situation too, you may wish to fight your ticket, either for economic reasons or because you're just plain mad at being singled out for what most people do without getting caught. This book is for you, whether or not you're an innocent victim. However, you should understand that:

- Being singled out isn't normally a defense unless you can establish that the discrimination was for vindictive purposes (almost impossible to do).
- Being a little guilty still means you're guilty, although the judge may cut your fine.
- For the most part, the traffic court system is inefficient and corrupt, packed with police-oriented judges who care more about feathering their own nests than about justice. (More on this in Chapter 18.)

In short, to win a traffic ticket fight, you must either obtain a dismissal or convince the judge you were innocent.

Parking tickets have their own logic. These tickets are given more to fill the city's coffers than to regulate parking. The procedures for fighting parking tickets are quite different from the procedures for fighting traffic tickets.

Abbreviations Used in This Book

We use these standard abbreviations throughout this book for important statutes and court cases.

California Codes

B&P	Business & Professions
CCP	Civil Procedure
H&S	Health & Safety
PC	Penal Code
VC	Vehicle Code

Federal Laws

U.S.C.	United States Code

Cases

A. or A.2d	Atlantic Reporter
Cal. App.	California Court of Appeal
Cal. Rptr.	California Court of Appeal and California Supreme Court
Cal.	California Supreme Court
F. Supp.	United States District Court
F.2d or F.3d	United States Court of Appeal
P. or P.2d	Pacific Reporter
S. Ct.	United States Supreme Court
U.S.	United States Supreme Court

Rules of Court

CRC	California Rules of Court

Opinions

Ops. Cal. Atty. Gen.	California Attorney General Opinions

Overview Chart

The following chart shows the structure of the book in graphic form.

How to Use This Book

If you haven't received a ticket yet, read Chapter 17 on what to do if you're pulled over. If you already have a ticket, keep going.

↓

Determine what you're charged with and assess the possible consequences (Chs. 1, 2, and 3). Then, read the chapter that covers your violation.

Infractions:
Speeding tickets & radar (Ch. 4)
Other moving violations (Ch. 5)
Pedestrian & bicycle violations (Ch. 6)

Parking Tickets & Equipment Violations:
(Ch. 6)

Misdemeanors:
Drunk Driving (Ch. 8)
Other serious offenses: Reckless driving, speed contests, etc. (Ch. 7)

Fighting an Infraction:
Decide whether to fight. Review the options available (Ch. 9)

In Person:
Seek court clerk (Ch. 10)

By Mail:
(Ch. 10)

Fighting a Misdemeanor:
Decide whether to handle the case yourself or hire a lawyer (Ch. 9)

Set arraignment date (Ch. 10)

Bypass arraignment, set trial date (Ch. 10)

Request traffic school (Ch. 10)

Pay fine (Ch. 10)

Go to arraignment & pretrial motions (Ch. 10)

Write a letter: Plead not guilty, bypass arraignment, & set trial date (Ch. 10)

Go to arraignment, plea bargain, & file pretrial motions (Chs. 10, 13)

Conduct trial by mail (Ch. 10)

Request retrial (Ch. 10)

Trial by jury (Chs. 11, 13)
Trial without jury (Chs. 11, 12)

Prepare for trial (Ch. 11)

Trial (Ch. 12)

Sentencing (Ch. 14)

Appeal (Ch. 16)

How to Read Your Ticket

The first step in fighting your ticket is learning how to use the information on it. Most important is the charge against you, which you need to know to prepare a defense. And you might even find that the officer used the wrong kind of ticket or made some other procedural error that might get your case dismissed. This chapter tells you how to read your ticket and use it to your advantage.

What Are You Charged With?

Although not all tickets are alike (we'll explore the differences later in this chapter), every ticket contains the basic information you need to determine what you're charged with.

Near the middle of the ticket, usually under the heading "Violation(s)," the officer will have written a very short description of the law she says you violated. This consists of:

- Which "code" you violated. All laws passed by the legislature are collected in a set of books known as "codes" (VC for Vehicle Code, PC for Penal Code, B&P for Business & Professions Code, H&S for Heath & Safety Code, etc.). You will almost always be cited for a Vehicle Code violation.

- The section number of the code that identifies the violation. In legal notation, the symbol "§" means "section number."

- A short description of the charge when moving violations are involved (such as "speed charge," "reckless driving"). For example:

Code	Section	Description
VC	22350	basic speed law

In addition, on speeding tickets, you'll find the "approximate speed" at which the officer clocked your vehicle and the posted or "prima facie" (abbreviated "PF") speed limit (VC § 40503). The meanings of these legal terms are discussed in Chapter 4.

Notice to Appear

Shaded areas indicate spaces subject to modification for local or agency requirements.

Are You Really Guilty?

Just because a police officer has written some code section on your ticket doesn't necessarily mean you violated it. Most laws are rather complex, so it's not uncommon to find that what you did was not, technically speaking, illegal. By finding the code and section number of the law you allegedly violated on your ticket, you can look up the law yourself to see if you really are guilty. This may sound elementary, but even lawyers often forget to do it.

You need the exact language of the law you're accused of violating. Chapters 4 through 8 of this book include the exact language of many of the most commonly violated Vehicle Code sections. If we don't include the statute you're cited for, you can find a current copy of the Vehicle Code (or other applicable code) in a law library. Every county has a law library open to the public, and some law schools also allow public use of their law libraries. You can also purchase a copy of the latest Vehicle Code from your local DMV office (issued annually in mid-March) for $6. If you have access to the Internet, you can find the California Vehicle Code at www.leginfo.ca.gov/calaw.html. Make sure you're using the most recent version of the statute—that is, the section in the vehicle or other code that applies to your offense—you're charged with. (If you need help on how to do legal research, read Chapter 9.)

Once you've found the statute that is cited on your ticket, read it very carefully. Try to figure out which things the prosecution will have to prove "beyond a reasonable doubt." Ask yourself, *"What are the elements of the offense?"*

An "element" is lawyer's lingo for a particular fact that must be proven by the prosecution in order to find you guilty of the offense. Some elements are central to the crime. Others are what nonlawyers might call "technicalities." Either way, every element must be proven against you in order for you to be found guilty.

For example, our motorist in the first chapter was charged with making an illegal U-turn. The law prohibiting U-turns in residential districts, VC § 22103, states:

> No person in a residence district shall make a U-turn when any other vehicle is approaching from either direction within 200 feet, except at an intersection when the approaching vehicle is controlled by an official traffic control device.

At this point you should stop and read the statute again, more slowly. This time draw a line between each clause, and think about what it means. For example, this statute could be divided up as follows:

> No person/ in a residence district/ shall make a U-turn/ when any other vehicle/ is approaching/ from either direction/ within 200 feet,/ except at an intersection/ when the approaching vehicle/ is controlled/ by an official traffic control device.

To be found guilty of having committed this offense, the prosecution must prove all of the following "elements" of the offense beyond a reasonable doubt:

1. That you (a person) were driving in a "residence district";

2. That you drove your vehicle in a 180-degree or "U-turn";

3. That another vehicle was approaching within 200 feet or less from ahead or behind you; and

4. That you were not at an "intersection" controlled by an "official traffic control device."

Thus, you will want to show that the area wasn't a "residence district," *or* that the vehicles the officer claims were approaching may have been over 200 feet away, *or* that you were at an intersection controlled by an "official traffic control device." If you can disprove any of these elements, you'll be found not guilty.

You will notice that many of these terms, like "residence district" and "official traffic control device" are rather ambiguous. When you find words like this, you should immediately look for a definition of those terms somewhere else in the code you're working with. In the Vehicle Code, definitions are listed near the beginning of the book, starting with § 100.

At this point you may be wondering, *"Is a judge likely to follow such a technical reading of the law?"* The answer is yes. This style of technical, word-by-word reading is one of the most important skills lawyers are taught in law school. Here's why. The American legal system under the Constitution and Bill of Rights provides the defendants in criminal cases a considerable number of "breaks" in order to give them a fighting chance in their battle against the all-powerful State. Although lawmakers have made many of these rights inapplicable to traffic court, the courts still must interpret traffic laws very technically or "narrowly," because the government must be able to point to a law that clearly prohibits what you did, before you can be found guilty. This means that you can't be found guilty unless the government proves beyond a reasonable doubt that you violated every "element" of the traffic offense you're charged with.

For many violations, it must also be true that you either intended to commit every element of the violation, or that you were careless in doing so. Penal Code § 20 says, "In every crime or public offense (including infractions) there must exist a union, or joint operation, of act and intent, or criminal negligence." In plain English, this means that to convict you, the state must usually show that you:

- committed all the elements of the forbidden act described in the specific code section you're charged with, and
- had an intent to commit those acts, or were "criminally negligent" (careless) in committing them.

For example, you might be able to successfully maintain that you acted neither intentionally nor carelessly since the "No U-turn" sign at the intersection was not visible, the stop sign you accidentally ran was blocked from view by tree leaves, or even that your speedometer was reading too low. The key is showing you weren't reckless or even careless. Just saying you "didn't mean to" run the stop sign won't get you anywhere.

Finally, even if you really did commit every element of your violation, you still might not be guilty if you had a legal excuse for doing so. For example, if you were charged with driving too slowly in the left lane (VC § 21654), it is a legal defense (provided for in the statute) that you were planning to turn left. You're not denying that you were driving slowly in the left lane, but rather offering an additional fact that legally justifies your apparently unlawful action. Or, you might have committed an honest mistake, such as relying on an inaccurate speedometer that told you you were driving 55 mph, when in fact you were doing 70. However, it's up to you to introduce this fact at trial.

Other Information on Your Ticket

At the top of your ticket (in the case of moving or equipment violations), you'll find the information the officer has obtained from your driver's license—your name, address, license number, etc. There's also a place for the date, time, and place of the alleged violation, the make, model, and year of your vehicle, and the license plate number. If the officer has made enough mistakes in these entries, you may be able to challenge his powers of observation when you get to trial.

Occasionally, the officer will write his vacation dates on your ticket as a message to the court clerk indicating which dates he won't be able to appear at trial. As we'll see in Chapter 10, you may be able to use this information to your advantage by scheduling your trial to occur on one of those dates.

Finally, your ticket should indicate the name of the court in which you must appear to pay the fine or arrange for a court date, and the court's address. You will be cited to appear in the superior court nearest to where the offense supposedly occurred. The notice will also state a deadline by which you must appear. For juveniles, it may state "to be notified," or words to that effect. On parking tickets, there will be an address where you can mail your fine if you don't want to contest it.

Types of Tickets

There are basically three types of tickets: the Notice to Appear, Notice to Correct Violation, and Notice of Parking Violation.

The Notice to Appear—
Officer Observes the Violation

If you were stopped for speeding, running a red light, or some other kind of moving violation, you should have received a "Notice to Appear." This kind of ticket was created to speed up and simplify the judicial process from arrest through trial. When the officer turns on the red light to pull you over, he technically places you under arrest. (See *People v. Superior Court* (1972) 7 Cal.3d 186, 200; VC §§ 40500, 40501.) While you are "under arrest," the officer fills out the ticket. Then, rather than placing you under actual arrest and taking you to jail, he simply has you sign that part of the ticket that says you agree to appear in court. By signing the Notice

to Appear, you are released from arrest and do not have to post bail. You are not admitting guilt, nor are you waiving any of your rights. If you refuse to sign the ticket, the officer is required to take you to jail (VC § 40302(b)). When the officer files his copy of the ticket with the court, it is considered the equivalent of a "complaint," meaning, in the legal context, the formal charging papers that formally begin the proceedings against you (VC § 40513).

The forms may vary some among police departments. Some forms include space for the number of passengers in the vehicle (in order to preclude your bringing a "witness" who wasn't really with you), the color of the vehicle (if the officer gets this wrong, you might be able to discredit his testimony since it reflects negatively on his ability to observe), and the weather, road, and traffic conditions when a speed violation is involved. Sometimes the ticket will have a little intersection map for the officer to diagram the way various vehicles were positioned during the violation. Finally, there will be a place where the officer signs under penalty of perjury that everything he stated in the ticket is true. He can only fill this in if he actually observed the violation.

If you signed a Notice to Appear you have promised to appear at the court specified on the ticket, and failure to do so is a crime punishable by a fine of up to $1,000 (plus a few more thousand in "penalty assessments") and six months in jail. (See, generally, Chapter 7.) In Chapter 17, we explain that, before signing, you can demand that the officer specify the place to appear as the court at the county seat, if your business or residence address is closer to the county seat than to the local court where you would otherwise be told to appear (VC § 40502(b)). We're assuming for now, however, that you've already received your ticket and you probably weren't aware of this.

The Notice to Appear—At Accidents

When an officer is called to the scene of an accident and believes you committed a violation, he can issue you a Notice to Appear. Most Notices to Appear issued in this situation are mailed to the driver following an investigation in which an officer determines the driver committed the violation. When the notice is mailed to you, you did not promise to appear because you did not sign it. Therefore, you cannot be charged with failure to appear if you don't show. However, a warrant for your arrest on the original offense can be issued if you ignore a letter from the court, telling you to appear on the violation (VC § 40604).

The Mailed Notice to Appear— Other Situations

In years past, an officer could issue a notice to appear only after observing a driver commit a violation. Eventually, an exception was made to allow an officer to issue a notice to appear— even by mail—for a violation the officer *didn't* observe, but thinks you committed based on investigation of a traffic accident.

Unfortunately, another exception has recently been added, in which a Notice to Appear may be mailed to a driver even when *no one* observed the violation. Some cities, most notably Los Angeles and San Francisco, have begun using "automatic enforcement" systems that photograph the car and driver whenever a car runs a stoplight or green-arrow turn signal (VC §§ 21453 & 21455), makes an illegal turn at an intersection (VC § 22101), or drives past a railroad crossing despite a flashing red signal (VC § 22451). The camera photographs the car's license plate (and the driver) for identification. After a computer check of DMV records, the Notice to Appear is mailed to the owner. This process is now legal for citations issued for these violations (VC §§ 21455, 21455.6, 40518).

An automatic enforcement system is *not* yet legal, however, to cite drivers for speeding in conjunction with automated "photo-radar" equipment. Since there is no provision in VC § 40518—or anywhere else in the Vehicle Code—that allows automated photographs to form the basis for speed violations, many judges will not enforce Notices to Appear based on "photo-radar." (We show you in Chapter 10 how to object to a photo-radar Notice to Appear.)

The Notice to Correct Violation

You could be cited for an equipment violation (such as a burnt-out tail light), or a minor license or registration violation other than an expired driver's license or vehicle registration (such as license or registration not in possession). If so, you may receive a Notice to Correct Violation (VC § 40303.5) or a Notice to Appear with a notation on the back stating that the charge will be dismissed if you submit certified proof that the violation has been corrected. Both tickets have a place for you to sign, promising that you'll take care of the problem within a specified time period. If you ignore these tickets, the penalties can be severe.

Sometimes an officer issuing a parking ticket will notice an equipment violation and note it on the parking ticket. Since you don't sign a parking ticket, your failure to correct may not be punished as severely, but you will still be fined for the violation, and you should be able to get the charge dismissed if you show certified proof of correction. (Read Chapter 6 for further information about equipment violations.)

The Notice of Parking Violation

A parking ticket is called a Notice of Parking Violation. It is placed on your vehicle when you're not present. There's no place for you to sign so you can't be charged with a misdemeanor for ignoring the ticket. However, the DMV may refuse to renew your vehicle registration. (We discuss this in greater detail in Chapter 6.) ●

What Are the Consequences?
Fines, Jail, Your "Record," and Insurance

"Will it go on my record?"

"What's the maximum fine?"

"Is jail a possibility?"

"Will my insurance rates go up?"

If you're like most people, these are the first questions that go through your mind when you get a traffic ticket. It makes sense that you want to know what you're dealing with before making any decisions about whether to simply pay the ticket or invest the time and effort to fight it. With this information in hand, you'll be in a far better position to decide whether it is worth your while to fight. This chapter provides that information for the most commonly charged violations.

Generally

The severity of the consequences of your ticket and the difficulty of fighting it depend on whether it is an infraction, misdemeanor, or felony, and whether it goes on your record. Below, we tell you the maximum penalties provided for each type of offense. (In actuality, these maximums are rarely imposed.)

Types of Violations: Infractions, Misdemeanors, and Felonies

There are three types of criminal traffic offenses. From the least to the most severe, they are: infractions, misdemeanors, and felonies. Most automobile-related violations are either infractions or misdemeanors. Parking offenses are not criminal offenses, but involve "civil" fines. They are no longer handled by the court system, except that courts will hear appeals of tickets following "administrative review" by the city or county that issued the ticket. (See Chapter 6.)

Infractions include all registration violations, and all but the most serious moving violations. If you're charged with an infraction, you can't demand a jury trial, and you are not entitled to a court-appointed lawyer regardless of your inability to afford one. On the other hand, jail cannot be imposed as the original penalty, but you can be fined up to around $400 ($100 plus approximately $300 more in "penalty assessments" and fees) on most first-offense infractions—and even more for certain serious ones, such as driving over 100 mph. And, if you fail to pay the fine without sufficient justification, you can end up in jail. Most infractions can be fought through an abbreviated or more informal procedure. (See Chapter 10.)

Where you are charged with a fourth infraction within a one-year period, you can demand that the case proceed as a misdemeanor (see below) so that you have the right to a jury trial and/or appointed counsel. There are both risks and advantages to this procedure, however, and these are described in detail in Chapter 7.

Misdemeanors involve more serious offenses, such as drunk or reckless driving, drag racing, trying to outrun a cop, hit-and-run with property damage, failure to appear in court as promised (by signing a ticket), and failure to pay a fine. If you're charged with a misdemeanor, you're entitled to a jury trial and a court-appointed lawyer if you cannot afford one. Most misdemeanors are punishable by up to a year in jail and fines up to $1,000 plus several thousand more in "penalty assessments." Fighting a misdemeanor charge is more formal, difficult, and lengthy than fighting an infraction. To fight serious misdemeanors, like drunk driving, you will probably want to hire a lawyer.

Felonies are very serious crimes punishable by imprisonment in the state prison for more than a year. Obvious (nontraffic) felonies include murder, armed robbery, and rape. Very few Vehicle Code offenses are felonies, the most notable being drunk driving or hit-and-run where someone was injured or killed in an accident. This book is absolutely not intended for use in defending against a felony charge; anyone accused of a felony should definitely see a lawyer.

Your Record

The long-term consequences of your ticket primarily depend on whether the ticket goes on your "record." Your record is that infamous piece of computer-stored information listing most of your traffic convictions (including tickets you've paid). However, parking, registration, and most equipment violations are not reported to the DMV (VC § 1803). Your record is kept at the DMV in Sacramento, and is accessible by computer terminal from most DMV offices (VC § 1808). The information is not available to the general public, but is available to police agencies, courts, the driver herself, and those whom the driver has given written authorization to inspect the record. Ordinary moving violations are kept as part of your DMV record for three years. More serious violations—such as reckless driving, driving over 100 mph, or driving with a suspended license—are kept on your record for seven years. Drunk driving, as well as alcohol-related reckless driving violations, are kept on your record for ten years (VC § 12810). If you commit another violation within that period, the record of your prior violations can result in stiffer penalties.

When you get auto insurance, your insurer will ask you to authorize them to view your driving record at any further date. Thus, a new offense on your record may result in an insurance rate increase. How your rates are affected by your driving record depends on your individual company. You may want to call your insurance company (without giving your name) to get a general idea of how much your rates would rise for the violation you're charged with.

Another function of your record is to keep track of "points." Most moving violations count as a single point on your record. Two points over a three-year period will probably result in an increase of your auto insurance rates. Four points in a year, or six in two years, or eight in three years, can result in your license being suspended. The license suspension process is discussed in detail in Chapter 15.

Note: The DMV generally uses the conviction date, not the offense date, in counting points for suspensions. The DMV is not notified when you get a ticket; it is notified only when you pay it, are found guilty after contesting it, or fail to appear in court as promised. As a result, you may save your license—or avoid a costly insurance hike—simply by pleading not guilty and going to trial. Later, if you're found guilty, earlier convictions may have "dropped off" your record by then.

EXAMPLE:

Ronnie Racer has paid off three speeding tickets in the last nine months. Today, he just got his fourth. If he pays it before the 12th month, he'll have four points over a 12-month period. The DMV will then suspend his license. But if Ronnie pleads not guilty, staves off trial for a few months, and is later convicted, his fourth conviction will fall outside of the 12-month period.

Note: VC §§ 12810–12810.5 are unclear on whether offense or conviction dates are used. Some DMV employees claim their computer system is sophisticated enough to base suspension on violation dates. However, in our experience, this is not the case.

EXAMPLE:

Shantée paid a speeding ticket in November 2004. She got a second one in September 2006, but got it dismissed by going to traffic school. In October 2007, she got a third one, but was ineligible for traffic school. She asked for a trial, which occurred in February 2008. Although she was convicted, her November 2004 ticket had dropped off her record, being more than three years old. So, she now has only one point and won't face an insurance increase.

Fines and Penalty Assessments

A traffic fine consists of a base fine plus penalty assessments. The primary penalty assessment is 220% of the base fine. Thus a $100 base fine becomes approximately $400 after adding around $300 in penalty assessments.

The Base Fine

Suggested base fines for most traffic violations are listed in the Uniform Traffic Bail Schedule. Are you wondering why a schedule of fines is called a bail schedule? The answer lies in the way the money is collected. Originally, a traffic fine couldn't be paid until the driver had appeared in court and either pleaded guilty or was found guilty by a judge. But as traffic courts became more and more congested and counties began to rely on traffic fines as an important source of revenue, court administrators thought of a way to both empty the courtrooms and fill the tax coffers: Cited drivers can post "bail" for their infraction by sending the money to the court clerk. When the driver doesn't appear in court on the date and time noted on the ticket, the bail is declared forfeited (it becomes the court's property) and the motorist is declared guilty. The system then treats these bail forfeitures as convictions and the violations go on record at the DMV in Sacramento (VC §§ 40510–40512.5). The "bail"

Base Fines	
Infraction	**Amount**
Most equipment and registration violations	$25
Most moving violations not involving speed	$35
Speeding 1–15 mph over the speed limit	$25
Speeding 16–25 mph over the speed limit	$50
Speeding 26 mph and more over the speed limit	$100 (plus a mandatory court appearance)
Running stop sign/ stoplight	$100
For speeding tickets in construction or safety enhancement zones (VC §§ 42009–42010):	
• Speeding 1–15 mph over the speed limit	$35
• Speeding 16–25 mph over the speed limit	$60
• Speeding 26 mph and more over the speed limit	$100 (plus mandatory court appearance)

Note: An additional $10 is added to the base fine for each 1-point or 2-point moving violation conviction already on your DMV record within the 36 months prior to the date of the offense. (See Chapter 15.)

is the fine that would have been levied had the motorist appeared in court and lost (or pleaded guilty). If all you want to do is pay the fine (the bail), don't set up a trial date. (See Chapter 10.) If you do, and then don't show up, you may find yourself facing a failure to appear charge, a serious offense. (See Chapter 7.) In practice, however, most judges won't bother to do this, and will simply declare your bail forfeited.

Penalty Assessments for Moving Violations	
Amount of the Penalty Assessment	**Use**
$10 for each $10 (or fraction of $10 of fine)	Under PC § 1464 this money goes to a peace officers training fund, a corrections training fund, and a driver training penalty assessment fund.
20% of base fine	Under Penal Code § 1465.7 this additional 20% "state surcharge" is used for general state government funding.
$7 for each $10 (or fraction of $10 of fine)	Under Government Code §§ 76000, 76100-76106, this money goes to county funds for courthouse construction, criminal justice facility (jail) construction, forensic laboratory, automated fingerprint identification, DNA identification, and emergency medical services in proportions determined by the county Board of Supervisors.
$2 for every $10 (or fraction of $10) of fine	Under Government Code 76000.5, and when approved by County Board of Commissioners or Supervisors, this money may be used for local emergency medical services funds.
$5 for each $10 (or fraction of $10 of fine)	Under Government Code §§ 70372, this money goes for courthouse construction.
$35 ($50 for misdemeanors)	Under Government Code §§ 70373, this amount is also tacked on for courthouse construction.
$10	When approved by the county Board of Supervisors under Vehicle Code § 40508.6, this money is used to pay the costs of keeping track of your prior convictions.
$1 (in areas where arraignments are held at night)	This money is used, per Vehicle Code § 42006, for the cost of running the court at night.

The Uniform Traffic Bail Schedule suggests a basic fine according to the guidelines in the table "Base Fines," above. But these base fines don't necessarily apply if you fight a ticket and lose. The judge can fine you less, or even more, based on prior offenses or aggravating factors. However, most judges will stick fairly close to the bail schedule in assessing base fines, since they don't want to be accused of penalizing defendants who insist on their right to trial.

Increased Fine for Accident With Injury

If you're convicted of any moving violation arising out of an accident in which anyone (other than yourself) was injured, you could be found guilty of "unsafe operation of a motor vehicle with bodily injury" or with "great bodily injury," defined as a "significant substantial, physical injury." The base fine is $70 for the "bodily injury" offense; $95 for "great bodily injury" (VC § 21070, 42001.19, PC § 12022.7). With penalty assessments of 260%, the total fine would be $252 and $342.

Penalty Assessments

Penalty assessments are added to every base fine and have nothing to do with your driving record or the circumstances of your infraction. Penalty assessments are revenue-generating schemes, pure and simple. The money is used to modernize courthouses and jails, train government employees, and provide for more police officers.

As you can see from the table, on each $10 of basic fine, you will pay $26 more ($10 + $7 + $5 + $2 + $2 (20% of $10 base fine)) plus an additional $35 for courthouse contruction, plus $11 for record keeping and night court costs. An additional $5 to $7.50 in penalty assessments can be added to every parking ticket.

Penalty Assessments for Parking Violations	
Amount of the Penalty Assessment	**Use**
Two or three surcharges (depending on the decision of the county Board of Supervisors) of $2.50 apiece	For each county's jail and/or courthouse construction fund, and for additional projects as decided by the Board of Supervisors.

EXAMPLE:

Francine Fast was cited for going 82 mph on the 65-mph freeway, 17 mph over the limit. The base fine is $50. Since Francine has had two moving violation convictions in the past three years, her base fine is increased by 2 x $10, or $20, for a $70 base fine. To this is added a penalty assessment of $24 for each $10 base fine (7 x $24 or $168). There's an additional penalty assessment of 20% of the base fine ($14), and add in another $35 for courthouse contructions, plus $10 for prior conviction record keeping and $1 for night court costs. The total fine is $50 plus $20 plus $168 plus $14 plus $35 plus $11, or $290.

The above example is only a rough illustration of how fines are calculated. In addition many counties are allowed to impose higher fines, and, especially for misdemeanors like DUI, there are additional specific penalty assessments. A thorough (and highly complex) explanation is provided in a "Uniform Bail and Penalty Schedules," published by the California Judicial Council (CRC Rule 4.102) consisting of over 150 pages and available online at www. courtinfo.ca.gov/reference. Enter "uniform bail schedule" in the search box.

Insurance Consequences: Cancellations and Rate Increases

When you obtain auto insurance, your policy generally lasts for a fixed period of time, usually either six months or a year. During this time, an insurance company can't raise your rates or cancel your insurance unless you fail to pay your premium.

When it comes time to renew your policy, however, your insurance company might raise your rates or even refuse to continue insuring you if you've had more than a few violations, or at least one accident. You may qualify for regularly priced insurance after a few years without further violations or accidents. It pays to shop around.

Many insurance companies raise rates at renewal time by taking away a "safe driver discount." (This "discount" also tends to keep you from filing minor fender bender claims.) Since the law requires insurance companies to give a "good driver" discount, this practice is likely to come into play where the driver has three or more moving violation infractions, including any points for an "at-fault" accident, within a three-year period.

Some insurance companies raise rates by adding a "surcharge," and still others do this by refusing to insure you except through their own separate "indemnity" or "casualty" company, which specializes in "higher-risk" drivers—and charges a lot more. (This isn't the same as being on an "assigned-risk" plan; see

Chapter 5.) Insurance companies are required to offer a "good driver" discount of at least 20% off regular insurance rates (Insurance Code § 1861.02).

You will not be eligible for this discount, however, if you have more than one violation "point" over a three-year period or have been convicted of driving under the influence within the past seven years. We discuss the DMV's violation "point count" system in Chapter 15. In short, you will lose your good driver discount if:

- you are at fault in any injury-causing accident, or

- you are convicted of any serious two-point offense, such as reckless driving, driving over 100 mph, speed contest or driving under the influence. (For a DUI conviction, you'll be ineligible for such a discount for seven years.) A conviction for any of these offenses will prevent you from getting a good driver discount for at least three years (seven years in the case of driving under the influence).

Also, you will lose a good driver discount if you accumulate two or more points in any three-year period. Violations for ordinary traffic infractions (such as speeding, stop sign and stoplight violations) count as one point. So do property damage accidents in which you are at fault. Seatbelt violations (VC § 26315) and anti-gridlock law violations (VC § 22526) are not supposed to count for violation points.

EXAMPLE:

Dan Driver was at fault in a minor accident in June 2007. His insurance company paid off the other driver. In May 2009, Dan chose not to fight a speeding ticket he received that year. Since Dan has accumulated two points over a three-year period, he will lose his good driver discount until June 2010, when the June 2007 accident point should drop off his DMV record.

As you can see, a ticket for a moving violation can have serious consequences if not successfully fought. Depending on the timing of a previous point on your DMV record, it could cost you hundreds or even thousands of dollars in increased insurance rates over several years. In practice, a 30-year-old driver who travels 12,000 miles a year faces a liability-insurance premium hike of 60% to 200%, depending on the insurer, if he or she accumulates two or more points.

Finally, some insurance companies may refuse to reinsure you once your current policy expires if you've had a very serious accident in which you were at fault, or are convicted of driving under the influence. You then may have to seek limited—and more expensive—"assigned risk" coverage. We discuss this in Chapter 5.

Insurance companies obtain information about your driving record from their own files of claims made against your policy, random checks of DMV records (per your previously obtained written authorization), or their own questionnaires and renewal applications. Omitting any information from these applications is a bad idea, since it may give the company an excuse to avoid paying off a large claim later on. The details of this practice vary so much among insurance companies that it is difficult to generalize.

The criteria for refusing to renew your insurance are usually less strict than for deciding initially whether to insure you. (See Chapter 5.) In other words, just because a particular company won't insure someone who has had three violations in three years doesn't necessarily mean they'll refuse to renew your insurance if you wind up with that many violations on your record later on. Some companies even guarantee never to refuse to renew your policy once you've been with them for a certain number of years—unless you manage to be convicted of drunk driving, hit-and-run, or some other very serious offense.

Overview of Specific Violations

Now that you have general information about the consequences of your ticket, we'll turn to an overview of the most commonly charged traffic violations. Read only the summary section that covers your violation, and skip the rest. You can refer to the chart at the end of this chapter that further summarizes specific violations. Then go to the chapter (4, 5, 6, 7, or 8) that covers your violation in detail.

Speed Violations

Most speeding violations are infractions (unless they involve something additional like reckless driving, in which case they are treated as misdemeanors). They always go on your record. They can make your insurance rates go up, or make it difficult to get insurance in the future. Because they are infractions, you can use many procedural shortcuts should you decide to fight (see Chapter 10). Since the law of speeding in California is complex and filled with technicalities, it is great for ticket-fighting. This is especially true where the speed limit you're accused of exceeding is 60 mph or less. You'll find numerous ways to fight a speeding ticket in Chapter 4. In sum, speeding tickets are often worth fighting, and by using the suggested defenses and procedural shortcuts provided in this book, you have a decent chance of winning. If all else fails, you can hope that the officer doesn't show up at trial and your case will be dismissed.

As shown above, the base fine for speeding tickets depends on the speed limit and how fast you're accused of driving (the greater your speed, the higher the base fine). The fine may be higher if you drove a bus or tractor-trailer.

Moving Violations Other Than Speeding

Moving violations appear on your record, so they may cause your insurance rates to rise. Moving violations not involving speeding, reckless driving, or drunk driving are infractions. Therefore, if you fight, you can use the procedural shortcuts discussed in Chapter 10. Your chances of success depend on the statute in question: Statutes that prohibit "unreasonable" actions (like unsafe lane changes or turns) are based on subjective judgments, and thus you can argue that what you did was safe and reasonable. Violations like running red lights and stop signs can be fought by showing that the sign was blocked from sight or that the light changed so quickly that you could not have stopped in time. Chapter 5 contains specific information about how to argue defenses for these and other moving violations. Even if you don't have a good defense, you can demand a trial and hope the officer doesn't show. Total first-offense fines for these violations (basic fine plus penalty assessment) range from $120 to $200 for more serious violations (following too closely and failure to yield right of way), and $371 for running a stop sign or stoplight.

Illegal Parking

Parking violations are not considered criminal offenses and do not go on your record. Therefore, your insurance rates will not go up. Parking tickets are usually based on local ordinances, and generally there will be some kind of informal procedure where you can either pay your parking ticket or set up a court date by mail. Although it is usually procedurally easier to fight parking tickets than moving violations, the minimal consequences often make it not worth the bother. Fines typically range from $15 to $40, but can be as high as $250 for some violations, such as parking in a handicapped-only parking space or a bus zone. The fine is usually listed on the ticket. We say more about parking tickets in Chapter 6.

Pedestrian and Bicycle Violations

Pedestrian and bicycle violations carry small fines (less than $70) and do not appear on your record. They are infractions and are thus open to the procedural shortcuts listed in Chapter 10. However, the small fines and lack of insurance consequences generally make them not worth fighting. For further information, read Chapter 6.

Defective Equipment

All equipment violations are infractions. The procedure for dealing with most equipment violations is different than for other infractions. You are generally given an opportunity to correct the defect within a specified time period, have the correction "certified," present this certification to the court clerk or judge, and have the charge dismissed. Nothing goes on your record or affects your insurance rates. If you don't take care of the problem, however, the consequences can be severe, including a maximum fine of $500 and six months in jail.

If the equipment defect is causing an imminent traffic hazard or is the result of your "persistent neglect," you don't get a chance to correct it, and you'll be given a regular ticket that you'll have to fight or pay. But even if you get a regular ticket and are convicted or pay the bail, the violation will still not go on your record unless it is one of the following (listed by Vehicle Code section):

§ 24002	unsafe or illegal operating condition or illegally loaded;
§ 24004	unsafe operating condition after warning by police officer;
§ 24250	driving at night without proper lighting equipment;
§ 24409	improper use of high-beam headlights;
§ 24604	protruding load without safety lights or flag;
§ 24800	not having a lamp or flag on a projecting load;
§ 25103	driving with only parking lights lighted;
§ 26707	faulty windshield wipers;
§ 27151	modifying exhaust system to increase noise;
§ 27315	seatbelt violation (no point count);
§§ 27360–27360.5	child restraint law violation;
§ 27800	motorcycle improperly carrying passenger; or
§ 27801	too-high seat or handlebars on motorcycle.

Total fines for equipment violations are usually about $150, if not dismissed following correction.

Equipment violations are covered in detail in Chapter 6.

Registration and License Violations

When you have a valid license or registration, but can't find it or don't have it with you when you're pulled over, you can be cited for a "correctable" violation that is treated in the same manner as correctable equipment violations above. They do not go on your record. See Chapter 6.

Driving With Expired License

Driving with an expired (or nonexistent) license is a misdemeanor theoretically punishable by a fine of up to $1,000 plus over $2,400 in additional assessments. It isn't "correctable" by renewing your license, since you already committed the offense by driving without a current license. However, many judges will assess only a smaller total fine of $300 to $400 if you appear in court after having renewed your license and show it to the judge. See Chapter 7.

Driving While License Suspended

Driving with a suspended license is a misdemeanor. If charged with this, you have a right to a jury trial, which will give you leverage in plea bargaining. (See Chapters 8 and 13.) In some circumstances you can truthfully argue that you were unaware of the suspension and the charge should be dismissed. If you were aware of the suspension and drove anyway, you'll have more trouble fighting the charge. The penalties can be severe—fines up to $1,000 plus up to $2,600 more in "penalty assessments" and six months in jail for a first offense. Convictions go on your record, although they have little effect on your insurance. License suspensions are covered in Chapters 7 and 15.

Driving Without Insurance

You must be able to show proof of automobile insurance when you are stopped by a police officer or are involved in an automobile accident. Failure to have insurance in effect at the time the officer asks for proof of coverage is an infraction punishable by a fine of up to $200 plus up to $531 in additional assessments, for a total of up to $731. (VC §§ 16028, 16029).

If you're cited for not having proof of insurance in your possession—even though you

had insurance in effect at the time—you can show written proof to a court clerk, who will dismiss the violation. The clerk will not dismiss the insurance violation on the basis of insurance you obtained after the fact. Getting your citation dismissed when you had insurance at the time you were cited but simply lacked the proof is discussed in more detail in Chapter 5.

Monetary penalties aren't the only consequence for a conviction for not having insurance. If you're an uninsured driver who's involved in an accident that results in more than $750 in damages, or injury to a person, your driver's license can be suspended for a year. This can happen even if you did not cause the accident, but are an innocent victim of someone else's negligence. (See Chapters 5 and 15 for more information on revocations.)

Serious Offenses (Reckless Driving, Hit-and-Run, Etc.)

Offenses such as reckless driving or "exhibitions of speed" (including squealing your tires) are misdemeanors that carry total fines of $3,600 or more and the possibility of license suspension and six months in jail. If someone is injured as a result of your reckless driving, you definitely could face a six-month jail sentence. Failing to stop at an accident (commonly known as "hit-and-run") is also a misdemeanor. (It can be charged as a felony if someone is injured or killed.)

Convictions for these offenses always appear on your record and will definitely cause your insurance premiums to rise and possibly be canceled. Since these offenses are misdemeanors, you have a right to request a jury trial and maybe gain some plea bargaining leverage. You must appear before a judge even if you simply want to plead guilty and pay a fine. You should probably consider hiring a lawyer to handle the plea bargaining and jury trial. For more information about these offenses and how to conduct a jury trial on your own, or how to get a lawyer, read Chapters 7, 9, 10, 11, and 13.

Driving Under the Influence (DUI)

Drunk driving is a serious offense. It is a misdemeanor that remains on your record for seven years. You should at least consult a lawyer with experience in drunk driving cases before trying to handle it yourself. On a fourth offense, or if someone is killed or injured because of your drunk driving, you can be charged with a felony, and should definitely be represented by a lawyer. In a few cases there are ways of beating a drunk driving charge, and you may be able to plea bargain. Additional offenses within seven years are severely punished with maximum penalties of up to three years in state prison (four years if someone is killed or injured), and mandatory license suspension or revocation. See Chapter 8 for details.

Non-DUI Alcohol-Related Offenses (Open Container, Etc.)

Having an open alcoholic beverage container in your car or on your person while driving is not as serious as driving while drunk. But it's still fairly serious. Most of these offenses are reported to the DMV. It is an infraction, so you don't get a jury trial, but you can get a trial before a judge with the officer present. Total fines (including penalty assessments) can be as high as $351. A conviction for this charge will be reported to the DMV and may cause your insurance company to refuse to renew your policy after it expires. For more information read Chapters 5, 9, 10, and 11.

Ignoring a Ticket, Failing to Appear in Court, or Failing to Pay a Fine

If you ignore a ticket that you've signed, fail to show up for a scheduled hearing, or fail to pay a fine, watch out!

Ignoring a Ticket and Failing to Appear: If you ignore a ticket you've signed, you may be charged with a separate misdemeanor called a Failure to Appear. A Failure to Appear is punishable by a fine of up to $1,000 (plus $2,600 in additional assessments) and six months in jail (VC § 40508(a)). Also, under VC § 40310, the court may choose to add a 50% late charge onto the original fine. If you continue to ignore your ticket or you fail to appear at a scheduled hearing, the court can impose another $250 "civil assessment" against you ten days after mailing a warning notice. Or, the court can also issue a warrant for your arrest and/or notify the DMV, which will suspend your license. (See VC §§ 40509 and 40509.5.)

When you ignore a ticket or fail to appear at a hearing, some courts will even refuse to let you set up a court appearance until you pay all fines and penalties. This means you could face continued suspension of your license until you pay hundreds of dollars. Finally, the court can find you guilty of the original charge (if it is an infraction), even if you never asked that it be set for trial (VC § 40903).

Failing to Pay a Fine: If you are sentenced to pay a fine following a court hearing, but you fail to pay it within the time allowed, you can be charged with an additional misdemeanor and the court can have the DMV suspend your license for up to 30 days (VC § 40508(b),(d)).

Of course, it is always best to respond to the ticket and to pay the fine on time. If, however, after having failed to appear you decide to challenge the charge, you may be able to employ some defenses and plea-bargaining strategies. We show you how to do this in Chapter 7, Chapters 9 through 12, and Chapter 15. As you will see in those chapters, you might be able to plead guilty to the original charge or just the Failure to Appear charge.

Out-of-State Tickets

"Can I be physically arrested for committing a minor traffic violation in another state?"

"What if I ignore a ticket I get in another state?"

"Will an out-of-state ticket go on my California driving record?"

Arrests for Out-of-State Violations

In a few states, out-of-state drivers accused of traffic violations are taken to jail, or before a judge (or justice of the peace), and aren't released until either bail is posted or a fine is paid. This is done because the state has no way short of extradition (having the person arrested and sent back to the state in which the offense occurred) to guarantee the appearance or the payment of the fine of out-of-state residents. This practice is becoming less frequent, but still occurs in some localities. So, when doing extensive driving out of state, you might want to carry some additional cash (perhaps up to $500). Some nationally known auto clubs have plans whereby members are guaranteed bail bonds of up to several hundred dollars.

Your Driving Record

Usually the trouble and expense of traveling back to another state to fight a ticket will outweigh the benefits of not paying the fine. Most people will therefore either plead guilty and pay the fine or arrange to "forfeit bail." If you do this, it might appear on your California driving record maintained by the DMV in

Sacramento. More than half the states have a mutual agreement known as the "Driver's License Compact" under which each member state reports out-of-state residents' traffic violation convictions and bail forfeitures to the state that licensed the driver (VC § 15022). Member states are all states (and the District of Columbia) except for Alaska, Georgia, Kentucky, Michigan, North Dakota, Oregon, Rhode Island, South Dakota, Tennessee, and Wisconsin.

If the DMV receives the report of a conviction or bail forfeiture from a member state, the offense will appear on your record in the same way it would for a similar offense under California law. Thus, speeding violations will appear, while parking infractions will not.

If You Ignore an Out-of-State Ticket

In a state where you were physically arrested for a traffic offense, taken to jail or brought before a judge, and then released after posting bail, your bail will be considered forfeited. Then, one of two things might happen. On the one hand, the judge might choose to treat the matter as though you just paid the fine. This "conviction," if it occurred in one of the states listed above, will then be reported to the California DMV.

On the other hand, not all states allow this, and even in some states that do, it's left to the judge's discretion. It is thus possible that your bail could be declared forfeited plus a warrant would still be issued for your arrest whenever you drive through the state. The state might also suspend your driving privileges within its own borders, in which case you'll also be charged with unlicensed driving.

You will most likely not be arrested in California for ignoring a traffic ticket in another state. Police from other states have no jurisdiction to arrest you outside of that state, and it is unlikely that California law enforcement officers will spend their time and energy to detain you until you can be extradited to the other state to answer to a minor traffic charge.

Finally, ignoring that ticket probably won't affect your California driving record, since ignoring an out-of-state ticket doesn't usually result in a conviction or bail forfeiture (unless you actually posted bail) and since, generally,

only convictions and bail for by other states. Even if an out-to-appear charge were somehow Sacramento, the DMV will not su refuse to renew your license. The DI refuse, however, to renew it—and ma it—for a California failure-to-appear ch (See Chapter 15.)

...iture are reported
...of-state failure-
...eported to
...spend or
...AV will
...suspend
...arge.

	...de	Classification	Fines (add 260% plus $46 for penalty assessments)/Jail
		Infraction.	$25–$100 for first offense, depending on how much over speed limit. (See Chapter 3.)
	...36	Infraction.	$35–$50 for most violations. $100 for stop sign/stoplight violations.
...peed (...)	§§ 23103–23109	Misdemeanor. Felony if hit-and-run and someone is injured.	$145–$1,000 plus 90 days in jail plus license suspension. If injury: $220–$1,000 plus 6 months in jail.
...nk driving (Chapter 8)	§§ 23152–23153	Misdemeanor. Felony if person is injured or 4th offense.	Severe. Multiple violations drastically increase penalties. (See Chapter 8.)
Open alcohol containers or marijuana in your car (Chapter 5)	§§ 23220–23229.1 §§ 13202–13202.5	(Alcohol) infraction or (marijuana) misdemeanor if charged under Health & Safety Code.	(Alcohol) $50–$100 or (Marijuana) $100.
Parking ticket (Chapter 6)	Local ordinance— varies from city to city	Infraction.	$15–$250 total fine, including penalty assessments
"Correctable" equipment violations (Chapter 6)	§§ 24000–28085	Infraction.	$25 proof-of-correction fee, if proof of correction is given to the court. If ignored, failure-to-appear penalty can be $1,000 plus six months in jail. (See Chapter 6.)
Registration/expired license violations (Chapter 6)	§§ 4000–9982	Infraction.	Dismissal on proof of correction (with $25 proof-of-correction fee), only if registration was in effect at the time citation was issued.
Driving without license or while it is suspended (Chapter 7)	§§ 12500–15028	Infraction or misdemeanor. (See Chapter 7.)	1st offense: $1,000 plus six months in jail. 2nd offense within 5 years: $2,000 plus 1 year in jail and forfeiture of your vehicle. (See Chapter 7.)
Driving without insurance/ accident reporting requirements (Chapter 5)	§§ 16000–16560	Infraction and license suspension if there's an accident.	$100–$200.
Ignoring a ticket/failing to show up for a court date/failing to pay a fine (Chapter 7)	§ 40508	Misdemeanor. Prosecutor may elect to treat as infraction. (See Chapter 7.)	

Does It Go on Your Record?	License Suspension	Insurance Consequences	How to Fight It: (Procedure)
Yes.	Rare for 1st or 2nd offenses. Maximum: 1st—30 days 2nd—60 days 3rd in 3 years—6 months. (See Chapter 14.)	Rates may rise. Depends on the company. Cancellation is likely after many violations.	Chapter 9 Chapter 10 Chapter 11 Chapter 12
Yes.	No. But DMV may suspend license if 4 violations in 12 months, 6 in 24 months, or 8 in 36 months. (See Chapter 15.)	Same as above.	Chapter 9 Chapter 10 Chapter 11 Chapter 12
Yes.	Up to 6 months.	Rates will rise. Policy may be canceled.	Chapter 9 Chapters 10–13
Yes. Remains on record for 7 years.	Up to 3 years.	Same as above. Cancellation likely.	Chapter 8 Chapter 9 Chapter 13
Yes.	(Alcohol) No. (Marijuana) Yes, up to 3 years for a first offense.	Rates may rise, coverage may be canceled.	Chapter 9
No.	DMV can refuse to renew auto registration or driver's license for unpaid tickets.	None.	Chapter 6
No, except the following: §§ 24002, 24004, 24250, 24409, 24800, 25103, 26707, 27151, 27800, 27801. (See Chapter 3.)	No.	Generally none.	Chapter 6
No.	No.	Little effect, if any.	Chapter 6
Yes.	Will lengthen existing suspension.	Few.	Chapter 7 Chapters 9, 11–13, 15
Yes.	1-year suspension if in a $500-plus accident, or injury accident, while uninsured. Then 3-year reporting requirement after that.	Will be difficult to get insurance while license is suspended.	Chapter 3 Chapter 15
Yes.	DMV will suspend license until underlying offense and failure to appear charge is "adjudicated."	None.	Chapter 7 Chapter 14 Chapter 15

Speed Violations and Radar

Because more tickets are given for speed violations than for any other moving infraction, we're devoting an entire chapter to the subject. And since many speeding tickets are based either on a cop's use of radar or laser or on aircraft sightings, we show you how these law enforcement schemes work and the common defenses you can employ when you are victimized by them. We also explain how to fight speeding tickets based on:

- an officer's pacing you (following you and comparing your speed to hers) by patrol car or aircraft

- a speed trap involving the misuse of radar or laser, and

- "photo-radar," where a combined radar unit and camera was used to generate a ticket that was mailed to you.

Note: If you weren't charged with speeding, you can skip this chapter. If you were charged with violating a "speed contest" or "exhibition of speed" law, read Chapter 7.

Another note: If your ticket is for a violation of VC § 22349 (exceeding the 65 mph limit, 70 on some portions of freeways, or 55 on a two-lane undivided highway), read the section entitled, "Exceeding Speed Limits." Otherwise, if your ticket is for violating VC § 22350 (all other speed limits), read on.

We begin with the good-and-bad news that although California's speed laws are a little more complicated than you might expect, this gives you quite a bit more room within which to beat a ticket—especially if radar was used.

The "Basic Speed Law" (VC §§ 22350, 22351)

VC § 22350. No person shall drive a vehicle upon a highway at a speed greater than is reasonable or prudent having due regard for weather, visibility, the traffic on, and the surface and width of, the highway, and in no event at a speed that endangers the safety of persons or property.

VC § 22351(a). The speed of any vehicle upon a highway not in excess of the limits in § 22352 or established as authorized by this code (VC §§ 22354– 22358.4) is lawful unless clearly proved to be in violation of the Basic Speed Law.

VC § 22351(b). The speed of any vehicle on a highway in excess of the prima facie speed limits in § 22352 or established as authorized by this code is prima facie unlawful unless the defendant establishes by competent evidence that the speed in excess of said limits did not constitute a violation of the Basic Speed Law at the time, place and under the conditions then existing.

The Elements of the Offense and the Burden of Proof

Violation of the Basic Speed Law—driving over the speed limit, but less than the 65 mph or 70 mph maximum speed limit (55 mph on two-lane undivided highways)—is an offense for which most people have been ticketed at one time or another. However, surprising as it may seem, a person traveling over the speed limit— but less than the usual 65 mph maximum speed limit (55 mph for two-lane undivided highways)—isn't necessarily violating the law. On the other hand, in some rare circumstances, usually during a heavy fog or a driving rain- storm, you can actually be in violation of this law even though you were driving below the speed limit. Why? Because in these circumstances it may be imprudent and unreasonable to drive faster than a crawl.

What you are really being charged with is driving "at a speed greater than is reasonable or prudent…." The posted or otherwise defined speed limit is only *presumed* to be the "reasonable or prudent" speed. When you are ticketed for exceeding the posted speed, the officer is taking advantage of a legal "presumption" that anything above the posted speed is unsafe.

Now, let's look at the elements of § 22350, the offense:

1. You must be driving a vehicle;

2. Upon a highway (defined as a "way or place of whatever nature, publicly maintained and open to the use of the public for purposes of vehicular travel")—including a "street" (VC § 360); and

3. Your speed either must be "greater than is reasonable or prudent" or must "endanger the safety of persons or property."

This last element is obviously the one most open to interpretation. Those readers who have recently moved to California may be unfamiliar with this concept, as opposed to the law in many other states that says that "if you were going over the limit, you're guilty, and that's it." In California, this is only true if you exceed 65 mph (70 on certain freeways, or 55 on two-lane undivided highways), a different violation—see the section entitled, "Exceeding Speed Limits."

Section 22351 goes on to state that the law *presumes* that the reasonable or prudent speed is the one posted on the speed limit signs. This is called the "prima facie" speed limit.

If you were going over the posted speed limit, you have an opportunity to defeat the "presumption" that you were going over a reasonable and prudent speed. You might do this by proving that weather, visibility, road width, etc., did not make a higher speed unsafe. You should realize that even though you're presumed not guilty, you bear the burden of proving that a speed in excess of the posted limit was safe. You are saying, essentially, "even if Your Honor finds that I was exceeding the speed limit, I'm still not guilty because my speed was reasonable and prudent in light of the circumstances."

Note: It is entirely proper to advance inconsistent arguments, that is, to argue that (1) you didn't exceed the speed limit, and (2) even if you did, it was still safe to do so.

"Technical" Defenses to Basic Speed Law Charge

There are two basic types of defenses to a speeding charge under the Basic Speed Law. One type—the technical defense—is that the police used impermissible methods to catch you. The other—the substantive defense—is that the police were wrong in their conclusions. We discuss the technical defenses first, in this part, because you normally raise them first in a trial, when the police officer testifies before you do. The substantive defenses are discussed in the next section.

Illegal Use of Radar or Laser— "Speed Trap" Laws

There are certain rules restricting when a traffic officer may or may not use radar to detect violations of the Basic Speed Law. You'll soon discover that these rules don't make much logical sense. But they're great for fighting tickets. They contain lots of "technicalities" that can result in your ticket being dismissed.

Requirement That Prosecution Provide "Engineering and Traffic Survey"

Okay, now for the rules. On most streets, the police may not use radar at that location where the speed limit hasn't been "justified" by an "engineering and traffic survey." This is because state law defines the use of radar on streets with unjustifiably low speed limits as an illegal "speed trap." VC § 40802(b) defines a radar "speed trap" as:

> A particular section of a highway with a prima facie speed limit ... if that prima facie speed limit is not justified by an engineering and traffic survey and where enforcement of the speed limit involves the use of radar or other electronic device that measures the speed of moving objects.

What this definition means is that wherever radar is used, some city, county, or state agency should have, within the previous five years, examined traffic and road conditions, including prevailing speeds, accident records, potential hazards, and visibility, and come up with a speed limit "justified" by that study. If the speed limit hasn't been justified by such a survey, the road is a "speed trap" and it is illegal for a traffic officer to use radar at all (VC § 40801). Cities and counties cannot enact local ordinances to evade the traffic-survey requirements. (*People v. Stone* (1987) 190 Cal. App.3d Supp. 1, 236 Cal.Rptr. 140.)

Appeals courts have ruled that an officer's mere *statement* that such a traffic study was made is insufficient to prove that it actually was done—unless the officer personally participated in the study—and that summaries of surveys aren't enough either. (*People v. Sterritt* (1976) 65 Cal.App.3d Supp. 1, 135 Cal.Rptr. 552; *People v. Ellis* (1995) 33 Cal.App.4th Supp. 25, 40 Cal.Rptr.2d 111; *People v. Earnest* (1995) 33 Cal.App.4th Supp. 18, 40 Cal.Rptr.2d 304.) If the officer did not personally participate in the study, a "certified" (authenticated) copy of the study must be physically introduced into evidence by the prosecution (normally this will be the police officer, as very few prosecutors appear in traffic cases). In some courts, however, *you* may have to insist that a certified copy be produced, rather than relying on the judge to think of this requirement on her own. (See Chapter 11 for more on this issue.) Unless proper evidence of such a traffic study has been admitted, the courts are legally forbidden to find anyone guilty of a speed violation detected by radar. This is true even if the officer's testimony is limited to his "visual estimate" of speed. If he used radar, this testimony is not admissible. (*People v. Conzelman* (1995) 33 Cal. App.4th Supp. 6, 39 Cal.Rptr.2d 156.)

There are several exceptions to the above rule. It does not apply to:

- roads where the speed limit is 65 mph or higher, including freeways
- streets in school zones where the speed limit is 15 or 20 mph, in 25 mph school zones when children are present, near children's playgrounds while children are present (*People v. Goodrich* (1994) 33 Cal. App.4th Supp. 1, 39 Cal.Rptr.2d 154), and 25 mph zones near senior centers where a "SENIOR" sign is posted
- most streets with 15 mph speed limits, and
- "local streets and roads," as defined by § 40802(b).

For the "local streets and roads" exception to apply, the officer must show that, either:

1. The local street or road is referred to as such on "the latest functional usage and federal-aid system maps as submitted to the Federal Highway Administration";

Were You Caught in an Illegal Radar Speed Trap?

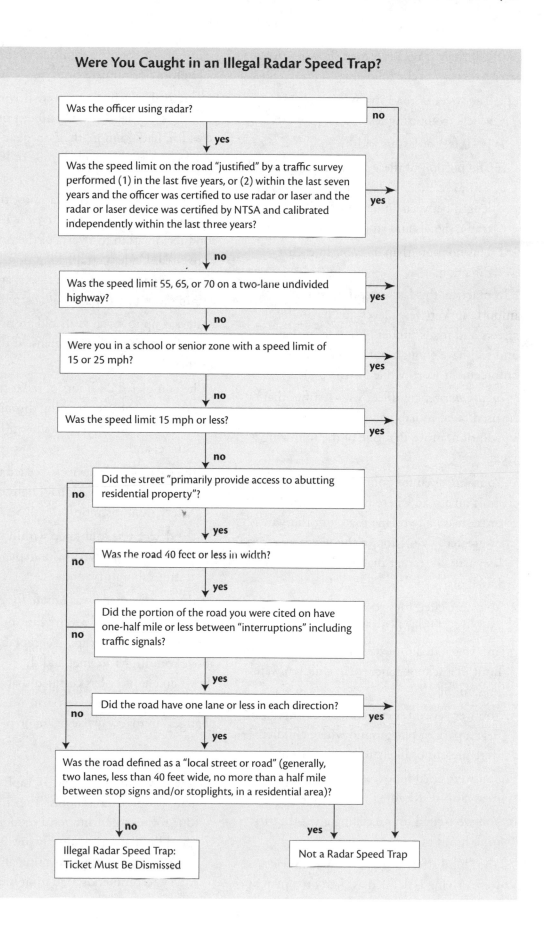

OR, if there is no FHA map showing the street, then *all* of the following:

2a. The street or road "primarily provides access to abutting residential property";

b. Is 40 feet or less in width;

c. The portion of the street or road on which you were cited is one-half mile or less in length between "interruptions" including traffic signals and stop signs; *and*

d. Has no more than *one lane* in each direction.

In practice, this last exception isn't too important. Very few places qualify as "local streets and roads" under either definition and still have enough traffic to make radar enforcement worthwhile for the police.

To summarize, an officer who testifies that he used radar to nab you for speeding must, in addition, prove that one of the following is true:

1. You were cited for going over the posted limit on a road where the speed limit was 55 or more on a two-lane road, or otherwise 65 or greater (a violation of the *maximum* speed law, actually, rather than of the Basic Speed Law); or

2. You were cited for exceeding the 15 or 20 mph speed limit in a school zone; or

3. You were cited for exceeding a 25 mph speed limit in a school zone where children were present; or

4. You were cited for exceeding a 25 mph limit near a park or playground where children were present or likely to be present; or

5. You were cited for exceeding a 25 mph limit in a "SENIOR" zone; or

6. You were cited for exceeding any other 15 mph limit; or

7. The "local street or road" on which you were driving is defined as such on a map of the city or county submitted to the Federal Highway Administration; or

8. The road on which you were driving was in a residential zone, was 40 feet or less in width, had no more than one lane in either direction, and had a half mile or less between "interruptions."

In addition, the officer must show that an engineering and traffic survey had been conducted within five years of the time you were cited. Under certain conditions, however, a survey done more than five years ago—but within seven to ten years—is acceptable.

Surveys up to seven years old are acceptable to challenge a speed trap defense if the officer testifies that:

- he completed 24 hours of radar training, or two hours of laser training through a Peace Officer Standards and Training (POST) course; and

- the radar or laser device exceeded the standards of the National Highway Traffic Safety Administration (NHTSA); and

- the device was calibrated within the last three years by a certified independent testing laboratory; and

- the driver's speed was unsafe for conditions.

A survey older than seven years, but done within the past ten years, is acceptable if all the above conditions are met and the prosecution shows an engineer has certified that within those ten years there have been "no significant changes" in roadway use or traffic patterns.

EXAMPLE:

You were cited for doing 35 mph on a four-lane road near no schools. The city council (due to pressure from local residents) set the speed limit at a ridiculously low 25 mph. Since an impartial engineering and traffic survey recommends a 30 mph limit, the speed limit isn't "justified" by the survey. Neither is the road considered "local," because it has four lanes and is 50 feet wide. Use of radar on this road to enforce the Basic Speed Law is forbidden as a speed trap.

When a police officer testifies that she used radar, but neither she nor anyone else mentions anything about an engineering and traffic survey, the "local streets" exception, or any of the other exceptions listed above, the judge must find you not guilty. Be warned, however, that some judges think that *you* have to raise this point during the trial in order to have it apply. To be on the safe side, it is best to raise an objection to any radar evidence at the moment the officer tries to introduce it at trial. We show you how to do this in Chapter 11.

Attacking a Survey Because It Doesn't "Justify" Posted Speed

In most trials involving radar speed violations, the prosecution must produce an engineering and traffic survey that complies with VC § 627 and engineering standards used by the State Department of Transportation to justify the posted speed limit. Frequently, however, such surveys do not adequately justify the posted speed.

In other words, if the survey does not properly justify the posted speed limit, the survey is inadequate, and the street is considered an illegal "speed trap" if radar is used. (*People v. Goulet* (1992) 13 Cal.App.4th Supp. 1, 17 Cal. Rptr.2d 801.)

In Chapter 11, we tell you how to determine whether the engineering and traffic survey the prosecution may use is adequate to justify the speed limit. Because this type of analysis requires a careful study of the survey, the best time to look into this is *before* trial, not during trial. For that reason, we strongly recommend

that you insist the prosecution provide you a copy of the survey before trial. You have that right, which we discuss in Chapter 10.

"Photo-Radar"—Radar Unit With Cameras

In 1988, the city of Pasadena became the first city in California to use a "Zelleweger-Ulster Photographic Doppler Unit" (a fancy name for an unmanned radar unit linked to a camera) to detect speeders. Not happy with the fact that live police officers may legally hide in the bushes with radar guns, Pasadena figured on raising revenue without having to pay police officers. Typically, an unmanned radar unit is set to activate a camera when it detects a vehicle traveling at a pre-set speed. The unit registers the vehicle's speed and takes a picture of the front of the vehicle, including the front license plate and driver. A notice to appear in court is mailed to the vehicle's registered owner. Many cities followed suit, but "photo-radar" has fallen out of favor in recent years, partly because of the high cost.

No law specifically authorizes or prevents the use of such Big Brother technology, and some city attorneys, therefore, believe it's legal for their cities to use these devices. However, all the speed trap laws definitely apply whenever radar is used—whether used by a live police officer or not. That means when photo-radar is used, the prosecution must still prove the road isn't an illegal speed trap, as discussed above.

If you receive a notice to appear in court on a photo-radar speeding charge, there will be no police officer to (1) identify you or (2) testify to the road, weather, and traffic condition. However, the local police department will have obtained a driver's license photograph of the person to whom the vehicle was registered, to compare with the photo that the photo-radar unit took.

In addition, as we note in Chapter 2, many judges believe photo radar is illegal because the Vehicle Code doesn't authorize it. In Chapter 10, we show you how to object in writing to a "photo-radar" ticket.

There is no legal rule that says the owner of a speeding vehicle was necessarily the person who drove it and committed the offense. Also, you have a Fifth Amendment right to refuse to admit you were the driver. This means that the photo taken must clearly identify you in the driver's seat. If glare, darkness, tinted windows, or other factors prevent a clear photo of the driver, the case should be dismissed without your having to testify. If you choose to be represented by a lawyer, and don't appear yourself (allowed per VC § 40507), your lawyer can point out that even a clear photo of *someone* driving a car registered to you is not enough to convict you, absent evidence of what you look like! This argument may work well if your driver's license photo does not closely match the photo that the radar unit took. That being so, you should exercise your right to insist on seeing the photographs *before* you appear before the judge. The police department is required to let you see the photographs first. Also, as we'll see later in this chapter, your testimony that you were driving safely under the circumstances may get you an acquittal. And, in photo-radar cases, there will be no officer to testify otherwise.

Note: More about radar—how it works and how it is used—is found in the section, "All About Radar."

Other "Speed Trap" Defenses

There's one other Vehicle Code definition of speed trap that's not of much importance, but which you should keep in the back of your mind. Before radar came into widespread use,

speeds were often determined by "clocking" the time it took a vehicle to drive over a marked road distance. Sometimes an actual hand-held stopwatch was used, and a frustrated or dishonest officer could fudge a little and get a higher speed by starting the stopwatch a little later or stopping it a little sooner, as the vehicle passed by the appropriate point on the road. This method of apprehending speeders is outlawed by VC § 40802(a), which also defines a speed trap as:

> A particular section of a highway measured as to distance and with boundaries marked, designated, or otherwise determined in order that the speed of a vehicle may be calculated by securing the time it takes the vehicle to travel the known distance.

This prevents police agencies from using not only the stopwatch method, but also "Prather" devices. These involve two rubber tubings (something like the kind you drive across at gas stations to alert the attendant) stretched across a lane and spaced about a car length apart. A built-in timer is turned on and off as the vehicle drives across the first and second hoses. (Whenever you see these devices, they are used for traffic-survey, not law enforcement, purposes.)

Also outlawed by VC § 40802(a) is a certain use of "VASCAR," which is an acronym ("Visual Average Speed Computer and Recorder") for a glorified electronic stopwatch connected to a simple distance/time computer. (VASCAR has absolutely nothing to do with radar, and does not emit electronic signals.) Simply stated, the officer travels a measured distance between two points on a road and this distance is fed into the computer. While parked out of sight, he then operates the timer controls based on his visual perception of when your car passes through those points, in the same manner as the buttons on old stopwatches were pushed.

However, for legal hairsplitting and exotic reasons beyond the scope of this book (and beyond reason), VASCAR can legally be used by a *moving* police vehicle. (The difference has to do with the idea that a moving police car does not use any one "particular" stretch of road to measure your speed.) Nevertheless, in view of the abandonment of VASCAR by nearly all police departments in favor of low-priced hand-held radar guns, cases involving the illegality of VASCAR as a speed trap almost never occur.

Substantive Defenses to Basic Speed Law Charge

The fact that the speed limit on a particular stretch of road has not been justified by an engineering and traffic survey does *not* mean that the speed limit is unenforceable. It just means that *radar* can't be used to enforce it. The police are free to use other methods of estimating the speed of a fast-moving vehicle, including "pacing" or following it while observing the patrol car's own "calibrated" (certified as accurate) speedometer. When faced with this type of law enforcement, you will need to prove that the officer's estimate of your speed was mistaken. Below, we explain how you can do this.

We'll also show you that even if you can't prove the officer incorrectly estimated your speed, you can still argue that the speed you were allegedly going was reasonable under the circumstances, so no laws were broken and your ticket should be dismissed.

Note: Of course, in cases where radar was legally used, you can try to challenge the accuracy of the radar measurements, but these arguments are tough to make and require some technical knowledge of how radar works.

Accordingly, that subject is covered separately in the section, "All About Radar."

Pacing

Many tickets for violation of the Basic Speed Law result from the police officer following the suspected speeder and using his own speedometer to clock the suspect's speed. This technique is known as pacing. Contrary to popular belief, there is no law stating that an officer must follow a vehicle a given distance, say one-eighth or one-fourth mile, before ticketing the driver. In practice, a cop will try to follow you for some reasonable distance if he can, to increase the effectiveness of his testimony should you contest the ticket. But cops who are out to fill their quotas sometimes present "evidence" based on tailing a speeding car less than a block, or even by guessing at the approximate speed. One Oakland judge convicted a supposed speeder on the officer's testimony that the driver's car "sounded like it was being driven at an excessive speed."

If you know an officer was behind you for only a short distance, your best tactic is to cross-examine the officer as to the distance he tailed you. If he admits it was, say, only one-eighth mile (between one and two city blocks), it will help to testify (if true) that while you were driving (at the speed limit) you noticed in your rear view mirror that the officer was closing the gap between your car and his very quickly, having the effect of giving him a high speedometer reading. This can be represented graphically as shown below.

You can see from this diagram that the faster police car bearing down on you will cover more distance in the same amount of time. The mathematical relationship between the two speeds (the officer's and yours), the distance the officer initially was behind you, and the distance your car traveled since the officer began following you, can be expressed by the formula:

$$\text{Your speed} = \cfrac{\text{Officer's speed}}{\left[1 + \cfrac{\text{Distance the officer was initially behind you}}{\text{Distance your car traveled until he was on your bumper}}\right]}$$

For the mathematically inclined, this formula is derived as follows: First, let "t" be the time it takes you going at speed "vyou" and the officer going at speed "vcop" to travel the respective distances "dyou" and "dcop." This time "t" will equal both (dyou/vyou) and (dcop/vcop), which are equal to each other. Therefore, (dcop/vcop) = (dyou/vyou). It is also true that if the officer drove faster in order to gain on you, then dcop = dyou + the distance the officer was originally behind you (we call this dcop behind). Also, from rearranging (dcop/vcop) = (dyou/vyou), we get dcop = (dyou × vcop)/vyou. These last two "dcop" equations are equal to each other, so dyou + dcop behind = (dyou and vcop)/vyou. Rearranging this last equation gives: vyou = (dyou × vcop)/(dyou + dcop behind). Dividing both numerator and denominator by dyou, we get: vyou = vcop/[1 + (dcop behind/dyou)].

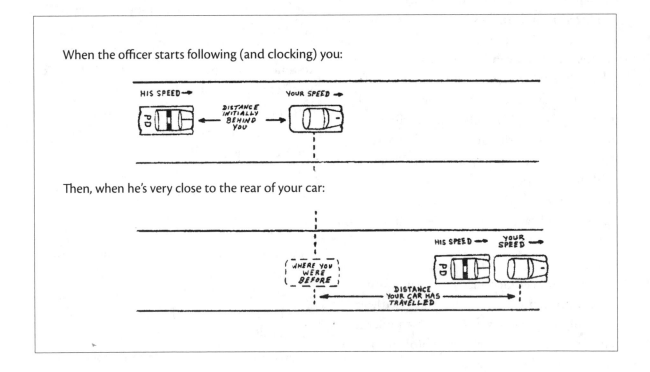

Here's an example of how this formula works. If the officer was going 75 mph on the freeway (they do it all the time) starting out one-quarter mile behind you and tailed you for one and one-half miles, finally bearing down on your rear bumper, he will say that since his speed was 75 mph and he was following you, your speed was 75 mph too. However, your speed works out to:

$$\frac{75 \text{ mph (officer's speed)}}{\left[1 + \left[\frac{\frac{1}{4} \text{ mile initially behind you}}{1\frac{1}{2} \text{ miles you drove as he followed you}}\right]\right]} = \frac{75 \text{ mph}}{1 + \frac{1}{6}} = 64.3 \text{ mph}$$

If the officer testifies, on cross-examination, to speeds and distances which, when put into the formula, show you were driving under the speed limit, your case is almost won. If the officer testifies to distances that won't calculate in your favor, you might be able to truthfully testify to ones that will. When your turn comes to testify, emphasize (if true) how you initially saw the patrol car some distance back in your rearview mirror, then saw it bear down on you so fast that you thought it was going to rear-end your car.

You should also testify (if true) that you were periodically glancing at your speedometer, that it indicated a certain speed, and that you held steadily to this speed—without slowing down—before and after you saw the patrol car.

You can get a certified speedometer calibration from a speedometer shop (look under "speedometers" in your yellow pages). This is excellent proof that your own speedometer was accurate, but it's fairly expensive. You can also check your speedometer's accuracy on the freeway by using a stopwatch while going exactly "60 mph," according to the speedometer, between mile markers. These are white strips about a foot wide and several feet long,

painted on the paved shoulder of the road, perpendicular to the direction of travel. Officers in slow-flying aircraft use these markers to calculate their own speed as they pace vehicles from the air. When you travel at exactly 60 mph between mile intervals, your speed is 88 feet per second, and you travel the 5,280 feet (or one mile) in exactly 60 seconds. If the number of seconds between mile markers at "60 mph" is something *other* than 60 seconds, use the following chart to calculate the true speed:

Seconds elapsed between mile markers	Your true speed (MPH)
50 seconds	72.0 mph
55 seconds	65.5 mph
60 seconds	60.0 mph
65 seconds	55.4 mph
70 seconds	51.4 mph
75 seconds	48.0 mph

You can also use the following formula to calculate your true speed:

$$\text{Speed, mph} = \frac{3{,}600}{\text{seconds between mile markers}}$$

A speedometer inaccuracy that makes yours read too high will help you. If, for example, your speedometer reads 60, but your watch says that 70 seconds passed, you were really going 51.4 mph. Your speedometer reads about 9 mph lower (at 60) than it should. Your testimony to this effect would indicate that you were going *slower* than you thought you were when you looked at your speedometer. Just because it reads 8 mph lower when you're going 55 mph does not mean it reads 8 mph lower at 35—that is, 28 mph. Speedometer calibration inaccuracies are never the same at each speed.

If, on the other hand, your speedometer read 60, but your stopwatch indicated that only 55 seconds had passed, you were really doing 65.5 mph. So here your speedometer reads *lower* than it should, fooling you into believing you're doing 60 when you're actually doing 65. If you testified to this, it would be almost an admission you were going over the speed limit. But, this too is a legal defense *if* you had no reason to believe your speedometer was in error. (If you'd noticed that the pace of traffic had seemed to be unusually slow whenever you drove, that might give you reason to believe your speedometer reading was too low. Of course, you have no obligation to volunteer information about your speedometer's accuracy.)

Proving an Over-the-Limit Speed Safe

As we saw earlier, you can defend against a charge of violating the Basic Speed Law not only by showing you weren't exceeding the speed limit, but also by establishing that even if you were over the limit, your speed was nevertheless "safe" under the circumstances.

EXAMPLE:

You were clocked by radar going 43 mph on a street where 35 mph signs are properly posted. The law presumes that you were driving faster than was reasonable or prudent. To fight this ticket you might advance two arguments (depending, of course, on the facts):

1. The police officer misused the radar and his clocking was therefore inaccurate (discussed later in this chapter); and

2. The weather was perfect, the road was dry and unobstructed, the traffic was very light—or if it was heavy, that you had to drive over the posted speed limit in order to keep up with traffic.

If you establish the first point to the judge's satisfaction, you will win. But even if you lose on this point, you may be able to establish that the speed you were driving was safe under the Basic Speed Law—assuming you get an open-minded and fair judge.

The important things to remember when fighting the presumption created by the posted speed limit under the Basic Speed Law are:

1. The prosecutor or police officer has the burden of proving what the speed limit was, and that you were driving at a certain speed over that; and

2. You have the burden of proving that such a speed was nevertheless safe (in addition, of course, to any evidence you can truthfully present to show that you weren't going over the limit).

Proving your case becomes more difficult, of course, as your speed increases. For example, proving that 38 mph in a 35 mph zone was safe may not be very difficult. Indeed, it's precisely for this reason that some judges automatically dismiss tickets—and few officers bother giving them—for driving 5 mph or less over the speed limit.

"Proving" that it was perfectly safe to drive over the speed limit depends solely on testimony given by you and possibly others who were in the car with you. Remember to address the following facts:

- **Weather:** It will count in your favor if you were driving during the *daytime* and there was no fog or rain, nor a cloud in the sky.

- **Visibility:** If you were driving on a straight stretch of road with very few or no visual blocks such as trees, parked cars, and curves, you can use these facts to help establish that it was safe for you to go over the posted speed limit.

- **Neighborhood:** It helps if there were no side streets from which cars might have suddenly appeared or residential areas where children could have run out into the street.

- **Traffic:** This is one that might work in your favor either way. If there was a lot of traffic and everyone was going about the same speed (and over the speed limit), you could argue that you might have endangered yourself and others by slowing down the flow of traffic. In fact, you might be able to argue that, had you driven more slowly, you would have been illegally impeding traffic. (As discussed in Chapter 5, this defense would be particularly effective if traffic was too heavy to allow you to get into the slow lane, or if you were on a two-lane road with a line of cars behind you and no place to turn out.) Also, if there was a lot of traffic, and radar was used, you may be able to successfully argue that the officer's radar unit was focused on another vehicle instead of yours. If there was little or no traffic on the road, and the posted speed limit was designed with average traffic flow in mind, you might be able to justify going 5 to 10 mph over the limit.

- **Road Width:** There are some roads designed for safe driving at 35 to 45 mph, but on which for some reason (usually pressure on local city councils from nearby residents), the speed limit is a ridiculous 25 or 30 mph. When you've been caught for speeding on such roads, there are two things working in your favor: First, your testimony as to the very large road width, along with other

testimony regarding weather, visibility, and traffic, may convince a judge that you were driving safely, even though over the posted limit. Second, as discussed above, if radar was used, it may have been used illegally.

Speeding on Bridges, Tunnels, and Overpasses (VC § 22405)

VC § 22405(a). No person shall drive a vehicle on any bridge, elevated structure, tube, or tunnel constituting a part of a highway, at a speed that is greater than the maximum speed that can be maintained with safety to such structure.

VC § 22405(b). Upon the trial of any person charged with a violation of this section ... proof of the determination of the maximum speed by the Department of Transportation or local authority and the erection and maintenance of the speed signs shall constitute prima facie evidence of the maximum speed that can be maintained with safety to the bridge, elevated structure, tube, or tunnel.

Once in a while, a ticket will be given for driving over the speed limit posted on a bridge, freeway overpass, or tunnel. This violation is similar to the Basic Speed Law in that it forbids driving faster than a "speed that can be maintained with safety." Again, the posted speed limit isn't absolute; any speed over it is only *presumed* to be unsafe, and this presumption can be rebutted. Therefore, everything we said about arguing that your speed was safe under the circumstances with respect to the Basic Speed Law applies here too. However, the police may use radar even though an engineering and traffic survey hasn't been made, though they almost never do—it's too dangerous to use while parked on bridges, tunnels, and overpasses.

Exceeding Maximum Speed Limits—55 to 70 mph (VC §§ 22349, 22356)

VC § 22349(a). Except as provided in Section 22356 (which allows the California Department of Transportation to fix 70 mph limits on certain freeways), no person shall drive a vehicle upon a highway at a speed greater than 65 miles per hour.

VC § 22349(b). … no person shall drive a vehicle upon a two-lane undivided highway at a speed greater than 55 miles per hour unless that highway … has been posted for a higher speed ….

The "maximum speed limit" used to mean that you could drive at 65 mph on roads for which the speed is not legally defined or posted. These days, however, the law is a little less clear. It is a violation of VC § 22349—the "Maximum Speed Law"—to do any of the following:

- drive over 70 mph on a freeway posted for that speed limit

- drive over 65 mph on a freeway (not posted at 70 mph) or on any other highway, or

- drive over 55 mph on a two-lane undivided highway (even if the speed limit isn't posted), unless the road is posted for a higher speed limit.

Basic Speed Law Defenses Are Not Available

Under this statute, the prosecution need only prove you were going faster than 65 mph, or 70 mph if posted on certain freeways in rural areas, or that you exceeded 55 mph and there was only one lane in each direction with no median or barrier. The relative safety of your speed under the circumstances is beside the point and the Basic Speed Law defense covered above cannot be used.

Common radar defenses will often be of no use under the maximum speed law, for two reasons. First, the "radar speed trap" defense usually does not apply to violations of this statute. Second, most tickets for maximum speed law violations are commonly given by the Highway Patrol on freeways, and the Highway Patrol relies more on pacing or aircraft than radar. (The speed trap laws set out in VC §§ 40802–40805 seem to apply only to violations of the Basic Speed Law (VC § 22350) under some circumstances, and not to the maximum-speed law (VC § 22349). Even so, the cases of *People v. Flaxman* (1977) 74 Cal.App.3d Supp. 16, and *People v. DiFiore* (1987) 197 Cal.App.3d Supp. 26, say the speed trap rules do apply if you are charged with violating the Basic Speed Law (VC § 22350)—even if your speed was over 65. These cases are binding only in Los Angeles County, but are followed by many other courts. An Orange County appellate court ruled the same way in *People v. Studley* (1996) Cal. App.4th Supp. 52 Cal.Rptr.2d 461.

Don't think that you cannot fight the ticket, however. Several means are still available: The officer may not show up for trial (see Chapter 12), or you may be able to establish enough doubt about your speed because the officer was measuring it while gaining on you from behind.

Defense Against Aircraft Patrol Sighting

If your ticket was based on a reading from an aircraft patrol, there are several ways you may be able to challenge it. Increasingly, drivers on California highways are receiving their tickets from a CHP unit that has been alerted to your speed by radio reports from airplanes. The aircraft is supposed to pace the car and measure the speed according to the time it takes the aircraft to pass between two markers on the highway set a mile apart. However, sometimes the aircraft measures the speed by the time it takes the car to pass between these markers. Either way, if a car is found to be speeding, a waiting ground patrol car is radioed. It, in turn, will either independently check your speed by pacing you, or will pull you over solely on the basis of the aircraft report.

If the ground patrol car did not independently verify your speed, your chances of successfully fighting this ticket are increased. Why? Both the aircraft officer and ground officer will have to be present—the aircraft officer to testify about your speed, *and* the ground officer to testify that you were the driver. If the ground officer fails to appear in court, prosecutors cannot prove their case because they must prove you were the driver. You do not have to admit you were driving. Thus, if either officer fails to appear, you can ask the court to dismiss the case. If you are asked to allow an absent officer's police report or other written record into court in place of live testimony, you have a right under the hearsay rule to refuse and insist that the case be dismissed if the officer is not personally present.

Even if both officers show up, it is possible for you to win. First, ask the judge to exclude one officer from the courtroom while the other is testifying. This will help prevent them from taking cues from each other. The aircraft officer will usually be the first to take the stand. He or she will testify that the car's speed was computed either from the speed of the aircraft passing through the marks, or from the speed of the car passing through the marks. In the first case, there is plenty of room for error (such as angle of flight, shortcut straight flight path along curving highway, inconsistent distance while pacing, and inaccuracy in ascertaining reference points from the air). In the second

situation, they have used a "speed trap," illegal under VC § 40802(a). (See *People v. Darby* (1979) 95 Cal.App.3d 707, 157 Cal.Rptr. 300.)

After testifying about how the speed was computed, the aircraft officer will next tell about radioing the ground unit. Here it is possible that he got the wrong car. License plate numbers are too small for the airborne officer to see, and many modern cars tend to look alike from above. Also, aircraft officers relay information on several cars at the same time, raising the possibility that the ground officer might confuse the report. If the ground-unit officer is excluded from the courtroom, and takes with him the copy of the ticket—which he, not the aircraft officer, issued—the aircraft officer won't be able to use the ticket to "refresh his memory" while testifying. In this situation, it isn't difficult to get the aircraft officer to admit, on cross-examination, that he can't remember details of particular cars he observed from the air.

The aircraft officer typically records the time, speed, vehicle color, and make, along with brief notes on each car, on an "observation log." You have the right to request a copy of this before trial by way of an "Informal Discovery Request." (See Chapter 10.) This log may show that the spotter was pacing more than one car at the same time, with hard-to-believe identical speeds for each. You may also see that the "pacing" occurred over less than a minute, or even that your car was described as being a different make or color than it really is. Obviously, tidbits like these are quite useful for casting doubt on the reliability of the pacer's observations.

If the ground officer testifies that he independently checked your speed, you can argue that he was prejudiced by the radio report and too eagerly bore down on you at a high speed—hence *his* high speedometer reading.

All About Radar

The majority of moving violations are given for speed violations. Since many involve the use of radar, it makes sense to examine how radar works, how it is used, how it malfunctions, and even how dishonest cops can put false readings on radar equipment.

It can be an uphill battle trying to convince judges (and most other people with little or no scientific training) that sophisticated electronic gadgetry is *not* infallible and *not* always superior to human observation. Nevertheless, after you've read this section, you'll know more about radar than most police officers and judges, and may be able to use that advantage in court. Tickets based on radar readings can be beaten.

How It Works

The word "radar" is an acronym for "radio detection and ranging." In simple terms, radar uses the rate at which radio waves are reflected off a moving object to determine its speed. With police radar, that moving object is your car. In more specific terms, radar units have a "transmitter" to generate radio waves and a receiver to amplify the reflected waves (make them stronger) and analyze them. The analysis is then reflected in a speed readout device.

Radar uses waves similar to those involved in AM and FM radio transmissions, but with a higher frequency (that is, more waves within a given period of time). Although it may seem mind-boggling, the frequency of the radio waves you pick up on an AM radio is about one million per second. FM involves 100 million cycles a second. UHF television waves use frequencies of approximately one billion cycles per second. By comparison, radar uses frequencies up to 24 billion per second.

Why so high? Because the higher the frequency, the straighter the beam and the truer the reflection. Ordinary radio frequencies can't be used for radar, and only such higher frequencies give radar its accuracy. As we discuss below, the primary defenses to speeding tickets based on radar involve attacking this accuracy.

To best understand radar it will be helpful for you to journey back to your childhood and imagine yourself with a new peashooter. You are standing behind a motionless car with a regular peashooter. You can't shoot a few billion peas per second, but you can shoot one every second without much trouble. If you bounce the peas off the back window at the rate of one each second, they will come bouncing back to you (if you blow hard enough), one at a time, at the same rate of one every second. It will take each pea a little time to make the trip from your peashooter to the car and back to you, and assuming you blow with the same force each time, it will take the same amount of time for each pea. This will allow you to say to yourself, for reasons you'll better understand in a minute, "Because there's no difference between the rate at which the peas are leaving the peashooter and the rate at which they're coming back—the car is standing still."

Now, let's say the car is moving forward at a very slow 2 mph (about three feet per second). That means that before the second pea hits, the car will have moved forward about three feet from the spot where the first one hit. So the second pea will have to travel three more feet to the car than did the first pea, *plus* three feet on the rebound. That's six feet altogether. If the peas are traveling at, say 12 feet per second, it will take that second pea an extra half second to travel that extra six feet. What this means is that instead of the second pea coming back to you one second after the first pea, it will come back

1½ seconds later. Assuming the car continued to move slowly forward, the third pea will come back 1½ seconds later than the second pea, and so on, even though you're still shooting one each second. Similarly, if the car were doing 4 mph instead of 2 mph, the peas would come back every two seconds, even though you were shooting one every second. If you didn't know how fast the car was going, you could calculate it by comparing the time it took for each pea to come back (1½ seconds for 2 mph, two seconds for 4 mph) with the time it took to shoot each one (one second). In this example, the car's speed in miles per hour would equal four times the difference between the number of seconds between peas coming back and the number of seconds between peas being shot.

What does all of this have to do with police radar? Think of a police radar transmitter as an extremely fast repeating peashooter sending out tiny balls of energy (instead of peas) at the rate of several billion per second.

A modern radar device is composed of (1) a transmitter whose frequency is set at 10.525 ("X-band") or 24.150 ("K-band") billion cycles (or little bouncing balls of energy) per second, (2) an antenna to both transmit the impulse and receive the reflected impulses, and (3) a special receiver.

The receiver measures the transmitter frequency and the very-slightly-different frequency of the bounced waves reflected back from the target vehicle. It then electronically subtracts the second from the first to get the difference in frequencies. An electric current representing this frequency difference is converted into miles per hour and appears on a meter or digital readout. The greater the difference between the transmitted and reflected waves, the greater the relative speed or *difference* of speed between the target vehicle and the police car. If the police car is not moving while clocking you, your speed is obtained by multiplying the difference in frequencies by a number dependent upon whether the X-band or K-band is used. The X-band frequency difference is 31.4 cycles per second for every mile per hour of speed, and the K-band difference is 72 cycles per second for each mile per hour.

Almost all car-mounted police radar sets can be used while the police car is moving. But moving radar presents a whole new set of technical problems. One major problem is the need to calibrate the "relative" speed detector (used on the target vehicle) and the "absolute" speed detector, which calculates the speed of the patrol car.

One final point: although radar signals can be bounced off stationary or moving objects, they cannot be bent over hills or around curves. In order for a cop to clock your speed with radar, the radar signals must travel in a straight line from her car to yours and back, or, in other words, you must be in her "line-of-sight." This doesn't necessarily mean you will always be able to see the radar unit ahead of you in time to slow down, however. Either the radar-equipped police vehicle will be hidden behind roadside shrubbery through which radar beams can easily pass, behind a parked car with just the radar sticking out, or, by the time you do see the radar unit, the officer will already have clocked your speed.

Many people are so awe-inspired by any sort of electronic wizardry that when they see a "Speed Checked by Radar" sign they tend to imagine something out of *Star Wars*. Some people even believe that somehow they are under constant police surveillance from some central control panel similar to that in an air traffic control tower. This is not possible. Radar beams travel in straight lines, and in police radar, that straight line has to be more or less in the same direction as you travel. Thus police radar can only clock the speed of a vehicle at which the antenna is pointed.

Types of Equipment

The use of radar for determining automobile speed started in the early 1950s with huge, but delicate and awkward, vacuum tube circuitry operable only by skilled technicians. The radar unit was so bulky and unstable, in fact, that there had to be a separate chase vehicle to pull the speeder over. With the advent of transistors in the late 50s and early 60s, integrated circuits in the late 60s, and compact microchips in the 70s and 80s, radar units became highly compact, durable, and even relatively inexpensive. But they are not necessarily any more accurate than the early models. Modern technology hasn't changed the basic problem with police radar—the radar beams unavoidably diverge (spread out) with distance and can track objects other than those at which they're aimed.

Although dozens of types of radar units can be purchased with your tax dollars, with prices ranging from $300 to $3,000 per unit, there are essentially three types of units in common use: car-mounted stationary radar, hand-held stationary radar "guns," and car-mounted "moving" radar.

Car-Mounted Stationary Radar

This type of radar device is currently the most common type used in patrol cars. The radar antenna is shaped something like a side-mounted spotlight without the glass reflector on the front. If you're really sharp-eyed and know what to look for, you can see it sticking out a little from a line of parked cars; it's usually mounted on the rear left window of the police car and faces toward the rear. Often an officer finds a nice tight parking spot in front of another vehicle, and sticks the antenna out past that vehicle in order to track the speed of moving traffic.

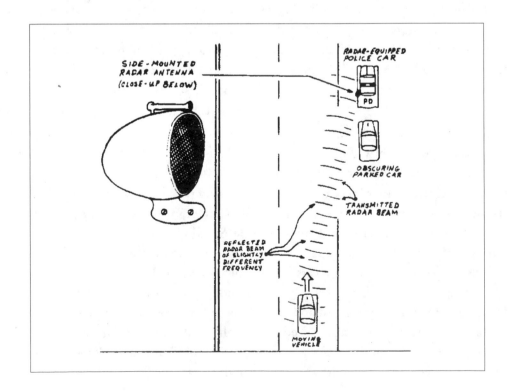

Sometimes the radar antenna will be placed inside the police car so that the beam travels through the rear window. But this has the disadvantage of not allowing the officer to park in front of a vehicle that hides his car, as the rear window must face the traffic flow without obstruction by stationary vehicles.

Once an officer gets set up and clocks your speed, he reads that speed on a little console about the size of a CB radio, which is either mounted under the dashboard or resting on top. On older models, the console has a meter that indicates the speed of the vehicle. This type of unit is equipped with a "hold" switch to keep the needle at the highest-read speed during the pass.

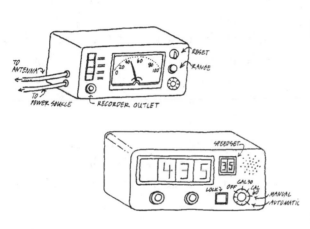

Later console units have a digital readout that will display the highest speed read during the second or two the target vehicle passes through the beam. This means that once your speed is recorded, slowing down does no good at all, and hitting the brakes only lights your stoplights and causes the front of your car to dip (front brakes grab hold better than rear brakes), so as to tell the officer that you knew darn well you were speeding.

These units also have a "speed set" switch that is set to the speed at which the officer has decided a ticket is appropriate. This allows the officer to direct his attention elsewhere while your car travels through the beam. If the speed reading exceeds the "speed set" value, a sound alarm goes off. The officer looks at the readout, then at your car, and takes off after you.

A Typical Radar Gun

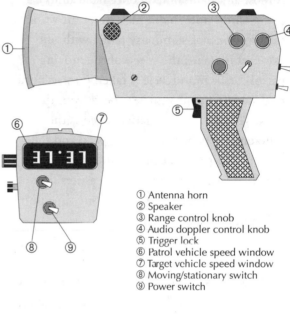

① Antenna horn
② Speaker
③ Range control knob
④ Audio doppler control knob
⑤ Trigger lock
⑥ Patrol vehicle speed window
⑦ Target vehicle speed window
⑧ Moving/stationary switch
⑨ Power switch

Hand-Held Radar

Hand-held "radar guns" are rapidly gaining in popularity, particularly among motorcycle officers. A "radar gun" is simply a gun-shaped plastic molding in which the transmitter, receiver, and antenna are all mounted. The antenna is mounted at the front of the gun, and a digital speed readout, as well as the controls, are mounted on the back. The designers even included a trigger switch so as to activate the radar beam only when needed, namely when the officer sees a car that appears to be traveling fast enough to spark his interest.

Note: The intermittent operation afforded by the trigger also tends to foil radar detectors and minimizes radar officers' worries about possible health hazards involved in the repeated day-to-day operation at close range.

Radar guns generally have a cable of wires leading either directly to the police vehicle's 12-volt power supply, or possibly even into the car's cigarette lighter outlet.

Moving Mode

Almost all car-mounted police radar units can operate in a "moving mode." The unit works the same way as stationary radar, with one extra refinement: the speed of the moving patrol car or motorcycle is taken into account to determine your vehicle's speed from the "relative" speed. The relative speed is the difference between your car's speed and the officer's. This is what the radar unit actually measures. This kind of radar measures the speed of traffic coming from the opposite direction or going in the same direction.

EXAMPLE 1:

Two cars are going in opposite directions on a two-lane road—one is a police car going north at 50 mph, and the other is going south at 45 mph. The relative speed is 95 mph because the two speeds are added to get the relative speed. This means that a radar unit in the 50-mph patrol car with its beam pointed at the 45 mph car will receive a reflected radar signal indicating a 95 mph relative speed. After the police vehicle's 50 mph speed is subtracted from this relative speed, your *actual* speed of 45 mph is obtained.

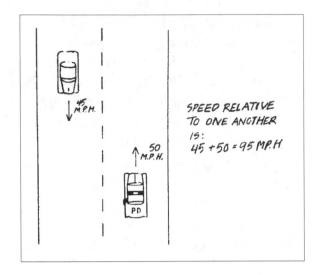

EXAMPLE 2:

Just ahead of the 50 mph radar-equipped patrol car is a truck doing 70 mph. The relative speed between the two vehicles is 20 mph, which the radar unit detects and adds to the patrol car's 50 mph speed. The result is a reading showing that the truck ahead is doing 70 mph.

One further note—many hand-held radar guns have the moving radar option, but almost all of them are operated from a fixed or stationary position.

Qualifications for Radar Use

Unlike the old days when police radar units had to be operated by skilled technicians, today's units can be operated by nearly anyone. Officers using radar do not have to hold any kind of certificate or license, but the agency employing them has to be licensed by the Federal Communications Commission. The license will specify the number of units in operation and the authorized frequencies. Most law enforcement agencies are licensed, but often they'll buy more units than authorized without updating their license. In addition, sometimes they'll only be licensed for the older X-band, but buy new K-band equipment. Even so, this sort of violation of federal regulations does not affect the validity of any speed law prosecutions in which the offending equipment was used.

If you're charged with violating a "prima facie" speed limit, the officer used radar or laser, and the engineering and traffic survey justifying the speed limit is more than five years old, but less than seven years old, the officer must testify as follows:

- he completed 24 hours of radar training, or two hours of laser training through a Peace Officer Standards and Training (POST) course
- the radar or laser device exceeded the standards of the National Highway Traffic Safety Administration (NHTSA)
- the device was calibrated within the last three years by a certified independent testing laboratory, and
- your speed was unsafe for conditions.

A survey up to ten years old is legal if all the above conditions are met and the prosecution shows an engineer has certified that there have been "no significant changes" in roadway use or traffic patterns.

In the absence of such testimony for a survey over five years old, you have a "speed trap" defense.

Malfunctions and Inaccuracies

Contrary to police department propaganda, the latest technology has *not* completely ironed out problems known to cause malfunctions and interferences on radar units. Most malfunctions result from the radar's operation in "real world" conditions, which are less than ideal. As you will see, you'll need a clear recollection of the traffic and weather conditions existing at the time you were stopped to successfully argue that the radar might have malfunctioned in your case.

While it's certainly true that radar units of the 50s and 60s suffered from more calibration and accuracy problems than do the units of today, there is absolutely no way, technologically or otherwise, to remove all sources of interference and inaccuracy in order to get the "perfect" radar unit. The necessity of human interaction with such a device also leaves plenty of room for error. Modern computers may be nearly infallible, but the people who program and feed data to them are not. The same goes for the police officer operating the radar unit. Following is a description of common malfunctions and sources of inaccurate readings.

More Than One Target

Police radar transmitters do not transmit a tight, narrow, laser-like beam that can be precisely aimed at a particular vehicle. Instead, radar beams are much like flashlight beams— the further the beam travels, the more it diverges—or spreads out. The more it diverges, the more likely it will hit more than one moving object, such as a vehicle in an adjacent lane. The typical beam angle or spread is 12 to 16 degrees, or about 1/25th of a full circle.

The result is that the beam will have a width of one foot for every four feet of distance from the radar antenna. The beam width will be two lanes wide (about 40 feet), only 160 feet distant from the radar antenna. Thus, if you're in one lane and a faster vehicle is in another, the other vehicle will contribute to a high reading on the officer's radar unit, yet he may mistakenly attribute it to you. The mistaken reading of another vehicle (and attributing its speed to you) is especially likely to occur if the other vehicle is larger than yours. In fact, the vehicle contributing to the officer's high radar reading needn't even be in another lane; if a larger vehicle, such as a truck, is rapidly coming up from behind you in your lane, the officer could see your car, but his radar could be reading the truck's speed. Inability of the equipment to distinguish between two separate objects is called lack of "resolution."

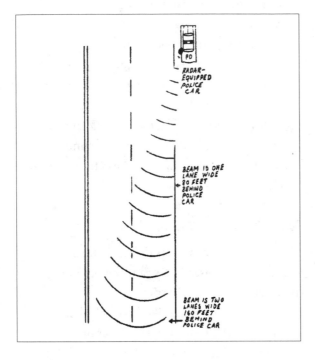

At a distance of a mere one-eighth mile, the radar beam will be four lanes wide, which means that the officer may well be reading the speed of cars on the other side of the road while trying to read yours as you're coming up behind him. In a situation where the officer merely puts the radar unit on automatic and waits for a buzzer to sound, and hasn't aimed at a specific vehicle, this inaccuracy in resolution can be very important.

Wind, Rain, and Storms

Although metal surfaces reflect radar beams better than most surfaces, pretty much anything will reflect radar waves, at least to some extent. On windy days, windblown dust or tree leaves can be "read." These spurious readings can be attributed to you. You may have read the

newspaper story about the state legislator who pointed a hand-held radar gun at a tree and "clocked" it at 70 mph!

Windblown rain will even reflect enough energy so as to give false signals, particularly if the wind is strong enough to blow the rain at a substantial angle to the ground. The more rain or wind blowing it, the more likely an erroneous radar reading.

It may also be possible for prethunderstorm atmospheric electrical charges to interfere with a radar unit. Electrically charged storm clouds are great radar reflectors and can reflect a signal back to the radar unit even though the storm clouds are high up in the sky. This is possible because the beam increases in width farther away from the radar unit's antenna. (It gets larger vertically as well as horizontally.) If such a storm cloud is being blown by the wind at sufficient speed, a false radar reading may result. One New Mexico justice court speeding case was dismissed when testimony showed that a high radar speed reading was obtained immediately prior to a thunderstorm.

If you're serious about trying to point out all the perils and pitfalls of radar readings when you get to trial, you may want to subpoena the instruction manual that comes with the radar unit that was used to clock your speed. (See Chapter 11.) The manufacturer will usually include a page or two on inaccurate readings and how to avoid them. This gives you a chance to point to this page and say, "Look, Your Honor, even the manufacturer, who is no doubt optimistic about his product, states that radar readings can be wrong in cases similar to this one." Police departments have been known to tear this page out before sending a subpoenaed manual, so be warned.

Calibration Problems

Every scientific instrument used for measuring a physical quantity needs to be "calibrated" to check its accuracy. (The Connecticut case of *State v. Tomanelli* (1965) 216 A.2d 625 indicates that certified tuning forks are the only scientifically acceptable method of calibration.) Radar equipment is no exception. This means that the radar equipment must be checked for accuracy against an object traveling at a known (not radar-determined) speed. If the speed on the radar equipment matches the known speed, the unit is properly calibrated. In practice, radar officers use a tuning fork as their moving object. While this may seem a far cry from a moving car, the use of a tuning fork is scientifically sound; tuning forks, when struck against a hard object, vibrate at a certain frequency (which we hear as an audible tone). Each fork has not only a unique frequency, but also a unique back-and-forth speed of vibration, this speed corresponding to a particular radar-determined speed.

Tuning forks are supplied by the manufacturer of the radar equipment and "certified" to correspond to the speed printed on the fork. According to most operations manuals, the radar unit should be calibrated with the tuning forks before each and every working shift and also before and after each violation. Ideally, several tuning forks of different speeds should be used to check the radar unit's accuracy over a given range.

Note: Tuning forks can easily become inaccurate unless they're kept in a little box and protected from mechanical damage; a good scratch or drop of a few feet can render one inaccurate.

As you might have figured, it's probably too much trouble for most officers to repeatedly open the boxes, remove the metal forks, strike them, hold them in front of the radar unit, and then return them to their boxes before and after each of the many violations they process every day. Most officers therefore do not calibrate their units with any regularity.

But if you go watch a few traffic court trials, you'll notice that quite a few officers swear they calibrated the radar unit immediately prior to and after the violation. Here's the catch. While often not an outright lie, this small oath usually means that the officer flicked on a "calibrate" or "test" switch built into the radar unit itself, read the proper calibrate reading, and switched it back to regular operation. It almost never means that the officer used a tuning fork. There's a big difference and it may be important to you.

The calibrate or test switch merely causes an internal frequency-setting device (called a "crystal") to generate a signal. The crystal's pulses are counted according to a preset ratio of pulses counted to pulses generated. The number of pulses counted in a certain period is indicated on the readout, and this number is supposed to correlate with a certain predetermined speed. But here's the problem with this sort of testing. There is a frequency circuit as well as a counting circuit, and only the counting circuit is tested in the so-called "calibrate" mode. This means that if the counting circuit is okay but the frequency circuit is off, the unit will be inaccurate, but this defect will not be detected by the officer. In other words, the accuracy of the unit will be affected, since frequency differences are indicative of a certain speed.

The fact that this limited test is mislabeled a "calibrate" test by most manufacturers misleads many officers into thinking that it's a substitute for a test with a certified tuning fork. It isn't— and thus it's extremely important in any traffic trial involving the use of radar to cross-examine the officer and see whether he really did use a tuning fork. Don't dwell on this, just in case he claims he did. If he says he didn't, then it's time to belabor the point. If you were able to ask the officer some of the questions listed in Chapter 17 when he stopped you on the road, you will be better prepared for trial.

Electrical Interference

This type of interference is pretty rare, but it's worth mentioning. Occasionally a passing motorist's CB transmitter will generate "harmonics" that interfere with the radar unit and cause a false reading. A harmonic is a numerical multiple of a basic signal frequency at which a transmitter is transmitting.

CB rigs utilize basic radio frequencies of about 27 million cycles per second. The second harmonic has a frequency of 54 million cycles, the third a frequency of 81 million cycles, and so forth. Although each successive harmonic frequency signal gets progressively weaker the higher the harmonic, poorly electrically filtered CB rigs are capable of generating 400th and higher harmonics to interfere with X-band, and 900th and higher harmonics to interfere with K-band radar. But this requires an unusual set of conditions—namely a poorly electrically filtered CB transmitter and a poorly filtered radar receiver unit. The more recent car-mounted radar units are fairly well filtered. Radar guns are not as well filtered and are therefore slightly more susceptible to such interference.

It also requires that the passing vehicle's CB rig be transmitting (not merely receiving) while passing near the radar unit. The kind of reading such interference would cause is hard to say. It could either be higher or lower, depending on the harmonic frequency of the interference.

False "Ground Speed" Reading in "Moving Mode"

As we said earlier, a radar unit used while the patrol car is moving must take into account both (1) the speed of an oncoming vehicle *relative* to the patrol car, and (2) the speed of the patrol car *relative* to the ground. If the patrol car's speed is 50 mph, the speed of an oncoming 45 mph car relative to the patrol car is 50 + 45, or 95 mph. In the radar unit, this value gets converted back to the 45 mph reading by electronically subtracting the patrol car's 50 mph speed.

This means that the moving radar unit can incorrectly attribute an erroneously high speed to the oncoming vehicle either (1) by measuring too high a relative speed for the oncoming car, or (2) by measuring too low a speed for the patrol car. This latter speed is determined by a patrol car-mounted radar unit pointed at the ground. Once in a while, however, the portion of the radar unit that is supposed to measure the speed or the ground whizzing by will instead measure the speed of a passing truck.

EXAMPLE:

If a patrol car is doing 53 mph in the right-hand lane of a four-lane divided highway, and a truck is slowly passing it in the left lane, doing 55 mph, the ground reading unit that improperly locks onto the truck will read a difference or relative speed of 2 mph. The electronics of the radar unit will then subtract this incorrectly low value for the reading for the relative speed (105 mph) of an oncoming car (its own 55 mph plus the patrol car's 50 mph, for a total of 105 mph) so that its speed will be read as 105 – 2, or 103 mph, when it's only doing 55.

Aiming Angle of the Beam

Unless the officer is directly in front of or behind you, there is no way he can avoid aiming his radar beam at some angle to your direction of travel. He will then be reading, depending on the angle, some "component" or fraction of your speed. For a 45-degree angle between the beam and your vehicle, he will read only 71% of your actual speed. Unfortunately, this error can only work against you. Since the radar unit's reading will be lower than your actual speed, exposing this error will only tend to prove that you were really going faster than the radar reading.

Someone Else's Speed

If the officer who pulls you over shows you a reading very different from what you thought your speed was, it may not really have been your speed, but someone else's. As we explained earlier in this chapter, the farther away your car is from a radar beam, the more likely that beam will intercept a nearby vehicle, especially one that is larger than yours. If this larger vehicle is moving faster than your vehicle, you might well be cited for its speed, the officer being unaware of the error.

On streets where traffic naturally flows at a speed over the limit, some especially zealous officers will take a reading on a "lead" vehicle and then pull over not only that vehicle, but also one or two others following behind. (Officers can, and do, single-handedly pull over several cars at once.) Then he'll use the reading for the lead vehicle as the speed for everyone else. He may even be up front about it, saying that he saw the vehicles behind following at the same speed (with no change in bumper-

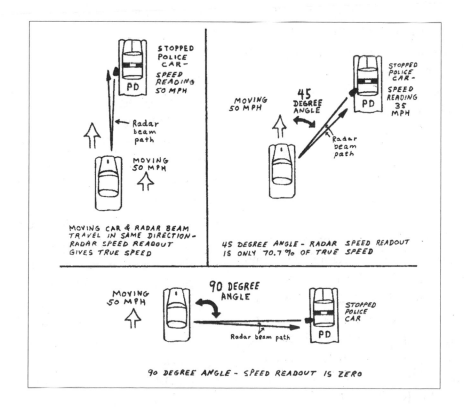

to-bumper distances), or that when the second and/or third cars passed, there was no change in the reading. This is all pretty shaky evidence. The officer would have had to note the lead car's reading while very carefully looking at the other cars. If the driver of the second car can truthfully testify as to how the lead car was going faster and increasing the distance, it should help in court.

Conversely, an officer might have inadvertently locked onto a higher reading of a second or third vehicle gaining on the one(s) in front and improperly attributed the speed to those in front. The larger the second or third gaining vehicles, the more likely this will occur. It may help the driver of the lead car if he or she can truthfully testify to seeing (in the rear or side mirror) the second vehicle quickly gaining from behind and suggest that the radar reading was really for that vehicle.

The most dishonest tactic, of course, is simply to obtain a high speed reading and show that same reading to every driver cited. If you suspect this (it's pretty rare but it has happened), you should go to the police station the next day and ask to see all the tickets the officer wrote that day. If all the tickets before and after yours show the same speed, you should either get photocopies or subpoena the tickets and bring out this interesting coincidence in court.

Radar Detectors

No chapter on radar would be complete without a few words on the technological ways of beating it, primarily with a radar detector. Usually this is a little black box you clip to your sun visor or put on your dashboard and plug into your cigarette lighter outlet. It is nothing more than a very sensitive radio receiver for signals in the radar frequency range. Instead of powering a loudspeaker, though, this type

of radio circuit trips a little relay when a radar signal is received. The relay then activates a buzzer or light to warn that your speed is being monitored. Many of the commercially available detectors have a sensitivity control that can be adjusted to give the best compromise between detecting faint, far-away signals and rejecting interfering off-frequency signals that come from sources other than police radar.

They're Legal

Radar detectors are perfectly legal. Although a few places, most notably Virginia and the District of Columbia, have experimented with laws making it illegal to drive a radar detector–equipped vehicle, California has no such law.

Therefore, you needn't worry about trying to hide your radar detector. In fact, with the exception of the specially designed "remote" units whose sensor is mounted under the hood, you should not hide it because the placement of a radar detector anywhere other than near the front windshield will shield it from incoming signals.

Problems

Folks who equip their cars with radar detectors are often lulled into believing they will never be caught for speeding. But radar detectors are not foolproof. Some will fail to give warning, and others will not give it in time. Here are a few reasons why:

- Many police radar units, and all hand-held radar guns, have push-button switches that allow the radar beam to be switched on and off at will. So instead of transmitting a steady, constant beam that can be picked up by a detector, the officer simply waits for an obviously speeding car, then activates the beam. A good radar detector will then warn the driver, but it will be too late to slow down before the officer takes his reading.

- Some radar detectors are not sensitive to all police radar frequencies. As mentioned earlier, police radar utilizes both the X-band and the newer K-band, but some of the cheaper or older "single-channel" detectors will only detect X-band signals. The newer "dual channel" (also called "stereodyne" or "heterodyne") and the scanning-type detectors—which scan back and forth between the X and K bands—are sensitive to both frequencies.

- The more sensitive detectors, particularly the scanning-type units, even though tuned or containing electronic filters, can give "false alarms" due to nearby strong signals from airport radar, telephone microwave links, and TV transmitters. As with "the boy who called wolf," enough false alarms will result in ignoring a real alarm.

- It is possible (though a violation of federal law) for police technicians to use a radar unit so that it operates off-frequency and goes undetected by properly tuned detectors. The practice has apparently become frequent enough for the Federal Communications Commission to issue a public warning noting the practice is illegal and could "cause interference to other licensed and important users of the [radio frequency] spectrum." (FCC Public Notice No. 1517, 1/15/87.) The scanning-type detectors, however, will still detect tampered radar units.

- Some of the cheaper units have a limited range. This means that by the time you're close enough to a radar unit for the light or buzzer to come on, you may be within the officer's range and your speed already determined. If there's another vehicle ahead of you, you're probably safe. But if your car is the "lead" car, you may get cited. The better radar detectors, of course, have a range such that they "see" the radar beam before the beam "sees" the car they're in. But even with these, an officer's cunning use of road features, such as bends in the road and crests of hills, may prevent detection of her beam until it's too late.

Other Devices

Finally, a few words about the supposed methods of beating radar. First and foremost, the long-held belief that you can "jam" police radar by putting balls of tin foil in your hubcaps or "chaff" in or on other places of your car is quite simply a myth. The only way to jam police radar is to utilize your own radar transmitter to broadcast signals of specific frequencies strong enough to override the reflected signal the officer reads, so as to produce a false reading on his equipment. This is expensive, impractical, technologically tricky, and illegal.

It would be nice if your car simply absorbed the officer's radar waves and reflected nothing back. A few people have actually spent hundreds of dollars to have their cars painted with an effective, but expensive, radar-absorbing paint called "Echo-sorb." Unfortunately, all metal surfaces—chrome, bumper, and grill included—have to be covered to be completely effective. This, of course, is not likely to win any beauty awards for your car.

"Laser" Detectors

"Laser detectors" are the most recent addition to the traffic cop's arsenal of speed-measuring devices. Built to look and act like a hand-held radar gun, a laser detector uses a low-powered beam of laser light that bounces off the targeted vehicle and returns to a receiver in the unit, whose electronics calculate the speed of the targeted vehicle. Laser detectors are supposedly more accurate than radar units.

One advantage of laser guns over radar is that a laser beam is narrower than a radar beam and can be more precisely aimed. This feature reduces (but does not eliminate) the chance that the speed of a nearby car will be measured, instead of the speed of the car at which the operator aims the gun. But even if the officer succeeds in holding the laser on a single car, there is room for error. Here's why.

Laser detectors measure distance (between the gun and the target car) using the speed of light and the time it takes the light, reflected off the target vehicle, to return. The detector makes about 40 of these distance measurements over a third of a second, then divides the light's round-trip distance by the time, to get the speed. To be accurate, the officer must hold the beam on the same part of the car during the test. However, it's impossible to make sure that the laser beam (which the officer can't see) continuously hits the same spot. When the beam moves from one spot on an oncoming car—like the windshield—to a nearer spot— like the front bumper a few feet ahead—it adds about four feet to the total distance during the one-third second measurement. Then, as far as the laser detector is concerned, the car appears to have traveled faster than it really has. In this case, the gun would read four feet per

one-third second, or 12 feet per second or 8 mph, too high. The basic problem here is that, unlike a radar unit which can be mounted atop a police cruiser's dashboard to measure speeds irrespective of the officer's steady hand, a laser gun must be perfectly aimed by the human operator in order to work properly. Thus, its measurement is highly subject to error.

Another problem with laser guns is that some laser detectors use more than one laser beam. A detector that uses three laser beams means that each strikes a slightly different part of the target vehicle. That's okay, but it's also possible (especially in heavy traffic) for one beam to hit the target car, and another beam to hit a nearby car. If the two cars are traveling at different speeds, the laser detector will read incorrectly.

Laser detectors have not won universal acceptance. As reported in the May 1997 *Car & Driver Magazine*, "Laser Loses a Legal Test," one New Jersey judge ruled laser so unreliable that the New Jersey State Police have taken heed and stopped using laser guns.

Speed trap note: If you've been cited in a speed trap and the officer used a laser detector, you can use all of the arguments regarding the definition of illegal speed traps. That's because VC § 40802(b) defines "speed trap" in terms of "the use of radar *or other electronic devices* that measure the speed of moving objects." This definition includes radar and laser speed detectors.

Other Moving Violations

While more citations are given for speeding than for any other single moving violation, a large number of tickets are given for nonspeeding violations. Like speeding violations, convictions for these other "moving" violations will wind up on your driving record. This chapter deals with the elements for each of the most common moving violations besides speeding.

Although space limitations don't allow us to list all moving violations here, we cover the most common ones for which people are cited. (Speeding is covered in Chapter 4.)

Not Stopping

This section covers failing to stop at stop signs and stoplights.

Going Through a Stop Sign (VC § 22450)

A common violation involves stop signs (Oh, those rolling stops!). Cops love to give tickets for this at quota time. The law simply says:

> **VC § 22450 (a).** The driver of any vehicle approaching a stop sign at the entrance to, or within, an intersection, or railroad grade crossing shall stop at a limit line, if marked, otherwise before entering the crosswalk on the near side of the intersection. If there is no limit line or crosswalk, the driver shall stop at the entrance to the intersecting roadway or railroad grade crossing.

The elements of this offense are *all* of the following:

1. You must drive a vehicle and approach a stop sign;

2. The stop sign must be at the entrance to or within an intersection or railroad grade crossing;

3. You must fail to come to a *complete stop* at:

- a limit line (a white stripe painted halfway across the street from the stop sign), if marked

- a crosswalk, if any, or

- the entrance to the intersection or railroad grade crossing if there was no marked limit line or crosswalk.

Occasionally, an officer will park on a cross street so that all she sees is the stop sign and limit line, and maybe a few feet of road in front of the line or sign. A conscientious driver might well come to a complete stop a few feet behind the line where the officer can't see; then, having already stopped as required, drive ahead into the intersection. If this happens to you, you should try to find out where the officer was parked. Later you can take pictures from that location to show just how limited the officer's view was.

It may happen that local conditions made the stop sign invisible—for example, leaves from adjacent trees covered or obscured your view of the sign until it was too late to stop. This too can be shown with photographic evidence, and establishes the defense that you were neither willful nor criminally negligent in driving through it.

One other good (if rare) defense applies to newly installed stop signs. It's all too easy to miss seeing a recently installed stop sign on a familiar road. In one case, a Monterey driver beat a ticket by admitting that he didn't see the stop sign but defending on the basis that it had been installed during his absence from the area for several months. The judge understood and found him not guilty.

Willfulness or carelessness is an implied essential element of every violation and a judge should find you not guilty if the stop sign wasn't visible until too late, or you didn't realize it had just been put there after being used to its absence.

People sometimes get a ticket because they stopped in front of the limit line or crosswalk, rather than behind. If this happens to you, perhaps you can truthfully testify that it hasn't been repainted for so long that it was unnoticeable. Here again, a picture is truly better than a thousand words.

Going Through a Stoplight (VC § 21453)

This is almost like going through a stop sign. The very similar law on stoplights reads:

> **VC § 21453(a).** A driver facing a steady circular red signal alone shall stop at a marked limit line, but if none, before entering the crosswalk on the near side of the intersection or, if none, then before entering the intersection, and shall remain stopped until an indication to proceed is shown.

Although the elements of this offense are pretty much the same as those for driving through a stop sign, more needs to be said about this one because stoplights have a nasty habit of changing from green to yellow to red before you know it.

It is not illegal to deliberately drive through a *yellow* light. VC § 21452(a) says that a yellow light means only that traffic facing the light is "warned" that a red light will soon follow. As long as the front of your vehicle *entered the intersection* or passed the crosswalk or limit line before the light turned red, you haven't broken the law. And unless the officer is sitting right at the intersection on the cross street and has a view unobstructed by other waiting vehicles, you're in a better position than he is to judge that.

Reminder: Never tell the officer who stops you that it was a really short yellow light. That comes pretty close to admitting that you did indeed enter the intersection when the light was red.

Improper Turning (VC §§ 22100–22106)

Since tickets are less frequently handed out for unsafe turning and related offenses, we'll briefly cover the possible infractions and offer a few pointers.

Note: As you read these sections remember that the term "highway," as used throughout the Vehicle Code, means *any* public road or street (VC § 360).

The Turn Itself

You can be cited for failing to make a proper turning movement, as the following (sub)sections describe.

Staying to the Right or Left Edge of the Road (VC § 22100)

This violation consists of failing to keep as close *as practicable* to the right or left edge of the road when respectively turning right or left, except at certain intersections when you're initially on a one-way street.

> **VC § 22100.** Except as provided in Section 22100.5 or 22101, the driver of a vehicle intending to turn upon a highway shall do so as follows:
>
> **(a) Right Turns.** Both the approach for a right-hand turn and a right-hand turn shall be made as close as practicable to the right-hand curb or edge of the roadway ... [except at certain unusual intersections].
>
> **(b) Left Turns.** The approach for a left turn shall be made as close as practicable to the left-hand edge of the extreme left-hand lane or portion of the roadway lawfully available to traffic moving in the direction of travel of such vehicle, and, when turning at an intersection, the left turn shall not be made before entering the intersection. After entering the intersection, the left turn shall be made so as to leave the intersection in a lane lawfully available to traffic

moving in such direction upon the roadway being entered ... [except at other unusual intersections].

Though you should read the entire code section if you're cited for this, a key element is usually the phrase "as close as practicable." Local conditions at the time (such as bike riders several feet out from the curb) may make "as practicable" pretty far away from the curb.

Turns Prohibited by Signs or Marked Lanes (VC § 22101)

VC § 22101(a). The Department of Transportation or local authorities, in respect to highways under their respective jurisdictions, may cause official traffic control devices to be placed or erected within or adjacent to intersections to regulate or prohibit turning movements at such intersections.

(b). When turning movements are required at an intersection, notice of such requirement shall be given by erection of a sign, unless an additional clearly-marked traffic lane is provided for the approach to the turning movement, in which event notice as applicable to such additional traffic lane shall be given by any official traffic control device.

(c). When right- or left-hand turns are prohibited at an intersection, notice of such prohibition shall be given by erection of a sign.

(d). When official traffic control devices are placed as required in subdivisions (b) or (c), it shall be unlawful for any driver of a vehicle to disobey the directions of such official traffic control devices.

This law forbids prohibited right, left, or other specified turns when "notice" of special turning requirements is given by either (1) a sign, or (2) a *clearly marked* traffic lane *plus* a traffic signal (that is, red or green arrows on a stoplight), which requires or forbids a certain type of turn. If you got a ticket at a particularly bad intersection where the sign or signal was difficult to see (for example, the sign was obscured by a pole or was not visible during darkness), then "notice" had not been given. The same is true if a right- or left-turn traffic lane is not "clearly marked." Photographs may help convince a judge.

Prohibited U-Turns (VC §§ 22100.5, 22102–22105)

There are three types of illegal U-turns. Let's look at each.

U-Turn in Business District (VC § 22102)

VC § 22102. No person in a business district shall make a U-turn, except at an intersection, or on a divided highway where an opening has been provided...

You can always make a U-turn at an intersection or opening in a divided highway unless a *visible* sign prohibits it. A "business district" is defined as a place where over 50% of the property fronting the street is "in use for business" along 300 feet of the highway—or 600 feet if the business area is only on one side (VC § 235). At intersections with stoplights, any U-turn must be made from the far-left lane (VC § 22100.5).

U-Turn in Residence District (VC § 22103)

VC § 22103. No person in a residence district shall make a U-turn when any other vehicle is approaching from either direction within 200 feet, except at an intersection when the approaching vehicle is controlled by an official traffic control device.

As we saw back in Chapter 2, the elements of this one are all of the following:

1. You were driving in a "residence district." This is where there are "dwelling houses" and "business structures" numbering at least 13 on one side of the road or 16 on both sides, over a quarter of a mile (VC § 515);

2. You made a full 180-degree or U-turn;

3. Another vehicle was *approaching* (not merely *stopped*) within 200 feet or less in front of or behind you;

4. You were not at an intersection controlled by an "official traffic control device" (sign or signal).

As stated earlier, you need only show *one* missing element to beat this one. The best way to do this is to raise doubt about whether another vehicle was *approaching* within the 200 feet or, if applicable, whether the area was a "residence district."

U-Turns in Nonresidential, Nonbusiness Districts (VC § 22105)

> **VC § 22105.** No person shall make a U-turn upon any highway where the driver of such vehicle does not have an unobstructed view for 200 feet in both directions along the highway...

This refers to areas of "highway" (that is, any street or road) that are neither residence nor business districts. You can make a legal U-turn across a double yellow line, provided you have 200 feet of unobstructed view (VC § 21460). It doesn't matter whether other vehicles are approaching within 200 feet, so long as you have an unobstructed view for that distance. If the officer claims the view was obstructed, it's up to him to prove that in court. He can use very precise testimony or pictures. The burden of proof is on him, not you. You cannot, however, cross two double yellow lines that are two or more feet apart or a highway divider strip.

Note: A U-turn does not include a left turn into a driveway, backing out, then driving off in the opposite direction. This is legal, according to the state Supreme Court. (See *People v. McGuire* (1978) 80 Cal.App.3d Supp. 1, 145 Cal.Rptr. 514.)

Unsafe Turns and Lane Changes

Two Vehicle Code sections deal with making unsafe turns or lane changes.

Pulling Onto a Road and Backing Up (VC § 22106)

> **VC § 22106.** No person shall start a vehicle stopped, standing, or parked on a highway, nor shall any person back a vehicle on a highway until such movement can be made with reasonable safety...

Unless your violation of this section caused an accident, this one is almost always worth fighting. Your own testimony as to the precautions you took prior to starting from a complete stop should raise a reasonable doubt that you proceeded without "reasonable safety."

Other Turns (VC § 22107)

> **VC § 22107.** No person shall turn a vehicle from a direct course or move right or left upon a roadway until such movement can be made with reasonable safety and then only after the giving of an appropriate signal in the manner provided in this chapter in the event any other vehicle may be affected by the movement.

The same sort of fuzzy and subjective aspects of "reasonable safety" mentioned just above apply here too. And remember that it's up to the officer or prosecutor to prove you proceeded *without* reasonable safety, not for you to disprove it. You do have the responsibility to rebut the officer's testimony on this point. (See Chapter 11 on preparing for trial.)

Signaling a Turn (VC §§ 22108, 22109, 22110)

> **VC § 22108.** Any signal of intention to turn right or left shall be given continuously during the last 100 feet traveled by the vehicle before turning.

VC § 22109. No person shall stop or suddenly decrease the speed of a vehicle on a highway without first giving an appropriate signal in the manner provided in this chapter to the driver of any vehicle immediately to the rear when there is opportunity to give the signal.

VC § 22110. The signals required by this chapter shall be given either by means of the hand and arm or by a signal lamp, but when the body or load on any vehicle or combination of vehicles projects 24 inches or more to the left of the center of the steering wheel so that a hand and arm signal would not be visible both to the front and rear of such vehicle or combination of vehicles, or under any condition when a hand and arm signal would not be visible both to the front and rear of the vehicle or vehicles, then the vehicle or vehicles shall be equipped with, and signals shall be given by, a signal lamp, except that implements of husbandry need not be equipped with signal lamps, but drivers of implements of husbandry shall give a hand and arm signal when required by this chapter.

Without going into too much detail, these jumbled sections taken together say you have to give the proper turn signal "continuously during the last 100 feet traveled by the vehicle before turning." To violate one or more of these code sections, all of the following must be true:

1. You either "turned your vehicle" from a direct course; or moved the vehicle right or left. (This includes changing lanes and even making a U-turn.)

2. You did this on a "roadway" (same as a highway—any road or street).

3. You failed to give an electrical or hand turn signal continuously during the last 100 feet of the turn, and there was another vehicle nearby that *may* have been affected by the (turning) movement.

When changing lanes, a signal is required if there is anyone behind you in any lane in your direction.

Most officers are not likely to give tickets for failing to signal unless you cut someone off or caused an actual or near-accident. At trial, the issue will usually be whether or not there was:

- another vehicle near where you turned, which
- may have been affected by your turn.

EXAMPLE:

You're making a right turn from the right-hand lane at an intersection. Usually the only other vehicle that could be affected by your failure to signal would be the one on the opposite side of the intersection if the driver were planning to turn left onto the same street in the same direction as you.

Possible defense strategies might include that you never really turned the vehicle, you were not on a "roadway" (perhaps on a private lot in a shopping center), or you were in an emergency situation in which you didn't have time to signal.

If your turn signals aren't working and you're aware of it, you should use hand signals. They're just as legal as electric signals. If you're not aware of a burnt-out turn signal and you get stopped for this, the officer will usually merely cite you for a correctable equipment violation (VC § 40610). This will not result in a violation on your record provided you correct the problem within the specified time and get the item "checked off." (More about this in Chapter 6.)

Dashboard turn signal indicators may still blink even though a front or rear signal lamp is burned out. If that's the case, you should suggest to the officer that you did signal and *maybe* the light's burnt out. It is obviously unwise from a strategic point of view to admit that you were aware of a defect. If you say you didn't signal because your turn signals aren't working, you'll be told something like, *"You should have signaled by hand then."* Also, the officer may cite you for an equipment violation as well as failure to signal. As we'll see in Chapter 6, you can probably get the court to dismiss the equipment violation once you've replaced the signal lamp.

If your turn-signal lamp was burnt out and you are cited for a moving violation, you should contest the ticket. Give as your basis VC § 40610, under which you should have been cited for the equipment violation instead, and provide proof that you've since replaced the burnt-out lamp.

Being Rude (Miscellaneous Violations)

A few conscientious officers write tickets only when they honestly feel a driver is endangering life or property, *or* is being outright rude to other drivers. "Being rude" includes offenses such as failure to yield the right-of-way to other drivers or pedestrians, improper passing, tailgating, driving so slowly as to obstruct traffic, and changing lanes abruptly in front of someone else. Let's look at some of these violations.

Failure to Yield Right-of-Way

Numerous Vehicle Code sections punish different types of failures to yield the right-of-way.

Traffic Accidents

Several Vehicle Code sections say when and where you should yield to a pedestrian or another vehicle. A large number of tickets for right-of-way violations are written by officers called to the scene of an accident. If the officers have not witnessed either the accident or the alleged violation, all they have to go on are the positions of the collided vehicles, other people's statements to them, and *your* admissions. Your own admissions, of course, can be used against you by the officer later on in court. Obviously, then, it's unwise to admit fault. If you are unsure of what to say, it's perfectly proper and legal to tell the officer you simply don't wish to talk about it.

But what about the statements of bystanders or others involved in the accident? Even if you remain silent, can't these be repeated in court by the officer? No. They are inadmissible "hearsay" evidence. The people who actually made the statement would have to personally testify against you. Such people, even when subpoenaed, will often fail to show up to testify. Therefore, tickets for right-of-way violations are almost always worth fighting when the officer bases her information on an accident she hasn't seen.

Yielding to Other Vehicles, Generally

The following is a brief rundown on the most common violations for failing to yield to other vehicles.

VC §§ 21451, 21453 (right-of-way in intersections). Before you lawfully go through a green light or turn on a green arrow, you must give the right-of-way to vehicles already in the intersection. However, you don't have to wait until the intersection is completely clear before entering it, so long as you don't deliberately crowd the other vehicles. This is a matter of subjective interpretation.

EXAMPLE:

You entered the intersection fairly cautiously, anticipating that a vehicle already legally there would be moving on. But its driver couldn't seem to figure out which way to turn. You had no way of knowing this would happen.

VC § 21800 (uncontrolled four-way stop sign intersections). This applies only at intersections that have:

1. no traffic signal, stop sign, or yield-right-of-way sign (the dangerous sort of intersection where accidents are likely to occur)

2. four stop signs, one for each street and in each direction, or

3. stoplights that are inoperative because of a power or other failure.

At any of these types of four-way uncontrolled intersections, whoever gets to the intersection first has the right-of-way, and if two cars get there at the same time from cross streets, the one on the other's *right* has the right-of-way. At intersections with four-way stop signs or with inoperative stoplights, each vehicle must come to a complete stop first.

The elements include all of the following:

• You were driving a "vehicle approaching a four-way intersection;"

• The intersection had four stop signs, one for each street in each direction *or* had no yield sign, stop sign, or operative traffic light on *any* street approach;

• Another vehicle also entered the intersection from "a different highway" (that is, not directly across from you, but usually to your right or left);

• The other vehicle either entered the intersection first or, if you both entered at the same instant, the other vehicle entered from the street or road to your right;

• You failed to yield to the other vehicle.

This particular violation is the one officers most often cite after they're called to an accident they didn't see. If you *admit* that the other car was there first or admit that the other one came in from your right when you both entered at the same time, you're through. The obvious defense, then, is to contend (if true) that *you entered the intersection first.*

At three-way or "T" uncontrolled intersections, the rules are different. The driver on the road that dead-ends must *always* yield to the other driver (the one crossing the "T"), no matter who got to the intersection first.

VC § 21801(a) (left turn or U-turn). The driver of a vehicle intending to turn to the left or to complete a U-turn upon a highway, or to turn left into public or private property, or an alley, shall yield the right-of-way to all vehicles approaching from the opposite direction that are close enough to constitute a hazard at any time during the turning movement, and shall continue to yield the right-of-way to the approaching vehicles until the left turn or U-turn can be made with reasonable safety.

This one is also pretty subjective. It states that when you're turning left or making a U-turn (and not in a special left-turn lane controlled by a green arrow signal), you have to yield to traffic coming straight ahead from the opposite direction until your left turn can be made "with reasonable safety." All of these elements must be met:

• You "intended" to turn to the left or make a U-turn or to turn left onto a driveway or alley from the street;

• One or more vehicles were approaching from the opposite direction;

• Such approaching traffic was "so close as to constitute a hazard" at any time during the turning movement. (If the traffic moved fairly slowly or was some distance away, or even if you drove fairly fast, this won't be true);

• You made the left turn anyway, and it wasn't done "with reasonable safety." (Unless the other car had to suddenly brake or swerve to avoid collision—or you had a collision— you should be able to raise "reasonable doubt" on this one.)

Once you start a U-turn, Section 21801(b) says you have the right-of-way to complete it.

VC §§ 21802, 21803 (stop signs and yield signs). Even though you may have stopped as required at a stop sign, you still might have failed to yield the right-of-way to another driver when you should have. The elements are:

- You either entered an intersection where a stop sign required you to stop, or encountered a yield-right-of-way sign;
- One or more other vehicles approached on an intersecting street or road;
- Such approaching traffic constituted "an immediate hazard" (it probably didn't unless you had an actual or near-collision); and
- You went through anyway.

EXAMPLE:

After signaling your intention to turn right, you stop at a stop sign. If you rush into that right turn and a car approaching from the left on the cross street has to suddenly slow down to avoid rear-ending you, you're probably guilty. On the other hand, if because of obstructions (such as hills or bends) you couldn't see the traffic from your left, or the other driver was driving too fast, you may have been in the right.

Yielding to Pedestrians

Here are the most common violations for failing to yield to pedestrians:

VC § 21950(a) (pedestrian in a crosswalk). The driver of a vehicle shall yield the right-of-way to a pedestrian crossing the roadway within any marked crosswalk or within any unmarked crosswalk at an intersection …

This section requires you to yield to a pedestrian crossing the road not only at a crosswalk but at an "unmarked crosswalk" and is the source of California's somewhat undeserved reputation for going to extremes to protect pedestrians. An unmarked crosswalk at an intersection is defined as "that portion of a roadway" defined by the "prolongation" of sidewalk boundaries across roads meeting at right angles (VC § 275(a)). This means that whenever two streets or roads (but not including alleys) cross each other at an intersection, imaginary "unmarked crosswalks" connecting sidewalks on opposite sides of a street are deemed to exist. So it doesn't help you to maintain that you were at an intersection without a marked crosswalk.

The elements of this one are:

- You drove a vehicle;
- You approached either a *marked* crosswalk anywhere, or an *unmarked* crosswalk at an *intersection*;
- There was a pedestrian actually crossing or trying to cross (there's plenty of room for doubt as to whether he was just standing there waiting or leisurely thinking about crossing); and
- You failed to yield to the pedestrian by either refusing to stop (even though there's no stop sign or traffic light) or coming very close to running the pedestrian down. There may be some room for doubt here, too.

EXAMPLE:

If a pedestrian walks from your right to your left across the street, you may continue to drive along at a slow speed, since she will have already passed in front of your car's path. This is not a "failure to yield" to the pedestrian, even though she may still be in one part of the crosswalk while you drive across another part. Contrary to what many think, it's not necessarily illegal, as it is in some states, for you to drive in one part of a crosswalk when another part of it is occupied by a pedestrian. It's enough that you yield to the pedestrian to allow her to cross safely.

VC § 21951 (passing vehicle stopped at crosswalk). Whenever any vehicle has stopped at a marked crosswalk or at any unmarked crosswalk at an intersection to permit a pedestrian to cross the roadway, the driver of any other vehicle approaching from the rear shall not overtake and pass the stopped vehicle.

This means you cannot pass another vehicle already stopped at either a marked or an unmarked crosswalk (at an intersection) while a pedestrian is crossing. In this situation, you must wait for the pedestrian to pass and the other car to proceed. You can't breeze past the adjacent stopped vehicle just because the pedestrian isn't in front of your car yet.

VC § 21952 (pedestrians on sidewalks near driveways). The driver of any motor vehicle, prior to driving over or upon any sidewalk, shall yield the right-of-way to any pedestrian approaching thereon.

This means it's illegal for you to:

- drive over any part of a sidewalk (for example, to enter a driveway), while
- failing to yield to a pedestrian "approaching" that portion of the sidewalk.

Driving Too Slowly

There are several ways a person can illegally slow or impede traffic by driving too slowly or failing to yield to a long line of vehicles behind.

Driving Too Slowly in Left Lane (VC § 21654)

VC § 21654 (a). Notwithstanding the prima facie speed limits, any vehicle proceeding upon a highway at a speed less than the normal speed of traffic moving in the same direction at such time shall be driven in the right-hand lane for traffic or as close as practicable to the right-hand edge or curb, except when overtaking and passing another vehicle proceeding in the same direction or when preparing for a left turn at an intersection or into a private road or driveway.

VC § 21654 (b). If a vehicle is being driven at a speed less than the normal speed of traffic moving in the same direction at such time, and is not being driven in the right-hand lane for traffic or as close as practicable to the right-hand edge or curb, it shall constitute prima facie evidence that the driver is operating the vehicle in violation of subdivision (a) of this section.

You are not permitted to drive in any lane other than the far-right one (unless you're preparing to turn left) if you're driving at a speed "less than the normal speed of traffic moving in the same direction." The elements are:

- You drove at a speed "less than the normal speed of traffic"; and
- You didn't drive "as close *as practicable* to the right-hand edge or curb." This usually means in the right-hand lane, unless there are unusual circumstances (like a farm tractor was going 15 mph in the far right lane).

Note: Don't think that you're safe from being cited for this if you're sticking steadfastly to the posted speed limit while in the left lane. Unless the speed limit is 55 mph on a two-lane road, or otherwise 65 mph (70 on parts of some interstate freeways), you have a duty to drive the same speed as other traffic *even if you have to go slightly over the speed limit*. Still, your speed has to be "safe" so that you don't violate the Basic Speed Law. However, this does not mean that you can exceed a maximum 55, 65, or 70 mph. However, the fact that you were planning to *turn left* from the street on which you supposedly drove too slowly in the left lane can be used as a defense. This defense is particularly effective if the officer observed you for a few blocks or less.

EXAMPLE:

It's a damp, drizzly day, and you're doing 35 mph. The speed limit is 35 mph. You want to turn left after a few blocks, and you move over into the left lane in preparation. Rip Snorter, the village idiot and drag racer, comes roaring up behind you, followed by his two buddies, horns blaring. A nearby officer ignores Rip and cites you for not keeping up with traffic. While perhaps you might have driven a little faster on another day, anything over 35 mph during bad weather conditions would be unsafe. Also, the fact that you were going to turn left justifies your being in the left lane.

Remember, this is a defense, which means *you* must raise it at trial. Once the officer shows that you were driving slowly in the left lane, she's satisfied her burden of proof. It's up to you to show a legal excuse for your action.

Impeding Traffic (VC § 22400(a))

VC § 22400(a). No person shall drive upon a highway at such a slow speed as to impede or block the normal and reasonable movement of traffic, except when reduced speed is necessary for safe operation, because of a grade, or compliance with the law.

The code section makes it illegal to drive "at such a slow speed as to impede or block the normal and reasonable movement of traffic." This is subjective. An officer trying to make this one stick should testify that there was a long line of frustrated, finger-gesturing drivers behind you trying to pass on a narrow road and that your speed was less than the legal speed limit. The section excuses slow driving if either you were traveling at the posted speed limit or that your lower speed was "necessary for safe operation." Be prepared to testify as to poor weather or visibility and road conditions, or steepness of the road, which might have

rendered a higher speed unsafe or impossible. Also, a fragile load you're carrying might make your slow speed "necessary for safe operation."

EXAMPLE:

Jake was cited for this offense, but defended on the basis that a fragile load of china he was carrying to his grandmother's house rendered the low speed "necessary for safe operation." In view of his having kept as far as possible to the right at all times, he was found not guilty.

Vehicle Code Section 22400(b) allows the Department of Transportation to post minimum speed limits (for example, "Minimum Speed 45 mph"), but this is pretty rare. Even so, slower driving is still allowed "when necessary for safe operation."

Failing to Use Turnouts (VC § 21656)

VC § 21656. On a two-lane highway where passing is unsafe because of traffic in the opposite direction or other conditions, a slow-moving vehicle, including a passenger vehicle, behind which five or more vehicles are formed in line, shall turn off the roadway at the nearest place designated as a turnout by signs erected by the authority having jurisdiction over the highway, or wherever sufficient area for a safe turnout exists, in order to permit the vehicles following it to proceed. As used in this section, a slow-moving vehicle is one that is proceeding at a rate of speed less than the normal flow of traffic at the particular time and place.

This section requires you to pull over into a "turnout" when driving a slow-moving vehicle that's slowing down a line of at least five other vehicles behind. In order to be guilty of this, all of the following must be true:

- You were driving a "slow-moving vehicle," meaning one that is going slower "than the normal flow of traffic" at the time;

- You were on a highway with two lanes, one in each direction;

- There were at least five other vehicles in a line behind yours, all slowed down because of you;

- You failed to pull over at a "turnout" marked as such by a road sign or other widened area to the right where you could safely pull over.

With this violation, it's no defense that you had to drive slowly in order to do so safely. Only your inability to pull over safely is a defense, and the law assumes you can do so at a specially marked turnout.

Tailgating (VC § 21703)

VC § 21703. The driver of a motor vehicle shall not follow another vehicle more closely than is reasonable and prudent, having due regard for the speed of such vehicle and the traffic upon, and the condition of, the roadway.

This code section makes it illegal to follow too closely, taking into account the speed, traffic, and road conditions. If you were following at a distance closer than one car length (15 feet)—the *very* minimum for each 10 mph of speed, particularly on the freeway—you were not reasonable. Even so, an officer's determination of what was "reasonable and prudent" may be different from the judge's. Also, the officer may have observed the short distance between your car and another that was only a temporary situation—such as when another car pulls in front of you, and you have to adjust to it by slowing to increase the distance. Where a ticket for this is given following an accident in which the driver rear-ended the vehicle in front, the officer cannot testify to the violation unless he saw the accident happen. You should always contest the violation in this situation. (See Chapter 2 on citations given at accidents.) The

other driver may not have noticed you in his rearview mirror, and the fact that an accident occurred doesn't necessarily prove you weren't driving safely, just that all your prudence didn't help.

Unsafe Lane Changes (VC § 21658(a))

VC § 21658. Whenever any roadway has been divided into two or more clearly marked lanes for traffic in one direction, the following rule applies:

(a) A vehicle shall be driven as nearly as practicable entirely within a single lane and shall not be moved from the lane until such movement can be made with reasonable safety.

Whenever the road is divided into two or more lanes, you shouldn't move from the lane until you can do so with *reasonable safety*. Even if you signal beforehand, you may still be making an unsafe lane change. CHP quota-hounds love this one and often pounce when a freeway driver moves quickly into an adjacent lane in traffic. To establish that the lane change wasn't made with reasonable safety, the officer should testify that she saw the other car's brake lights flash as it slowed down to accommodate your lane change.

The necessary elements are:

- The road had two or more lanes for traffic in the same direction;

- Lane boundaries were clearly marked;

- You either failed to drive "as nearly as practicable" within the lane, or changed lanes without regard for "reasonable safety." (This violation occurs when the driver either straddles a lane—safely or not— or changes lanes unsafely. *People v. Butler* (1978) 81 Cal.App.3d Supp. 6, 146 Cal.Rptr. 856.)

EXAMPLE:

You're doing 65 mph on the freeway in the right-hand lane. To avoid cars entering from an upcoming on-ramp, you decide to move into the center lane. Preparing to change lanes, you flick on your left turn signal and look in your rear- and sideview mirrors. You see another car in the middle lane, but it's about eight car lengths back, so you change lanes. You did your part by signaling and checking your mirror. If the other car has to slow down, it's because it's going over the 65 mph speed limit, and any unsafe conditions are due to the other driver's high speed, not your lane change.

Crossing Into a High-Occupancy Vehicle Lane (VC §§ 21655.5–21655.9)

It is an infraction to drive on a highway or freeway "high-occupancy vehicle" lane (also known as a carpool lane) in violation of posted restrictions limiting the use of the lane to vehicles having a minimum number of occupants or specially designated "low-emission" vehicles. The law says such lanes must be marked by "signs and other official traffic control devices to designate the exclusive or preferential lanes, to advise motorists of the applicable vehicle occupancy levels," and "to advise motorists of high-occupancy vehicle usage" (VC § 21655.5). For example, the far left lane of some freeways is marked with diamonds painted on the road surface every few hundred yards and with signs on the median indicating the "diamond lane" is to be used only by vehicles with a minimum of two or three occupants during posted days and hours.

This law also says that special surveys must be conducted before these carpool lanes may be designated. You may be able to successfully argue (as did one of our readers) that the prosecution must prove, as part of its case, that such a survey was conducted. (See Chapter 12.)

Where such a lane is separated from other lanes by a double solid line, it is also against the law to enter or exit the lane across those solid double lines, even if your vehicle is eligible to be in the carpool lane. (The only exception is for yielding to an emergency vehicle that uses a siren or flashing emergency lights.) So, once you're in such a lane, you must stay there until the double lines end (VC § 21655.8).

A first conviction of either of the above offenses is punishable by a fine of $100 to $150 plus a several-hundred-dollar penalty assessment. For a second offense within one year, or a third or subsequent offense within two years, the fines are $150 to $200 and $250 to $500, respectively plus the penalty assessment (VC § 42001.11).

Improper Passing

Five Vehicle Code sections basically define three unlawful ways of passing unsafely.

Endangering Those You Pass (VC §§ 21750, 21751)

You are forbidden from "interfering with the safe operation" of any vehicle or bicycle you pass, and any vehicle coming from the opposite direction on a two-lane highway. Unless you cause an actual or near-accident—either by forcing the car you pass to veer to the right toward the road shoulder, or by causing a vehicle approaching from the other direction to slow down or pull off safely to the right—you should probably fight this ticket. Your obvious defense would be that you simply didn't interfere with the other vehicle's safe operation.

Unsafe "Blind" Passing (VC § 21752)

This section forbids you to drive on the left side of the road (while passing) when approaching the top of a hill or a curve, so as to "create a hazard" to vehicles that *might* approach from the other side. However, this, too, is somewhat subjective. It doesn't matter that there were no other vehicles approaching; it's enough if there *might* have been, creating the possibility of a head-on collision. The section further prohibits passing within 100 feet of a bridge, tunnel, or railroad crossing, but the officer's estimate of your distance from such places may be uncertain. (Remember, the *officer* has the burden of proving that the distance was less than 100 feet.)

Passing on the Right (VC §§ 21754, 21755)

You are prohibited from passing on the *right* unless one of the following applies:

- The passed vehicle is about to turn left (note that you can't drive onto the unpaved shoulder of the road);
- The street or road is wide enough to accommodate two lanes of traffic (that need not be marked off in a business or residence district), not counting widening of the paved area at intersections; or
- You're on a one-way street or a divided highway.

Even if passing on the right is allowed under one of the above exceptions, you must do so "under conditions permitting such movement in safety."

Failure to Change Lanes on Freeway Near Parked Emergency Vehicle (VC § 21809)

This new law, enacted in January 2007, makes it an offense to fail to pull over into another available lane (or slow down if that can't be done safely) if you're driving on a freeway in a lane adjacent to a parked emergency vehicle (police, fire, or ambulance) or tow truck with flashing lights (red or blue, or amber in the case of a tow truck). The elements of this are:

- you were driving in a vehicle
- on a freeway
- in a lane immediately adjacent to a parked emergency vehicle or tow truck
- whose emergency or amber lights are flashing, and
- you failed to change lanes into another available lane, if that can be done safely and is practicable or, if not safe and practicable, you also failed to slow "to a reasonable and prudent speed that is safe for existing weather, road, and vehicular or pedestrian traffic conditions."

This means that if you're driving in the far-right "slow" lane on the freeway and you see a police car, fire vehicle, ambulance or tow truck with flashing lights, you must try to get over to the next lane and if you can't, you slow down to a reasonable speed.

This law also applies to those unusual situations where the emergency vehicle with flashing lights is parked on the left shoulder and you're in the far-left "fast" lane. In that case, pull over to the lane to your right, if you can, or slow down.

The base fine is $50, which means $180 with penalty assessments.

The "Anti-Gridlock Act" (VC § 22526)

You may not "enter an intersection" (or a railway or "railway transit" crossing) unless there is "sufficient space on the other side" to pull into without "obstructing the through passage of vehicles from either side." This is called the "Anti-Gridlock Act of 1987." Simply put, in crowded traffic, you have to make sure there will be space for your car to fit into so that you don't block the intersection. A wrong guess is punishable by fines of $50 to $100 on a first offense, $100 to $200 on a second offense, and $250 to $500 on a third—plus the 260% penalty assessment. (These enhanced penalties only apply where signs about the law are posted at the intersection by local authorities (VC § 42001.1).) This violation is reported to the DMV, but does not count as a point toward your violation point count (VC § 12810.4).

Cellular Phone Use and Texting While Driving

It is now against the law to use a cellular or other "wireless telephone" while driving unless it's "specially designed and configured" to allow hands-free listening and talking and is used in that manner while driving, except for emergency calls (police, fire, and health care provider) (VC § 23123.5).

It is also against the law to write, send, or read a text-based communication—whether that is an instant message, text message, or email—while driving. However, it is legal to glance down at a cellular phone in order to read a name or number and dial it (by name or number), so long as that doesn't involve reading an actual message (VC § 23123.5). Of course, you should be using that cell phone with a hands-free device such as a Bluetooth device or a speaker system.

The base fines are $20 (first offense) and $50 (second and subsequent offenses), plus penalty assessments. These violations are also reported to the DMV but do not count as points towards your violation point count (VC § 12810.3).

Non-DUI Alcohol-Related Offenses

The serious offenses of driving under the influence of liquor and drugs are covered in Chapter 8. However, there are also some so-called minor offenses having to do with alcohol. These can be nasty, since the violations are considered minor—so you can't have a jury trial or court-appointed attorney—but the fines are often at or near the maximum for the first offense, and may be even higher for repeaters. Moreover, some insurance companies will cancel your insurance, or at least raise your rates for violations involving a driver drinking or having an open container, which are reported to the DMV. In addition, traffic school is not an option for these offenses (California Rules of Court, Rule 851). Thus, you will have a real incentive to fight these tickets.

Note: All of the non-DUI alcohol-related offenses listed below forbid alcohol-related violations on streets and highways and also when using an off-road vehicle—such as all-terrain vehicles, dune buggies, or dirt bikes—driven on any publicly maintained lands.

(See *People v. Squadere* (1978) 88 Cal. App.3d Supp. 1, 151 Cal.Rptr. 616; *People v. McCloskey* (1990) 226 Cal.App.3d Supp. 5, 277 Cal.Rptr. 509.)

Open Container on Person of Driver (VC § 23222(a))

VC § 23222(a). No person shall have in his or her possession on his or her person, while driving a motor vehicle upon a highway ... any bottle, can or other receptacle, containing any alcoholic beverage that has been opened, or a seal broken, or the contents of which have been partially removed.

This is the most common "minor" alcohol-related offense. Convictions for this offense *are* reported to the DMV.

The elements of this violation are all of the following:

- You drove a motor vehicle;
- You drove the vehicle "upon a highway"—any public road, but private roads or parking lots don't count;
- You kept a container, such as a bottle, can or glass *on your person* (that is, you held it in your hand or kept it in a pocket or purse);
- The container held *any* amount of an alcoholic beverage when the officer found it;
- The seal, if any, on the bottle was *broken, or* the container's contents were "partially removed."

Police frequently cite a vehicle's *driver* when a *passenger* has the open container on his or her person. This can be the basis of a good defense, as a bottle held by a passenger as his own is not "on the person" of the driver, so the passenger, not the driver, should be ticketed under VC § 23226. (See Section 4, below.) If the legislature had intended to hold the driver responsible for a passenger's drinking, the law would have forbidden the driver to "allow" a passenger to drink or have an open container.

EXAMPLE:

You and your friends are on the way to the beach with a few unopened six-packs of beer. Unbeknownst to you, one of your friends in the back seat can't wait, and opens a can of beer before you get there. When an officer pulls you over for an expired registration, he notices the open beer can in the back and tickets *you*, the driver. Your defense is that you didn't have the open container on your person, and the officer should have cited your passenger instead.

Open Container Kept in Vehicle by Driver or Owner (VC § 23225(a))

VC § 23225(a)(1). It is unlawful for the registered owner of any motor vehicle, or the driver if the registered owner is not then present in the vehicle, to keep in a motor vehicle when the vehicle is upon any highway... any bottle, can or other receptacle containing any alcoholic beverage that has been opened, or a seal broken, or the contents of which have been partially removed, unless the container is kept in the trunk of the vehicle....

This second most common "minor" alcohol-related offense differs from the first in that the container need not be "on the person" of the driver. This section prohibits a driver or a passenger from keeping an open alcoholic beverage container (or one with a broken seal) in a place other than the trunk—while the vehicle is "upon any highway." Also, an owner who isn't driving but is in the car—perhaps when parked on the road or letting someone else drive—can be cited.

The elements of this offense are all of the following:

- You were a driver or owner of a vehicle;
- You were in the vehicle;
- The vehicle was "upon any highway," but the vehicle doesn't have to be driven for the owner to be cited;
- You kept a container, such as a bottle, can, or glass somewhere in the vehicle *other than the trunk*. (For vehicles without trunks—such as pickups and liftbacks—the container must be kept in some area of the vehicle not normally occupied by the driver or passengers, but *not* in the glove compartment);
- The container held *some* amount of an alcoholic beverage when the officer found it;

- The seal, if any, on the bottle, etc., was *broken*, or its contents were "partially removed";
- The container was not in the "living quarters of a house-car or camper."

Driver Drinking in Vehicle (VC § 23220)

This law forbids drinking "any alcoholic beverage while driving a motor vehicle upon any highway." The elements of this one are pretty obvious; however, the citing officer must testify that he actually *saw* you raise the bottle or can to your mouth and drink from it. Even if your breath smells of alcohol, *that alone* is no proof you drank while *driving* the vehicle, even if you are carrying an open container.

Alcohol Violations Involving Driver or Owner (VC §§ 23223, 23226, 23221)

The three laws mentioned above (VC §§ 23222(a), 23225, and 23220) apply to an owner or driver who has an open container in the vehicle. However, persons other than the owner or driver may be cited under other sections of the Vehicle Code. VC §§ 23223 and 23226, respectively, forbid *any* person (whether or not he or she is an owner or driver) to have "on his or her person" or to "keep" an open container in a "motor vehicle upon a highway." Vehicle Code Section 23221 prohibits drinking "any alcoholic beverage while in a motor vehicle upon a highway." Since these offenses don't include driving or ownership of a vehicle as an element, they apply to passengers, as well as to situations where no driving is involved—such as when the vehicle is parked on a public street. They do not apply to passengers in taxis, limousines, or buses, however (VC § 23229). With these exceptions, the elements of violation under these sections are essentially the same as those covered above (VC § 23222(a)—open container on person, VC § 23225—open container "kept" in vehicle, and VC § 23220—drinking in vehicle).

People Under 21 (VC §§ 23224, 23136–23140)

Persons under age 21 who drive with an open alcoholic-beverage container in the vehicle, transport even unopened alcoholic beverages (except in the course of employment), or who possess an open container while a passenger, can be convicted under VC § 23224, which is a misdemeanor punishable by a $500 fine (plus penalty assessments) and/or up to 30 days in jail.

Also, if a person under 21 is convicted of this or any other offense involving drugs or alcohol (including VC §§ 23222–23226), the court is required to suspend his license for a year, or delay for a year the person's ability to get a license if he or she doesn't have one yet. On written request, the court can issue a restricted license—for example, to allow driving to school or work. This mandatory license suspension also applies to nondriving offenses, such as mere possession of alcohol by a person under 21 (B&P Code § 25662), being drunk in public (PC § 647(f)), or possession of marijuana or other illegal drugs. It also applies to vandalism by graffiti (PC § 594).

Besides being subject to a one-year license suspension for any alcohol-related offense, a person under age 21 can be punished for "almost-drunk" driving—having a blood alcohol level of 0.05% or higher while driving. (For adults, it's illegal to drive at 0.08% and above.)

Illegal Drug Use/Possession

Driving with one ounce or less of marijuana in your vehicle is a misdemeanor. So is ordinary possession of an ounce or less, whether in a vehicle or not. Either way, you're entitled to a jury trial, but the offense is not punishable by imprisonment. The maximum fine that can be imposed is $100, plus "penalty assessments" (VC § 23222(b), H&S § 11357).

However, any conviction of a drug offense (including possession of prescription drugs without a valid prescription)—whether or not driving or a vehicle is involved—*may* be punished with a license restriction or suspension for six months, or for a year if the person convicted was under age 21 at the time of the offense. A person whose license is suspended can request a "restricted" license allowing him or her to drive to and from school or work, but only if the judge rules that mass transit to and from work or school is inadequate. If a motor vehicle was "involved in, or incidental to," the violation, this can be punished with a suspension or revocation for up to three years (VC §§ 13202, 13202.3, 13202.5).

In 2000, voters passed the Substance Abuse and Crime Prevention Act (also known as Proposition 36). It says that a person convicted of a nonviolent drug-possession must be given probation, drug treatment, and dismissal of the charges on the successful completion of probation, except for people convicted of possession for sale or driving under the influence of drugs (PC § 1210.1.).

If you are convicted of any crime that comes under Proposition 36, it does not prevent the DMV from suspending your driver's license during treatment. But you may, depending on the offense, be able to regain your driving privilege by petitioning the court if you successfully complete treatment and any other terms of your probation.

Motorcycle Helmet Laws (VC § 27803)

Under newly amended VC § 27803, you can be cited for (1) driving a motorcycle (or a "motor-driven cycle" having a 150 cc or smaller engine, or a "motorized bicycle" (moped)) on a highway while not wearing an approved helmet, (2) driving a motorcycle on a highway while a passenger is not wearing a helmet, (3) riding a motorcycle on a highway, as a passenger, if you are not wearing a helmet, or (4) riding a motorcycle on a highway, as a passenger, if anyone else on the motorcycle isn't wearing a helmet. Regardless of how many of these situations may have existed, each person, driver, or passenger can be cited for only one violation of this law.

There are no defenses to this, other than that you weren't on a public "highway" (which includes a street) or that you and any other person(s) on the motorcycle were all wearing helmets.

Violations Involving Accidents and Insurance

Drivers involved in accidents—even those who are completely blameless—have a legal duty to prove that they're insured, to file accident reports in certain situations, and to communicate specific information to other drivers. We'll look at each obligation below.

Proof of Insurance

Under VC § 16028, a police officer may ask you for proof that the vehicle you're driving is insured. She may not stop you solely for the purpose of finding out whether you're insured, but she can demand proof at the same time as she cites you, or just questions you, for some other violation or suspected violation, moving or not. Even if you're in an accident as merely the unlucky victim of someone else's dangerous driving, you'll have to have proof if asked. If you don't have it, you can be cited. Let's look at how the law works.

There are two ways to run afoul of the proof-of-insurance law:

- you have insurance, but don't have written proof, or
- you don't have insurance at all, let alone written proof.

The penalties vary according to your situation.

You have insurance but no proof. You can get the insurance violation dismissed by giving a copy of your current insurance policy or policy card (issued by your insurance company) to the court clerk. If you fail to do this, the violation is an infraction, punishable by a fine of around $1,800 (including a penalty assessment).

You didn't have insurance when you were cited. If you weren't insured when you were stopped or involved in an accident, or for any other reason cannot prove insurance coverage, you have a big problem. First, you will face a fine, including penalty assessments, of approximately $600 to $800.

If you are an employee driving your employer's vehicle and are unable to provide the necessary insurance information, you can sign the Notice to Appear on behalf of your employer, who must then establish that the vehicle was insured when you were driving it. (VC § 16028(d).) This won't work if you're just driving the car of a friend or acquaintance and are asked to produce insurance. You must be able to prove you're insured while driving your friend's car, either through your own or your friend's policy.

Giving wrong information about insurance is a misdemeanor punishable by a base fine of up to $500 (plus penalty assessment) and imprisonment of up to 30 days.

What do you need to show to the officer to avoid violating the proof-of-insurance law? Your word alone (*"Of course I'm insured!"*) won't satisfy the officer. You'll need written evidence of the name of your insurance company and your policy number.

The best way to comply with the law is to stop whatever you're doing right now, make a copy of your insurance policy, put it with your vehicle registration card, and carry it with you whenever you drive. By law, insurance companies must issue special cards providing the necessary information, but not all companies do.

Mandatory Reporting of Certain Accidents

Vehicle Code § 16075 provides that if an accident involves personal injuries or property damage in excess of $750, all drivers must file an accident report giving their side of the event and providing evidence of insurance. Failure to be covered by insurance in this circumstance will result in a one-year license suspension by the DMV. If you don't file the required report with the DMV, your license will be suspended (assuming the accident is reported to the DMV by someone else) until you do submit a report. (See Chapter 15.)

If you're driving someone else's vehicle and are involved in a reportable accident, you may face a suspension if you don't show proof of the owner's insurance. To prompt owners to cooperate, the law makes it an infraction for an owner to fail to provide insurance information under these circumstances (VC § 16050.5).

Exchange of Information at Accidents (VC § 16025)

Drivers involved in an accident are required to give each other their names, residence addresses, driver's license numbers, vehicle identification numbers, and insurance information. Refusal to give such information is an infraction, punishable by a $250 fine, plus the usual penalty assessments.

A Few Words About Getting Insurance

As long as you have a driver's license, you can always get auto insurance. The trick is to get it at a rate you can afford. You won't qualify for a good driver discount if you've had two or more moving violations plus at-fault accidents over the past three years, and most companies won't insure you at even regular rates if you've had three or more such "points" over the past three years, an accident or violation in the past year, or if you've had any drunk or reckless driving convictions within the past five years. Also, if you've recently had your license suspended, been refused insurance by another company, or had your policy canceled, many companies will refuse to insure you at their regular rates.

If you can't get regular-rate insurance, you'll have to apply for what's called the "assigned risk plan." This is an arrangement by which a "high risk" driver with too many accidents or violations is assigned to a particular company. Each insurance company is assigned a number of assigned-risk drivers in proportion to how much regular business it does in the state. The company is required to sell liability insurance (but not collision, fire, or theft insurance) to drivers assigned to it at rates regulated by the California Department of Insurance. These rates are very high, on the order of $1,000 per year, just for minimum liability insurance. After paying this for several years without getting any more violations or accidents on your record, you should be able to get the rates reduced.

As you can see, the system can really grind you under if you don't have automobile insurance. Imagine becoming the victim of a vicious cycle in which (1) your insurance rates are raised because of traffic violations on your record, and (2) you can't afford insurance any more, so you do without. Then (3) you're involved in an accident in which you're not at fault. Because fault doesn't matter, you (4) lose your license for being uninsured during an accident, and (5) find that in light of your violations, accident, and license suspension, no one will insure you—even after the year suspension—for less than $2,000 per year. Still, you (6) have to drive in order to get to work (you can't afford to move closer to work and there's no decent mass transit), so you (7) drive without a license, (8) get caught, (9) forfeit your car to the state if you've had a prior conviction, (10) go to jail, and (11) lose your job while you're there. This means you (12) can't make your rent and (13) lose your home, and (14) your mate leaves you and takes the kids. Your life is ruined—all because of those tickets you sheepishly paid off without a fight. Is this an exaggeration? Sure. But many folks have experienced at least some parts of this vicious cycle.

Tickets That Don't Appear on Your Record

Parking, pedestrian, bicycle, and most equipment violations will not affect your driving record, as long as you take care of them. But if you ignore them, these minor violations can balloon into a difficult and costly situation. In fact, if you ignore them long enough, you may even lose your driver's license or car registration.

Parking Tickets

Parking tickets, contested (challenged) or uncontested, are no longer processed by the courts (except for appeals). If you contest your parking ticket, your hearing will now be handled by the city or county that issued it to you, or by a private business that handles tickets for the city or county. Before 1993, you could often get a parking ticket dismissed by challenging the ticket in court and insisting that the "meter maid" or "parking control officer" who wrote it show up in court. This would have worked in your favor simply because that person would be too busy writing more revenue-generating parking tickets to show up and sit for several hours waiting for a case to be called. Unfortunately, you can no longer insist that the person who issued the parking ticket be present at a trial.

What Happens If You Ignore Them?

There is no criminal penalty for ignoring parking tickets, and no warrant will be issued for your arrest if you ignore one or more of them. Unlike tickets for moving violations, parking tickets have no place for you to sign. But eventually (as we will see in more detail in Chapter 15), the city or county will notify the DMV, which will refuse to let you renew your vehicle registration or driver's license until you pay an increased fine plus additional administrative fees as high as $30 or $40.

If you ignore five or more parking tickets, or if your car has no valid license plates, your car can be immobilized or towed and stored by the authorities until you pay up (VC §§ 22651(i) and (j), 22651.7). Your car can be immobilized by fastening a lock called a "Denver Boot" around one of the front wheels, which prevents it from being driven away without severe damage.

If you have not responded to a parking ticket within 21 days, you will receive a mailed notice demanding that the parking ticket be paid. This is called a "Notice of Delinquent Parking Violation," which will also threaten a DMV "hold" on your vehicle registration and possibly your driver's license. If the original parking ticket had either blown off the vehicle or been stolen, this will be your first notice of the ticket. If your only objection is that you didn't receive the ticket and don't think you should have to pay an increased fine for that reason, relax. The law allows you to pay the original fine if you do it within 14 days of the mailing date of the Notice of Delinquent Parking Violation (VC § 40207). Also, you are entitled to a photocopy of the original ticket on request (VC § 40206.5).

Procedures for Contesting Parking Tickets

The registered owner of the vehicle will either pay the parking fine or contest the citation. The procedures for paying or contesting should be indicated on the parking ticket, along with the date, time, type of violation, and location of the offense (VC § 40202(a)). Procedures for contesting parking tickets are more informal than for contesting moving violations because parking violations are no longer handled in court. However, strict time deadlines apply. If you want to contest a parking ticket, you must act within 21 days of the date the ticket was issued, or 14 days from the date of mailing of the "Notice of Delinquent Parking Violation," whichever is later (VC § 40215(a)). Otherwise, the parking fine is considered due, and you have no right to a hearing after this deadline has passed. Your vehicle registration (or even driver's license) renewal will be held up until you pay all parking penalties, plus administrative fees, to the DMV.

Step One: Requesting an "Investigation"

In order to contest a parking ticket, you first need to contact the office indicated on the ticket and try to explain the situation. The law says you can do this by "written request, telephone, or in person." Essentially, this contact is a request, by you, that they "investigate" the matter in light of your explanation—for example, to check the broken parking meter or obscured no-parking sign you complained about. The office may investigate the matter and dismiss the ticket. If they won't, they should notify you of that in writing.

Note: This step is called an "investigation" (VC § 40215(a)). (Some agencies erroneously refer to this step as an "administrative review.") It is not a hearing. You are entitled to a hearing ("administrative review") only if the agency refuses to dismiss the ticket as a result of the investigation (VC § 40215(b)).

Step Two: Requesting a Hearing ("Administrative Review")

If, following the first-step "investigation," the agency insists the parking ticket was proper, you can then request a hearing to contest the ticket further. However, at this point, you must first pay the ticket. The agency is not allowed to charge any hearing fee. (See *Tyler v. County of Alameda* (1995) 34 Cal.App.4th 777, 40 Cal. Rptr.2d. 643, modified 35 Cal. App4th 813.)

The agency must receive the fine and your request for an "administrative review hearing" within 21 days of the date it mailed you the notice that the ticket would not be dismissed. Considering the time this notice might take to get to you, plus the time your fine and request will take to get through the mail to the agency, this doesn't allow you much time. If you can't afford to prepay the fine to get a hearing, you should ask the agency to waive the requirement. Under VC § 40215(b), each agency must adopt procedures to waive the prepayment requirement for those who can show "verifiable and substantial proof" of inability to pay.

In your letter requesting an "administrative review," you should state whether you want a review "by mail" or by "personal conference." Such a letter might look something like this:

June 30, 20xx

Alameda County Sheriff
c/o Parking Hearings
4400 MacArthur Blvd.
San Leandro, CA 94619

Re: Parking Citation A123456

Dear People:

Having been notified of the results of your investigation and decision not to dismiss the above-referenced parking citation in your letter dated June 21, 20xx, I hereby request an administrative review under VC § 40215(b). Enclosed is a check for the $250 parking penalty. I prefer a personal conference [or a review by mail]. Please advise me of the hearing date.

Sincerely,

Patti Parker

Patti Parker
123 Peachtree Place
Berkeley, California 94710

Should you request an administrative review "by mail," you should include a detailed summary of why you believe you should not be responsible for the ticket.

If you opt for an in-person hearing, you will have an informal meeting with a "hearing officer." The person who issued the ticket will not be present. Basically, you will have the opportunity to explain why you should not be responsible for the ticket.

Bring any witnesses with you who can testify to the facts. If they cannot appear at the hearing, bring their written statement, which should be signed under penalty of perjury.

Good defenses include:

- obscured, missing, or worn parking signs or curb/pavement markings

- vehicle breakdown resulted in having to park overtime or illegally

- vehicle was "boxed in" by other cars, making it impossible to move the car before sign or metered time limit, and

- parking meter was broken or defective.

Defenses that usually will not work include:

- *"I was trying to get change for the meter."*
- *"I had to go to the bathroom."*
- *"I left the motor running."*
- *"I left someone with the car."*
- *"I didn't see the sign" (even though it was clearly visible).*
- *"My car was only a little bit in the red zone."*
- *"It hasn't been enforced in the past."*

You will receive a notice of decision either at the hearing or in the mail. If the decision is in your favor, the money you paid will be refunded to you.

Step Three: A New Trial

After an "administrative review," the agency will notify you of the decision at the hearing (in person) or by mail. If you wish to take the matter further, you have the right to request a new trial. You have 30 days from the date you are notified that you have been found liable for the ticket. The fee for the new trial is $25. The fee and the parking fine you paid in order to get a hearing are refundable if the court eventually finds you not liable for the ticket. However, even in this new trial, the person who issued the parking ticket does not have to appear in court. Like the "administrative review," the city's or county's case is based on the information in the ticket, and you have no right to cross-examine the person who issued the ticket. No further appeal is allowed after this. (See *Lagos v. City of Oakland* (1995) 41 Cal.App. 4th Supp. 10, 49 Cal.Rptr.2d 203.)

Equipment, License, and Registration Violations

Tickets for correctable equipment violations or for not having your license or registration with you (provided they were valid and up to date when you were driving) must be dismissed when you show a timely "proof of correction" to the judge or court clerk and pay a $10 fee. A "correctable violation" is any equipment violation that:

- is not the result of "persistent neglect" (bald tires, for example, would be)

- doesn't show "fraud" (that is, a forged license or registration), and

- doesn't present an "immediate safety hazard" (a broken windshield or no headlights would be considered such a hazard). (See VC § 40610.)

Regular Tickets— The Notice to Appear

When an officer cites you for equipment, registration, or license violations on a regular ticket or Notice to Appear (on which he usually also cites you for a *moving* violation), the ticket will usually indicate on the back that the charge can be dismissed by showing "proof of correction" to the appropriate court. If you're unlucky enough to get slapped with a mechanical violation ticket while driving someone else's car, though, you may have trouble if the owner fails to correct the defect. *You*, not the owner, must deal with the ticket. (Of course, you have nothing to lose by fighting the ticket and pointing out this unfairness to the judge, who might dismiss the charge.)

The procedure for getting equipment violations corrected is straightforward. Any type of violation can be certified as corrected by the Highway Patrol or by *any* sheriff or police department. It doesn't have to be the same agency that issued the Notice to Appear (VC §§ 40303.5, 40522, 40610). But don't stop a Highway Patrol or other officer on the freeway; it's dangerous and they don't appreciate it. Instead, call the nearest Highway Patrol office or police or sheriff's department, and ask them when it's convenient to obtain a certification.

Note: The Highway Patrol, police, and sheriff's department will often refuse to certify corrections of misaligned headlights, bad brakes, faulty mufflers, and other defects where special equipment or training is necessary. You'll have to go to an authorized gas station or auto repair shop, which may charge you between $50 and $100.

For a license or registration violation, you can also have a DMV employee certify that you have a valid driver's license or registration. There is a space at the bottom of the reverse side of the Notice to Appear for the police officer or DMV employee to certify that the equipment, license, or registration violation has been corrected.

When you show this "Certificate of Correction" (or a valid driver's license or registration) to the court clerk or judge and pay a $10 fee, she will dismiss the violation.

The "Notice to Correct Violation"

An officer who stops you and is convinced that an equipment, license, or registration violation (other than failure to renew registration on time) isn't the result of "persistent neglect" or fraud, and isn't an immediate safety hazard, can issue you a Notice to Correct Violation, instead of listing a Vehicle Code violation on a regular Notice to Appear ticket (VC §§ 40303.5, 40522, 40610). By signing it you don't promise to make a court appearance, but only to correct the violation within the amount of time the officer specifies on the notice. Thus, you don't have to deal with the court.

After you get the violation certified as corrected, deliver or mail it to the court named on the notice, along with a $25 fee. If you don't, you may find yourself facing both the equipment, license, or registration violation—charged as a regular infraction— plus a misdemeanor charge of failure-to-correct as promised. Make a copy of the correctable certification and note when and where you mailed or delivered it, in case it gets lost. If you mail it, use certified mail with a return receipt. If you ever wind up in court, remind the judge that the law forbids imposition of a fine where "proof of correction has been timely and properly secured" (VC §§ 40522, 40610(e)).

(Name of Agency and Jurisdiction)

CONTINUATION	☐ NOTICE TO APPEAR		☐ MISDEMEANOR	
OF CITATION	☐ NOTICE TO CORRECT VIOLATION	☐ Traffic	☐ Nontraffic	(Citation No.)

Date of Violation	Time	☐ AM	Day of Week	Case No.
1 / /		☐ PM	S M T W T F S	

Name (First, Middle, Last)
2

Veh. Lic. No. or VIN	State

Correctable Violation (Veh. Code, § 40610)

Yes	No	Code and Section	Description	Misdemeanor or Infraction (Circle)
4 ☐	☐			M I
5 ☐	☐			M I
6 ☐	☐			M I
7 ☐	☐			M I
8 ☐	☐			M I
9 ☐	☐			M I
10 ☐	☐			M I
11 ☐	☐			M I
12 ☐	☐			M I
13 ☐	☐			M I
14 ☐	☐			M I
15 ☐	☐			M I
16 ☐	☐			M I
17 ☐	☐			M I
18 ☐	☐			M I
19 ☐	☐			M I
20 ☐	☐			M I

21 ☐ Violations not committed in my presence, declared on information and belief.

I declare under penalty of perjury under the laws of the State of California the foregoing is true and correct, and a continuation of the enforcement document noted.

22 _____
       Arresting or Citing Officer   Serial No.

23 /   / _____
     Date   Name of Arresting Officer, if different from Citing Officer   Serial No.

WITHOUT ADMITTING GUILT, I PROMISE TO APPEAR AT THE TIME AND PLACE INDICATED.
24 X Signature

Judicial Council of California Form
Rev. 01-01-04 (Veh. Code, §§ 40500(b), 40513(b), 40522, 40600, 40610(d), 40618; Pen. Code, § 853.9)

SEE REVERSE
TR-108

IMPORTANT—READ CAREFULLY

This form is used when multiple offenses are charged and the original Notice to Appear/Notice to Correct Violation form does not provide sufficient space for the listing of all the charges. PLEASE REFER TO THE REVERSE OF THE ORIGINAL NOTICE TO APPEAR/NOTICE TO CORRECT VIOLATION FOR IMPORTANT INFORMATION REGARDING YOUR LEGAL OBLIGATIONS.

CORRECTABLE VIOLATIONS ON A NOTICE TO APPEAR: Those driver license, vehicle registration, and mechanical violations cited in accordance with Vehicle Code section 40610(a) will be dismissed by the court if PROOF OF CORRECTION and payment of a transaction fee are presented to the court by mail or in person on or before the appearance date. Proof of correction should be obtained for driver license, registration, and equipment violations. CORRECT EQUIPMENT VIOLATIONS IMMEDIATELY.

Violations of Vehicle Code section 16028 (automobile insurance) will be dismissed only upon (1) your showing or mailing to the court evidence of financial responsibility valid at the time this notice to appear was issued and (2) your payment of a transaction fee.

CORRECTABLE VIOLATIONS ON A NOTICE TO CORRECT VIOLATION: Those driver license, vehicle registration, and mechanical violations cited in accordance with Vehicle Code section 40610(a) must be corrected and PROOF OF CORRECTION must be provided to the law enforcement agency's office designated on the reverse side of the Notice to Correct Violation form within 30 days in order to have the violation cleared. Proof of correction should be obtained for driver license, registration, and equipment violations. CORRECT EQUIPMENT VIOLATIONS IMMEDIATELY.

METHODS FOR OBTAINING CERTIFICATION OF CORRECTION (Veh. Code, § 40616):
1. Pollution control device violations must be certified by a smog check station licensed by the California Bureau of Automobile Repair.
2. Lamp, brakes, and exhaust system violations may be certified as corrected by an authorized inspection and installation station for the specific violation(s).
3. Registration and driver license violations may also be certified as corrected at an office of the Department of Motor Vehicles or by any clerk or deputy clerk of a court.
4. Proof of correction, except for violations that must be cleared at a certified inspection and installation station, may be obtained at _____ (fill in location) during regular business hours.

CERTIFICATE OF CORRECTION (MUST BE RETURNED TO: ☐ COURT, ☐ CITING AGENCY)

Section(s) Violated	Signature of Person Certifying Correction	Serial No.	Agency	Date

Shaded areas indicate spaces subject to modification for local or agency requirements.

Ignoring Correctable Violations

If you ignore a Notice to Appear, on which you signed a promise to appear in court or offer proof of correction, you'll face a failure-to-appear charge, punishable by a maximum fine of $1,000 (plus penalty assessments) and six months in jail. Also, the judge will probably not dismiss the charges even if you've corrected the problem, and you'll have to pay the fine for that violation too.

If you ignore a Notice to Correct Violation, on which you promised the police you'd correct the violation, the police agency will complain to the court. The court will then formally charge you with the violation *and* with the offense of failing to correct a violation as promised. The maximum penalty for this one is also a $1,000 fine (plus penalty assessment) and six months in jail (VC § 40616).

Also, if you ignore a Notice to Appear, a warrant may be issued for your arrest or the DMV will be notified and you will be prevented from renewing your driver's license.

Noncorrectable Violations

If the officer fails to list a particular equipment, license, or registration violation (except driving with a suspended or revoked license) as correctable, you should get the violation corrected and fight the ticket. Even if the officer notes on the ticket that the violation is not correctable, a judge can disagree. Judges often dismiss the violation if you've corrected the problem. If the judge is hesitant to dismiss, you should present evidence showing that you met all three conditions that required the officer to give you a chance to correct it, namely that:

- the violation isn't the result of "persistent neglect" (bald tires, for example, would be)

- there was no "fraud" involved (that is, a forged license or registration), and

- the violation doesn't present an "immediate safety hazard" (a broken windshield or no headlights would be considered such a hazard).

EXAMPLE:

You are stopped and cited for having a burnt-out tail light. Unlike having burnt-out headlights or bad brakes, this isn't really an "immediate safety hazard." Your testimony that you didn't know about the faulty tail light until the officer told you about it will establish that you weren't guilty of "persistent neglect." Then, if you show the judge that you fixed the tail light promptly after the officer told you about it, the charge will most likely be dismissed.

Equipment or Registration Violations Written on Parking Tickets

When an officer who issues a notice of parking violation also sees a vehicle-registration or equipment violation on the parked vehicle, he may also list the violation on the parking citation. This type of ticket must be initially processed by the agency that handles parking tickets (VC § 40225). The county, city, or private contractor handling the parking ticket must dismiss equipment violations on a showing of proof of correction, just as a court would, but can charge $10 for doing so. For license-plate violations, this dismissal process is only available if you can prove the car was legally registered at the time the ticket was issued. Otherwise, the fine for an equipment violation on a parking ticket is $30. If you want to contest the equipment violation written on the parking ticket, you will have to do it in the same way a parking ticket is contested.

Other Nonmoving Violations

This section covers miscellaneous Vehicle Code violations that are either not reported to the DMV, or reported but have a zero-point count, meaning that the violation cannot be used to suspend your license or insurance rates.

Violations by Pedestrians

Violations committed by pedestrians are not reported to the DMV. Neither are they subject to the laws that increase the fines for repeated violations, or possibly charge you with a misdemeanor on the fourth offense in 12 months (VC §§ 40000.28). They are, in effect, less serious than parking tickets; the fines, plus penalty assessments, are approximately $100.

Still, if you're one who wants to fight, keep in mind that all the pedestrian violations are listed in the Vehicle Code. This means that you can demand the officer specify the place to appear as the court at the county seat. (See Chapter 17.) If the officer has nothing better to do than bust pedestrians, make him drive a few miles to make the charges stick!

Here are a few of the violations for which pedestrians are most commonly cited.

VC § 21955 (jaywalking). Between adjacent intersections controlled by traffic control signal devices or by police officers, pedestrians shall not cross the roadway at any place except in a crosswalk.

The elements are:

• The pedestrian walked across a roadway *between* (not *at*) two intersections;

• The area walked over was not within a marked crosswalk; and

• *Both* intersections were controlled by traffic signals (not just stop signs) or police officers. (Neither need have had a painted crosswalk.) Just one stoplight-controlled intersection is not enough.

VC §§ 21950(b), 21953, 21954 ("immediate hazard"/ unnecessarily stopping traffic). These sections make it unlawful for a pedestrian to dart out into a roadway, to "unnecessarily stop or delay traffic" even while in a crosswalk, or when not in a crosswalk to fail to yield to an oncoming vehicle when the oncoming traffic is "so near as to constitute an immediate hazard." It may be easy to raise a reasonable doubt as to whether there was an immediate hazard or whether the stop or delay of traffic was unnecessary.

EXAMPLE:

You are cited for darting out into a street between two intersections controlled by stop signs. Only if the officer establishes that you caused a vehicle to suddenly swerve or come to a screeching halt should the judge find you guilty.

Violations by Bicyclists

Violations committed by bicyclists—even though classified as moving violations—are not supposed to be reported to the DMV (VC § 1803(b)(6)).

Violations by bicyclists can, however, count as prior offenses for the purpose of increasing a fine for a subsequent Vehicle Code violation within a year or for elevating a fourth infraction in a year to a misdemeanor. But if bicycle violations aren't reported to the DMV, they won't be on your record, so the judge shouldn't know about them unless you bring them up.

EXAMPLE:

You just got your second ticket within six months for bicycling through one of those ridiculous four-way stop signs at a deserted intersection in a residential neighborhood. Also, some quota-anxious rookie officers busted you a little less than a year ago for jaywalking, and you paid the fine. Although the present ticket means it's your third infraction in less than a year, you don't have to worry about an increased fine. Previous jaywalking tickets don't count toward increasing the maximum fine. And although your prior bicycle stop-sign-running ticket theoretically *does* count toward raising the possible fine on your present offense, it won't be on your DMV record. So the judge won't know about it unless you admit to it. Thus, the maximum fine won't be more than the first-offense maximum of $100 plus penalty assessments, and will probably be less. Finally, the violation won't be reported to the DMV.

Specific Violations

Vehicle Code Section 21200 makes all traffic laws that apply to motor vehicles applicable to bicycles. However, VC § 21202 requires a bicyclist moving at a speed "less than the normal speed of traffic moving in the same direction" to "drive as close as practicable to the right-hand curb or edge of the roadway" except when passing, turning left or right, approaching any place where a right turn is allowed, or when essential to avoid a collision.

Vehicle Code Sections 21650 and 21650.1 also permit bicyclists to ride on the shoulder of the road, if there is one, as long as they ride in the same direction as the traffic.

Speed laws apply to bicyclists. So do laws requiring stops at red lights or stop signs. Demoralizing as it is for a cruising bicyclist to have to stop and restart at a deserted four-way intersection, bicyclists are frequently cited for running stop signs. Bicycling while drunk is also against the law. (See Chapter 8.) And it is not hard for a bicyclist to speed in a 25-mph zone without realizing it. On the other hand, it is possible to argue that exceeding the speed limit with a bicycle was safe under the circumstances, even if doing so in a car might not have been safe.

Seatbelt and Child Restraint Violations

Seatbelt and child-restraint violations are reported to the DMV, but seatbelt violations have no "point value" and therefore can't be used as a basis for suspending your license as a "negligent operator" (VC § 12810.2). However, child-restraint violations do count for one point and can be used by the DMV for license-suspension purposes.

Seatbelt Violations

Any driver of an automobile in which all persons (passengers and driver) are not buckled in may be cited for violating VC § 27315.

Because of the way the law is written, a driver commits only one violation no matter how many passengers are unbuckled. One violation occurs while driving "unless that person [the driver] and all passengers four years of age or older..." have seatbelts fastened. However, each passenger over 16 not wearing a seatbelt can be separately charged. (Passengers under 16 need to be buckled in, but only the driver will be cited.) Exceptions to this law include emergency vehicle operators, newspaper or postal carriers making deliveries, and anyone who has been excused by a doctor because of a medical condition or disability.

An auto owner who doesn't keep every seatbelt originally sold with the vehicle "maintained" can also be cited, even if no passengers are in the vehicle to be endangered by this fact. This includes tucking the seatbelts under the seat where they can't easily be reached.

The total fine per individual ticketed is $20 for a first offense and $50 for a second or subsequent offense, plus penalty assessments.

Note: Police officers can stop you for the sole reason that you are not wearing a seatbelt.

Child Restraint Violations

Vehicle Code Sections 27360 and 27360.5 require that all child passengers under six or weighing less than 60 pounds be restrained in special child-restraint safety seats that contain a sort of harness and fit onto a passenger seat. The law applies to any parent or guardian of such a child, who is present in the vehicle, either as a driver or passenger. A first violation is a correctable one that must be dismissed by a court on showing proof (a receipt) that such a seat was purchased or that a class on its use was attended.

If the child's parent or guardian is not in the car at all, seatbelts are sufficient restraints for the child. But if seatbelts aren't used, the parent or guardian passenger can be cited. If no parent or guardian is in the car, the driver can be cited. This violation is not correctable.

Federal Government Tickets

Despite the absence of state authorities from federal lands, such as national parks and military bases, you can be cited by federal authorities for violating state traffic laws or federal traffic regulations on federal land.

Traffic Laws on Federal Lands

The United States government issues traffic and parking tickets for violations that occur in national parks and on military bases and other federal property. In national parks, you can be ticketed for disobeying specific national park traffic regulations, including disobeying the speed limit and driving under the influence (see Title 36, Code of Federal Regulations, § 4). On other property owned and operated by the federal government in California, including military bases, you can get a ticket for violating California law (Title 18, U.S. Code, Section 13). These tickets are issued by federal civilian or military police, and must be contested in federal court.

Even when California traffic laws apply on federal property in the state, the procedures involved in the issuing of the ticket and in fighting it are governed only by federal law. For example, the law may be different on what the federal police can do when they first stop you (like radioing for warrant checks) and on getting a ticket dismissed because the federal police did not properly comply with the law. (See Chapter 10.) Also, since federal tickets are tried in federal court rather than in a California court, you cannot demand the county seat. (See Chapter 17.) In fact, most counties don't have

a federal court, and you might find yourself traveling a great distance to fight the ticket.

There is no law saying that federal violations have to be reported by the federal courts to the California DMV. However, some federal magistrates will do so anyway. Therefore, whether a conviction or bail forfeiture will go on your driving record will depend on the particular court.

Arraignment and Trial

To contest a federal ticket of any kind, you must make at least two court appearances. First, you must go to the arraignment on the day, time, and place listed on the ticket and plead not guilty. Then, you must return for the trial.

In federal court, "misdemeanors" are those offenses punishable by up to a year in jail, in which case the defendant has a right to a jury trial. "Petty offenses," on the other hand, are those punishable by up to six months in jail, and there is no right to a jury trial. Where you are charged with a state offense, the punishment imposed by the federal court can be no greater than the maximum penalty under state law. Since under California law, ordinary moving violations, being infractions, are punishable by a fine only and no jail, they are classified as "petty offenses" and there is no right to a jury trial. In fact, many Vehicle Code misdemeanors are punishable by six months in jail at most, rather than a year. In federal court, these are "petty offenses" and there is no right to a jury trial. Therefore, first-offense drunk driving charges do not entitle you to a jury trial, because the maximum penalty is "only" six months in jail.

The inside of a federal courtroom looks pretty much like the inside of a courtroom in state court, except the furnishings are fancier and there's no California flag—just an American flag. (See Chapter 12.) Often there is a podium facing the judge, at which you must stand while addressing the court. The judge (called a "magistrate judge") sits on the same type of high wooden box-throne and wears the well-known dreary black robe, and a court clerk and bailiff (deputy U.S. marshal) are present.

Although a little more formal, procedures at arraignment and the actual conduct of the trial are pretty much the same as in California courts. (See Chapter 10, but ignore anything having to do with pretrial. Also see Chapters 11 and 12.) The case will almost always be prosecuted by an attorney or law student who works for the local U.S. Attorney's Office. Also, the sentencing procedures mentioned in Chapter 14 do not apply to federal courts.

There are other important differences between California and federal court procedures, if the trial is for a speed violation in a national park. If you are charged with a speed violation in a national park, you cannot use the defense that your speed, though above the posted speed limit, was safe, because national park regulations flatly prohibit driving over the speed limit.

In speeding cases where federal police used radar, the prosecution might claim it doesn't have to show that an engineering and traffic survey was made on the road, as it must in California state courts. (See Chapter 4.) It depends upon whether this requirement is considered "procedural" or whether it relates directly to the violation. You should argue the latter, saying that California's VC § 40803(b) specifically makes this requirement an element of the offense in radar cases.

Fines

The federal statute that "assimilates" all of the states' criminal law into federal criminal law provides for "like punishment" as under state law. This means that the maximum fine for infractions under California law cannot ordinarily exceed $100, $200, or $250 for respective first, second, or third Vehicle Code offenses. As we'll see in Chapter 14, a prior offense can't be used to raise your fine unless the prosecutor initially alleges the offenses in a complaint—seldom done in federal courts—or you admit to having committed the prior offense, which you should take care not to do. So, the maximum permissible fine will almost always be $100 and the actual fine will usually be less. Also, a federal court can't add state penalty assessments to the fine, since these are state-imposed taxes on the fine, not part of the "punishment" itself.

The Serious Offenses (Misdemeanors)

Generally

While most Vehicle Code offenses are classified as infractions, a few are considered to be more serious "misdemeanors." This chapter deals with the most common misdemeanor violations. The most serious one—driving under the influence, or "drunk driving"—is covered in Chapter 8.

Arrests and Notices to Appear

You can be physically arrested and taken to jail for most misdemeanors. However, the normal procedure is to release you upon your promise to appear at a later time in court to answer the charge. (We cover Notices to Appear in Chapter 2.)

The Vehicle Code *allows* an officer to physically arrest you for reckless driving, property damage hit-and-run, speed contests ("drag racing") or "exhibitions," trying to evade arrest (that is, outrun the patrol car or motorcycle), driving with a suspended or revoked license, trying to evade an officer, or other misdemeanors not listed in the Vehicle Code.

Police officers are *required* to take you to jail if you are arrested for the misdemeanor of driving under the influence of alcohol or drugs or for any felony. Should you be taken to jail, the police have the right to search the entire passenger compartment of your car and open any unlocked containers they find inside, such as suitcases and paper bags. (They do not have the right to open locked containers in a trunk, however.) Any incriminating evidence can be seized and used against you (*N.Y. v. Belton* (1981) 453 U.S. 454).

Marijuana Note: You can't be physically arrested for possession of one ounce or less of marijuana, even though the offense is a misdemeanor (H&S § 11357(b)). However, the officer can arrest you if he has probable cause to believe you are driving under the influence of marijuana.

When you're charged with any misdemeanor, you have the right to a jury trial and, if you're indigent, to a court-appointed lawyer.

Misdemeanor Trials

The main aspect of trials for misdemeanor violations (as opposed to trials for infractions) is that you have the right to a jury trial. We believe you should almost always assert this right. Why? Because judges are often a lot more cynical and "case-hardened" than people who serve on juries. To state the matter as straightforwardly as possible, you have a better chance with 12 jurors than with one judge, since if even only one juror agrees with you, you can't be convicted.

Whether or not you opt for a jury trial, your misdemeanor trial will be more formal than if you were charged with an infraction. A prosecuting attorney will represent the state, and procedural requirements, such as rules of evidence, will be strongly adhered to. Unless you're an unusual person who is experienced in conducting yourself in courtrooms, you are probably best advised to hire an attorney, or to ask the court to appoint a lawyer for you if you can't afford one. (See Chapter 9.) When first confronted by the rules of conducting a case in a court of law, it's all too easy for an inexperienced person—even with an excellent case—to feel like a toddler trying to cross a freeway.

Normally, judges do not give much help to people representing themselves, on the theory that this would be unfair to the prosecutor. If you represent yourself, you will need to understand how a trial works, how to introduce evidence, how to question witnesses, and how to make opening and closing statements to the jury. For help in addressing these and other issues, we provide a procedural outline of the process and a list of resources that are available in most law libraries (see Chapter 13).

Fines and Jail Sentences

Most Vehicle Code misdemeanors carry the threat of a jail term for up to six months and a fine of up to $1,000 plus $1,900 in penalty assessments (VC § 42002). A few misdemeanors prescribe different maximum penalties. For example, second-offense driving with a suspended license (VC § 14601) carries a maximum fine of $2,000 (plus "penalty assessments"), while first-offense exhibition of speed (VC § 23109) carries a maximum jail sentence of 90 days. There is also the possibility that your license will be suspended. (Punishments for the more common misdemeanors are listed later in this chapter.)

While rare, a judge can order a person sentenced to pay a fine to work off the fine at the rate of $100 per day spent in jail (VC § 42003(b)). (This is not allowed for infractions. (VC § 42003(a)).) Higher courts have ruled that you can't be imprisoned for nonpayment of a fine you can't afford, but many judges disregard this (*In re Anzano* (1970) 3 Cal.3d 100, 89 Cal. Rptr. 255). If you face this prospect because you are truly broke, you should tell the judge you are unable to pay, that you object to going to jail for a fine you can't pay, and that you would like the judge to appoint a public defender for you.

Sealing Your Record

Most employment and other types of applications expect you to list misdemeanor offenses but not "minor traffic violations." Misdemeanors may keep you from getting a particular job. However, you can get some misdemeanors legally purged from your record. Then you can truthfully say on employment applications that you have not been convicted of the offense.

The procedure works like this. You file a form requesting to have the record of a misdemeanor conviction or guilty plea retroactively changed on the court records to look as if you pleaded not guilty and the charges were dismissed. If you were granted probation, you must wait until the probationary period expires and you have fulfilled all the terms of probation. If no probation was given, you must wait a year from the date you were sentenced before you can make the request (PC §§ 1203.4, 1203.4a).

Unfortunately, the procedure does not erase the conviction from your driving record, and the DMV can still consider it for the purpose of suspending your license (VC § 13555). Also, for misdemeanors carrying a heavier penalty on a second or third offense, the erased conviction can still be used as a prior offense to raise the penalty in a subsequent legal procedure.

Common Vehicle Code Misdemeanors

Aside from driving under the influence (which is covered in Chapter 8), the following are the most commonly charged Vehicle Code misdemeanors.

Reckless Driving (VC §§ 23103, 23104)

The most serious of these driving-related misdemeanors is reckless driving.

The Violation

> **VC § 23103(a).** Any person who drives any vehicle ... in willful or wanton disregard for the safety of persons or property is guilty of reckless driving.

This law applies to driving on "a highway"—which includes any public road or street—and an "offstreet parking facility"—which includes most public and private parking lots (VC § 12500(c)). It does not apply to private roads.

Reckless driving is covered in one of the most vaguely worded statutes in the Vehicle Code. Court decisions over the years have interpreted "willful or wanton disregard for the safety of persons or property" to mean that:

- you were driving so dangerously as to be in danger of causing an accident, *and*
- you were, or should have been, aware that you were driving dangerously.

Thus, you can be found guilty even if you didn't know you were driving dangerously (that is, you lacked "willfulness"). The test is whether a "reasonable and prudent person" in your situation (driving your car, having your knowledge of the road conditions, etc.) *should have known* that driving the way you did was dangerous.

Examples of reckless driving include rounding corners at excessive speeds, weaving in and out of slower-moving traffic, driving through a school zone on a weekday at 50 mph, or driving when you know you can't stay awake. It's one of those things that is difficult to define exactly, but most people know it when they see it. Many police officers go by a rough rule of thumb that three moving violations, committed in rapid succession by a driver, constitute reckless driving. The courts, however, do not recognize that rule, preferring to require that the driving be "willful and wanton." In plain terms, this means knowing but not caring that you may kill or injure someone.

Reckless driving is a "discretionary arrest" misdemeanor, meaning that the officer can either give you a ticket or place you under physical arrest and take you to jail. Clearly then, if you're ever stopped for reckless driving, your attitude should be civil, without making admissions, and you should tell the officer that you'd be happy to sign the Notice to Appear.

Penalties

Reckless driving is punishable by:

- a fine of $145 to $1,000 (plus penalty assessments)
- a jail sentence of up to 90 days, and/or
- having your car impounded for 30 days.

As with speeding violations, the court can order a license suspension of up to one, two, or six months respectively for the first, second, and third offenses committed within the time the DMV keeps them on your record (VC § 13200). For this purpose, ordinary speeding violations count as prior offenses, so that a person convicted of reckless driving after having previously been convicted of speeding faces a two-month suspension.

If someone other than you was injured as a result of your reckless driving, the penalty increases to:

- a mandatory license suspension for up to one year (VC § 13350); and
- a fine between $220 and $1,000, plus penalty assessments; and
- a jail sentence of up to six months (VC §§ 23104, 23105).

If the injury is very serious and you were previously convicted of reckless or drunk driving or engaging in a speed contest or exhibition, you can be charged with and convicted of a felony.

Finally, police have the power to impound a vehicle for 30 days when the driver uses it to drive recklessly (VC § 14602.7). See Chapter 17 for more information.

Speed "Contests" and "Exhibitions" (VC § 23109)

VC § 23109(a). No person shall engage in any motor vehicle speed contest on a highway.

VC § 23109(c). No person shall engage in any motor vehicle exhibition of speed on a highway.

This code section is primarily aimed at people who drag race and show off—for example, by screeching their tires.

Speed Contests

Vehicle Code Section 23109(a) prohibits any "motor vehicle speed contests," such as racing with another vehicle on a highway, or even against a clock. (It does not include legitimate auto rallies where the course is 20 miles or more and posted speed limits are not exceeded.)

To convict you, the prosecution must prove that you:

- were driving a motor vehicle on a "highway" (including a public—but not private—street or road)

- were driving at a high rate of speed in relation to the applicable speed limit, or were at least accelerating very quickly, and

- intended either to pass, or avoid being passed by, one or more other vehicles or to beat a clock or other timing device, so as to demonstrate that your vehicle is capable of a higher speed or acceleration.

A "speed contest" does not have to be prearranged or formal. Two drivers who meet, dart daggers at each other at a stoplight, rev their engines and zoom off are just as engaged in a speed contest as are those who arrange their race a week in advance.

It's not necessary for the officer to nab more than one "drag racer" to make a case. Even though a "contest" seems to require that there be more than one driver, testimony by an officer or bystander that there was someone else involved is sufficient to establish that element. Also, a race against a timing device is considered a speed contest.

It is illegal under this section to "aid or abet in" a speed contest. This includes people who came to watch an illegal, prearranged drag race, since the presence of spectators is deemed to encourage the actual participants. It is also illegal to help place a barricade or obstruction in the highway as part of organizing a speed contest or exhibition of speed (VC § 23109(d)).

Exhibition of Speed

Even if you aren't found guilty of engaging in a speed contest, you may still be convicted for an "exhibition of speed" under Subdivision (c) of VC § 23109. The elements of this misdemeanor are all of the following:

- You were driving a motor vehicle on a "highway" (or any public road or street);

- You were either driving very fast or accelerating very quickly, usually causing a screeching of tires;

- You thought someone else would probably be watching or hearing and you were showing off for their benefit, or even to irritate them;

- The spectators do not have to be anyone you know.

While the violation is called an "exhibition of *speed*," courts have ruled that sudden acceleration (getting up to a high speed from a standstill in a very short time) "so rapid as to break the traction between a vehicle's tires and the pavement" is an exhibition of speed even though the car does not continue at a high speed (*People v. Grier* (1964) 226 Cal.App.2d 360, 38 Cal.Rptr. 11; *In re F.E.* (1977) 67 Cal.

App.3d 222, 136 Cal.Rptr. 547). Thus, tire screeching done as part of showing off how fast the car can accelerate or take corners is covered by this statute. Unfortunately, many police will cite people who accidentally screech their tires; a ticket in this situation should be vigorously contested because only intentional conduct of this sort violates the law.

Since exhibition of speed is a fairly serious offense, many people try to plea bargain down to a regular speed violation. But you will have more bargaining power if you insist on a trial by jury, since prosecutors often don't want to bother with a jury trial. If you fail to have the charge reduced and you go to trial, you should argue that although you might have been speeding (without actually admitting that you were), you didn't intend to screech your tires for someone else's benefit. For example, if it was a very hot day, you may be able to argue that the stickier road surface made it harder for your tires to hold traction—hence the screeching was accidental. This happens because a very thin layer of semiliquid hot asphalt on top acts as a sort of imperfect lubricant between the tires and road surface. Or, if you were driving someone else's car, you may be able to successfully claim that you were unfamiliar with its acceleration characteristics.

Penalties

The maximum penalty for taking part in a *speed contest* is:

- a $1,000 fine
- 90 days in jail
- a six-month license suspension, and
- having your car impounded for 30 days.

On a second offense, the maximum jail sentence is six months (with a 48-hour minimum), and a six-month license suspension or restriction is required (VC § 13352(a)(8), (9)).

Also, when a person other than the driver is injured, this offense can be charged as a felony.

The maximum sentence for exhibition of speed is:

- a $500 fine, plus penalty assessments
- a jail sentence of 90 days, or both, and
- a license suspension for up to six months. For a second or third conviction within five years, a six-month suspension is required (VC § 13352(a)(8)).

In addition to the usual misdemeanor penalties, a judge must order that you complete 50 hours of community service if convicted.

As with reckless driving, police have the power to impound a vehicle for 30 days when the driver uses it in a speed contest (VC § 23109.2). See Chapter 17 for more information.

While it's rare for a court to suspend someone's license for occasional speeding infractions, judges commonly do it for drag racing and "showing off your wheels."

Ignoring Tickets and Not Paying Fines (VC § 40508)

You should never ignore a ticket you signed promising to appear in court. Nor should you "forget" to show up for a court appearance. Dealing with the fallout from the original violation is bad enough without going through the harassment and indignities involved in having a warrant issued for your arrest.

If you can't make a scheduled court appearance because you're unavoidably delayed (stuck in traffic) or because of an illness or emergency, phone the traffic division of the court. The phone number is in the county listings of the phone book under Superior Court. Make a note of the time you called, who you spoke with, and what was said.

Finally, be sure to pay any fine on a charge you fought and lost.

If you violate a written promise to appear in court (which you sign on a Notice to Appear before the officer lets you go) or neglect to pay a fine, a warrant can be issued for your arrest, your license may be suspended, and you will be charged with a misdemeanor—even if the ticket you ignored or fine you didn't pay arose out of an infraction. This means that you then face the prospect of a $1,000 fine plus penalty assessments and the theoretical possibility of going to jail for six months. Now let's look at the specific violations.

Failure to Appear as Promised

VC § 40508(a). Any person willfully violating his written promise to appear or a lawfully granted continuance of his promise to appear in court or before a person authorized to receive a deposit of bail is guilty of a misdemeanor, regardless of the disposition of the charge upon which he was originally arrested.

Most nonfelony Vehicle Code moving violations begin with a Notice to Appear, the standard "ticket" that the officer asks you to sign. By signing, you promise to appear at the court listed on the ticket, either to forfeit bail or set up a court date. This does not apply to parking tickets.

Failing to appear in court as promised on a Notice to Appear can have many adverse consequences. Aside from being charged with the new misdemeanor of failure to appear, these include:

- being convicted "in absentia" (in your absence) of the underlying infraction, and thus becoming liable (responsible) for the fine *and* having the conviction on your DMV record
- being liable for an additional 50% late charge tacked onto the fine
- being liable for an additional $250 "civil penalty" if you still fail to appear following a warning letter from the court (PC § 1214.1)
- having your driver's license suspended until you appear in court and have the case resolved, and
- having a warrant issued for your arrest (VC §§ 40509, 40509.5).

In addition to the above, you can be charged with violating the above-quoted law. The language of VC § 40508(a) says that "any person *willfully* violating his written promise to appear" is guilty of a misdemeanor. However, failure to appear can also be charged as an infraction punishable only by a fine of up to $100, plus penalty assessment, unless at arraignment you object and insist it be charged as a misdemeanor (PC §§ 17(d), 19.8). (See Chapter 10.)

Willfully violating "a lawfully granted continuance" is also a misdemeanor. This means that you violate VC § 40508(a) by failing to show up in court not just the first time you must appear to deal with your ticket, but also for any subsequent appearance required. For example, if you go to the court clerk to set up a future court date, that later date is legally regarded as a "continuance" or postponement of the case. Also, if you appear before a judge at an arraignment, but then don't show up for the trial, you may be charged with failure to appear, even though technically you didn't promise in writing to show up at the trial.

The elements of "failure to appear" are both of the following:

- You signed a written promise to appear, whether on a Notice to Appear given to you as part of the ticket or on a form supplied by the court clerk when you set a court date;

- You *willfully* failed to show up at the court, either at the clerk's window (to pay the ticket or set a court date), or in court before a judge as lawfully directed on a later date.

"Willfully" sounds as if you must have *intended* not to show up. Perhaps, then, you might think you're not guilty if you just forgot. While it might be technically true to claim that forgetting to appear is not willful, it probably won't work as a defense. You will have a hard time convincing a judge or jury that you were so preoccupied with other things that you were not a willful violator. Your excuse for forgetting will have to be a very good one—like a major earthquake or the death of a close relative.

The excuse of having lost the ticket will probably not work. You still have a duty to follow the matter up with the personnel at the courthouse. If you've ever walked into a busy court clerk's office without your ticket and tried to get them to look it up for you, you may have learned just how slow and unhelpful some traffic clerks are. Nevertheless, the burden is on you to try. If you try to have them locate your file and are unsuccessful, you may be able to convince a judge or jury your failure wasn't willful. Be prepared to testify in detail about whom you spoke to and the dates.

If you mailed a fine to the court in lieu of a personal appearance, and the fine got lost in the mail or by a court clerk, that *is* a valid defense. Your failure to come to court wasn't willful because you understood you didn't have to appear, since you mailed in the fine, if that's what a "courtesy notice" said, or a clerk told you so over the phone.

Some Strategy

Unfortunately, most folks who get pulled in on a failure to appear charge sheepishly plead guilty and pay fines—sometimes totaling several hundred dollars on both violations—without realizing the consequences. It's not just an increased fine on the original violation; you now have a misdemeanor on your record. In most cases (except when the DMV refuses to renew an about-to-expire license until the case is concluded), you should plead not guilty on both the underlying charge and the failure to appear and demand a jury trial on the misdemeanor failure-to-appear charge and on any original charges that are misdemeanors.

There are a couple of reasons for this. First, a jury is more likely than a judge to acquit you. Judges have heard hundreds of lame excuses for failures to appear, and often don't believe them. Second, jury trials require a lot more time, work, and energy on the part of judges and prosecutors. As a result, the prosecution is much more likely to be willing to plea bargain. For example, you might be offered the chance to plead guilty to the original traffic violation (which will then appear on your record) in return for a dismissal on the failure to appear charge. Or, if you think another moving violation will jack up your insurance rates or result in a license suspension (see Chapter 15), you might instead want to plead guilty to the failure to appear charge (which will go on your record, but it's not a moving violation and has no "point" value), and have the traffic charge dropped, provided it's understood in advance that there will be no jail sentence. If failure to appear was originally charged against you as an infraction, and you didn't object, jail isn't a possibility. (See PC §§ 17(d), 19.8.)

Of course, having several failure-to-appear convictions can hurt you in the future, if you're ever arrested for a serious offense, such as drunk or reckless driving. A judge who might otherwise release you from jail without your having to post bail may be inclined to insist you pay a very high bail if she sees a lot of failures to appear on your record.

Finally, if you're charged with failure to appear, you may have a reasonably good chance of having the ticket for the original offense dismissed. Chances are that a lot of time has passed, perhaps a year or two, since the officer issued the ticket on the original traffic charge. Sometimes, because of storage limitations, police agencies only keep records of tickets issued (including the officer's notes) for a certain length of time, often 18 months, after which they're destroyed—sometimes without regard to whether or not the charges are still pending. Without such notes to refresh the officer's memory, he's not likely to remember the circumstances surrounding his long-ago encounter with you. Moreover, it's possible that the officer may not even be with that particular police agency any more, and they might not even know how to contact him. This is especially true of Highway Patrol officers, who are routinely transferred around the state. Nevertheless, even if you're found not guilty on the underlying offense, you still can be found guilty on the failure to appear charge.

Failure to Pay a Fine (VC § 40508(b))

VC § 40508(b). Any person willfully failing to pay a lawfully-imposed fine for a violation of any provision of this code or a local ordinance adopted pursuant to this code within the time authorized by the court and without lawful excuse having been presented to the court on or before the date the fine is due is guilty of a misdemeanor regardless of the full payment of the fine after such time.

A "fine" is the amount the judge orders you to pay *after* you plead guilty or are found guilty in court. "Bail" is what you pay if you don't fight the ticket. (See Chapter 3.) In addition to being assessed a $250 "civil penalty" for failing to pay a fine (PC § 1214.1), you can be charged with the offense of willfully failing to pay a lawfully imposed fine. This offense consists of all of the following:

- You appeared before a judge on a Vehicle Code or local ordinance violation;
- You pleaded or were found guilty;
- The judge "lawfully" ordered (sentenced) you to pay a fine;
- You willfully failed to pay the fine.

The most important element of this violation is whether your failure to pay was "willful."

Willful Nonpayment

If you are sentenced to pay a traffic fine and cannot afford to pay it because doing so would seriously jeopardize your ability to support yourself or your family, you are not acting "willfully." A "willful" act is defined as an act done consciously, knowingly, and with "stubborn purpose" (*Helme v. Great Western Milling Co.* (1919) 43 Cal.App. 416). Explain your circumstances to the judge and, if you can, offer to pay it in installments. If even that would be a hardship, ask the judge to hold a hearing on your ability to pay the fine, taking your income, expenses, and other factors into account. (We'll go over this in more detail in Chapter 15.)

The judge may fail to give an immediate ruling in the hearing on your ticket, and instead will "take the matter under submission" (or "advisement"). You do have the right to make the judge tell you her finding immediately (see *People v. Kriss* (1979) 96 Cal. App.3d 913, 158 Cal.Rptr. 420, and Chapter 12). If this happens, you will be notified of the verdict by mail and told the amount of the fine, if any. Naturally, until you receive this notice, or otherwise learn of the result and fine, your failure to pay is not willful. Since the courts don't send such notices by mail providing for a return receipt, they have no way of knowing if you received the notice. Unfortunately, they will assume the worst of you and charge you with failure to pay, and it will be up to you to convince a judge or jury otherwise.

Again, if you mailed in the fine in time for it to be received in the court's mail before any deadline is imposed, the court's failure to receive it does not make your conduct willful. If a judge tells you differently, insist on a jury trial!

Penalties

The possible penalties for ignoring a ticket (other than a parking ticket) and failing to pay a fine include an additional fine, and even jail if the offense is charged as a misdemeanor. Your driver's license can also be suspended by the DMV until you resolve the matter.

Fines and Jail

The maximum fine for the failure to appear or failure to pay a fine is $1,000, plus penalty assessments. The longest possible jail term is six months. In most situations, though, jail sentences are extremely rare, and fines vary from $200 to $600.

Your Driver's License

If you ignore a ticket (other than a parking ticket) or neglect to pay a fine, the law allows the DMV to refuse to renew, or sometimes to suspend, your license, and sometimes allows a judge to "impound" your license. If you fail to appear, the court reports that fact to the DMV. The DMV may then refuse to renew your license until you "adjudicate"—or resolve— both the traffic offense for which you were originally cited and the failure to appear charge (VC §§ 12808(a), 40509(a)). (See Chapter 15.)

If you fight a traffic infraction charge and are found guilty, but don't pay the fine, the judge can "impound" your license for up to 30 days—regardless of whether your failure to pay is willful or whether you can afford the fine (VC § 40508(c)). Also, this failure to pay is reported to the DMV (VC § 40509(b)). The DMV will not only refuse to renew your license, but can even suspend it right away upon receiving notification of your failure to appear or pay a fine (VC § 13365).

Noncompliance With Court Order (VC § 40508(c))

> **VC § 40508(c).** Any person willfully failing to comply with a condition of a court order for a violation of this code, other than for failure to appear or failure to pay a fine, is guilty of a misdemeanor, regardless of their subsequent compliance with the order.

This is a catch-all law requiring you to do the things the judge, traffic referee, or commissioner orders you to do in relation to a violation. For example, a person convicted of a Vehicle Code infraction might be ordered to perform community service instead of paying a fine, to attend traffic school, or even to surrender a driver's license the court suspended. If you fail to comply, you may be charged with this new misdemeanor offense. Once again, you must deliberately fail or refuse to comply with the court's order in order to be punished under this law. However, suppose you tried to perform the community service or attend traffic school but were prevented from or not allowed to do so. Or perhaps you were unable to surrender your license to the court because you had lost it. Such explanations should help show that you weren't acting willfully.

And, as with misdemeanor failure-to-appear and failure-to-pay charges discussed above, the same misdemeanor penalties apply, and you have the right to a jury trial.

Driving While Your License Is Suspended (VC §§ 14601–14601.5)

Of course it's illegal to drive if your license has been suspended, or if your license has been restricted in some way. This would be the case if you were caught driving to a party at night when your license only allowed you to drive to and from work. The seriousness of this offense depends on the reason for the original suspension.

The Offense

What happens if you get caught driving while your license is suspended or revoked? It's not a defense that your livelihood depends on getting to and from work in the face of an inadequate or nonexistent mass-transit system.

The elements of this offense are simply:

- You drove a motor vehicle;
- Your license was suspended or revoked (but not "impounded") at that time, either by a court or the DMV;
- You knew about the suspension or revocation.

This last element requires a little explanation. To convict you of driving with a suspended or revoked license, the prosecution must prove that you knew your right to drive had been taken away. This is pretty easy to prove if your license was suspended by a judge when you appeared in court. But if the DMV suspended or revoked your license, the prosecution must prove that the DMV mailed or otherwise sent you a notice of that fact. Then you have the burden of proving to a jury (if true) that you never received the notice. *Never* waive the right to a jury trial on this one.

Penalties

The potential penalties for driving while your license is suspended are severe:

The *maximum* penalty for a first offense is a $1,000 fine, plus penalty assessments and/or jail for six months. For a second offense within five years, the maximum penalty is a $2,000 fine plus up to one year in jail.

The *minimum* fine for a first offense is $300, plus penalty assessments. For a second offense in five years, it is $500. It is rare to receive a jail sentence for a first offense, but in some cases, a judge is required to impose one.

Original Reason for License Suspension	Penalty If You Drive While License Suspended
Reckless driving or having too many violations on your record.	Mandatory 10 days in jail if you're caught driving with a suspended license for a second time within five years (VC § 14601).
Driving under the influence.	A first offense of driving while under suspension must be punished by at least 10 days in jail. A second offense within five years carries a mandatory minimum jail term of 30 days (VC § 14601.2). If your driving (while license suspended) caused an accident in which anyone was injured, you will not be allowed work release or community service, but must do "straight time" behind bars (VC § 14601.4).
Any reason.	If your driving during the suspension occurred while you had a "point count" (see Chapter 15) of three or more over a possible 12-month period, you can be prosecuted as a "habitual traffic offender." As such you will face a possible $1,000 fine and 30-day jail sentence for a first such offense. A second such offense in seven years is punishable by a fine of up to $2,000 and a jail sentence of up to two months (VC § 14601.3).

Sometimes the severity of the sentence depends on why your license was suspended in the first place.

If your license was suspended for driving under the influence, or your driving caused an accident resulting in injury, the judge can only let you own a motor vehicle if it is equipped with an "ignition interlock device," which prevents the vehicle from starting until you blow an alcohol-free breath sample into it.

If your license was suspended for something other than driving under the influence—for example because of a failure to appear (VC § 14601.1)—the judge or the district attorney may reduce the charge to an infraction punishable by a fine of up to $250 plus penalty assessments. You don't have to agree to this, however, and may insist it be treated as a misdemeanor with a right to a jury trial (PC §§ 17(d), 19.8).

These violations now have a "point count" value of two points for license-suspension purposes. (See Chapter 15.) This is true even for violations reduced to infractions. This means driving with a suspended license can be part of the basis for a further suspension by the DMV.

People who drive while unlicensed will face yet another penalty—forfeiting their vehicle to the state—if they own it and if they have been previously convicted of driving with a suspended license (VC §§ 14601, 14601.1, 14601.2, or 14601.5) or driving while unlicensed (a "lesser" misdemeanor violation—VC § 12500(a)). This "civil forfeiture" is enforced by the civil court system, and not through the criminal or traffic court system. (See Chapter 17.)

Fourth Offense Within a Year (VC § 40000.28)

> **VC § 40000.28.** Any offense that would otherwise be an infraction is a misdemeanor if a defendant has been convicted of three or more violations of this code within the 12-month period immediately preceding the commission of the offense and such prior convictions are admitted by the defendant or alleged in the accusatory pleading. For this purpose, a bail forfeiture shall be deemed to be a conviction of the offense charged. This section shall have no application to violations by pedestrians.

An Infraction Can Be a Misdemeanor

If you were convicted of three or more violations within 12 months prior to another alleged violation, that fourth offense can be charged as a misdemeanor, even if it's an infraction.

The three prior Vehicle Code or local-ordinance violations need not be moving violations of the type reported to the DMV, though pedestrian violations don't count. If you were convicted of three Vehicle Code violations of any kind, even equipment violations (or merely forfeited bail by paying off the tickets) within a 12-month period, a fourth Vehicle Code violation of any kind could be treated as a misdemeanor. Since parking violations are no longer considered criminal offenses, they no longer count as prior offenses for this purpose.

Prosecution as a Misdemeanor

In practice, fourth offenses classified as infractions are almost never prosecuted as misdemeanors. It is just too much of a bureaucratic nightmare for prosecutors to deal with. They are too busy to spend their time on what is still basically a minor offense. Besides, even if the charge remains an infraction, you can still be fined $250, plus up to $425 in penalty assessments.

Insisting on a Misdemeanor Jury Trial

You may have noticed that VC § 40000.28 says a fourth offense infraction is a misdemeanor when the three "prior convictions are admitted by the defendant." Does this mean that if you had three convictions or bail forfeitures within the 12 months before you were cited for a fourth offense that you could insist on being charged with a misdemeanor and demand a jury trial? Amazingly, yes, as long as you can produce the records (*People v. Shults* (1978) 87 Cal.App.3d 101, 150 Cal.Rptr. 747). But subjecting yourself to a maximum $1,000 fine, plus penalty assessment, and a six-month jail sentence, is a very high price to pay for getting a jury trial. And if the jury finds you guilty, the judge may be disposed to give you a rough time. While judges are not supposed to penalize you for asserting your right to a jury trial, the fact that you have used a lot of court time over a minor offense won't count in your favor.

Warning: If you are on formal or even "court" nonreporting probation for a prior misdemeanor or felony offense, DO NOT MAKE THIS DEMAND.

When you are on probation for violation of a misdemeanor or felony, one of the conditions of your probation is to "obey all laws." Generally, an infraction charge or conviction will not trigger a charge against you that you violated this condition of your probation. The courts and jails are too crowded for the system to worry about such technical details.

But where you are faced with a new misdemeanor charge, the system is likely to take this more seriously. You will face not only the new misdemeanor charge, but also an additional charge of violating the terms of your probation.

As to this latter charge—that you violated the terms of your probation—you have no right to a jury trial. You will still face a possibly hostile judge without a jury—the very thing you were trying to avoid in the first place.

Tactical Advantages and Strategic Considerations

One of the best reasons for demanding that your case proceed as a misdemeanor is to avoid a driver's license suspension. If you go to trial in traffic court, you run the risk of losing, having a fourth point go onto your driving record, and then having your license suspended by the DMV. On the other hand, if you insist that the case proceed as a misdemeanor, you can demand a jury trial. If you are unable to afford a lawyer, you have the right to court-appointed counsel (usually the public defender). Your chances of obtaining a favorable plea bargain (which may save your license) through this process may actually be better than your chances of winning an infraction trial before a traffic commissioner.

Here, your goal is not necessarily to go to trial and "beat" the charge (unless you've got a very good case) because, as discussed above, if you lose, the system might retaliate against you for exercising your rights. Instead, your goal may just be to force the system into entering into a favorable plea bargain with you, under which you might avoid that fourth point within a year. For example, you might be allowed to plead to a no-point violation, like not having your seatbelt fastened or your vehicle registration in your possession.

For a detailed discussion of conducting appeal negotiations, see Chapter 13.

The easiest way to demand that the case be tried as a misdemeanor is to have copies of your records of conviction (a DMV printout might even be sufficient), and then make an oral (verbal) motion after pleading guilty at your arraignment. The best way to make your demand for the case to proceed as a misdemeanor is to file a formal motion with the court. You may want to prepare the motion well in advance of your arraignment in traffic court and file it so that it will be heard on the actual date of your arraignment. For a detailed discussion of how to do that, see Chapter 10.

Driving Under the Influence (DUI)

One of the most serious driving offenses is that which we call "drunk driving." Since you don't have to be "drunk" to be convicted of this offense, many people call it "Driving Under the Influence" (DUI). Because this charge is so serious, and because factual and legal issues in such cases can be very complicated, we don't intend here to tell you how to conduct your own DUI defense—that would take a book in its own right. Here we simply give you the basic information you will need to understand your options and to deal intelligently with your lawyer, if you decide to hire one.

Under California law, this class of offense includes not only driving while "under the influence" of alcohol and/or drugs (legal or illegal), but also includes driving with a blood-alcohol level of 0.08% or greater—0.05% or greater, for people under 21 years old (VC § 23140)—whether you were feeling any "influence" of the alcohol or not. Both offenses are treated equally severely. They are the most serious, as well as the most frequently charged, Vehicle Code misdemeanors.

Though much of this book is designed to help you handle your own traffic court case, you should decide to be more cautious about handling your own DUI case, since the stakes are very high. Even a first conviction will result in a large fine, *plus* at least two days in jail, plus at least a 30-day license suspension followed by a five-month restriction that forbids you from driving other than to and from work, and a requirement to complete a minimum three-month alcohol treatment program (the program will be ten months long if your blood alcohol level was 0.20% or above; VC §§ 23160, 23161, 23536, 23538, 13352(a)(1), 13352.1, 13353.2, 13352.4, 13353.7). A second conviction within ten years means you will definitely serve at least ten days in jail (probably more) and have your license suspended for a year, without allowing you to drive to and from work. And those are the *minimum* penalties—which judges frequently exceed, especially in sentencing repeat offenders (VC §§ 23540, 23542, 13352(a)(3), 13353.2, 13352.5).

The *maximum* penalties for a first offense include a $1,000 fine—*plus* over $2,400 in penalty assessments—and six months in jail. For a second offense you can be put in jail for up to a year. In addition, your insurance may be canceled, or at least the rates drastically increased. And a drunk-driving charge stays on your driving record for *ten years*. (Minimum and maximum penalties for first and repeat offenses are listed in detail in this chapter.)

Before you read further, we wish to emphasize general rules that you should understand when dealing with the subject of DUI:

1. You will almost always be better off taking the blood or breath test when it is requested by the police.

2. Your chances of beating a DUI charge are exceedingly slim if the chemical test result is substantially over the limit (0.08% alcohol by weight).

Read the rest of this chapter with these two points firmly in mind.

Editor's Note: The subject of driving under the influence stimulates much passion in those who wish to stamp it out. In fact, we have previously been accused by these people of abetting drunk driving by explaining the different ways to defend against this offense. We believe that every criminal defendant is presumed innocent until convicted and should have the benefit of the information we provide here. Our job, as we see it, is to disseminate information about the law in a form that can be understood and utilized by nonlawyers. We leave it to others to implement the law and change it if they believe it doesn't go far enough.

The Offenses

In this section, we explain the elements of several different types of DUI offenses. (For less serious alcohol-related offenses, such as "open-container" violations, see Chapter 5.)

Driving Under the Influence

VC § 23152(a). It is unlawful for any person who is under the influence of an alcoholic beverage or any drug, or under the combined influence of an alcoholic beverage and any drug, to drive a vehicle.

The elements of this misdemeanor offense are:

- You drove a vehicle—that is, you steered and controlled it while it was moving; and

- At the same time, you were "under the influence" in that your ability to drive safely was affected to an appreciable degree by an alcoholic beverage you drank, a drug that you took, or the combination of the two.

Driving

The first element—"you drove the vehicle"—is usually not in dispute. Even when it is, it can be proved in court by "circumstantial" or indirect evidence. In one case, for example, a person accused of drunk driving had been discovered passed out in a car with its engine running. The jury was allowed to infer from the running engine that he had been driving.

Sometimes a drunk driver and a sober (or, at least, less drunk) passenger will try to switch places in their seats just before the officer approaches the car. This tactic almost always fails to fool the officers, and can often make the situation worse if the officer later testifies in court as to all the "furtive movements" occasioned by this awkward and desperate ploy.

In sum, the defense that you weren't driving (or that no one saw you drive) can sometimes be a fairly difficult one. You should definitely talk to an attorney experienced in drunk-driving defense if you think you might be able to use it.

Simultaneous Driving and Intoxication

Though it may sound obvious, both the driving and the under-the-influence elements must occur at the same time for a person to be guilty. For example, if you gulped down a double martini just before you started to drive and drove only a few minutes before being stopped and arrested, you might have been sober enough while driving. However, by the time a blood sample is taken a half hour later, it may show a substantial alcohol content. In other words, if your blood-alcohol level was rising because of drinks you had before you started to drive, your blood-alcohol content (BAC) may have been lower while you were driving than when you were tested later. (This is often referred to as the "rising-blood-alcohol" defense.)

A more unusual, yet similar, situation occurs when a driver who has had nothing to drink gets into an accident, and then walks into a nearby bar to get a drink and calm his nerves. This is a terrible idea, because when the police arrive to investigate the accident, they smell alcohol on his breath and arrest him. By the time he submits to a chemical test of his blood or breath, the alcohol will have worked its way through his body and he will be erroneously charged with having driven under the influence. But we use this extreme example to illustrate the idea of a "rising-blood-alcohol" defense.

It is important to understand that the delay between the time a person was driving and the time he gave a blood or breath sample can be used to his advantage. Once you stop drinking, your blood alcohol level decreases as time passes. This means that it was higher when you were driving than when the blood or breath sample was taken. Indeed, prosecutors use this fact to their advantage. For example, if your BAC was measured at 0.07% one hour after you were stopped, the prosecutor can argue to the jury that an hour before the test, when you were driving, your BAC was 0.09% and "burned off" to 0.07% by the time you were tested. That's because alcohol levels in the body fall at approximately 0.02% per hour, as the prosecution will tell the jury. We'll learn more about this later in this chapter.

Being "Under the Influence"

You don't have to be drunk to be "under the influence." (In a sense, the phrase "drunk driving" is a misnomer.) The question is whether your ability to drive was "impaired" so that you weren't as cautious or alert as a sober person would have been in similar circumstances.

A 1970 court decision (*People v. Schoonover*, 5 Cal. App.3d 101, 85 Cal.Rptr. 69) still applicable today defined the state of being "under the influence" as follows:

> *"A person is under the influence of intoxicating liquor when as a result of drinking such liquor his physical and mental abilities are impaired so that he no longer has the ability to drive a vehicle with the caution characteristic of a sober person of ordinary prudence under the same or similar circumstances."*

How is this determined? Well, the arresting officer will testify about your driving behavior that led him to stop your car, your symptoms (slurred speech, red eyes, dilated pupils, flushed face, strong alcoholic-beverage odor on your breath, unsteadiness on your feet after getting out of your car, etc.), and your inability to pass the roadside coordination test. The coordination test may involve saying the alphabet, closing your eyes and touching one index finger to the other or to your nose,

counting forward and backward using your fingers and thumb, patting one palm rapidly with the front and back of your other hand, balancing on one foot, and the well-known walking a straight line (usually a sidewalk cement line), etc.

Finally, "scientific" evidence—the concentration of alcohol in your blood or breath shortly after you were arrested—allows the judge or jury to infer, perhaps after hearing the testimony of an "expert witness," that you were under the influence while driving. However, this kind of evidence isn't absolutely necessary to convict you. Many people who have refused to submit to blood or breath tests for alcohol have been convicted of driving under the influence solely on the basis of the testimony of police officers that they drove erratically or flunked coordination tests.

Blood Alcohol Levels

As we'll see later in this chapter, the law requires a person arrested for driving under the influence to give a blood or breath sample to be tested for alcohol content—when asked. Your refusal to do so will result in a one-year license suspension by the DMV, and a three-year revocation of your license if you have been in trouble before (see Chapter 15)—even if you're eventually found innocent of the charge. Because of this, most people submit to the tests. As a result, the prosecution is usually armed with "scientific" evidence of a defendant's supposed intoxication. The more alcohol in your blood, the more likely it is that you were under the influence. But it is important to realize that you can be convicted of driving under the influence even though your blood alcohol level is fairly low—particularly if your drove erratically, slurred when you spoke, or staggered around. As we'll see, some people are more intoxicated at a given blood alcohol level than are others.

To make it easier for a jury to decide whether you were "under the influence," the legislature has come up with a set of "presumptions" that are based on the amount of alcohol the jury determines to have been in your blood while you were driving. The jurors do this by considering the chemical test evidence (VC § 23610).

If your blood alcohol content (BAC) is found by a jury to have been *less* than 0.05%, the law "presumes" that you were *not* under the influence (VC § 23610(a)(1)). This means that unless there's other strong evidence against you (such as testimony that you were erratically weaving all over the road), you should be acquitted. Prosecutors will almost always drop the charge when the BAC results come out this low.

If your BAC is found to have been between 0.05% and 0.08%, the law says that there's no presumption either way. In this range, most prosecutors are willing to plea bargain down to a lesser charge, such as reckless driving, if you are over 21 years old (VC § 23610(a)(2)). However, for persons under 21, driving with a BAC of 0.05% or more is a criminal offense. For persons under 21, driving with a BAC of 0.01% or more—or refusing a roadside breath test—is punishable with a one-year "civil" or "administrative" license suspension (VC § 23136).

However, your plea of guilty to a reckless driving charge will go on your record as having been plea bargained down from drunk driving. Then, if you're charged with DUI again within ten years, you will face the same increased penalty you would face on a second drunk-driving charge (VC §§ 23103.5, 23540, 23546).

An attorney can be of assistance here, but if you know what you're up against, you may be able to do it yourself. Indeed, many overburdened prosecutors may also be willing to plea bargain the charge down to reckless driving if your blood alcohol level is only slightly over 0.08%.

Finally, a jury is told at trial that if they determine your blood alcohol level, while driving, to have been 0.08% or more, they must presume you were under the influence. This means that the jury must find you guilty unless you raise a "reasonable doubt" as to whether you really were under the influence. But even if you win this way, you still can be found guilty of the separate offense of driving with blood alcohol of 0.08% or more, as we'll see shortly.

Drugs: Legal or Illegal

Vehicle Code Section 23152(a) also makes it illegal to drive under the influence of a drug, or under the combined influence of alcohol and a drug. Subdivision (c) of this same law makes it illegal to drive while addicted to a drug—other than methadone for treating heroin addiction—even though not under the influence at the time.

Most folks are surprised to learn that the "drug" doesn't even have to be an illegal one. You can be arrested and convicted for driving under the influence of legally prescribed tranquilizers, or even over-the-counter nonprescription drugs, like antihistamines or other decongestants, if they adversely affect your ability to drive (VC § 23630).

Driving While Blood Alcohol Is 0.08% or Higher

The law flatly prohibits anyone with a blood alcohol concentration of 0.08% (eight one-hundredths of one percent by weight) or more from driving, whether or not any driving is impaired.

VC § 23152(b). It is unlawful for any person who has *0.08% or more,* by weight, *of alcohol* in his or her blood *to drive a vehicle.*

In any prosecution under this subdivision, it is a rebuttable presumption that the person had 0.08% or more, by weight, of alcohol in his or her blood at the time of driving the vehicle *if the person had 0.08% or more, by weight, of alcohol in his or her blood at the time of the performance of a chemical test within three hours after the driving.*

The elements of this offense are:

- You drove a vehicle; and
- Alcohol was present in your blood at a concentration of 0.08% or greater *while you were driving.*

The latter is legally "presumed" if a blood test taken within three hours of the driving showed your blood alcohol to be 0.08% or more, but the presumption can be rebutted. This is normally done with evidence relating to the time and amount of drinking, or your condition and behavior at the time of driving, which suggests that your blood alcohol level might have been lower while driving than when taking the chemical test. For example, if you took a stiff drink just before driving, its alcohol didn't work its way into your bloodstream until after you were arrested and took the chemical test. Or, your friend who was with you before you drove testifies to your lack of slurred speech or staggering—so as to suggest a high-result blood test to be in error.

What this law means is that regardless of whether you have been "driving under the influence," you can still be found guilty of the offense of driving with a BAC of 0.08% or more. In most cases, the jury will be given a choice of finding a defendant guilty of driving under the influence (VC § 23152(a)) and/or driving with a blood alcohol level of 0.08% or higher (VC § 23152(b)). So, even if you and

your witnesses could convince a jury that your ability to drive was superb and that you were just as cautious and conservative a driver as a person who'd had nothing to drink, the jury can still find you guilty of what we call "drunk driving" if it believes your blood alcohol was 0.08% or more while you were driving. The penalty is the same whether you are convicted of one or the other, or both.

EXAMPLE:

Tom Tippler, just out of a late business meeting, was driving down the freeway at 9 p.m. Although he'd had two stiff mai tais at Pete's Plateau, his reflexes and muscular coordination were close to normal because, quite frankly, he drank like that every day and his system was used to it. When he leaned over to light a cigarette, his car swerved just a bit inside his lane. A zealous CHP officer pulled him over, smelled the alcohol on his breath, and asked him what he'd had to drink. Tom replied truthfully and the officer arrested him. A blood sample he gave showed an alcohol concentration of 0.09%. Even if the jury believes Tom's business associates when they testify to his apparent total sobriety when he left them, it may still convict Tom under § 23152(b)— driving with a blood alcohol level of 0.08% or more—if the jurors believe Tom's blood alcohol level was 0.09%, or even 0.08%, while driving.

"Attempted" DUI

You probably know that attempted murder, burglary, etc., are crimes. This is because Penal Code Section 664 makes it a crime to attempt to commit a crime. An appeals court ruled that this rule applies to driving under the influence as well (*People v. Garcia* (1989) 214 Cal.App.3d

Supp. 1, 262 Cal.Rptr. 915). The offense can occur when a person under the influence merely attempts to start or drive a vehicle.

In circumstances like this, your offer to plead guilty to attempted DUI—instead of DUI or driving with an over-0.08% BAC—may be a good bargaining chip to avoid more serious consequences. However, even if you succeed, you will still face DMV license-suspension proceedings if your BAC tested at 0.08% or more.

Felony DUI

If you *kill or injure* anyone as the result of driving while you are under the influence of alcohol, *or* while your blood alcohol is 0.08% or more, you can be found guilty of a felony and could go to state prison for over a year, and possibly for up to five years, depending on whether it's your first, second, or third offense (VC §§ 23153, 23554, 23556, 23560, 23562, 23566). Prior convictions for misdemeanor under-the-influence or over-0.08% driving count as prior offenses for the purpose of increasing the prison sentence. So do prior convictions of alcohol-related reckless driving (VC §§ 23560, 23566). The jury (and sometimes the judge) will have the option of reducing the offense to a misdemeanor, but even in such cases, the person convicted could still spend up to a year in the county jail—and probably will, since judges take DUI extremely seriously under these circumstances. Also, a person faced with a fourth drunk-driving charge over a ten-year period may be charged with a felony, even where no one was injured as a result of the offense (VC § 23550).

This is all we'll say about felony drunk driving. Needless to say, no one should ever attempt to handle a felony charge without a lawyer, and anyone accused of felony under-the-influence or over-0.08% driving should use

this book only as a very limited introductory resource.

Penalties the Court Can Impose

This part of the chapter lists the state-imposed penalties for drunk-driving convictions. There's no need to read this section word for word. (It's pretty boring if you do.) Use it as a reference, reading only that part that pertains to your offense. However, you may want to skim these pages to get an overall view of how drunk drivers are treated in California. Keep in mind that in addition to these penalties, your insurance company may cancel your policy or increase your rates dramatically. If you lose your insurance (or can't afford it) you will not be able to drive until you obtain it again.

Note: There are also separate license-suspension penalties imposed by the DMV, including, at minimum, a four-month or one-year suspension for a first, or subsequent, offense. These suspensions are in addition to the penalties listed here, which are imposed by a court after conviction.

Editor's Note: These penalties are subject to frequent change by the legislature, almost always in the direction of greater severity. While we do our best to keep this book completely up-to-date, penalties for drunk driving is the one area where we may occasionally fall behind.

DUI Not Involving Bodily Injury or Death

The range of penalties for DUI depends largely upon whether it's your first, second, third, or fourth offense within ten years. Note also that the range of penalties is the same regardless of whether you were driving while dead drunk or were merely driving while alert but with a blood alcohol level of 0.08% or higher. (Of course, within the permitted range of sentences, judges can and do sentence those who were very drunk more harshly than those with borderline blood alcohol levels.)

The provision for fines, jail sentences, and other penalties follow.

First Conviction

Maximum Penalties

The maximum penalties for a misdemeanor first conviction (within ten years) of VC § 23152 (DUI or 0.08% or more BAC) are as follows:

- a $1,000 fine plus over $2,600 in penalty assessments (see Chapter 3)

- six months' imprisonment in the county jail (VC § 23160)

- a six-month license suspension (VC § 13352(a)(1)); ten months for blood alcohol level of 0.20% or more (VC § 3352.1)

- having your vehicle "impounded" (stored at your expense) for 30 days (VC § 23594), and

- being required to attach an "interlock" breath device to your vehicle that will not allow the car to start if there is any alcohol on your breath. This will cost you about $800 (VC § 23246).

Minimum Penalties and Probation

In reality, almost all first offenders are placed on probation for three to five years. During that time, they are restricted by the terms of the probation. If they violate their probation during that time, they can face a nonjury hearing where additional penalties can be applied.

These minimum terms are as follows:

- A $390 fine plus over $1,000 in ordinary penalty assessments, plus additional DUI-only assessments for a total of approximately $1,800.

- A 48-hour jail sentence or a 90-day license restriction allowing you to drive to and from your work—and at your work—if required, and to an alcohol treatment program. If the 90-day restriction is imposed, it begins after your DMV four-month suspension or 30-day suspension followed by a five-month restriction (VC §§ 23538(a)(3)(A), 13352(a)(1)).

- Attendance and completion of a $500, three-month alcohol-treatment program (nine months if your blood alcohol level was 0.20% or higher (VC § 23538(b)). Completing the program is a requirement for ever being able to drive again following a "per-se" DMV license suspension and for minimizing that suspension to 30 days (plus five or eight months of restricted driving) instead of the six- or ten-month flat suspension that would otherwise be imposed.

- Loss of your driver's license for at least 30 days, followed by either a five-month restriction to drive to, from, and in your work and to and from the program, or an additional two-month restriction that allows you to drive only to and from the program.

Of course, these are just the minimum penalties. In practice, most judges typically impose a total fine of $1,800 to $2,000 and five to ten days in jail (more if the BAC was high, like over 0.15%). These penalties are in addition to attending the three- or six-month-long first-offender program, plus the standard conditions of probation, which include:

- not driving with *any* measurable amount of alcohol in your system

- submitting to a blood or breath test on request of a police officer, and

- refraining from further violations of the law (VC § 23600).

In practice, this last condition means no further misdemeanors. Ordinary traffic infractions don't count.

Keep in mind that even on a first offense, a judge has the power to order your car impounded for up to 30 days, and require that you have an expensive "interlock" device placed on all cars you own. This is likely if your blood alcohol level was 0.20% or higher.

Second Conviction in Ten Years

Maximum Penalties

The maximum penalties for a misdemeanor second conviction within ten years of a prior conviction (counted from the date of the previous offense to the date of the second offense) are as follows:

- a $1,000 fine plus penalty assessments for a total of approximately $3,000

- one year in jail

- a two-year license suspension by the DMV (VC §§ 23542, 13352(a)(3))

- impoundment of your vehicle for up to 30 days at your expense (VC § 23195), and

- required installation of an "interlock" device on all vehicles you own (VC § 23575(f)).

Minimum Penalties and Probation

Even for a second offense, the above maximum penalties are seldom imposed. Most often, second-offenders get probation. However, the terms of probation are more severe (VC §§ 23542, 13352(a)(3)). First, the judge will impose the standard conditions listed above. Then he can impose the following:

- A $390 fine plus penalty assessments for a total of approximately $1,800

- Ten days in jail or 96 hours (including two 48-hour sessions)

- Completion of an 18- or 30-month second-offender alcohol-treatment program, which costs about $1,800, as a condition of probation. You must complete this program if you ever want to drive again. Enrollment in this program also allows you to reduce the two-year suspension to one year, followed by a two-year license restriction that allows you to drive to, from, and in your work, and to and from the program—after the first year of suspension.

- You must install an "interlock" device on all vehicles you own (VC § 13352.5).

Once again, these are only the minimum penalties, and the ones a judge imposes could, and probably will, be greater, especially in terms of the jail sentence. This will especially be true if you were still on probation for a first offense when you were arrested for a second, or if your BAC was 0.20% or more.

Third and Subsequent Offenses Within Ten Years

Maximum Penalties

The maximum penalties for a third and fourth offense within ten years are as follows:

- a $5,000 fine plus over $13,000 in penalty assessments for a total of $18,000

- one year in jail for a third offense; 16 months in state prison for a fourth offense, if charged as a felony (VC §§ 23546, 23550)

- impoundment of your vehicle for up to 90 days (VC § 23195), or even forfeiture and loss of your vehicle (VC § 23596)

- revocation of your driver's license for three years (third offense) or four years (fourth offense) (VC § 13352(a)(5), (7), and

- a 30-month alcohol treatment program before getting your license restored (VC §§ 23548, 23552).

Minimum Penalties

Along with the standard probation require-ments listed above, the minimum penalties are as follows:

- a $390 fine plus over $1,000 in ordinary penalty assessments, plus additional DUI-only assessments for a total of approximately $1,800

- 120 days in jail for a third offense, 180 days for a fourth offense (VC §§ 23548, 23552), and

- revocation of your driver's license for three years (third offense) or four years (fourth offense), and completion of a 30-month multi-offender program to get your license back (VC §13352(a)(5), (7)).

Once again, these are the minimum penalties. Judges take third and fourth offenses extremely seriously, and are not likely to impose the mini-mum, except in most unusual circumstances. You can likely expect your car to be impounded or forfeited also.

Additional Penalties

If a defendant refused to take a blood or breath test, the court must impose an additional continuous jail term of 48 hours for a first offense, 96 hours for a second offense, and ten days for a third offense, in addition to the above penalties (VC § 23577).

Similarly, in addition to the penalties listed above, the court must impose additional jail time if there was a passenger under age 14 in the vehicle at the time it was being driven by the defendant. This additional jail time is two, ten, 30, and 90 additional days in jail on a first, second, third, and fourth offense, respectively (VC § 23572).

Finally, the court must impose 60 days addi-tional jail time if it finds that, while driving under the influence (or with a blood alcohol level of 0.08% or more), the defendant drove in a "willful and wanton" manner and at least 20 mph over the posted speed limit (30 mph on freeways) (VC § 23582).

How Alcohol Interacts With Your Body

Just as the amount of gasoline in your fuel tank depends on how often you fill it and how much you burn off as you drive, the amount of alcohol in your bloodstream is determined by a balance between how fast alcohol is absorbed into your blood and how fast it's eliminated from it. Elimination occurs when most of the alcohol is "burned" or "oxidized" in your body, while the rest of the alcohol is excreted in breath, urine, and perspiration. Since alcohol is eliminated from the bloodstream at a fairly steady rate, the degree of intoxication depends a lot on the rate of absorption. If alcohol is absorbed rapidly into the bloodstream, the blood alcohol level will get high fast—and so will you. If it is absorbed slowly enough to be eliminated before it builds up, you won't feel very high.

Absorption Into the Bloodstream

When you take a drink, the alcohol is absorbed into the blood through the mucous lining of the entire gastrointestinal tract: the mouth, the esophagus, the stomach, and the small intestine. The rate of absorption increases as the drink moves down the tract. Absorption from the stomach into the bloodstream (by way of blood-carrying capillaries in the stomach lining) is faster than from the esophagus or mouth. The street wisdom, which says that drinking on an empty stomach will get you higher, faster, is true because there is nothing else in your stomach to compete with the alcohol in terms of getting absorbed. The fastest rate of absorption is from the upper end of the small intestine.

For an "average individual," about 60% of the alcohol consumed at a given time will have been absorbed into the bloodstream a half-hour later. About 90% will have been absorbed in an hour, and all of it will have been absorbed in an hour and a half. However, this is just for an "average" individual with an "average" stomach food load, drinking "average" drinks. In fact, the rate of alcohol absorption depends on all sorts of things—the quantity of alcohol ingested, the concentration of alcohol in the drink, the rate of drinking, and the nature and amount of diluting material already in the stomach.

Elimination From the Body

Alcohol is eliminated from the body in two ways. Ninety to 95% of it is oxidized, mostly in the liver, to form water and carbon dioxide (a gas that dissolves in the blood, goes to your lungs, and is exhaled). The rate of its oxidation is pretty much the same over time, but varies, depending on how well a person's liver functions. People who drink regularly burn alcohol faster than casual drinkers. Chronic alcoholics burn it even faster. The remaining 5% to 10% of the alcohol is eliminated unchanged by perspiration, in urine by way of the kidneys and bladder, and in the breath by way of the blood as it reaches the lungs.

Calculating Approximate Blood Alcohol Levels

Since driving with a BAC of 0.08% or more is illegal, it can be helpful for you to be able to estimate your own blood alcohol at any given time, based on the number of drinks you had and the time you had them. Although a person's exact blood alcohol level depends on a number of factors, there's a simple, reasonably accurate way you can figure what your highest possible blood alcohol level could be (for example, if you drank very fast on an empty stomach).

If you divide the number 3.8 by your body weight in pounds, you should obtain a number between 0.015 and 0.040. Call this your own personal "blood-alcohol-maximum-per-drink" number. This is the maximum percentage alcohol that will be added to your blood with each "drink" you take. For the purposes of this calculation, a "drink" is a 12-ounce, 4%-alcohol, bottle of beer, or a 4-ounce glass (a small wine glass) of 12%-alcohol wine, or a one ounce shot glass of 100-proof liquor (most bars' mixed drinks have this amount of alcohol). (Micro-brewery beer, malt liquor, *pint* bottles of beer, large (6 oz.) wine glasses, 20%-alcohol ("fortified") wines, and very stiff or large mixed drinks should be counted as "one and a half" drinks.) For each such "drink," your blood alcohol concentration will be increased by about the following percentages.

Likely Maximum Blood Alcohol Level (%)

Your Weight in Pounds	Drinks Consumed in One Hour				
	1	2	3	4	5
100	0.038	0.076	0.114	0.152	0.190
120	0.032	0.064	0.096	0.128	0.160
140	0.027	0.054	0.081	0.108	0.135
160	0.024	0.048	0.072	0.096	0.120
180	0.021	0.042	0.063	0.084	0.105
200	0.019	0.038	0.057	0.076	0.095
220	0.017	0.034	0.051	0.068	0.085
240	0.016	0.032	0.048	0.064	0.080

Legend:

☐ over 0.05%; subject to prosecution for driving under influence

▨ over 0.08%; guilty of misdemeanor if you drive a vehicle

$$\text{Approx. Blood Alcohol Level (\%) over time} = \frac{3.8 \times \text{\# of drinks}}{\text{body weight}} - \frac{.01 \times \text{\# of minutes} - 40}{40}$$

Note: The numbers in the chart above may vary depending on the sex and physical condition of the person drinking. Numbers may be higher for females and people in poor physical condition.

EXAMPLE:

Linda Light, weighing a petite 100 pounds, could possibly have had a blood alcohol level of up to 0.038% from just one drink and up to 0.076% from two drinks. Three drinks could put her over the 0.08% blood alcohol level, especially if she drank them quickly on an empty stomach.

Hans Heavy, on the other hand, weighs in at 240 pounds, and his maximum blood alcohol increase per drink is only 0.016%. He's barely feeling the effects of the first one. To get past 0.08% blood alcohol, he'd have to down at least six drinks in an hour.

Now let's look at how long the alcohol elimination process takes. *After* about 40 minutes have passed, your body will begin eliminating alcohol from the bloodstream at the rate of about 0.01% for each *additional* 40 minutes. So, once you multiply the number of drinks you've had by your blood alcohol maximum per drink, subtract 0.01% from that number for each 40 minutes that have passed since you began drinking—but don't count the first 40 minutes.

Note: If you are so addled by alcohol that you cannot do the math, you are probably too drunk to drive.

For those of you who like mathematical shorthand:

EXAMPLE:

100-pound Linda Light's blood alcohol level after two drinks gulped down rather quickly could be as high as 0.076%. But if she drank them over a period of an hour and 20 minutes (or 40 minutes beyond the first 40 minutes) her blood alcohol would be about 0.010% less, or 0.066%. Forty minutes later, it would be down to about 0.056%, and so on. (Keep in mind that these are only approximate calculations.)

Finally, for those of you who prefer bar graphs over numbers and formulas, a reproduction of a set of graphs printed by the Department of Motor Vehicles is shown below.

Effects of Alcohol

Alcohol affects you because of its presence in the brain cells. It reaches your brain within seconds after it has been absorbed into your bloodstream.

ALCOHOL IMPAIRMENT CHART
DRIVING UNDER THE INFLUENCE OF ALCOHOL AND/OR DRUGS IS ILLEGAL*
There is no safe way to drive while under the influence. Even one drink can make you an unsafe driver.

Drinking alcohol affects your **Blood Alcohol Concentration (BAC).** It is illegal to drive with a **BAC** that is .08% or more (.04% or more if you drive commercial vehicles; .01% or more if under 21). However, a **BAC** below .08% does not mean that it is safe or legal to drive. The charts below show the **BAC** zones for various numbers of drinks and time periods. **Remember:** "One drink" is a 1 ½-ounce shot of 80-proof liquor (even if mixed with non-alcoholic drinks), a 5-ounce glass of 12% wine, or a 12-ounce glass of 5% beer. These "one drink" equivalents change if you are drinking ale, malt liquors, fortified wines, port, brandy, different proof liquor, **or** if you are drinking on an empty stomach, are tired, sick, upset, or have taken medicines or drugs.

How to use these charts: Find your weight chart. Then, look for the total number of drinks you have had and compare that to the time shown. If your **BAC** level is in the grey zone, your chances of having an accident are 5 times higher than if you had no drinks, and 25 times higher if your **BAC** level falls in the black zone.

BAC Zones:	90 to 109 lbs.	110 to 129 lbs.	130 to 149 lbs.	150 to 169 lbs.	170 to 189 lbs.	190 to 209 lbs.	210 lbs. & Up
TIME FROM 1st DRINK	TOTAL DRINKS	TOTAL DRINKS	TOTAL DRINKS	TOTAL DRINKS	TOTAL DRINKS	TOTAL DRINKS	TOTAL DRINKS
	1 2 3 4 5 6 7 8	1 2 3 4 5 6 7 8	1 2 3 4 5 6 7 8	1 2 3 4 5 6 7 8	1 2 3 4 5 6 7 8	1 2 3 4 5 6 7 8	1 2 3 4 5 6 7 8
1 hr							
2 hrs							
3 hrs							
4 hrs							

Technical note: These charts are not legal evidence of actual BAC. Although it is possible for anyone to exceed the designated limits, the charts have been constructed so that fewer than 5 persons in 100 will exceed these limits when drinking the stated amounts on an empty stomach. Actual values can vary by body type, sex, health status, and other factors.

Legend: ☐ (.01%–.04%) Possible DUI—*Definitely unlawful if under 21 years old* ▨ (.05%–.07%) Likely DUI—*Definitely unlawful if under 21 years old* ■ (.08% Up) Definitely DUI

* VC §§23152, 23153, 23136, 23140 DUI=Driving under the influence of alcohol and/or other drugs.

DL 606MO (REV. 10/2004)

The three serious types of impairment resulting from the "depressant" effects of alcohol on the brain are:

- less efficient vision and hearing
- lack of muscular coordination (clumsiness), *and*
- deterioration of judgment and self-control (euphoria and loss of inhibitions).

Again, the extent of impairment will vary from person to person, and the above figures represent only a range of averages. Some people, particularly regular drinkers, will have a sort of built-up immunity to alcohol. Still, their BAC may be 0.08% or more, making it illegal to drive even if they can do so safely. At the other extreme, people who normally abstain from alcohol begin to suffer slight impairment at a blood alcohol level as low as 0.02%! Moderate drinkers begin to show mild symptoms at 0.04 to 0.07%, while some heavy drinkers require 0.07 to 0.09% to suffer any impairment at all.

Effects of Blood Alcohol

% Blood Alcohol	State	Symptoms
0.01–0.05	relaxation	mild feeling of relaxation, very little effect
0.05–0.12	mild euphoria	slower reflexes, less coordination, lowered inhibitions, and increased self-confidence
0.08–0.25	impairment	memory and muscular coordination greatly reduced
0.15–0.30	great impairment	dizziness, disorientation, confusion
0.27–0.40	drunken stupor	inability to stand or walk; vomiting likely
0.35–0.50	coma/near death	body temperature fails and death from respiratory paralysis may result

Some persons, who over long periods of time consume large amounts of alcohol on a daily basis, may never be seriously affected in terms of muscular coordination—although alcohol can still cloud their judgment. (Of course, claiming that your 0.27% blood alcohol had no effect on your driving because you've been an alcoholic for years is not a recommended line of defense, since you must be found guilty if the jury believes your blood alcohol was 0.08% or more while you were driving.)

What does "under the influence" really mean? Do you wonder why the exact figure of 0.08% blood alcohol is used to define an offense under VC § 23152(b)? Is it because everyone is drunk at that level, or is it just a nice convenient round figure having little to do with reality? The truth lies somewhere in between. Here's the story.

In 1939, the American Medical Association had a "Committee to Study Problems of Motor Vehicle Accidents" look into the blood alcohol level at which a person is "under the influence" as far as driving is concerned. As a result of the study, the AMA and the National Safety Council concluded that:

- A person whose blood alcohol was 0.05% or less is definitely not under the influence;

- A person whose blood alcohol was between 0.05% and 0.15% might be under the influence, depending on the individual and the circumstances;

- A person with over 0.15% blood alcohol was definitely under the influence.

California uses only the first of the above conclusions in the form of a presumption that a person with less than 0.05% blood alcohol is not under the influence (VC § 23155(a)(1)). But the range of alcohol levels between which a person legally may or may not be under the influence is conservatively set at 0.05% to 0.08% (VC § 23155(a)(2)) rather than at the range suggested by the AMA study, namely 0.05% to 0.15%. For years, the law defined 0.10% and above as under the influence, even though many experts believe that this cutoff level should be 0.15%. However, in more recent years, special-interest groups and vote-hungry politicians have lowered the 0.10% cutoff to 0.08%.

The truth is that some people really are poor drivers at a particular blood alcohol level, but many others are not. Nevertheless, the legislature in 1969, after intense lobbying by district attorneys, police officers' associations, insurance companies, and other special-interest groups, adopted the 0.10% standard as the level at which a driver would be presumed to be "under the influence." After more intense lobbying by these same groups in 1981, the Legislature took away even the right to prove one's innocence when a blood alcohol exceeds a certain level. What this means is that some sober—and "innocent"—drivers may be unjustly convicted. And, once again in 1989, these same lobbying groups got the level lowered from 0.10% to 0.08%.

Blood or Breath Tests for Alcohol

Most drunk-driving arrests result in the arrested person taking a "chemical test" for the presence of alcohol in his blood or breath. This section briefly explains the law that requires this, as well as the tests themselves.

The "Implied Consent" Law

California's "implied consent" law requires any person lawfully arrested for driving under the influence to give a blood or breath sample when taken to the jail or police station. (This means the officer had a "reasonable suspicion" to pull you over, and then "probable cause" to arrest you. An officer has a reasonable suspicion to stop you if he saw you commit a violation or drive erratically. If, after he pulls you over, he notices the obvious symptoms of intoxication, he will then have "probable cause" to physically arrest you and charge you with driving under the influence.) If you refuse, your driver's license will be suspended by the DMV for a year, or more if you've previously suffered a "drunk-driving" conviction or previously received a similar suspension. (See also Chapter 15.) This is true even if you're eventually found not guilty of the current drunk-driving charge. If you have been convicted of drunk driving (or plea bargained reckless driving), or have suffered a similar suspension within seven years prior to your refusal to take the test, your license will be revoked for two years.

In addition, if you refuse to take *any* test, the police may forcibly hold you down while a technician sticks a needle into your arm to withdraw blood. (*People v. Ford* (1992) 4 Cal. App.4th 32, 5 Cal.Rptr.2d 189.) Although most police departments have a policy of involuntary testing only if an injury accident is involved, they may, in theory, forcibly withdraw blood in nonaccident cases as well. Finally, if the police successfully force you to submit to a blood test, your license will still be suspended because of your refusal to take the test voluntarily.

Your Right to a Choice of Tests

Even though you must submit to some kind of test, you have the right to choose between a blood or breath test (VC § 23577). If one of the tests is unavailable, you are required to take the other available test. For example, if the police department's breath tester is broken, you will be required to take a blood test. You may only opt for the less-accurate urine test in the highly unlikely situation where both blood and breath tests are not available.

Which test should you choose? It depends on the circumstances. If you had only one beer, glass of wine, or mild drink, your blood alcohol will be under 0.05%, a level so low that no sane prosecutor would try the case. Since results from a breath test (unlike those from a blood test) can be directly displayed on the measuring device right away, it will become clear that you're sober and the police might therefore let you go. On the other hand, if it's been less than an hour since you've finished your last drink (more, if you've eaten food), your body is still absorbing alcohol. When your body is absorbing alcohol, a breath test will give an erroneously high value. I once observed a test in which a person drank a few ounces of tequila; half an hour later, she took a blood and a breath test. The blood test showed 0.05% alcohol, but the breath test read 0.10%.

The reason for this result is that while your body is absorbing alcohol, your arterial blood alcohol level is higher than your venous blood alcohol level, and a breath test measures the higher arterial blood alcohol. So, if you last drank less than an hour before you're tested, don't take the breath test. Choose the blood test if you're sure you're below 0.08%. (However, if you choose the breath test, and it gives a low or zero alcohol reading, and if the police still have a "reasonable belief" that you're under the influence of *drugs*, they can insist, again under penalty of losing your license if you refuse, that you take a blood or urine test.)

Despite the requirement that the police offer you a choice between the two tests, the courts have refused to effectively enforce this provision. In one case, the police refused to give the suspected drunk driver a choice and insisted on a blood test. The court refused to exclude evidence based on a coerced blood test, thereby gutting the law allowing such a choice of any enforcement mechanism. (See *People v. Pucinelli* (1976) 63 Cal.App.3d 742, 135 Cal. Rptr. 34; *In re Garinger* (1987) 188 Cal.App.3d 1149; *Carleton v. Superior Court* (1985) 170 Cal.App.3d 1182 (six police officers allowed to hold down refusing driver and extract blood); *People v. Ryan* (1981) 116 Cal.App.3d 168; *People vs. Fite* (1968) 267 Cal.App.2d 685; and *Schmerber v. California* (1966) 384 U.S. 757, 86 S.Ct. 1826.) The general trend is that the courts will wink at police misconduct in this respect, for anything short of forced stomach-pumping.

Other Rights

The rule is that you do not have the right to have your attorney present for the test. You do have the right to an additional blood or breath test performed by an independent doctor, nurse, clinical lab technologist, bioanalyst, or any other person of your choosing. You have the right to have this person come down to where you're being held to collect your blood, breath, or urine sample at your expense. Still, this is difficult to arrange, and is not usually useful, unless your own test results are much lower than the police test—a rarity unless the sample taken by the police got mixed up with someone else's—and can be expensive if you want to use the results at trial, since you need to pay witnesses to testify.

This test is not, however, a substitute for the test done by the police, and you cannot delay the test until the person you call comes. If you do, your delay will be treated as a refusal and you will lose your license (*Payne v. Director of DMV* (1990) 235 Cal.App.3d 1514, 1 Cal. Rptr.2d 528). You must submit to the police-administered test of your choosing when they ask you to do so. If your independent test results come out much lower than the results

of the one the police made you take, the police tests will appear more questionable to a jury. If they don't, your lawyer doesn't have to use the results (VC § 23158(b)).

Finally, after the results are in on your blood, breath or urine test, you have the right to "full information concerning the test" (VC § 23158(c)). This means you're entitled to a copy of the results, *plus* a written explanation of the manner by which the analysis was performed. You or your attorney should request this information by letter within a week or two of your arrest. Also, if a blood test was taken, you have the right to have part of the preserved sample collected by the police tested by an independent laboratory. (*People v. Hitch* (1974) 12 Cal.3d 641.) If the police administer a breath test, they must advise you of your right to give an extra "back-up" sample for this sort of retesting, since a breath sample can't be saved easily. Unfortunately, the failure of the police to do this cannot be used to keep the breath test results from being used as evidence (VC § 23614).

The Chemical Tests: How They Work, How They Fail

In this section, we introduce you to how the different tests work, and some of the ways they go wrong.

Blood Tests

Other than directly measuring the alcohol content of your brain cells (which can be dangerous), the most accurate test to determine the possibility of alcohol affecting your driving is the blood sample test. Challenging the accuracy of this test is not as easy as challenging the accuracy of the breath or urine tests. Also, a blood sample is a very good indicator of whether you had taken any drugs.

However, if you have submitted to (or were coerced into taking) a blood test, there are several ways you may be able to challenge its accuracy.

The most common modern method for analyzing alcohol in a blood sample utilizes a "gas chromatograph," a device that vaporizes a liquid sample and passes the vapor through a "column" of dry chemicals that separate the vapor. Different vapors come out of the other end of the column at different times, and when the alcohol vapor comes off, its amount is measured by a detector whose output is displayed on a graph or digital readout. This method also relies on the use of standard solutions containing known amounts of alcohol to "calibrate" the gas chromatograph. Still other tests involve reaction of the alcohol with an enzyme.

A much older (and rarely used) procedure for the chemical analysis of blood samples for alcohol involves distilling the alcohol out of the blood and reacting it with a chemical called an "oxidizing agent." The more alcohol there is, the more oxidizing agent is used, allowing the analyst to calculate the alcohol from the amount of chemical required to oxidize all the alcohol. This oxidizing agent is really a solution of potassium dichromate ($K_2Cr_2O_7$) in distilled water. Its concentration has to be known with great precision in order for the result to be accurate.

In challenging any type of chemical analysis, a good defense lawyer should know how to cross-examine the analysts to shed doubt on the accuracy of the result. Did the analyst prepare the "standard" solution herself, or just take someone else's word for its content? Does the analyst periodically check the solution concentration to make sure it hasn't changed? Are tests periodically performed on samples of known alcohol concentration?

Also, most laboratories that analyze blood samples run numerous samples every day, making some errors on some samples (maybe yours!)—more probable than if an analyst were carefully concentrating on just one. Proper record keeping and laboratory organization are necessary to guard against sample mix-ups, as different parts of the analyses are carried out in different bottles and beakers. You may be able to cast some doubt on the test readings by raising questions about their record keeping.

Finally, blood samples that aren't properly preserved and sit around a long time before being analyzed have a tendency to either coagulate or decompose. If the sample coagulates, so that the red blood cells separate out from the liquid blood portion, the alcohol is further concentrated in the remaining liquid portion—contributing to a false high reading. If the sample decomposes, a false high reading will also be obtained because one of the chemical products of this decomposition is alcohol. Therefore, it is important that the analysis be done shortly after the sample is taken, and that the sample be properly preserved to minimize decomposition.

These are only remote possibilities, however. More than likely, the analysis of a blood sample will be correct, and a very good indicator of the blood alcohol in your system, at least at the time the sample was taken. Also, the prosecution's science-trained "expert witness" will almost always favorably impress a jury.

Breath Tests

Usually, you should only take the breath test if you finished your last drink at least an hour before the test. However, if you've had very little to drink, and it's been at least an hour since you stopped drinking, you may want to opt for the breath test. With this test, the police will know your approximate blood alcohol level immediately, and if the reading indicates less than 0.05% blood alcohol, they may release you right away. But don't count on it. They may simply keep you in custody until someone bails you out. Also, after seeing the low alcohol reading, and still being convinced your driving ability truly was impaired, they may think you're on drugs instead, and insist on a blood sample after that.

An analysis of breath gas gives only an indirectly determined value for blood alcohol. A breath test determines how much alcohol is in some portion of exhaled air, not how much alcohol is in the blood. To calculate content of blood alcohol from those of exhaled air, the content of alcohol in the air is normally multiplied by the number 2,100. This number, known as a "partition coefficient" or "partition ratio," is used because the lung air exhaled by an "average" person usually has 1/2,100th the amount of alcohol of an equal volume of blood. Using this "average" figure amounts to little more than scientific guesswork. For example, one study showed some people have lung-air alcohol concentrations 1,500 times smaller than their blood alcohol values, while other people have lung-air alcohol concentrations 3,000 times smaller. Also, the value varies for the same person over time and depends on body temperature and even respiration rate. As with results from a urine alcohol analysis, the calculated blood alcohol level (already printed or displayed on a readout on the machine) may be erroneous.

EXAMPLE:

Based on an "average" for all persons studied, the law assumes your blood alcohol content to be 2,100 times the content of alcohol in your breath. (Actually, this calculation is already done inside the breath-analyzing device.) So, if your breath contains 0.00004% alcohol, this number multiplied by the "partition coefficient" of 2,100 will give a calculated percentage of 0.08. But if your own "blood-to-breath" ratio is really 1,500 to 1, the 0.00004% breath alcohol content really means a blood alcohol level of 0.06%. Thus, the results could "prove" your blood alcohol was an illegal 0.08%, when in fact it was less than that.

Formerly, a person with a "borderline" breath alcohol level was allowed to use the "erroneous partition coefficient" defense to show a breath test inaccurate. However, VC §§ 23152 and 23153 now define the offense in terms of grams of alcohol per 210 liters of breath (a value consistent with a 2,100:1 partition coefficient), as well as grams of alcohol per 100 milliliters of blood. Thus, any evidence tending to show a partition coefficient other than 2,100:1 will have no bearing on the concentration of alcohol in the breath gas itself, and will be disallowed. (*People v. Bransford* (1994) 8 Cal.4th 885, 35 Cal.Rptr.2d 613; *People v. Ireland* (1995) 33 Cal.App.4th 680, 39 Cal.Rptr.2d 870.)

Alcohol-containing substances in your *mouth* can also produce falsely high readings, since the amount of alcohol vapor given off by anything in your mouth is much greater than any amount you exhale from your lungs. This includes stomach fluid vomited or regurgitated up within 20 minutes of taking the test, some toothache medicines, mouthwashes, and breath fresheners. Even a burp just before or while you blow into the breathalyzer tube may cause a falsely high reading. For this reason, the person administering the test is supposed to watch you for at least 20 minutes prior to taking the test to make sure you don't burp, belch, regurgitate, vomit, or put anything into your mouth.

There is also the possibility of a malfunction in the breath-testing devices. To assure accuracy, the device must be calibrated with air containing known amounts of alcohol vapor every 100 tests or ten days, whichever is more frequent. The police department's records should indicate how often the device has been calibrated, serviced, and used. A lapse in record keeping and/or police memory as to calibration and preparation of sample solutions can help your attorney establish reasonable doubt about the accuracy of the instrument. Other errors may result from the particular type of breath gas analyzer used.

Finally, because breath gas analysis is often inaccurate, you may be asked to take the tests two, or even three, times to produce a consistent result. Your failure to give them all the breath samples they want will result in your license being suspended by the DMV. (In *Hasiwar v. Sillas* (1981) 118 Cal.App.3d 295, the police measured 0.10% alcohol on the first try, then 0.15% on the second. They then insisted on a third breath test, which was refused. The DMV suspended his driver's license for failing to "complete" the test, and the court approved the suspension.)

Breath Gas Analyzers: The most common device uses a beam from an infrared heat source. When the beam encounters alcohol vapor, some of its energy is absorbed by the alcohol molecules. The more infrared energy absorbed, the higher the blood alcohol.

This method measures alcohol to the exclusion of other organic materials (like acetone on the breath of diabetics) better than some older devices, but is easily subject to the same interferences from alcohol-containing substances in your mouth. Also, the measuring devices have to be periodically maintained and standardized.

Urine Tests

The law no longer allows you to choose a urine test. You can choose only a blood or breath test.

Only if the officer is unable to access a breath-testing device *and* unable to locate a trained technician to take a blood sample, can the officer insist on such a test.

The urine test is less accurate than the blood or breath tests, which is why the law was changed in 1999 to allow use of the test only when the blood and breath test are unavailable. For example, you can only take a urine test when a police department's breath-analyzing machine is out of order and there is no professional available to take a blood sample. Indeed, you must take a urine test under these circumstances, since it's the only test available.

The urine test is the least accurate primarily because urine isn't blood, which actually contains the alcohol. So assumptions have to be made from a urine test on how much alcohol was ingested. Thus, the urine alcohol level has to be "correlated" to an "equivalent" blood alcohol level. An "average" 1.33:1 ratio of urine alcohol to blood alcohol is generally used. However, studies have shown that some people have alcohol levels only 40% as high in their urine as in their blood, while others have twice the alcohol content in their urine as in their blood. The urine test will give an erroneously high result if your urine has a higher concentration of alcohol than usual. Your urine may have a higher concentration of alcohol even if it's been a few hours since you last drank and your body is eliminating alcohol that is still in your system. This means that the blood alcohol level the prosecution infers from a urine alcohol analysis might be incorrect in some cases.

EXAMPLE:

The prosecutor assumes your urine alcohol to be an "average" 1.33 multiple of your blood alcohol. If a sample of your urine is found to contain, say, 0.133% alcohol, the prosecutor would divide this value by 1.33 to calculate a blood alcohol value of 0.10%. But if your kidneys actually pump out urine with an alcohol content *twice* that of your blood, a 0.133% urine alcohol content, divided by two, corresponds only to a 0.066% blood alcohol value. Thus the prosecutor would try to "prove" your blood alcohol level was 0.10%, when in fact, it was under 0.07%.

Also, a specimen of bladder urine only represents a composite of a continuously changing blood alcohol content. The pool of urine in the bladder at any given time is an accumulation of secreted urine since the last emptying of the bladder. It therefore tells much less about a person's blood alcohol at a particular moment than does a blood sample. This can work for or against you. If you had a lot to drink several hours beforehand and hadn't urinated since that time, the urine test result may be misleadingly high. If your drinking was relatively recent, though, say within an hour of the time you gave the sample, and especially if you'd had any nonalcoholic liquids before that, the urine test would give a misleadingly low result. Because of this, the only way to properly test a person's urine is to have him or her void the bladder and then produce a second urine sample. The police know this, and will insist that you also produce a second sample 20 minutes later.

Urine samples are analyzed for alcohol in almost the same way as blood samples. The results are therefore also subject to some of the same laboratory errors. (See above.)

If you do take the urine test, the police are required to give you "such privacy in the taking of the urine specimen as will insure the *accuracy of the specimen*, and at the same time, maintain the *dignity of the individual involved*" (VC § 23158(e)). In other words, you have the right to some privacy, but you can't insist on going alone into a bathroom where you might be able to secretly dilute the sample with tap, or toilet, water. At the very least, though, they have to exclude all persons of the opposite sex from the room in which you give the sample.

In sum, then, most chemical analyses of your breath, blood, or urine will give an accurate indication of your actual blood alcohol level. However, the tests are not infallible, and an experienced criminal defense attorney may be able to cast enough doubt on borderline test results to convince a jury that you might not be guilty.

License Suspension Penalties and Procedures

Years ago, a person convicted of driving under the influence did not necessarily face a driver's license suspension for one conviction of driving under the influence. The DMV would suspend a person's driver's license only if the person's driving record showed other violations as well.

Then, in response to changing attitudes toward drunk driving, license suspensions became automatic for a first offense unless the person was granted probation, was required to attend an alcohol treatment program, and was given a 90-day restriction, allowing the person to drive to and from work for work-related reasons, and to and from the alcohol treatment program. Actual license suspensions were imposed by the court, or by the DMV, after the person had violated probation. Naturally, this occurred *after* the person was convicted.

Now, however, your license is suspended *before* any conviction, and your suspension notice—effective 30 days from the date of your arrest—is handed to you by a police officer. Suspension is then automatic, unless you request a hearing from the DMV within ten days. If you can't convince the DMV to overturn your suspension, your license is suspended—even if the court dismisses or reduces the charges.

After arresting you for driving under the influence, a police officer will take away your driver's license and present you with a notice that your license is suspended effective 30 days later, and a temporary license to allow you to drive within that 30-day period.

The request for hearing must be made to the DMV within ten days, or the suspension will go into effect, even if the charges are later reduced or dismissed in court. For that reason, every person arrested for driving under the influence should request a hearing in the event that they later prevail in court, and should do it within ten days of the arrest. For further information on how to request a DMV hearing when you receive a notice of suspension, see Chapter 15.

Whether you default or show up at the hearing and lose, your driver's license will be suspended for a period of time that depends on a number of factors, including:

- whether you refused a chemical test, or, if you submitted to one, whether it showed your blood alcohol was 0.08% or more
- the total number of prior convictions of driving under the influence (or plea-bargained reckless driving) over the past ten years
- suspensions you have received for driving under the influence on any separate occasions, and
- previous suspensions for refusing blood, breath, or urine tests within the previous ten years. (VC §§ 13353–13354.)

Prior DUI convictions (or suspensions) plus suspensions for refusal over previous 10 years	0	1	2 or more
Suspension for driving with blood alcohol over 0.08%	4 months (10 months if over 0.20%	1 year	1 year
Suspension for refusal of chemical test	1 year	2 years	3 years

Persons 21 and older who receive first-offense suspensions for driving with blood alcohol levels over 0.08% (but not for refusing a chemical test) may receive a five-month restricted driving privilege to drive to and from work, and to and from an alcohol treatment program, if they enroll in such a program, after serving 30 days of straight suspension.

Persons under 21 also face one-year license suspensions for either driving with a blood alcohol level of 0.01% or more, as measured by a hand-held police "preliminary alcohol screening (PAS) device or other chemical test," or for refusing to submit to such a roadside test. (VC §§ 13353.1, 13353.2, 23136–23138.) This is in addition to any criminal penalties for driving under the influence.

Dealing With a DUI Charge

The following is only a very brief summary of what you need to consider if faced with a drunk-driving charge.

Evaluating Your Case

After you've been arrested for driving under the influence, and have been released from jail, you should try to objectively evaluate your case. Your alternatives include:

- simply pleading guilty as charged
- trying to plea bargain down to a reduced charge
- asking for a trial before a judge, or
- demanding a *jury* trial.

The general rule is that if you choose to fight the charge, you should usually insist on a *jury* trial—you'll have a better chance than with a case-worn and possibly cynical judge who has seen a lot of guilty people. The only exception to this general rule is when your defense is fairly unusual or technical. For example, if you staggered out of a bar and into your car, and fell asleep—but you didn't drive—a judge might be more receptive to your defense than a jury.

(The U.S. Supreme Court has ruled that a person accused of drunk driving punishable by up to six months in jail isn't entitled, under the U.S. Constitution, to a jury trial (*Blanton v. City of North Las Vegas* (1989) 489 U.S. 538, 109 S.Ct. 1289, 103 L.Ed.2d 550). However, under California's own state constitution, the right to trial by jury exists for any offense punishable by any imprisonment whatsoever (*Mitchell v. Superior Court* (1989) 49 Cal.3d 1230, 1242–1243, 265 Cal.Rptr. 144).) As with any jury trial in a criminal case, the prosecutor must convince *all 12* jurors of your guilt, as opposed to just one judge in a nonjury trial.

Still, even jury trial conviction rates for driving under the influence are high, though they vary in different parts of the state. (Sadly, this is partly because special-interest groups have, over the years, fostered a public attitude to the effect that eradicating the drunk-driving problem is more important than having fair trials.) Part of the money you're paying your lawyer is for the value of her experience in knowing what a local jury is likely to do in a given situation.

Generally, the more a jury is likely to find you guilty of driving under the influence (or with an over-0.08% blood alcohol), the more you will want to plea bargain, or negotiate a settlement, with the prosecutor. Since drunk-driving juries unfortunately put a lot of faith in the blood test results (and the prosecutor's scientific mumbo-jumbo that goes along with it), it is these results that are most likely to affect your choice of options.

As a general rule, a person whose blood alcohol test results are higher than 0.12% will have a very low chance of winning at trial. This is especially true since an over-0.08% blood alcohol level is sufficient to convict you—whether you were drunk or not (VC § 23152(b)). The only way you can be acquitted of such a charge is to shed doubt on the validity of the test results so that either the jury entirely disbelieves them, or thinks that after adjusting for possible errors in your favor, your blood alcohol *might* have been less than 0.08%. It is very difficult for even a trained and experienced lawyer to do this. Therefore, a confident prosecutor is not likely to enter into a plea bargain where you agree to plead guilty to a reduced charge like reckless driving.

If your blood alcohol tested out at between 0.08 and 0.11%, your chances of winning in a trial are slightly better, but not much. You still have to convince a jury that the test results are at least inaccurate enough to raise a reasonable doubt as to whether your blood alcohol was 0.08% or higher at the time you were driving. And, if the prosecutor also charges you with driving under the influence (VC § 23152(a)), you'll also have to establish that you weren't "under the influence" at whatever blood alcohol level you had.

Whether you have a decent chance of convincing a jury you weren't under the influence will depend largely on the type of testimony your lawyer can elicit from anyone who was with you either before or while you were driving. The types of witnesses who can testify as to your sobriety may range from local "pillars of the community" the jurors might believe to barroom buddies who were also enjoying plenty of sauce (good luck!).

EXAMPLE 1:

Irwin spent an entire evening in a bar—9 p.m. to closing time at 2 a.m. He drove home alone, was pulled over, and admitted to the mythical "two beers," though he probably had a lot more. Although his drinking buddies at the bar, as well as the bartender, would say Irwin wasn't under the influence, none of them saw him take the "field sobriety" or coordination tests. The results of his blood test showed an 0.11% alcohol level. When interpreted ("extrapolated") back to the time he was driving, his blood alcohol worked out to about 0.13%.

In this situation, Irwin (if he represents himself) or his lawyer should probably try to get the best possible deal for a guilty plea—perhaps a minimum fine, or a 90-day license restriction in lieu of a jail term. If the prosecutor refuses to bargain, Irwin may not have much to lose by going to trial, except a higher lawyer's fee—which may not seem so large when compared to the extra costs he'll incur over the next few years should he be convicted. And who knows? He might get lucky.

EXAMPLE 2:

Suppose instead that Irwin had just left a "business lunch" where more than one person who *hadn't* been drinking could testify they saw Irwin with his wits about him. Or suppose Irwin drove back to work with at least one other person who saw him perform the sobriety test successfully. In these situations, he should see what the prosecutor will offer in a plea bargain. It may be just a slap on the wrist, though Irwin would then have a "prior"—even if he pleaded guilty to only reckless driving. If no favorable plea bargain is forthcoming, Irwin should seriously consider getting a lawyer and fighting his case.

If your blood alcohol was measured at less than 0.08%, your chances of beating a drunk-driving charge are better. First, you won't be convicted of having blood alcohol of 0.08% or more, and the prosecutor will have to establish that you were under the influence at the below-0.08% level. However, if your blood alcohol level was found to be slightly under 0.08%—say 0.06% or 0.07%—measured about an hour after you were driving, the prosecutor would then claim that it was higher—namely 0.08%—when you were driving, and fell below that level before the blood or breath sample was taken. A skilled attorney should be able to properly cross-examine the prosecutor's expert witnesses to show that the likelihood of one's driving ability being affected at a blood alcohol level of less than 0.08% is small. Naturally, the farther below 0.08% your blood alcohol was, the better your chances are of being acquitted and the more likely the prosecutor will be willing to plea bargain.

What if you refused to submit to a blood or breath test? Your chances of beating the drunk-driving charge at trial might be slightly better than if you had submitted to the test and the results showed a very high blood alcohol level. (However, your refusal to take the test can be used against you, and jurors may consider this to be a damning admission on your part.) The prosecutor may be unable to convict you for having a blood alcohol level of 0.08% or more, but she still may be able to convict you of having been under the influence. This will depend almost entirely on how much weight the jury gives to the testimony of the police officer and prosecution witnesses, compared to how much the jurors will believe any testimony you can present. And, of course, your refusal to take the test will result in an automatic license suspension for at least a year. If you've had one or two prior alcohol-related reckless driving and/or drunk-driving convictions, or separate DMV suspensions based on 0.08% or more blood alcohol, within seven years, the suspension will last for two years or three years respectively (VC § 13353).

Getting a Lawyer

As mentioned earlier, defending yourself against a drunk-driving charge in a jury trial is not recommended. Once you've been released from jail and have had a chance to evaluate your case, you should think about getting an attorney to represent you (see Chapter 9), in addition to putting in an automatic hearing request to the DMV. If you're unable to afford an attorney, you should ask the judge to appoint a lawyer for you when you first appear in court. Even if your case seems hopeless, you have nothing to lose by taking advantage of free legal representation. If you aren't poor enough to qualify for a court-appointed lawyer, and believe that your case falls in the narrow range where you may be able to win a jury trial, begin by making an appointment with an attorney experienced in criminal defense work. Even though you may be unable to afford to pay her to defend you in a jury trial (the fee for this could be as high as several thousand dollars), you should be able to afford

the fee for one or two office visits. At the very least, you can hire her for the limited purpose of fully explaining your options to you, or perhaps to try to work out a plea bargain with the prosecutor. Defense attorneys' statistics show that the chances of beating a drunk-driving charge by going to trial are low. If your case is rife with hopeless circumstances (for example, blood alcohol over 0.15%, dismal failure on coordination tests, etc.), you should be wary of an overly optimistic lawyer who tells you your chances are excellent while demanding more and more money as the case drags on.

Plea Bargaining

Plea bargaining (sometimes also referred to as "sentence bargaining") is a process where a criminal defendant (or his or her lawyer) and the prosecutor reach a compromise, then the defendant enters a guilty plea to a reduced charge or, sometimes, in exchange for the promise of a reduced fine or jail sentence. Plea bargaining generally takes place over the phone or at the prosecutor's office, and often at a "pretrial conference" in the judge's chambers before trial. As part of the process, the judge informally tells you—or your lawyer—the sentence that he or she will impose if you plead guilty.

The "bargain" of a plea bargain is that the prosecutor avoids having to try a questionable case, but still gets to rack up a conviction, while the person accused of drunk driving receives the minimum sentence or, perhaps, only a less serious conviction for reckless driving.

Plea bargains in drunk-driving cases, however, are no longer as common as they were many years ago. Since driving with a blood alcohol level of over 0.08% or more is illegal—regardless of whether the driver is under the influence—it is easier for prosecutors to obtain convictions in the formerly borderline cases

(0.08% to 0.12% alcohol levels). And from the accused's perspective, the incentive to plead guilty to reckless driving is far less under the new law, since the law now requires that a statement be placed on your record that alcohol was involved in the offense (VC § 23103.5), and since your license will be suspended by the DMV for four months or a year even in the face of such a lesser conviction. Also, your insurance company may treat records of such guilty pleas as drunk-driving convictions and cancel, or refuse to renew, your policy anyway. Also, if you're charged with drunk driving again within the next seven years (after having plea bargained a previous drunk-driving charge down to reckless), the earlier plea will be used against you for the purpose of increasing both the minimum and maximum penalties if you're convicted—just as if you had been convicted of drunk driving the first time.

EXAMPLE:

The first time Bill Blotto was accused of driving under the influence, he faced a minimum penalty of a $390 fine (plus penalty assessments) plus either two days in jail or a 90-day license restriction whereby he would have been allowed to drive only to, from, and in work. Instead, Bill was allowed to plead guilty to reckless driving and pay a smaller fine. Two years later, Bill was charged with drunk driving again. Although it will be his first drunk-driving conviction, if he pleads or is found guilty, he will face the same penalty as would a second-offense drunk driver—mandatory minimum penalties of two days in jail (probably more), an 18-month alcohol treatment program, and a one-year license suspension followed by a two-year license restriction.

Despite the attempts of "law-and-order" types to forbid plea bargaining, it will always be with us. Without it, defense attorneys would have nothing to lose by pleading each and every one of their clients not guilty and demanding a jury trial all the time. When you consider that only about 10% of all serious criminal cases ever go to trial, and that nearly all the remaining cases are plea bargained, an end to plea bargaining would increase five-fold the number of trials in the criminal courts. This would require more courts, judges, court personnel, and taxes.

Although more will be said in Chapter 13 about conducting your own plea bargaining negotiations, you may wish to hire a lawyer to do it for you. A prosecutor may not be as willing to enter into a plea bargain with an inexperienced defendant who might well do a poor job of representing herself. Also, an experienced lawyer who regularly handles drunk-driving cases will be more familiar with local practices, prosecutors, and judges than you can ever hope to be. Nevertheless, many defendants who have taken the time to educate themselves both as to the law and to the nuances of bargaining have done every bit as well as, and sometimes better than, lawyers, and have saved themselves a big fee.

Pretrial Court Proceedings

Pretrial court procedures for offenses other than drunk driving are covered in detail in Chapter 10. However, since drunk-driving cases are more complex and should generally be handled by an attorney, this section is designed to give you information you'll need to intelligently participate in your attorney's defense of your drunk-driving case.

Arraignment

Some time after you're arrested, you will appear before a judge for arraignment (Chapter 13). You will be asked to plead to the charge, either guilty or not guilty. Arrangements will also be made regarding your right to counsel and bail. If you tell the judge you can't afford to hire a lawyer, she will probably ask you to fill out a financial disclosure form and refer you to the Public Defender's office. In smaller counties, the judge may appoint a private defense lawyer to represent you (Chapter 9). Most defendants charged with misdemeanors who have not already posted bail are released on their own recognizance at arraignment. Having an attorney represent you at arraignment is normally unnecessary. At this stage, you are only entering a plea, and you can plead not guilty and insist on a jury trial. You do not have to specifically request a jury trial; it is assumed you want one unless you expressly waive that right. You can always change your plea to guilty or nolo contendere (see Chapter 10), or drop the demand for a jury trial later. If you're also charged with having prior under-the-influence convictions, you should deny them so that you or your attorney can challenge their validity later. At arraignment, the case will also be set for a "pretrial conference."

Getting the Best Judge

If you hire an experienced attorney to defend you against a drunk-driving charge, he will generally know which judges to avoid because they usually favor the prosecution or sentence harshly. Lawyers can use various procedures (such as changing pleas, dropping the demand for a jury trial, asking for continuances) to minimize the chance that such a judge will hear your case. If all else fails, the attorney can use one "peremptory challenge" to disqualify a judge, indicating that he "believes" the judge to be prejudiced. True, you could do this yourself (see Chapter 10), but an attorney experienced in drunk-driving trials will be more likely to know which judge, if any, to challenge.

Motions to Suppress Evidence

If the police illegally arrested you and/or obtained any evidence against you in an illegal manner, your attorney can schedule a special pretrial hearing to suppress certain evidence (PC § 1538.5). The prosecution is then prevented from using it at trial. For example, if you consented to give a blood sample only after the police beat you into submission, your attorney may want to make a "motion to suppress" the test results, thereby keeping them from being introduced into evidence at trial.

A motion to suppress is heard several weeks (sometimes months) before the trial actually takes place. It is only heard before a judge, perhaps one who will not be presiding at your trial. This type of motion is fairly technical and complicated, and will probably involve cross-examining the officer who arrested you. You're advised not to try to handle it yourself.

Motions to "Strike a Prior"

A person who pleads guilty to, or is convicted of, a second or third offense of driving under the influence can suffer a far heavier penalty than a first offender. In order to obtain the heavier penalty—a mandatory jail sentence and license suspension—the prosecution must "charge" the prior conviction against you. When you initially plead "not guilty" to the offense, *never* admit any priors charged against you. (A court cannot require that you discuss uncharged prior convictions if and when you plead guilty (*Municipal Court v. Superior Court* (1988) 199 Cal.App.3d 19, 244 Cal.Rptr. 519).)

Simply "deny" them. This is perfectly legal. If you "admit" them, you destroy any chance of challenging their validity on technical grounds.

If your attorney is unable to successfully challenge the validity of the priors you denied, the prosecution gets to introduce them into evidence. The judge is supposed to warn the jury that the evidence of a prior is admitted only for the purpose of increasing your sentence if found guilty of the current charge. But the jury is likely to use this information as an indication that you probably also committed the current offense. For this reason, if your attorney is unable to get the priors stricken before trial, it may be best to ask for a "bifurcated" (two-part) trial where the jury considers your priors only if, and after, it finds you guilty of the offense (see *People v. Bracamonte* (1981) 119 Cal.App.3d 644, 174 Cal.Rptr. 191). Another approach is to admit them just before trial out of hearing of the jurors. This renders the prosecution's evidence of your priors irrelevant and inadmissible.

By having a prior conviction "stricken," you face a less severe penalty if convicted on the current charge. The procedure to strike a prior is based on whether you were properly informed of and/or intelligently waived (gave up) certain rights at any hearings related to the prior offenses. Again, this type of motion is extremely technical and better left to your attorney.

The Pretrial Conference

In most counties, a "pretrial conference" is scheduled some time before a jury trial. The pretrial conference usually occurs inside a judge's chambers, and is where most plea bargaining (and sentence bargaining) occurs. (See Chapter 13.) The prosecutor usually begins by emphasizing the blood alcohol test results and summarizing what the police officer and any other witnesses will testify to. This is to establish that he or she has a very strong case, implying that the defendant might as well plead guilty, or at least accept any offer of a plea bargain. To sweeten this prospect, the prosecutor might also offer to recommend a minimum sentence to the judge in exchange for a guilty plea. The judge might indicate whether or not he or she will accept such a recommendation; if the judge says he'll accept it, this will tell you or your lawyer what your sentence will be if you plead guilty to the original or a reduced charge.

If the prosecutor refuses to consider offering you the prospect of pleading guilty to a lesser charge and/or recommends more than the minimum sentence if you plead guilty, this is the time for you or your lawyer to briefly summarize your defense to the judge and prosecutor. You should emphasize the proposed testimony of any witnesses you may have regarding how sober you were just before you were driving. Also, if the blood alcohol test results are not much above 0.08%, indicate that you're prepared to cross-examine the chemist or breath gas analyzer operator regarding the scientific validity of the results. (This is especially important where a urine or breath test is involved.)

Then, depending on the judge's personality, she may try to convince you, your lawyer, or the prosecutor, to compromise. (Some judges are very forceful in this regard and even take pride in insisting on compromise, so as not to have to do as many jury trials.) If a compromise is worked out, a time will be scheduled (possibly right then and there) for you to plead guilty to the original or a reduced charge in the courtroom. If not, a trial date will be set if one hasn't been already.

The Trial

The trial of drunk-driving cases is similar to the trial of any other misdemeanor offense. (Misdemeanor jury trial procedure is explained in Chapter 13.) The selection of jury members is very important, however, and a lawyer should try to exclude all nondrivers, all nondrinkers, and all MADD-sympathizers from the jury. Lawyers can do this by using peremptory challenges, where no reason need be given for excusing a juror. ●

Should You Fight Your Ticket/ Should You Get a Lawyer?

Now that you've read all about the type of ticket you received, you probably want to jump into your trusty old steed, drive (slowly, of course) down to traffic court and demand your right to contest it. Unfortunately, the procedure isn't that simple. As the following chapters will explain, before you can have a trial, you need to contact the court clerks, possibly post bail, decide whether you want an arraignment, and determine whether you need to make any pretrial motions.

So, the first thing you should do is go home, pour yourself a glass of wine (or bowl of chicken soup, if you prefer), curl up in a chair, and think things over. Above all, relax; anger won't help you to think clearly and you won't be able to do anything about the ticket for several days after you get it anyway.

Note: If you're facing a misdemeanor charge (see Chapters 7 and 8) you should consider contesting it, or a plea bargain. You should also seriously consider getting a lawyer to assist you. This chapter offers advice on how to find a good lawyer to represent you.

Things to Consider

Before deciding whether or not to contest your ticket, you should consider whether you are, in fact, guilty, what's involved in contesting it, the chances of successfully doing so, and the possible consequences.

Are You Really Guilty?

In deciding whether to fight, you should begin by determining whether you really are guilty. Examine the ticket for the code section the officer says you violated. (See Chapter 2.) Then, study the exact language of that code section, set out in the appropriate chapter of this book (Chapter 4 for speeding violations, Chapter 5

for other moving violations, etc.). If we don't reprint the code section that you were cited for, look it up in the Vehicle Code that you got from the DMV, go to your local law library (see Chapter 2), or look online at http://dmv.ca.gov.

Carefully read and reread each "element" of the offense, as we instruct in Chapter 2. If you are not guilty of each and every element, you are not guilty of the offense. Also, don't overlook the possibility of arguing that you lacked willfulness or criminal negligence.

Pay particular attention to elements that require a subjective judgment on the part of the officer. For example, reckless driving involves driving "in *willful* or *wanton* disregard for the safety of persons or property." What seems like willfulness or wantonness to one person may appear to be the height of caution to another. Another example: The "Basic Speed Law" requires that you not be driving "at a speed greater than is *reasonable* or *prudent*...." What seemed like a lack of prudence to the police officer may in fact have been the height of prudence from your viewpoint (and hopefully the viewpoint of any witnesses to the event).

On the other hand, violations that require only objective observations by the cop, like going over the 65 mph speed limit or running a stop sign, will turn solely on which version of the facts the court believes—yours or the cop's. (Good luck!) These kinds of arguments are rarely successful, but you might get lucky.

Finally, pay close attention to any defenses you might be able to raise to legally justify your action. In Chapter 5, for example, we noted that driving slowly in the left lane is legally justified if you were planning to make a left turn. These kinds of defenses are generally more successful because they raise some additional fact or legal point that precludes a conviction, rather than simply contradicting what the officer saw.

Will the Officer Show at Trial?

Whether you are guilty or not, you should consider whether it is likely the officer will appear at trial. If he or she does not, the case probably will be dismissed. The great majority of tickets that are beaten are done so on this basis.

If you asked for a trial at the county seat (see Chapter 17), there is a good chance that the officer won't show. Also, in some places, such as San Francisco, that encourage people to agree to "informal" hearings without the officer present (see Chapter 10), officers aren't used to showing up for trial—and might not do so, even if you opt for a regular trial.

Finally, the more serious the violation the more likely it is the officer will show up in court. An officer will be more inclined to appear in court to testify against someone who zipped through a school zone at 45 mph than against someone she cited for doing 42 mph in a 35 mph zone. (This writer once noticed that a CHP officer failed to show for a trial where he wrote someone up—at quota time on the last day of the month—for the heinous crime of doing 60 mph on the 55-mph-limit freeway.)

Will Your Insurance Rates Rise?

You should also consider whether your insurance will rise as a result of this ticket should you be convicted or pay the fine. Given the law's requirement for a "good driver discount," this is more likely now than in years past for a second moving-violation infraction in three years. We discuss this at length in Chapter 3.

Were You in an Accident?

If you were cited for a moving violation at the scene of an accident in which you were involved, you should *never* plead guilty. A guilty plea can be used against you later in a civil lawsuit by anyone else involved in the accident. But the guilty plea must be before a judge; merely paying off the ticket by forfeiting bail to a clerk is not considered pleading guilty for this purpose. Nor is pleading nolo contendere (no contest) a guilty plea. A not-guilty plea, of course, cannot be used against you in a civil action, and neither can a conviction following a not-guilty plea (VC § 40834).

How Much Time and Effort Will It Take to Fight?

The time and effort it will take to fight your ticket depends on (1) the kind of violation you're charged with, (2) the extent to which you want to fight it, and (3) other factors, like the distance between the court and your home.

Parking Violations

Parking violations are handled by a unique procedure that involves relatively little hassle. You can handle some of the steps by mail. (Parking ticket procedure is fully described in Chapter 6.) Since parking violations do not go on your driving record, you may want to look at the matter simply in terms of balancing your time lost from work versus the fine.

Infractions

Infractions (other than parking tickets and equipment violations) allow for numerous fighting options. These options are summarized here from the most ambitious to the least ambitious. You may want to refer to the flowchart at the end of Chapter 1 to get an overview of how these options fit together.

Infraction Option #1: Fight Your Ticket to the Hilt. If you want to pull out all the stops, you can insist upon every procedural formality to which you're entitled. The idea is to make the state give up before you do.

This tactic gives you the most chances for success, but also requires the most amount of time and energy. You must appear at an *arraignment*. You should insist on receiving a copy of the officer's notes about the circumstances of your supposed violation. You may need to type up your procedural requests (called "*motions*") and argue them before a judge. (Read Chapter 10 to find the kind of requests you can make. Determine if any apply to your situation.) If your requests are granted your case might be dismissed at this stage, but the chances are rather slim.

If your requests are denied, you must prepare for trial. At trial, you hope the officer doesn't show. If he doesn't, you win. If he does, you try to cast a reasonable doubt on his version of the events through your cross-examination, for which you've prepared in advance. You also must prepare to make specific legal "objections" to the officer's testimony, to get certain evidence excluded—like radar evidence, for example. Finally, you present your own side of the story through your own testimony and that of witnesses you've arranged to be there. This too requires advance preparation to be done effectively.

This option is best suited for those who have a valid legal excuse or who qualify for a procedural dismissal of their ticket. Note, however, that by pleading not guilty, you give up your right to attend traffic school and have the charges dismissed. (See Option #4.) If traffic school is not an option for your violation, or not available in your county, you might as well fight.

Infraction Option #2: Bypass Arraignment and Go to Trial. If you don't want to take the time to request every pretrial procedural formality at arraignment, but still want to have a trial with the officer present, you can bypass the arraignment and proceed directly to trial.

(However, you should still insist on getting a copy of the officer's notes, as we discuss in Chapter 10.) Most court clerks won't tell you about this option.

There are two ways to bypass arraignment. You can go to the court clerk and say that you're pleading "not guilty" and that you want your next appearance to be a formal trial with the officer present. If you don't want to go to the courthouse and wait in line, you can plead not guilty by mail, and state in your letter that you'd like to have a formal trial with the officer present. However, if you choose this option, you will have to post the fine with the court in advance, the fine being refundable if you are found not guilty.

Bypassing the arraignment is a sensible option for those who want to fight, but who want to minimize the number of court appearances they have to make. But remember, once you've pleaded not guilty, you have forfeited your opportunity to attend traffic school.

Infraction Option #3: A "Trial by Written Declaration." If you wish, you can conduct your trial by mail, through a procedure called a "trial by declaration" (see Chapter 10). In a trial by declaration, you lay out your side of the story in a carefully drafted letter to the court. If you lose this trial by mail, you still get a chance to win at an in-person trial with the officer present.

Also, under this option, you must pay the fine to the court in advance and it will be refunded to you if you are found not guilty.

Infraction Option #4: An "Informal Hearing." Some traffic courts—most notably in San Francisco—offer "informal hearings" in which you give up the right to call the officer to court and simply explain your side of the case. Many people who don't want the hassle of a formal trial elect to settle for this type of hearing before the judge at arraignment. (See Chapter 10.)

Beware. This is not always a wise move. At an informal hearing, you give up many of your most important rights—like your right to have the police officer appear at your hearing. Furthermore, your chances of talking your way out of a conviction at an informal hearing are generally slim at best.

Many people end up pleading "guilty with an explanation" in hopes of getting a lower fine. They may get the lower fine, but they still end up with a conviction on their driving record, which can result in higher insurance rates and stiffer penalties next time they get a ticket.

The only time this option makes sense is when you're charged with an offense that does *not* go on your record, and you simply want to argue for a lower fine.

Infraction Option #5: Traffic School. For most minor moving violations not involving alcohol or exceeding the speed limit by more than 25 miles per hour, you can go to the court clerk (in most counties) and request traffic school instead of admitting guilt. (In some counties, you may have to go to an arraignment to make this request.) However, you still have to pay the amount of the fine, a $49 to $59 "administrative fee," and $25 to $30 to the traffic school itself. After you complete traffic school, the case is dismissed and no conviction record is sent to the DMV. (All that results on your DMV record is a notation that you went to traffic school—information disclosed to courts only, but not insurance companies.)

If you were cited for an ordinary one-point, non-alcohol, non-drug-related moving-violation infraction not involving speed more than 25 miles per hour over the posted limit, you can keep it off your driving record by attending traffic school. You must meet the following requirements:

- have a valid driver's license from any state
- did not fail to appear for any court date on this ticket (or, if you did, you've paid the failure-to-appear penalties), and
- at least 18 months have elapsed between the date of your last citation for which you attended traffic school and the date of the current citation (VC § 1808.7 and Rule 4.104, Calif. Rules of Court).

This rule has been in effect since 1997, but some local court clerks have not caught on. So if a court clerk tells you can't attend traffic school because of a local court policy, you should ask to be arraigned before a judge. Once there, tell the judge you want to attend traffic school, and that you're entitled to under Rule 4.104 of the California Rules of Court.

Traffic school is a reasonable option for people charged with an infraction that would appear on their record but who either don't want to take the time to fight, or know that they're guilty. The time it takes to attend traffic school—a Saturday or a few weeknights—may not be much more (or even less) time than it takes to fight your ticket to the hilt. And with traffic school, you can rest assured that the violation will not appear on your record, while your chances of beating a ticket by contesting it are uncertain, at best, if the officer shows at trial.

Note: Traffic school cannot be chosen as an option more than once in an 18-month period.

There's some hassle involved in opting for traffic school. You have to attend it—usually on a weekend—and in some counties you may have to make an extra trip down to the courthouse for arraignment to request it.

On the other hand, since traffic schools are often privately run (for profit), they also are frequently more interesting than any government bureaucrat could make them. And the information presented can be very valuable:

Traffic safety, intelligently presented, has a lot going for it.

Keep in mind that there is a wide variety of traffic schools out there, each using a slightly different approach. You should shop around for one that best suits your interests, schedule, and financial needs. For example, some traffic schools are taught by comedians and others by police officers, some require a high level of participation and others require only attendance. Some traffic school courses are offered in languages other than English. For a complete list of traffic schools in your county, ask the court clerk.

Regardless of which traffic school you choose, remember to be on time. Because a certain number of hours of attendance are required, latecomers are often turned away. And remember to bring a copy of your ticket and your driver's license. After you have completed the course, you will be given a certificate to fill out and return to the DMV, to verify that you have attended.

Many courts have now authorized the use of Internet-based online traffic school. However, some of the counties that allow this require you to take an exam at a local library or auto insurance broker's office before passing the course. Since the list of courts that allow use of online traffic schools—and the special rules applicable to each—is constantly changing, check www.webtrafficschool.com, www.trafficschool.com, www.trafficschoolonline.com, and www.hmall.com to see which courts allow use of their programs. You can also check with the clerk's office at your local courthouse.

Infraction Option #6: Pay the Fine (Don't Fight). You can always simply pay the fine and suffer the consequences. This of course involves the least amount of hassle. The system makes it as easy as possible. You can even pay by mail in most cases. But think carefully about the effects of "giving up" before you finally decide. Especially consider the long-term consequences of having a conviction on your record: higher insurance rates, points on your record, and stiffer penalties on future tickets.

In sum, then, you have lots of choices when it comes to fighting an infraction. Read the selections cross-referenced in the above summaries to get a better idea of what each option entails.

Equipment Violations

Equipment violations, as we saw in Chapter 6, are dealt with by a unique procedure. You really have no choice but to have the defect corrected and show certification of the correction to the court within a specified time. Failure to do so can result in a misdemeanor charge against you. If you feel the equipment wasn't defective in the first place, getting certification of that fact shouldn't be difficult.

Misdemeanors

Misdemeanor defendants have different options. You must appear at arraignment even if you simply want to plead guilty. If you want to fight, you have the choice of either a jury trial or a trial before a judge. Conducting a jury trial is almost always the best choice, but it is very difficult to conduct one successfully on your own. Plea bargaining is also an important part of handling a misdemeanor charge. You should seriously consider hiring a lawyer skilled in such matters if you're charged with a misdemeanor.

The Big Picture

If you're still undecided, you may want to consider this: Only a vigilant and aggressive attitude by the motoring public will ever take the profit out of the ticket business. If everyone fought unjustified tickets, the police establishment would be too busy testifying in court to continue raising revenue for politicians. At the very least, if a traffic cop knew he'd have to back up every citation with a court appearance, before a fair and honest judge, ticketing activities would be limited to serious violations, as they should be. (See Chapter 18.)

Do You Need a Lawyer?

Within the past decade, people have become more sophisticated in dealing with legal problems. Many people present their own cases in court. If you face a fairly minor infraction punishable by no more than a $200 fine, it might not make sense for you to get a lawyer.

When serious offenses are involved, such as driving under the influence, reckless driving, driving while your license is suspended, or other misdemeanors punishable by time in the county jail, you should consider hiring a lawyer, or, if you can't afford one, getting the public defender to represent you. Even if you previously represented yourself in a civil proceeding, such as a divorce, name change or simple lawsuit, and know something about criminal law, it often isn't wise to represent yourself when you're charged with a misdemeanor punishable by jail.

What Lawyers Can Do for You

There are three basic ways a lawyer can help you when you're charged with a traffic violation.

Consultation and Advice

The lawyer can listen to the details of your situation, analyze it for you, and advise you on your position and best plan of action. Ideally, she will give you more than just conclusions—she can educate you about your whole situation and

tell you all the alternatives available from which you can make your own choices. This kind of service is the least expensive since it only involves an office call and a little time. A charge of more than $75 to $100 for a half-hour consultation might be considered excessive. Find out the fee before you go in.

Negotiation

When you're charged with serious violations, the lawyer can use her special talents, knowledge and experience to help you negotiate with the prosecuting agency (the district or city attorney's office) to your best advantage. Often she will be able to do this more successfully than you could. If the lawyer specializes in criminal law, she may even have a good working relationship with several prosecuting attorneys. Without spending much of her own time, she can sometimes accomplish a lot through even a letter or phone call.

Represent You in Court or Before the DMV

If you're charged with a serious offense such as driving under the influence, or if you face loss of your driver's license, a lawyer can present your defense in court, or perhaps represent you in a DMV driver's license suspension hearing. When you're faced with a heavy sentence if you lose, you're under a lot of pressure to present your case, and that alone can cause you to do it poorly. You'd be surprised at how many people can come across like Perry Mason while fighting a speeding ticket on principle but will stutter, stammer and fall into quiet, disorganized desperation when they're charged with drunk or reckless driving. But a person not facing those consequences, particularly one with some experience in criminal defense work, can do a fairly good job. This is probably the reason all modern cultures—and many ancient ones— have invented lawyers in the first place.

Types of Lawyers

Now let's look at the various kinds of lawyers and lawyer services that are available.

Private Attorneys

Not every lawyer in private practice is adequately equipped to defend you against a misdemeanor or even an infraction traffic charge. Like physicians, many lawyers specialize, and you don't want a lawyer who mostly handles divorces defending you in a criminal case (all traffic tickets are handled criminally) any more than you'd want a plastic surgeon prescribing something for your stomach upsets. Since very few lawyers specialize in traffic ticket defenses (it just doesn't pay enough), the next best thing might be a competent criminal defense lawyer, provided you can afford it. Use the same sorts of common-sense techniques that you use to find quality services in other areas. Start by asking a lawyer you know, a friend, or a business associate for a referral to a good criminal defense lawyer who practices locally. You will want to seek out a person who spends at least a third of his or her time on criminal cases because a "full-time" criminal lawyer is more likely to know all the subtleties of the most recent criminal cases. If you're charged with driving under the influence, you should try to find a lawyer who has tried at least several "drunk driving" cases and who knows when and when not to "plea bargain" a case. (See Chapter 8.) You should also try to find a local lawyer because he will be in a position to know the idiosyncrasies of the judges and prosecutors who will handle your case and who have great discretion in disposing of it.

Note: We generally do not recommend referral panels set up by local bar associations. Lawyers are given only minimal screening as to their expertise in traffic cases in order to be listed on these panels. For the most part, the attorneys listed there are either new to the practice of law or don't have enough business. If you try an attorney referred by one of these panels, be sure to ask the attorney a lot of questions about her qualifications. (How many cases like yours have they done? Are there any former clients you could contact? And so on.)

Once you have the name of a lawyer or, preferably, several lawyers, who handle criminal cases, you will want to meet them and see if you feel comfortable with their approach. Remember, it's your case—not the lawyer's—and you want to be sure to hire a person whom you respect and who will respect you enough to explain fully what is going on at all times. If a lawyer is not open and frank with you at the first interview, it is unlikely that his communication skills will improve later. Remember, the Latin root of the word client is "to hear, to obey." (The word was invented with the idea that the one who *has* the client is supposed to hear and obey the *client*, not vice versa.) It is easy to find a lawyer who encourages that kind of relationship, but if you want some say in your own case, you will have to be a bit more choosy.

Probably the best way to approach payment with a lawyer you don't know is to agree on a price for an initial consultation. Some lawyers will briefly discuss your case for free, or for as little as $30 for a half hour. For a more detailed discussion of the facts of an average misdemeanor case and the lawyer's suggestions about a defense strategy, something in the range of $75 to $100 would seem fair. If you don't like the lawyer, you haven't wasted much money. One way to judge whether a lawyer will satisfy you in the long run is to pay attention to how straightforward he is willing to be at the beginning.

Group Legal Practices and Prepaid Legal Services

A new but rapidly growing aspect of California law practice is the group legal practice program. Many groups, including unions, employers and consumer action groups, are offering plans to their members whereby they can get legal assistance for rates that are substantially lower than offered by most private practitioners. Some of these plans are good, some mediocre, and a few are not worth much, but most are better than nothing. It really depends on whether you end up with an attorney with any expertise in handling traffic cases. Because the group practice area of the law is changing so rapidly, we can't give you a statewide list of group legal plans.

The Public Defender

If you're charged with a misdemeanor and cannot afford the hundreds of dollars for a criminal defense attorney, you can request a court-appointed lawyer, usually a deputy public defender, to represent you. In most counties, you fill out a financial declaration in court, and the judge then refers you to a public defender. In other counties, you make an appointment with the public defender's office to discuss both your case and financial situation.

The legal determination of whether or not you can afford a lawyer depends upon the requirements specified by the particular county. If you have a relatively low-paying job, or no job, if your family is living on a tight budget, and if you do not have a savings account large enough to pay a lawyer to represent you, most judges will allow the public defender to represent you or authorize a private attorney to do so.

Even if you do have some financial resources but not thousands of dollars, the county will often provide you a lawyer if you insist you can't afford one. The county does not want to risk having to prosecute your case a second time if appellate judges determine later that you could not afford a lawyer and were thus deprived of your constitutional right to counsel at your first trial. However, the county can require you to pay back the cost of your legal services after your trial, using a fee schedule based on your income.

When you're charged with a misdemeanor, trying to qualify as an "indigent" so that a court-appointed lawyer can represent you is often a sensible way to proceed. Although there are a few (very few) incompetent public defenders with little training in criminal law, the public defender system is better than you might think. Many public defenders chose their careers because they genuinely want to help people. As a result of handling so many criminal cases, they are generally both experienced and competent. Indeed, you have a far greater chance of finding a mediocre lawyer at criminal defense by looking blindly through the yellow pages, than you do by consulting a public defender. Even if you don't qualify for free representation, the public defender's office may refer you to a relatively inexpensive but competent private criminal defense lawyer if you ask.

Perhaps the biggest drawback of being unable to afford a criminal defense attorney is that you risk getting an appointed lawyer to represent you with little experience or interest in criminal law. Another less serious disadvantage of having public representation is that public defenders are almost always overworked and may not give your case—especially if it is a minor one—the attention that you feel it deserves. If you think that your case is not getting enough attention or that it is not being handled with sufficient care, ask the lawyer to explain to you exactly what is being done. If his explanation doesn't satisfy you, try to get another lawyer.

Note: You do not have a right to a lawyer paid by the county if you are charged only with an "infraction." For example, if you are cited for doing 95 mph on the freeway, punishable only by a $281 total fine (plus penalty assessments), the county is not required to provide you with a lawyer. Only when the offense is punishable by a jail sentence, or is called a "misdemeanor," are you entitled to a court-appointed lawyer—and then, only if you truly can't afford a lawyer.

Getting the Most Out of Your Lawyer

Once a lawyer agrees to represent you, she has a duty to represent you to the best of her ability, whether or not you are guilty. Indeed, except under the most unusual circumstances, a criminal defense lawyer has a moral responsibility to continue to defend you, even if you say that you have committed the act with which you are charged. Because your lawyer is not the judge or the jury, she cannot rely on her "opinion" of your guilt, or even on your own "opinion" of whether you are guilty. Unless you want to plead guilty, the attorney's job is to provide you with the best possible defense, short of allowing you to lie under oath.

It is important to emphasize that if you want to participate in your defense, you should make this agreement with your lawyer before she begins to represent you. If you are a participating type, you should try to find a lawyer who feels comfortable explaining to you the legal aspects of your case and consulting with you about your case. There are some decisions, such as whether to object to evidence or how to cross-examine a witness, that are appropriate for the lawyer to make. There are other choices, such as whether to plead guilty or accept a plea bargain, that should be yours. As a general rule, tactical decisions about procedure should be explained to you, but you should be willing to pay close attention to your lawyer's advice. Think of it this way: If you hire a carpenter to build a bookshelf, you will want to go over the plans carefully, but you will probably rely on the carpenter's experience when it comes to choosing and placing the nails.

There is no substitute for finding a lawyer whom you can honestly trust. Honesty is important because to defend you against the state's prosecution, your lawyer must know the whole truth about your activities. If you cannot be completely honest and forthright with your lawyer, then find another one. Finding another lawyer is easy if you can afford to hire one, but if the judge has appointed you a lawyer, then you must convince her to appoint a different one. To persuade a judge to do this, you will have to give very specific good reasons why you do not want to work with the lawyer. The fact that she is not spending enough time on your case is a good reason.

Legal Research

Much of what lawyers know about law they didn't learn in law school. Instead, they researched it. Legal research isn't all that difficult. You sure don't need a law degree to do it. In fact, many basic techniques of legal research can be learned in several hours. An excellent resource for helping you find your way around the law library is *Legal Research: How to Find & Understand the Law*, by Steve Elias and the Editors of Nolo (Nolo). This section will very briefly note some of the techniques discussed in that book.

The tattered Vehicle Code you bought from the DMV a year or two earlier is a good starting point. But while it lists all the "statutes" (laws passed by the legislature), it doesn't list any of the appeals court decisions that determine what those laws mean. Sometimes these case decisions can make a big difference. (For example, decisions by California appeals courts have established that the misdemeanor offense of "exhibition of speed" can be committed

Examples of Case Citations

case name	year of decision	volume no.	3rd series Official Reports of California Supreme Court	page no.	volume no.	case is also listed in California Reporter, the "unofficial" reporter	page no.	volume no.	case is also listed in the 2nd series of Pacific Reporter	page no.
People v. McGaughran	(1979)	25	Cal.3d	577,	159	Cal.Rptr.	191,	585	P.2d	206

case name	year of decision	3rd series of Official Reports of the California Courts of Appeal, volume 60, page 24 of the supplement in the back of the volume	the case also appears in volume 160, page 531, of the Calif. Reporter
People v. Halopoff	(1976)	60 Cal.App.3d Supp. 24,	Cal. Rptr. 531

case name	year of decision	3rd series of Official Reports of California, Courts of Appeal, volume 167, page 534	case is also listed in the 2nd series of Pacific Reporter, volume 334, page 931
Smith v. Municipal Court	(1959)	167 Cal.App.3d 534,	334 P.2d 931

case name	year of decision	volume 384, page 436, of Official Reports of the United States Supreme Court	also published in volume 86, page 1062, of the Supreme Court Reporter, an "unofficial" source	also published in the 2nd series of "Lawyers' Edition" of the U.S. Supreme Court. Reports, volume 16, page 695
Miranda v. Arizona	(1966)	384 U.S. 436,	86 S.Ct. 1062,	16 L.Ed.2nd 695

not only by speeding, but also by deliberately accelerating so rapidly as to screech a car's tires—see Chapter 7.)

The best way to find written court decisions that interpret a particular law is to look in an "annotated code." An annotated code is a set of volumes of a particular code (Vehicle Code, Penal Code, Health & Safety Code, etc.) that list below the text of each law (also called "code section"), brief summaries of the court decisions that have interpreted the meaning of that law. These annotated codes—published by West Publishing Company (West's Annotated California Codes—blue volumes) and by Bancroft-Whitney (Deering's California Codes—brown volumes)—can be found in any law school library in the state. They have comprehensive indexes by topic, and are kept up-to-date each year with paperback supplements ("pocket parts") located in a pocket in the back cover of each volume. (Don't forget to look through these pocket parts for the latest law change or case decision since the hardcover volume was printed.)

The brief summaries of the court decisions are followed by the title of the case, the year of the decision and the "citation," so that you can find the case and read it. The "citation" is a sort of shorthand identification of the page, volume and series of volumes where the case can be found. The "official" volumes of cases are published by the appeals courts as *Official Reports of the California Supreme Court* (abbreviated "Cal.," "Cal.2d," "Cal.3d," or "Cal.4th," respectively representing the first, second, third, and fourth "series" of volumes) and as *Official Reports of the California Courts of Appeal* (similarly abbreviated "Cal.App.," "Cal.App.2d," "Cal. App.3d," and "Cal.App.4th"). The Courts of Appeal are California's "intermediate" level appeals courts, on a lower legal level than the California Supreme Court, but higher than the Superior and Justice courts of the counties.

There are six appellate districts in the state, with courts in San Francisco, Los Angeles, Sacramento, San Diego, Fresno, and San Jose. (The California Supreme Court resides in San Francisco, not Sacramento, with branch offices in Sacramento and Los Angeles.) The cases are also published in "unofficial" volumes by the West Publishing Company. These are *California Reporter* (abbreviated "Cal.Rptr." or "Cal.Rptr.2d," respectively, for the first and second series) and *Pacific Reporter* (similarly abbreviated "P." or "P.2d"). The case is the same whether you read it in the "official" or "unofficial" reporter.

This information should take some of the mystery out of legal research. If, in the course of your research, you still have questions, don't hesitate to ask a law librarian for assistance. As long as you don't appear to be asking for legal advice, and you look like you have some idea of what you're looking for, most law librarians will go out of their way to help you.

Some examples of case citations are shown above.

Legal Research on the Internet

It is now possible to look up the text of any California law from any computer connected to the Internet. If you do not have a computer of your own, most public libraries provide free access to the Internet. You can begin your search for the California Vehicle Code at Nolo's Legal Research Center at www.nolo.com/research/index.html. Click on "State Laws," click on "California," and check the section marked "Vehicle Code." You will then be taken to a complete and searchable copy of the state vehicle code.

RESOURCE

Other Internet Sites. There are a number of other useful Internet sites for help fighting your traffic tickets. They include:

- www.courtinfo.ca.gov/selfhelp/traffic, the official website of the Judicial Council of California, the administrative arm of the California court system

- www.dmv.ca.gov, the official site of the California Department of Motor Vehicles, and

- www.courtinfo.ca.gov/otherwebsites. htm, located on the official website of the administrative arm of the California courts, which links you to local court websites around the state.

There are also several other good websites where groups and individuals provide valuable ticket-fighting information and strategies. The ones we like best are:

- www.speedtrap.org, which lists the locations of speed traps nationwide

- www.mrtraffic.com, which is run by Los Angeles radio station host Kenny Morse and deals with many traffic-related issues, and

- www.motorists.org, the website of the National Motorists Association, an advocacy group for the driving public.

Fighting an Infraction Citation

This chapter covers the initial steps of fighting an infraction charge. If you're charged with a misdemeanor, skip this chapter and go directly to Chapter 13. If you're charged with an infraction, read this chapter carefully before deciding how you want to fight.

Preliminary Steps for Fighting an Infraction

There are numerous procedures you must follow before you can ever get to trial or even traffic school. For some people, however, most of these steps may be unnecessary. In this chapter, you learn how these procedures work, and how to bypass the ones you don't need, so you can save yourself a few wasted hours of waiting in line.

Note: As mentioned before, parking tickets are handled by a simpler procedure, which is fully described in Chapter 6. If you have a parking ticket, you probably don't need the information in this half of the book. The same is true for "correctable" equipment violations. (See Chapter 6.)

Phoning the Court for Information

You probably have noticed the little notation on the bottom of your ticket telling you to appear at a certain date, time, and place "before a judge of the Superior Court at …." This doesn't necessarily mean that any trial, or even a scheduled court appearance before a judge, will occur on that date. All it means is that if you don't see the court clerk before that date about paying the ticket or scheduling a court appearance, the system will start treating you as if you were a very small stone caught in a very large grinder. (See Chapter 7.)

But before you take that trip down to the courthouse to see the clerk, you should phone the clerk's office and ask some questions about the county's procedure. By asking a few questions in advance, you can save yourself a lot of time once you actually begin to fight. If your ticket doesn't list the court's phone number, look it up in the telephone book under the listings for the county in which the court is located, under "courts," or "Superior Courts." Unfortunately, more and more traffic courts are shifting to recorded phone-message systems (the kind where you hear an announcement but can't leave a message) and give no specific information over the phone, so as to require a trip to the courthouse and a long wait in line to get any information. Even in courts where clerks still answer the phone, you can probably expect to be put on "hold." Persist.

When you finally do get through to a live person on the telephone or after you have trekked down to the courthouse in person, be ready to ask some fairly simple questions. You might say something like this:

- *"I received a moving violation citation on* (Month, Day, Year), *and I would like to know whether I can arrange today for a court appearance to contest the violation, or do I have to wait until I receive a 'courtesy notice' in the mail?"* (A courtesy notice is a computer-printed reminder to do something about your ticket. See below.)

- You may also want to ask the clerk whether the county has a traffic school program. If the county does have such a program, ask whether you have to appear before a judge at arraignment to ask for traffic school, or whether you can arrange it with the court clerk.

Courtesy Notice

Superior Court
Palo Alto Branch
270 Grant Ave. Rm 204
Palo Alto, CA 94306

Traffic citation MV50864 issued on 01/13/20xx has been filed with the court. You may post and forfeit bail in the sum of $271 by mailing check or money order payable to the Municipal Court in the enclosed envelope within 20 days from the date of the citation. Bail forfeiture closes the case. If you wish to appear in court you must appear in this office within 20 days from the date of the citation to arrange an appearance date.

Office Hours: 8:30 a.m. to 4:00 p.m.

Failure to comply with the instructions within the specified time will result in a bail increase and you will not be permitted to renew your driver's license.

Please disregard this notice if this citation has been paid or you have appeared in court.

Failure to comply with these instructions may result in a warrant for your arrest with an increase in bail.

B0025640 D 03/26/20xx

DO NOT SEND CASH

Checking the Court's Website

Voice mail systems make it a frustrating and time-wasting process to speak with a live person. But you can access information on the Internet if you have a computer. If you don't, most public libraries offer free access to the Internet.

The value of court websites varies. Some only give you general information on paying your ticket, but little or no information on traffic schools or fighting your ticket. Los Angeles County provides the most comprehensive court website in California. It allows you to check the status of your ticket, the "bail" amount, whether it is past due, and even allows you to set up an arraignment date to appear in court. It is located at www.lasuperiorcourt.org/traffic.

To find the website for any other county court in California, go to www.courtinfo.ca.gov/courts/trial/courtlist.htm.

Deciding How to Plead

Before you go to the clerk's office, decide how you want to plead. There can be as many as five options to choose from: not guilty, guilty, nolo contendere, forfeiting bail without a plea, and accepting traffic school instead of a plea. By deciding ahead of time which way you want to plead, you'll know what kind of hearing to ask for when you get to the clerk's window. For example, if you want to plead "not guilty" you may want to bypass the arraignment and request a trial with the officer present. If you want to opt for traffic school, you may be able to tell the clerk immediately and be done with it.

Each of the possible plea options is discussed below.

Not Guilty

Under our legal system, it is always your legal right to plead not guilty whether or not you think you really are. You can do this by mail, at the court clerk's office, or at arraignment.

By pleading not guilty, all you're saying is that, since you're presumed innocent, you're going to insist on your right to have the prosecution prove *every* element of its case. For example, if you plead not guilty to a charge that you violated the Basic Speed Law by doing 38 mph on Market Street, where the speed limit is 25 mph, it's legally equivalent to saying:

- I wasn't driving a motor vehicle down Market Street, and

- the speed limit wasn't 25 mph, and

- I wasn't going over 25 mph.

Even if only one of these denials is true (or even if none of them are), you're not doing anything wrong by pleading not guilty. You're merely demanding that they prove every element against you.

Guilty Pleas

Formal guilty pleas to infractions are rare, but are more common in misdemeanor cases. Most people charged with infractions simply fork over the forfeited bail to the clerk without entering any plea at all.

One exception to this is the so-called "guilty with an explanation" plea, where a person pleads guilty but tells his or her story to the judge at an informal hearing at arraignment, hoping to get a reduced or suspended fine. Unfortunately, this is generally not a good idea. Even if a sympathetic judge reduces or "suspends" the fine, the offense still goes on your driving record if it's one of those types of violations that gets reported to the DMV, and your insurance rates may rise, depending on the offense. Thus, the "guilty with an explanation" plea is usually used by ill-prepared people who do not want to take another trip down to the courthouse for trial.

Just as a plea of not guilty constitutes a denial of the truth of every element of a charge, a guilty plea constitutes an admission of each element.

You should never plead guilty to a charge arising out of an accident in which you were involved. Should you be sued, your guilty plea can be used against you. Instead, you should

either forfeit bail (see below) or plead nolo contendere (no contest) if you don't want to fight the ticket.

Nolo Contendere

Remember how former Vice President Spiro Agnew pleaded nolo contendere (pronounced *no'lo con-tend'-er-ray*) to not paying income tax on the money he was accused of having received as bribes? Even though his nolo contendere plea had the same effect as a guilty plea for criminal purposes, it prevented the IRS from using a guilty plea against him in later civil proceedings over back taxes. Similarly, if you're ever cited for a nonfelony Vehicle Code violation arising out of an accident and you don't want to fight the ticket, you can plead nolo contendere, sometimes referred to as "no contest," at arraignment.

Bear in mind that a plea of nolo contendere has exactly the same consequences as a guilty plea with regards to the amount of the fine, extra penalties on future offenses, your driving record at the DMV, and the effect on your insurance rates.

Some judges do not like to see people plead nolo contendere and will try to prevent them from doing so. If the judge won't let you, tell her that there was an auto accident (if true). If that doesn't convince the judge, then plead not guilty; you can change it later if you get a more intelligent judge at trial. Of course, if you have to go that far, you may decide to fight it all the way.

"Forfeiting Bail" (Just Paying the Fine)

Showing up at the clerk's window to pay your ticket (or mailing in the fine, for parking tickets) has the same effect as pleading guilty, except that it cannot be used against you in a lawsuit arising out of an accident. This is because you are only forfeiting bail by arranging not to contest the ticket. You are not pleading guilty. If the violation is one of those that's normally reported to the DMV (see Chapter 3), it will appear on your driving record, and will count as a prior conviction for all purposes. Your insurance rates are also likely to rise.

Traffic School With Dismissal

In most counties, for nonalcohol-related moving violations, rather than fighting your ticket, you can sign up for traffic school and have the violation erased from your driving record. (All that goes on your record is a notation you've been to traffic school and when—information disclosed only to courts, to prevent people from using this option more than twice over a certain period.) Keep in mind that even if you opt to attend traffic school, you are still required to pay the fine, plus a $49 to $59 referral fee and a $25 to $30 fee to the school.

After you've successfully completed traffic school and a notice of completion is sent to the court, the traffic charge will not show up on your record. For more information on what to expect from traffic school, see Chapter 9.

Note: Entering a plea other than guilty or otherwise exercising your right to contest your ticket does not automatically make you ineligible for traffic school. That decision is at the discretion of the judge, who is not required, under California Rules of Court Rule 4.104, to state on the record a reason for granting or denying a traffic school request.

Warning: If you do opt for traffic school, "willful failure" to sign up for and complete it is a misdemeanor (VC § 42005). At the very least, since you must prepay the fine in order to be referred to traffic school, failure to attend after doing so will be treated as if you've "forfeited bail," and the violation will go on your DMV record. (For more on traffic school, see Chapter 9.)

Obtaining a Copy of the Officer's Notes and Traffic Survey in Radar Cases

Before presenting your case, or even before deciding whether to contest a ticket, it would be helpful to know what the officer will probably say in court if and when she testifies against you (PC § 1054, et. seq.).

Typically, police officers who issue traffic tickets will write themselves brief notes on the reverse of their copy of the citation. (The copy you receive does not have this information on it.) Because officers will write a number of other tickets in the several-month period between writing yours and testifying about the incident later in court, they will generally use such notes to refresh their memory at or before trial. It is not uncommon for police officers who testify in traffic court to do so while reading these notes to themselves.

You have the right to demand a copy of these notes, well before trial, from the prosecuting agency and/or the police agency involved, using an "Informal Discovery Request" form. (A sample version of this form is included here, and a blank form is in the back of the book.) This is because PC §§ 1054 through 1054.7, added by Proposition 115 in 1990, require the prosecution in any criminal case to provide the defendant with copies of all written statements made by witnesses, including police officer witnesses, and any written reports. (This includes infractions (PC § 19.7).)

You also have the right, under PC § 1054.1(f), to obtain a copy of the engineering and traffic survey that is used against you in a radar case at trial.

The prosecution, or the police agency if the prosecuting agency does not normally handle infractions, is required to provide this information to you within 15 days of receiving your written request. However, the law also requires you to disclose your evidence to the prosecution if you request "discovery" from the prosecutor. This means that you must include copies of written statements or notes in your possession, if you intend to use them at trial. (See Chapter 17.) You must also disclose the names and addresses of any persons, other than yourself, whom you plan to call as your own witnesses at trial.

To fill out the form, list your name and address at the top box in the space provided. In the box below that, list the full name and address of the court, including county and judicial district. In the box below that, list your name again, as it is indicated on the citation. Below that, list the court case number if you have it (it is printed on any courtesy notice you may have received from the court), and list the name of the police agency, the citation number, and the date the citation was issued, all of which should be indicated on the citation.

For tickets issued by the CHP, you will need to mail your request to the CHP office where the ticketing officer is stationed. To get this information, call any CHP office, give them the "area" number listed on the citation and ask for the mailing address.

If you are charged with a violation of the Basic Speed Law (VC § 22350), and you believe that the officer may have used radar to clock your speed, put a check in the box next to "[If checked] Any engineering and traffic survey …."

If you are charged with any speeding violation (VC §§ 22349, 22350) and you believe that an officer in an aircraft determined your speed (see Chapter 4), put a check in the box next to "[If checked] Any observation logs …."

At the bottom of the Informal Discovery Request, list the names and addresses of witnesses, not including yourself, whom you intend to call at trial. This obviously includes passengers or others who observed the situation and are willing to testify on your behalf. (If you neglect to list someone, you may not be allowed to call that person as a witness at your trial.) If you do not plan on calling any witnesses other than yourself, check the "None" box. Then, if you have any written statements, diagrams, or pictures you intend to use at trial, check the box next to the words "See attached," and attach photocopies of them to your request. Finally, have someone else—someone over 18 who resides or works in the county in which the papers will be mailed—mail a copy of the request and any attachments to *both* the district attorney (or city attorney in Los Angeles and other parts of L.A. County) who handles criminal cases in the applicable courthouse *and* to the police agency that issued the citation. You should also mail a copy to the city attorney of the city employing the officer who cited you; or, if a sheriff's deputy cited you, to the "county counsel" for the county. You can find both addresses in the government listings in the telephone directory for the area. Then, after your friend mails the copies, have her sign a Proof of Service by Mail similar to the one that follows (a blank form is in the back of the book), indicating that the Informal Discovery Request was mailed at a given date and place. Keep the original request and Proof of Service for your files. Do not file them with the court.

It's possible that your discovery request will be ignored, since most prosecuting agencies routinely disregard papers sent to them regarding traffic court cases, and police departments tend to shun requests for information other than subpoenas. Although you may be eager to get the information you requested, it may be even better if your request is disregarded. If your discovery request is ignored for over 15 days, you can make a written motion to dismiss the case or to preclude the officer who cited you from testifying. Or, if the prosecution or police agency does not send you a copy of

INFORMAL DISCOVERY REQUEST

Name: DANIELLE DEFENDANT
Address 123 Main Street
        San Jose, CA 95113
Defendant in Pro Per

SUPERIOR COURT OF CALIFORNIA
COUNTY OF SANTA CLARA
SAN JOSE–SANTA CLARA BRANCH
925 Ruff Drive, San Jose, CA 95113

THE PEOPLE OF THE STATE OF CALIFORNIA, Plaintiff

vs.

CASE NUMBER
C-1003456

Citing Agency: San Jose P.D.   Citation No.: SJ-12345   Date Issued: 6/15/20xx

INFORMAL DISCOVERY REQUEST (Traffic Infraction) PC 1054–1054.1, PC 19.7

TO THE DISTRICT ATTORNEY FOR THE ABOVE-REFERENCED COUNTY, AND TO THE ABOVE-REFERENCED POLICE AGENCY:

1. Pursuant to Penal Code §§ 1054 and 1054.5(b), the above-named defendant hereby requests that you provide disclosure of the following:

   a. Defendant's statements and any and all relevant written or recorded statements of witnesses, including any statements, diagrams, or drawings, made by the citing police officer on the reverse of the above-referenced Notice to Appear or on any piece of paper or other medium of information storage. YOU ARE SPECIFICALLY REQUESTED TO PROVIDE THE ABOVE-REFERENCED DEFENDANT OR ATTORNEY OF RECORD WITH A PHOTOSTATIC COPY OF THE REVERSE SIDE OF THE CITING OFFICER'S COPY OF THE ABOVE-REFERENCED NOTICE TO APPEAR, IF THE CITING OFFICER HAS MADE ANY NOTATIONS ON IT.

   b. The names and addresses of all prosecution witnesses who will testify at trial.

   c. (X) [If checked] Any engineering and traffic survey within the meaning of VC § 627(a), conducted within the last five years, which justifies the prima facie speed limit relevant to the alleged violation charged in the above-referenced Notice to Appear. IF THIS ITEM IS CHECKED AT LEFT, YOU ARE SPECIFICALLY REQUESTED TO PROVIDE A COPY OF THE ENGINEERING AND TRAFFIC SURVEY, MEETING THE DESCRIPTION ABOVE, WHERE SUCH SURVEY WILL BE PRODUCED AT TRIAL.

   d. ( ) [If checked] Any observation logs kept or maintained by CHP officer in aircraft speed cases. IF THIS ITEM IS CHECKED AT LEFT, YOU ARE SPECIFICALLY REQUESTED TO PROVIDE A COPY OF AIRCRAFT OBSERVATION LOGS KEPT OR MADE BY OFFICER WHO ALLEGEDLY OBSERVED DEFENDANT'S VEHICLE EXCEED SPEED LIMIT.

2. The following is disclosed to you pursuant to Penal Code § 1054.3:

   a. NAMES AND ADDRESSES OF WITNESSES (OTHER THAN DEFENDANT) WHO WILL TESTIFY AT TRIAL:

   ( ) None.

   (X) The Following: Wendy Witness, 123 State St., Sunnyvale, CA 94087

   b. RELEVANT UNPRIVILEGED WRITTEN OR RECORDED STATEMENTS OF WITNESSES:

   (X) NONE.

   ( ) See Attached

Dated   7-1-20xx   *Danielle Defendant*
                                    Defendant in Pro Per

PROOF OF SERVICE

PARTY WITHOUT ATTORNEY (My Name and Address): **MY TELEPHONE NO.:** David Defendant 310-555-6543 555 Oak St. Ramos, CA 90909	

NAME OF COURT: Superior Court of California **STREET ADDRESS:** County of Los Angeles **MAILING ADDRESS:** 1945 S. Hill St. **CITY AND ZIP CODE:** Los Angeles, CA **BRANCH NAME:** Metropolitan Branch	

PLAINTIFF/JUDGMENT CREDITOR: People of the State of California
                                         vs.

DEFENDANT/JUDGMENT DEBTOR: David Defendant

PROOF OF SERVICE BY MAIL (CCP Sections 1013a, 2015.5)	**CASE NUMBER** C1009999

I declare that:

1. At the time of service I was at least 18 years of age and not a party to this legal action.
2. I am a resident of or employed in the county where the mailing occurred.
3. My business or residence address is:
4. I served copies of the following paper(s) in the manner shown:

    a. Papers served [list exact titles of paper(s)]:

       Informal Discovery Request

    b. Manner of service: by placing true copies in a sealed envelope addressed to each person whose name and address is given below and:

       ☒ depositing the envelope in the United States Mail with the postage fully prepaid; or

       ☐ (If deposited at a business:) placing for collection and mailing following ordinary business practices. I am readily familiar with the business practice for collection and processing of correspondence for mailing with the United States Post Office. The correspondence will be deposited with the United States Post Office on the same date as the date of deposit (below) in the ordinary course of business.

       (1) Date of Deposit: _____

       (2) Place of Deposit (city & state; business address if deposited at a business):

5. I declare under penalty of perjury under the laws of the State of California that the foregoing is true and correct.

Executed on <u>October 1, 20xx</u> at <u>   St. Ramos   </u> California.

Print Name <u>Frederick Friend</u>   *Frederick Friend*
                                             [Signature of Person Who Served Papers]

Los Angeles Police Dept. Central Traffic Div. Central Facility Bldg. 251 E. 6th St. Los Angeles, CA 90014	Los Angeles City Attorney 200 N. Main St. #1800 Los Angeles, CA 90012	Los Angeles County District Attorney 201 W. Temple St. Room 18000 Los Angeles, CA 90012

                                                    ☐ Additional names and addresses on reverse

the Engineering and Traffic Survey, you can make a motion to preclude the prosecution from using the survey against you at trial. If that motion is granted, a radar speed case against you will likely have to be dismissed at trial. A sample motion is shown later in this chapter. If this motion is granted and the officer is prevented from testifying, you should ultimately win the case.

Deciding What Kind of Hearing You Want

If you decide to contest your ticket, there are several kinds of hearings available. You can have a formal "in-person" trial with the officer present. In some places, you can have an "informal hearing" at arraignment, although this is not something we normally recommend. Or, you can contest your ticket through the mail.

Formal Trial With Officer Present

As we've stated before, in most cases, you should insist on a trial with the officer present. By doing so, you get the advantage of being able to challenge the officer's assertions in court, and most importantly, you gain the very real possibility that the officer will not show up to testify against you, and your case will be dismissed.

A trial for an infraction is held in a court with a judge or "commissioner" presiding. You are notified where and when to appear. Be on time. When your case is called, you (and your witnesses, if any) and the officer walk up behind the table, raise your right hands and are "sworn in." There is usually no prosecutor. The officer tells his story first. His job is to testify to facts that establish all the required elements of the case. After he's finished, you have an opportunity to cross-examine him. You can ask him questions on matters he has testified

to, and on new matters that might help you establish a defense (for example, to establish the excellent weather and visibility in a Basic Speed Law case).

After you finish cross-examining, you get your turn to explain what happened. You will probably want to contradict the officer's testimony by establishing other facts that tend to disprove one or more elements of the offense. You may also want to establish facts that constitute a defense even if everything the officer said was true. Some judges will then give the officer a chance to cross-examine you.

After all the testimony has been given (including that of witnesses) the judge usually gives the decision. Some judges will instead try to "take the case under advisement," with your permission. If the judge finds you guilty, she will usually, at the same time, tell you what the fine will be. (You can, however, insist on the right to be sentenced between six hours and five days later. See Chapter 14.)

In a few places minor traffic cases are sometimes prosecuted by bored assistant district or city attorneys, but in most courts, the police officer prosecutes the case himself merely by testifying.

If you decide you want a formal trial be sure to read Chapters 11 and 12.

Informal Hearing

The second kind of hearing you can get—in some courts—is an informal hearing, which usually is held at the same time as arraignment. If you're ever asked by a court clerk, or by a judge at arraignment, whether you prefer a formal trial or an informal hearing, be careful. You may think that the distinction involves things like whether you testify from a witness stand or just tell your story from behind a table, or whether the case against you is presented by the police officer or by a deputy district or city attorney. An informal hearing will very likely sound good to you. Unfortunately, the nice-sounding word "informal" may mean little more than that you give up your right to insist on the officer's coming to testify against you. Indeed, you have very little to gain by giving up your right to a formal hearing. Since moving violations go on your record, you should usually insist on the formal trial with the officer present. A surprising number of tickets are beaten by people who insist that the officer show, and have their cases dismissed when he doesn't.

However, if you do go to arraignment and have signed up for an informal hearing, watch other people's cases and notice whether they are often found not guilty by a particular judge. If they are, you too may want to tell the judge that you want to go ahead with the "informal" hearing.

But if it appears to you that the judge is prone to finding people guilty, consider changing your mind when your name is called and asking for a formal trial with the officer present. Traffic court judges who want people to accept informal hearings won't get many takers if they convict everyone and assess heavy fines. But be careful. If the judge's "leniency" only takes the form of reduced fines or "suspended" sentences (you're found guilty and pay no fine—but it still goes on your record), forget it. You may save money on the fine now, but you'll pay more in increased insurance rates later. Also, insist on a formal trial if you see the judge consistently taking cases "under advisement." This usually means he found the defendant guilty but doesn't have the guts to tell the person directly.

In sum, an informal hearing is better than no hearing at all, but not much better. If you're serious about fighting your ticket, you may be better off by proceeding directly to formal trial with the officer present. If the choice is between paying the fine and putting up a little fight, you might want an informal hearing and hope to get a lenient judge at arraignment.

"Trial-by-Declaration" (VC § 40902)

The law also allows traffic-court "trials" without actually requiring anyone to show up in court. A person accused of a nonalcohol-related infraction (all moving violations other than open-container violations, etc.) may contest a ticket by telling his or her story in a letter to the court. This is called "trial by declaration."

One advantage of telling your story in writing is that you can take time to draft a convincing, well-thought-out defense, which may sound better to the judge than the oral testimony of an inexperienced, nervous defendant. A second, and even bigger, advantage is that you get two chances to be found not guilty. If you start off with written testimony and are found guilty, you have 20 days to demand and get a regular trial (called a "trial de novo") with the officer present. A third advantage is that if you're found guilty in a "trial by declaration," you can get a copy of the officer's declaration from the court file, and use it to prepare for the trial de novo. Thus you have nothing to lose.

CAUTION

In the past, some courts have developed schemes to trick you into giving up your right to a trial de novo, or to make it harder for you to demand one. One such scheme, used in Marin County, was to get you to agree to "Trial by Declaration on Stipulation," meaning you gave up your right to trial de novo if you were found guilty. This is now illegal (VC § 40902(a)(2)). The new law says that statewide rules—set out in Rule 4.210 of the California Rules of Court—supersede any local rules. Rule 4.210 allows you 20 days to request a trial de novo, and the law does not allow local courts to set other deadlines. If for some reason the court denies your demand, you can appeal that denial to the Superior Court Appellate Division using the procedures in Chapter 16.

TR-205

NAME OF COURT: SUPERIOR COURT OF CALIFORNIA, COUNTY OF ALAMEDA	FOR COURT USE ONLY
STREET ADDRESS: 39439 PASEO PADRE PARKWAY	
MAILING ADDRESS: PO BOX 5113	
CITY AND ZIP CODE: FREMONT, CA 94537	
BRANCH NAME: FREMONT-NEWARK BRANCH	

PEOPLE OF THE STATE OF CALIFORNIA

VS.

DEFENDANT: LENNY D. LEADFOOT

REQUEST FOR TRIAL BY WRITTEN DECLARATION
(Vehicle Code, § 40902)

CITATION NUMBER:
F-44123

CASE NUMBER:
A-036912-B

TO BE FILLED OUT BY COURT CLERK

A. **DUE DATE** (for receipt of this form and any unpaid bail) (specify):

B. Bail amount required: $

C. Bail amount already deposited by defendant: $

D. Date mailed or delivered by clerk:

E. Mail or deliver completed form, evidence, and mail to the Clerk of the (specify):   Court at (mailing address):

REQUEST FOR TRIAL

1. I have reviewed the *Instructions to Defendant (Trial by Written Declaration)* (form TR-200).

2. I request to have a trial by written declaration.

3. The facts contained in the Declaration of Facts on the reverse are personally known to me and are true and correct.

4. I know that I have the right not to be compelled to be a witness against myself. I understand and agree that by making any statement, I am giving up and waiving that right and privilege.

5. EVIDENCE   The following evidence supports my case and includes everything I want the court to consider in deciding my case:
   a. ☐ photographs (specify total number):
   b. ☐ medical record
   c. ☐ registration documents
   d. ☐ inspection certificate
   e. ☒ diagram
   f. ☐ car repair receipt
   g. ☐ insurance documents
   h. ☒ other (specify):   DECLARATION OF WITNESS

(Declaration continued on reverse)

Form Adopted by the Judicial Council of California TR-205 [New January 1, 1999] **Mandatory Form**	**REQUEST FOR TRIAL BY WRITTEN DECLARATION** (Trial by Written Declaration—Traffic)	Vehicle Code, § 40902

PEOPLE v. DEFENDANT (Name):	CASE NUMBER:
LENNY D. LEADFOOT	A-036912-B

6. **DECLARATION OF FACTS** (Type or print only. State what happened and explain all the items of evidence you checked in item 5 on the reverse and tell how they support your case. You may add additional pages.)

(Name):   LENNY D. LEADFOOT

(Current mailing address):   123 PLUMBUMPED DRIVE, SANTA BARBARA, CA 93101

STATEMENT OF FACTS (begin here):

Pursuant to Vehicle Code § 40902, I wish to exercise my right to trial by declaration with regard to a Vehicle Code infraction citation. As required, I enclose a check for $82 bail. Please refund the same to me in the event the court finds me not guilty.

On September 20, 20xx, at approximately 10:30 a.m., I was driving my 1966 Volkswagen, License No. 123ABC, west on Breezy Boulevard, a four-lane divided highway, between Drag Boulevard and Zoom Street. I was in the right-hand lane. The weather was clear and dry. There was no traffic in my direction other than a large panel truck (visible in my side view mirror) in the left lane, several car lengths behind me. The truck overtook and passed my vehicle shortly before I crossed the Zoom Street intersection.

Approximately two blocks past Zoom Street, Officer Stickler of the Fremont Police Department stopped me. He informed me that he had determined my speed on his hand-held radar unit to be 50 mph, the posted prima facie speed limit being 35 mph. He said that he had read my speed at the Breezy Boulevard-Drag Boulevard intersection from the intersection at Zoom Street, which a street map will show is 500 feet away. Officer Stickler responded to several of my questions by stating that the radar beam width was "about six degrees," and that his unit had been "calibrated recently with this little knob," pointing to the "calibrate" position on the controls of the unit. He said he hadn't used a tuning fork, and that he didn't have one in his possession. He also indicated that his unit was capable of reading speeds of both oncoming and receding traffic.

I believe that there exists a reasonable doubt as to the accuracy of Officer Stickler's radar reading. As can be shown by the attached diagram, a six-degree beam width at 500 feet will indiscriminately read speeds of vehicles across a width of 55 feet—all four lanes of traffic.

The radar unit may therefore have been reading both speeds of traffic in my direction (including a truck target much larger and more likely to reflect radar beams than my small Volkswagen) and the heavy traffic in the other direction. This being so, it is doubtful that the speed he recorded was mine. Furthermore, even if I were traveling at 50 mph, the weather was clear and dry, and there was very little traffic in my direction on a divided four-lane road. The intersections of Breezy Boulevard with Drag Boulevard and Zoom Street are both controlled by stoplights. Under these conditions, even 50 mph would have been a safe speed at which to drive (although I doubt that I was going that fast). The truck that overtook and passed my vehicle did so safely even at its higher speed.

Finally, my research efforts at City Hall have failed to yield any record of a traffic survey justifying the 35-mph speed limit within the past five years.

Also enclosed is the declaration of Wilhelmina D. Witness.

7. Number of pages attached: _2_

I declare under penalty of perjury under the laws of the State of California that the foregoing is true and correct.

Date: OCTOBER 2, 20xx

LENNY D. LEADFOOT

· ·
(TYPE OR PRINT NAME)

▶ *Lenny D. Leadfoot*

_____
(SIGNATURE)

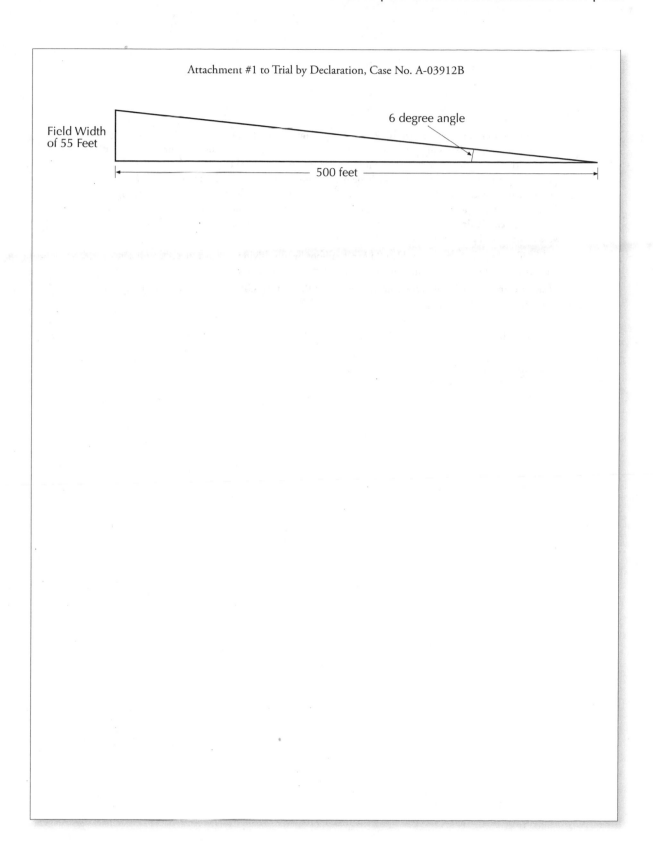

Attachment #1 to Trial by Declaration, Case No. A-03912B

Field Width
of 55 Feet

6 degree angle

500 feet

Attachment #2 to Trial by Declaration, Case No. A-036912-B

Declaration of Witness

I, Wilhelmina Witness, on September 20, 20xx, at approximately 10:30 a.m., was riding as a passenger in an automobile driven by Lenny D. Leadfoot. Mr. Leadfoot was relaxed and not driving very fast for conditions. There were no other cars on the road in our direction of travel that I could see, other than a large truck that passed us on the left shortly before we crossed the Zoom Street intersection. We were talking as we drove westbound on Breezy Boulevard in Fremont. As we drove past Zoom Street, Mr. Leadfoot said that a police officer was pulling us over. I was surprised because I didn't know why we were being pulled over. We drove to the side of the road and waited for the officer. I asked Mr. Leadfoot why we were being pulled over, and he said he did not know.

The officer approached the car. He told Mr. Leadfoot he was driving 50 mph in a 35-mph zone. I was surprised because I didn't think that we were going that fast. I still don't think so.

I declare under penalty of perjury under the laws of the State of California that the foregoing is true and correct.

DATED: October 2, 20xx

Wilhelmina D. Witness

In order to stand any chance of beating the ticket by "written declaration," you'll have to do more than just deny the charge. For example, in a typical radar speeding case, your written statement is going to have to show a little sophistication and might look something like the example earlier in this chapter. Use the "Request for Trial by Written Declaration" form in the back of this book.

With your declaration (including that of any witness), you must include a check or money order for the amount of the fine ("bail"), which should be stated on any "courtesy notice" mailed to you by the court. If you didn't receive such a notice within three weeks of receiving the ticket (or if, for some reason, the courtesy notice doesn't state the "bail"), try calling the court. If you can't get through on the phone or a court website to find out the amount, and absolutely can't travel to the courthouse to find out, you may have to try and calculate it using the information we provide in Chapter 3, Section A3. (Keep in mind that the total fine for speed violations depends on the speed you were cited for, plus penalty assessments.)

Several weeks after submitting your written declaration, you should receive a notice in the mail telling you of the judge's decision. If the notice says you were found not guilty, your fine ("bail") that you prepaid should be refunded to you. You are entitled to a full refund, but unfortunately, there are no rules as to how soon the court must do so. If you don't receive a refund within two months, you should either go to the courthouse and ask why it's taking so long, or write a letter to that effect.

If the notice says that you've been found guilty, you have the right to request a regular trial with the officer present, but you only have 20 days to do this. A sample form to file with the clerk to demand a regular trial is shown here, and a blank form is in the back of the book. Be sure to file this form with the clerk as soon as possible after you are found guilty following trial by declaration.

Although you could mail in the form, court clerks are notorious for losing or delaying the filing of documents sent in by nonlawyers. Because of this, you probably should go to the courthouse and file it in person, or, if you must mail it, do so by certified mail, return receipt requested. While you're there, ask for a photocopy of the officer's declaration. You are entitled to this for a nominal copying cost (usually 75 cents a page), since it's a public record. The officer's declaration will give you an idea of what he will say at the trial. You can look at your copy of the officer's declaration while he testifies. If he says anything that contradicts his testimony in the declaration, you can point that out to the judge. (Keep in mind that *your* declaration will be available to the judge or prosecutor to indicate discrepancies in *your* testimony, too.) Finally, if you want to use the testimony of a witness, that person must appear in court. You cannot use the declaration they wrote for your trial by declaration.

If the clerk fails to set a trial date that is within 45 days of the date you filed the Request for New Trial (Trial de Novo) form, you may wish to make a motion to dismiss for lack of a speedy trial. Rule 4.210(b)(7) of the California Rules of Court requires that a trial must be heard within 45 days after a new trial is requested.

If you make a motion to dismiss because more than 45 days have passed since you filed your request for a trial de novo, you should cite rule 4.210(b)(7). Point out that your request serves the same function as a not-guilty plea, and starts the 45-day period running. You can use the sample motion to dismiss set out later in this chapter, with the following variations:

TR-220

NAME OF COURT:	SUPERIOR COURT OF CALIFORNIA, COUNTY OF ALAMEDA
STREET ADDRESS:	39439 PASEO PADRE PARKWAY
MAILING ADDRESS:	PO BOX 5113
CITY AND ZIP CODE:	FREMONT, CA 94537
BRANCH NAME:	FREMONT-NEWARK BRANCH

FOR COURT USE ONLY

PEOPLE OF THE STATE OF CALIFORNIA

vs.

DEFENDANT: LENNY D. LEADFOOT

REQUEST FOR NEW TRIAL (TRIAL DE NOVO)
(Trial by Written Declaration—Vehicle Code, § 40902)

CITATION NUMBER: F-44123

CASE NUMBER: A-036912-B

1. The clerk mailed the court's *Decision and Notice of Decision* (form TR-215) in my trial by written declaration to me on *(date)*: November 2, 20xx

2. I am submitting this request to the court within 20 days of the date in item 1. *(The court must receive this request within 20 days of the date in item 1.)*

3. I am dissatisfied with the court's decision. I request a new trial (trial de novo) for the following violations *(specify)*:

Vehicle Code Sec. 2235

Date: OCTOBER 2, 20xx

LENNY D. LEADFOOT
....
(TYPE OR PRINT NAME)

▶ *Lenny D. Leadfoot*
_____
(SIGNATURE)

IF YOU WISH TO REQUEST A NEW TRIAL, YOU MUST SUBMIT A *REQUEST FOR NEW TRIAL (TRIAL DE NOVO)* WITHIN 20 DAYS OF THE DATE STATED IN THE CLERK'S CERTIFICATE OF MAILING (see item 1 above).

Form Adopted by the
Judicial Council of California
TR-220 [New January 1, 1999]
Mandatory Form

REQUEST FOR NEW TRIAL (TRIAL DE NOVO)
(Trial by Written Declaration—Traffic)

Vehicle Code, § 40902

- Change the Declaration to indicate that you had a trial by declaration, were found guilty, and then filed a request for a trial de novo. State that more than 45 days have elapsed without a trial since you filed your request, and so you are asking that the case be dismissed.

- Add a paragraph to the Memorandum of Points and Authorities, arguing that Rule 4.210(b)(7) states "the clerk shall set a trial date that shall be within 45 days of receipt of defendant's written request for a trial de novo."

The new trial is handled in exactly the same way as any traffic trial. However, two things should be kept in mind. First, if the judge is the same, file a "Peremptory Challenge" disqualifying her (see Chapter 11) as soon as you can, or ask the judge at trial to disqualify herself on the grounds that she has already decided issues in the same case. Second, never agree to an "informal" trial without the officer present; that's essentially what you had before—in writing—and you lost.

CAUTION

Handling tickets by mail. Whenever you handle a ticket by mail rather than going down to the clerk's window in person, be sure to send all of your correspondence, fines, or court papers by certified mail, return receipt requested.

Do this even if you're simply paying a fine. If you only use regular first class mail, you have no way of knowing whether your papers ever reached their destination. If they didn't, you may face additional fines and possibly additional charges against you for failing to respond to your ticket in time—and the court won't listen to your claims that your correspondence got lost in the mail. Paying the small fee for certified mail is cheap insurance against hundreds of dollars in fines in the future.

If You Want Things Delayed

Instead of proceeding right to trial—or even to a guilty plea, if that's what you're going to do—you may want to put things off for several weeks or months. One reason to do this might be to avoid a license suspension by postponing the future date of any convictions, that is, "spread out" the violation "points" over a broader time period.

If you want to delay things, go to the court clerk a few days before the appearance deadline listed on your Notice to Appear or Courtesy Notice and ask for an extension. Usually, the clerk will give you the first one without much coaxing. You can ask the clerk to simply extend the deadline date, or, failing that, to schedule your arraignment as far off as he or she is permitted to do. This will give you more time to prepare your defense and/or to postpone the date of any conviction.

When you finally have to show up in court for arraignment, you can take another shot at postponing the matter even more, if necessary, by explaining to the judge or commissioner that you do not want to enter a plea until you "have time to consult with counsel" or receive a reply to your discovery request. Here, the judge or commissioner may be impatient, but will usually allow a very short continuance (delay).

When you near the deadline given by the commissioner, again, you may want to try to prevail on the clerk, judge, or commissioner to give you one more extension. At this point, though, you are likely to have more difficulty than before. You may be required to "post bail" to get the case continued further. If the clerk or judge gives you a hard time, you can explain to him or her that you need more time to find a lawyer to discuss your case with.

When you finally go to arraignment, if you have still received no reply to your previously mailed informal discovery request, you should attempt to gain another continuance so that you can receive and review the officer's notes before you enter a plea. Simply explain to the judge or commissioner that you cannot enter a plea until you receive the discovery you requested, and that you wish to schedule a motion "to dismiss because of the prosecution's failure to respond" to your discovery request. It is impossible to predict how a court will respond to your request, but you have absolutely nothing to lose by trying.

Contacting the Court Clerk

Now that you've found out the county's procedure from your phone call, the Internet, or visit to the clerk's office, and now that you've decided how you want to plead and what kind of hearing you want, you're ready to see the clerk to take care of your ticket. At the clerk's window you can either pay your fine and go home, sign up for traffic school (if you qualify), arrange a date for your arraignment (if you want one), or set up a date for a formal trial.

You should probably wait at least a week after you receive the ticket before you visit the clerk's office. It sometimes takes this long for the officer's copy of the ticket to reach the court, and the court personnel will refuse to deal with the matter until they have received it. In some counties, you may even have to wait longer because the county waits to obtain your record from the DMV in Sacramento before it forwards the officer's copy of the ticket to the clerk. (In Los Angeles County, you can use the court website—www.lasuperiorcourt.org/traffic—to see if your ticket is in the system and also to set up an arraignment appearance in court.)

Note: Don't avoid seeing the clerk out of fear she'll have you arrested on the spot for a traffic warrant on this or another case. First,

most traffic-infraction failures to appear are nowadays just reported to a court-appointed private collection agency, rather than the DMV (at least initially). (The DMV can suspend your license until you get the matter resolved.) This usually occurs without any warrants being issued. Second, you can usually call the county sheriff in advance to see if they have any warrants against you. Third, even if there are minor warrants against you, most courts will give you time to post bail.

Should You Bypass the Arraignment?

The major decision you'll have to make at the clerk's window is whether you want to set a date for an arraignment. An arraignment is a brief proceeding where you are informed of your rights and of the charge against you (usually the Vehicle Code section number and a very brief explanation of where and when you allegedly violated it), and how you wish to plead—that is, guilty, not guilty, or nolo contendere (no contest). This is also where you can request traffic school, if the clerk has refused your request. If you plead not guilty, a date is set for your trial.

If you don't want to contest your ticket, there's no need to set up a date for arraignment. Merely go to the clerk's window and pay your fine or request traffic school if your county offers that option.

If you do want to fight your ticket, you can either set up an arraignment or bypass that step and proceed directly to a formal trial with the officer present. If you want to plead not guilty, you can enter your not-guilty plea at the clerk's window and set up a date for trial at that time, bypassing the arraignment. (See below.) In fact, you do not even need to go to the clerk's window—you can enter your not-guilty plea by mail, and have the court notify you of your trial date. Either way, you will have to post the bail in advance if you choose to bypass arraignment (V.C. § 40519). However, this way, you give up your right to a speedy trial.

However, before you decide to bypass the arraignment, be aware that it is an important step for assuring certain rights. You should attend it if you want any of the following:

- to have your rights read to you

- to request that the place of trial be changed to another court (usually the one at the county seat). This request must be made at the arraignment (PC § 1462.2)

- to demand that the charges be dismissed on the grounds that there has already been too much delay on the part of the court personnel. This motion does not have to be made at the arraignment, but the arraignment is the only time for you to ask the judge to set up a separate hearing, prior to trial, for a "speedy trial motion," and

- to object to the proceedings in photo-radar cases.

Other reasons for going to an arraignment include:

- not having the bail money to post under VC § 40519

- wanting to request traffic school in exchange for a dismissal of the charge if the clerk would not allow it, and

- pleading nolo contendere to a violation arising out of an accident.

In courts that allow it, some people elect to go to arraignment to have an "informal hearing," without the officer present, on the same day as the arraignment. As explained above, this is generally not recommended.

If you're still unsure whether you want an arraignment, read the section entitled, "Arraignment," below.

Setting Up an Arraignment Date

If you decide you do want an arraignment, ask the clerk to schedule one. Make sure that the time and date the clerk gives you is on the arraignment calendar, not the trial calendar. Some courts schedule arraignments at night, but clerks usually won't put you on the night arraignment calendar unless you specifically ask for it.

Bypassing the Arraignment (A Shortcut)

If you do not want an arraignment—that is, you wish to contest your ticket and don't plan to make any of the motions mentioned above— simply tell the clerk that you wish to plead "not guilty" right now as provided by VC § 40519(a), thereby "waiving" the arraignment. You have this right, as long as you assert it *before* the last day for appearance stated on your Notice to Appear. Emphasize that you want your next appearance to be a trial with the officer present, and that you're willing to post bail. You will probably have to pay the amount of the fine as bail. Unlike forfeited bail in traffic cases, this bail really is bail (that is, a deposit to guarantee your appearance) and will be returned to you if you're eventually found not guilty. If you're found not guilty, your bail should be refunded in six to eight weeks. If you simply don't show up, you'll lose your bail, be charged with an additional misdemeanor for failing to appear, or be found guilty "in absentia." (See Chapter 7.)

Note: In avoiding a separate court date for arraignment, you give up your right to insist on a trial within 45 days afterward. If you opt for this procedure, the court clerk may schedule your trial date months away.

The clerk is required to set a trial date—not merely an arraignment date—if you ask for it and post the bail in advance. If the clerk hassles you about this, be persistent and tell him to read VC § 40519(a). Or, ask to speak to a supervisor. Keep going up the ladder until you get results.

Bypassing Arraignment by Mail

You can also bypass your arraignment by mail (VC § 40519(b)). The procedure is similar to that just described, except it's all done in writing. You send a personal check for the proper amount of the bail. If you received a courtesy notice, the bail amount will be listed. Otherwise, you'll have to call the clerk and ask, or check the court's website. The amount should be the same as the bail to be "forfeited" if you were to choose to just pay the fine.

Along with your check, you send a note giving the case number of your ticket or courtesy notice, and clearly indicate that you are pleading not guilty. This should be mailed by certified mail (return receipt requested) at least five days before the deadline for you to appear (as stated on your ticket). The clerk's office is then supposed to notify you by mail (postmarked at least ten days before) of your trial date. (By bypassing the arraignment you give up your right to a speedy trial.)

Your note to the clerk should look something like this:

June 10, 20xx

Traffic Clerk
Superior Court
Los Angeles Metropolitan Branch
Traffic Division
1945 S. Hill St.
Los Angeles, California

RE: Los Angeles Police Dept.
Citation No. LA-12345
dated June 1, 20xx;
Your Docket No. L-123456789-A.

Dear Sir or Madam:

This is in regard to the above citation I received in Los Angeles on June 1, 20xx. I hereby waive the arraignment, and, in accordance with § 40519(b) of the Vehicle Code, plead not guilty to the charge of violating § 22350 of the Vehicle Code. I request a trial date for a trial with the officer present.

Pursuant to my telephone conversation yesterday with Ms. Donna Nuthin of your office, I am enclosing a check for bail in the amount of $271.

Sincerely,

Sara Speedaway

Sara Speedaway
123 Market Street
Santa Ana, CA 90123

Be sure to keep a carbon or photocopy of the letter for your records, and to save all certified mail receipts.

If your court district allows a "trial by declaration," you can handle your whole case by mail.

Arraignment

The rest of this chapter discusses the arraignment and the procedural requests (called "motions") you can make at arraignment. If you've already decided to bypass arraignment (see the previous section), you can go directly to the next chapter. If you are still undecided, keep on reading to get a better idea of what an arraignment involves.

Telling You Your Rights

One of the most important parts of the arraignment is to inform you of your basic legal rights. These include the right to be represented by an attorney, to cross-examine the officer, to subpoena witnesses, to have your case tried within 45 days, and to have a jury trial in a misdemeanor case.

Usually the judge will read these rights to the group of defendants in the courtroom when court begins, or a clerk will pass out a printed sheet containing this information. Rarely will the judge recite these rights to a defendant individually.

Note: By reading this book, you're already getting a pretty good idea of what those rights are, so there's no need to schedule an arraignment just to hear someone read them to you.

When your case is called, the judge will ask you whether you understand these rights. Answer yes only if you really do. If you say you understand something, but really don't, you won't be allowed to complain about it later. Similarly, don't sign forms until you know what you are signing. Below is a sample "Advice of Rights" form.

Occasionally, a judge may ask you to "waive" (give up) certain rights. She may, for example, announce that unless you object, it will be assumed that you want an informal hearing in which the citing officer will not be present for you to cross-examine. Or, due to a very crowded court calendar, your trial might be scheduled more than 45 days ahead, unless you object. (See below, "'Waiving Time' for Trial-Setting," for advice on when you should and shouldn't give up this right.) So listen carefully, and don't mistakenly give up these important rights. If the clerk or judge sets a trial date beyond the 45-day period and you don't object, you will have accepted what is called a "special waiver" of your right to a speedy trial and can't complain about it later. If the officer doesn't show up at trial, the judge can postpone trial for up to ten more days, even if you withdraw your special waiver of your right to a trial within 45 days of arraignment (PC § 1382(a)(3)(B)).

Entering a "Not Guilty" Plea

Once the charge is read to you and you have claimed or waived certain rights, the judge or clerk will ask you how you plead. Your answer should almost always be "not guilty." (If you intended to plead guilty, you should have just paid your fine to the clerk without taking time off work to go to an arraignment.) However, if the clerk has not allowed you to attend traffic school, you may want to tell the judge you prefer traffic school and refer him to Rule 4.104, California Rules of Court, to explain why you are eligible. If the judge won't allow you to attend traffic school, you have little to lose by pleading not guilty and going to trial.

You might be asked about prior offenses, or "priors" (earlier violations on your record), though in practice this is very rare. This is called "charging a prior," and lays a basis for raising your fine above that for a first-time offense in the event you're found guilty of the current charge. You should always deny the prior offenses. This is perfectly proper, even

ADVICE OF RIGHTS—TRAFFIC VIOLATIONS

The following represents a summary of the rights you have as a defendant in this Court. If you do not understand these rights, be sure to request a further explanation from the court.

Each defendant has the following rights:

1. To have the complaint or citation read in open court.

2. To be represented by legal counsel at all stages of the proceedings and to be allowed a reasonable time to obtain an attorney. If you are charged with a misdemeanor and are indigent, the Court will appoint an attorney to represent you.

3. To plead guilty or not guilty or nolo contendere. A plea of nolo contendere has the same effect as a plea of guilty except that it cannot be used against you in a civil action.

4. To confront and cross-examine witnesses who would testify against you.

5. To the use of subpoena power of the Court to compel the attendance of witnesses on your behalf.

6. A constitutional privilege against self-incrimination; you cannot be compelled to be a witness about the matter.

7. To have your case tried within 45 days of your plea.

8. If you are charged with a misdemeanor, you are entitled to a jury trial.

9. If you plead guilty or nolo contendere (no contest) you have the right to delay sentencing for six hours and sentence must be imposed within five days. Since it may be inconvenient to return to court for sentencing, the Court will assume that you prefer to be sentenced immediately unless you request a later date.

10. If you desire to admit guilt and to give an explanation to the Court, you may do so after entering your plea of guilty. Your plea of guilty, however, is an admission of each element of the offense, and your explanation will be considered only in determining the appropriate penalty.

MAXIMUM PENALTIES

If you are convicted of any infraction, you may be fined $270. For a second conviction within one year, you may be fined $540. A third conviction within one year carries a maximum penalty of $675. A fourth conviction may be treated as a misdemeanor. Your license may also be suspended as a consequence of a conviction for certain violations.

Misdemeanor convictions of §§ 23103 (reckless driving) and 23109 (speed exhibition or contest) carry possible sentences of 90 days in jail and a fine of $2,700, plus a possible license suspension. Other misdemeanors, including violations of §§ 12500 (driving while not licensed) and 40508(a) (failure to appear) are punishable by six months in jail and a fine of $2,700.

I HAVE READ THE ABOVE ADVICE OF RIGHTS AND UNDERSTAND THE SAME. I FURTHER UNDERSTAND THAT IF I SHOULD PLEAD GUILTY OR NOLO CONTENDERE, I WILL BE GIVING UP THE RIGHTS SET FORTH IN SECTIONS (2) THROUGH (8), ABOVE.

Signed _____

Address _____

City _____ Zip Code _____

Telephone _____

though you may really have forfeited bail or been convicted of the prior offense. You're not committing perjury (lying under oath) any more than when you plead not guilty. When they ask if you have any prior convictions, simply say, *"I deny the validity of any prior convictions."* All you're doing is requiring the prosecution to prove the existence of priors by locating the original court records, which is often difficult to do. (The Court of Appeal has held that a court violates a defendant's rights against self-incrimination when it asks him or her about prior offenses. See *Municipal Court v. Superior Court* (1988) 199 Cal.App.3d 19, 244 Cal.Rptr. 591, and Chapter 14.)

The Informal Hearing Option (Infractions Only)

Courts that allow "informal hearings" without the ticketing officer present sometimes encourage you to agree to this procedure on the same day you are arraigned. As we've said before, this is rarely in your best interest. You generally have a better chance of beating a ticket in a formal trial where the officer may well fail to appear. The only time you should agree to an informal hearing is when the judge conducting the informal hearings finds people not guilty at least half the time on moving violation charges, in cases called before yours.

Note: If the judge appears to be encouraging informal trials, make sure he doesn't assume that you want one. All you have to say is, *"I plead not guilty, Your Honor, and request a trial with the officer present."*

If you do decide to have an informal hearing, the procedure is simple; you merely tell your story to the judge. Your best shot at beating a ticket is to testify to facts that legally excuse you of the charge, as opposed to denying that you committed an "element" of the offense. The reason for this is that by agreeing to substitute the officer's copy of the ticket for his testimony,

you have basically admitted to the truth of what's stated on the face of the ticket. For example, if the ticket says you were doing 45 in a 35 mph zone, you stand a better chance of being found not guilty if you establish that 45 mph was a safe speed under the circumstances (road width, traffic, weather, visibility, etc.), rather than by arguing that you were only doing 33 mph. If you disagreed with what was stated on the ticket, you should have insisted on a trial with the officer present so you could have exposed his untruths by cross-examination. On the other hand, when you say that it was safe to go 45 mph, you're dealing with an issue not specifically addressed by the brief information on the face of the ticket, and the judge or commissioner isn't faced with a conflict between your story and the ticket. And since the officer isn't present to contradict you, you may have a decent chance of winning.

People sometimes confuse an informal hearing with "pleading guilty with an explanation." But these are very different procedures. In the informal hearing, you believe you are not guilty, and your explanation (that is, your defense) shows why. You could be found not guilty, in which case nothing is reported to the DMV, and nothing goes on your driving record. In pleading guilty with explanation, you're basically saying, *"Yes, I'm guilty"* (and that goes on your DMV record), *"but please give me a break on the fine."* In actuality, you should have gone to an informal hearing (if not a formal one) and seen whether you couldn't beat the charge altogether. Pleading "guilty with an explanation" is seldom a good idea.

"Waiving Time" for Trial-Setting

The law requires that a trial date be set within 45 days from the day you plead not guilty (PC § 1382(a)). Traffic court judges who are faced with too many trials within this time may try to get you to waive your right to a speedy trial. They may ask something like, *"Do you waive time for trial?"* If you say no, the judge is required to set it within the 45-day period. One reason for not waiving time is that if, on the trial date (usually pretty close to the end of the 45-day limit), you show up and the officer doesn't, it's difficult for the judge to arrange for resubpoenaing the officer and still have a trial within the 45-day limit. As a result, the judge must dismiss the charge against you. If you do agree to waive time, however, for one of the reasons set out below, the judge can reset the trial for a later date and force you to come in again. On the other hand, even if you have waived time, some judges will dismiss the case "in the interest of justice," since forcing you to appear three times—once for arraignment, and twice for trial—may be too much to ask. But this practice is entirely up to the judge.

The best strategy is to politely decline to waive time, which forces the judge to set your trial before the 45th day after you enter your plea. Then, you should ask for a trial very close to the end of the 45-day period. If the judge resists, tell him you need that much time because the prosecution has 20 days to respond to your request for the officer's notes (PC § 1054.5(b)) and you will need the rest of the time to prepare for trial.

Once the judge sets the trial date, send out your Informal Discovery Request, if you haven't already done so. The prosecution has 20 days to respond to your mailed request, but must respond at least 30 days before trial (PC § 1054.7). Chances are the prosecution won't meet both deadlines, even if your trial date is scheduled almost 45 days away.

Before trial, you can then move to dismiss if the prosecution fails to meet either deadline. At that time you should also be ready to argue that for the judge to give the prosecution more time *"would require me to choose between the right to timely discovery, and the right to a speedy trial, your Honor."* (See later in this chapter for the format of a discovery motion and how to argue it in court.)

If the trial date is inconvenient for you, tell the judge. She will very likely set a later date. If that later date is more than 45 days off, you should object. If you don't, you will have impliedly agreed to a "special waiver" of your right to a speedy trial within 45 days of arraignment and won't be able to use the delay to try to get your case dismissed later. If that happens, and the officer doesn't show at trial, then the judge can postpone trial for up to ten days and give the officer a second chance to show up. So unless you have a very good reason, we generally recommend that you not give up your right to a speedy trial.

You may want to postpone the trial if you know when the officer will take a vacation. Many standard-form tickets have a space for the citing officer to fill in his vacation dates. Most officers simply neglect to fill this in, but when they do, it's meant as a signal to the court personnel not to schedule the trial during that period. If at arraignment the court personnel aren't too wide awake, however, and the officer's vacation period is not too far off (two or three months at the most), you might want to ask for a trial date that happens to fall within the officer's vacation period. If the judge doesn't see what you're up to (even if he does, there is nothing he can do, other than refuse your requested date), the judge may agree to the proposed trial date on the condition that you waive time for trial. When the trial comes and the vacationing officer doesn't show, you are in a good position to protest vigorously about how you had to lose a day's pay and drive 25 miles (*"which is punishment enough, Your Honor"*) and request a dismissal "for lack of prosecution."

Seasoned trial lawyers often try to get trials delayed and then delayed again. The theory is that if the delay is long enough, memories fade, witnesses die or move away, and police records get routinely destroyed, with the result that the prosecution has a tough time trying to prove its case.

Requests You Can Make at Arraignment

In certain situations, there are issues you should raise at arraignment in order to protect your rights.

"Demurring" to Photo-Radar Tickets

In a few cities, a radar unit placed in a police vehicle is connected to a camera that photographs the license plate of the offending vehicle, as well as the driver. No police officer pulls you over. Instead, a computer-generated Notice to Appear is mailed to the registered owner of the vehicle.

Aside from fighting that sort of ticket on the merits, as discussed in Chapter 4, you may wish to try to nip the ticket in the bud before even pleading not guilty. Although no case law specifically provides for this, some attorneys have successfully beaten such tickets on the ground that, in this situation, a copy of the mailed Notice to Appear is not a legal substitute for the criminal complaint that is required to initiate prosecution. A Notice to Appear is a valid substitute for a complaint, but only when issued by an officer who observed the violation or issued it as the result of an accident. (See PC § 949 and VC §§ 20413 and 40600(d).) A few exceptions exist for tickets issued by "automatic enforcement systems" that take pictures of alleged traffic offenders and their cars' license plates. These exceptions, however, apply only to stop sign and stoplight violations, illegal turns at intersections, and bypassing railroad crossing gates (VC § 40518). No similar exception exists for speed violations, and VC § 21455.6(b) states that while it authorizes automatic enforcement systems, it "does not authorize the use of photo radar for speed enforcement purposes."

Again, the way to attack this lack of a complaint is by filing a demurrer. When your case is called, you should state:

"Your Honor, rather than entering a plea, I would like to file a demurrer with the court at this time on the basis that a Notice to Appear is not a legal substitute for a complaint in a photo-radar case such as mine. According to Penal Code Section 1003, a demurrer can be filed at arraignment, and so I would like to do that now."

You then hand your papers to the clerk. The judge may ask you if you've served a copy on the district attorney. If so, say:

"No, Your Honor. Section 1003 seems to require the demurrer be presented, and served on the prosecutor, at arraignment only."

If there's no prosecutor there (usually there isn't in traffic court), say:

"Since there is no prosecutor here, I believe the district attorney's office has impliedly given up the right to service."

If a prosecutor is present, hand her a copy of your papers. Then, you should say:

"Your Honor, Penal Code Section 1006 requires that the demurrer be heard immediately."

Even though this is true, the judge will probably set a hearing on it for another time, and may also require you to provide the district attorney's office with a copy.

When you do get a court hearing on your demurrer, you should say:

> *"Your Honor, the basis of this demurrer is that it's apparent from the court's file in this case that the supposed Notice to Appear was issued in a situation where only a verified complaint may be used. This is a photo-radar case in which there was no traffic stop, so that the Notice-to-Appear procedure in Vehicle Code Sections 40500 through 40502 is inapplicable, and no complaint has been filed."*

If the judge rules against you, plead not guilty. If the judge agrees, though, the district attorney might file a verified complaint. However, district attorneys' offices often will neglect to do so.

You might want to consider ignoring the mailed Notice to Appear. Since you didn't sign it, you never promised to appear in court. Of course, the city may then file a complaint and ask that a warrant be issued for your arrest (or your driver's license suspended), perhaps after being spit out by a computer unaware your citation was never signed. If no actual complaint is issued for a year, the statute of limitations will have expired.

A sample demurrer follows below.

Requests You Can Make After Pleading Not Guilty

At arraignment, after pleading not guilty, there are specific requests you should make in certain situations:

- Where you sent an Informal Discovery Request, and have received no response, you can ask the judge to set a date to hear your discovery motion before trial. At this hearing, you can formally ask the judge to dismiss the case for failure to comply with your request, or, if the judge won't dismiss the case, for an order requiring the police or prosecutor to disclose the information you requested.

- Where the offense can be charged as a misdemeanor or infraction (such as failure to appear (VC § 40508(a)) or driving without a valid license (VC § 12500(a)), or where it's your fourth infraction within a year, you can insist it be charged as a misdemeanor where you have a right to a jury trial. **Note:** See warning below.

- Where you insisted the officer cite you to appear in the court at the county seat (see Chapter 17) and he refused, you should ask that the case be transferred there. If the judge refuses, ask her to set a date for your motion for change of venue.

- Where there have been months of delay before arraignment, you can ask the judge to set a date for your motion to dismiss for violation of your right to a speedy trial.

In any of these situations, you should *briefly* summarize the legal basis for your request. Judges who hear traffic cases are often pretty impatient with defendants who make long statements. A bored, impatient judge might stop you before realizing the valid legal point you're making.

Note: Formal motions and legal arguments are rarely heard at arraignment. (Demurrers of the type mentioned above are supposed to be the only exception (PC §§ 1003, 1006).) The only thing you should do at arraignment is plead not guilty, briefly state your request (transfer to county seat, or dismissal), and ask the judge to set a hearing on the matter.

123 Main Street
Pasadena, CA 91100
Tel: (818) 555-1234

Defendant in Pro Per

SUPERIOR COURT OF CALIFORNIA, COUNTY OF LOS ANGELES

PASADENA BRANCH

THE PEOPLE OF THE STATE
OF CALIFORNIA,

    Plaintiff,

vs.

PHOEBE PHOTON,

    Defendant.

Case No. 123456

DEMURRER TO
"NOTICE TO APPEAR"
POINTS AND AUTHORITIES

(Penal Code § 1004(2))

Defendant hereby demurs, pursuant to PC § 1004(2), to the Notice to Appear herein, on the ground that it does not conform to the provisions of PC §§ 950 and 952, or VC § 40513. As the Notice to Appear indicates on its face that it was not issued pursuant to an arrest per VC §§ 40500 et seq., it is not a statutory substitute for a complaint under § 40513(b).

WHEREFORE, defendant prays that this demurrer be sustained.

DATED: March 15, 20xx

PHOEBE PHOTON
Defendant in Pro Per

POINTS AND AUTHORITIES

STATEMENT OF FACTS

This is a "photo-radar" speeding case. The defendant was mailed a copy of a purported "Notice to Appear." This form is not approved by the Judicial Council for this purpose. It is to be used only in conjunction with an "arrest" in which the citing officer apprehends the alleged violator. An officer's name is typed or machine-printed on the form, and defendant's signature does not appear in the promise-to-appear position of the form. No complaint has been filed.

ARGUMENT

I. DEFENDANT'S DEMURRER IS PROPERLY BEFORE THE COURT

A demurrer may be asserted in a criminal case. PC § 1002. Since a demurrer may be asserted in a misdemeanor case, it may be asserted in an infraction case. PC § 19.7. It "must be put in, in open court ... at the time of arraignment...." PC § 1003. One basis for a demurrer is that the complaint (or its equivalent) does not comply with PC §§ 950 and 952. PC § 1004(2).

II. INTRODUCTION

Only when a police officer observes a violation of a misdemeanor (or an infraction) is he or she empowered to make an arrest.* Pursuant to VC §§ 40500 et seq., the officer then issues a Notice to Appear, which the defendant signs and promises to appear in court; the officer then releases the defendant. Only where this form is used as intended by the Judicial Council does VC § 40513(b) provide that it is a legal substitute for a complaint. VC § 40513(b) allows it to be the legal substitute for a complaint.

The prosecution here was not initiated by a lawfully issued Notice to Appear presented to or signed by defendant. Instead, the matter was commenced by the mailing of a printed notice to defendant. This procedure is not authorized. Vehicle Code § 40518 authorizes "automated enforcement systems" *only* for violations of Sections 21453 and 21455 (stoplights), 22101 (illegal turns at intersections), and 22451 (railroad crossing violations). It does not authorize this method for violations of Section 22350 or 22349. The prosecution in the instant case could only have properly initiated either by 1) filing of a formal complaint, or 2) the issuance to defendant (at the scene, following apprehension by an officer who observed the alleged violator's

---

*For the purpose of apprehending traffic violators, such an "arrest" occurs when the officer merely pulls over the suspect on the highway. *People v. Superior Court* (1972) 7 Cal.3d 186, 200.

identity) of a Notice to Appear signed by the officer and on which the defendant promised to appear. Since neither has occurred, the Court is without jurisdiction to hear the case.

III. A NOTICE TO APPEAR, ISSUED IN A DEFENDANT'S ABSENCE, UNSIGNED BY AND MAILED TO HIM, IS NOT A LAWFUL SUBSTITUTE FOR THE COMPLAINT REQUIRED TO INITIATE A MISDEMEANOR OR INFRACTION PROSECUTION.

There are two ways for a police officer to initiate a prosecution against a person the officer believes committed a misdemeanor or infraction Vehicle Code violation. The first, and usual, way is to issue a "Notice to Appear" to the motorist whom the officer has allegedly observed commit the offense. The officer observes the alleged violation, and the alleged perpetrator, and apprehends that person. The officer then prepares a Notice to Appear, which the alleged violator must sign to obtain his or her release following this type of "arrest" (stated as such in §§ 40500 et seq.). The original of the true Notice to Appear, filed with the court, constitutes a lawful substitute for a verified complaint, even in the face of a not-guilty plea. VC § 40513(b). This method is only intended for the situation where the officer immediately stops and apprehends the alleged violator. The second way, more common for offenses that are not traffic infractions, is to file a complaint on which a warrant is issued by a magistrate for the defendant's arrest.

The Notice to Appear is authorized by § 40500 of the Vehicle Code. It is supposed to be used only where a person is "arrested for any violation of [the Vehicle] Code not declared to be a felony." The Notice to Appear cannot be used unless there is an arrest in this sense. As an officer generally may arrest a person suspected of having committed a misdemeanor or infraction only when he has observed the offense and the perpetrator, and as a Notice to Appear can be issued only by an officer who has "arrested" the suspected offender, it follows that a Notice to Appear can be issued only when the citing officer has observed the violation and the perpetrator and apprehended the latter.

There are two exceptions to this rule. A notice to appear can be issued for a violation arising out of an accident investigated by a qualified police officer (VC § 40600) or by an automatic enforcement system relating to nonspeeding violations (VC §§ 21453, 21455, or 22101), as allowed per VC § 40518. See also VC §§ 40520, 40521. But no such exception exists for speeding violations via "photo-radar" or anything of the like. Indeed, VC § 21455.6(b), in referring to the authority to use such automatic enforcement systems contained in VC § 21455.5, says that VC § 21455.5 "does not authorize the use of photo radar for speed enforcement purposes by any jurisdiction."

It is only when the Notice to Appear is properly used in accordance with § 40500 et seq., on a form intended for that purpose by the Judicial Council, that it is a lawful substitute for a complaint. VC § 40513(b).

The Judicial Council Notice to Appear form was never intended for use as a citation to be issued in a defendant's absence and mailed to him or her in this situation. That form is intended to be filled out by the arresting officer at the scene of a traffic-stop, noncustodial arrest, to be signed by the officer under penalty of perjury, and then to be signed by the defendant as a promise to appear. Only VC §§ 40600 et seq. provide for the issuance of such notices after the fact, and then only in accident cases.

In other words, a formal complaint is necessary unless a proper Notice to Appear has been prepared on "a form approved by the Judicial Council." However, the Judicial Council has not promulgated a form to be mailed to the defendant in nonaccident speeding cases, for the simple reason that no statute authorizes the mailing of any type of violation notice, or Notice to Appear, to the registered owner in photo-radar cases. The procedure erroneously used here is analogous to the procedure used where an officer mails a citation to a driver following an accident investigation, pursuant to VC §§ 40600. The analogy is important because the Attorney General has determined that in such cases a mailed "Notice to Appear" is not a lawful substitute for a complaint. An excellent discussion in this regard can be found in 59 Ops. Cal. Atty. Gen. 355 (1976). Following a detailed analysis of the three ways (Notice to Appear, Notice of Violation, and verified complaint) by which misdemeanor or infraction prosecutions can be initiated, the writer concluded that "[t]he terms 'notice of violation' and 'notice to appear' as contained in VC § 40600 are not synonymous" and that the mailing of a "Notice to Appear" to a driver "does not fully comply with legal requirements." Id. at 356. The opinion concludes that a mailed Notice to Appear, used in a situation for which it was not intended by the Judicial Council (namely other than after an officer apprehends an alleged violator for a violation allegedly observed) is not a lawful substitute for a complaint.

Since a complaint (or legal substitute) is essential for jurisdiction (see PC § 949; VC §§ 40513, 40603; Anger v. Municipal Court (1965) 237 Cal.App.2d 69; Gavin v. Municipal Court (1960) 184 Cal. App. 712), the court is without jurisdiction.

CONCLUSION

For the foregoing reasons, the notice filed herein is not a lawful substitute for a complaint under VC § 40513(b), because it is not the form the Judicial Council prescribed in the situation where an officer does something other than apprehend the violator and then and there determines his or her identity. As no actual complaint has been filed, the Court is without jurisdiction to hear the matter.

DATED: March 15, 20xx

Phoebe Photon

PHOEBE PHOTON
Defendant in Pro Per

Requesting a Hearing on a Motion Regarding Discovery

You have the right to request and receive a copy of any notes the officer made regarding the alleged violation, including the notes officers commonly make on the back of their copy of the ticket. That section also includes a sample Informal Discovery Request used for this purpose. Unfortunately, prosecutors, officers, and police agencies often ignore these requests, but you can turn this to your advantage by making a motion to dismiss (or, in the alternative, getting a court order that the information you requested be produced) on account of this failure.

If you sent your Informal Discovery Request at least 20 days before your arraignment and received no response, you should ask the judge at arraignment to schedule a "motion" hearing before the trial date. After you plead not guilty, say:

> "Your Honor, since the prosecutor and police agency have ignored my Penal Code Section 1054 discovery request, I would like the court to set a hearing on my discovery motion. I would like this heard well before trial, so that I have time to prepare, in the event I do receive the materials in response to my motion."

The judge should set a hearing date, but may ask you a few questions. If the judge mutters something about discovery being inapplicable to traffic cases, you may have to remind him that the case of *Hobbs v. Municipal Court* (1991) 233 Cal.App.3d 670, 284 Cal. Rptr. 655, holds that discovery applies in misdemeanor cases, and PC § 19.7 applies all misdemeanor procedures to infractions in the absence of a law to the contrary.

If the judge wants to hear your motion on the date of trial, you should object by saying, *"Your Honor, I won't have enough time to prepare my case if I receive the discovery materials a few minutes before I have to go to trial."*

After the judge gives you a hearing date and time for your motion, you should prepare a motion as shown in the section below, "Motions After Arraignment."

Demanding a Jury Trial in Certain Cases

A very few offenses, most notably failure to appear (VC § 40508(a)), driving with an invalid license (VC § 12500(a)), or driving with a license suspended for failure to appear (VC § 14601.1), can be charged as misdemeanors (punishable by up to six months in jail and a $2,700 or $2,900 total fine) or as infractions. Many courts have begun charging these offenses as infractions. The advantage to you is a lower maximum possible penalty; the disadvantage is that you have no right to a jury trial.

You do have the right, under PC §§ 17(d)(1) and (2) to "elect to have the case proceed as a misdemeanor" (after having been "informed of (your) rights," which rarely occurs), and to have the matter tried as an infraction, only "with the consent of the defendant." This means that when you are charged with any of these offenses, you can have a jury trial. The advantage is that prosecutors will then be forced to deal with you in order to avoid what is, for them, a low-priority item.

EXAMPLE:

You're charged with violating the Basic Speed Law (VC § 22350), an infraction. Since you waited too long to respond to the citation, you're also charged with failure to appear (VC § 40508(a)). Because the system wants to keep the case in high-volume, low-cost traffic court, the failure-to-appear is charged as an infraction. You can insist it be charged as a misdemeanor and demand a jury trial (and even a public defender, if your income is low enough).

The case will then be assigned to a real judge (not a "commissioner" or "referee") and a prosecutor, and set for a "pretrial conference." Once you tell them you'll insist on your right to a jury trial, the judge and prosecutor may offer to drop one charge if you'll plead guilty to the other for a promised low fine.

Warning: When you raise the stakes this way, you also risk being sentenced to jail, if found guilty, by a vindictive judge angry at you for bogging down the system. On the other hand, few judges are really this bad, and county jails are usually so filled to capacity as to discourage judges from jailing people for first-offense minor misdemeanors such as these. The choice is up to you. However, if you are currently on probation for a misdemeanor offense, do not do this for any reason. The judge or prosecutor will likely use the new misdemeanor to violate your probation on the first misdemeanor. A judge would then conduct the hearing, which was what you were trying to avoid in the first place.

Vehicle Code § 40000.28 (as well as the case of *People v. Shults* (1978)) establish your right to insist that a fourth infraction committed in a year be charged as a misdemeanor. When you plead guilty, and claim you've had at least three other infraction convictions based on three prior offenses that occurred within a year of your receiving this fourth ticket, the judge is required to hold a hearing to determine if you've really had the three prior convictions. At such a hearing, a certified copy of your DMV printout should suffice for this purpose.

Again, though, this can be dangerous. A judge who has just spent two days on a jury trial for your fourth speeding offense in a year may convince himself that a few days or months in jail would slow you down.

If you prepare beforehand, you may be able to succeed in having your demand granted at the arraignment, rather than later. What you will need is "certified" copies of the records of convictions of your prior offenses.

Note: A DMV printout or a notice from the DMV containing a list of your priors may suffice. You can get certified copies of your prior offense records from the court where you were convicted. Just go to the clerk's window and pay the small fee.

Bring your certified copies of the convictions to your arraignment. When you are asked to enter a plea, say "not guilty." Then raise your motion for the case to proceed as a misdemeanor by saying something like this:

> *"Your Honor, I admit to having been convicted of three prior infractions within the last year, and, pursuant to Vehicle Code Section 40000.28 and under the authority of the case of People v. Shults (1978) 87 Cal.App.3d 101, I request that my case proceed as a misdemeanor. I have in my possession certified copies of my records [or a DMV printout showing the convictions] of conviction for those offenses. If the court will not rule on my request today, I ask that a hearing be set for me to file and argue a formal motion on this issue."*

At this point, the judge may ask to see the certified copies and might look up the law. If she does so and grants your motion, the case will then be transferred to another court, where misdemeanors are heard. We refer you to Chapter 13 for a detailed discussion of handling misdemeanors, including conducting plea negotiations. If the judge does not issue a ruling on the spot, but sets a hearing for the motion, you will have to prepare, file, serve, and argue legal papers supporting your demand that the court charge you with a misdemeanor. Instructions on how to do this can be found in the section, "Motions After Arraignment," below.

Demanding Transfer to the County Seat

As we discuss in Chapter 17, a person being cited for a Vehicle Code offense often has the right to demand of the officer writing the ticket that they go to court at the "county seat" rather than at some other court nearer to where the offense supposedly occurred. And almost all police officers—with the exception of Highway Patrol officers—either are ignorant of that law or simply refuse to follow it.

When this happens, the person cited will probably have to make a formal motion to transfer the case to the county seat court.

Note: You have a right to have this motion granted *only* if you demanded the county seat from the officer when you were stopped. To preserve your right to make such a motion, you must demand transfer at arraignment. (PC § 1462.2.) This would be done by saying something like this:

> *"Your Honor, I plead not guilty, and, pursuant to Penal Code Section 1462.2 and Vehicle Code Section 40502(b), I request that this case be transferred to the county seat. I live/work closer to the county seat than to this court, and I made a timely demand of the officer for the county seat, which he refused. If Your Honor won't transfer it now, I request the matter be set for my motion for change of venue."*

The judge should then either order the case transferred or set a date for such a motion. If the judge sets a motion hearing for the same day as the trial, but a few minutes before, he's setting you up to deny the motion and find you guilty. Ask him to set it several weeks beforehand. If he won't, then you probably should disqualify that judge from hearing your motion, by filing a peremptory challenge. (See Chapter 11.)

Requesting a Hearing on a Motion to Dismiss for Lack of a Speedy Trial

Occasionally, in courts in larger cities, court clerks faced with crowded dockets will refuse for months to allow a person charged with a traffic offense to attend arraignment. This is often because the law requires that you be given a trial date no later than 45 days after the arraignment and not-guilty plea, unless you "waive time" for trial. (PC § 1382(a)(3).) In places where the system is so bogged down, clerks would rather delay the date your statutory right to a speedy trial begins.

However, if this forced waiting goes on for too long, the clerk is still denying you a speedy trial. Under the state and federal constitutions, you have a right to a speedy trial even though no clear-cut law requires trial within a certain number of days. This means that if any sort of lengthy "prearraignment" delay occurs, and your ability to defend your case suffers as a result, you have a right, after arraignment, to make a motion to dismiss the case on the basis that your constitutional right to a speedy trial was violated before arraignment.

This motion is proper in some cases, even where you've failed to appear in response to a ticket, if the system has taken no action against you for over a year (*Serna v. Superior Court* (1985) 40 Cal.3d 239).

So, if at arraignment you think you should make a motion to dismiss on the basis that your right to a speedy trial was denied because of prearraignment delay, you should ask the judge to set a date for hearing on your motion.

Asking That a Reporter or Recorder Be Used

According to the case of *In re Armstrong* (1981) 126 Cal.App.3d 565, a misdemeanor defendant has the right to insist that a court stenographer (reporter) be present to take verbatim notes of the proceedings, or that a tape recorder record them. Since there is no law specifically allowing infraction proceedings to proceed without a reporter or recorder present, the *Armstrong* rule applies to infractions as well. (Penal Code § 19.7 says that unless there is a law that specifically provides otherwise for infractions—such as PC § 19.6, removing the right to a jury trial in infraction cases—misdemeanor rules apply to infractions. The case of *People v. Matthews* (1983) 139 Cal.App.3d 537, 188 Cal.Rptr. 796, says that PC § 19.6 even incorporates misdemeanor "case law" into infraction procedure. Thus, the *Armstrong* rule requiring recorded proceedings should apply to infractions.)

The purpose of this rule is to allow a transcript of the trial proceedings to be prepared later if you need to appeal. A sample form for requesting a recorder or reporter, preferably at arraignment (or at least a few days in advance of trial), is shown here and a blank form is in the back of this book. If for some reason you are unable to file the written demand at arraignment, file it with the clerk at least a few weeks before trial. At the arraignment, simply state, after pleading not guilty, *"Your Honor, I wish to file this request for a court reporter or tape recorder, so that the trial proceedings will be recorded."* If the judge thinks that such things are not available in traffic court, tell her that PC § 19.7 and *In re Armstrong*, as indicated on the form, require this even for an infraction.

If the judge refuses to provide a court reporter or tape recorder, ask to be allowed to use your own pocket tape recorder, if you have one. Unless the judge has a good reason to deny this, she must allow it (California Rules of Court, Rule 1.150). In *People v. Ashley*, (1990) 220 Cal. App. 3d 919, 269 Cal.Rptr. 769, one court ruled that it was an illegal "abuse of discretion" for a judge to refuse to allow a hand-held recorder, even though the proceedings were transcribed. Although that case involved a murder, the court based its decision on Rule 980, not on the seriousness of the charge.

Other Motions

The above is certainly not a complete list of the types of technical issues you can raise at and/or after arraignment. Pretrial motions in criminal cases are often brought on numerous other grounds, such as motions to suppress evidence based on an unlawful search by a police officer. (PC § 1538.5.) However, other than those listed above, there are few motions applicable to traffic cases.

Motions After Arraignment

If your request at arraignment resulted in the judge setting a hearing date on a motion, you will have to prepare for the hearing on that motion. Also, if the judge refused to set a hearing date, or otherwise brushed you aside without setting a hearing, you will have to schedule such a hearing through the court clerk.

Most courts hear such motions one or two days during the week on what's called a "law-and-motion calendar." Almost all such motions deal with criminal matters more serious than traffic infractions. Some courts schedule motion hearings in traffic cases during the same period they conduct arraignments. To find out which days motions are heard in traffic cases, call the court clerk. If the person has no idea what you're talking about (which is very likely), ask to speak to a supervisor! Keep going up the ladder until you get results. If this fails, contact the "criminal" court clerk for this information.

Once you get a date and courtroom number for your motion to be heard, you'll have to write them in on the Notice of Motion form you file. Try to prepare the motion papers at least two weeks before the hearing date so that the district

FERN FASTIDIOUS
123 State St.
Gilroy, California

SUPERIOR COURT OF CALIFORNIA, COUNTY OF SANTA CLARA
SOUTH COUNTY BRANCH

THE PEOPLE OF THE	)	No. B987654
STATE OF CALIFORNIA	)	
Plaintiff,	)	
	)	**DEMAND FOR COURT REPORTER**
vs.	)	**OR ELECTRONIC RECORDING**
	)	**OF PROCEEDINGS**
DEBORAH DEFENDANT,	)	
	)	
Defendant.	)	
	)	

The above-named defendant in the above-entitled action hereby requests that the Court provide for attendance at trial proceeding herein by a stenographic court reporter, or that the proceedings be electronically recorded. Or in the alternative, that defendant be allowed to record such proceedings under Rule 1.150 of California Rules of Court.

DATED: 1-2-20xx

Fern Fastidious
_____
FERN FASTIDIOUS
Defendant in Pro Per

POINTS AND AUTHORITIES

According to case law set forth in *In re Armstrong* (1981) 126 Cal.App.3d 568, all misdemeanor proceedings must, on the defendant's request, be recorded electronically or by a *stenographic* court reporter. This requirement is incorporated into infraction proceedings by Penal Code Section 19.7, which states, "Except as otherwise provided by law, all provisions of law relating to misdemeanors shall apply to infractions…" According to *People v. Matthews* (1983) 139 Cal.App.3d 537, this statute incorporates into infraction procedure all constitutional procedural protections applicable to misdemeanor procedure, even where not required by the Constitution for infraction procedure per se. Thus, infraction trials must be recorded or reported at the defendant's request.

DATED: 1-2-20xx

Fern Fastidious
_____
FERN FASTIDIOUS
Defendant in Pro Per

(or city) attorney's office won't be able to complain about insufficient time to prepare and respond to the motion.

General Rules on Preparing Motions

The best way to tell the judge about the facts and legal reasons why your motions should be granted is to put it all in writing in a standard legal format, properly "serve" it on the prosecutor, and file it with the court clerk. The standard legal format for this requires all of the following:

- a "Notice of Motion" to tell the prosecutor's office that you're going to have your motion heard at the date, time, and place of arraignment

- a "Declaration" listing certain facts entitling you to the granting of the motion (for example, you asked the citing officer to send the ticket to the "county seat," but he refused)

- "Points and Authorities," a fancy name applied to a short legal essay, citing laws or court cases as to why, in light of the facts presented in the Declaration, the judge should grant the motion, and

- a "Proof of Service," on which a person other than you states she mailed a copy of all the above to the prosecutor's office.

All this looks nice if typed double-spaced on line-numbered legal paper, as are the samples that follow. You can usually get line-numbered legal paper at any good quality office supply store or it is available as an option on many word-processing programs. But it's okay to type neatly on ordinary typing paper. After you sign the papers, make two sets of photocopies, one set for yourself and one for the prosecutor's office. Then have someone else put the copies in a stamped envelope addressed to the Office of the District Attorney nearest to the court

where your motion will be heard (or in some cases the office of the city attorney of the city in which you were ticketed—call the court clerk to find out which), and mail the envelope. This process is called "serving" the papers. You are not allowed to do this for yourself.

The person "serving" your papers must be over 18 and either work or reside in the county in which she mails the letter. When the papers have been mailed, this person must also fill out a Proof of Service, stating under penalty of perjury that she mailed the copies, is over 18, and lives or works in the county where they were mailed. A blank Proof of Service form is in the back of this book.

Once all this is done, you should file the original motion papers and Proof of Service with the traffic court clerk. Do this at least two weeks before the arraignment date. You may get a few strange looks from clerks who aren't used to people filing motion papers in traffic cases. If so, be firm and insist the paper be accepted.

Common Sense Note: Most judges are very comfortable dealing with attorneys and very uncomfortable when facing a nonlawyer who makes legal arguments. In the following pages we offer guidelines, suggestions, and sample legal documentation, for the purpose of allowing you to advance your legal rights without the need for a lawyer. The judge may react to your presentation in any number of ways, from hostile questioning about fine points of law, to bored indifference, to complete interest. Obviously we can't predict how your judge will react. The point is, don't worry if things go awry when you appear before the court on your own behalf. The fault is not necessarily in you or in this book. Just keep plugging ahead the best you can.

Now, let's see how to prepare the papers that are necessary for each kind of motion.

Checklist for Filing a Motion

(Follow *all* steps.)

☐ 1. Type up a Notice of Motion from the sample we provide, substituting your name, the court's name (Superior or Municipal Court), county, judicial district and courtroom number, your case number, and motion date assigned by the arraignment judge or obtained from the clerk.

☐ 2. Tailor the Declaration and the Points and Authorities to fit the facts of your case, making sure everything you say in them is true.

☐ 3. Don't forget to sign and date them.

☐ 4. Type a Proof of Service with the prosecuting agency's address listed, but don't fill it out or sign it.

☐ 5. Make *two* sets of photocopies of the above documents.

☐ 6. Have an adult friend mail one set of photocopies to the office of the prosecuting agency (district attorney or city attorney), mailing it in the county where she lives or works. Then she should fill out and sign the original of the Proof of Service.

☐ 7. Go to the court clerk and file the original of your set of papers (the set with the Proof of Service filled out by your friend). Ask the clerk to "file-stamp" your remaining set of photocopies, so you'll have proof that you filed the originals.

☐ 8. When you go to arraignment, remind the judge of your motion and ask for a dismissal (or transfer, depending on the motion), or—if the judge doesn't want to hear the case then and there—for a postponement of the motion hearing to another date.

☐ 9. Be prepared to answer any questions the judge may have about what you said in your papers.

Various Types of Motions

The following motions are the most common types made after pleading not guilty at arraignment. Each one may or may not apply to your particular situation.

Motion to Preclude Testimony (or Exclude Evidence) on Account of Prosecution's Failure to Provide "Discovery"

As we discussed earlier in this chapter, you have a right to request a copy of the officer's notes. You also have the right to obtain a copy of any engineering and traffic survey that will be produced at trial in a radar case (PC § 1054.1(f)). If the prosecution and police agency refuse to respond with the requested information within 15 days of a personally delivered request (20 days for a mailed request), you should request, at arraignment, a pretrial hearing date for your discovery motion. In this motion, you should ask the court to preclude the officer from testifying and from using any engineering and traffic survey because he or she failed to respond to your Informal Discovery Request or, at the very least, you should ask the court to order the prosecution to turn the material over to you before trial.

Preparing the Papers

The papers for your discovery motion should look something like what follows.

Note: This motion contains legal arguments and headings for a motion where the prosecution has failed to supply both the officer's notes and the engineering and traffic survey. If your motion is only in reference to the officer's notes (that is, yours is not a radar speed case or the prosecution supplied the survey but not the notes), then you must omit all of the text that appears between the brackets that look like this: { }. If, however, your motion is also concerned with the survey, you should simply omit the brackets and include the text that appears in between them.

Note: After this, include copies marked "Exhibit A" at the bottom of both the Informal Discovery Request (with any attachments of written notes *you* disclosed) and the Proof of Service.

What to Say in Court

At the hearing on your motion, say to the judge:

> *"Your Honor, both the prosecuting and police agencies, to whom I sent a written discovery request under Penal Code Section 1054, have refused to respond within 20 days as required by Penal Code Sections 1054 through 1054.7. Because this is a minor traffic case, I am requesting dismissal, or preclusion of the officer's testimony (and exclusion of any engineering and traffic survey), as a sanction. In the alternative, I am requesting $250 in fees imposed against the district attorney and an order that the material I requested be produced. The legal basis for this request is stated in my Declaration and Points and Authorities, which Your Honor has on file."*

At this point, the judge may do a number of things. If you're really lucky, he may dismiss the case! (A few of our readers have reported this result.) In that event, you've won! If you're just plain lucky, the judge may "preclude" the prosecution from using the evidence they didn't disclose—the officer's testimony (if the officer's notes weren't produced) or a radar-speed-case engineering and traffic survey. (If that happens, you should win later at trial, in the absence of the essential officer's testimony or survey in a radar speed case.) More than likely, though, the judge may simply order the prosecution to produce the missing notes and/or survey.

If you're unlucky (or the judge is just plain lazy), the judge may try to put off a decision until the day of trial. If that happens, remind the judge that the purpose of discovery is to allow you to see the evidence well before trial so that you have time to prepare, and that PC § 1054.7 requires disclosure at least 30 days before trial. The case of *Sandeffer v. Superior Court* (1993) 18 Cal.App.4th 672, 22 Cal. Rptr.2d 261, says that disclosure should occur well before trial and that late disclosure defeats the whole purpose. To this, the judge might offer to postpone the trial, in which case you should note that you should not be required to choose between your right to "discovery" (the legal word for the disclosure process) and a speedy trial.

If the judge does grant any of your requests (short of dismissal), you should get him or her to sign a written order to that effect. If the judge does not wish to do so, simply say, *"Your Honor, there is no way for your order to have any legal effect unless it is signed and properly served on the opposing party, and that is why I have prepared a proposed order, which I have right here."* At this point, the judge should sign the appropriate order.

Note: For each order, there is an "order granting the motion" and the order itself. The judge should sign both.

If the judge indicates his willingness to sign the order, you should ask to approach the clerk so that you can give him/her your copies of the appropriate orders.

What follows are some sample written orders of the form that a judge might agree to sign for Dan Defendant after granting his motion.

Be sure to follow all the steps outlined in the Motion Checklist appearing above.

Once the judge signs your order(s), make sure you receive a file-stamped copy of that order or orders with the judge's signature or stamp

DAN DEFENDANT
626 Grey Bar Ln.
El Sobrante, CA 94803
Tel: (510) 555-1212
Defendant in Pro Per

SUPERIOR COURT OF CALIFORNIA, COUNTY OF CONTRA COSTA

MOUNT DIABLO BRANCH

THE PEOPLE OF THE STATE OF CALIFORNIA,

Plaintiff,

vs.

DAN DEFENDANT,

Defendant.

No. 1234567

NOTICE OF MOTION FOR PRECLUSION OF TESTIMONY {; FOR EXCLUSION OF EVIDENCE} OR IN THE ALTERNATIVE FOR DISCLOSURE AND MONETARY SANCTIONS; DECLARATION; POINTS AND AUTHORITIES

[P.C. Sections 1054 et. seq.]

TO: PLAINTIFF, THE PEOPLE OF THE STATE OF CALIFORNIA, AND TO THE DISTRICT ATTORNEY FOR THE WITHIN-NAMED COUNTY:

PLEASE TAKE NOTICE that on February 15, 20xx, at 9:00 A.M. in the above-entitled court at 2970 Willow Pass Road, Concord, California, County of Contra Costa, Defendant will move the court for an order precluding the testimony of the citing police-officer witness {, and for excluding introduction of any engineering and traffic survey,} for the trial of the above-entitled case, or in the alternative, for an order for disclosure of discovery and other sanctions.

This motion is made on the ground that the People, upon having been served with an informal Discovery Request under Penal Code Sections 1054 et. seq., have failed and refused to respond to the same for at least 20 days.

This motion is based on the pleadings, records, and files in this action, the accompanying Declaration and Points and Authorities, and on oral and documentary evidence to be presented at the hearing on the motion.

DATED: January 20, 20xx

Dan Defendant

DAN DEFENDANT,
Defendant in Pro Per

POINTS AND AUTHORITIES

INTRODUCTION

In this infraction case, the People have failed to comply with a "Proposition 115" discovery request under Penal Code Section 1054.5. The following argument will show that the provisions of Penal Code Sections 1054 through 1054.7 do indeed apply to traffic-infraction cases, and that the Court should impose the sanction of preclusion of the police officer's testimony { and exclusion of any and all traffic and engineering surveys within the meaning of Vehicle Code Section 40802(b), } or, in the alternative, should order disclosure of the evidence requested by defendant in his Informal Discovery Request and require the district attorney or the citing police agency to pay monetary sanctions to defendant.

ARGUMENT

1. **THE PROVISIONS OF PENAL CODE SECTIONS 1054 THROUGH 1054.7 DO APPLY TO INFRACTION PROCEEDINGS.**

Penal Code Sections 1054 through 1054.7 (as added by Proposition 115, effective June 6, 1990) provide for discovery "in criminal cases" (P.C. Section 1054(e)). This has been held to include misdemeanor prosecutions (*Hobbs v. Municipal Court* (1991) 233 Cal.App.3d 670, 284 Cal.Rptr. 670.) It also includes infraction prosecutions by virtue of Penal Code Section 19.7, which states in pertinent part, "Except as otherwise provided by law, all provisions of law relating to misdemeanors shall apply to infractions...." Such exceptions do exist with respect to the right of trial by jury and the appointment of counsel (P.C. Section 19.6). However, no such provision exempts discovery laws from application to infraction proceedings. Penal Code Section 19.7 incorporates into infraction procedure all statutory law (and even constitutional law not *per se* applicable to infractions), absent an express statutory declaration to the contrary (*People v. Matthews*, 139 Cal.App.3d 537, 188 Cal.Rptr 796 (1983)). Thus, the provisions of Penal Code Sections 1054 through 1054.7 apply to infraction procedures.

Under Penal Code Section 1054.5, parties to criminal actions—including infractions—may engage in informal discovery. Pursuant to an "informal discovery request," the defendant may request the People to disclose, among other things, "Relevant written or recorded statements of witnesses or reports of the statements of witnesses whom the prosecutor intends to call at trial" (P.C. Section 1054.1(f)). This obviously includes, in traffic-infraction matters, any written statements the officer(s) has made about the alleged violation, on his or her copy of the Notice to Appear, or elsewhere, at least if the officer will testify at trial. { This also includes any engineering and traffic survey that will be used as evidence against the defendant in a radar case. Clearly such a survey is a "result of [a] physical ... examination, scientific tests, experiments, or comparisons that the prosecutor intends to offer in evidence at trial," and, hence, explicitly falls within the purview of Penal Code Section 1054.1(f). }

It is a universal police practice for officers who issue Notices to Appear for moving violations to write brief notes about the circumstances surrounding the alleged violation, including any admissions of the defendant, on the reverse side of the officer's copy of the Notice to Appear. Most if not all officers refer to such notes when testifying in court about the alleged violation. These notes are the equivalent of a police report, but are not normally supplied to the defendant. Fortunately, Proposition 115 has codified discovery procedures, which clearly apply to infractions. Just as it is essential in a misdemeanor case for an attorney preparing for trial to review the officer's police report, it is essential in traffic-infraction cases for the defendant to review the notes made by the officer. More importantly, such notes fall directly within the purview of P.C. Section 1054.1(f).

A. *A defendant in a traffic-infraction case involving radar is entitled to discovery of a copy of any engineering and traffic survey that will be introduced against him at trial.*

This case involves the use of radar and, hence, in order for the prosecution to establish a prima facie case against the defendant, V.C. Section 40803(b) requires the prosecution to introduce a valid engineering and traffic survey into evidence at the trial to show that no evidence was obtained in violation of the speed-trap prohibition contained in V.C. Section 40802.

Such a survey is explicitly discoverable under Penal Code Section 1054.1, which reads, in pertinent part:

The prosecuting attorney shall disclose to defendant all of the following materials ... (f) ... any reports or statements of experts made in conjunction with a case, including the results of ... scientific tests, experiments, or comparisons which the prosecutor intends to offer in evidence at the trial.

An engineering and traffic survey is, most certainly, a "report," "statement," based on "scientific tests, experiments, or comparisons..." that the prosecutor intends to introduce at trial. As such, the prosecution is obligated by law to provide the defendant with a copy of such a survey upon a proper request made under Section 1054.5(b). Defendant herein made such a request, which is a prerequisite to seeking court enforcement of the discovery provisions of P.C. Sections 1054 *et. seq.*

The defendant must also disclose information when he or she attempts to obtain discovery from the People. See P.C. Sections 1054.3 and 1054.5(b). Where the defense discloses Section 1054.3 discovery in an informal discovery request to the People for Section 1054.1 discovery, the People must disclose within 15 days the information sought by the defense in that request (P.C. Sections 1054.5(b) and 1054.7). Where the People ignore such a request, the defense may move for sanctions "upon a showing that a party has not complied with the informal discovery procedure...," and "a court may make any order necessary

to enforce the provisions of this chapter, including, but not limited to immediate disclosure, contempt proceedings, delaying or prohibiting the testimony of a witness or the presentation of real evidence, continue the matter, or any other lawful order." No motion to compel is required as a prerequisite to such sanctions (*People v. Jackson* (1993) 15 Cal.App.4th 1197, 19 Cal.Rptr.2d 80).

II. **IN TRAFFIC INFRACTION CASES, WHERE THE PEOPLE HAVE FAILED TO COMPLY WITH THE INFORMAL DISCOVERY PROCEDURES IN PENAL CODE SECTIONS 1054.1 AND 1054.7, THE PEOPLE SHOULD BE SANCTIONED WITH PRECLUSION OF THE TESTIMONY OF ANY POLICE-OFFICER WITNESSES {AND WITH PRECLUSION OF ADMISSION OF ANY ENGINEERING AND TRAFFIC SURVEY.}**

Here, the defendant made the appropriate disclosures under Section 1054.3, and requested disclosure from the People under Section 1054.1, but the People ignored the request. Defendant sent the request to both the district attorney and the police agency involved, the latter being notified directly in light of the fact that the prosecutors often do not participate in traffic-infraction prosecutions. A copy of the request is attached to the within declaration as exhibit "A." The appropriate sanction in this type of case is preclusion of the citing officer's testimony { and exclusion of any engineering and traffic survey. } A court may properly exclude the testimony of a witness whose paperwork has been unreasonably withheld (*Sandeffer v. Superior Court* (1993) 18 Cal.App.4th 672, 22 Cal.Rptr.2d 261).

This, after all, is a traffic-infraction matter. Even if the court were to order disclosure just before trial, the defendant would, most likely, require more time to prepare for trial after having read the officer's version on the reverse of his or her Notice to Appear. {Additionally, due to the complexities of the requirements for a valid engineering and traffic survey, it would be patently unfair to defendant to allow disclosure of the survey just before trial, without giving defendant time to properly examine the survey for compliance with Vehicle Code Section 627 and other legal requirements.} Thus, continuing this matter and requiring the defendant to come to court for an extra appearance would be unfair, especially in light of the fact that the People would be responsible for the delay by virtue of their failure to disclose.

Since the People have failed to comply with the statutory provisions of Proposition 115, sanctions are absolutely necessary to penalize the People's initial transgression and, more importantly, to deter future abuse of the discovery process. Pro-Per, traffic-infraction defendants should not have to bring a written motion such as this to secure their compliance.

The People may argue that sanctions are not necessary or required where the defendant eventually receives the information requested sometime before trial. Their reasoning would be that the defendant is not prejudiced and/or that there is "no harm done" by the People's initial refusal to perform their duties under Proposition 115. There are many flaws in this argument and there is a substantial amount of authority in opposition to these contentions.

The clear and unequivocal policy of our State's Legislature and Judiciary is that traffic-infraction proceedings must be simple, speedy, and inexpensive to conduct (*People v. Carlucci* (1979) 23 Cal.3d 249, 152 Cal.Rptr. 439; *In Re Dennis B.* (1976) 18 Cal.3d 687, 135 Cal.Rptr. 82). In *In Re Dennis*, Justice Mosk wrote:

> The chief reason for classifying some prohibited acts as infractions is to facilitate their swift disposition. (cite omitted) ... This type of flexibility benefits all parties: defendants gain a swift and inexpensive disposition of their cases without the risk of major penalties; and the prosecution, the court system, and ultimately the public benefit because judicial and law enforcement resources are freed to concentrate on serious criminal behavior (*Id.* at 695).

The *justification* for this policy is further explained in *People v. Carlucci* (1979) 23 Cal.3d 249, where the court stated,

> Inasmuch as these cases ordinarily entail the imposition of small fines, it is neither economically feasible nor warranted by the relatively limited monetary exposure of the defendant for counsel to be employed or *multiple appearances* to be made for arraignment and trial. As noted in *People v. Battle* (1975) 50 Cal.App.3d Supp. 1, 7, 123 Cal. Rptr. 636, 640... "In the overwhelming majority of infraction cases the primary interest of the accused will be served by expedition in disposal...." (cite omitted) (Emphasis added) (*Id.* at 258).

The above-cited policy is obstructed, the defendant is prejudiced, and the integrity of the court is threatened when prosecuting agencies do not respond to a legitimate discovery request. Defendants must move the court to issue an order for disclosure of the essential information in order to obtain lawful and adequate discovery. As a result, a procedure that is required to be swift, inexpensive, and uncomplicated becomes complex and plagued by delays.

The defendant is prejudiced because he or she is forced to expend time and money on multiple pretrial court appearances, rather than on preparing a defense to the charges. The trial court itself is harmed by the prosecution's nonconformance with Proposition 115 because it is required to expend precious judicial resources on enforcing Proposition 115's intended, self-executing provisions. In fact, two of the law's stated purposes for this discovery procedure are to reduce the expenditure of judicial resources on pretrial discovery issues in criminal cases:

> This chapter shall be interpreted to give effect to all of the following purposes: ... (b) To save court time by requiring that discovery be conducted informally between and among the parties before judicial enforcement is requested. (c) To save court time in trial and avoid the necessity for frequent interruptions and postponements .... (Penal Code Section 1054).

Whenever these provisions are not enforced by the imposition of sanctions, the law's explicit purpose is subverted and judicial resources are wasted by the errant party. This is because the statutory scheme of

Proposition 115 obviates the need for judicial intervention into the discovery process unless there is a bona fide question of law regarding the material requested by a party. (See *People v. Jackson* (1993) 15 Cal. App.4th 1197, 19 Cal.Rptr.2d 80.) No such question exists in this action.

If this Court allows prosecuting agencies to engage in such unlawful conduct, the likely result will be *routine* noncompliance with informal discovery requests. This is because a message will be sent to the People that such noncompliance will be ignored and even tolerated. Such a result, even on a small scale, will not only subvert the well-established and strongly promoted judicial and legislative policies underlying the current traffic-infraction and criminal discovery procedures, but will also erode the confidence our citizens have in the fairness and impartiality of the entire criminal justice system.

In *Carlucci, supra*, the California Supreme Court emphasized the long-standing principle that courts are *required* to "...avoid, as much as possible, the appearance of impropriety" (*People v. Carlucci*, 23 Cal.3d 249, 259). A court's adherence to the above-stated principle of avoiding the appearance and fact of impropriety is even more essential in traffic court than in any other forum. In *People v. Kriss* (1979) 96 Cal.App.3d 913, 921; 158 Cal.Rptr. 420, the Court of Appeals stated:

> So long as traffic violations are adjudicated in court, the letter and spirit of misdemeanor procedure should be followed. ... This is often the *only* contact citizens have with the court system. It is *important* that the proceedings appear to be fair and just. An appearance of arbitrariness is to be avoided, even in the crowded conditions of traffic court.

In *People v. Goulet* (1992) 13 Cal.App.4th Supp. 1, the court recently reiterated this point, stating:

> Traffic rules account for most of the contact by average citizens with law enforcement and the courts. Enforcement of laws which are widely perceived as unreasonable and unfair generates contempt toward those who make and enforce those laws.

Nothing could appear to be more improper, be more opposed to the spirit of the law, or generate serious contempt for law enforcement agencies than a court's practice of strictly enforcing the technical provisions of the Vehicle Code against traffic-infraction defendants, while, at the same time, refusing to enforce discovery provisions against prosecuting agencies.

The sanction of preclusion of police officer's testimony, in serious cases involving malum in se crimes, should be reserved for those situations where the abuse of the discovery process is particularly egregious. In traffic-infraction cases, however, where the charges involve only malum prohibitum offenses, the sanction of preclusion of the officer's testimony [and exclusion of an engineering and traffic survey in a radar case] is the most appropriate under existing law. Preclusion [and/or exclusion], in most instances, will undoubtedly result in the failure of the prosecution to be able to establish a prima facie case against the defendant. This is tantamount to ordering dismissal. Such a ruling, however, would not be a departure from long-established procedures for handling prosecutorial/trial court errors in traffic infraction matters.

In support of this position is a large body of case law ruling that error on the part of the People or the trial court, at the trial level or on appeal, *necessitates* dismissal of traffic-infraction cases. *People v. Kriss* (1979) 96 Cal.App.3d 913 (sentencing error mandates dismissal on remand following reversal); *People v. Ruhl* (1967) 63 Cal.App.3d Supp. 6; *People v. Bighinatti* (1975) 22 Cal.App.3d Supp. 5; *People v. Jenkins* (1976) 55 Cal.App.3d Supp. 55 (appeal delay caused by People or trial court mandates reversal and dismissal on remand); *People v. Hernandez* (1985) 166 Cal.App.3d Supp. 1 (explaining *Bighinatti, supra,* and *Ruhl, supra,* as meaning that dismissal following reversal for error or delay on the part of the trial court should be granted in *minor* traffic infractions); *People v. DiFiore* (1987) 197 Cal.App.3d Supp. 26 (citing *Bighinatti, supra,* for the proposition that dismissal is appropriate remedy for trial court's error); *People v. Marcroft* (1992) 6 Cal.App.4th Supp. 1 (reversal and dismissal is appropriate remedy for trial court's error in minor traffic infractions).

In a case involving prosecuting agencies who failed to comply with Proposition 115, a court of appeal has ruled that dismissal, *in and of itself,* is an appropriate sanction where the government's refusal to provide lawful discovery results in a denial of due process to the defendant (*People v. Brophy* (1992) 5 Cal. App.4th 932, 937-938, 7 Cal.Rptr.2d 367). { The failure to produce the most essential and controversial piece of evidence in the exclusive control of the prosecution, such as an engineering and traffic survey, constitutes an even more egregious due process violation than that of refusing to produce relevant written statements of the citing officer. Such is the case herein. }

Justice must be administered equally. This means that prosecuting agencies must be held accountable for their violations of the law just as strictly as accused citizens are made to answer for their alleged violations—if not more so—because of their *sworn duty* to enforce and uphold the law.

CONCLUSION

It is for these reasons and based on the foregoing authorities that defendant humbly requests this Court to order that the citing police officer be precluded from testifying { and/or the engineering and traffic survey be excluded } such that the matter must be dismissed for lack of prosecution. In the alternative, defendant humbly requests this Court to order disclosure of such evidence and payment by the People, to defendant, of monetary sanctions in the sum of $250 to compensate defendant for the time and effort spent in researching, drafting, and arguing this motion to compel discovery.

DATED: January 20, 20xx

Respectfully submitted,

Dan Defendant
_____
DAN DEFENDANT,
Defendant in Pro Per

DECLARATION

I, DAN DEFENDANT, declare:

1. I am the defendant in the above-entitled action.

2. On October 15, 20xx, I received the Notice to Appear herein.

3. On November 5, 20xx, I caused both the district attorney and the citing police agency to be served with copies of an informal discovery request, a copy of which is attached hereto, with a copy of the Proof of Service, as "Exhibit A."

4. More than 20 days have elapsed since I caused said request to be mailed, and I have received no response to the same from anyone.

I declare under penalty of perjury under the laws of the State of California that the foregoing is true and correct.

DATED: January 20, 20xx

Dan Defendant

DAN DEFENDANT,
Defendant in Pro Per

---

on it. If the judge ordered that the prosecution produce the notes of survey by a particular date, it can only be enforced if you have a copy of it "served" on the prosecution.

Serving the Orders

A copy of an order that requires the prosecution to disclose evidence should be "personally served" on the prosecution or police agency. But you do not actually have to personally deliver the order to the officer and the district attorney himself. You should have your friend leave a copy of the order with the receptionists at the police station and at the prosecutor's office. When you have your friend deliver the documents, he or she should obtain the name of the person who accepted the papers and then fill out and sign a "Proof of Service," which

should look something like the sample that follows the orders.

What to Do If the Order Is Ignored

If the order is ignored, the police and/or the prosecutor could actually be in trouble. In theory, they could be held in contempt of court, but that isn't likely: Your request that they be held in contempt may force the judge toward a "middle ground" of *now* ordering the case dismissed. You can make this request any time after the expiration of the time period for the police and prosecutor to respond. Be sure to bring blank copies of the order for monetary sanctions—you may get lucky and have a judge that takes personal offense at having his orders ignored.

DAN DEFENDANT
626 Grey Bar Ln.
El Sobrante, CA 94803
Tel: (510) 555-1212

Defendant in Pro Per

SUPERIOR COURT OF CALIFORNIA, COUNTY OF CONTRA COSTA
MOUNT DIABLO BRANCH

THE PEOPLE OF THE STATE
OF CALIFORNIA,

    Plaintiff,

vs.

DAN DEFENDANT,

    Defendant.

No. **1234567**

ORDER FOR PAYMENT OF MONETARY SANCTIONS

[P.C. Sections 1054 *et. seq.*]

TO: People of the State of California; District Attorney for the County of Contra Costa; and, the officer with badge #123 of the Concord Police Department.

    GOOD CAUSE APPEARING and it having been established that you have failed to comply with defendant's lawful and proper informal discovery request, YOU ARE HEREBY ORDERED to pay defendant DAN DEFENDANT monetary sanctions in the sum of $250, no later than March 1, 20xx.

DATED: _____

_____
COMMISSIONER OF THE SUPERIOR COURT

DAN DEFENDANT
626 Grey Bar Ln.
El Sobrante, CA 94803
Tel: (510) 555-1212

Defendant in Pro Per

SUPERIOR COURT OF CALIFORNIA, COUNTY OF CONTRA COSTA
MOUNT DIABLO BRANCH

THE PEOPLE OF THE STATE
OF CALIFORNIA,

    Plaintiff,

vs.

DAN DEFENDANT,

    Defendant.

No. **1234567**

ORDER GRANTING DEFENDANT'S MOTION TO COMPEL DISCOVERY

[P.C. Sections 1054 *et. seq.*]

    Defendant's motion to compel discovery came on for hearing in Department 3 of the above-entitled court on February 15, 20xx, defendant appearing in propria persona and the People (appearing/not appearing). The matter having been submitted,

    IT IS HEREBY ORDERED that defendant's motion to compel discovery of the citing officer's notes { and any engineering and traffic survey } is granted.

DATED: _____

_____
COMMISSIONER OF THE SUPERIOR COURT

DAN DEFENDANT
626 Grey Bar Ln.
El Sobrante, CA 94803
Tel: (510) 555-1212

Defendant in Pro Per

SUPERIOR COURT OF CALIFORNIA, COUNTY OF CONTRA COSTA
MOUNT DIABLO BRANCH

THE PEOPLE OF THE STATE
OF CALIFORNIA,

Plaintiff,

vs.

DAN DEFENDANT,

Defendant.

No. 1234567

**ORDER GRANTING DEFENDANT'S
MOTION FOR MONETARY SANCTIONS**

[P.C. Sections 1054 *et. seq.*]

Defendant's motion for monetary sanctions came on for hearing in Department 3 of the above-entitled court on February 15, 20xx, defendant appearing in propria persona and the People not appearing. The matter having been submitted,

IT IS HEREBY ORDERED that plaintiff's motion for sanctions in the sum of $250 be, and, the same is, granted. The sum shall be payable to defendant by the District Attorney within 30 days.

DATED: _____

_____
COMMISSIONER OF THE SUPERIOR COURT

DAN DEFENDANT
626 Grey Bar Ln.
El Sobrante, CA 94803
Tel: (510) 555-1212

Defendant in Pro Per

SUPERIOR COURT OF CALIFORNIA, COUNTY OF CONTRA COSTA
MOUNT DIABLO BRANCH

THE PEOPLE OF THE STATE
OF CALIFORNIA,

Plaintiff,

vs.

DAN DEFENDANT,

Defendant.

No. 1234567

**ORDER GRANTING DEFENDANT'S
MOTION FOR PRECLUSION OF
TESTIMONY [AND PRECLUSION
OF ADMITTANCE OF ANY ENGINEERING
AND TRAFFIC SURVEY }**

[P.C. Sections 1054 *et. seq.*]

Defendant's motion for preclusion of testimony [and preclusion of admittance of any engineering and traffic survey } came on for hearing in Department 3 of the above-entitled Court on January 15, 20xx, defendant appearing in propria persona and the People not appearing. The matter having been submitted,

IT IS HEREBY ORDERED that plaintiff's motion for preclusion of testimony of all police-officer witnesses, and for exclusion of any engineering and traffic survey, is granted, and this action is dismissed based upon lack of prosecution.

DATED: _____

_____
COMMISSIONER OF THE SUPERIOR COURT

DAN DEFENDANT
626 Grey Bar Ln.
El Sobrante, CA 94803
Tel: (510) 555-1212

Defendant in Pro Per

SUPERIOR COURT OF CALIFORNIA, COUNTY OF CONTRA COSTA, MOUNT DIABLO BRANCH

THE PEOPLE OF THE STATE OF CALIFORNIA,

    Plaintiff,

vs.

DAN DEFENDANT,

    Defendant.

No. 1234567

ORDER COMPELLING DISCOVERY OF THE CITING OFFICER'S NOTES {AND OF ANY ENGINEERING AND TRAFFIC SURVEY}

[P.C. Sections 1054 *et. seq.*]

TO: People of the State of California; District Attorney for the County of Contra Costa; and, the officer with the badge # of: 123 of the Concord Police Department:

GOOD CAUSE APPEARING and it having been established that you have failed to comply with defendant's lawful and proper informal discovery request,

YOU ARE HEREBY ORDERED to deliver to defendant by United States Mail, within 30 days of service of this order, the following:

1) A photostatic copy of the reverse side of the citing officer's copy of the Notice to Appear #A-12345, issued on October 10, 20xx; { and,

2) A photostatic copy of any engineering and traffic survey, within the meaning of Vehicle Code Section 627(a), which will be used against defendant herein at trial. }

DATED: _____

_____
COMMISSIONER OF THE SUPERIOR COURT

RE: PEOPLE V. DAN DEFENDANT
CASE NO.: 1234567

Proof of Service

I, SARAH SERVER, declare:

1. I am over the age of eighteen and not a party to the within action.

2. On July 18, 20xx, I served the within Order Compelling Discovery by leaving true copies thereof with persons apparently in charge of the following offices:

Office of the District Attorney
County of Contra Costa
456 Prosecutor Place
Concord, California

Concord Police Department
Willow Pass Road and Parkside Drive
Concord, California
ATT: _____

I declare under penalty of perjury under the laws of the State of California that the foregoing is true and correct.

DATED: July 18, 20xx

Sara Server
_____
Sarah Server

You can either schedule a hearing renewing your discovery motion, or you may simply wait until the date set for trial (unless the judge scheduled another hearing when he or she signed the order).

When you show up at that hearing, be sure to bring the proofs of service for the orders and copies of the signed orders that your friend served. Also, as mentioned above, you may want to bring blank copies of the order for monetary sanctions in case the judge is willing to make an example out of the officer or prosecutor.

What to Say in Court

"Your Honor, the citing police officer and the district attorney's office were personally served with your order to provide discovery. Both agencies have ignored the court's order. I hereby request that you either hold them in contempt of this court, or dismiss this action and order the police agency and district attorney to pay monetary sanctions in the amount of $250 for the expense, time, and effort required by me to file, serve, and argue this motion, as well as to personally serve your order on them."

Here, again, if the judge orders anything in addition to dismissal, such as monetary sanctions, you must get the judge to sign the appropriate order. Once signed, you will then need to have it personally served on the citing officer and on the district attorney.

Motion for a Transfer to the County Seat

As discussed in Chapter 17, one of the best strategies in fighting a traffic ticket involves getting your case transferred to a different court—the one at the county seat.

Vehicle Code Section 40502(b) requires a citing police officer to list on the ticket as the "place to appear" the court at the county seat, if requested by the person getting the ticket. Unfortunately, many local police officers are unaware of this requirement and will refuse to specify the county seat court on the ticket. This means you'll have to go to arraignment at the court the officer specified, and request a "change of venue" to the county seat.

You must request the transfer at arraignment, otherwise you'll lose the right. (PC § 1462.2.) Also, if you failed to make such a request at the time the officer gave you your ticket, you can't request it for the first time at arraignment.

Los Angeles Area Note: In Los Angeles County, the entire City of Los Angeles is the county seat. Any of its branch courts qualifies as a "county seat" court. If you receive a citation in the Los Angeles area "cities" of Chatsworth, San Fernando, San Pedro, Van Nuys, or East Los Angeles (which are not separate cities at all, but are parts of the City of Los Angeles), and are cited to appear at the local court there, instead of the downtown "Metropolitan" Los Angeles court on Hill Street, you're already being cited to appear at a county seat court. For this reason, you won't be able to get your case transferred to the downtown "Metropolitan" Branch, which is simply one of several county seat courts.

Preparing the Papers

The papers for your motion to change venue to the county seat should look something like the sample below. The papers are prepared, served, and filed in accordance with the instructions above. Don't forget to prepare a Proof of Service to be signed by the person who mails the papers to the prosecutor's office.

Michael Mover
950 California Street
Mountain View, CA 94010
Tel: (650) 555-5678

Defendant in Pro Per

SUPERIOR COURT OF CALIFORNIA, COUNTY OF SANTA CLARA
PALO ALTO BRANCH

THE PEOPLE OF THE STATE
OF CALIFORNIA,

    Plaintiff,

vs.

MICHAEL MOVER,

    Defendant

Case No. A1234567B

NOTICE OF MOTION FOR CHANGE OF VENUE TO COUNTY SEAT; DECLARATION; POINTS AND AUTHORITIES

TO: PLAINTIFF, THE PEOPLE OF THE STATE OF CALIFORNIA, AND TO THE DISTRICT ATTORNEY FOR THE WITHIN-NAMED COUNTY:

PLEASE TAKE NOTICE that on the date set for arraignment herein, July 16, 20xx at 9:00 a.m. in Department 33 of the above-entitled Court at 270 Grant Avenue, Palo Alto, California, Defendant will move the Court for an order transferring the place of trial in this action to the Municipal Court at San Jose, California.

This motion is made on the ground that Defendant, upon having been arrested for the offense charged, requested that the court at which he be directed to appear be specified as the court at the county seat, and that pursuant to § 40502(b) of the Vehicle Code, the said court is therefore the proper court for trial of this action.

This motion is based on the pleadings, records, and files in this action, the accompanying Declaration and Points and Authorities, and on oral and documentary evidence to be presented at the hearing on the motion.

DATED:

                      MICHAEL MOVER
                      Defendant in Pro Per

DECLARATION

I, MICHAEL MOVER, declare:

1. I am the Defendant in the above-entitled action.

2. On May 15, 20xx, I was driving my vehicle in a westerly direction on California Street in Mountain View when I was stopped by Officer J. Friday of the Mountain View Police Department. Officer Friday got out of his vehicle and indicated his intention to cite me for a speed law violation. I immediately told Officer Friday that I desired to have the court at which I would be directed to appear be the one at the county seat, namely the court at San Jose, pursuant to Section 40502(b) of the Vehicle Code. I informed him that the court at the county seat in San Jose was closer to my principal place of business at 123 Silicon Street, Santa Clara, California, which was and is my principal business address where I am employed as an electronics technician. Officer Friday told me he would not do so because the address of the Palo Alto court was already printed on his citations. He told me to "take it up with the court clerk."

3. I then told Officer Friday that he was required to specify the court as the one in San Jose, and I offered him a photocopy of Vehicle Code Section 40502(b), but he refused to read it, replying, "I already know all I need to know in the Vehicle Code." He then indicated again that he would specify the Palo Alto court as the one at which I should appear.

4. Officer Friday then prepared a traffic citation or Notice to Appear in which the court at which I was directed to appear was, contrary to my repeated requests, the Palo Alto court. I was then handed the citation book so that I could sign the citation and promise to appear.

5. I then signed my name on the citation, promising to appear as directed, and wrote the words: "COUNTY SEAT REQUESTED AND REFUSED."

I declare under penalty of perjury under the laws of the State of California that the foregoing is true and correct.

DATED:

                      MICHAEL MOVER
                      Defendant in Pro Per

POINTS AND AUTHORITIES

ARGUMENT

I. WHEN A NOTICE TO APPEAR IS ISSUED BY A PEACE OFFICER FOR VIOLATION OF THE VEHICLE CODE, THE OFFICER MUST SPECIFY THE PLACE FOR APPEARANCE AS THE COURT AT THE COUNTY SEAT, IF SO DEMANDED BY THE PERSON CITED.

When a peace officer cites a person for violation of the Vehicle Code and issues a Notice to Appear, the place for appearance is governed by Section 40502 of that Code, which states in pertinent part:

§ 40502. [*Place to Appear*] The place specified in the Notice to Appear shall be...:

(b) Upon demand of the person arrested, *before a municipal court judge or other magistrate having jurisdiction of the offense at the county seat* of the county in which the offense is alleged to have been committed... [Emphasis added]

Subdivisions (a) and (c) of Section 40502 respectively name the "nearest or most accessible" magistrate or a "person authorized to receive a deposit of bail" as other places that may be specified as the place to appear. With respect to these two choices, the decision lies within the arresting officer's discretion. Subdivision (b), however, requires the place to appear to be the county seat whenever (1) the arrested person's residence or business address is closer to the county seat than to the nearest municipal or justice court, and (2) the arrested person demands that the place to appear be the county seat. In *Smith v. Municipal Court* (1959) 167 Cal.App.2d 534, 538, the similar wording of former Section 739(c) of the Vehicle Code was construed to require that "[i]f a demand therefore is made by the arrestee, the officer must specify *as the place of appearance a municipal court within the judicial district at the county seat* or at the demand of the arrestee, before a magistrate in the judicial district..." [Emphasis added].

Whichever court is so demanded is the proper court for trial. Here, defendant requested that the court at the county seat be that place, but the citing officer refused to comply.

II. WHEN THE ARRESTING OFFICER HAS REFUSED TO COMPLY WITH A DEMAND FOR APPEARANCE AT THE COUNTY SEAT COURT, THE ACTION MUST BE TRANSFERRED THERE FROM THE NON-COUNTY-SEAT COURT WHEN SUCH TRANSFER IS REQUESTED AT ARRAIGNMENT.

Section 1462.2 of the Penal Code states that "*Except as provided by the Vehicle Code*," the proper court for the trial of a misdemeanor is in the judicial district in which the offense is alleged to have occurred. The fact that this section specifically refers to the Vehicle Code shows that the Legislature contemplated provision of Vehicle Code Section 40502 as determining trial venue for Vehicle Code offenses where a Notice to Appear is issued. Section 1462.2 states that when the action is commenced in a court other than the proper court for trial, it may nevertheless be tried there, "unless the defendant, *at the time he pleads*, requests an order transferring the action or proceeding to the proper court." It continues, "If after such

request it appears that the action or proceeding was not commenced in the proper court, the court shall order the action or proceeding transferred to the proper court." The proper time for making the motion is therefore immediately following a not-guilty plea at arraignment. In *Smith*, the court stated that the respondent court "was without discretion to deny the motion to transfer..." [167 Cal.App.2d at 541].

The court at the "county seat" is a court located *within the city limit of the city* in which the *seat of government of the county* is located (Government Code Section 23600). See also *People v. Beltran* (1981) 124 Cal.App. 3d 335. In this county, that city is San Jose.

DATED: June 25, 20xx

MICHAEL MOVER
Defendant in Pro Per

What to Say in Court

At the hearing on your motion, say to the judge:

> *"I request a change of venue to the Municipal (or Justice) Court at the county seat. I already made this request at arraignment, as required by Penal Code Section 1462.2. The legal basis for my request is stated in my Declaration and Points and Authorities, which Your Honor has on file."*

At this point, the judge should grant your request to transfer the case. If someone from the district attorney's office is there, she may argue the legal merits of your request. Nevertheless, the law is pretty clear. If the judge refuses to transfer, and insists on a trial in his court, you will have grounds for an appeal if you're eventually found guilty. (See Chapter 16.)

Be sure to follow all the steps outlined in the Motion Checklist.

Disqualifying the Trial Judge

One of the least known surprises in California law is that everybody gets one free shot at disqualifying a judge. You don't have to prove that the judge is unfair or biased, you just have to believe it. You might have heard that a particular judge is unfair or rude, sides with police officers over defendants, metes out heavy fines, or worse. If you anticipate that the judge at arraignment will assign your case to such a judge, § 170.6 of the Code of Civil Procedure allows you to file a "Peremptory Challenge." This is simply a typed statement in which you say you think that the particular judge is "prejudiced," either against you personally or against your "interest."

Although the law refers to this type of written request as a "motion," it does not require a hearing. You just file it with the court clerk prior to trial. (You can also wait and file it just before trial, if the case hasn't been specifically assigned to a particular judge or commissioner before that. See Chapter 12.)

You should only use this Peremptory Challenge when you're really certain that you do not want to appear before that particular judge or commissioner and you're not worried about getting someone even worse (since you're only allowed one challenge of this kind). Also, many judges take a dim view of defendants disqualifying one of their colleagues, and the second judge might, perhaps unconsciously, hold this against you.

A sample form is shown below, and a blank fill-in type form for this purpose is in the back of the book.

When you must file the Peremptory Challenge depends on how your case is assigned to a particular judge. If your case is assigned for trial or other hearing to a particular courtroom presided over by a judge you don't want, it's best to file your Peremptory Challenge as soon as possible afterward. If the judge tells you that your case is assigned to him "for all purposes"—or words to that effect—you must file your Peremptory Challenge within ten days of this statement. But judges and traffic commissioners often forget to tell you this, so you can simply ask the judge if the case is assigned to him "for all purposes." If he says it is, you should visit his courtroom within ten days to decide if you want to file a peremptory challenge. If you determine the judge is a "hanging judge" after that visit, you must file the peremptory challenge within ten days of the time the judge said he would hear the case "for all purposes."

If a judge does not assign the case to himself "for all purposes," you should have the right to file the peremptory challenge just before trial. (See *Bouchard v. Insona* (1980) 105 Cal.App.3d 768, 164 Cal.Rptr. 505; *Retes v. Superior Court* (1981) 122 Cal.App.3d 799, 176 Cal.Rptr.

DEBORAH DEFENDANT
123 Fell St.
San Francisco, CA 94137
(415) 555-1234

Defendant in Pro Per

SUPERIOR COURT OF CALIFORNIA, CITY AND COUNTY OF SAN FRANCISCO
SAN FRANCISCO BRANCH

THE PEOPLE OF THE STATE OF CALIFORNIA
 	
        Plaintiff,
 	
vs.
 	
DEBORAH DEFENDANT,
 	
        Defendant.
_____
	) No. A-123456-F
	)
	)
	) PEREMPTORY CHALLENGE
	) [CCP § 170.6]
	)
	)
	)
	)
	)

I, the above-named defendant, declare:

I believe the Hon. _____, the judge or commissioner before whom the above-entitled matter is assigned to or pending before, is prejudiced against my interest, so that I cannot have a fair trial before such judge or commissioner.

WHEREFORE Defendant requests, ex parte, per CCP Section 170.6, that the said judge or commissioner be disqualified from hearing the above-entitled matter.

I declare under penalty of perjury under the laws of the State of California that the foregoing is true and correct.

DATED: October 10, 20xx

Deborah Defendant
_____
Deborah Defendant

160.) Unfortunately, many traffic court judges and commissioners will ignore the rules and reject your challenge. Since this issue is hard to raise in an appeal, they feel they can get away with this. (See *People v. Hull* (1991) 1 Cal.4th 266, 2 Cal.Rptr.2d 526, and Chapter 16.)

Simply file the Challenge (filled out with the name of the judge you don't want) with the clerk. You don't have to have a copy mailed to the prosecutor beforehand, and you don't have to prepare a Notice of Motion or Proof of Service.

At this point, your case should be assigned to a different judge.

Motion to Dismiss—Long Delay Before Arraignment

If an unusually long amount of time (at least four months: see *Rost v. Municipal Court* (1960) 184 Cal. App.2d 507) is allowed to pass between the time you were ticketed and your arraignment, and you diligently tried to get a court date earlier, you can make a motion at the arraignment for a dismissal of the charge on the ground that you were unconstitutionally deprived of your right to a "speedy trial." Court clerks in some counties absolutely refuse to begin processing a case, and won't assign you an arraignment date, until you receive a courtesy notice in the mail and bring it to them. If there's a delay of several months in getting this out, an unconstitutional "prearraignment delay" will have occurred, and you will be entitled to a dismissal. Also, if you can show in your Declaration that this delay "prejudiced" (hurt) your case, your chances of getting your case dismissed will be higher.

EXAMPLE:

Your Aunt Agatha was riding with you when you were cited, in January, for doing 45 mph in a 35 mph zone. If you'd been able to go to trial in February or March, Aunt Agatha would have been able to testify to your approximate speed, that you were just keeping up with traffic, and that the weather and road conditions made your speed safe. However, various court clerk delays that were not your fault caused your trial to be scheduled for May. Unfortunately, Aunt Agatha moved to her sister's home in Missouri in April and will not be available to testify. Your inability to get the early trial date has therefore hurt your case.

Preparing the Papers

Below is a sample of what the papers for a "Motion to Dismiss" should look like in this situation.

The Declaration should list the pertinent facts relating to the delay, and should be written to truthfully reflect what happened in your case. (We suggest that you use your own words and not copy the example word for word.) Finally, you will have to make at least two sets of copies of the motion papers. A friend of yours will have to fill out and sign the original of a Proof of Service and mail one set of the copies to the district or city attorney's office. Then you'll have to go down to the courthouse and file the set of originals.

What to Say in Court

When you get to the courtroom, sit down and wait until your case is called. Then step forward. The judge will ask you to enter a plea. Respond with:

DECLARATION

I, PATIENCE FAULTLESS, declare:

1. I am the defendant in the above-entitled action.

2. On January 15, 20xx, I was stopped while driving my motor vehicle, and was cited by a police officer for a violation of § 22350 of the Vehicle Code. I was presented a copy of the Notice to Appear in this action by that officer.

3. While so driving, I was accompanied by Mrs. Agatha Aardvark, who would have been able to testify on my behalf to the speed of my vehicle and to the traffic, weather, and road conditions at the time.

4. On January 16, 20xx, I appeared at the office of the Clerk of the Municipal Court at 2120 Martin Luther King, Jr. Way, Berkeley, California, as directed, and requested a court date for arraignment. The deputy clerk to whom I spoke refused to assign me a court date, made a notation on the Notice to Appear that the matter was "Continued to February 28, 20xx." I again appeared at the office of the above-mentioned Clerk of the Municipal Court, as directed, and requested a court date for arraignment. A deputy clerk again refused to assign me a court date, made a second notation on the Notice to Appear that the matter was "Continued to April 11, 20xx," and told me to come back on that date. She informed me that I would be unable to obtain a court date until I had received a "courtesy notice" in the mail.

5. On April 2, 20xx, Mrs. Agatha Aardvark moved permanently to Joplin, Missouri, and will therefore be unable to testify at any trial of the within matter.

6. On April 9, 20xx I received a "courtesy notice" in the mail. This was fifty-three (53) days subsequent to my first appearance before a deputy clerk of the Municipal Court.

I declare under penalty of perjury under the laws of the State of California that the foregoing is true and correct.

DATED: April 10, 20xx

Patience Faultless
PATIENCE FAULTLESS

PATIENCE FAULTLESS
950 Parker St.
Berkeley, CA 94710
(415) 555-1234

Defendant in Pro Per

SUPERIOR COURT OF CALIFORNIA, COUNTY OF ALAMEDA
BERKELEY-ALBANY BRANCH

THE PEOPLE OF THE STATE OF CALIFORNIA,

    Plaintiff,

vs.

PATIENCE FAULTLESS,

    Defendant.

No. B 0025640 D

NOTICE OF MOTION TO DISMISS; DECLARATION; POINTS AND AUTHORITIES

TO: PLAINTIFF, THE PEOPLE OF THE STATE OF CALIFORNIA, AND TO THE DISTRICT ATTORNEY FOR THE WITHIN-NAMED COUNTY:

PLEASE TAKE NOTICE that on the date set for arraignment herein, May 9, 20xx, at 9:00 a.m. in Department 2 of the above-entitled Court at 2120 Martin Luther King, Jr. Way, Berkeley, California, Defendant will move the Court for dismissal of the above-entitled action.

This motion is made on the ground that Defendant has been denied a right to a speedy trial under Article I, § 15, of the California Constitution and the Sixth Amendment of the United States Constitution.

This motion is based on the pleadings, records, and files in this action, the accompanying Declaration and Points and Authorities, and on oral and documentary evidence to be presented at the hearing on the motion.

DATED: April 10, 20xx

Respectfully submitted,

Patience Faultless
PATIENCE FAULTLESS
Defendant in Pro Per

So you should use this motion—making appropriate changes in wording your Declaration and Points and Authorities—even if you can't show that a witness moved away or some other type of "prejudice" to your case.

[Note: Even though some earlier California appeals courts say you need to show your ability to defend was hurt by the delay, this is no longer the only factor (see Points and Authorities on next pages). Courts are supposed to consider four factors, including the length of and reasons for the delay, your record of insistence on a speedy trial, and finally, prejudice to your case. In the face of a long delay for no good reason, you might not have to show prejudice.]

POINTS AND AUTHORITIES

ARGUMENT

I. THE CONSTITUTIONAL RIGHT TO A SPEEDY TRIAL IS SELF-EXECUTING AND IS NOT LIMITED OR RESTRICTED BY STATUTE.

Although the various provisions of Penal Code Section 1382 constitute the Legislature's implementation of the constitutional right to speedy trial after arraignment, that implementation does not necessarily encompass all the constitutional protections. The courts have held that the constitutional provision for speedy trial is "self-executing." In *Barker v. Municipal Court* (1966) 64 Cal.2d 806, the California Supreme Court stated: "It is unnecessary that petitioners, in asserting their constitutional rights to a speedy trial, rely on specific statutory provisions."

Citing *Barker*, the court in *Zimmerman v. Superior Court* (1967) 248 Cal.App.2d 56, stated that certain Penal Code Sections (§§ 686, 802, 1050) "are merely 'supplementary to and a construction of' the Constitution [citation omitted]. So, too, are Sections 1381, 1381.5, 1382, and 1389 establishing maximum periods within which defendants must be brought to trial."

In *People v. Flores* (1968) 262 Cal.App.2d 313, the Court held that "(e)xcessive, unexcused delay is a ground for dismissal of a criminal charge, even though the particular delay is not specifically covered by a statute requiring mandatory dismissal. The defendant ... repeatedly insisted upon the prompt disposition of this cause." (In the instant case, defendant did precisely this, but was thwarted by court personnel at every turn.)

II. THE CONSTITUTIONAL RIGHT TO A SPEEDY TRIAL ATTACHES AT THE TIME AN ACCUSED IS STOPPED ON THE HIGHWAY AND CITED FOR A TRAFFIC VIOLATION.

The People will perhaps argue that, even for constitutional purposes, the right to a speedy trial runs only from the date of filing of a criminal complaint. This oft-cited rule, however, is only an example of the general principle that the time begins to run when a person becomes an accused (see *Serna v. Superior Court* (1985) 40 Cal.3d 239). When an arrest is made pursuant to a warrant, this will always be the case. But virtually all arrests' arising out of traffic violations occur before any complaint is filed. In traffic infraction cases, an arrest occurs when the officer determines there is probable cause to believe that an offense has been committed and begins the process of citing the violator to appear in court (*People v. Superior Court* (1972) 7 Cal.3d 186, 200).

In the case of *In re Mugica* (1968) 69 Cal.2d 516, the California Supreme Court stated, "The basic policy underlying the constitutional guarantee to a speedy trial is to protect the accused from having criminal charges pending against him an undue length of time." The interest in not prolonging the pendency of criminal charges requires that such time should begin to run when the defendant is

unequivocally informed that a criminal charge will be brought. This is what a Notice to Appear does. It is issued in conjunction with an arrest, and constitutes a statutory substitute for a complaint (Vehicle Code § 40513(b)). This being so, an arraignment within a reasonable time of arrest is still required, even when the accused is not in custody. Therefore, an unreasonable delay between the time of issuance of a Notice to Appear on a traffic violation and the time the accused is allowed to appear at arraignment will require dismissal upon the making of a timely motion.

III. A SHOWING OF PREJUDICE CAUSED BY THE DELAY IS NOT REQUIRED.

[*Note: Use this paragraph, or something similar, only if your case has been hurt by clerk-caused delay.*]

A three-month delay from the time defendant was cited to the time she was permitted to request arraignment for a traffic citation is not reasonable, and has prejudiced her ability to present her case; a potential witness has moved away. However, such prejudice need not always be shown. Rather, it is only one of four factors that a court must consider.

The United States Supreme Court, in *Moore v. Arizona* (1973) 414 U.S. 25, 26-27, rejected the requirement of a showing of prejudice to one's defense as a necessary element in reversing a conviction for an unconstitutional abridgment of the Sixth Amendment right to a speedy trial, stating:

The state court was in fundamental error in its reading of *Barker v. Wingo* and the standard applied in judging petitioner's speedy trial claim. *Barker v. Wingo* expressly rejected the notion that an affirmative demonstration of prejudice was necessary to prove a denial of the constitutional right to a speedy trial...

* * * * * *

Moreover, prejudice to a defendant caused by delay in bringing him to trial is not confined to the possible prejudice to his defense in those proceedings. Inordinate delays may...create anxiety in him, his family, and his friends...(quoting *Barker v. Wingo* (1972) 407 U.S. 514).

In *Barker v. Wingo, supra,* the court listed four factors to be considered in evaluating a speedy-trial motion: (1) the length of the delay; (2) the prosecution's justification for it; (3) the defendant's insistence on a speedy trial, and (4) prejudice to defendant's case, a factor not determinative if the other three militate in favor of dismissal.

In *Serna v. Superior Court* (1985) 40 Cal.3d 239, the California Supreme Court, citing *Moore*, stated, "The defendant need not establish actual prejudice as a prerequisite to a hearing at which the evidence relevant to this balancing process is heard."

Finally, it makes little difference whether the delay is the fault of court personnel or the prosecution itself. *People v. Kerwin* (1972) 23 Cal.App.3d 466, 469. Accordingly, the within action should be dismissed.

DATED: April 10, 20xx

Respectfully submitted,

Patience Faultless
PATIENCE FAULTLESS
Defendant in Pro Per

PROOF OF SERVICE

I, JOHN SMITH, declare:

1. I am over the age of eighteen and not a party to the within action.

2. My residence address is 1234 El Monte Ave., Berkeley, California, in the county within which the mailing herein mentioned occurred.

3. On April 25, 20xx, I served the within Notice of Motion to Dismiss, Declaration, and Points and Authorities on the plaintiff by placing true copies thereof in a separate sealed envelope, with the postage thereon fully prepaid, in the United States Postal Service mailbox at Berkeley, County of Alameda, California, the said envelope being addressed to:

Office of the District Attorney
County of Alameda
2120 Martin Luther King Jr. Way
Berkeley, CA

I declare under penalty of perjury under the laws of the State of California that the foregoing is true and correct.

DATED: April 26, 20xx

John Smith
JOHN SMITH

"I am making a motion to dismiss for lack of a speedy trial. The legal basis for my request is stated in the Declaration and Points and Authorities that Your Honor has on file, and copies of which have been served on the district (or city) attorney. They indicate that over three months have passed since I was able to get this arraignment date."

After that, you should mention how your case was hurt by the delay, or emphasize that the U.S. Supreme Court in *Moore v. Arizona* and the California Supreme Court in *Serna v. Superior Court* said that a showing of "prejudice" isn't necessary to prevail under a constitutional speedy trial theory. At this point, if someone from the district attorney's office is present, she will probably object. That person may say something like *"The time for speedy trial should be counted from the time of arraignment, not from when you were cited."* You should respond that the cases you cited in your Points and Authorities deal with a constitutional right to speedy trial beginning from the time of arrest, which, for traffic ticket purposes, is when you were ticketed.

If you are fortunate enough to have been assigned a conscientious, intelligent judge, you might just have to answer a few questions relating to your legal theories. If the judge hasn't read the papers, he may quickly go over them, or you may be asked to briefly summarize the legal basis of your motion. Never read directly from your Points and Authorities. It's simply too boring. To prepare yourself, spend an hour or two the night before going over your main points. Be sure you are prepared to state them to the judge succinctly. If you are afraid of forgetting a point and feel more secure with notes, write your principal points on an index card for quick reference. Relax. You are not being judged on your speaking abilities—only on the law.

If the judge grants your motion, your case will be dismissed and you win. If not, he may postpone the hearing on the motion to another date. If the judge simply denies the motion, he will set a trial date.

Motion to Dismiss—Long Delay Before Arrest for Misdemeanor

You can also claim your right to a speedy trial was violated because the police took too long to arrest you after you ignored a ticket. If you ignore a ticket or refuse to pay a fine, you can be charged with a misdemeanor and a warrant can be issued for your arrest. Fortunately, neither the police nor the prosecutor's office take the trouble to go to your home and arrest you. (It's much easier—and cheaper—to send you threatening notices and have the DMV put a "hold" on your driver's license renewal.) The charge might remain pending for several years, whether your driver's license is suspended or not.

If you haven't been arrested within a year after being charged with failure to appear, you should move for a dismissal on the ground that your right to a speedy trial has been violated. In this case, you do not have to convince the judge that your ability to defend against the charge has been compromised ("prejudiced") because of the delay. If it's been less than a year but more than four months since you were charged with failure to appear, you still might be able to have your case dismissed if you can convincingly show that your ability to defend yourself has been seriously prejudiced by the delay.

Note: When you're finally arrested on an old charge, or voluntarily go to court because the DMV either suspends or won't renew your license until you do, you should make your Motion to Dismiss at your arraignment.

Preparing the Papers

The papers you will have to prepare for this kind of speedy trial motion are very similar to the ones you just saw in the previous example. The Notice of Motion and Proof of Service forms are prepared the same way. The Declaration and Points and Authorities for this kind of motion should look something like the form below.

Finally, the Proof of Service goes on the last page. It should look like the one at the end of the previous set of speedy-trial motion papers. All these papers are prepared with copies mailed to the prosecutor and the original filed with the court clerk.

What to Say In Court

When your case is called at arraignment, you simply say:

"Your Honor, I plead not guilty and request dismissal for lack of a speedy trial under the rule of Serna v. Superior Court. My Declaration and Points and Authorities indicate that over a year has elapsed since the complaint was filed, and no attempt has been made to arrest me."

Again, either mention how the delay has hurt your case, or that the *Serna* case says you don't have to show that it did. It will then be up to the prosecution to explain why they didn't arrest you. Unless they respond with something to the effect that you changed your address and were concealing yourself, the judge should dismiss the case.

Note: If you were arrested, taken to jail, and not released on bail, you would go directly to

---

DECLARATION

I, LANE TURNER, declare:

1. I am the defendant in the above-entitled action.

2. On February 1, 20xx I became aware that a misdemeanor complaint charging me with a violation of Vehicle Code Section 40508(a) had been filed in the above-entitled court on January 2, 20xx.

3. Since June 12, 20xx and until the present date, I have regularly resided at 950 Parker Lane, El Cajon, California, the address on file with this court.

4. Since April 3, 20xx and until the present date, I have been employed at 123 Industrial Drive, El Cajon, California, and was there regularly during working hours.

5. I made no attempt to avoid any arrest.

I declare under penalty of perjury under the laws of the State of California that the foregoing is true and correct.

DATED: February 14, 20xx

Lane Turner
LANE TURNER

POINTS AND AUTHORITIES

I. THE CONSTITUTIONAL RIGHT TO A SPEEDY TRIAL IS SELF-EXECUTING AND IS NOT LIMITED OR RESTRICTED BY A STATUTE

[This section should be the same as part 1 of the previous Points and Authorities, excluding the last paragraph.]

II. THE CONSTITUTIONAL RIGHT TO A SPEEDY TRIAL ATTACHES AT THE TIME A PERSON BECOMES AN ACCUSED, AND THE POLICE HAVE AN AFFIRMATIVE DUTY TO SERVE ARREST WARRANTS IN A TIMELY FASHION, WHERE THEY CAN DO SO THROUGH ROUTINE, UNCOMPLICATED INVESTIGATION.

For constitutional purposes, the right to a speedy trial runs from the date of arrest or filing of a criminal complaint. A Notice to Appear, signed by a police officer charging a Vehicle Code violation, is the equivalent of a complaint under Vehicle Code Section 40513(b). If the prosecution thereafter makes no serious attempt to physically arrest the defendant on a warrant within a year, after the Notice is filed with the court, that delay is "presumptively prejudicial" to the defendant's right to a speedy trial, and the charges must be dismissed on motion (*Serna v. Superior Court* (1985) 40 Cal.3d 239). In *Serna*, the court summarized its holding by stating, "Delay between the filing of a misdemeanor complaint and the arrest and prosecution of a defendant which exceeds the statutory period of limitation is unreasonable and presumptively prejudicial…" The same standard applies to delay between the filing of a Notice to Appear and trial.

In this case, over a year has elapsed since the Notice to Appear was filed with this court, and since a bench warrant was issued as a result of the failure to appear, the defendant has made no attempt to evade arrest. The defendant has lived at the same address, and has held steady employment at the same business address. The authorities could have easily served the defendant with the arrest warrant at either location but failed to do so. In such circumstances, where the State has failed to fulfill its affirmative duty to serve its warrants, the court should dismiss the charges. See *People v. Mitchell* (1972) 8 Cal.3d 114, 104 Cal. Rptr. 348; *Jones v. Superior Court* (1970) 3 Cal.3d 734, 737, 91 Cal.Rptr. 578, 580.

In *Jones v. Superior Court, supra,* the court found a delay in service of an arrest warrant to be unreasonable. The court noted that "there was no evidence that [Jones] attempted to avoid arrest" (*Jones, supra,* 3 Cal.3d at p. 738). "He was under no obligation to go to the police station, and his failure to appear cannot justify an otherwise unreasonable delay in apprehending him.… Petitioner was not in hiding and his whereabouts could have been discovered by routine, uncomplicated investigation" (*Jones, supra,* 3 Cal.3d at p. 741).

Finally, it makes little difference whether the delay is the fault of court personnel or the prosecution itself (*People v. Kerwin* (1972) 23 Cal.App.3d 466, 469). Accordingly, the within action should be dismissed.

DATED: February 14, 20xx

Respectfully submitted,

Lane Turner
LANE TURNER
Defendant in Pro Per

court for arraignment, without having had time to prepare a written motion. If that happens, you can (and should) make the motion orally at arraignment, remembering to tell the judge about the 1985 California Supreme Court case of *Serna v. Superior Court*. Also, you should ask the judge to let you testify under oath as to how the delay hurt your ability to defend against the charge. If all else fails, ask the judge to reschedule the hearing on your motion for another day.

Summary

The procedures for setting up the motion for hearing at arraignment, and for preparing, filing, and serving the papers on the prosecutor, are the same as those in the Motion Checklist provided earlier in this section.

Motion to Dismiss—Long Delay After Arraignment

Another type of "speedy trial" motion for dismissal has to do with delay occurring after arraignment. It should be made if you haven't gone to trial within 45 days after your arraignment and you didn't waive your right to have a trial within that time.

In this case, of course, your arraignment will already have occurred without your having obtained a hearing date from the judge and you will have to obtain such a date from the clerk.

Your motions papers should look something like the ones that follow.

What to Say to the Judge

When your motion is called, and it seems that the judge has read your papers, you probably will only need to respond to any questions asked. There's no use repeating what you've already said. If, however, the judge hasn't read your papers, simply say:

> *"Your Honor, I'm moving for a dismissal under Penal Code Section 1382. More than 45 days have passed since I was arraigned, I never waived time for trial, and I still haven't had a trial."*

Unless the prosecutor can show a very good reason for the delay, your case will probably be dismissed.

DANIEL DEFENDANT
950 Parker St.
San Jose, CA 95129
(408) 555-6789

Defendant in Pro Per

SUPERIOR COURT OF CALIFORNIA, COUNTY OF SANTA CLARA

SAN JOSE BRANCH

THE PEOPLE OF THE STATE) No. A5675675B
OF CALIFORNIA,)
) **NOTICE OF MOTION TO**
Plaintiff,) **DISMISS FOR LACK OF**
) **PROSECUTION; DECLARATION;**
vs.) **POINTS AND AUTHORITIES**
)
DANIEL DEFENDANT,) **[Penal Code § 1382]**
)
Defendant.)
)

TO: PLAINTIFF, THE PEOPLE OF THE STATE OF CALIFORNIA, AND TO THE DISTRICT
ATTORNEY FOR THE WITHIN-NAMED COUNTY:

PLEASE TAKE NOTICE that on August 1, 20xx at 9:00 a.m., in Department 12 of the above-
entitled Court at 955 Ruff Drive, San Jose, California, Defendant will move the Court for dismissal of the
above-entitled action.

This motion is made on the ground that more than 45 days have elapsed since the arraignment, and
that Section 1382 of the Penal Code therefore requires that the action be dismissed.

This motion is based on the pleadings, records, and files in this action, the accompanying
Declaration and Points and Authorities, and on oral and documentary evidence to be presented at the
hearing on the motion.

DATED: July 17, 20xx

Daniel Defendant
DANIEL DEFENDANT
Defendant in Pro Per

DECLARATION

I, DANIEL DEFENDANT, declare:

1. I am the defendant in this action.

2. I was arraigned in Department **8** of the Municipal Court for the Santa Clara County Judicial
District (San Jose Branch) on June 2, 20xx and pleaded not guilty to the charges pending against me. The
presiding judge, Hon. Timothy Handimafine, set the trial for July 15, 20xx at 2:00 p.m. in Department 9.

3. On July 15, 20xx at 2:00 p.m., I appeared for trial in this action in Department 33 of the said
court, Commissioner Raymond Cunningone presiding. The said commissioner informed me that Officer
Greg Gettem, who was scheduled to appear as a witness against me, was on vacation and that trial would
have to be postponed. He continued the trial to August 5, 20xx over my objection.

4. More than 45 days have elapsed since I was arraigned on June 2, 20xx and I have still not had a
trial in this action.

5. I have not been responsible for any of the delay herein mentioned, and have not waived time for
trial under Section 1382 of the Penal Code.

I declare under penalty of perjury under the laws of the State of California that the foregoing is true
and correct.

DATED: July 17, 20xx

Daniel Defendant
DANIEL DEFENDANT
Defendant in Pro Per

POINTS AND AUTHORITIES

Defendant is charged with a violation of the Vehicle Code constituting an infraction. PC § 17 requires that "all provisions of law relating to misdemeanors shall apply to infractions," the only exceptions being that infractions are not triable by a jury, nor is a defendant entitled to the assistance of a court-appointed attorney.

Section 1382(c) of the Penal Code requires that a criminal action must be dismissed "when a defendant in a misdemeanor (and hence also an infraction) case in an inferior court is not brought to trial ... within 45 days after his arraignment ... unless the defendant requests or consents to a later date." See *Arreola v. Municipal Court* (1983) 139 Cal.App.3d 108; *Beasley v. Municipal Court* (1973) 32 Cal.App.3d 108; *Casteneda v. Municipal Court* (1972) 25 Cal.App.3d 588; *Hankla v. Municipal Court* (1972) 26 Cal. App.3d 342.

Accordingly, more than 45 days having passed without trial since defendant was arraigned, and defendant not having waived time for trial or caused the delay, the complaint herein must be dismissed.

DATED: July 17, 20xx

Respectfully submitted,

Daniel Defendant
_____
DANIEL DEFENDANT
Defendant in Pro Per

Motion to Demand That Infraction Proceed as a Misdemeanor

As discussed earlier, in Chapters 3 and 7, you have the right, when charged with a fourth infraction within a year, to demand that the case proceed as a misdemeanor. Before you make such a demand, however, we urge you to go back to our previous discussions and consider both the benefits and pitfalls.

Preparing the Papers

The papers for your motion to have the case proceed as a misdemeanor should look some-thing like the ones below. You should attach the certified copies of your convictions, or a DMV printout or warning notice indicating your convictions, to your motion.

What to Say in Court

As far as what to say in court, we refer you back to Section D2b, where we noted that this type of request could be made at arraignment. If the judge grants your motion, the case will most likely be set for a "pretrial conference." We refer you to Chapter 13 on how jury-triable misdemeanor cases are handled.

DAN DEFENDANT
3044 Grey Bar Lane
Berkeley, CA 94703
Tel: (510) 845-2999

Defendant in Pro Per

SUPERIOR COURT OF CALIFORNIA, COUNTY OF ALAMEDA,
OAKLAND-PIEDMONT-EMERYVILLE BRANCH

THE PEOPLE OF THE STATE OF CALIFORNIA,	)))	No. 1945-993-6
Plaintiff,	))	**NOTICE OF MOTION TO CHARGE INFRACTION AS MISDEMEANOR**
vs.	))	**DECLARATION; POINTS AND AUTHORITIES**
DAN DEFENDANT,	))	
Defendant.	))	[V.C. Section 40000.28]

TO: PLAINTIFF, THE PEOPLE OF THE STATE OF CALIFORNIA, AND TO THE DISTRICT ATTORNEY FOR THE WITHIN-NAMED COUNTY:

PLEASE TAKE NOTICE that on October 10, 20xx, at 11:00 A.M. in Department 2 of the above-entitled court at 661 Washington Street, Oakland, California, County of Alameda, Defendant will move the court for an order to charge the alleged violation of V.C. Section 22350 an infraction, as a misdemeanor.

This motion is made on the ground that defendant has been and admits to having been convicted of three prior infractions within the last twelve months.

This motion is based on the pleadings, records, and files in this action, the accompanying Declaration, Exhibits, Points and Authorities, and on oral and documentary evidence to be presented at the hearing on the motion.

DATED: September 15, 20xx

Daniel Defendant
DANIEL DEFENDANT,
Defendant in Pro Per

DECLARATION

I, DAN DEFENDANT, declare:

1. I am the defendant in the above-entitled action.

2. On April 25, 20xx I received the Notice to Appear herein.

3. The Notice to Appear charges a violation of V.C Section 22350, an infraction.

4. I have been and hereby do admit to having been convicted of three prior infractions within the twelve-month period immediately preceding the date of the Notice to Appear herein.

I declare under penalty of perjury under the laws of the State of California that the foregoing is true and correct.

DATED: September 15, 20xx

Daniel Defendant
DANIEL DEFENDANT
Defendant in Pro Per

POINTS AND AUTHORITIES

I. **WHERE AN INFRACTION DEFENDANT ADMITS TO HAVING BEEN CONVICTED OF THREE PRIOR INFRACTIONS WITHIN THE PRECEDING TWELVE MONTHS OF ALLEGEDLY COMMITTING A FOURTH, HE IS ENTITLED TO HAVE THE CASE PROCEED AS A MISDEMEANOR.**

Vehicle Code Section 40000.28 requires that a fourth infraction proceed as a misdemeanor where the defendant has been and admits to having been convicted of three prior infractions within the twelve months preceding alleged commission of the fourth. The relevant portion of that statute reads as follows:

> Any offense which would be an infraction is a misdemeanor if a defendant has been convicted of three or more violations of this code … within the 12-month period immediately preceding the commission of the offense and such prior convictions are admitted by the defendant …. For this purpose, a bail forfeiture shall be deemed to be a conviction of the offense charged.

In *People v. Shults* (1978) 87 Cal.App.3d 101, 150 Cal.Rptr. 747, the court ruled that where the convictions have in fact occurred within the preceding twelve months and the defendant admits them, it is *mandatory* that the case proceed as a misdemeanor. The trial court has no discretion to order otherwise, stating:

> Vehicle Code Section 40000.28 appears to have a single meaning on its face and requires no interpretation. (citations omitted) The plain meaning of the relevant portion of the section is that there are two requirements for elevation of an infraction to a misdemeanor: (1) three prior convictions within twelve months, and (2) defendant's admission of the priors ….

Id. at 105.

Here, defendant admits to having been convicted of three prior infractions within the preceding twelve months (see Exhibit "A"), and is therefore entitled to be treated as a misdemeanant and accorded a jury trial.

CONCLUSION

For the foregoing reasons and based on these authorities, defendant hereby demands that the case proceed as a misdemeanor.

DATED: September 15, 20xx

Respectfully submitted,

Daniel Defendant

Daniel Defendant
Defendant in Pro Per

After Your Motion Is Granted or Denied

After your hearing on a motion, the judge might give the decision right away, or may want to read the papers and think it over. The decision will either be to "grant" or "deny" the motion.

Denied Motions

If your motion is denied by the judge, you can bring the judge's error to the attention of a higher court in one of two ways. The easier choice is simply to go to trial. If you're found guilty, you can then appeal to the Superior Court Appellate Division and raise the errors, in the hope of getting your case reversed. One problem with this (especially if you're complaining about having been denied the right to a speedy trial) is that, in addition to showing that the judge was legally wrong in denying your motion, you may also have to show that you were put at a serious disadvantage because of the ruling (for example, that your key witness moved away during the excessive delay). Appeals are also fairly complicated, and the chances of success aren't high.

The alternative is to bring a separate lawsuit, requesting the Appellate Department to order the court to grant your motion. This is called a "mandate" or "prohibition" proceeding, and is extremely complicated. It is only worth the trouble in very serious cases.

Granted Motions

Obviously, if you win a Motion to Dismiss, it's the end of the case—you win without having to go to trial. If you win a Motion for Transfer to the county seat, prepare to wait. Then prepare to wait some more. If you're lucky, the judge's order to the clerk to transfer the case will baffle and befuddle the clerks, and may cause your case to be delayed for several months. This kind of delay works to your advantage because it increases your chances of eventually winning at trial (memories fade, police officers quit the force or transfer), and maybe even of getting your case dismissed for delay.

Still, unless your successful motion was one for dismissal, you'll need to prepare for trial. That's what the next few chapters are about.

Courts Refusing to Hear Motions Before Trial

When this book was first published in 1982, people rarely made written motions in traffic court. Since then, many readers have used the motions in this chapter to assert their rights. Unfortunately, not a few lazy or biased judges—and clerks—have responded by making it harder for people accused of traffic violations to assert their rights. One of the ways they have done this is by refusing to separately set (or "calendar") motions for hearing, by insisting that your motions be heard on the day and at the time of trial.

There are practical and tactical reasons for demanding separate motion and trial dates. For example, consider a motion to dismiss on account of the prosecution's refusal to give you a copy of the officer's notes. If the motion is heard at least a day before trial and you win the motion and the officer complies, you'll have time to study his notes before trial. But if your motion is heard and granted just before trial is set to start, you won't have this preparation time.

There's a psychological reason, too, to separate your motion from the trial. It's far better to argue your motion without the sight of the uniformed, impatient officer cooling his heels in the courtroom. Why? If hearing your motion (even if it's not granted) will delay the trial, this will mean that the officer will have to return a second time for the actual trial—an order that many efficiency-minded (and officer-friendly) judges will be loathe to make. And if your motion to dismiss is granted (or you've successfully moved for a change of venue), the officer will have made a trip to court for nothing. In short, there is enormous pressure on the judge to start trial when the witnesses are present, and your chances of winning your motion go way up if you can argue it before they're assembled. So it's very important that any motion you make, requesting dismissal for failure of discovery, lack of a speedy trial or some other ground, or for a change of venue, be heard separately from and *before* the date set for trial.

The best time to request a separate motion date is at arraignment. If the judge refuses to set a motion hearing at all, politely ask, *"Your Honor, is my understanding correct that you are denying the motion at this time, without being willing to hear it on a contested motion calendar?"* If the answer is yes, you may have grounds for appeal. Or, you might suggest, *"Your Honor, I realize there is no separate motion calendar in traffic court. Could it be heard three weeks from now, on the arraignment calendar?"* With that, you're inviting the judge to hear your motion at a convenient time, when he'll be in court anyway.

If the judge persists in refusing to take your request for a separate motion calendaring seriously, and mutters something about hearing it "at trial," you should politely object with a little speech that is calculated to do two things:

- **Convince the judge.** The reasons explained above for hearing your motion before and separate from the trial are completely legitimate concerns that judges hear from

lawyers every day. Every litigant needs time for preparation. Obviously, you'll need to tactfully phrase your fear that the presence of the officer (and his annoyance if he's ordered to return) will sway the outcome.

- **Set up your appeal.** If the judge denies your request and you eventually take an appeal based on that denial, you'll have to have proof that you asked for separate dates and gave the lower court judge all of the reasons why he should grant your request. Your word alone in an appellate brief won't suffice, and you can't raise this issue for the first time in an appeal. When your argument is taken down by the court stenographer (or tape recorder), you'll have proof that you raised the issue before the lower judge (lawyers call this "making a record").

Here are some suggestions for what to tell the judge when asking for a separate motion date for your motion to dismiss, change venue, or other motion:

> *"Your Honor, if this motion is heard directly before trial (unless the Court grants the motion to dismiss) and orders the officer to produce his notes, I'll need time to prepare after I receive them. That will result in a continuance, inconveniencing the officer. Or, if you don't continue the case, I won't have adequate time to prepare for trial after I receive the notes. I therefore object to hearing the motion at trial and request a separate setting for this motion."*

If your motion is for a change of venue, you might also remind the judge that, if it's granted on the day of trial, the officer will have appeared unnecessarily.

Another way to force a traffic court to hear a motion before trial is to simply set it on a day and time that arraignments are heard. For example, if the court in which you must appear has arraignments on Mondays at 8:30 a.m., write Monday at 8:30 a.m. as the date and time of your motion and have it served on the city attorney's or district attorney's office by mail—with a proof of service signed by the mailer—at least 20 days before the hearing. Then, file it with the clerk, telling her, *"It's a written request to the Court, for placement on the arraignment calendar."* If the clerk balks, ask if she's really refusing to file your papers or to put your case on the arraignment calendar. If she reminds you that you've already been arraigned, tell her you want to be "rearraigned." If she still refuses, prepare a written memo to her, as below.

Of course, ultimately nothing can force a hostile bureaucrat or biased judge, intent on taking away your rights, to treat you fairly. Their fear that they'll be reversed (and embarrassed) on appeal is just about your best weapon. Short of that, the procedures in this section should increase your chances, however.

Moe Motion
123 Main Street
Santa Clara, California

March 10, 20xx

Carrie Clerk
Deputy Clerk
Superior Court of Santa Clara County
South County Court Facility
12425 Monterey Road
San Martin, California
HAND DELIVERED

RE: People v. Moe Motion
Case No. B-1234567

Dear Clerk:

I insist my case be placed on the arraignment calendar for April 30, 20xx at 8:30 a.m., notwithstanding my having been arraigned earlier, on April 20, 20xx. I also request the moving papers submitted herewith be filed, and that you file-stamp my copies.

If you refuse to do either, please so indicate with your signature at the bottom of this letter and return it to me. Thank you.

Sincerely,

Moe Motion

Preparing for Trial

In this chapter, we tell you how to prepare for a formal trial with the officer present. This is the type of proceeding you think of when you hear the word trial, where both sides present evidence and a judge decides who should prevail. Other types of proceedings—such as "informal hearings" and "trials by declaration"—that don't involve the give and take of an adversarial proceeding in a courtroom are covered in Chapters 9 and 10.

Overview of Formal Infraction Trial With Officer Present

In most cases where you choose to contest your infraction ticket, you should insist on a formal trial with the officer present. By doing so, you get the advantages of being able to challenge the officer's assertions in court and, most importantly, you gain the very real possibility that the officer will not show up to testify against you. In that case, your ticket could be dismissed. Before we tell you to how to prepare for this kind of trial, it will be helpful to get an overview of the entire process.

A trial for an infraction is, in most areas, held in a Superior Court. In Los Angeles and a few other counties, trials are held in Municipal Court. The trial is held before a judge, commissioner, or traffic referee. Here we will use the word "judge" for all three.

In any court you will be notified where and when to appear. Be on time. When your case is called, you (and your witnesses, if any) and the officer walk up behind a table or podium, raise your right hand and are "sworn in." There is usually no prosecutor. The officer tells his story first. His job is to testify to facts that establish all the required elements of the case. After he's finished, you have an opportunity to cross-examine him. You can ask him questions on

matters he has testified to, and on new matters that might help you establish a defense. Don't argue with him.

After cross-examining the officer, you get your turn to explain what happened. You will probably want to contradict the officer's testimony by establishing other facts that tend to disprove one or more elements of the offense. You may also want to establish facts that constitute a defense even if everything the officer said was true. Some judges may then give the officer a chance to cross-examine you, or ask a few questions themselves.

After all the testimony has been given (including that of witnesses) the judge usually gives the decision. Some judges will try to delay making a decision by saying they want to "take the case under advisement," with your permission. If the judge finds you guilty, he will usually tell you what the fine will be at the same time. You can, however, insist on the right to be sentenced between six hours and five days later (see Chapter 14).

There are several variations to this scenario. For example, a few courts expect you, the officer, and all witnesses to testify from the witness stand instead of from behind a table or podium. This may seem like a small matter, but you'll be surprised how many people capable of doing a good job in the somewhat relaxed atmosphere behind a table, stumble, stutter, and mumble incoherently when they must speak from a witness stand. Often people who will use notes when standing behind a table will abandon them when testifying from a witness stand, thinking somehow it's impermissible. This is a mistake. Nobody cares whether you use notes. In fact, you're probably a lot better off using them to make sure you don't omit important details. The judge may even be impressed that you are so well organized.

Getting Your Materials Together

Many people who defend themselves in traffic court think that all they need to do is tell a good story to the judge and they will be found not guilty. They couldn't be more wrong. Although it is true in theory that the "burden of proof" in a traffic case is on the prosecution, in practice, almost everything a police officer says is believed and you have the heavy burden of proving him wrong. Your job is made even more difficult by the fact that police officers are very skilled at giving courtroom testimony and at stretching the truth when they have to.

To overcome these difficulties it's important that you be well prepared. This chapter will show you how to prepare for the two most important things you must do at trial. These are:

1. Putting on a very convincing display, using your own testimony and other evidence to raise a "reasonable doubt" about whether you are guilty. Depending on the situation, you may have to prepare notes, research laws, take pictures of the scene, bring witnesses, and practice giving your own testimony beforehand.

2. Showing through cross-examination of the officer that his story has holes in it that raise some doubt about whether you are guilty.

Gathering Your Notes and Research

The first step in preparing for your trial is to write down everything you can remember about the traffic violation. It's best to do this while it's still fresh in your memory, preferably as soon as you or the officer leave the scene or as soon thereafter as possible. (Of course, we realize that many readers will only be resorting to this book long after the fact of the ticket being given. If you want to be better prepared, in the event you receive a ticket in the future, read Chapter 17.) You may also want to take pictures of the scene from different angles and locations, if it's relevant to your case. In Chapters 4 through 8, we showed you how to figure out the elements of your violation and determine your best defense. You should try especially hard to remember the details of those facts that relate to your defense.

Preparing Diagrams and Maps

Diagrams or maps of the place where you allegedly committed the violation are always useful, particularly in speeding cases. Many officers use diagrams, and a few ticket form books are even printed with a little intersection for the officer to fill in. If you use a diagram, you'll be better equipped to illustrate inaccuracies in the officer's testimony. In radar cases, you can show how the radar beam might have intercepted targets other than your vehicle. Where radar wasn't used, you can indicate how the officer's vehicle overtook yours at a higher speed. In defending against traffic signal and stop sign violations, you can point to the place where the green light turned yellow or where you stopped at the sign. For turning violations, you can show how far away the oncoming or cross traffic was when you made your turn.

Your diagram should include the intersection, stop signs or signals, dividers, crosswalks, limit lines, and the location of parked vehicles, and should indicate the approximate widths of the streets and lanes. The locations of moving vehicles—yours, the officer's and maybe of oncoming or cross traffic—can be indicated either with movable markers cut out of colored paper or cardboard or by drawing an arrow with a felt-tipped pen as you testify. Some courtrooms have chalkboards or large pads of drawing paper you can use, but don't count on it. Here's a sample diagram of an intersection:

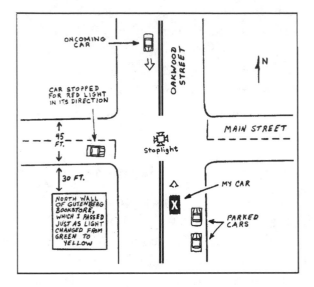

For speed violations where you were paced by the officer over a long stretch, a diagram of the road should show intersections and familiar buildings or other landmarks, and should also indicate the distance traveled between the place where you first saw him and where he stopped you.

TIP

Never try to draw your diagram in court. The result is sure to be time-consuming and klutzy. Instead, carefully prepare it beforehand. Use a large piece of thick white paper and several thick felt-tip pens. Use black or dark blue to denote roadways and intersections and other colors for vehicles and traffic signals. If you are artistically challenged, have a more talented friend help.

You'll obviously want to refer to your diagram in court as part of presenting your testimony. To do this, inform the judge that you have a visual aid that you would like to use when you testify.

EXAMPLE (How to testify with a diagram):

You made a left turn at a stoplight, and were then pulled over and charged with running a red light in order to make the turn. You claim you entered the intersection when the left-turn arrow light was turning from green to yellow. In court, you testify as follows:

"As I approached the intersection and got into the left-turn lane, I saw a green-arrow signal, which changed to yellow just as I crossed the final line of the crosswalk at the entrance to the intersection. As I made the turn, I saw the officer's car behind two other cars. I proceeded because the light was yellow in my direction and because a car was right on my tail, making a quick stop unsafe. I have a diagram of the intersection. I made it last week just after I went back to the intersection. May I please show it to the court?"

At this point, if a prosecutor is present, you show it to her (otherwise to the cop). Then hand it to the court clerk (who may mark it Exhibit #1 before handing it to the judge). If the courtroom has an easel or blackboard, place your diagram there, facing the judge. If not, find a place to prop it up so that it can be seen clearly. (The judge or clerk will probably help by telling you how to do this.)

Your testimony should continue something like this:

"Your honor, my car is shown on this diagram in green. The dotted green arrow shows my path as I completed the turn. The officer's vehicle is indicated in red. The roadway is outlined in black, and its curvature is shown, indicating that if the officer had been 100 feet behind me as he testified, he would not have been able to see my vehicle around the curve. The road

is marked to scale, as I've confirmed with a photocopy of that portion of a city map, which I'd like to have marked as Exhibit #2 and present to the court. At this time, I ask that Exhibits #1 and #2 be introduced into evidence."

Using Photographs in Court

In addition to diagrams, you may want to use photographs. Photos are best used to show conditions like:

- obscured traffic signs or signals
- the view from where the cop was sitting when he claimed to have seen your vehicle
- road obstructions such as curves and hills, or buildings that restrict visibility, and
- road width and straightness to show that an over-the-limit speed was safe, if you're charged with violating the Basic Speed Law (see Chapter 4).

TIP

Have key photos enlarged. It's hard to look at 3" x 5" photos, especially in a courtroom where you are trying to explain why the photo helps establish your case. It is far better to present 8" x 10" enlargements that the judge can see without a magnifying glass.

There are some things photos don't show well, including situations where road and traffic conditions rapidly change, so that what happened when you were ticketed can't really be replicated. It also rarely helps to show the judge photos of an accident scene taken after the vehicles have been moved. You must personally take any photograph you intend to use in traffic court or, if someone else is the photographer, have that person come to court with you. This is because you—or the photographer—must testify where and when the picture was taken.

To refer to a photo and show it to the judge, formal trial court rules require you to have it marked as an exhibit and formally introduced into evidence. But in most traffic courts, judges will simply look at your photo without the need for a lot of gobbledygook. Here's an example of what to say (if the judge is not a stickler for formality, leave out the part about marking it for identification):

"Your Honor, I would ask that this photograph be marked for identification as Exhibit #1." (Show it to the officer (or prosecutor), then hand it to the clerk, who will mark the exhibit.) *"I took this picture along Main Street, at the same place where the officer indicated in his notes—and just now testified to—that he was parked when he says he saw me fail to stop at the stop sign on Market Street at its intersection with Main. I took it just two weeks after he issued me the citation, at the same time, 4:45 p.m., during the same rush-hour conditions on a weekday. I believe it accurately shows the impaired visibility the officer had of traffic coming in my direction, and it shows why he couldn't have had a very clear view of where he claims I ran the stop sign. I request that this Exhibit #1 be introduced into evidence."*

Deciding on Witnesses

You have the right to bring as a witness anyone who was present and observed the situation in which you allegedly committed a violation. This will usually be someone who was in the car with you.

Before you go to trial, ask your potential witness to tell you her version of what happened. Then go over your version of the facts to make sure you won't be contradicting each other. This does not mean your witness should lie to adjust her story to fit yours. However, if your stories are too far apart, you probably shouldn't ask this person to testify.

Later, in the section, "Testimony Presented on Your Behalf," we also show you how to prepare a witness for trial after you have interviewed him or her and decided their testimony will help your case. (There is nothing wrong with going over testimony with your potential witness. Attorneys would never go to court without first preparing their witnesses.)

Subpoenaing Witnesses

A subpoena (now officially called an "Order to Attend Court or Provide Documents") is a document that requires a witness to appear in court at the time and place of your trial. Failure to appear can result in arrest and jail or a fine for contempt of court.

There are two situations where you may want to "subpoena" a witness:

1. If a witness wants to testify on your behalf but needs to be excused from work or school, or

2. If the testimony of a reluctant witness is absolutely essential for winning your case.

If the testimony of an unwilling witness is not absolutely essential, you probably should not subpoena her. You don't want to be stuck with a hostile witness who might seek revenge by damaging your case.

To have the court issue a subpoena, go to the clerk as far ahead of the trial date as possible—preferably two to three weeks before—and ask that a subpoena be issued. Give the clerk your case name, case number, your scheduled trial date and courtroom number, and the name and address of the people you're having subpoenaed. The clerk may prepare the subpoena, or may simply hand you a blank form

(see the appendix) on which to fill in the appropriate information. After the information is placed on the subpoena, the clerk should sign it, put the court's seal on it, and give it to you.

There is another kind of subpoena besides a regular subpoena—a "subpoena duces tecum." (This is where the "or Provide Documents" name of the form comes into play.) The subpoena duces tecum orders the witness not only to appear in court, but also to bring certain papers, books, items, or other type of evidence along. (See the appendix.) For a subpoena duces tecum, you will also need to indicate on a separate written statement, or declaration, attached to the subpoena, what items you want the subpoenaed person to bring, and why it's necessary to subpoena the items. A sample declaration follows.

Note: The subpoena or subpoena duces tecum must be "served" on the person subpoenaed. Any person who is over 18, other than you, can do this. (A defendant cannot serve a subpoena in her own case.) You can even insist that a police agency—which has jurisdiction over the area in which the subpoena is to be served—serve the subpoena at no charge. (PC § 1328.) For unincorporated areas of a county, that's the sheriff, and for cities, it's that city's police department. To do this, you must mail or deliver the original and a copy of the subpoena to the police agency, with instructions to serve the copy at the address you give. You should instruct them to fill out the Proof of Service on the back of the original, which is returned to you for filing with the court. But be warned: Many law enforcement agencies are backlogged, and your subpoena may still be sitting in an officer's in-basket long after your trial has been held.

A copy of the Proof of Service is shown here and is included as the back page of the subpoena form in the appendix.

CR-125/JV-525

ATTORNEY OR PARTY WITHOUT ATTORNEY (Name, State Bar number, and address):

Stanley Safespeed
950 Parker Street
Berkeley, CA 94710
TELEPHONE NO.: 415-555-1234   FAX NO. (Optional):
E-MAIL ADDRESS (Optional):
ATTORNEY FOR (Name): Defendant in Pro Per

SUPERIOR COURT OF CALIFORNIA, COUNTY OF Alameda
STREET ADDRESS: 2120 Grove Street
MAILING ADDRESS: Berkeley, CA 94704
CITY AND ZIP CODE:
BRANCH NAME: Berkeley-Albany Branch

CASE NAME: The People of the State of California v. Stanley Safespeed

ORDER TO ATTEND COURT OR PROVIDE DOCUMENTS: Subpoena/Subpoena Duces Tecum	CASE NUMBER: A-123456-B

You must attend court or provide to the court the documents listed below. Follow the orders checked in item 2 below. If you do not, the judge can fine you, send you to jail, or issue a warrant for your arrest.

1. To: (name or business)

2. You must follow the court order(s) checked below:
   a. ☐ Attend the hearing.
   b. ☐ Attend the hearing and bring all items checked in d. below.
   c. ☐ Provide a copy of these items to the court (Do not use this form to obtain Juvenile Court records):
      (1)
      (2)
      (3)
   d. ☐ If this box is checked, provide all items listed on the attached sheet labeled "Provide These Items."
      If someone else is responsible for maintaining the items checked in c. above, that person (the Custodian of Records), must also attend the hearing.
   e. ☐ If this box is checked and you deliver all items listed above to the court within 5 days of service of this order, you do not have to attend court if you follow the instructions in item 5.

3. Court Hearing Date:
   Date: May 1, 20xx   Time: 3:00 pm   The court hearing will be at (name and address of court):
   Dept.:   Rm.:   2120 Grove Street, Berkeley, California 94704
   Call the person listed in item 4 below to make sure the hearing date has not changed. If you cannot go to court on this date, you must get permission from the person in item 4. You may be entitled to witness fees, mileage, or both, in the discretion of the court. Ask the person in item 4 after your appearance.

4. The person who has required you to attend court or provide documents is:
   Name: Phone No.:
   Title:
   Address:
   Number, Street, Apt. No.
   City   State   Zip

   Date: _____   ▶ _____
                                      Signature

Form Adopted for Mandatory Use
Judicial Council of California
CR-125/JV-525 [New January 1, 2007]

ORDER TO ATTEND COURT OR PROVIDE DOCUMENTS:
Subpoena/Subpoena Duces Tecum
(Criminal and Juvenile)

Page 1 of 2

STANLEY SAFESPEED
950 Parker St.
Berkeley, CA 94710
(510) 555-1234

Defendant in Pro Per

SUPERIOR COURT OF CALIFORNIA, COUNTY OF ALAMEDA

BERKELEY-ALBANY BRANCH

THE PEOPLE OF THE STATE
OF CALIFORNIA,

          Plaintiff,

vs.

STANLEY SAFESPEED,

          Defendant.

NO. A-123456-B

DECLARATION IN SUPPORT OF
ISSUANCE OF SUBPOENA
DUCES TECUM

I, STANLEY SAFESPEED, declare:

1. I am the defendant in the action of *People v. Safespeed*, No. A-123456-B, pending before the Superior Court for the Berkeley-Albany Branch.

2. I seek to have the clerk of the court issue a subpoena duces tecum requiring Officer Terrence Ticketer of the Berkeley Police Department to appear at the time and place for the trial in this action, set forth on the said subpoena duces tecum, and bring with him the following items:

   a. The hand-held radar unit with which he alleges he determined my speed.

   b. The instruction manual stating how the said radar unit is to be operated.

   c. The tuning forks or other devices with which he calibrated the said radar unit on the day of the alleged violation.

3. It is essential to my defense that the above items be produced at trial in order that I may demonstrate with them that radar speed measuring units produce false and spurious readings and do not accurately measure speeds of moving objects, including the vehicle I was driving when cited for the alleged violation.

   I declare under penalty of perjury under the laws of the State of California that the foregoing is true and correct.

DATED: April 1, 20xx

                              Stanley Safespeed
                              Stanley Safespeed

CR-125/JV-525

CASE NAME:

CASE NUMBER:

5. a. Put all items checked in item 2c and your completed *Declaration of Custodian of Records* form in an envelope. (You can ask the person in item 4 where to get this form.) Attach a copy of page 1 of this order to the envelope.

 b. Put the envelope inside another envelope. Then, attach a copy of page 1 of this form to the outer envelope or write this information on the outer envelope:

 (1) Case name
 (2) Case number
 (3) Your name
 (4) Hearing date, time, and department

 c. Seal and mail the envelope to the Court Clerk at the address listed in item 3. You must mail these documents to the court within five days of service of this order.

 d. If you are the Custodian of Records, you must also mail the person in item 4 a copy of your completed *Declaration of Custodian of Records.*

— *The server fills out the section below.* —

Proof of Service of CR-125/JV-525

1. I personally served a copy of this subpoena on:

 Date: _____ Time: _____ ☐ a.m. ☐ p.m.

 Name of the person served: _____

 At this address: _____

 After I served this person, I mailed or delivered a copy of this Proof of Service to the person in item 4 on (date): _____

 Mailed from (city): _____

2. I received this order for service on (date): _____ and was not able to serve (name of person) _____ after (number of attempts) _____ attempts because:

 a. ☐ The person is not known at this address.
 b. ☐ The person moved and the forwarding address is not known.
 c. ☐ There is no such address.
 d. ☐ The address is in a different county.
 e. ☐ I was not able to serve by the hearing date.
 f. ☐ Other (explain): _____

3. Server's name: _____ Phone no.: _____

4. The server (check one)
 a. ☐ is a registered process server. d. ☐ works for a registered process server.
 b. ☐ is not a registered process server. e. ☐ is exempt from registration under Business and Professional Code
 c. ☐ is a sheriff, marshal, or constable. section 22350(b).

5. Server's address: _____
 If server is a registered process server:
 County of registration: _____ Registration no.: _____

I declare under penalty of perjury under the laws of the State of California that I am at least 18 years old and not involved in this case and the information above is true and correct.

Date: _____

_____ ▶ _____
TYPE OR PRINT NAME OF SERVER SIGNATURE OF SERVER

CR-125/JV-525 [New January 1, 2007] **ORDER TO ATTEND COURT OR PROVIDE DOCUMENTS:** Page 2 of 2
Subpoena/Subpoena Duces Tecum
(Criminal and Juvenile)

If you want to subpoena the radar unit or manual of the officer who cited you, two copies of the subpoena must be delivered to that officer's supervisor. If you want to subpoena police records of any kind, the two copies must be delivered to the supervisor of whoever has control of the records. You can also insist that the police department serve the subpoena on its own appropriate employees. To do this, you give the police agency the original and two copies, plus a letter of instruction. In this case, your original and copies must reach the police agency at least five days before the court hearing (PC § 1328). Here are some sample letters to accomplish this:

Dan Driver
123 Main Street
Salinas, CA 93900

April 1, 20xx

Monterey Police Department
Pacific & Madison Streets
Monterey, CA 93940

RE: People v. Driver
Monterey Court No. 1234567

Dear People:

Enclosed are an original and a copy of a subpoena for service on Wilma Witness, of 1200 9th Street, Monterey. The best time to serve Ms. Witness is between 6:00 p.m. and 8:00 p.m. on weekdays.

Please fill out the Proof of Service on the back of the original and return to me. Thank you for your anticipated cooperation.

Sincerely,

Dan Driver
Dan Driver

Rhonda Roadrunner
456 7th Street
Los Angeles, CA 90010

May 1, 20xx

Los Angeles Police Department
251 E. 6th Street
Los Angeles, CA 90014

RE: People v. Roadrunner
Los Angeles Metropolitan Branch Superior Court No. 23456789

Dear People:

Enclosed are an original and two copies of a subpoena duces tecum for service on your custodian of records. Please give two copies of the subpoena duces tecum to his/her immediate supervisor and return the original to me with the Proof of Service filled out. Thank you for your anticipated cooperation.

Sincerely,
Rhonda Roadrunner
Rhonda Roadrunner

If a police department fails to comply with a subpoena—such as by refusing to produce the radar manual—you should ask at trial that the case be continued and that the officer be directed to produce the items sought. (See below. Obviously, if no officer shows up to testify against you, you should instead ask the judge to dismiss the case against you.)

Motions You May Want to Make Before Trial

Depending on the circumstances, you may wish to make certain requests of the judge before trial.

Requesting a "Continuance" (Postponement)

A "continuance" is a postponement of a scheduled court appearance (usually a trial). You might want your trial date postponed because you won't be prepared on the scheduled trial date, you'll be out of town, or are ill, or, better still, you've just discovered the days the officer will be on vacation and you want the trial held then.

Unless you've informed the prosecutor or officer in advance, most requests for a continuance that are made on the day of trial will be denied. However, it is usually not difficult to arrange for a continuance if you plan ahead. You should make your written request at least several weeks before trial whenever possible. Send a copy to the officer's police agency, or to the district or city attorney's office if it prosecutes traffic cases, or if your case involves a misdemeanor violation. Such a letter might look like this:

---

123 Parker St.
Berkeley, CA 94710

May 5, 20xx

Clerk, Alameda County Superior Court
Berkeley-Albany Branch
2120 Martin Luther King, Jr. Way
Berkeley, California 94710

RE: People v. Safespeed, Case No. A-123456
Trial Date: June 1, 20xx

Dear Sir or Madam:

I am scheduled to appear for trial in the above matter on June 1, 20xx. Unfortunately, I will be out of town on that date due to my employer's insistence that I attend a two-week seminar in New York between May 28 and June 11. I therefore request that trial be continued to June 15, or as soon as possible thereafter as it can be scheduled. Please inform me as to whether the continuance will be granted and any new trial date and time.

Sincerely,

Shirley Safespeed

Shirley Safespeed
cc: Officer G. Growlski
Berkeley Police Department

If you don't receive a reply at least a week before the scheduled trial date, call the court clerk. If the continuance hasn't been granted (or if dealing with the clerks proves fruitless), you'll have to appear in court on the trial date. It is best to be prepared to go to trial, although you can ask for a continuance again. The continuance will probably be granted if you show your copy of the letter as proof that you notified the police and/or the district/city attorney of your request well in advance. Of course, there is always a chance that if the officer doesn't show, and the judge doesn't notice your letter in the file, he might dismiss the case (since it will look like you showed up ready for trial but the officer didn't). So, you may want to wait to see whether the officer shows before raising your request.

You may also want to ask for a continuance when the officer who cited you shows up and, either (1) he or another officer you've subpoenaed have failed to produce material you've demanded in your subpoena, or (2) a witness you've subpoenaed simply failed to show. For example, the officer failed to bring the manual for the radar unit, which you subpoenaed earlier. (Of course, if the officer who cited you doesn't show, you should ask that the case be dismissed.) The best time to request a continuance on this basis is when your case is called before the trial starts, after having asked the officer or other person if they brought all material listed in the subpoena duces tecum.

Responding to a Prosecution Request for a Continuance

Occasionally, because of an officer's scheduled vacation or other anticipated reason for his absence, the district attorney or police agency will ask for a postponement of the trial date and will notify you by mail. If you receive such a notice, figure out whether the letter indicates that the court has already granted the continuance, or whether the agency is merely stating that the officer won't be showing up and you needn't go. If the court date has been changed, you should receive a notice from the court, not merely the prosecuting or police agency. If the letter only indicates that the prosecution wants a continuance, you may want to show up in court on the trial date—ready

for trial—to object. Be prepared to point out that you had to make arrangements well in advance to take time off from your job (at a loss of pay) on the day originally scheduled for trial and that you don't relish the thought of doing it again. If you're lucky, the judge may then dismiss the case.

Preparing a Motion to Disqualify the Judge

As we noted in Chapter 10, you can disqualify a particularly unfair or hard-line judge merely by preparing and using a "Peremptory Challenge." This is your right under Code of Civil Procedure § 170.6. The time to use the challenge depends upon whether your case is assigned to a particular judge "for all purposes" at the outset (usually at arraignment), or is specifically assigned ten days or more in advance to a particular judge (as opposed to a particular courtroom or department). If neither of these is true, you can move to disqualify the judge just before your trial begins, by telling the judge—before any witnesses are sworn in—that you wish to file the Peremptory Challenge. Otherwise, you must file this document with the court either (1) within ten days of an "all-purpose" assignment (again, usually at arraignment), or (2) at least five days before trial, if a specific judge was assigned at least ten days before the trial date.

If you are able to make your Peremptory Challenge only on the day of the trial (because your case wasn't assigned to a particular judge sufficiently in advance of trial), fill out your challenge in advance, except for the name of the judge. Then, when you show up at the courthouse for your trial and discover the name of your judge, fill it in at that time. Once presented with the Peremptory Challenge, the judge will have to transfer the case to another courtroom. If no other judge is available, the case will have to be postponed to another day when one is available. Once you find out this information the trial date information can be filled in.

Hedge Note: Assuming your case is not the first to be heard, you can observe the judge who will be hearing your case and decide whether he seems to be dealing fairly with other cases. If so, leave your Peremptory Challenge in your briefcase and have your trial. If you decide, before your case is called, that the judge is more likely than not to find you guilty, produce the Peremptory Challenge when your case is called.

Another Hedge Note: If traffic court trials are regularly held by one judge—so that you know in advance where your trial will be held and which judge will hear it—it might be helpful for you to go to the courthouse and watch traffic trials held by the same judge several days before your case is to be heard. If the judge seems unfair or finds people guilty even when they have a good defense, you may want to prepare and file your Peremptory Challenge.

Note: If the officer doesn't show up—even if you dislike the judge—you should not use the Peremptory Challenge, but rather should just ask the judge to dismiss the case.

Preparing to Deal With the Officer's Testimony

In traffic offense trials, the testimony of the police officer who cited you is the most important part of the prosecution's case. The officer's story will usually follow this pattern: he will testify that he was parked or driving, minding his own business ("writing a report" or "observing traffic") when he observed you committing all the elements of the particular violation. He may also embellish this with testimony relating to traffic and road conditions, to establish why the violation was hazardous to other vehicles, pedestrians, etc. That testimony will usually sound, in part, something like this:

> *"I was parked observing traffic, when I observed the defendant enter the intersection at Maple and Pearl Streets, heading south on Maple after the light had turned red. There was heavy traffic at the time and several cars had to apply their brakes to avoid an accident. The road was also wet from a rain storm earlier in the day."*

You should listen closely to what the officer says and focus on ways to challenge his testimony. Depending on what the officer says, you may be able to:

- make a legal objection that results in the officer's testimony being excluded from your trial, or
- successfully ask the officer questions (called cross-examination) to cast doubt on the officer's version of the facts.

When and How to Object to Testimony

Few people have the legal knowledge to raise picky technical objections. Fortunately, in most traffic trials, you don't need it. In fact, raising lots of objections in traffic court can quickly become counterproductive, as it's more likely to raise the hackles of the judge than to help you win your case.

Objecting to testimony is a tactical decision. Always ask yourself: *"How likely am I to succeed?"* As part of doing this, you should also consider how damaging the testimony is to your case. For example, if the officer is providing background detail about the weather or road conditions that has little to do with whether you committed a particular violation,

DARLENE DISQUALIFIER
950 Parker Road
Los Angeles, CA 90000
(213) 555-6789

Defendant in Pro Per

SUPERIOR COURT OF CALIFORNIA, COUNTY OF LOS ANGELES
LOS ANGELES METROPOLITAN BRANCH

THE PEOPLE OF THE STATE OF CALIFORNIA Plaintiff, vs. DEBORAH DISQUALIFIER, Defendant.	) No. M123221-B))) PEREMPTORY CHALLENGE) [CCP § 170.6])))))

I, DARLENE DISQUALIFIER, declare:

1. I am the defendant in the above-entitled action.

2. On September 12, 20xx, the date of trial herein, it became known to me that the Hon._____ _____ was scheduled to try the above-entitled matter as judge or commissioner.

3. I believe that the aforesaid judge or commissioner, before whom the trial in the above-entitled matter is pending, is prejudiced against my interest so that I believe that I cannot have a fair and impartial trial before such judge, court commissioner, or referee.

WHEREFORE, Defendant requests ex parte, per C.C.P. Section 170.6, that the said judge or commissioner be disqualified from hearing the above-entitled matter.

I declare under penalty of perjury under the laws of the State of California that the foregoing is true and correct.

DATED: September 12, 20xx

Darlene Disqualifier
DARLENE DISQUALIFIER
Defendant in Pro Per

you gain little by objecting—even if your objection is technically correct.

But a few well-placed objections can serve a major purpose. That's because the testifying police officer probably expects you to be unprepared and nervous and he is likely to be overconfident. (After all, he has probably testified many times before, in cases against unprepared defendants.) If you are able to surprise him with even a few valid objections, you may well throw him off-balance and weaken his testimony.

Here are four valid tactical objections that might help you disconcert the officer:

Radar or Laser Evidence and the Engineering and Traffic Survey Requirement

For Basic Speed Law violations (except in 15 mph two-lane roads, 55 mph, 65–70 mph, and 15 and 20 mph school zones, 25 mph "senior" zones, and on "local streets and roads"), the officer may not properly testify about the use of radar or laser, or even about his visual estimate of your speed if he was using radar or laser, until he has introduced into evidence a certified copy of an engineering and traffic survey justifying the speed limit where you were nabbed (see Chapter 4). If he tries to testify without doing this, object by saying something like:

> *"Your Honor, I object to the introduction of radar testimony on the ground that Officer Gettem has failed to lay the foundation by proving an engineering and traffic survey as required by Section 40803 (b) of the Vehicle Code."*

It is not enough for the officer to just testify that such a survey was conducted, unless he helped conduct it. Mere testimony about the study should be objected to on the basis that it's "hearsay" and not the best evidence. (The "best evidence" rule requires production of

the survey itself.) Neither are mere summaries of surveys acceptable evidence. (See *People v. Sterritt* (1976) 65 Cal.App.3d Supp. 1, 135 Cal.Rptr. 522; *People v. Ellis* (1995) 33 Cal. App.4th Supp. 25, 40 Cal.Rptr.2d 111; *People v. Earnest* (1995) 33 Cal.App.4th Supp. 18, 40 Cal.Rptr.2d 304.)

Some courts will allow radar speed convictions without introduction of a survey, unless you insist that one be introduced. If you object about the absence of a survey, the judge will probably quickly mumble something about "judicial notice" of a copy of the survey filed with the court. If this happens, you should at that time politely object to the judge taking judicial notice of the document without it being produced in court, and you should insist on seeing the survey itself. It must then be produced. Don't settle for anything less than a certified copy. (A true certified copy bears an original signature of some city or county employee stating the copy is a true copy of the original.)

A few courts have been known to try to take shortcuts by keeping only a list of streets that have been surveyed. But under the case of *People v. Peterson* (1986) 181 Cal.App.3d Supp. 7, 226 Cal.Rptr. 544, this is improper; such a list should be objected to as "hearsay," and a "violation of the best-evidence rule." The actual survey itself might not be located anywhere near the courtroom. If the judge seems inclined to postpone the case to allow the prosecutor or officer to produce the survey, you should argue that the prosecution should have come to court prepared, and you might also want to complain of the hardship of having to stay longer or come back another day.

If you followed the procedures in Chapter 10 for making the prosecution disclose a copy of the engineering and traffic survey in a Basic Speed Law case involving radar or laser, then the prosecution either ignored your request or sent you such a copy.

If the prosecution ignored your "Informal Discovery Request" for the survey, you hopefully made a "Motion for Exclusion of Evidence" or for dismissal (see Chapter 10); if the judge ordered the nonproduced survey "excluded," you still have to point that out at trial, if and when the prosecution produces it. If, on the other hand, you have not made this sort of motion in writing before trial, you can still do that orally, at trial, if the prosecution tries to introduce it into evidence at trial, or even to refer to it. To do this, your objection at trial should be:

> *"Your Honor, I object to the introduction of any engineering and traffic survey, because the prosecution did not disclose it in my written Informal Discovery Request, which was served on both the police agency and the district [or city] attorney's office. Because the prosecution is first showing it to me at this late stage, I have not had time to review the survey, to see if it complies with the requirements of Vehicle Code Section 627 and the Department of Transportation requirements. It is unfair to expect me to do that at trial. Since the prosecution would not produce it in response to my Informal Discovery Request, it should be excluded."*

Note: At this point, if the court previously made a written order requiring disclosure of the survey or excluding its introduction into evidence, be sure to show the judge a file-stamped copy, noting "and the court previously ordered that the evidence be disclosed" (or "precluded," if that was the order). If no such order was made, at least show the judge the Informal Discovery Request you made, with the Proof of Service indicating copies were mailed to the police and prosecuting agencies.

On the other hand, the survey may have been disclosed to you before trial. If so, you should review it well before trial to see if it truly "justifies" the posted speed limit. The police or prosecution can usually point to a survey completed within the required previous five years (or seven or ten years in some cases; see Chapter 4), but frequently, the survey itself will be legally inadequate. An inadequate survey will not "justify" the posted speed limit in accordance with the methods determined by the Department of Transportation.

To justify the posted speed, the survey must include consideration of:

1. 85th-percentile "prevailing speeds";

2. traffic accident records; and

3. specified "road and/or traffic conditions not readily apparent to the driver."

In one case (*People v. Goulet* (1992) 13 Cal. App.4th Supp. 1, 17 Cal.Rptr.2d 801), an appeals court reversed a speeding conviction because the survey was inadequate in not following the 85th-percentile rule. Under this rule, the 85th-percentile speed is the speed at or below which 85 percent of motorists travel. The speed limit must be set at or slightly below that speed in the absence of unusual conditions. The court in the *Goulet* case, citing Vehicle Code § 627 and the Department of Transportation's own Traffic Manual (now located in the California Department of Transportation's *Manual on Uniform Traffic Control Devices* (MUTCD)), ruled:

"... [T]he general rule [is that speed limits are to be] set at the 85th-percentile speed or within five mph under that speed. Some speed limits may be justified because they are set five mph below the general rule, based on higher than expected accident rates or listed hidden hazards. Some speed limits may appear unjustified because:

1. The speed limit is set 10 or more mph under the 85th-percentile speed;

2. The speed limit makes violators of large percentage of drivers;

3. 'Conditions' listed are not hidden hazards, that is, they are readily apparent to a driver;

4. There is no explanation of how the conditions listed require the speed limit set; or

5. The accident rate is not higher than would be expected statistically."

In the *Goulet* case, the defendant successfully argued that a 35-mph speed limit was not justified by the traffic survey because the 85th-percentile speed was 48 mph, and the survey did not mention any hidden conditions or higher-than-expected accident rates that would justify a lower speed limit. The conviction was reversed and her ticket was ordered dismissed.

Although the *Goulet* case is binding authority only in Ventura County, it can be cited in any court as persuasive authority to support an argument that a particular speed limit is not justified by the engineering and traffic survey introduced against you. Also, you can argue that the *Goulet* case is based upon the Department of Transportation's Traffic Manual, which was enacted in response to Vehicle Code § 627, and, as such, speaks with the force of statutory authority.

If you are faced with a traffic survey that doesn't seem to justify the speed limit, you should analyze the survey to see if the survey itself provides the facts (statistics and/or diagrams) necessary to justify any reduction of the speed limit much below the 85th-percentile speed. (This is extremely hard to do during the hurried and tense atmosphere of a trial, which is one more reason why you should request a copy of the survey in advance with an Informal Discovery Request.) Conclusions made by traffic engineers, such as unspecified "conditions" requiring a reduced speed, are not

sufficient to justify the lowered speed limit. In court, you should argue that since it is the prosecution's burden to submit a valid survey and to show the absence of a radar/laser speed trap, it follows that the factual basis for an engineering opinion must be stated on the survey itself. Without this factual information appearing on the face of the survey itself, the prosecution will not be able to meet its burden of proof under Vehicle Code § 40803(b), because the survey doesn't "justify" the speed limit in accordance with the requirements of Vehicle Code § 627.

If the traffic survey purports to justify a speed limit of more than 5 mph below the "85th-percentile" speed of traffic, but fails to contain specific enough references to accident records, your preparation should include how to explain this rather complicated issue to the judge. Unfortunately, folks are rushed through traffic court and have only a limited amount of time allotted to their case. We have prepared a legal brief on this issue on the next few pages, in case you don't feel comfortable explaining this complicated subject in the time allotted. If you are going to argue that the survey is invalid as not truly justifying the speed limit, you should at least read the survey and understand it well before the day of trial. Then, you will be able to adapt the argument (that the speed limit isn't justified) to the specific facts. A proper objection might sound something like this:

"Your Honor, I object to the introduction of testimony requiring radar (or laser), which is inadmissible under Vehicle Code Section 40803(a), and to any testimony from the officer, who under Section 40804 is incompetent as a witness. This is because, despite this survey, the prosecution has still not proven the absence of a speed trap, as they must, under Section 40803(b). The survey doesn't justify the posted speed limit

3044 Grey Bar Lane
Berkeley, CA 94703
Tel: (510) 845-2999

Defendant in Pro Per

SUPERIOR COURT OF CALIFORNIA, COUNTY OF ALAMEDA, FREMONT-NEWARK BRANCH

PEOPLE OF THE STATE OF CALIFORNIA,

 Plaintiff,

vs.

DARLA DEFENDANT,

 Defendant.

Case No. A-123-456-7

MEMORANDUM OF POINTS AND AUTHORITIES ON INADEQUACY OF ENGINEERING AND TRAFFIC SURVEY.

Introduction

Defendant is charged with a violation of the Basic Speed Law under the Vehicle Code. The citing officer used radar to measure the alleged speed of defendant's vehicle. This argument will show that the use of radar to enforce the posted speed limit, on the stretch of road where the defendant is alleged to have committed the violation, constitutes an illegal speed trap within the meaning of V.C. Section 40802. This is true even though an engineering and traffic survey that has been conducted within the five years immediately preceding the issuance of this citation purports to justify the speed limit.

The general rule regarding prima facie speed limits is that they must be set at or within 5 MPH below the speed at which 85 percent of the motorists travel, as indicated by the survey. The 85 percentile is the standard promulgated by the Department of Transportation under the direction of V.C. Section 627. This standard must be met unless there are special and enumerated conditions described in the engineering and traffic survey that justify a further reduction of 5 MPH below the 85 percentile. (See Traffic Manual, State of California, Department of Transportation, Chapter 8, Sections 1-2, and *People v. Goulet* (1992) 13 Cal. App.4th Supp. 1, 17 Cal.Rptr.2d 801.) Relevant portions of the TRAFFIC MANUAL are included in the Appendix to the Court's opinion in *Goulet, supra.* There are no appropriate conditions mentioned anywhere in the relevant survey that could justify a speed limit that is more than 5 MPH below the 85th-percentile speed on this particular stretch of road.

Since the posted speed limit is not justified by the survey, the use of radar to enforce that limit constitutes an illegal speed trap under V.C. Section 40802. Consequently, the citing officer herein is incompetent to testify in this matter under V.C. Section 40804(a). Further, this court is without jurisdiction to render a judgment of guilty in this action under V.C. Section 40805. As a result, the citing officer must be precluded from testifying in this action, and the matter must be dismissed.

Argument

I. WHERE THE POLICE UTILIZE RADAR TO ENFORCE A PRIMA FACIE SPEED LIMIT THAT IS NOT PROPERLY JUSTIFIED BY AN ENGINEERING AND TRAFFIC SURVEY, SUCH ENFORCEMENT CONSTITUTES AN ILLEGAL SPEED TRAP.

The California legislature has, as far back as 1923, declared a strong public policy against the maintenance of illegal speed traps by local municipalities. (See *People v. Sullivan* (1991) 234 Cal.App.4th Supp. 1; *People v. Halpoff* (1976) 60 Cal.App.3d Supp. 1; *People v. Goulet* (1992) 13 Cal.App.3d Supp. 1, 1-2.) One motivation behind this policy is to encourage universal adherence to speed laws by maintaining a highly visible law enforcement presence, rather than using clandestine enforcement techniques designed to punish a few motorists for violating the law. (See *Sullivan, supra,* at p. 60; *Halpoff, supra,* at Supp. 5; *Fleming v. Superior Court* (1925) 196 Cal. 344, 349; and *Goulet, supra,* at Supp. 2. See also V.C. Section 40800, requiring traffic enforcement officers on duty for that specific purpose to wear distinctive uniforms and to use vehicles with distinctive markings.) A further motivation behind this policy is eloquently described by the Court in *Sullivan, supra,* as follows:

Commentators have suggested that the Legislature was also motivated by a desire to eliminate clandestine methods of traffic enforcement designed to augment local revenues through exorbitant fines.

Id. at p. 59. (See also *Goulet, supra,* at Supp. 2).

The relevant definition of an illegal speed trap can be found in Vehicle Code Section 40802(a) and (b), both of which read:

[A speed trap is a] ... particular section of a highway with a prima facie speed limit that is provided by this code or by local ordinance ... if that prima facie speed limit is not justified by an engineering and traffic survey ... and where enforcement of the speed limit involves the use of radar ...

(See also *Goulet, supra,* at Supp. 13).

The "local streets and roads" exception to V.C. Section 40802 does not apply to the facts herein because the stretch of road relevant to this particular offense does not meet any of the criteria established under V.C. Section 40802.

Since the enforcement of the speed limit on this particular stretch of road involves the use of radar, and because a survey has been conducted, the primary issue here is whether or not the posted prima facie speed limit is legally and scientifically justified by the survey. In addressing this very same question, with respect to a different stretch of road, the court in *Goulet, supra*, stated that, "[a] speed limit is not justified by a survey unless the survey [itself] proves or shows the speed limit to be just and based upon a sufficient lawful reason" (Id. at Supp. 16).

Thus, an engineering and traffic survey conducted within five years is not, in and of itself, enough to demonstrate that the use of radar is not an illegal speed trap. As will be demonstrated below, the relevant speed limit must, by law, be set at or within 5 MPH below the speed at or above which 85 percent of the motorists travel on that road. There is an exception, however, when certain and definite conditions exist to scientifically justify an additional 5 MPH reduction and are actually and particularly described in the engineering and traffic survey. In any event, however, the prima facie speed limit must not be set below 10 MPH under the 85-percentile speed (*Goulet, supra*, at Supp. 24 n. 20).

A. In order for a prima facie speed limit to be justified by an engineering and traffic survey, it must be set at, or within 5 MPH below, the speed of which 85 percent of the motorists travel on that road, unless there are certain specific and enumerated conditions in the engineering and traffic survey that scientifically justify a lower speed.

The general rule regarding *prima facie* speed limits is that they must be set at speeds that will facilitate the orderly movement of traffic and that are also reasonable and safe. (See *Goulet, supra*, at Supp. 16, citing V.C. Section 22358.) Throughout this argument, defendant cites the *Goulet* case, which is a convenient summary of the law regarding traffic surveys. While it is true that the *Goulet* case is not binding authority outside of Ventura County, the law cited in the case itself, specifically, that which is found in the TRAFFIC MANUAL, is binding authority as a valid delegation of legislative authority.

As such, the TRAFFIC MANUAL has the force of statutory authority and is binding on the courts of this State. (See *Wilson v. Civil Service Comm. of L.A. County* (1964) 224 Cal.App.2d 340, ruling that legislative delegations of regulatory power speak with the force of law.) Vehicle Code Section 627(a) states that an engineering and traffic survey must comply with methods determined by the Department of Transportation. In accordance with the legislative delegation of authority in V.C. Section 627(a), the Department of Transportation has published a manual ("TRAFFIC MANUAL"). The TRAFFIC MANUAL details the methods by which such surveys shall be conducted, and, more importantly, describes the criteria that are to be used in determining what speed will achieve the goal of the general rule regarding prima facie speed limits as stated in *Goulet, supra*, and in V.C. Section 22358.

The court, in *Goulet, supra*, quotes the TRAFFIC MANUAL as requiring that:

Speed limits should be established preferably at or near the 85 percentile speed, which is defined as that speed at or below which 85 percent of the traffic is moving. … Speed limits below the 85 percentile are not generally considered safe and speed limits below the

85 percentile do not facilitate the orderly movement of traffic. Speed limits established on this basis conform to the consensus of those who drive highways as to what speed is reasonable and safe; [for purposes of V.C. Section 22350] and are not dependent on the judgment of one or a few individuals.

Id. at Supp. 17-18.

This standard is wholly consistent with the policies underlying the basic speed law and with the policies underlying the Legislature's prohibition against illegal speed traps. The court, in *Goulet, supra*, went on to quote the Department of Transportation's reasoning, as follows:

The basic speed law states that no person shall drive at a speed greater than is reasonable or prudent. The majority of drivers comply with this law, and disregard regulations that they consider unreasonable. It is only the top fringe of drivers that are inclined to be reckless and unreliable, or who have faulty judgment and must be controlled by enforcement. Speed limits set at or slightly below the 85 percentile speed provide law enforcement officers a means of controlling the drivers who will not conform to what the majority considers reasonable and prudent.

Id. at Supp. 18.

Consistent with Vehicle Code Sections 627(b)(2) and (3), there are two types of circumstances that will allow a municipality to set a speed below the Department of Transportation's 85 percentile standard, namely: (1) an unusually higher accident rate in comparison to a similar stretch of road, and (2) "highway, traffic, and roadside conditions not readily apparent to the driver." (See also *Goulet* at Supp. 24, n. 20, and TRAFFIC MANUAL at Section 1.) However, the Department of Transportation advises that any such reduction be done with caution, stating:

The establishment of a speed limit of more than five miles per hour below the 85 percentile (critical) speed should be done with great care as this may make violators of a disproportionate number of the reasonable majority of drivers.

Goulet, supra, at Supp. 19, citing TRAFFIC MANUAL.

In view of this fact, the TRAFFIC MANUAL only allows for a *further* reduction of an additional 5 MPH (for a total of 10 MPH) under the 85th-percentile speed where "engineering [judgment] may indicate…" the need (Id. at Supp. 33, citing TRAFFIC MANUAL). Thus, there is no authority or any engineering justification that will allow for a speed limit reduction of up to an additional 5 MPH (for a total of 10 MPH) below the 85 percentile speed.

In summarizing the TRAFFIC MANUAL and in review of the relevant Vehicle Code sections pertaining to the establishment of prima facie speed limits, the *Goulet* court lists the situations in which a prima facie speed limit is not justified by a survey. Id. at Supp. 24 n. 20. These circumstances are as follows:

... 1. The speed limit is set 10 or more mph under the 85th percentile speed; 2. The speed limit makes violators of a large percentage of drivers; 3. "conditions" listed are not hidden hazards, that is, they are readily apparent to a driver; 4. There is no explanation how the conditions listed require the speed limit set; or 5. The accident rate is not higher than would be expected statistically.

Id. (See also V.C. Section 22358.5, which forbids speed limit reduction for conditions such as curvature, which are, in fact, apparent to the driver.) It is not enough for the People to simply argue that such conditions exist based upon a conclusory statement of opinion regarding the need for a reduced speed that might appear in the survey. According to *Goulet*,

To support such a reduced speed limit, the survey must contain sufficient information to document other conditions not readily apparent to the driver.

Id. at Supp. 21.

This requirement is also stated by the Department of Transportation in the TRAFFIC MANUAL* in Section 2:

Whenever such factors are considered to establish the speed limit, they should be documented on the speed zone survey or the accompanying engineering report.

Id. Additionally, where an unusually high accident rate is used as a basis for a speed limit below the 85th-percentile figure, an actual statistical comparison must appear on the face of the survey (*Id.* at Supp. 21). In the words of the *Goulet* court, such documentation is "...not a mere technical nicety [.] ... the trial judge must determine *if the facts stated in the survey justify* the speed limit set." (Emphasis added) *Id.* at Supp. 22-23.) A trial judge cannot possibly make such a determination based upon mere conclusory opinions in the survey.

It is the prosecution's burden to prove that evidence of the defendant's speed was not obtained from the maintenance of an illegal speed trap (*Halpoff, supra*, at Supp. 7). This means that the prosecution must first prove that an engineering and traffic survey, *with the proper contents*, has been conducted within five years preceding the date of the alleged violation. *Id.* (See also V.C. Section 627 and V.C. Section 40803(b).) Under V.C. Section 40802(b), such contents include a *justification* of the posted, prima facie speed limit. It follows that the prosecution, having the burden of proving the absence of a speed trap, must prove that the posted speed limit is justified by the information contained in the relevant survey (*Halpoff, supra*, at Supp. 7); *Goulet, supra*, at Supp. 16. No such burden can be met without the inclusion of specific factual data that supports a conclusion that a reduction of the prima facie speed limit below the 85th-percentile speed is warranted (*Goulet, supra*, at Supp. 19, 23-24).

* The applicable portion of the California Department of Transportation's former Traffic Manual is now contained in its *Manual on Uniform Traffic Control Devices* (MUTCD).

Therefore, in order for a trial judge to evaluate the justification for a speed reduction and for the prosecution to meet its burden, there must be specific factual data, contained in the actual survey itself, which form the basis of any engineering opinions asserting a necessity for a reduction of the prima facie speed limit (*Id.* at Supp. 24). No such factual data appears in this survey.

Here, the speed limit is set at 25 MPH. This is 11 MPH below the 85-percentile speed, as indicated by the survey in question. There are no statistical comparisons on the face of the survey that would justify a reduced speed limit in light of unusually high accident rates. Further, there are no conditions not readily apparent to drivers that are listed on the survey (IF APPLICABLE: or the conditions listed relate to curvature or some other condition(s) that is (are), in fact, readily apparent to the driver).

(IF APPLICABLE: More importantly, given the fact that the speed limit is set at more than 10 MPH under the 85 percentile, it is, on its face invalid. As shown above, the court, in *Goulet, supra*, and the Department of Transportation in the TRAFFIC MANUAL, clearly mandate that such a major reduction will not be justified by any of the situations that allow for only an additional 5 MPH reduction (*Goulet, supra*, at Supp. 24 n. 20; TRAFFIC MANUAL at Section 2).)

Given these facts, the 25 MPH speed limit makes violators out of a disproportionate number of reasonable drivers, it does not facilitate the orderly movement of traffic, and it generates contempt for law enforcement and the courts. Consequently, such speed limit is not reasonable, nor is it justified by an engineering and traffic survey. Hence, the use of radar to enforce this speed limit constitutes an illegal speed trap under the definition of Vehicle Code Section 40802(b).

The importance of the Department of Transportation's 85th-percentile rule, and the Legislature's prohibition against illegal speed traps, cannot be underestimated. The *Goulet* court emphasizes this view, stating:

Traffic rules account for most of the contact by average citizens with law enforcement and the courts. Enforcement of laws that are widely perceived as unreasonable and unfair generates contempt toward those who make and enforce those laws.

Id. at Supp.

2. This sentiment, in the context of traffic enforcement, was also emphasized by the Court of Appeal in *People v. Kriss* (1979) 96 Cal.App.3d 913 at 921.

Citizens must obey the law. So should municipalities. It generates contempt for law enforcement when local governments use radar illegally to enforce unreasonably low speed limits. This is so particularly in light of this state's 71-year-old policy of enforcing speed laws by visible deterrence, rather than through punitive selective enforcement.

II. WHERE EVIDENCE OF A "SPEEDING" VIOLATION IS OBTAINED THROUGH THE MAINTENANCE OF AN ILLEGAL SPEED TRAP UNDER V.C. SECTION 40802(b), THE CITING OFFICER IS INCOMPETENT TO TESTIFY AT TRIAL, NO EVIDENCE OF THE SPEED OF THE VEHICLE MAY BE ADMITTED BY THE COURT, AND THE COURT IS WITHOUT JURISDICTION TO ENTER A JUDGMENT OF GUILTY AGAINST THE DEFENDANT.

A. Where any evidence of the speed of a vehicle is obtained during the maintenance of an illegal speed trap, the citing officer is incompetent to testify and no evidence of the speed of the vehicle may be admitted by the court.

Where as here, evidence of a speed violation is the fruit of an illegal speed trap, no witness is competent to testify in the case against the defendant, if such testimony is based upon the maintenance of an illegal speed trap (V.C. Section 40804(a).)

The People may attempt to avoid this prohibition by arguing that the officer's use of radar, in this instance, may have only been employed to augment his visual estimate of the vehicle's speed. Their conclusion, then, would be that while evidence of the radar reading could be excluded, the officer's visual estimate of defendant's alleged speed must be admitted. Hence, a demurrer is inappropriate on this possibility. This conclusion is clearly in error and there is a substantial amount of authority to the contrary.

This state's Legislature and our courts have emphatically rejected the above argument. Vehicle Code Section 40803(a) explicitly states that:

No evidence as to the speed of a vehicle ... shall be admitted in any court upon the trial of a person in any prosecution under this code upon a charge involving the speed of a vehicle when the evidence is based upon, *or obtained from or by the maintenance or use of a speed trap* (Emphasis added).

Id. at Supp. 63.

In *Sullivan, supra,* the Court of Appeal for the Sixth District emphasized and upheld the broad and sweeping scope of the language of that statute, ruling:

We believe [that Section 40803(a)] ... pertains not only to a radar reading obtained through maintenance of a speed trap but also to the independent observations of the officer operating the speed trap.

Id. at Supp. 63.

In *Goulet, supra,* the court specifically rejected the argument that visual estimates of speed could be allowed even where a radar reading is required to be excluded:

We conclude that such a distinction is in error. ... Sections 40802, subdivision (b) and 40803, subdivision (b) and both apply "where enforcement involves use of radar." These sections do not say that they apply *only* where enforcement is *exclusively* based on radar (Emphasis added).

Id. at Supp. 8-9.

Most recently and directly on point, the court, in *Hutchinson v. City of Sacramento* (1993) 17 Cal. App.4th 791 at 798, restated the rule that *all* evidence regarding the speed of a vehicle that is obtained during the maintenance of an illegal speed trap must be excluded.

Thus, even if it were true that the officer's radar reading was used only to confirm a visual estimate of the vehicle's speed, V.C. Section 40803(a) and the cases construing it, clearly require the exclusion of any such estimate the officer might have made while maintaining an illegal speed trap. (See also V.C. Section 40801, which flatly prohibits the use of a speed trap for "securing evidence" for prosecutions under the Vehicle Code.) Also, the officer is "incompetent as a witness" under these circumstances (V.C. Section 40804(a)).

Given these authorities, and in light of the arguments in Part 1 above, it is clear that all evidence regarding the speed of defendant's vehicle herein must be excluded. As a result, the prosecution will not be able to introduce *any* evidence to prove its case.

B. Where any evidence of the speed of a vehicle is obtained through the use or maintenance of an illegal speed trap, no court has jurisdiction to render a judgment of conviction for a speeding offense.

Vehicle Code Section 40805 states that a court is without jurisdiction to render a judgment of conviction for speeding where the court admits any evidence secured in violation of Sections 40800 through 40808. This section clearly incorporates V.C. Section 40801, which prohibits the maintenance of an illegal speed trap to secure any evidence related to a vehicle's speed—even if that evidence is a visual estimate that is merely confirmed by a radar reading. (See also *Sullivan, supra,* at 63; *Goulet, supra,* at Supp. 8-9; and V.C. Section 40803(a).)

This application of the evidentiary issues as well as the jurisdictional question is supported by a substantial amount of authority, which is summarized by the court in *Goulet, supra:*

As in this case, *People v. Peterson* (1986) 181 Cal.App.3d Supp. 7 [226 Cal.Rptr. 544] and *People v. DiFiore* (1987) Cal.App.3d Supp. 26 [243 Cal.Rptr. 359] applied the speed trap sections to cases in which officers also testified to visual estimates. (See also *People v. Sullivan, supra,* 234 Cal.App.3d at pp. 60-62.)

Id. at Supp. 14.

Clearly, then, it matters not whether the officer was utilizing radar to augment a visual or other estimate of speed, or whether the officer relied solely on the radar reading. The fact is that an officer's use of radar where the speed limit is not properly justified by an engineering and traffic survey invokes both the evidentiary and jurisdictional provisions of V.C. Section 40800 *et. seq.*

C. The "Right to Truth-in-Evidence" provision contained in the California Constitution does not abrogate any of the statutory remedies for violations of speed trap rules contained in V.C. Sections 40800 through 40808.

For a time, the "Right-to-Truth-in-Evidence" provision of the California Constitution (Art. I, Section 28(d)) was argued to have abrogated the exclusionary provisions of the relevant Vehicle Code sections pertaining to speed trap evidence. (See *People v. Munoz* (1992) 11 Cal.App.4th 1190, 1191, n. 1.) This argument, and the cases accepting it, were emphatically rejected by the Legislature in:

> ... [T]he adoption of section 40808 by Statutes 1992, chapter 538, section 2. The measure passed the Senate 35 to 0 and the Assembly 57 to 3, both well in excess of the two-thirds majority required by Proposition 8.

Goulet, supra, at Supp. 27.

Today, V.C. Section 40808 is still effective and explicitly exempts the speed trap evidentiary exclusions from Proposition 8:

> Subdivision (d) of Section 28 of Article I of the California Constitution shall not be construed as abrogating the evidentiary provisions of this article.

V.C. Section 40808.

As has been shown in Part I above, the officer's use of radar to measure the speed of defendant's vehicle, or even merely to confirm any supposed visual estimate of that speed, constitutes the maintenance of an illegal speed trap under V.C. Section 40802. This is so because the prima facie speed limit of 25 MPH on the road in question in this case has been set below the 85-percentile speed, without lawful justification for this reduction being contained in the relevant survey.

Conclusion

Since the prosecution will not be able to introduce any evidence as to the speed of defendant's vehicle, and because the court is without jurisdiction to render a judgment of conviction in this case, there is no plausible legal theory on which the prosecution could argue for the defendant to be convicted of the charged offense. Consequently, defendant must be found not guilty.

Respectfully submitted,

DATED: March 15, 20xx

Darla Defendant

DARLA DEFENDANT,
Defendant in Pro Per

of 25 mph, more than 5 mph below the 85th percentile speed of 32 mph, and there is nothing specific in the survey regarding accident records or road hazards not readily apparent to the driver. I have prepared a brief on this issue, which I would like to submit to the court." [Hand it to the clerk, with a copy to the officer or prosecutor.] *"Since the survey does not justify the posted speed limit, the area is a speed trap under Section 40802(b), radar (or laser) evidence is not admissible, and the officer who used radar (or laser) is incompetent as a witness."*

In summary, in a Basic Speed Law case involving the use of radar, remember the following:

- If the officer begins to testify about radar without producing a traffic survey in court, you should object to his testimony;

- If the survey is produced, but you never received a copy of it in response to your Informal Discovery Request, object to its consideration by the court as unfair, and argue it should be "precluded";

- If no survey is produced, or if one is produced that either was not conducted within five years (seven or ten years in some situations; see Chapter 4) of the date of the alleged violation, or if the survey does not justify the speed limit as indicated above, if radar or laser was used, then a "speed trap" was involved. You should object to testimony of radar or laser under VC § 40803(a), to the officer's testimony about any matter, since he is incompetent as a witness under VC § 40804, and you should state that under VC § 40805, the court is "without jurisdiction" to convict you of a speed violation in such circumstances.

Finally, the judge might say that a 1991 appeals court decision (*People v. Sullivan* (1991)

234 Cal.App.3d 56, 285 Cal.Rptr. 553) has removed the requirement that the prosecution produce an engineering and traffic survey in radar speeding cases. This is untrue. The *Sullivan* case was later invalidated by the 1992 enactment of Vehicle Code § 40808, which legally excludes speed-trap evidence, despite the "truth-in-evidence" provisions of Article I, § 28(d), of the California Constitution. Be prepared to make that argument if necessary. (In *People v. Munoz* (1992) 11 Cal.App.4th 1190, 15 Cal.Rptr.2d 21, a different court ruled that even before 1993, when VC § 40808 became effective, the 1992 passage of that law was important enough to convince the court that the *Sullivan* case no longer validly stated the law.)

Hearsay Evidence in Aircraft Speed Detection

In situations where an officer in an aircraft radios your car's speed and description to an officer in a patrol car, the patrol-car officer cites you for going at a speed he may not have personally observed. When tickets given in this type of situation are contested, both officers have to show up in court—the one who issued the ticket, and the one who determined the speed, without whose testimony the first officer's evidence would be insufficient. Be prepared to object to such evidence as hearsay if one officer starts testifying about something the other officer—who isn't also in court—told him.

This type of hearsay testimony may take any one of the following forms:

1. The ground-based officer testifying as to what the aircraft-based officer told him your speed was; or

2. The aircraft-based officer testifying as to his knowledge of the distance between highway markings on the ground (by which he calibrated his aircraft speedometer); or

3. Either of the two officers testifying by written statement.

Be ready to object to any evidence of this kind as "hearsay."

Officer Reading From Notes

As we saw in Chapter 10, police officers usually make notes on the back of their copies of the citations they issue. They do this so that later, if there is a trial, they can be specific about what happened. But it is technically improper for the officer to simply read directly from his notes (or from any other document) while testifying in court, unless he first follows several important procedural steps. (Lawyers call this "laying a proper foundation." See Evidence Code § 1237.) The officer must first testify that:

- he can't remember all the details of the violation

- he recorded them shortly after issuing the citation, and

- he needs to refer to them to refresh his memory.

Because most people who get tickets never object to note reading, most officers don't know how to follow these "foundation-laying" technical procedural steps. If the cop at your trial does not lay the proper foundation, you can object as follows:

> "Objection, Your Honor; the witness is clearly reading from a writing, and he has not laid the proper foundation for the use of a writing under Evidence Code Section 771 or 1237. He has not testified as to whether he needs to refer to the notes to refresh his recollection. In any event, I have the right to inspect any writing the officer will use or has used under those sections, and I ask the court to instruct the witness to show me the writing, while he lays the proper foundation."

In all likelihood the judge will simply tell the officer to lay the proper foundation as outlined above and, if he succeeds (sometimes with coaching from the judge), proceed with his testimony, using the notes. But you should try to get the notes away from the officer so that he can't just keep reading them. You want to show the judge that the officer either can't remember the incident he cited you for, and is just reading from his notes, or that the officer's memory is such that he needs the notes to refresh his memory. When you see that the officer is peering down at notes, you should object that the officer is reading notes you haven't seen and politely request that you should be allowed to see them. (Under Evidence Code Section 771, you have a right to see any notes a witness uses to refresh his or her memory.) At that point, the judge should direct the officer to hand the notes to you. Don't give them back unless the judge tells you to do so.

If the judge does tell you to give the notes back to the officer, you should politely remind the judge that under Evidence Code § 771, you're entitled to see if the officer has an independent recollection of the incident without looking at his notes, or if he needs them to refresh his recollection. The judge should then require the officer to testify without the notes, unless the officer admits he has "no independent recollection" and needs to refer to them.

Sometimes the judge will attempt to "coach" the officer and help him or her lay the proper foundation for using the notes; if so, you should politely object to the court's assuming the role of prosecutor by asking "leading" questions. If the judge begins to coach the officer, you should object by saying:

> "Objection, Your Honor; with all due respect, it appears as though the court is assuming the role of prosecutor in conducting direct examination of the

witness, which is prohibited by the California Supreme Court's ruling in People v. Carlucci *(1979) 23 Cal.3d 249, 259. Also, and again with all due respect, the Court is also asking improper leading questions on direct examination. I again ask the Court to instruct the witness to lay a proper foundation for the use of the writing."*

If the judge "overrules" your objection, you have won two important things:

1. You have gotten to read the officer's notes, if you had been denied that right before trial;

2. You can claim in your closing argument that the officer has a poor memory for events, and can't really contradict any evidence you present, which should, of course, raise a reasonable doubt as to your guilt.

If you are nevertheless found guilty, you may be able to use a judge's improper rulings as ammunition in an appeal to a higher court. (See Chapter 16.)

If the officer lays a foundation by testifying that he cannot adequately recall the events leading up to the citation, and that his notes will refresh his recollection, you can allow him to look at the notes. But then he must testify from memory. (You may have to remind the judge of this fact with another objection.) In order for the officer to read from his notes, he will have to lay a more complicated foundation, namely that he can't remember the circumstances of the violation, but he wrote them down correctly at that time (Evidence Code § 1237). However, it is not very likely that an officer will tell the truth on this point, by admitting that he doesn't remember anything about the circumstances.

Assuming Facts Not in Evidence/ Lack of Personal Knowledge

Another favorite and improper ploy that officers use while testifying to initially seeing your vehicle is to say something like, *"I saw the defendant's vehicle …."* Here the officer is improperly tying you (the defendant) to what he initially observed by looking at a vehicle, which may or may not have been yours.

The proper way for the officer to testify is that he observed "a vehicle" (rather than "the defendant's vehicle") commit a violation, and that he then pulled over that vehicle and identified you by asking you to produce your driver's license and noting the license photograph looked like you. When, however, you allow the officer to shortcut the process by testifying that he observed "the defendant's" vehicle, you've allowed him to improperly establish that you were the driver of the wayward vehicle the officer says he saw.

An objection on this basis is appropriate if:

- there is some question as to whether the vehicle the officer initially saw was really the one you were driving, or

- you simply want to fluster the officer a bit, and bring him down from his lofty, self-assured perch.

In many situations, making this objection is not frivolous. There may really be some doubt about whether the offending vehicle the officer observed was yours, especially if the officer saw it from a distance or in poor light. For example, when an officer on the freeway first sees a speeding vehicle, it is often a half mile or more away (and at night he may really see no more than the offending vehicle's tail lamps). And if the offending vehicle is small—a compact car or a motorcycle—the officer may have periodically lost sight of it behind a bigger vehicle. This of course raises the possibility that the ticketed vehicle was the wrong one. Similarly, if there is a curve in the road, a hill, or even heavy traffic, the cop may have lost sight of the offending car and stopped the wrong one.

In objecting to the officer's "assuming facts not in evidence" or "lack of personal knowledge," you say something like this:

> *"Objection, Your Honor. This testimony assumes facts to which the officer hasn't testified. There is no evidence before this court as to who was driving the vehicle that this officer claims to have seen. The officer could not possibly have personal knowledge of the identity of the owner of a vehicle he merely saw traveling on the road. I move that his testimony not be considered."*

(Lawyers would ask that it be "stricken," but you may be better off sticking to plain English.)

Here the judge will probably do one of two things: "Sustain" (grant) your objection and then "strike" (disregard) the officer's testimony (by often saying something like, *"So stricken. Continue, Officer Jones"*). Or, the judge may ask the officer to "rephrase" his testimony (sometimes coaching him to say that he first saw the offending vehicle and then identified you).

Cross-Examining the Officer— Basic Strategy

After the officer finishes testifying, you have the right to ask him questions in order to get him to clarify his testimony or to bring out other facts. But be careful. Cross-examination can often backfire, because the person you're questioning has a lot of experience in testifying in court. The last thing you want is for the officer to elaborate and embellish his story.

Preparation is the key to successfully questioning (cross-examining) the officer—with an eye toward raising a reasonable doubt as to your guilt. You can ask almost anything you want, so long as the answer you're seeking is in some way relevant to your effort to prove you didn't commit a particular element of the violation or to some other valid defense. Develop your cross-examination step by step, beginning with the least important background questions and ending with the ones that go to the heart of your defense.

Note: Don't go fishing. If you don't have a specific reason to ask a particular question, don't ask it. Unfocused questions rarely result in answers that will help your case and they commonly give the officer a chance to repeat damaging facts likely to convict you. Also, be sure your questions do not include an admission of guilt, such as, *"Where were you when I ran the stop sign?"* Instead, they should always be noncommittal, such as, *"Where were you when you claim you saw me run the stop sign?"*

The types of questions you'll want to ask in trials involving common traffic violations are listed in Section 3 below. If your situation is not covered, use what you learn here to develop a set of your own questions, designed to show how the officer could have been mistaken in his observations.

However, don't simply read through the questions below. Traffic judges and police officers have told us, over the years, that too many folks use this book almost mindlessly by droning on, reading each question one after the other, without any thought as to whether each question asked/read is designed to elicit any useful information. Instead, put some thought into it beforehand. Make a double-spaced list of questions you intend to use and bring that list with you to trial. Then, depending on the officer's testimony earlier in your trial, pencil in any necessary additions and changes. But remember, even after you ask a question, you'll want to retain as much mental flexibility as possible. That's because your next question should often be keyed to the officer's response. For example, if the officer's answer is evasive, be prepared to bear down with more specific questions until you either get the answer you want or force the officer to lie.

The best way to cross-examine is to ask specific—not open-ended—questions. For example, avoid questions such as, *"What happened then?"* or *"Why did you stop me, anyway?"* (The officer could seriously tarnish your defense by replying, *"Because you broke the law."*) Far better to ask questions such as, *"Isn't it true that there was a large hedge between your location and mine?"* (If the officer denies it, be prepared to confront him with a photo of that hedge.) Another good question is: *"Isn't it true you stopped me because of a radio report from an aircraft, and didn't determine my car's speed yourself?"*

Your goal in cross-examination is to show the judge:

- the officer's powers of observation were not perfect
- one or more legal elements of the particular offense are missing
- the existence of a defense, such as "mistake-of-fact" where you didn't know the stop sign was there until too late because the sign was obscured by trees
- the officer was doing several things at once, or
- the officer may have lost sight of your car between the time he observed the offense and the time he pulled you over.

Of course, you may occasionally get an unexpected answer. If you do, you'll have to rely on your broad understanding of the facts to decide whether to ask more detailed questions, or quickly switch to the next line of questions.

💡 **TIP**

It is almost always a mistake to adopt an antagonistic stance toward the officer. And it never makes sense to try to argue with him. Even if the cop answers a question untruthfully, or gives a ridiculous answer, it's your job to try to expose his fabrication by politely asking more direct questions, not by saying, "That's just not true" or "How could you tell such a whopper?"

EXAMPLE:

Your Question: *Officer, how far were you from my vehicle when you initially took your radar reading?*

Officer's Answer: *500 feet.*

Your Bad Response: *Officer, you know darn well that the radar beam width at that distance can't differentiate between vehicles in adjacent lanes. This whole deal is a sham.* (This is argument, and isn't allowed during the cross-examination phase.)

Your Good Response: (in the form of a second question) *Officer, you previously testified that your radar unit has a beam width of 12 degrees. Isn't it true that at 500 feet from your radar unit this means the beam will be about 100 feet across?*

Your Good Follow Up: *On the road where I was ticketed, aren't the individual lanes about 15 feet in width?*

Your Very Good Follow Up: *So, isn't a 100-foot-wide radar beam equivalent to the width of over six traffic lanes?*

Nonresponsive Answers

More often than not, when you ask the officer a good question—one to which a truthful answer might prove damaging to the prosecution—the officer will avoid answering directly. Another frequent annoyance is where the officer properly answers your question but then starts to give a speech. This can be unnerving—and it is improper. You may want to "rein in" the officer, showing him that you are in control of the examination. Also, you want to force the officer to answer the question directly, and stop him from giving unsolicited speeches that just bolster his side of the story. You can achieve this goal by raising the objection that the officer's testimony is "nonresponsive" to your question. (Evidence Code § 766.)

EXAMPLE:

You are testing a motorcycle officer's powers of observation by attempting to show that he was not wearing any eye protection while "pacing" your vehicle with his motorcycle. You are trying to establish that the wind, which was blowing into the officer's unprotected eyes, obscured his vision, so that he may have lost sight of the vehicle committing the offense, before pulling over your similar-looking vehicle:

Your Question: *"Isn't it true, officer, that you were not wearing any eye protection while you were riding your motorcycle on the day in question?"*

Officer: *"Well, I could see very well and the windshield on my motorcycle..."*

Here, you would interrupt the officer by saying:

"Objection, your Honor; that is nonresponsive. I move to strike the witness's answer, and ask the court to instruct him to answer the question as stated."

When the officer does answer your question, but starts giving a speech, you want to cut him off with the same objection. Using the above example, suppose the officer instead answers with something like, *"No, I wasn't; however, the windshield on my motorcycle..."* Here, you would interrupt saying, *"Objection, your honor; that is nonresponsive. The witness has already testified. I ask the court to instruct the witness to confine his answers to the questions directly put to him. I move to strike all of the testimony after his response regarding his eye protection."*

Here, the judge may or may not sustain your objection, depending on the particular context of the questioning. The judge may say something to the effect that the witness should be allowed to explain his or her answer. If the judge says this, just let it go.

Cross-Examination Questions to Test the Officer's Power of Observation

The basis for all citations for traffic violations lies in the perceptions of the officer. Thus, the more you can establish that there are some things he doesn't remember as to where, why, and how he stopped you, the more doubt you raise as to the truth of those parts of his story that seem to establish the elements of the violation. The following is a list of some of the types of general questions you might want to ask in order to test the officer's knowledge of the location and conditions where he observed you. Review these sample questions before trial, and leave out those that would be irrelevant in your case. Don't ask them in a boring, monotonous way either, lest you put the judge to sleep. Also, be prepared to leave out any questions that the officer answered in his initial testimony.

Sample Questions

1. *"Where were you located when you first saw my vehicle?"*
2. *"Where was my vehicle when you first saw it?"*
3. *"Was your car (or motorcycle) parked or moving at the time?"*

If parked:

4. *"Was your engine idling, or was it off?"* (If idling, you can later argue that he was already intent on stopping someone regardless of whether he saw a violation or not.)

If the engine was off:

5. *"What did you do to start your vehicle?"*

6. *"Did you turn on your lights?"*

7. *"Did you use your two-way radio?"* (These questions are aimed at showing the police officer was too busy doing other things to watch you for more than a second before deciding you were speeding.)

8. *"Did you start your engine just before you saw the alleged violation, or while it was occurring?"* (If just before, you can argue in your closing statement that he made up his mind to stop you before he saw any violation. If during, he might have been too busy starting the engine to observe things very well.)

If moving:

9. *"In which lane were you traveling?"*

10. *"In which direction were you going?"*

11. *"How fast were you driving?"* (Leave this one out for speeding violations. You don't want the cop to say he had to go 90 mph to catch you.)

12. *"Did you have a clear view of the traffic on the road when you claim you observed the violation?"*

13. *"Was there any other traffic on the road other than your vehicle and mine?"* (Your goal here is to ask questions regarding the number and types of other vehicles on the road and their movements. The less he remembers, the better your later argument will be that he can't remember much of what happened that day. On the other hand, if he describes other vehicles in great detail, you may be able to later claim that he may not have observed your car accurately, since he was so busy watching everything else.)

14. *"Could you describe the make, model,*

or colors of the vehicles in front of your vehicle?" (They usually can't.)

15. *"Could you describe the make, model, or colors of the vehicles on either side of you?"* (Again, they usually can't. If they say they can, it's usually not in the officer's notes, and you can then ask about that.)

16. *"How fast was the flow of traffic?"*

If slower than your vehicle, ask:

17. *"Did you see my vehicle passing any others?"*

Note: Here is an example of how you should use the cop's answers to frame subsequent questions. If he says you passed other vehicles, ask him for specifics (type of vehicle, color, make). He probably won't remember. If he says other traffic was slower than you, but also has said you weren't passing other vehicles, he's contradicting himself and you'll want to point this out in your closing argument. If he says he was traveling at the same speed as, or faster than your vehicle, your over-the-limit (but under-65) speed might have been safe, and therefore legal. (See Chapter 4 on the "Basic Speed Law.") Follow up with questions on this point, such as those listed below. If he says there was no other traffic, again, your under-65-mph but over-the-limit speed might be considered to have been safe under the circumstances.

If you're charged with violating the Basic Speed Law (Vehicle Code § 22350), you can ask:

18. *"Do you consider yourself to have fairly well-developed powers of observation and memory for details concerning weather and road conditions?"*

Then, ask the officer about every possible detail and hazard on the road, leaving out all hazards that were really there. This way his answers will make it seem like the roadway was pretty safe, or that he can't remember all the details. Road conditions you'll want to ask about can include:

- **Highway width.** *"Officer, isn't it true that there were two lanes in each direction?"*

- **Divider strips or islands.** *"Isn't it also true that there were divider islands present, so as to separate opposite directions of traffic? Isn't it true that this island minimizes the possibility of a collision with traffic in the opposite direction?"*

- **Sharp curves.** *"Isn't it true there were no sharp curves over the area you say you determined my speed?"*

- **Dips or hills.** *"Isn't it true there were no dips or hills over the area you say you determined my speed?"*

- **Railroad crossings.** *"There were no railroad crossings either, were there?"*

- **Road repairs in progress.** *"There were no road repairs in progress, were there?"*

- **Obstructions on the road.** *"There weren't any other obstructions in the road, were there?"*

- **Soft shoulders.** *"There weren't any soft shoulders that you saw, were there?"* (If the answer is yes, it probably isn't indicated in the officer's notes; if not, your next question should bear this out.)

- **Pedestrians, bicyclists, or animals in the road.** *"There were no pedestrians present, were there?"* (If he answers *"Yes,"* ask him to describe where they were and what they looked like. If it's not in his notes, he likely won't recall.)

Note: The more the officer says he can't remember, the better, since you can later use his poor memory to cast doubt on the accuracy of his testimony about your violation when you make your final argument. In this regard, it is often a good idea to ask questions you know the officer won't be able to answer. The best way to prepare to do this is to look at his notes beforehand.

Cross-Examination Questions for Specific Violations

The remainder of your cross-examination of the officer should be directed at undermining his testimony on the specific elements of the offense you are charged with, or getting him to admit circumstances justifying your violation. It follows that these cross-examination questions depend greatly on the violation charged. For example, in radar speeding cases, you might want to bring out the officer's lack of familiarity with his radar unit. But where you were cited for speeding after an officer paced your vehicle with hers, it would make no sense to make this inquiry.

Note: Don't read the questions out of this book. Ask questions that really apply to your case. Hopefully you'll be able to fine-tune some of the ones you find here, but, if necessary, be prepared to start from scratch. For example, don't ask the officer about high-voltage power lines affecting radar readings unless you really can show there were nearby high-voltage lines.

Speed Violations in General

The following questions deal with how the officer measured your speed. (See Chapter 4 for more on measuring speeds.) The officer will undoubtedly testify as to the method he used. It will then be up to you to cast doubt on the accuracy of his claims through cross-examination.

Visual Speed Estimation

If the officer estimated your speed only through visual observation, without pacing your vehicle or using radar or laser, ask questions like these:

1. *"Over what distance did you see my vehicle travel?"* (If the officer says it was short— or you can introduce evidence such as the location of a hill, curve, or traffic lights

proving it was short—you can later argue he couldn't have arrived at an accurate speed estimate.)

2. *"Did my speed change after you observed me?"* (If he says you slowed down after you apparently saw his car, you can later argue that the original high estimate was good only over a tiny distance and, therefore, inherently unreliable. If he says your speed suddenly went up or down, ask him to explain exactly where. Few officers have that good a memory, a fact you may be able to use in your final argument to cast doubt on the accuracy of the officer's other observations. (See the end of this chapter, for more on how to make a closing argument.)

3. *"Was my vehicle traveling toward you, away from you, or across your line of vision?"* (Perhaps you can say, in closing argument, that it is more difficult for the officer to estimate the speed of vehicles moving in a more or less direct line toward or away from his, than if vehicles are traveling across his field of vision. Do this only if you can later introduce evidence, during the prosecution of your case, on this point.)

4. *"Have you ever participated in controlled tests where you were asked to estimate vehicle speeds?"* (Most officers will say no—a point you can bring up on your closing argument. If the officer says he has participated in such tests, ask whether he always guessed the exact speed correctly. If he says *"Yes,"* he's obviously lying—no one is that good; if he says *"No,"* you can later point out that he admitted how difficult it is to estimate correctly.)

Speed Estimated by Pacing Your Car

If the officer's estimate of your speed was based on his looking at his own speedometer while following or "pacing" you, the following questions are usually helpful. (Also see Chapter 4, where we discuss possible defenses to tickets based on pacing.)

1. *"Over what distance did you follow my vehicle at a steady rate of speed?"* (The shorter the distance, the better your argument that he made an inaccurate reading.)

2. *"Was the distance between your car and mine always constant?"* (If he says *"Yes,"* he may be mistaken, since eventually he almost surely had to close in on you to pull you over. What he wants to say is that the distance was the same over the entire time you were being paced, at which point he sped up to stop you.)

If he seems to deny that at some point he speeded up, follow up with questions like these:

3. *"Did you observe your speedometer while you were following me?"*

4. *"How many times did you observe it?"*

If he says he was watching it almost constantly, follow up with a question like this:

5. *"When pacing at a constant speed is it important that you watch the subject vehicle continuously?"*

If he says *"No,"* you can follow up with a question like this:

6. *"If you don't watch a vehicle continuously during pacing, isn't it possible to lose track of the car you are pacing and focus on a similar looking vehicle?"* (If the officer continues to deny the need to look at the vehicle continuously, move on and attack his methods in your closing statement. See Chapter 4 for more on pacing.)

7. *"Was there other traffic?"* (Ask only if there was.)

8. *"Which lanes were the other vehicles in?"*

9. *"Can you describe any of the other vehicles by make, model, or color?"*

10. *"Were you paying attention to the other traffic in order to drive safely?"*

11. *"How often did you observe my vehicle?"*

If he testifies that he was watching his speedometer carefully, and testifies in detail to other traffic on the road (he may do this to try to impress the judge), follow up with:

12. *"So you were watching my vehicle, other traffic, and your speedometer all at the same time?* (If he says no, he was mostly watching your vehicle, ask, *"And you were watching other traffic too, correct?"* (Then, during your closing argument, you can argue that he was mostly watching your car and others, without much time to glance down at his speedometer.)

13. *"How far behind my vehicle were you while you were pacing it?"*

If he was pacing from more than a few hundred feet back, ask:

14. *"Do you agree that the ability to pace depends on good depth perception, so that you can follow at a constant distance?"*

15. *"Do you also agree that the farther away an object is, the more difficult it is to pace it?"* (If he says no, ask him which is more accurate—a pace at 100 feet, or a mile behind.)

16. *"Have you recently participated in controlled tests where you paced a vehicle a known speed from (whatever distance he claims to have paced you)?"* (The answer will almost always be "No.")

If at night or dusk, ask:

17. *"Officer, you paced my vehicle at night (or dusk), correct?"*

18. *"Would you agree it's harder to keep a constant distance, in order to conduct an accurate pace, at night (or dusk) than in the daytime?"*

He should agree. If not, continue with questions like this:

19. *"Isn't it harder to accurately pace at night, when you can see only two tail lights, as opposed to driving in the day when you can see the whole car body?"*

In attacking the accuracy of his speedometer, you can ask:

20. *"How long before you cited me was the speedometer in your patrol car (or motorcycle) last calibrated?"* (If the officer tries to simply say, *"It was accurate,"* he's bluffing, and you'll want to ask him to "Please answer the question." If the officer's vehicle's speedometer hadn't been calibrated recently, this is definitely a fact you'll want to use as part of your final argument.)

21. *"Did you bring a record of the most recent speedometer calibration with you today?"* (He often won't.)

22. *"Are you aware that speedometer accuracy is affected by tire circumference?"* (He will probably say *"Yes."*)

23. *"Are you also aware that tire circumference is affected by tire pressure and wear?"* (Again, he will probably agree.)

24. *"Then isn't it fair to say that speedometer accuracy is affected by tire pressure and wear?"* (He may try to hem and haw, but eventually should concede the point if you repeat the question.)

If he just doesn't seem to get it, ask this next question:

25. *"If you had such tires on your car, the odometer would erroneously read high, correct?"*

26. *"Were your tires' pressures checked when your speedometer was calibrated?"* (Probably not.)

27. *"Were they checked on the day you cited me?"* (Probably not.)

28. *"Are you aware that a tire's air pressure depends on its temperature?"*

29. *"Have the tires on your patrol car been rotated, or have any of them been changed since the last speedometer calibration?"* (See Chapter 4 for more on tire-wear and pressure problems.)

Speed Detected From Aircraft

Where your car's speed was detected from an aircraft, your cross-examination should shed doubt on the speed the officer determined for the aircraft (and therefore your car as he followed you), the officer's knowledge of distance between highway markings (based on hearsay?), his identification of your vehicle, and the patrol car officer's having picked out the right vehicle from among other traffic. Here are a few sample questions:

1. *"Officer Aircop, you used a stopwatch or other timing device to time the passage of the aircraft between the two highway markings, correct?"*

2. *"Isn't it true that you timed the passage of the car over a fixed distance?"* (The answer will always be *"Yes."*)

3. *"Did you actually measure the distance between the highway markings on the ground?"* (The answer should be *"No,"* at which point you should ask the judge to *"strike"* his previous testimony. Simply

say, *"Your Honor, I move to strike the officer's testimony as to the speed of the vehicle, since it was based on a distance-divided-by-time, which distance was not within this officer's personal knowledge."* If the judge strikes the testimony, you have won your case, as there is no other evidence of your speeding. If the judge refuses, you must, regretfully, move on.)

Note: If the officer in the aircraft simply timed the passage of your vehicle between two highway markings—as opposed to following you (from above)—after using the markings and a stopwatch to determine the aircraft speed, he has used an illegal speed trap prohibited by Vehicle Code § 40802(a), and you should ask the judge to dismiss the case. In practice, though, most officers know this and won't admit to this.

4. *"Did you watch my vehicle that whole time without looking away?"*

If he says *"Yes,"* ask:

5. *"Did you have a stopwatch and a log to read my speed?"*

If he answers *"Yes,"* ask:

6. *"Didn't you look down at them and write log entries?"*

If *"Yes,"* ask Question 7 below. (The point you want to make in the next two questions is that the officer was doing many things, including looking at a stopwatch and log, and watching many cars, so that he could easily have lost sight of a particular car.)

7. *"Did you report other vehicles for speeding at or near that time?"*

8. *"How many cars were you monitoring?"*

9. *"How much time passed between the time you calibrated the speed of the aircraft, and the time you paced my vehicle?"*

10. *"If a headwind had slowed the aircraft after you timed its passage between the highway*

markings, wouldn't you have had to again time your passage between the markers to determine your speed relative to the ground?"

11. *"Did you do that?"*

12. *"Are you certain the wind speed did not change during this time?"* (The answer will almost have to be "No.")

13. *"To determine the aircraft speed, what reference point on the aircraft did you use to check the aircraft passage over each line?"* (Usually it will be a wing or wing strut.)

14. *"How far was that object from you?"* (Usually ten to 15 feet.)

15. *"If you had moved your head forward or backward while observing your reference point passing the first or second marker, the elapsed time on your stopwatch would be incorrect, isn't that so?"* (If he denies this, ask him to hold up a pen at arm's length against a distant object in the courtroom about 20–30 feet away. Then ask him to move his head one foot forward or back while holding the pen steady. Finally, ask if the pen doesn't seem to line up a few feet off. The shorter the distance between the two reference points on the highway, the more significant this type of error is—over long distances it won't affect the reading of your speed enough to matter.)

Additional questions to ask the air officer, which can be used with either speed measuring method:

16. *"When you identified what you say was my vehicle, you didn't read a license plate, did you?"* (This can't be done from 500 feet in the air.)

17. *"You didn't radio down the make or model of vehicle, did you?"* (Only ask this if the air officer's log doesn't mention this. It

often won't, since they often can't tell this from 500 feet up either.)

If there was other traffic:

18. *"Were there other vehicles on the highway?"*

If he answers *"Yes,"* ask:

19. *"Could you describe the other vehicles by make or color?"* (If he can't describe the make and model of your vehicle or other vehicles, you can question his memory in your final argument and raise the possibility that he stopped the wrong vehicle.)

20. *"Did you report other vehicles for speeding, along with mine?"* (If the officer answers *"Yes,"* you can argue that his attention was divided among several vehicles, opening up the possibility that he was confused and mixed up your safe speed with another car's speeding.)

Questions for the Ground Officer

Only ask these questions if Officer Aircop says he radioed Officer Groundcop.

21. *"Officer (Groundcop), isn't it true you were first alerted to my vehicle only because of the radio report from Officer (Aircop)?"*

If he says *"Yes,"* and the ground officer in the patrol car didn't testify he paced you after hearing the report from the air officer, ask:

22. *"So then, your knowledge of the vehicle's speed was based solely on the radio report, correct?"* (If he says "Yes," you should ask the judge to "strike" his testimony because it is based on "hearsay," what the air patrol officer told him through the radio. Even if the judge denies your request, you should argue in your closing statement that the officer who actually ticketed you was acting on second-hand information, which is inherently unreliable.)

Speed Estimated by Radar

If the officer used radar to measure your speed, use some or all of these questions. Your goal is to show:

- He doesn't really know how radar works;

- He was not careful about maintaining his unit's accuracy;

- The speed he measured may not have been your vehicle's.

 CROSS-REFERENCE

For more on radar, please read Chapter 4.

Only ask these questions if the officer did not show you the radar readout at the time you were stopped.

1. *"Does your radar unit have a control that allows you to "lock in" the targeted vehicle's speed onto the readout?"*

If yes:

2. *"Did you show your unit's speed to me when you stopped me?"* (Assuming the answer is *"No,"* claim in your final argument that because he could easily have shown you your speed, there must be some reason he chose not to do so.)

3. *"Could you please describe briefly how speed-determining radar works?"* (If he can't do this—or gets it wrong—consider using this admission as part of your final argument.)

4. *"Isn't it true that delicate and sensitive electronic measurement instruments such as radar units must be calibrated often to make sure they're accurate?"*

5. *"Did you calibrate your unit immediately before and after you measured my claimed speed?"* (Usually the answer will be *"No,"* as radar officers typically calibrate only at the beginning and end of their shifts.)

If no, use this point in your final argument. If yes, ask:

6. *"How exactly did you calibrate the unit?"*

If he says he turned on the unit's "calibrate" switch:

7. *"You mean, you didn't use a tuning fork?"*

8. *"Doesn't the radar unit's manufacturer recommend calibration with a tuning fork?"*

9. *"Isn't a tuning fork, certified as accurate by a testing laboratory, a better way to check the unit's accuracy than using the unit's own internal electronics, which may be faulty?"*

If he says he used a tuning fork:

10. *"What was the certified speed for the tuning fork you used?"*

If it's much different from the speed he says he clocked you at—for example, 25 mph, but your car clocked at 60 mph—follow up with:

11. *"Isn't it true that tuning-fork-checked accuracy at one speed is not a guarantee of accuracy at a different speed?"*

12. *"When was the tuning fork itself last calibrated by an independent testing laboratory?"*

13. *"Do you have a certificate of accuracy for this particular tuning fork?"*

No matter what calibration method was used:

14. *"Has your radar unit ever malfunctioned in any way?"* (A *"No"* answer is an obvious lie.)

If he says no, ask:

15. *"Then it's never been repaired, or taken to the shop, as far as you know?"*

If he says it hasn't, ask:

16. *"You mean, not even for routine maintenance?"*

17. *"What's the maximum range, in thousands of feet, of your radar unit?"*

Note: At this point, you can calculate the approximate width of the beam at the end of its range by using the formula: beam width (feet) = 17.4 x maximum range (thousands of feet) x beam width (degrees). [This is derived as follows: At low angles, the sine or tangent of an angle approximately equals the angle, in "radians" (6.28 or 2 x π [3.14] "radians" = 360 degrees of arc). Therefore, the angle (in radians) about equals the beam width divided by the distance. Or, the beam width about equals the angle (in radians), multiplied by the distance. If we use degrees (360 in a circle) instead of radians (only 6.28 in a circle), we must multiply by 6.28/360 (about 0.0174). If we use thousands of feet for distance, the overall conversion factor becomes 17.4.]

18. *"What is the beam width of your radar unit in degrees?"* (Don't settle for an answer in "lanes." As discussed in detail in Chapter 4, the beam width will get longer the farther the unit is from your vehicle, and you want to emphasize this point. If he doesn't know the beam width in degrees, ask him how much wider the beam gets for each hundred or thousand feet of distance from the radar unit. Be prepared to quickly calculate the beam width at the maximum range, so you can follow up with this question:)

19. *"So then, at the maximum range, where you can still determine a target's speed, the width of the beam is about* [calculate here] *feet, isn't it?"*

20. *"Isn't that much wider than one lane of traffic?"*

21. *"Isn't this wide enough to reflect beams from other nearby vehicles or even a low-flying aircraft or nearby trains?"* (Obviously, only use this last part if you were cited near railroad tracks or an airport.)

22. *"When you aim your radar unit at a nearby object, your unit's antenna will pick up signals reflected from other more distant sources, won't it?"* (He may say *"Yes,"* but that the unit is made to track the strongest reflected signal.)

If so, follow up with:

23. *"Did you know that a more distant, but larger, vehicle may reflect a stronger signal than a smaller nearby vehicle?"*

Only ask the next four questions if it was windy the day when you were cited:

24. *"Have you ever obtained what turned out to be a false speed reading by aiming a radar unit at, for example, another vehicle, or a tree blown by the wind?"*

25. *"And if those surfaces are in motion, they can cause a false reading on a radar unit, can't they?"*

26. *"Isn't it true that windblown tree limbs, or even leaves, can sometimes reflect radar signals so as to generate a false reading?"*

27. *"Even blowing dust or rain can sometimes do this, can't it?"*

28. *"Do you know what a harmonic frequency is?"*

29. *"Are you aware that harmonic frequencies of nearby radio transmissions, for example from CB sets, can cause false radar readings?"*

30. *"Did you know that electrical interference from nearby power lines or transformers, or even high-voltage neon lights, can generate false radar readings?"*

31. *"When you estimated my vehicle's speed, were you first observing my vehicle with your eyes, or were you using your radar unit to determine this?"*

If the officer was looking at your vehicle:

32. *"So, then, you had already assumed I was exceeding the speed limit before you took a radar reading?"*

If the officer was looking at the radar unit:

33. *"So, you had already formed an opinion of my speed before looking up at my vehicle?"*

34. *"Could a completely untrained person use your radar unit accurately?"* (The answer should always be *"No."*)

35. *"Could you please describe the training you've had in the use of radar?"* (Many officers will try to pretend that a radar unit salesman's two-hour pep talk they probably received on how to use a particular radar unit was an intense "seminar.")

36. *"How long ago were you given this training?"*

37. *"How long did the training last?"*

38. *"Was this training conducted by a salesperson for the radar-device company?"*

39. *"Did you have supervised 'hands-on' instruction out on the road?"*

40. *"Have you participated in any tests where you used radar to measure a vehicle's speed, then were told the correct speed?"* (Almost never; if he says *"Yes,"* try to get him to give precise details.)

Speed Estimated Using Laser

 CROSS-REFERENCE

For more on lasers read Chapter 4.

In your cross-examination of an officer who used a laser gun to estimate your speed, you want to bring out the following points:

- The officer doesn't really know how laser works;

- The laser unit might not have been aimed and used correctly.

1. *"Officer, how does laser work?"* (This is harder to describe than radar, and the officer may not do a good job.)

2. *"Isn't it true that the laser unit works by measuring distances, using the speed of light and the time it takes a reflected beam to return, between the laser unit and the target vehicle?"* (The officer will probably agree that it sounds right.)

3. *"How many distance measurements does it make in a second?"* (He probably won't know.)

4. *"Isn't it true that the laser unit emits three separate light beams? And that each beam hits a different spot on the target vehicle?"*

5. *"And isn't it also true that when you aim the laser unit to get an accurate reading, you must aim it at the same part of the target vehicle during the entire time of the measurement?"*

6. *"Isn't it also true that if, over the measurement period, you first aim it at the passenger area, then move the gun slightly so the beams hit the hood, that at least part of your measurement will take into account the five or so feet difference between those two points?"* (If he admits this, you can later argue in your closing statement that this caused an error. See Chapters 11 and 12 on "closing arguments.")

7. *"Have you read the instruction manual for this unit?"*

If *"Yes,"* ask:

8. *"Doesn't it refer to this type of possible error?"*

If the cop seems confused, follow up with:

9. *"Was it possible you made this type of error?"*

10. *"Was there other traffic in my direction?"* (Ask only if there was—a point you can make in your testimony if he doesn't admit it.)

11. *"Isn't it also true that if one of the three beams reflected off a vehicle near mine, going at a different speed, and another beam reflected off my vehicle, your laser gun would have produced an incorrect result?"*

12. *"And isn't it possible, if you're, say, a quarter of a mile away, and an adjacent car going in my direction passed me, that one of the three beams might have hit my car, with the others hitting the second car?"*

Especially if he says this is unlikely, follow up with:

13. *"But isn't it true that the possibility of this type of error is also mentioned in your instruction manual?"*

Speed Measured by a Stationary Radar/ Laser, Visually Estimated First

Officers often testify that they visually estimated your speed and then used stationary radar (or a laser) to measure your speed more precisely. If the officer testifies to this, ask the officer the following three questions:

1. *How many feet were you from my vehicle when you visually estimated its speed?*

2. *How many feet were you from my vehicle when you first took the radar (or laser) reading?*

3. *How many seconds elapsed between these two events?*

Using the answers the officer gives you, subtract the distance from question 2 (feet from the vehicle when radar reading was taken) from the distance in question 1 (feet from vehicle when speed was estimated), and divide the result by the number of seconds in question 3 (time elapsed between the two events). The resulting number will give you a speed, in feet per second. If you divide this number by 1.47 (1.5 is close enough), this should give your speed in miles per hour; if that result is less than the speed the officer says you were going, in closing argument you can argue to the judge that by the officer's own testimony, either the officer's visual estimates or the radar/laser reading was faulty.

EXAMPLE 1:

As Stan Speedo cross-examines Officer Olsen, the officer testifies that: (1) he was 500 feet away when he first visually estimated Stan's speed at 65 mph (in a 50 mph zone), and (2) 300 feet away when he first took a radar reading of 63 mph, and that (3) about 3 seconds elapsed between these two events. So, Officer Olsen is really saying that Stan drove 200 feet (500 feet – 300 feet) in 3 seconds, or 200 feet ÷ 3 seconds, or 67 feet per second. To convert feet per second to miles per hour, divide by 1.47. So, 67 ÷ 1.47 = 45 miles per hour. Later, in his closing statement, Stan can argue that according to Officer Olsen's testimony and some pretty simple math, he was really doing 45 mph, well within the 50 mph speed limit.

EXAMPLE 2:

Francine Fast cross-examines Officer O'Malley, who testifies that: (1) she was 500 feet away when she first visually estimated Francine's speed at 60 mph (in a 50 mph zone), and (2) 200 feet away when she first took a radar reading of 59 mph, and that (3) about 2 seconds elapsed between these two events. She's saying Francine traveled the difference in distance, 300 feet, in 2 seconds, or 150 feet per second, which, divided by 1.47, gives a speed of 102 mph. Later, in her closing statement, Francine can argue that she couldn't have been going 102 mph, so the officer's observations were faulty.

"Basic Speed Law" (VC § 22350) Questions

If you were cited for going over the posted speed limit but under the maximum speed limit of 65 mph (55 mph on two-lane undivided highways), it's still possible to be acquitted if you can show that it was safe under the conditions at the time to drive at a higher-than-posted speed. This doesn't mean you have to admit you were going over the limit—just that it would have been safe to do so.

In preparing your cross-examination questions, start by thinking of the actual road, traffic and weather conditions when you were cited. Then use this information to edit and fine-tune the following questions. For example, if it was raining or foggy, the less said about the weather, the better. Also, don't ask about traffic conditions if traffic was fairly heavy (unless you believe you can use this information to cast doubt on whether the cop paced, or radared, or lasered the right car). Similarly, it usually makes sense to ask next about highway conditions if you were ticketed on a two-lane winding, hilly road.

Here are some sample questions:

If the traffic was light:

1. *"Was there a lot of traffic in my direction?"*
2. *"How many vehicles were there in my lane?"*
3. *"How many were behind me?"*
4. *"How many were in front of me?"*
5. *"Can you describe them by make, model, or color?"*
6. *"What was the average distance between vehicles?"*

The point of many of the following questions is to establish that it was safer to exceed the limit in order to keep up with the flow of traffic around you.

7. *"Was I ticketed at rush hour?"*
8. *"Was most of the traffic going at about the same speed you say I was going?"*
9. *"Did you see my vehicle pass any others?"* (Don't ask if you did pass other vehicles.)

If he says *"Yes,"* follow up with:

10. *"Could you describe the vehicles I passed, by make, model, or color?"* (He probably can't—a fact you may be able to use later in your final argument to cast doubts on the accuracy of his testimony.)

Then, only if he says you weren't passing other cars, ask:

11. *"So then, it's true that I was going slower than, or at least at the same speed as, the other traffic?"*

Ask all the following questions that fit in an effort to show that even if you did slightly exceed the speed limit, it was safe to do so.

If there was no rain:

12. *"Was the road pavement dry?"*

If there was no fog or rain:

13. *"Was the visibility good?"*

If it was a clear day:

14. *"Was the sun shining? Were clouds obscuring the sun?"*

If you were cited at night but visibility was good:

15. *"Are there street lights along this stretch of road?"*
16. *"Were the lights on?"*

If the road had at least two lanes in your direction:

17. *"How many lanes did the road have in my direction?"*

If the road was divided by a median or barrier:

18. *"Did the road have a divider or barrier down the middle?"*

If there were no intersections near where you were cited:

19. *"Were there any intersections nearby?"*

If there were intersections but all were controlled by stop lights:

20. *"Were there any uncontrolled intersections nearby?"*

If there were no blind curves:

21. *"Were there any sharp turns in the roadway?"*

If the road was flat:

22. *"Were there any hills obscuring the view from the roadway?"*

If there were no pedestrians:

23. *"How many pedestrians were in the area?"*

24. *"Were any pedestrians crossing the road? Trying to cross?"*

TIP

Don't forget to make these points in your testimony. If the road, traffic, and weather conditions really were good, the above line of cross-examination questions should help your case. But remember, the best time to convince the judge that you really were driving safely is when you present your testimony along these lines. But if you can get the officer to agree that traffic was light and road conditions were good, you'll certainly want to refer to his statements in your final argument as part of your claim that the officer agreed with your description of conditions.

CROSS-REFERENCE

See Chapter 5 to review the most common defenses to traffic light violations.

Running a Stoplight (VC § 21453)

The defense to this one is usually fairly straightforward. Since it's legal to enter an intersection on a yellow light, the main job of cross-examination is to cast doubt on whether the officer accurately observed that the traffic light was red when the front of your car drove across the "limit line" or cross street.

1. *"Did you see my vehicle at the time the green light first turned to yellow?"* (If he says he didn't, then he could have seen you only a few seconds before he says you ran the red light, creating at least doubt as to his ability to see something happen so fast.)

2. *"For how many seconds does the yellow light stay on?"*

If he says he doesn't know how long the yellow light was lit, follow up with:

3. *"Can you estimate how long the yellow light was lit?"* (If he still won't volunteer an answer, you can contend in your final argument that his powers of observation weren't that good.)

It can pay to know more than the officer. Of course, you should always time the light so you know the answer. That way, if the officer guesses too brief a duration for the yellow light, you can follow up by asking the questions below:

Questions related to your speed

Only ask these if you weren't speeding, and if the ticket itself and the officer's notes are silent about this point. The point here is to show that if you were going the speed limit, the duration of the yellow light was too short to allow you to come to a complete stop before the yellow light turned to red. Believe it or not, traffic signals are not all timed to allow a proper stop given the speed limit (see below after question 7).

4. *"In your opinion, was I traveling at or near the speed limit?"*

5. *"What was that speed limit?"*

6. *"How many feet from the intersection was my vehicle when the green light turned yellow?"*

7. *"What is the normal stopping distance at that speed limit?"*

Once the officer testifies as to your speed and location when the light turned yellow, you will want to make a quick calculation with a pocket calculator. Multiply the speed in miles per hour by the number 1.47, giving your speed in feet-per-second. (One mile per hour is 5.280 feet per hour, or 5,280 feet per 3,600 seconds—60 seconds for each of 60 minutes in an hour—or 5,280/3,600 feet per second, or 1.47 feet per second.) Next, divide this number into the number of feet he said you were from the intersection when the light turned yellow. This will give you the number of seconds you had to enter the intersection before the light turned red. If this number is less than the number of seconds the yellow light was on (based on your timing or the officer's estimate) then you would have entered the intersection while the light was still yellow. You can introduce your timing test during your own testimony and refer to it in closing arguments.

If the officer was on the cross street (at right angles to the one you were on), he probably assumed that when he saw the red light change to green, the yellow light had changed to red in your direction. If this seems to be the case, ask:

8. *"Could you see the color of the light facing me from your location?"* (If he says *"Yes,"* stop here.)

But if he says *"No,"* ask:

9. *"Why do you say I entered the intersection on a red light if you couldn't see my light?"* (He will undoubtedly say because his light went green.)

10. *"You mean you assumed my light turned from yellow to red at exactly that time?"* (He will most likely answer "Yes.")

11. *"Did you promptly examine the signal to determine whether the light in my direction was properly synchronized so as to turn red when the one in your direction turned green?"* (Very few officers check the lights for synchronization. If the officer did not, you can contend in your final argument that it sheds doubt as to whether the light was really red when you entered the intersection. This argument is bolstered if you can also establish that the officer was not in a good position to see exactly when you entered the intersection. If you have established this, you should hit this point hard in your closing arguments.)

If the officer was at an angle that would have made it difficult to observe, you might ask this:

12. *"Isn't it true that you couldn't see the color of the signal facing me from where you were?"*

Tactics When Automated Enforcement Devices ("Red Light Camera") Are Used

A new twist in defending against red light tickets has occurred in recent years with the introduction of photographic "automated enforcement systems," also known as "red light camera" devices. These consist of a camera triggered by vehicles passing over a sensor in the intersection when the traffic signal is red. The camera takes pictures of the vehicle's front license plate and the driver. A Notice to Appear is then mailed to the vehicle's registered owner, supposedly after a police officer checks the photo of the driver against the driver's license photo of the registered owner.

Though these systems are legal throughout California (Vehicle Code §§ 21455.5–21455.7, 40518, 40520), the law says that the driver, not the vehicle's registered owner, is liable for the ticket. If the owner was not driving the vehicle when the pictures were taken, he can fill out a Declaration of Nonliability (included with this kind of Notice to Appear), stating this under penalty of perjury. The form requires the registered owner to reveal who was driving the vehicle. However, the law does not specifically require you to "snitch" on the real driver. (Where the form asks you for the driver's name, some people write "decline to state" or even "not me!"). Even if you do list the true driver, the worst that will usually happen is that he or she will receive what some people call a "snitch ticket," without the court's address, which is only a bluff, to which, unfortunately, many people respond and pay fines. The difference between a "snitch ticket" which you can legally ignore, and a real ticket, is that a real ticket will tell you to contact the court, giving a real address, whereas a phony "snitch ticket" will not tell you to contact the court, and may even say, "Do not contact the court," or words to that effect, saying only to contact the police department.

TIP

Want to know more about "snitch tickets"? Visit www.highwayrobbery.net for more information.

The first step to take in fighting a ticket issued by a red light camera device is to get the photographs by serving an Informal Discovery Request (see Chapter 10), if copies of the pictures weren't already included with the Notice to Appear that was mailed to you. (Many police departments automatically mail you copies of such pictures taken by the device.) When you get the pictures, examine them to see if the picture of the driver bears any likeness to you or your driver's license photo, and whether the license plate number can be read clearly.

At a trial, the prosecution must present evidence on how the device works, and that it was working properly on the day the particular citation was issued. The prosecution must also present photos showing the vehicle's license plate, the driver, and the driver's license photo of the registered owner.

If the images are clear, you can consider mounting the following defense: If no employee of the company that maintains the red light camera device shows up to testify, you should object to the photos being admitted into evidence, saying, *"Your Honor, since no one has appeared to authenticate the photographic evidence, I object to such evidence for lack of foundation."* If the photographs are excluded, there is no evidence to convict you. (On the other hand, if the judge allows the photos in evidence over this quite proper objection, you may later have a basis for an appeal if found guilty—see Chapter 16.) If the judge allows the photographs into evidence, you might then concentrate on claiming that the photo of either the license plate or the driver (or both) is unclear.

If a company employee does appear at your trial, object as follows: *"Your Honor, I object to the introduction of the photographic evidence, as the witness has not testified that he personally took the photos, or saw them being taken, so there's no evidence of authentication."* Again, if the photographs are excluded, there is no evidence to convict you. We think, however, that if the employee testifies as to how the device works, and that it was properly working on the day you were cited, most judges will overrule this objection. (Still, it's worth a try, because some judges are hostile to this technology and thus might look for an excuse to rule against it on some ground.)

If the photos are allowed into evidence, but the images are not clear, you can consider challenging the photo's clarity, arguing that it is not clear enough to legally convict you. You can say, *"I submit there is a reasonable doubt as to whether the driver of that vehicle is in fact me."* You should not agree to testify unless you can truthfully say that you were not driving the vehicle at the time the picture was taken. (After all, it sure doesn't help you to admit you know you ran the light, and saying you *"don't remember"* isn't really testimony that you didn't run it.) If you choose not to testify, and the judge nevertheless asks you whether it was your car or whether you were the driver, you can reply, *"Your Honor, I respectfully decline to testify, and I ask that you dismiss, for lack of proof beyond a reasonable doubt, that I was driving the vehicle at the time."*

If the duration of the yellow light preceding the red light was too short, the case may be dismissed. Under VC § 21455.7, yellow light durations must be in accordance with California Department of Transportation (CalTrans) *Manual on Uniform Traffic Control Devices* (MUTCD) § 4D-11 and Table 4D-102.

The table below shows the minimum yellow light duration for the posted speed limit. You may want to go back to the intersection, find a safe place to stand (or legally park), and time the yellow light duration with a stopwatch. Take at least five readings and average them, also noting the location, date, and time. Better yet, have a friend do it—as long as your friend agrees to testify at trial for you. If the yellow light duration is less than that required in the table below, you should be prepared to testify to that effect and to ask for a dismissal based on VC §§ 21455.5(a)(2) and 21455.7, which require the yellow light duration to "meet the criteria" set by CalTrans in the MUTCD.

Even if the yellow light duration is at least as long as required in the table below, you may want to check the city's engineering and traffic survey used to set the speed limit on that street. Such surveys typically note an "85th percentile" speed (the speed that 85% of the traffic does

Table 4D-102. Minimum Yellow Light Change Interval Timing	
Posted Speed (miles per hour)	**Minimum Yellow Interval (seconds)**
25 or less	3.0
30	3.2
35	3.6
40	3.9
45	4.3
50	4.7
55	5.0
60	5.4
65	5.8

California MUTCD, Page 4D-50. If you decide to use this chart in court, you may want to print it out directly from the California MUTCD. You can find it on the CalTrans website, currently at www.dot.ca.gov/hq/traffops/signtech/mutcdsupp/pdf/camutcd/CAMUTCD-Part4.pdf

not exceed), which traffic engineers use to set realistic speed limits. In some cases, city governments impose low speed limits but the 85th percentile speed is quite a bit higher than the posted speed limit. If the 85th percentile speed is at least five miles per hour (mph) over the posted speed limit, then calculate the minimum yellow light duration based on the nearest five-mph increment posted speed in the table above. *If the actual yellow light duration is less than the corresponding recommended yellow light duration, you can argue that the 85th percentile speed should apply because traffic engineers—being concerned about safety rather than city revenue—want to take actual speeds into account.* If the yellow-light duration is shorter than that corresponding to the nearest 85th percentile speed in the table above, you should ask for a dismissal under VC §§ 21455.5(a)(2) and 21455.7.

Another possible defense is that of missing or non-visible posted signs that are supposed to warn of "photo enforcement." Such signs must "clearly indicate the system's presence, and [be] visible to traffic approaching from all directions," or be posted "at all major entrances to the city, including, at a minimum, freeways, bridges, and state highway routes." (VC § 21455.5(a)(1)) Find out if and where such signs are posted. If signs are not clearly visible at all intersection approaches, *and* also do not exist at all freeways, state-highway, and bridge city entrances, take photographs that show the lack of signs and be prepared to show the photos at trial.

There are other defenses as well. For example, the city might not have issued only warnings notices for a camera's first 30 days of operation, as required by VC § 21455.5(b). The law appears to state that this is a defense, even if you were not one of the persons cited within the first 30 days. In fact, a recent court case (People v. Fischetti, 2008) found that the 30-day warning period applies to each photo-enforcement camera, as it is installed.

This 30-day warning requirement, as well as the yellow light duration compliance requirement and photo-enforcement warning sign requirement, are "foundational," meaning that the city, or prosecution, being more likely than you to be in possession of this type of information, has to produce testimony or other evidence on these points as part of its case. If any of this evidence is missing from the prosecution's case, namely (1) yellow light duration compliance, (2) posting of warning signs, or (3) issuance of only warning notices for the first 30 days of a camera's operation, you should move to dismiss for "lack of foundation" at the close of the prosecution's case.

In addition, only a "governmental agency, in cooperation with a law enforcement agency,

may operate an automated enforcement system." (VC § 21455.5(c)) But some of the operational functions of the automated system may be, and generally are, contracted out to the private companies that supply and maintain the cameras. (VC § 21455.5(d)) Under this statute, city contracts with such private businesses may not contain clauses which pay the business "based on the number of citations generated, or as a percentage of the revenue generated," if the contract was made or renewed after January 2004. According to the excellent website on red light cameras, maintained since 2002 at www.highwayrobbery.net, a great many cities (all listed on the site) have such contracts, and their citations may be subject to dismissal on that basis.

In 2002, a San Diego judge dismissed 292 such tickets (*People v. John Allen, Et. al.*, San Diego County Superior Court No. 57927-SD) because $70 of each then-$271 fine (the fine is up to about $400 now) was paid over to Lockheed Martin, the camera provider. This legal issue is currently pending before the California Supreme Court in the case of *In re Red Light Photo Enforcement Cases*, Calif. Supr. Ct. No. D-048882, superseded court of appeal opinion at 163 Cal.App.4th 1314 (2008). Check www.highwayrobbery.net to see if your city is on the list of cities with clauses where payment to the private company is based on the number of tickets issued or convictions. If it is, go to City Hall and ask to see a copy of the contract, which is required by law to be publicly available. You may then wish to ask the judge to delay the trial until the California Supreme Court rules in that case.

Cities are now more aggressively using red light cameras to ticket for a relatively minor class of red light offense, namely failing to come to a complete stop on a red light before making a right turn, a violation of VC § 21453(b) rather than § 21453(a). Though running a red light is dangerous, failing to come to a complete stop at a red light before turning right is a lot less so, at least where the driver looks to make sure no traffic is approaching from the left. Even though no yellow light is usually involved with this type of offense, the yellow light and other defenses above apply to this offense as well.

TIP

More information is available online. If you're facing a red light camera ticket, visit www.highwayrobbery.net to learn more about fighting your ticket.

Running a Stop Sign (VC § 22450)

CROSS-REFERENCE

See Chapter 5 for more discussion on stop-sign defenses.

Defending this type of case almost always comes down to a choice between your claim that you stopped and the officer's assertion that you didn't. Here there are commonly only two defenses aimed at raising reasonable doubt:

- Whether you came to a complete stop behind the "limit line" or the imaginary line at the corner where a painted line would go;
- Whether there was a regulation stop sign controlling traffic in your direction.

Your questions of the officer will depend on where he observed you. If he testified he was on a cross street, or on the other side of the intersection, not at the entrance to the intersection, ask:

1. *"When you observed my vehicle, were there other vehicles in front of you?"*
2. *"How many?"*

3. *"Can you describe them by make, model, and color?"* (Unless his notes indicate, he probably won't remember the number of vehicles in front, or their descriptions.)
4. *"How far down the street could you see?"*

CAUTION

Don't cross-examine when a stop sign is hidden. As noted in Chapter 5, you can sometimes defend a stop-sign charge by claiming the sign was obscured. If that is your claim, it's probably best not to cross-examine the officer. That's because he will probably say he saw the sign clearly. Better to simply tell your story—backed up by a diagram and, if possible, a witness—when it's your turn.

Illegal Turns (VC §§ 22100–22106)

CROSS-REFERENCE

Illegal turn defenses are discussed in Chapter 5.

Here we look at a few questions you might ask when ticketed for an unsafe turn. Whether a particular driver is really guilty beyond a reasonable doubt of making an unsafe turn is usually a subjective judgment, unless there is a clearly visible sign absolutely prohibiting the turn. Therefore, you should ask the same sorts of questions you would ask for speeding in violation of the Basic Speed Law, in order to show that under real-world conditions your turn was done safely. The following questions should be helpful.

If the turn was at an intersection:

1. *"Was the intersection controlled by a traffic signal?"*
2. *"Did you see the color of the signal when I entered the intersection?"* (Unless the officer was directly behind you, he could not have seen the signal.)

3. *"Did I come to a complete stop in the intersection before turning?"* (Ask only if you did—it tends to show you were being careful.)

4. *"How many feet was the oncoming vehicle from me when I made the left turn?"*

5. *"How fast was the oncoming traffic moving?"*

Based on the answers to 4 and 5, the time you had, in seconds, to make the turn before being hit by the oncoming traffic is equal to the speed in number of feet the oncoming vehicle was from yours, divided by the speed of the oncoming vehicle, in feet per second. (Multiply the speed in miles per hour by 1.47 to get the speed in feet per second, then divide the distance in feet by that number.) If this works out to five seconds or more, you can later argue that there was plenty of time for you to turn safely.

6. *"Was my turn signal flashing?"* (Ask only if it was.)

7. *"For how long?"*

8. *"Did any vehicle blow its horn in response to my turn?"* (Ask only if none did.)

9. *"Did the oncoming vehicle slow down, in your opinion, because of my turn?"* (He will almost always answer "Yes.")

10. *"Did that vehicle screech its tires?"* (Ask only if it didn't.)

If the cop says *"No,"* you should ask:

11. *"Could the oncoming vehicle have slowed down because the driver was waving me to turn?"*

12. *"Isn't it true that many safe drivers slow down at intersections out of general caution, whether or not someone up ahead is turning?"*

Testimony Presented on Your Behalf

Defendants who know what to say and when to say it are far more likely to win than are defendants who just stand up and hope to tell a convincing story. In short, if you've come this far, you want to be well prepared. One big key to doing this is to carefully practice your presentation.

Although you're not required to testify, it's almost always a good idea. Judges won't admit it, but they generally assume that a defendant who tries to claim that the prosecutor hasn't proven her case, while at the same time asserting the Fifth Amendment right to silence, must be guilty. Or put another way, if you think you will be proven guilty by answering questions on the witness stand, it usually makes sense for you to go to traffic school. Even if the only reason you went to court was the hope the officer would not show up (but he did), you'll almost always do better by explaining your version of what happened as clearly, honestly and forcefully as you can than you will by clamming up. The only exception to this is when you know you committed the offense, and simply want to cast doubt on the prosecution's testimony that you did; it's perfectly legal to do that, but in that situation, you won't want to testify.

After you have practiced making your presentation enough times that you are getting pretty good, have a tough-minded friend or family member play the part of the judge. Ask them to try to poke holes in your case by occasionally interrupting your presentation with questions (many judges do this). Do this several times until you feel comfortable answering questions about your version of what happened and the evidence you present to back it up. When you are done, ask your skeptical friend for a verdict. If your friend convicts you, the judge is likely to do so. Keep practicing until you convince your volunteer judge that you are innocent.

One good approach to presenting traffic court testimony is to outline the key points you want to make on a note pad or file card well in advance of your court date (leave space between entries for later additions). Be sure your testimony establishes an adequate defense to the violation (for example, it clearly demonstrates you didn't commit at least one key element of the violation). Use your notes as you practice making your presentation. (It's fine to glance at your outline, but it is a mistake to simply read it.) Then in court, after you cross-examine the officer and learn new facts, quickly add to or edit your outline. This way, when it's finally your turn to testify, you should be prepared to tell a smooth and well-thought-out story.

For those who have never previously appeared in traffic court, it is a great idea to drop by and watch a few cases. Sure, this takes a couple of hours, but you are almost sure to learn more than enough to make this a wise use of the time. There is not enough space to provide sample testimony for every possible violation, but the following examples provide a road map to preparing your testimony, no matter what charge you face.

Unlike the prosecution, which has to prove all the elements of the offense, your testimony need only raise a reasonable doubt about just one element the prosecution has to prove. For example, with speeding violations, your best approach might be to establish that the officer's estimate of your speed was incorrect. With Basic Speed Law violations, you might want to establish that the speed the officer says you were going was safe. (Actually, your burden is only to establish a reasonable doubt as to whether your speed was unsafe. This is because,

under Evidence Code § 607, you need only "raise a reasonable doubt as to the existence of the presumed fact." Since the Basic Speed Law includes a presumption that you were driving unsafely if going over the "prima facie" speed limit—see Chapter 4—you need only raise a reasonable doubt as to whether you were driving at an unsafe speed.)

Preparing Your Witnesses

You have the right to present witnesses who were present and observed the situation that caused you to be ticketed. This will usually be someone who was in the car with you, but could be a pedestrian or the driver of another vehicle. But before you ask a potential witness to testify for you, you'll obviously want to be sure he agrees with your version of what happened.

If you have more than one witness, write down all their names. Then write a description of what each will say and how their testimony will help your case. Decide in what order they should testify to present a logical sequence of events.

CAUTION

Don't let a witness bend the truth. Occasionally a friendly witness will volunteer to stretch the truth on your behalf. Even though the crime of perjury is rarely prosecuted in traffic cases, lying is a bad idea. Aside from the moral implications of lying, a skilled prosecutor can expose even one small lie and it will usually destroy the credibility of everything else your witness says, even if much of it is true.

Witnesses who are organized and prepared are far more convincing than those who are neither. Start by acquainting your witness with the various legal elements of the case and the strategy of your defense. Her testimony should support one or more key aspects of it. Just as you did when you prepared your own testimony, have someone pretend to be the judge and have your witness practice her testimony several times. Incidentally, helping your witness prepare in this way is completely legal and routine. Every lawyer rehearses witnesses. In case the judge (or any prosecutor) asks your witness whether he has discussed his testimony with you, he should simply be prepared to say something like this: *"Yes, I was a little nervous and wanted to do a good job of telling the truth."*

It is also wise to put yourself in the role of a prosecutor, and ask the witness some tough cross-examining questions. We discuss how to cope with cross-examination in the section entitled, "Cross-Examination by the Prosecution," below. Have your witness read that section.

Explain to your witness that there's a possibility he will be asked to step outside the courtroom when you testify, in order to prevent him from adjusting his testimony to be consistent with yours (of course, to avoid this problem, you have the right to call your witness first, before you testify.) (You also have the right to insist on this, should two or more prosecution witnesses testify against you.)

Testimony for Specific Violations

Here are some examples of possible testimony for specific violations.

Exceeding Maximum Speed Limits (VC § 22349)

If you're charged with exceeding the 65 or 70 mph maximum speed limit (55 mph on undivided two-lane highways unless otherwise posted), you should focus your testimony preparation on arguing that you were not speeding at all. But you need to do more than simply say what your under-the-limit speed was; if you simply say you were going 64 mph and the officer testifies it was really 73 mph, the judge will almost always choose to believe the cop's version. However, there are some good defenses you can mount that could even the odds a little. In preparing your testimony, you should consider the following approaches:

- *"The officer didn't keep a constant distance between our vehicles when he 'paced' me. I could see him in my rearview mirror bearing down on me fast. It took him just a few seconds to close from about half a mile back to being right behind me, which is when he activated his lights. In fact, after glancing at my speedometer and seeing that I was going at the speed limit, I was convinced the officer was speeding to an emergency farther down the road. When I realized he was after me, I was genuinely surprised."*

- *"There was other traffic in my direction in front (or back) of me. The officer's wide radar beam could have hit the other traffic at the distance he was from me. Some of this other traffic was going faster."*

- *"The road wasn't straight. Visibility was poor due to curves and hills. He could not have seen me for the time necessary to determine if I was speeding, which I was not."*

- *"There were other vehicles similar to mine on the road at the time. One, the same make and color as mine, passed me. After the officer rounded the curve, he pulled me over by mistake."*

Here is example of how you might prepare your testimony in an "absolute" speeding case:

"When the officer stopped me for speeding, it was 5:15 p.m. I had just left work to go home. I wasn't in a hurry. I drive Highway

4 home every day and I know the speed limit's 55 mph. Just before Officer Kwota pulled me over, I had slowed going around a curve, because I needed to move from the left to the right lane, to prepare to turn right onto Market Street. I had to pause for a moment because another red 1995 Chevy Blazer, almost identical to mine, passed me in the right lane at a high rate of speed and exited at Market Street. By this time, I had slowed to about 35 mph because I was still trying to move over to the right. At this point, I saw Officer Kwota's car come around the curve in the right lane. I was going to wait to allow him to proceed past me before getting in the right lane, but, to my surprise, he got into the left lane behind me and turned on his emergency lights. After I pulled over, the officer asked me if I knew why he had stopped me, and I said, "No, I think you stopped the wrong car." I told him that a similar looking car had sped past me just after coming around a curve. He then asked me if I knew how fast I was going, and, not knowing where and when he was referring to, I said, 'somewhere between 35 and 50 mph'."

Notice how the testimony in these sections is specific and detailed. The more detail and specifics, the more convincing your testimony —a lot more convincing than simply saying, *"I wasn't speeding, man. I was doing 50. I was cool."*

"Basic Speed Law" Violations (VC § 22350)

When you're charged with going over the speed limit, but less than 65 mph, you can attack both the officer's estimate of your speed and attempt to show that a speed over the limit would have been safe. And you don't have to admit that you were going over the limit—that's for the prosecution to prove. After you testify as to what you thought your speed actually was, you might then point out that, *"even if I was going slightly faster than that, it was safe to do so because…"* As we say in Chapter 4, this claim should be backed up with testimony as to favorable road, weather, and traffic conditions.

Here you should focus your testimony preparation on arguing that you were not speeding, but that, even if you were, it was only a few miles over the limit in a situation where this was safe. But always start by understanding that unless it was obvious you were over the limit, your best approach is to admit nothing and make the prosecution prove it. (Assuming it's true, you can testify—in detail—that you were going at or below the limit.)

If you really were going slightly over the limit, you should consider making as many of the following points as fit your situation:

- *"Even if I was going slightly faster than 30 mph, it was safe to do so because:*
- *"There was very little vehicle or pedestrian traffic on the road."* (This is a particularly good argument if you can truthfully tell the judge you were ticketed at 6 a.m. or some other time when traffic is known to be light)
- *"There was little or no other traffic in my lane, in my direction"* (or in both directions) *"for at least a half mile."*
- *"There was no cross traffic or uncontrolled intersections."*
- *"There were several lanes in each direction and there was no one else even in my lane."*
- *"Even if I did exceed the speed limit, it was by less than 5 mph."*
- *"The road in question has an artificially low speed limit."* (Here, a picture of a wide, straight two-lane road with no traffic but a 25 mph limit might be convincing).

- *"The weather was clear (no rain, fog, hail, etc.)."*
- *"The road was dry."*
- *"The road was well lighted by regularly spaced street lamps."*
- *"There were no sharp curves, hills, dips, or other such 'natural' road defects requiring a slower speed."*

Here is one example of how you might prepare your testimony against charges of speeding with a "presumed" speeding violation:

"I'm sure I didn't exceed the speed limit, but even if I did, it must have been by a small amount. Certainly by the time I saw Officer Ticketem and checked my speedometer I was going right at the 35 mph limit. But even assuming I was going a little faster before that, it was very safe to do so. Please let me explain. I was in the left of two lanes in my direction, there was no traffic ahead in my direction—except for one vehicle that suddenly passed me on the right. The road is a four-lane divided highway, two lanes in each direction, and it was straight, and slightly downhill in my direction, so that I could see ahead for about a half mile. The next intersection, with Market Street, was about a quarter of a mile ahead, I could see the green light, and there was no cross-traffic waiting at the intersection. There were no pedestrians either. It was 6:45 p.m. in July, and most people were home eating dinner. It was still daylight, the weather was clear, and the road was dry. In fact, it was the kind of situation where even going 45 or 50 mph would have been safe, even though I wasn't going nearly that fast."

Running a Stoplight (VC § 21453)

When you're accused of running a red light, the issue is usually whether your vehicle entered the intersection after the light changed from yellow to red. To be guilty, the front bumper of your vehicle must have passed into the cross street after the light changed (see Chapter 5). In preparing your testimony, consider the following approaches:

- *"I was driving at (or below) the speed limit."*
- *"I was only several car lengths from the intersection when the green light turned yellow."*

Both of these defenses are based on the idea that the yellow light must last long enough for a car traveling at the speed limit to make it through the intersection before the light turns red. If you testify you were a few car lengths from the signal when the light turned yellow, you are, in effect, saying that you must have entered the intersection when the light was yellow, since you were so close.

- *"I looked up at the light and noted that it hadn't yet changed to red as my car entered the intersection."* (A diagram might be very useful.)
- *"I didn't think I could safely stop the car because I feared being rear-ended by someone tailgating me."*
- *"I proceeded through the yellow light cautiously."*

Here is one example of how you might prepare your testimony against charges of running a stoplight:

"I was driving at the speed limit, 35 mph on Warren Street. I know this because I looked down at my speedometer just as I began slowing to prepare to turn at the intersection with Maple Street. The green

light changed to yellow as I was only about two car lengths in front of the entrance to the intersection. So, I continued and the light was still yellow as my car crossed over the crosswalk and entered the intersection. As is my habit, I glanced up at the traffic signal overhead—which continued to stay yellow until it passed out of sight over the top of my windshield. At all times the cross-traffic heading in both directions on Maple Street was stopped, so my turn did not create a dangerous situation."

Be as specific as possible. Go back to the scene and attempt to determine the exact distance you were from the light when it changed from green to yellow (for example, maybe the car in front of you just turned into a gas station), the duration of the yellow light, and your car's speed. With the help of a diagram, based on the facts you present, you could argue that you only could have entered the intersection while the light was still yellow. If you show you were 100 feet away from the intersection at a gas station entrance—going 35 mph when the light turned from green to yellow—you can figure out how many feet-per-second you were traveling and prove you were well into the intersection before the light turned yellow.

Running a Stop Sign (VC § 22450)

The issue is simply whether you came to a complete stop behind the limit lines or entrance to the intersection. The more you go into detail about what happened while you were stopped, the more believable your testimony. Things like this, if true, might help:

- You saw the stop sign, slowed down, and came to a complete stop.
- You stopped behind the white limit lines painted on the road, or, if none, behind the entrance to the intersection.

- You noticed a slight amount of cross traffic, and inched forward a few feet for a better look at it, where you stopped again.
- You looked left and right, waited until it appeared safe, and drove forward.

A defense that occasionally works is that the stop sign was obscured and you couldn't see it until it was too late. Perhaps untrimmed tree leaves or branches obscured the stop sign. If you were unable to see it, you can argue that you made a reasonable "mistake of fact," and thus should be found not guilty.

Illegal Turns (VC §§ 22100–22106)

When you're accused of having made an "unsafe" or "hazardous" turn at an intersection, you might want to testify—to the extent you truthfully can—as follows:

1. The road had two or more lanes in your direction, you had to change lanes to turn, and you signaled and looked in your rear or sideview mirror before doing so;

2. You used your turn signal at least 100 feet (six to eight car lengths) before turning;

3. You had the right of way, either because the light was green for a left or right turn, or because you stopped on a red light before turning right;

4. You proceeded into the intersection cautiously, watching oncoming traffic if you were turning left, or for cross traffic from the left if you were turning right;

5. You came to a complete or near stop in the intersection (or at least proceeded cautiously) for a left turn, or at the entrance to the intersection for a right turn on a red light;

6. There was no oncoming traffic (for a left turn) within several car lengths of the other side's entrance to the intersection, or no cross traffic from the left (for a right turn);

7. Your turning movement was smooth, neither too sharp, nor too wide;

8. You finished your turn in the proper lane of the street you turned onto—the far right lane for a right turn, and the left or middle lane for a left turn.

Other Offenses

To list detailed summaries of proper testimony for all the offenses listed in Chapter 5 would take more space than would be justified. Generally, in order to outline your "direct" testimony for other offenses, the first step should be to carefully analyze the Vehicle Code violation you're charged with, breaking the offense down into its "elements." Then, try to plan your testimony—to the extent you can truthfully testify—around those elements. You should especially concentrate on any elements (for example, "posing a hazard," driving "unsafely") that call for a measure of subjective interpretation. Finally, outline your testimony.

Cross-Examination by the Prosecution

In regular criminal trials, where procedure is more formal than in traffic court, the prosecuting attorney gets a chance to cross-examine any person who testifies. This seldom occurs in most traffic court trials because infraction cases are usually prosecuted by police officers instead of prosecuting attorneys. A few judges give the police officer the opportunity to cross-examine, an opportunity most officers decline, if only because they're so sure they'll win without it. If the officer does try to cross-examine you or a witness, you might want to object on the grounds that he's not an attorney. It should be remembered that the officer doesn't really represent the state as a prosecutor.

He's only a witness there to tell his side of the story. A person can prosecute a case by cross-examining a witness only if he is a plaintiff (one who files charges) or a defendant, or the proper attorney. (You can cross-examine the officer because you're the defendant.) If you wish to object, say something like the following:

> *"Your Honor, I object to Officer Shultz cross-examining me on the ground that he is neither the true plaintiff nor its attorney—he's just a witness."* (If the judge suggests you're out of line, you might ask whether he will permit your nonattorney witness to cross-examine police officers.)

Assuming you or your witnesses have to respond to cross-examination questions, keep the following things in mind:

- Keep your cool—don't respond in an evasive, hostile, or argumentative manner.

- It's often wise to keep your answers to nondamaging questions short. The reason is so that you don't end up unnecessarily volunteering information that turns out to hurt your case.

- Although you can be told to answer *"Yes"* or *"No"* to a question, you have the right to fully explain any answer you give. It can be a good idea to do this if the prosecutor asks you a seemingly damaging question. For example, if you are asked whether you exceeded the 25 mph posted speed limit, you can answer *"Yes,"* but you have the right to add that doing so was safe because you were only doing 30 mph and no cars were on the road.

- Tell the truth. Obvious as this may sound, many people think they can get away with "stretching the truth." The last thing you'll want is for a judge or prosecutor to expose a lie (or even get you to retract a minor point). This is likely to happen when you are less than truthful in response to a question to which the prosecutor already knows—and can prove—the answer.

- If you don't know, say so. Many people are so afraid to admit ignorance that they trip themselves up, often needlessly. If your witness was talking and didn't notice whether two cars turned ahead of you on a yellow light (but can say you crossed the limit line when it was still yellow), make sure he knows it's okay to respond *"I don't know"* when he does not.

Final Argument

After you (and your witnesses, if any) have completed testifying, or after any cross-examination by the prosecution, you should have a chance to summarize your case. This is where you explain to the judge (or jury in a misdemeanor case) why there's a reasonable doubt as to whether you had committed at least one of the elements of the offense, and possibly also how you have proven a defense. Basically, you are reviewing and summarizing the main points you had been trying to make all along at trial. You can also argue points of law, citing cases or statutes that support your position.

Before trial, outline your final argument on a sheet of paper, but don't feel bound by it. Be sure your outline is flexible enough to include unexpected statements made by the officer during his testimony.

Unfortunately, many judges are quite narrow-minded about allowing traffic court defendants to "argue" their case in a closing statement. Such judges have developed the view that only lawyers are capable of understanding and making legal arguments, and will jealously try to keep everyone else out.

If the judge refuses to let you make your final arguments or cuts you off before completion, you should politely but firmly assert your right to make a legal argument. If he still refuses, or constantly interrupts during your attempt at argument, let it go. Better to let a hostile judge—who's going to rule against you, final argument or not—commit an error that might well get your conviction reversed on appeal. In the case of *People v. Douglas* (1973) 31 Cal.App.3d Supp. 26, 106 Cal.Rptr. 611, an appellate court reversed a conviction for running a stoplight because the traffic court judge refused to allow the defendant to argue his case. Also, see the U.S. Supreme Court case of *Herring v. New York* (1975) 422 U.S. 853, 95 S.Ct. 2550.

Trials Before a Judge (Without a Jury)

Introduction

Since jury trials are available only for misdemeanors and not for infractions, most traffic violations are heard before a judge alone. As a general rule, these judge trials are conducted relatively informally. However, if a prosecutor is present (usually in a misdemeanor case where you didn't ask for a jury or in the few places which still use prosecutors), the trial will be more formal. First we provide you an overview of each type of trial. Then we get into specifics.

Traffic Trials Without a Prosecutor (Infractions Only)

In traffic trials without a prosecutor, the clerk first calls the case and you and the police officer go forward. Before testimony begins, you may wish to make any of the last-minute motions (such as for continuance, dismissal, judge disqualification) that we discuss in Chapter 11, if you feel it's necessary. You can also "move to exclude" multiple prosecution witnesses from the courtroom while the remaining witness testifies.

The judge allows the officer to tell his side of the story in narrative form, perhaps asking a few questions afterward. You then should be given an opportunity to cross-examine the officer with relevant questions. Some judges may not remind you of this, but they must let you do so if you insist. At this time, you tell your side of the dispute, and any witnesses you have tell their version, after which the judge might ask a few questions.

Finally, the judge announces his verdict of guilty or not guilty. If he finds you guilty, he will usually pronounce sentence (a fine) right away, unless you ask for a postponement.

Nonjury Trials Prosecuted by a District (or City) Attorney (Misdemeanors and Infractions)

All misdemeanor cases are prosecuted by district or city attorneys. While trials in infraction cases almost always are prosecuted just by the officer, occasionally a prosecutor will appear. In such infraction cases, and in misdemeanor cases where the defendant has given up the right to jury trial, here's how the trial proceeds.

The clerk calls the case, and you and the prosecutor go forward. Again, this is the time to make any last-minute motions to request a continuance, a dismissal, a change of venue, the disqualification of the judge, and to ask for the exclusion of multiple prosecution witnesses from the courtroom.

The prosecutor, then you, are permitted to make opening statements summarizing what you each intend to prove. (These are often dispensed with in trials without a jury.)

The prosecution puts on its case by asking questions of its witnesses. After each prosecution witness testifies, you are given the chance to cross-examine her.

After the prosecution's witnesses have testified, you can give an opening statement, if you did not make one at the opening of the trial. But you must remember to tell the judge at the beginning of the trial that you want to "reserve" the right to make your opening statement when you present your case.

You also have the right to ask the judge to dismiss the case after the prosecution ends its case against you, if you believe the evidence is not strong enough to convict you. However, the judge may disagree. In that case, you can proceed to present your case in a narrative form. If a prosecutor is present, he has the right to cross-examine you and any witnesses you present. However, it is not proper for the police officer to ask you questions.

A prosecutor, then you, make the final closing arguments, summarizing the testimony and relating it to the applicable law. After your argument, the prosecutor can make another "rebuttal" argument. A police officer is not allowed to make a closing statement. The judge then announces his verdict. Unless you want to be sentenced right away, the judge will set a later time for sentencing.

Although the above formats are found respectively in police-officer-prosecuted infraction trials and D.A.-prosecuted misdemeanor trials, some courts are run more formally (or informally) than others. Each of these formats is discussed in greater detail below.

Understanding the Courtroom

Traffic court trials are generally conducted in standard courthouses in courtrooms that look much like those on television. In addition to the judge (or commissioner), a clerk and a bailiff will normally be present. They sit at tables near the judge's elevated bench, or slightly off to the side. The clerk's job is to keep the judge supplied with necessary files and papers, and to make sure that proceedings flow smoothly. In more formal trials, there also may be a court reporter present, who keeps a word-by-word record of proceedings. Such records are seldom kept for infraction trials.

Courtrooms are divided about two-thirds of the way toward the front by a sort of fence known as "the bar." The judge, court personnel, and lawyers use the area on one side of the bar, and the public, including people waiting for their cases to be heard, the other side. You are invited to cross the bar only when your case is called by the clerk. Then you come forward and sit at the long table, known as the counsel table, facing the judge. What happens next depends on whether yours is a formal or informal trial. In informal trials, your witnesses accompany you to the counsel table. At more formal trials, they remain behind the bar (as does the officer) and testify at the witness stand only when their names are called. In some informal traffic court hearings, you will be asked to raise your right

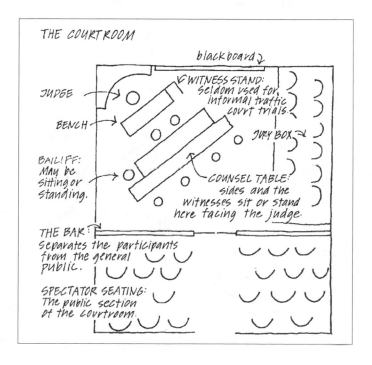

THE COURTROOM

blackboard

JUDGE

BENCH

WITNESS STAND: seldom used for informal traffic court trials.

JURY BOX

BAILIFF: May be sitting or standing.

COUNSEL TABLE: sides and the witnesses sit or stand here facing the judge.

THE BAR: Separates the participants from the general public.

SPECTATOR SEATING: The public section of the courtroom.

hand and swear to tell the truth before the judge arrives. In others, and in all formal trials, you or your witnesses will only be sworn in just before testifying.

In nearly all traffic court trials, you, your witnesses, and the prosecution will present the case from the long table; you do not sit in the witness box next to the judge. Many people feel that it is polite to stand while addressing the judge, but this is not a requirement and you should do what feels most comfortable to you.

Common Sense Note: Many people react to the negative experience they have had with our traffic court system by appearing hostile and angry in court. This sort of attitude, while understandable, is almost sure to be counter-productive. Judges are used to "lawyerly attitudes"—that is, to people who separate themselves emotionally from the cause they are arguing—and will often punish (decide against) people who make "a scene." A little conviction that you are right can be refreshing against this background of workaday cynicism, and can be very effective, but don't overdo it. As a general rule, judges have a low tolerance for emotion.

Also, when you address the judge, you should say, *"Your Honor."* Silly as it sounds, many judges have fragile egos, and are so used to being addressed this way that it grates on them to be addressed any other way.

Trial Procedure

This section takes you step-by-step through a traffic court trial, with information on your options at the various stages of the proceedings.

Note: Throughout this section, the terms "prosecutor" and "the prosecution" will be used as general terms referring to whoever is doing the prosecuting against you, whether that be the police officer or a district or city attorney.

Clerk Calls the Case

The trial begins when the clerk calls your case, usually by saying *"People v. [your name]."* The clerk (or sometimes the judge) might then recite the bare facts of the case, perhaps something like, *"You are charged with a violation of Sec. 22350 of the Vehicle Code—the Basic Speed Law—on October 24, 2004, by driving 45 mph in a 35-mph zone on the 400 block of Main Street in the City of Ventura."*

Last-Minute Motions

Before the prosecution begins its case, you might want to make one or more of the motions discussed in Chapter 10. These include requesting a continuance, disqualifying a judge, asking for dismissal (or to preclude testimony) based on the prosecution's failure to provide "discovery," asking for dismissal because of delay, and moving the trial to the county seat.

Lack of Prosecution (If the Officer Fails to Show Up)

Since you're presumed to be innocent until proven guilty, your case should be dismissed if no one is able to testify to your guilt—namely the officer. If the officer fails to show, you should ask the judge to dismiss the case "for lack of prosecution," perhaps complaining about how you've been severely inconvenienced by having to take time off work. Such requests are usually granted. They are denied, and the case postponed to another date, only where the officer has a very good excuse, both for not showing and not notifying the court beforehand—such as when the officer's wife had to be rushed to the hospital to give birth.

Disqualifying the Judge

If, when your case is called, you have decided you probably cannot get a fair shake from the judge, commissioner, or traffic referee, and the officer is present, this is your last opportunity to disqualify the judge by presenting a Peremptory Challenge if you haven't done so already. Simply say, *"Your Honor, I wish to file this Peremptory Challenge,"* and hand it to the clerk.

If the judge is a volunteer lawyer serving as "pro tem" judge, you do not need to do this. Simply tell him you don't consent to his hearing the case—if the officer shows. If the officer does not appear, you simply ask for dismissal.

Excluding Multiple Witnesses

Once in a while the prosecution will have more witnesses than just a police officer. In addition to freeway aircraft patrol situations involving two officers, this may happen if you encountered two police officers on patrol when you were cited. Also, if you were involved in an accident, other drivers or bystanders—in addition to the officer—may be asked to testify against you. Needless to say, it will work against you if each of the prosecution witnesses recites a similar version of the facts but a version different from yours. On the other hand, if the testimony of a witness is inconsistent with another's, it will help your case.

If the witnesses are allowed to stay inside the courtroom and watch each other testify, their stories may indeed become very similar. For this reason, you should make a motion to exclude multiple witnesses from the courtroom. Such a request will always be granted, and will mean that while any prosecution witness testifies, all others must wait outside.

Note: A "Motion to Exclude" works both ways. Any witnesses you have must also then wait outside while you or another testifies. (You can minimize this disadvantage by waiting until after they testify to give your own testimony; you can't be excluded from the courtroom because you're the defendant and you cannot be forced to testify before your witnesses do.)

Asking That a Reporter or Recorder Be Used

As we saw in Chapter 10, the case of *In re Armstrong* (1981) 126 Cal.App.3d 565 and PC § 19.7 work together to give an infraction defendant the right to insist that a court stenographer (reporter) be present to take verbatim notes of the proceedings, or that a tape recorder record them.

Hopefully, you requested a reporter or recorder in writing at arraignment, or at least a few weeks before trial, by filing the written request shown in Chapter 10. But even if you didn't, you can still make this demand at trial—if the officer shows up, of course. If you did make the demand but it was ignored, reiterate the demand by saying, *"Your Honor, I did file a request that a court reporter or tape recorder be present, and I do request that at this time again."*

Again, if the judge refuses, you might ask to be allowed to use your own pocket tape recorder, if you have one. The judge is required to allow that, absent a good reason, by Rule 980(c), California Rules of Court.

Requesting a Continuance If Your Subpoena Is Not Obeyed

If you've subpoenaed a witness for trial and that person does not appear, you should request a continuance—but only if the officer who cited you shows up. Also, if a person on whom you served a subpoena duces tecum ordering him to produce certain documents fails to do so, you can ask the judge to postpone the case and order that person to bring the requested material.

Opening Statements

Before testimony is presented, both the prosecution and the defense have an opportunity to make an opening statement, stating how they intend to prove each element of the case.

The Prosecution's Statement (Only in Trials Prosecuted by a Lawyer)

In trials prosecuted by the deputy district or city attorney, the prosecution may give an "opening statement," stating how he intends to prove each element of the case. But since almost all infraction trials are prosecuted by a police officer, opening statements are rare. Police officers cannot make them, and prosecutors usually "waive" them.

An opening statement indicates what the prosecutor intends to bring out when he questions the officer on "direct examination." The prosecutor doesn't testify that the defendant committed the offense, but simply lays the groundwork for the officer (or maybe other witnesses as well) to testify to that effect.

Your Opening Statement

Technically, you have the right to make an opening statement at the outset or "reserve" it for when you begin to put on your testimony. As a practical matter, you probably should not make an opening statement at the outset. By saving your opening statement until you begin your defense, you have the opportunity to work it around the officer's testimony. Also, by giving your statement right after the prosecution's, you'll be revealing your strategy in advance. (A sample reserved opening statement is given below.)

Even when no prosecuting attorney makes an opening statement, you still have the right to present an opening statement before you testify.

Some people feel an opening statement helps them organize their presentation. On the other hand, an opening statement has less effect on judges, who pride themselves on following the evidence, not arguments. This is why opening statements are usually only made in jury trials.

The Prosecution's Testimony

After any opening statements, the officer who cited you will testify. In most traffic trials, he will be testifying from the counsel table. In more formal trials, he will testify from a witness stand.

You can interrupt if you have a legitimate legal objection to the propriety of particular types of testimony (see below). However, you should never interrupt with *"He's lying!"* or *"That's not true!"* You'll get the chance to testify later.

Your Objections to Certain Types of Testimony

Keep in mind that you should not make technical objections just for the sake of making them. Most objections to testimony are made on one of six grounds:

1. The testimony is irrelevant to anything that needs to be proven;

2. The testimony relates to something or someone other than what the officer testifying observed, and is therefore "hearsay";

3. The testimony of an officer assumes facts not in evidence (for example, when an officer testifies that "the defendant's vehicle" exceeded the speed limit, but hasn't testified how he knew it was your vehicle, he's assuming a fact—that you drove the vehicle—that hasn't been testified to yet);

4. The officer's testimony does not answer your question to him during cross-examination,

and/or he adds statements not having to do with your question;

5. The officer offers evidence—such as an engineering and traffic survey in a radar speed case—that you requested well before trial in an Informal Discovery Request, but which the prosecutor or police ignored; or

6. The foundation necessary to testify to a particular fact hasn't been introduced. For example, a photograph of the scene of the alleged offense, by itself, proves nothing. However, your testimony that you took the picture at a certain day and time representative of traffic conditions at the time you were stopped establishes a "foundation" of fact that gives meaning to the photograph.

The two most important objections likely to be made in traffic court are objections 5 and 6, listed above.

Watch the officer carefully to see if he's using notes. Many officers use notes scribbled on the back of their copy of the ticket to refresh their memories. If the officer does this, you have a right to object on the basis the officer hasn't "laid the foundation" necessary to use the notes. First he must testify he needs the notes to refresh his memory, at which point you have a right to see them.

In the last chapter, we told you how to prepare to make an objection to radar evidence in speeding cases. It is important that you object whenever a police officer starts testifying about his radar unit's speed reading, unless the original or certified copy of a traffic and engineering survey justifying the speed limit has already been introduced into evidence. (See Chapter 11.) Making this type of objection in formal trials is fairly easy—you just wait for the officer to mention "radar," or if there's a prosecutor present, for him or her to ask any question relating to radar. Immediately object before the officer can say anything further, on the ground that the prosecution hasn't "laid the foundation under Vehicle Code Section 40803(b)" for the introduction of radar evidence.

Unfortunately, in most trials involving speed violations the officer just tells his side of the story instead of responding to questions. This makes it very difficult to stop him before he testifies to the speed reading on his radar unit. You should therefore be ready to jump in with your objections at the slightest hint from the officer that he is going to try to get in his radar evidence without providing a traffic study. Your objection might be phrased like this:

"Excuse me, Your Honor, I would like to object to, and move to strike, Officer Growlski's testimony on his use of radar, on the ground that he hasn't laid the foundation by introducing a traffic and engineering survey justifying the speed limit. Under Sec. 40803(b) of the Vehicle Code, he is required to do this."

Of course, once the officer or prosecutor produces any survey, you should:

1. Object to its introduction into evidence if the prosecution failed to provide you with a copy of it in response to your Informal Discovery Request. (See Chapter 10.)

2. Check to see if it was conducted. (See Chapter 4.)

3. Review it to see if it "justifies" the posted speed limit. (See Chapters 4 and 11.)

If the survey is too old or does not justify the speed limit, you should continue to object to the introduction of testimony about radar, or to the testimony of the officer who used radar.

Your Cross-Examination

After the officer is finished, you get to cross-examine him along the lines suggested in the previous chapter. If you haven't read the section in Chapter 11, "Preparing to Deal With the Officer's Testimony," you should do so now. Remember to be polite and nonargumentative. If he gives an unexpected answer, don't argue with him. Either ask more detailed questions if you think he's lying, or just go on to the next line of questioning. Ask him simple questions that require short and direct answers—don't ask vague questions that give him a chance to tell more of his story. If he tries to do that, politely interrupt with, *"Thank you,"* or, *"I think you've answered my question."* If he persists in trying to tell more of his story—rather than responding to the question—remind him that he already had a chance to do that when he gave his direct testimony.

If the case is handled by a prosecuting attorney, he will have the chance to ask more questions of the officer after you finish. This is called "redirect examination," and the questions are supposed to relate only to the matters you brought up during your cross-examination. If the prosecutor takes advantage of his right to redirect examination, you, too, get another turn—called "recross-examination"—to ask more questions of the officer. Again, the scope of your questions is limited to matters brought out by the prosecutor on redirect examination. Theoretically, this could go on forever, but since the scope of the questions is limited to what the other side asked just before, it eventually ends. Of course, since almost all traffic infractions are handled without prosecutors, this is usually a moot point.

Motion for Acquittal

Once in a while, particularly where the violation is complex, the officer may forget to testify about one of the elements. Keep a little checklist of the elements of the charged offenses in front of you. Check off each element as he testifies to it after you've finished cross-examining the officer and ask yourself whether he has failed to testify to one or more of the elements. If so, turn to the judge and say something like:

> *"Your Honor, I move for an acquittal on the ground that Officer Gettem has failed to establish all the elements of the offense."*

What will happen when you make such a motion depends upon the particular judge. Quite probably, the judge will ask you to specify what part of the prosecution's *prima facie* case was lacking.

Chances are good that if you tell the judge what's wrong with the prosecution's case, he'll have the officer correct that problem. On the other hand, if you don't explain the defect in the prosecution's case, you may not be giving the judge enough information to understand the problem, and the judge will deny your motion. To avoid this double-edged sword, we recommend the following procedure:

1. Before trial, go to the law library and make copies of the *Belton* and *Martinez* cases (*People v. Belton* (1979) 23 Cal.3d 516; *People v. Martinez* (1982) Cal.App.3d 119). Give them to the judge at trial when you make your motion for acquittal. Explain to the judge that these cases strongly imply that a court must rule on a motion for acquittal by only looking at evidence presented up to that point. Further, explain that based on these holdings, you believe you should not have to specify the defect in the prosecution's case;

2. Be sure the proceedings are being recorded;

3. In moving for an acquittal on the ground that the officer failed to establish all the elements of the offense(s) you're charged with, you may want to say the following:

"Your Honor, I move for acquittal under Penal Code § 1118, on the ground that the prosecution has failed to establish a prima facie case. In the case of People v. Belton (1979) 23 Cal.3d 516, at 520–522, the California Supreme Court ruled that a defendant need not state the specific defect in the prosecution's case because that would force the defendant to assist the prosecution in making its case.

"In the case of People v. Martinez (1982) 132 Cal.App.3d 119, at 129–130, the Court of Appeal suggested that courts establish procedures by which trial courts could make proper and informed rulings on motions for acquittal, without the prosecution gaining such an advantage. The court said a trial court should rule that the prosecution would not be allowed to reopen its case after the defendant presented the exact grounds for his motion. In light of these authorities, I ask this court to rule that the prosecution will not be allowed to reopen its case, so that I may freely argue this motion for acquittal here, rather than on appeal. I have copies of those cases if you wish to review them before making your decision." [Give the copies of the cases to the clerk to give to the judge];

4. If the judge rules in your favor, you may then explain what elements were missing from the officer's testimony;

5. If the judge does not explicitly agree to grant your request, you will have to decide whether to "rest" your case (and appeal), or whether to testify to your side of the story, thus perhaps supplying the missing testimony yourself and spoiling any future chance for retrial by an appeals court. (We discuss the appeal procedure in Chapter 16.) You could try a middle approach at that point, by testifying to your side of the story, with the hopes of later appealing if the judge finds you guilty. (Such an appeal will be on the ground that the verdict was not supported by the evidence. See Chapter 16.) However, you must be careful not to supply the missing element in your testimony, or during your cross-examination of the officer. Otherwise, you may lose any appeal.

In radar speed violation cases, the requirement of the introduction into evidence of a valid engineering and traffic survey that justifies the posted speed is considered an "element" of the case. (See VC § 40803(b) and Chapter 4.) Rather than immediately objecting to the officer's testimony regarding the use of radar, you may wait until the officer has finished testifying. The problem with waiting this long to object, however, is that the judge may rule that you "waived," or gave up, the right to object, by not doing so right away.

Thus, it may be safer to object sooner rather than later. When you do object to the testimony, you should move to have the judge "strike" (disregard) it. If the judge strikes the testimony, you then make the motion for acquittal. Again, as stated above, the case of *Belton* requires that the court's ruling on the motion be made on the evidence as it stands at the time you make the motion. Thus, even if the judge later allows the officer to produce the survey, you should be able to successfully appeal his ruling on the motion.

Note: You should, however, object to the judge if he attempts to avoid your motion and allow the officer to produce the survey. Be persistent, cite *Belton,* explain *Martinez,* and insist that the judge rule on the motion before he or she allows the officer to proceed.

"Reserved" Opening Statements

If, at the beginning of the trial, you reserved your opening statement, now is the time to make it, before you give your testimony. If you decide to give an opening statement, summarize what you (and your witnesses, if any) intend to prove. Stan Safespeed's opening statement might sound something like this:

> *"Your Honor, I will show, primarily through my own testimony, that I ascertained my speed to be approximately 35 miles per hour on Wilshire Boulevard, by occasionally glancing at my speedometer as I was driving, and that my speedometer, as shown by a subsequent calibration, was accurate at that speed reading. I will also testify to the fact that Officer Ticketem suddenly raced up behind me, nearly rear-ending my vehicle, and that is the sole cause of his own high speedometer reading.*
>
> *"Finally, I will show that the road was well constructed and lit, that the traffic was moderate, that the weather was clear and dry, and that therefore, even if I was going over 35 miles per hour, I was still traveling at a safe speed."*

Notice that this statement is only a preview of the testimony that will follow. It is important not to confuse the opening statement (a summary of what you intend to prove) with the proof itself.

You may also skip the opening statement and go straight to testimony, which is usually the case.

Your Testimony

In most informal trials, you will simply stand up at the counsel table, look at the judge, and present your testimony. Don't hesitate to look down at your notes, but if possible, don't read directly from them. In more formal trials, you'll be testifying from a witness stand.

When you're finished giving your testimony, pause for an instant. If a prosecutor is present, wait for him to cross-examine you. Then, if you have any other witnesses, introduce them. Your witnesses can either testify in the same narrative fashion in which you testified, or, if you prefer, you can ask them to respond to your questions.

In more formal trials, the prosecutor may insist that your witnesses' testimony only be in response to your questions. Unless you were going to question them anyway, you should object to this request. Simply say that you're unfamiliar with "direct examination" techniques, and that (if there's no jury) the judge will be able to disregard objectionable testimony anyway. If you choose—or are required—to have your witnesses respond to questions, and particularly if a prosecuting attorney is conducting the case, here are some hints that will make things go easier:

1. Think about the key facts to which your witnesses will testify, and arrange them in topical or chronological order. Try to save the more important questions for last.

2. Build a foundation for later questions using the expected answers from earlier questions.

3. Avoid irrelevant details.

4. Don't ask questions that assume facts "not in evidence." (This means, don't ask *"How hard was it raining?"* unless there has already been testimony that it *was* raining.)

5. Don't ask leading questions. In other words, don't put words in your own witnesses' mouths or ask questions that seem to instruct them on how to answer. (Instead of asking *"The road surface was dry, wasn't it?"* or *"Was the road dry?"* ask *"What was the condition of the road surface?"*)

Don't ask questions that call for "hearsay." Don't ask your witness to recite what she was told by someone else, unless that someone else was the police officer and it helps your case.

Cross-Examination by Any Prosecuting Attorney

After you and any witnesses have testified, the prosecutor (if present), or sometimes the judge, may question any or all of you. If the police officer tries to do this, you should object on the ground that he is only a witness, not licensed to practice law, and that courtroom cross-examination certainly constitutes the practice of law. (See Chapter 11.) If your objection is overruled, you must answer the officer's questions.

Any response by you or your witnesses on cross-examination should be given courteously, truthfully, and as briefly as possible. Contrary to old Perry Mason episodes, you don't have to give a *"Yes"* or *"No"* answer. After all, what if the prosecutor asked you whether you knew you were speeding? Both *"Yes"* and *"No"* are bad answers. You have a right, for example, to say you knew you weren't speeding because you were continually glancing at your speedometer, or to briefly explain your answer.

> **CAUTION**
>
> **Don't be hostile toward the person cross-examining;** it may hurt your case. You do have the right, however, to politely object to any question which is abusive, assumes facts not in evidence, or asks irrelevant information or is based on hearsay. Keep your objections to a minimum, objecting only when your or your witness's response to the question would be damaging to your case—not just for the sake of proving you would have made a dynamite lawyer if you hadn't decided to be a professional

bowler, or whatever. Finally, remember that any matters brought up during cross-examination can be clarified by your giving further testimony.

Closing Statements

After all the evidence is presented, both the prosecution and defense will have opportunity to make a closing statement.

The Prosecution's Statement

In trials conducted by a prosecuting attorney, she will probably give a closing argument as to why you're guilty. She will explain how the officer's testimony (and maybe even some cross-examination testimony given by you or your witnesses) "proves beyond a reasonable doubt" each element of the offense and disproves any defenses you've raised.

If a police officer tries to give a closing statement, you can object on the ground that this involves the practice of law. If the officer is nevertheless permitted to make a statement, listen closely. The officer is definitely not permitted to introduce new testimony. If he does, object.

Your Closing Statement

Whether or not a prosecutor or police officer gives a closing argument, you have an absolute right to make one. Unfortunately, and unfairly, this fact is often ignored by traffic court judges. If the judge tries to deny you this right, politely but firmly insist on it, unless it is absolutely clear that you have won your case. If the judge interrupts to tell you a closing argument isn't allowed, you have two choices. You can cite *People v. Douglas* ((1973) 31 Cal.App.3d Supp. 26, 106 Cal.Rptr. 611) as authority that a closing statement must be allowed in traffic cases, or you can simply submit to the judge's unlawful refusal to hear a final argument. Then you'll have a good chance of getting your conviction reversed on appeal. (In *People v. Douglas*, an appeals court reversed a conviction for running a red light because the trial judge "ignored, talked-over, and otherwise refused to acknowledge the defendant when he attempted to make a closing summation." See Chapter 16.) However, all you'll win on appeal is a right to a new trial.

Your closing statement should basically summarize how at least one of the elements of the offense hasn't been proven beyond a reasonable doubt or how you have proven a defense. It might help to explain first how the law you're accused of having violated can be broken down into its various elements. Then explain how:

1. The officer's testimony failed to show that one or more of the elements was present; or

2. Your own testimony (and that of any other witness) has shown that one or more elements did not exist despite the officer's testimony; and/or

3. Testimony has established one or more defenses to the charge.

To begin your closing argument, say to the judge: *"My closing argument is as follows: …"* (You always give your closing argument standing up at the counsel table, even if you testified from the witness stand.)

Prosecution's Rebuttal

In formal trials with a prosecutor, the prosecution gets to make a *second* closing statement after you've given yours. He gets two shots at convincing the judge, but you only get one. This is usually justified on the ground that the prosecution has the burden of proving you guilty and thus should have the last word.

The Verdict

After all the evidence and closing statements have been presented, the judge must announce her verdict. When the judge doesn't have the guts to tell you to your face that you've just been found guilty (or sincerely wishes to think the matter over), she may try to take the case "under advisement." But she cannot do this without your permission. If the judge makes the mistake of "taking the matter under advisement" without asking you if it's okay, don't remind her of this mistake. You can appeal if you're found guilty. The conviction will almost certainly be reversed, and the case will probably be dismissed. (*People v. Kriss* (1979) 96 Cal.App.3d 913, 158 Cal.Rptr. 420. Also, see Chapter 16.)

If the judge takes the case under advisement, call or visit the court about once a week to find out the verdict. You must appeal within 30 days from when the judge files the verdict with the court clerk. Court clerks sometimes may wait two or three weeks before notifying you by mail. With the mail as slow as it sometimes is, this can leave you with very little or no time in which to appeal.

If the judge finds you not guilty, you don't have to pay any fine and are entitled to a refund of any bail you may have posted. Such refund should reach you (speedily) in two to six months.

The Sentence

Most traffic court judges will try to assess a fine immediately after announcing a guilty verdict. However, you have the right to wait at least six hours before sentencing, unless you agree otherwise (PC § 1449). If the judge doesn't ask your permission, you have grounds to have the sentence vacated and be resentenced. (See Chapter 14.) Obviously, then, you wouldn't want to exercise this option unless the sentence is too harsh. Your sentence is not automatically stayed if you appeal. This means you must pay any fine even if you intend to appeal. If you don't, you can be charged with the serious crime of failing to pay a fine.

Reporting Obnoxious Judges

Unfortunately, quite a few judges take offense at nonlawyers who represent themselves competently and thoroughly in traffic court. Unfortunately, many judges in traffic cases have cut off, or even refused to allow, cross-examination and final argument, interrupted repeatedly, stared off into space while the defendant presented his or her case, ridiculed the defendant, and commented on how honest and believable the police officer is compared to the defendant.

Even in the face of this sadly too-frequent behavior, you can have the last word. Anyone, whether accused of a traffic violation or not, has the right to complain about the behavior of the official presiding over the trial, by simply writing a letter. If your complaint is about a "commissioner," "traffic referee," or "pro-tem judge" (lawyer filling in as a judge, with your consent), your complaint should be to the "presiding judge" of the Superior or Municipal Court.

You can also complain to the Commission on Judicial Performance. This agency has the power to censure or even remove judges and commissioners for misconduct. Although it has a reputation for being lax, and although it often acts only in the face of repeated complaints, the Commission on Judicial Performance has disciplined a tiny handful of judges for extreme misconduct—including one for going on record as stating he always believes police officers over traffic-court defendants. The Commission's

address is 455 Golden Gate Avenue, Suite 14400, San Francisco, CA 94102-3660. Its telephone number is 415-557-1200.

One word of caution. Anyone in authority who receives a complaint about a judge or commissioner is wary of disgruntled people whose primary complaint is that the person complained of didn't believe their story at trial. This doesn't mean that if you lose in traffic court you shouldn't complain about a judge's or commissioner's improper behavior. However, you should be ready to point to specific things he or she did, in your own case or perhaps even in other cases you saw in court the day you were there, which showed a biased, prejudiced, or tantrum-oriented judge or commissioner. This would include:

- assisting the prosecution to extremes, in the prosecution of the case

- yelling, shouting, or repeatedly snapping at you, or anyone, in the face of appropriate objections

- repeatedly cutting off—or disregarding—your right to thoroughly cross-examine the officer with relevant questions

- genuine inattentiveness as you presented your side of the case (staring off into space, pushing your exhibits off to the side without looking at them, etc.)

- refusal to allow you to give a closing statement, or repeated hostile interruptions during it, and

- frequent comments that suggest the judge or commissioner believes all traffic-court defendants guilty and/or always believes police officers over other individuals.

If you were found guilty by such a judge or commissioner, don't hesitate to say so, but be sure to give a factual basis for believing your complaint may be valid nevertheless. Be sure to give specific facts such as dates, times, case names and/or number, and perhaps a few direct quotes from the judge or commissioner, if you can recall them.

If you do complain, feel free to send a copy of your letter to the judge or commissioner, though you don't have to. In fact, sending a copy to the judge, while noting at the bottom of your letter that you are doing so (for example, with "cc: Judge O.B. Noxious") will give your complaint letter a little more credibility. You cannot be held in contempt of court for doing so, and if nothing else, you may have an effect on that judge's behavior in the future.

Handling a Misdemeanor Charge: Arraignment to Jury Trial

Introduction

When you're charged with a misdemeanor, you have the right to a trial by jury. As a general rule, a person accused of committing a misdemeanor stands a better chance of being acquitted by a jury than by a judge. That's why defendants accused of driving under the influence almost always demand a jury trial.

The format of a jury trial is similar to a formal nonjury trial (described in Chapter 12). The chief differences are that jury trials always involve prosecutors and require the selection of jurors prior to trial, and the jury must be "instructed" (after testimony and closing statements) on how to determine whether you're guilty.

However, before you start thinking about doing your own jury trial, keep the following in mind: First, jury trials in misdemeanor cases are much more difficult than ordinary nonjury trials for infractions. This is especially true since the state will be represented by an experienced prosecutor—who knows all sorts of subtle and underhanded ways to sway juries. Second, the stakes are higher. A misdemeanor conviction for such offenses as drunk or reckless driving or speed contests or exhibitions will give you a criminal record and will cause your insurance to be canceled or the rates drastically increased. Doing your own jury trial should be a last resort, and only because you can't find an attorney you can trust or afford. (See Chapter 9.)

Arraignment

The first courtroom appearance in a misdemeanor case is arraignment. Unlike infraction arraignments, misdemeanor arraignments cannot be waived. The most important thing that occurs at arraignment is pleading not guilty.

Entering Your Plea

An arraignment in a misdemeanor case is similar to that for an infraction, *except* you can't bypass it and you aren't allowed to have an "informal hearing" (described in Chapter 10). With misdemeanors, the time you're arraigned depends on whether you were issued a Notice to Appear (see Chapter 2) or were released on bail. If you were issued a Notice to Appear, the matter is handled in much the same way as an infraction, in that you must show up in court on or before the date and time indicated, to arrange with the clerk for an arraignment. (The appearance date and time on your ticket is more likely to mean an actual arraignment date and time—not merely a deadline to see the clerk—when a misdemeanor is charged.) If you were released on bail from jail after having been arrested, your release papers should indicate your arraignment date. If you're jailed and not released (perhaps because you can't make bail), your arraignment must occur on a court day within 48 hours of your arrest, excluding Sundays and holidays (PC § 825). It is a brief proceeding where you are informed of your rights and of the charge against you (usually the Vehicle Code section number and a very brief explanation of where and when you allegedly violated it). You are also asked to enter a plea—that is, guilty, not guilty, or nolo contendere.

Guilty pleas are more common in misdemeanor cases than in infractions, since a court appearance is required. You can't just forfeit bail to the clerk as you can with an infraction. If you don't want to fight the charge, you still have to go before a judge and plead guilty or no contest.

But you should think carefully about pleading guilty to a misdemeanor at arraignment. It's usually better—and more common—to plead not guilty and then try to work out a deal later to either plead guilty to a "lesser offense" in exchange for a prosecutor's promise not to charge you with a more serious offense, or to at least get an indication from the judge (at a later "pretrial conference") as to your likely sentence. (If you plead not guilty at the arraignment, you can always change your plea after that.) If you're charged with drunk driving, for example, you might be well advised to offer to plead guilty to the less serious misdemeanor of reckless driving instead. Since that choice may not be offered until later in the proceedings, you might want to plead not guilty at that point. Or, if the initial charge was reckless driving, you might offer to plead guilty to the infraction of violating the Basic Speed Law. (See below, on "making deals.")

You should never plead guilty to a charge arising out of an accident in which you were involved. Should you be sued, your guilty plea can be used against you. Instead, you should plead nolo contendere (no contest) if you don't want to fight the ticket.

If you need time to consult an attorney for advice, tell this to the judge, who will postpone the arraignment for several days (PC § 990). Simply say, *"Your Honor, I haven't had time to consult with a lawyer. Could I please have this arraignment continued for several days?"*

Demanding a Jury Trial

Once you plead not guilty, you should request a jury trial. In theory, when you're charged with a misdemeanor, the case should be set for a jury trial, without your having to specifically demand one. In theory, you'll wind up with a nonjury trial in a misdemeanor case only if you expressly waive (give up) that right. However, mistakes do happen. Some judges automatically set some less serious misdemeanors (such as failure to appear or reckless driving) for nonjury trial because they assume that people representing themselves prefer it. Don't go along with this. If you're charged with a misdemeanor, it doesn't hurt to add, *"And I*

request a jury trial" after the initial, *"Your Honor, I plead not guilty."*

Also, be wary if the judge asks you if you want a "court trial." Among lawyers and judges, the phrase "court trial" doesn't mean a trial in a court(room), it means a *trial without a jury.* So if the judge asks you if you want a "court trial," be sure to answer, *"No, Your Honor, I want a jury trial."*

Often, the judge won't give you a trial date right away, but will set a date for a court appearance called a "pretrial conference." In fact, pretrial conferences are so common in jury cases that if the judge simply sets the case for trial, she may have mistakenly assumed you waived a jury trial; if that happens, you should remind the judge you requested a jury trial since the offense is a misdemeanor, and ask whether a pretrial conference should be scheduled.

As with infractions, the case must be tried within 30 days of your arraignment, unless you specifically "waive time" (PC § 1382(a)(3), and see Chapter 10). If you don't waive time, the judge will probably schedule the trial date within the 30 days, but will also schedule a pretrial conference.

Other Requests You Can Make at Arraignment

The arraignment is also the place at which you can request any of the following:

- the place of trial changed to another court (usually the one at the county seat)—see Chapters 10 and 17

- a court-appointed lawyer (only in misdemeanor cases if you haven't enough money to pay for a lawyer)—see Chapter 9

- your case moved from a particular judge you feel will be prejudiced against you—see Chapter 10, or

- scheduling of future motions you intend to make. (See Chapter 10.)

Read the passages referenced above to decide whether you might want to make any of these requests. Also, read the sections on legal research in Chapter 9.

Making Deals

Since jury trials can be time consuming for all concerned, the prosecutor (and maybe the judge, too) has an incentive to work out a deal with you. For example, the prosecutor might offer to drop some charges if you plead guilty to one or two others. Thus, she may agree to reduce a serious misdemeanor charge (such as driving under the influence) to a less serious one (like reckless driving—if your blood alcohol wasn't too high) or reduce a misdemeanor (reckless driving, or speed contest, or exhibition of speed) to an infraction (ordinary speeding).

Negotiating

Most such negotiations occur either at a "pretrial conference" in the judge's chambers, or are sometimes held impromptu just before trial, in a corner of the hallway outside the courtroom or in a nearby office.

But even though most "plea bargaining" occurs just before trial, there's nothing to prevent you from approaching the prosecutor before then to see if she is willing to reduce or dismiss one or more charges (and "recommend" a lenient sentence to the judge) in exchange for a guilty plea. About a week after you've pleaded not guilty and demanded a jury trial, you should try to find out the name of the prosecutor who will be handling your case. This information should be available from the district (or city) attorney's office, a branch of which might be located in or near the courthouse building. Once you have the prosecutor's name, you will find it easier to get past the receptionist whenever you phone that office regarding your case.

If you plan to negotiate with the prosecutor, whatever you do, remember: It's important to let her know that you're well prepared to go through with a jury trial, but you're willing to listen to alternatives other than pleading guilty to everything you're charged with. For example, if you're charged with a speeding infraction and a failure-to-appear misdemeanor for which you've demanded a jury trial, you might offer to plead guilty to just one charge, provided a low fine is recommended to the judge and the other charge is dismissed. Or, if you're charged with a misdemeanor such as a speed contest, or exhibition of speed or reckless driving, you might offer to plead guilty to a reduced charge of simple speeding.

Other points to remember while negotiating are:

- Be careful about pleading guilty to everything you're charged with, on the promise of a lesser fine and/or no jail sentence. If you're charged with two or more offenses, at least one of which is a jury-triable misdemeanor, you have a lot of bargaining power; you can insist on going to a jury trial if the prosecutor won't dismiss one charge in exchange for pleading guilty (or nolo contendere) to the other.

- Do not lay everything "on the table" by telling the prosecutor every detail of your defense strategy.

- On the day set for trial, never agree to plead guilty to anything when the police officer hasn't shown up to testify. (This will be rare, however, in misdemeanor cases.)

- Never make any admission of guilt before a deal is formalized (see below).

EXAMPLE:

You talk to a deputy district attorney who says *"Come on now—just between us—you were drunk as a skunk, weren't you?"* Don't say, *"Sure."* If you do and a deal is not made, the prosecutor can testify to your admission in court. Even if a deal is made, there's still no reason to admit any facts about your case to anyone. So don't. All you should do to keep your part of the bargain is plead *"guilty"* when the judge asks you how you plead.

How a Deal Is Formalized

Without plea bargaining, the courts would become so clogged with cases where jury trials were demanded that many cases would have to be dismissed for not being tried within the 30-day time limit. Still, no one wants to talk much about this "necessary evil," and formal records of plea bargains are not kept. What happens once a deal is made is simply that a prosecutor requests permission to dismiss or reduce one or more charges "in the interests of justice," and indicates your intention to plead guilty to a reduced charge. Sometimes the prosecutor may also recommend a particular punishment.

Although the judge does not have to agree to the dismissal or reduction of charges, nor to the recommended punishment, he almost always will. If the judge does not agree, he will say so and give you a chance to withdraw your offer to plead guilty. Then the judge asks you a few questions to find out if you understand that you're giving up your right to trial by pleading guilty (to the reduced charge), and that the prosecutor's "recommendation" in regard to your sentence is just that and does not bind the judge. Although this statement seems to give the judge free rein to sentence you more harshly than you bargained for, that almost never will happen. If it does, you will be given

the opportunity to withdraw your guilty plea, plead not guilty instead, and go to trial before a different judge without any reference being made to your withdrawn plea.

Selecting the Jury

In this section, we'll look at the jury-selecting process—basic procedures, questions you ask potential jurors, presenting challenges to disqualify a prospective juror who you believe is strongly prejudiced against you, and making peremptory challenges to exclude certain types of people without having to prove prejudice.

The Basic Procedure

Many lawyers believe that selecting the members of the jury is the single most important phase of the trial. It begins as soon as your case is called, after any preliminary motions are taken care of.

Before trial, the potential jurors will normally be seated in a "jury assembly room" waiting to be called. However, in some courts, they may be milling around in the corridors or be seated inside the courtroom with you before court begins. If you find that the people sitting around you are potential jurors, don't try to influence them. But be your pleasant and charming best. Brief idle conversation won't hurt, as long as you don't talk about your case. Don't tell anyone you're a defendant unless asked.

When your case is finally called and it's clear that no compromise can be reached, the first 12 people from the group of potential jurors will take their seats. If the court provides you with a list of all the names (and occupations) of the potential jurors, write down the name of each juror on a chart as they are seated. (Usually they are seated in two rows of six chairs each.) Later

JURY PANEL CHART			Peremptory Challenges							Only for offenses punishable by over 90 days in jail			
			No.	1	2	3	4	5	6	7	8	9	10
Date	Case No	People of State of Calif.	Plaintiff										
		vs.	Defendant										

1	2	3
4	5	6
7	8	9
10	11	12

in the selection process, if a juror is disqualified and a new one takes the seat, you can cross out the name of the person who left and enter the new name. (Many lawyers prefer to write the jurors' names on small adhesive "post-it notes" attached to the appropriate place on a jury seating chart. This allows easy removal of the post-it note and replacement with a blank one when a juror is excused, a method superior to crossing out and rewriting juror information in the small space provided.)

Since 2001, judges have had to allow for limited questioning of prospective jurors by the prosecution or defense. (C.C.P. § 223.) You may wish to do this since many judges ask prospective jurors only perfunctory questions relating to occupation, spouse's occupation, previous experience with the criminal justice system, and acquaintance with police officers and attorneys. This procedure is called "voir dire" ("vwar deer," French for "to speak the truth"). The questions will be to the entire panel and to individual jurors. If the answers to any of these questions indicate blatant prejudice, you or the prosecutor can ask the judge to excuse that person "for cause." If the prejudice is more subtle, or you or the prosecutor just doesn't like the potential juror's attitude, a "peremptory challenge" can be used to excuse the juror.

When you are allowed to ask questions of prospective jurors, start by asking the entire panel particular questions related to their possible prejudices or biases that the judge or prosecutor have not asked. (A sample list is shown below.) If there are any potential jurors with serious prejudices against defendants (or in favor of police officers), the answers to your questions will hopefully reveal this and the judge will excuse that particular juror "for cause." (This way, you don't have to use one of your peremptory challenges.) The answers given by the potential jurors (including the tone of voice, hesitancy to answer particular questions, scowls, bad or good vibes in general) may guide you in deciding whether to exercise a peremptory challenge to get rid of someone you don't want to hear your case. Questioning jurors also gives you the opportunity of educating them about general principles of law.

After you've used "for cause" and/or peremptory challenges to affect the makeup of the jury, it becomes the prosecutor's turn again. (This means that if after you've excused several jurors, you're satisfied with the jury makeup and "pass" the selection to the prosecutor, then, if the prosecutor excuses no more jurors, the selection is over. It might be over before you think, so you'd better be sure that you're satisfied with the jury makeup each time you "pass" to the prosecutor.) The prosecutor will be particularly concerned about the new jurors who have replaced those you excused. If he or she excuses any of the jurors, you have another turn. This goes on until both sides are satisfied with the makeup of the jury, or run out of challenges.

Questions to Ask on "Voir Dire"

If you are permitted to question the potential jurors, start by asking their name, occupation and place of employment, whether they're married, and if so, their spouse's occupation (unless you've already been given this information by the court, or the judge or prosecutor has established it). After you've noted all this on a jury seating chart, you should ask the panel general questions, similar to the following:

1. *"Do any of you have any objections to sitting here as jurors in a misdemeanor traffic violation case? Please raise your hand if you do."*

2. *"Do any of you object to the fact that I will be representing myself without an attorney?"*

3. *"Are any of you aware of the fact that in order to find me guilty of the offense I'm charged with, the prosecution must prove beyond a reasonable doubt every single element of its case?"*

Note: This sort of question is designed more to "educate" prospective jurors, than to lead to an answer that will give you useful information. One important aspect of voir dire is to inform jurors—some of whom may assume you're guilty, or you wouldn't have been arrested in the first place—that you're "presumed innocent," that the prosecution must prove you're guilty, that the prosecution must prove everything it is required to prove, and that it must do so "beyond a reasonable doubt." Some prospective jurors do not realize this, and may need such gentle reminders. Of course, if a juror's answer suggests disagreement with, or total ignorance of, all these rules, the answer may help you decide to exercise a peremptory or for-cause challenge against the juror. (See below.)

4. *"Are there any of you who have trouble believing that a person is innocent until proven guilty beyond a reasonable doubt on the basis of the evidence?"*

5. *"Will you each commit yourself to honor the constitutional guarantee that a person is not guilty, unless the prosecution proves each element of the offense beyond a reasonable doubt?"*

Note: As with question 3 above, the purpose of questions 4 and 5 is mostly to educate the jurors by reminding them of their obligations in this regard. Each should at least nod his or her head. If any juror gives you bad vibes in this regard, you may want to use a peremptory challenge.

6. *"Do you all understand that my being accused of a violation is no evidence at all of guilt?"*

7. *"Have any of you ever been employed as a law enforcement officer or security guard?"*

8. *"Do any of you have friends or relatives who have been employed as law enforcement officers or security guards?"*

9. *"Do any of you have friends or relatives who have been employed in a district attorney's office?"*

10. *"Are there any among you who would believe the word of a police officer solely because he is a police officer, over my own testimony?"*

11. *"Do any of you believe that police officers are incapable of mistaken observations?"*

12. *"Do any of you believe police officers always tell the entire truth?"*

13. *"Have any of you ever sat on a jury previously where the defendant was charged with the offense I'm charged with?"*

14. *"Have any of you ever been involved in an automobile accident that you believe was caused by someone breaking the law?"*

15. *"Are there any of you who don't drive at least ten thousand miles each year?"*

16. *"Are there any among you who have never been cited for a moving traffic violation?"* **Note:** *You might want to reject a juror who's never been subject to the indignity, or you may want to reject a person who too-quickly paid the fine because he "knew he was guilty."*

The above questions are only examples. Depending on the facts of your particular case and the offense with which you're charged, you could come up with others. For example, in drunk driving cases, you might ask general questions as to whether any of the potential jurors occasionally take a drink. (You would want to exclude a teetotaler.)

If any of the jurors indicate, whether by nodding, raising a hand, or even by a facial expression, an affirmative answer to a question, be prepared to follow up. Address the particular juror by name, if possible. You might say:

> *"Ms. Jones, I noticed you seemed to nod yes when I asked you if you had any friends or relatives who were police officers. Could you elaborate on that?"*

Depending on the answer, you might want to ask further questions to expose a possible anti-defendant or pro-police prejudice. If you decide to excuse that particular person, use one of your peremptory challenges. If the juror's prejudice is blatant, ask the judge to excuse the juror for cause.

Challenges for Cause

If a prospective juror *strongly* indicates that he is prejudiced against defendants, would believe the word of a police officer over yours no matter what, or thinks you have to prove yourself innocent, you should ask the judge to disqualify that person for cause. Be polite when you do so, or you'll only succeed in alienating the remaining jurors. However, you're likely to find that it's a rare person who will outright admit his prejudices so clearly that you can successfully challenge that person for cause. Also, the law of disqualification for cause is complicated and beyond the scope of this book. If you believe a juror is so prejudiced that he should be disqualified for cause and the judge doesn't disqualify that person, you will have to trust your instincts and use one of your peremptory challenges. Don't cause a scene with the judge.

Peremptory Challenges

You have the right to excuse prospective jurors for any reason or for no reason. You should exercise peremptory challenges with care, however, because you only have a limited number of them—six or ten. Though you should rely on your instincts, you probably would be wise to consider exercising peremptory challenges to exclude the following types of people:

1. Present and former police officers and security guards;

2. Anyone who has ever worked in a prosecutor's office, including lawyers;

3. Relatives or close friends of the above;

4. Teetotalers in drunk driving cases;

5. Anyone who has ever been involved (or has a close friend or relative who has been involved) in an accident caused by someone else charged with the offense you're charged with (especially if it's drunk driving);

6. People whose dress and/or lifestyles are much more conservative than yours;

7. People who don't drive or who have never received a traffic ticket;

8. People who obviously resent being called for jury duty;

9. People you feel uneasy about but don't know why.

When you excuse a prospective juror, be polite. Simply say something to the judge like, *"The Defense would like to thank and excuse the fifth juror, Ms. Smith."*

Trial Procedure

After the jury is selected, the 12 jurors are "sworn in." Then, the trial proceeds in much the same way as a trial before a judge. (See Chapter 12.)

Opening Statements

The opening statements are presented in the same way noted in the previous chapter, but you address the jury instead of the judge. Since jurors obviously know less about the law than most judges, an opening statement is advisable. You can give it right after the prosecutor gives (or waives) hers, or you can reserve it until just before you put on your testimony. If you want to make an opening statement, don't read it while shuffling or stooping—look at the jury members directly. Refer to your notes only from time to time. Be sure you have already practiced it at home with friends. The important thing to remember is that your bearing will probably have a much greater effect on a jury than it would have on a judge.

The Prosecution's Testimony

In jury trials, the officer will always testify in response to the prosecutor's questions, never by narrative. You should avoid all but the most crucial objections. Studies have shown that jurors are more likely to rule against the side that makes the most objections, everything else being equal. Jurors resent anyone trying to keep them from hearing evidence and even if you do successfully object and keep certain evidence out, they are likely to be able to guess the answer to the question objected to, and will probably attach a lot more importance to the answer than they would if you'd just let it pass.

There are several areas where the general rule of not objecting may not be appropriate. These include:

1. When the prosecutor tries to introduce radar evidence of your speed without having first introduced into evidence a traffic and engineering survey justifying the speed limit. (**Note:** Only when a speeding offense is charged as a misdemeanor because of

three prior violations in a year will a jury be involved.);

2. Where questions are extremely vague, confusing, or unintelligible;

3. Where a prosecution witness is asked questions which are so "leading" that the prosecutor is really supplying all the testimony in the question. A leading question is one that implicitly "instructs" the witness how to answer. To cite the Chapter 12 example, questions stated as *"The road surface was dry, wasn't it?"* or *"Was the road dry?"* are leading; *"What was the condition of the road surface?"* is not.

Note: Do not use this objection unless the overall pattern of the prosecution's questions are leading. If you object to each leading question, you will not only make the judge and jury impatient, but also, when it's your turn to ask questions, the prosecutor may probably fight fire with fire, harassing you with objection after objection about the form of your questions. Prosecutors can play this game a lot better than you can, so think twice before you object.

Your Cross-Examination

When you cross-examine the prosecution's witnesses, be courteous but firm. If the officer tries to tell more of his story, you might gently interrupt with *"Please answer the question— you've already had a chance to tell your story; I'd appreciate it if you wouldn't try to influence the jury any further."* (Juries hate to be influenced.) Otherwise, the cross-examination should be pretty much the same as in trials before a judge, as discussed in the previous chapter.

Motion for Acquittal

A motion for acquittal is used when the prosecution has failed to establish the elements of the violation. Since jury trials are always handled by trained prosecuting attorneys (who use checklists to make sure they don't forget anything important), this will almost never occur.

"Reserved" Opening Statement

If you "reserved" your opening statement at the beginning of the trial, this is the time to make it—before you present your testimony. (See Chapter 12.)

Your Testimony

Your testimony in a jury trial should also be pretty much the same as it would be before a judge, with two important exceptions:

- Be sure to look directly at the jury from time to time while you do your best to look sincere without being phony. Throughout your trial, your demeanor should reflect that you are an honest, law-abiding citizen who has been wrongly accused.

- You may be able to exert subtle influences on the jury by sprinkling your testimony with slightly relevant personal details with which one or more members of the jury might identify. For example, if you were on your way to a church function when you were pulled over, and there are a few churchgoers in the jury, casually mention the fact, but don't overplay it. Jurors also tend to like firefighters, medical personnel, and teachers. However, if you're an undertaker, bill collector, or insurance salesman, you may be wise to keep your occupation to yourself.

Finally, while judges often train themselves to remain totally expressionless even while hearing the most blatant lie (lest they be accused of being prejudiced), at least some of the jurors will probably be a little more transparent. Be alert for signs on jurors' faces that might suggest confusion or disbelief, and adjust your conduct accordingly. For example, if a part of your testimony evokes snickers, don't refer to that part in your final argument.

When your testimony is completed, and after the prosecutor has cross-examined you (see below), introduce any other witnesses who will testify on your behalf. As we saw in the previous chapter, the prosecutor might insist that your witnesses testify only in response to questions you ask, as opposed to the narrative fashion in which you testified. You should object to this request and tell the judge you're unfamiliar with the way such questions should be asked. You should be prepared to ask non-objectionable questions just in case the judge sides with the prosecutor in this point.

Cross-Examination by the Prosecution

When it's your time to be cross-examined by the prosecutor, listen carefully to the question. Do not guess at an answer you don't know. Ask the prosecutor to repeat questions you don't understand. On the other hand, do not purposely avoid answering reasonably clear questions; otherwise the jury will think you are being evasive. Do not show discourtesy or anger toward the prosecutor, even if she tries to irritate you. If she is obnoxious and you remain polite, it may well arouse the jurors' sympathies on your behalf. Otherwise, your response to cross-examination should be the same as in nonjury trials. Explain this to any witnesses you will be calling.

Jury Instructions

After you present your evidence, but before the beginning of closing arguments, you can (and should) submit proposed "jury instructions" to the judge to be read to the jury. If you don't, the judge will most likely read a number of standard instructions, plus one or more relating specifically to the offense(s) you're charged with. These jury instructions are listed in a book referred to as "CALCRIM," or *California Criminal Jury Instructions,* which can be found at any law library, or on the Internet. This book contains jury instructions appropriate to all sorts of criminal trials, and are referred to by number. The standard instructions include how jurors are to understand the duties of the judge and jury, types of evidence, weighing evidence and determining credibility of witnesses, and the most important one, the presumption of innocence.

TIP

You can find CALCRIM online. The full text of the *California Criminal Jury Instructions* (CALCRIM) are available online (in downloadable pdf format) at www.lawca.com/juryinst/CALCRIM .html.

Somewhere in the middle of all this, the judge inserts instructions about the particular offense(s) charged. The judge must also add other instructions suggested by you or the prosecutor if they accurately reflect the law and are relevant to the charge and the evidence presented at the trial.

To request one or more jury instructions, submit a written form to the judge before the closing statements to the jury begin. Your request for jury instructions should be prepared in advance before the day of your trial, and might look something like the one which follows the lists of instructions.

Jury Instructions Useful in Misdemeanor Traffic Cases	
Pretrial Instructions	
Number	**Purpose of Instruction**
100	Summary of trial process, before jury is selected.
101	Cautionary admonitions, after jury is selected.
102	Instructions on the taking of notes.
103	Meaning of "reasonable doubt."
104	What is, and is not, evidence.
105	Evaluating witness testimony.
Pre-deliberation General Instructions	
Number	**Purpose of Instruction**
200	Duties of judge and jury.
201	Cautionary instruction to avoid conducting investigations.
202	Note taking, in more detail; notebooks.
220	Reasonable doubt defined.
222	Evidence defined.
223	Direct and circumstantial evidence, defined.
224	Circumstantial evidence and sufficiency of evidence.
225	Circumstantial evidence relating to intent or mental state.
226	Evaluating the testimony of witnesses.
250	General intent crimes, union of act and general intent.
251	Specific intent crimes, union of specific intent or mental state.
257	Criminal negligence, union of act and intent.
300	Production of all available evidence is not required.
301	Sufficiency of single witnesses' testimony.
302	Evaluating conflicting evidence.
355	Defendant's right not to testify. (*Use only if defendant did not testify.*)

Jury Instructions Useful in Misdemeanor Traffic Cases (cont'd)

Pre-Deliberation Instructions as to Particular Offenses

Number	Purpose of Instruction
2110	Duties of judge and jury.
2111	Driving with a blood-alcohol greater or equal to 0.08%.
2125	Prior DUI over 0.08% convictions.
2126	Prior DUI convictions, bifurcated trial.
2130	Refusal to take tests, and consciousness of guilt (DUI). (*Do not request this, the prosecution will ask for this instruction in DUI test-refusal cases.*)
2140	Hit-and-run, with injury.
2142	Hit-and-run, lesser included offenses.
2150	Hit-and-run, property damage only.
2180	Evading peace officer.
2182	Evading police officer.
2200	Reckless driving.
2201	Speed contest.
2202	Exhibition of speed.
2220	Driving with suspended or revoked license.
2221	Driving without a valid license, but license not suspended.
2240	Failure to appear.
2241	Driver and driving defined.

Pre-Deliberation Closing Instructions

Number	Purpose of Instruction
3500	Requirement for it unanimous verdict.
3530	Judge's comments on the evidence.
3550	Final closing instructions.

The full text of the *California Criminal Jury Instructions* (CALCRIM) is available online at www.lawca.com/juryinst/CALCRIM.html.

RALPH LEADFOOT
950 Parker Road
Berkeley, CA 94710
(510) 555-1234

Defendant in Pro Per

SUPERIOR COURT OF CALIFORNIA, COUNTY OF ALAMEDA
BERKELEY-ALBANY BRANCH

THE PEOPLE OF THE) No. A-123456
STATE OF CALIFORNIA)
     Plaintiff,)
) REQUEST FOR JURY
vs.) INSTRUCTIONS
)
RALPH LEADFOOT,)
)
     Defendant.)
_____)

Defendant, RALPH LEADFOOT, hereby requests that the jury be instructed with the following CALCRIM instructions:

100	105	220	226	2200
101	106	222	251	2240
102	200	223	300	3500
103	201	224	301	3530
104	202	225	302	3550

DATED: March 31, 20xx   *Ralph Leadfoot*
            _____
            RAPLH LEADFOOT
            Defendant in Pro Per

Closing Arguments

After all the evidence is presented, both you and the prosecutor will have the opportunity to present closing arguments. Here we give you a sample closing argument that you can adapt to suit your own particular case.

The Prosecution's Argument

During the prosecutor's closing argument, remain calm—poker-faced if you can. Don't express outrage, indignation, derision, or any other emotion, no matter how horribly the prosecutor distorts the truth. Just listen carefully to the prosecution's arguments so that you can respond to them in your own closing argument, which comes next.

Your Argument

Your closing argument to the jury serves two purposes. First, you should explain how the evidence isn't sufficient to prove your guilt (or actually disproves it), and second, you should rebut statements made by the prosecutor in her arguments. Reread the closing statement information in Chapter 12.

Be sure to emphasize to the jurors that each element of the offense must be proven "beyond a reasonable doubt," which is something in between a "great" doubt and a "mere" or insignificant doubt. But with a little glib talk, you can infer that a "reasonable" juror (everyone considers him/herself to be reasonable) who has any doubt at all about any element of the offense must find you not guilty. Remember, it only takes one stubborn juror to produce a "hung" jury. Part of your argument might go something like this:

"Ladies and gentlemen, since I know that I'm innocent of the offense(s) charged, I'm contesting it/them here. Attorneys are very expensive, and so I'm defending myself. Not being familiar, as is the prosecutor, with all the legal technicalities and rules of trial procedure, I researched the nature of criminal trials, since I wanted to present the case as best I could. The most important thing I learned about American criminal trials—and we are all taught this—is that the prosecution must prove a defendant guilty—as to each and every element of the offense—beyond a reasonable doubt. [Now, describe the elements of the offense and how, in light of the evidence presented, why doubt remains. This is the most important part of your argument!]

"The doctrine of "reasonable doubt" means that if you have any doubt as to whether any of those elements is true, and you feel that such doubt is reasonable, you must find me not guilty. You are not necessarily saying, "I'm absolutely sure he's innocent," but rather, "The prosecution has failed to prove everything it has to prove beyond a reasonable doubt."

"I submit that the evidence indicated sheds a reasonable doubt on my guilt. The prosecutor, in her statement to you, merely repeated the police officer's testimony. But this is only part of the evidence. I (and my witnesses) also testified, and I know I was telling the truth. You must not believe a police officer's powers of observation to be infallible just because he's a police officer, or that he's incapable of exaggerating a little. When the prosecutor repeated what the officer said, she didn't disprove any of the evidence I (and my witnesses) presented. She wants you to give the officer's word complete credibility, and my word none. If the law required this, we wouldn't need trials at

all! We could all just have automatic guilty verdicts.

"I'm asking you to consider all the testimony—mine and that of my witnesses included.

"Now, when the prosecutor argues the case again—she gets another chance while I only get this one—she may tell you that I have a lot to gain, and that therefore the officer's story is more believable than mine. I ask you to take this with a grain of salt. Even though official "quota systems" were supposedly outlawed quite a few years ago, it's no secret that police officers are promoted at least partly on the basis of the average number of violations they charge people with every month. [Some prosecutors may object to this. If this happens, simply drop the point and go on.]

"I have no hard feelings toward the officer, and I know that part of the reason he's on the roads is to protect us from hazardous drivers, but he's not infallible, and in this particular case, he was mistaken. [Now, briefly reiterate the key areas in which he was mistaken, and also rebut any of the points the prosecutor made in the initial argument to the extent you feel it will help you.]

"Since I'm not an attorney, I could not present this case as smoothly and professionally as the prosecutor; nor did I know when to object to any evidence she might have improperly introduced [use this only if you made no objections and the prosecutor made some]. *Still, I hope you will examine all the evidence and apply it to each element the prosecution has to prove.*

"You may recall that in the beginning of this case, you each indicated you would

honor the constitutional guarantee that a person is not guilty until and unless the prosecution proves each element beyond a reasonable doubt. Indeed, in this case, the prosecution has come up far short in doing this. In retiring to the jury room, I ask you to do your duty in this regard and to enter a verdict of not guilty. Thank you."

This may seem a bit long-winded but it goes pretty fast when you're talking. Feel free to change it to suit your particular case. It's wise to practice this sort of statement a number of times before you go to court.

TIP

What Is reasonable doubt? To be convicted of a traffic violation in most states, you must be found guilty beyond a "reasonable doubt." The legal definition goes like this: "Reasonable doubt is not a mere possible or imaginary doubt, but that state of the evidence where you do not have an abiding conviction, to a certainty, of the truth of the charge."

Now that's as clear as mud, isn't it? Here is a real-life example of reasonable doubt that may help: John is tried for murder and all the jurors vote "guilty" except Jake, who holds out for a not-guilty verdict. The jury is hung. A local citizen later confronts Jake, saying, "How could you say John didn't do it?"

"I didn't say John didn't do it, I'm just not sure that he did," Jake replies.

The Prosecution's Rebuttal Argument

Since the prosecution has the burden of proof, it gets two shots to argue its case to the jury. The second one is intended to allow a rebuttal to the things you covered in your argument. Sometimes the prosecutor won't exercise this opportunity.

The Judge Instructs the Jury

Finally, the judge will instruct the jury from the standard instructions, plus any that were accepted from suggestions by you or the prosecutor. Then the bailiff will take the jury into the jury room to deliberate. The longer they take, the better for you. When they come back, they will announce a verdict. The judge will thank and excuse them. If you are found guilty, the judge will set a time for you to appear for sentencing. It's improper for her to sentence you right then and there unless you agree to it, and in many cases you shouldn't. ●

Sentencing

Time for Sentencing

The law provides for a cooling-off period between the time you're found (or plead) guilty and the time the judge (or traffic commissioner) sentences you. Unless you agree otherwise, the judge must wait at least six hours before sentencing you (PC § 1449).

Usually, though, traffic court judges will ignore this rule and sentence people immediately. Since most people are unaware of the requirement, very few object. But the law is clear. If you are sentenced too soon, you can ask the judge to "vacate" the sentence on the ground that she hasn't waited the six hours (unless you have waived this right). If the judge refuses, the sentence can be reversed on appeal. Unfortunately, however, the fact that the sentence will be reversed doesn't mean that the underlying conviction is wiped out. It is not, and you will simply be resentenced.

There are two advantages to insisting the judge wait at least six hours before sentencing. First, it gives you a chance to figure out whether you have legal cause to ask for a new trial. When you come back for sentencing, you have the right to orally make a "motion for a new trial" and explain your legal reasons why. Second, if you face a license suspension, the postponement will give you time to contact a friend who can drive you home from court.

Now that we've told you of the advantages of insisting on a six-hour delay, here is one large disadvantage. By requesting the court to set up another court appearance, you are creating trouble for the court bureaucracy. Recognizing this, the judge may decide to exercise her discretion and impose a larger fine than would have otherwise been the case (even though she's not supposed to punish you for exercising your rights). Our advice is to insist on your six-hour delay only when it will truly serve a purpose, and not just to throw a monkey-wrench into the court machinery.

Remember: If you agree to have the judge "think your case over" and decide on your guilt or innocence in your absence, none of the above applies. You just receive a notification by mail indicating whether you are guilty, and if so, what the sentence will be.

Possible Sentences

In Chapters 3 through 8, we set out the possible penalties for the main traffic offenses. Go back to your section and review the maximum and probable penalties for your violation. Absent a plea bargain, the sentences listed in those chapters are what you should expect at your sentencing hearing.

Repeat Offenses

As we pointed out in Chapter 3, the fines are higher for a second or third Vehicle Code infraction within 12 months. Fortunately, though, a judge may not increase an infraction fine beyond the first-time limit on the basis of prior offenses unless either the prosecution initially alleged that you had prior convictions (almost never done in traffic court) and provides court records showing convictions (see Chapter 10), or you admit the prior violations shown on your driving record (VC § 42004. See also *In re Tahl* (1969) 1 Cal.3d 122, 81 Cal. Rptr. 557). A prior offense based on a guilty plea is not valid for the purpose of increasing your sentence unless you expressly waived your right to trial, the right of confrontation, and the right against self-incrimination (*People v. Matthews* (1983) 139 Cal.App.3d 537, 188 Cal.Rptr. 796). If the prosecution does not attempt to prove the constitutional validity of your prior offenses (they rarely do), the judge can only raise your fine above that for a first-time offense if:

1. He looks at your DMV record;

2. Then asks whether you've had any prior violations within the last 12 months; and

3. You answer "Yes" (VC § 42004).

If something like this happens, you do not have to answer, and you probably should not unless your driving record is spotless. An appeals court has ruled that questions by the court about whether you have prior convictions violate your Fifth Amendment right against self-incrimination. (*Municipal Court v. Superior Court* (1988) 199 Cal.App.3d 19, 244 Cal. Rptr. 591. PC § 19.7 applies this case law to infractions. See *People v. Matthews* (1983) 139 Cal.App.3d 537, 188 Cal.Rptr. 796.)

If you have prior convictions, don't lie and say that you don't. The judge can tell from your DMV printout. So why is he asking? It could be because the DMV printout is not legal proof of your prior convictions unless you admit them, and, if you do that, the judge can then get you with a fine higher than the first-offense maximum. So you should *not* admit to having any prior convictions and you should remind the judge that it's improper for him or her to ask you.

If the judge asks you if you've had any prior violations within the last 12 months, you may want to say the following.

> *"Your Honor, I object to this court's question and decline to answer on the grounds that the question violates my right against self-incrimination. In the case of* Municipal Court v. Superior Court *(1988) 199 Cal. App.3d 19, at page 28, the court ruled on that basis that a criminal defendant may not be questioned with regard to convictions."*

If the judge overrules your objection and takes your objection as an "admission," you will have strong grounds for appeal if he or she fines you more than the first-offense maximum. (See Chapter 16.) More importantly, you still do not have to answer "*Yes*" to this question. What you should say instead, is *"At this time, Your Honor, I hereby deny the validity of any and all prior convictions that might appear on any DMV printout."*

At this point, the judge should let it go. If you have a particularly vindictive and/or surly traffic judge, he or she might order the clerk to get the records of your convictions and set another hearing to "prove" the validity of the priors. Again, you will want to object to this as well—otherwise, you will not be able to raise the issue on appeal. To do so, you would say something like: *"I object to this court's actions of seeking out prior convictions and of conducting an independent evidentiary investigation, which, under the rule of* People v. Handcock *(1983) 145 Cal. App.3d Supp. 25, is not appropriate."*

If after all of this resistance, the judge still sentences you to a fine higher than the maximum for a first offense that reflects any prior convictions, you should move to vacate the sentence on the ground that you did not admit any priors. If that fails, you can and should appeal the sentence. (See Chapter 16.)

Inability to Pay

If you're sentenced to pay a fine you cannot afford, tell the judge. The judge can authorize that the fine be paid in installments or at a later date. If the judge grants you time to pay a fine for an infraction, she must also set a date to allow you to explain why you were unable to pay, if that's the case (VC § 42003(a)). You can't be sent to jail for inability to pay a fine, but you can be jailed for either refusing to pay or for failing to come to court with a sufficient explanation of your inability to pay (*In re Antazo* (1970) 3 Cal.3d 100, 89 Cal.Rptr. 255; VC §§ 40508(b), 42003(a). Also, see Chapter 7.) "Inability to pay" does not mean you have to be totally destitute, but rather that you and/or your family would have to do without the basic necessities of life—food, clothing, and shelter—if you were forced to pay the fine. Be prepared to tell the judge about your earnings, expenses and property, and why payment of a fine or installment would be a real hardship on you and/or your family.

If you are able to pay a fine for an infraction but refuse to do so, you can be cited for contempt of court or charged with the misdemeanor of failure to pay (VC § 40508(b)). For misdemeanors, the judge can order you to spend one day in jail for each $30 of the fine you don't pay. The judge cannot do this for failure to pay an infraction fine (VC § 42003(a), (b)).

If you can't afford to pay the fine, the judge can restrict your driving for up to 30 days until it is paid (VC § 40508(c)). This can only be done for one period of up to 30 days, even if you still can't pay the fine after that. If this penalty prevents you from earning a living, either because it is impossible for you to get to and from work or because you have to drive as part of your job, ask the judge immediately to modify the order to allow you to drive at least for that purpose. Driving while your license is impounded is punishable by fine (or even five days in jail) as contempt of court.

Note: The DMV will also refuse to renew your driver's license if notified by the court that you "willfully failed to pay" your fine. The court will notify the DMV of this on all reportable Vehicle Code violations (see Chapter 6 for violations *not* reported to the DMV), unless the judge determines that you were unable to pay the fine (VC §§ 12807(c), 40509(b)).

Traffic School

In Chapter 9, we indicated that in most counties you can go to traffic school, as an alternative to being tried, and the violations you are charged with will then not appear on your DMV record. When you plead or are found guilty of a violation, the judge may tell you it's "too late" to attend traffic school to keep the case off your record. In fact, it doesn't hurt to ask to pay the fine and attend traffic school for that purpose. You might remind the judge that the law says a judge can't routinely apply a policy against traffic school for those who go to trial and lose (*People v. Wozniak* (1987) 197 Cal.App.3d Supp. 43, 243 Cal.Rptr. 686; *People v. Enochs* (1976) 62 Cal.App.3d Supp. 42, 43-44, 133 Cal.Rptr. 363).

Judge-Imposed License Suspensions and Restrictions

As we mentioned in Chapters 4–8, some infractions and all misdemeanors can result in court-ordered license suspensions from up to 30 days (for first-time infractions) to up to three years for some drug and alcohol related offenses.

Note: In practice, license suspensions are extremely rare for first- or even second-offense speeding infractions, except where your speed is very high—like 100 mph on the freeway or 50 mph in a school zone.

A judge cannot suspend your license for a period longer than he would for a first-offense violation unless you admit the prior offense (or it is proved by the prosecution). So, for example, with a reckless driving (without bodily injury) or speed violation charge, the judge can only suspend your license for longer than the 30-day maximum for a first offense if you admit to the prior offense or the prosecution proves its constitutional validity.

Note: Driving while your license is suspended is a misdemeanor punishable on a first offense by a fine of up to $1,000 (plus penalty assessment) and up to six months in jail. (See Chapter 7.)

Jail and Probation

As we saw in Chapters 3 through 8, you cannot be sentenced to jail for committing an infraction, but you can be for committing a misdemeanor. Six months is the maximum sentence authorized for most Vehicle Code misdemeanors (one year for repeat DUI offenses), but sentences that long are rarely given.

Some misdemeanors, like reckless driving, provide for a mandatory jail sentence of "not less than" a certain number of days. However, the judge usually has the discretion to grant you probation and suspend all or part of the jail sentence. But there are some exceptions. For example, a person convicted of driving while her license was suspended for an under-the-influence violation must go to jail for at least 10 days. (VC § 14601.2. See Chapter 7.)

In many cases, judges will allow persons sentenced to jail to serve the time on weekends or through a sheriff's "work alternative" or "work release" program. You or your attorney should request this if you would otherwise lose time from work.

If you are sentenced to jail for a Vehicle Code misdemeanor, you are entitled to have your sentence "stayed" for at least 24 hours, on request (VC § 42004.5). The judge can only refuse this request if she believes that you would not return to serve the jail sentence.

For most offenses, a judge can grant probation, usually by imposing a sentence and "suspending" all or part of it. However, you should clearly understand that if the terms of probation are violated, you have to serve the original sentence. The judge can also grant probation without imposing a sentence, and if the terms of the probation are violated, you go back before the judge to be sentenced.

Probation terms may also include going to jail or paying a fine. For example, a person convicted of driving under the influence must be sentenced to a suspended sentence of six months in jail, with probation, the conditions being the payment of a $375 fine plus penalty assessments, spending 96 hours in jail, and staying out of trouble for the next three years. Probation can last for three years, but if the judge doesn't specify, it only runs for one year.

Motions to Vacate Sentence

If the judge sentences you harshly, you can move to "vacate" the sentence if:

1. you were sentenced over your objection within six hours after being found guilty, or

2. you were assessed a penalty higher than the maximum for the first offense and you didn't admit to any prior offenses and the prosecution didn't prove them.

You should make this motion right after the judge improperly sentences you. However, if for some reason you had failed to object then, you should file a written motion to vacate the sentence as soon as possible thereafter.

The procedure for preparing and filing such a motion is the same as that given in Chapter 11 for other motions. First, a court date is obtained from the clerk. Then, you type a Notice of Motion, Points and Authorities, and Proof of Service, preferably on numbered legal paper. Make two sets of copies, and have a friend mail one set to the district (or city) attorney. The original set (including a Proof of Service signed by your friend) is then filed with the clerk.

The following sample motion papers list two separate grounds for moving to vacate the sentence. The first is that the judge refused a request to postpone sentencing for at least six hours. The second ground is that the fine

PATRICIA PRIOR
950 Parker St.
Berkeley, CA 94710
(510) 555-1212

SUPERIOR COURT OF CALIFORNIA, COUNTY OF ALAMEDA
BERKELEY-ALBANY BRANCH

THE PEOPLE OF THE STATE
OF CALIFORNIA,
    Plaintiff,

vs.

PATRICIA PRIOR,
    Defendant.

NO. A-123456 - B

**NOTICE OF MOTION
TO VACATE SENTENCE;
POINTS AND AUTHORITIES**

TO: PLAINTIFF, THE PEOPLE OF THE STATE OF CALIFORNIA, AND TO THE DISTRICT ATTORNEY FOR THE WITHIN-NAMED COUNTY:

PLEASE TAKE NOTICE that on March 6, 20xx at 9:00 a.m. in Department 2 of the above-entitled Court, at 2120 Martin Luther King, Jr. Way, Berkeley, California, defendant PATRICIA PRIOR will move to vacate the sentence imposed in the above-entitled action, on the grounds that:

1. Sentence was imposed immediately after pronouncement of verdict without defendant's consent, in violation of Section 1449 of the Penal Code; and

2. The sentence imposed is in excess of that permitted by law in the absence of allegation and proof, or admission by defendant, of prior Vehicle Code infractions.

This motion is based on this Notice of Motion and attached Points and Authorities, and on the pleadings, records, and files in this action.

DATED: March 1, 20xx

Patricia Prior

PATRICIA PRIOR,
Defendant in Pro Per

POINTS AND AUTHORITIES

STATEMENT OF FACTS

On February 22, 20xx, defendant was convicted of violating Section 22350 of the Vehicle Code, an infraction. No prior offenses were alleged in the complaint. The verdict of guilty was pronounced in open court by the Honorable Hugo Humorless, who sentenced defendant to a $200 fine immediately thereafter. Judge Humorless neither requested defendant to waive time for sentencing, nor did defendant waive such time. She did, however, deny any prior Vehicle Code offenses when asked by Judge Humorless, who replied, "Well, I see one here on the form from the Department of Motor Vehicles. This being your second offense in a year, I'm fining you $200 plus a $280 penalty assessment."

ARGUMENT

I. A SENTENCE IMPOSED ON A PRO PER DEFENDANT WITHIN SIX HOURS OF A GUILTY VERDICT MAY BE SET ASIDE ON MOTION, ABSENT A WAIVER OF TIME FOR SENTENCING BY DEFENDANT.

When a defendant has been convicted of a misdemeanor, the court must set a time for sentencing that is between six hours and five days from the time of pronouncement of the verdict (Penal Code § 1449). The same post-conviction procedures apply to infractions. See Penal Code § 19.7.

While time for sentencing can be waived, there can be no waiver by a pro per defendant unless the right is explained to her and she consents to be sentenced immediately (*People v. Wilson* (1963) 60 Cal.2d 139, 32 Cal.Rptr. 44).

If the defendant is sentenced earlier than the statute allows, the sentence may be vacated on motion. See *In re Elsholz* (1964) 228 Cal.App.2d 192, 39 Cal.Rptr. 356.

Accordingly, since the record shows defendant appeared in pro per and did not indicate a knowing waiver of the time for sentencing, the sentence herein must be vacated.

II. THE MAXIMUM FINE FOR A VEHICLE CODE INFRACTION IS $100 PLUS PENALTY ASSESSMENT, ABSENT ALLEGATION AND PROOF OR ADMISSION BY DEFENDANT OF A PRIOR CONVICTION OF SUCH AN INFRACTION.

The maximum fine for conviction of a Vehicle Code infraction is $100 for the first offense, $200 for the second, and $250 for the third, plus any penalty assessments (VC § 42001(a)). In general, a defendant cannot be given the higher maximum penalty for a second or later offense unless the prior offense is (1) alleged in the complaint, and (2) either proved at trial or admitted by the defendant. See *People v. Ford*

(1964) 60 Cal.2d 772, 794, 36 Cal.Rptr. 620; *People v. Ratner* (1944) 67 Cal.App.2d Supp. 902, 153 P.2d 790; 39 Ops. Atty. Gen. 13 (1962). The complaint herein, a police officer's citation or "Notice to Appear," obviously does not allege any prior infractions.

It is true that for Vehicle Code offenses, Section 42004 of that code authorizes the court to use a written report from the Department of Motor Vehicles showing prior convictions. However, the section states that "the communication is prima facie evidence of such convictions, *if the defendant admits them....*" [Emphasis added.]

By implication, the DMV report does not establish the prior convictions (or bail forfeitures) unless the defendant admits them. If the defendant denies such priors (or is not even asked about them), the DMV report is insufficient to establish such priors. In the instant case, defendant did not admit any priors. Accordingly, she may be fined only $100 (plus penalty assessments), and the $200 fine (plus penalty assessments) must be set aside.

DATED: March 1, 20xx

Respectfully submitted,

Patricia Prior

PATRICIA PRIOR
Defendant in Pro Per

PROOF OF SERVICE

I, JOHN SMITH, declare:

1. I am over the age of eighteen and not a party to the within action.

2. My residence address is 1200 Shattuck Ave., Berkeley, California, in the county within which the herein-mentioned mailing occurred.

3. On March 1, 20xx I served the within Notice of Motion to Vacate Sentence and Points and Authorities on plaintiff by placing true copies thereof in a separate sealed envelope, with the postage thereon fully prepaid, in the United States Postal Service mailbox at Berkeley, County of Alameda, California, the said envelope being addressed to:

Office of the District Attorney
County of Alameda
2120 Martin Luther King, Jr. Way
Berkeley, CA 94704

I declare under penalty of perjury under the laws of the State of California that the foregoing is true and correct.

DATED: March 1, 20xx

John Smith

JOHN SMITH
Defendant in Pro Per

is greater than that for a first-time infraction, even though no prior offenses were proved or admitted. If your situation involves only one of these grounds, you should prepare your Notice of Motion and Points and Authorities accordingly.

If your motion is to vacate the sentence because the judge sentenced you too soon, you should say:

> *"Your Honor, I'm moving to vacate the sentence on the ground that I was not sentenced between six hours and five days after conviction as required by Penal Code Section 1449. I call attention to the Points and Authorities I've submitted."*

If you're moving to vacate a sentence greater than that for a first-time offense because no prior offenses were proved by the prosecution or admitted by you, say something like this:

> *"Your Honor, I'm moving to vacate the sentence of a $500 fine on the ground that the fine is higher than the $100 maximum, plus $171 penalty assessments, or $271, for a first-time infraction, yet no priors were proven, nor did I admit to any. I call attention to the Points and Authorities I've submitted."*

If your motion is denied, you can appeal your sentence. But even if you win this appeal, the appeals court will still allow the conviction to stand and will merely order the trial court to sentence you properly.

If You Appeal

Appealing the decision does not automatically postpone the sentence. Judges will seldom, if ever, "stay" (postpone) a fine while your appeal is pending. They simply require you to pay and refund your money in the event the conviction is reversed. Jail sentences, license suspensions, and forced attendance at traffic school, however, cannot be so easily undone if your conviction is reversed. Ask the judge to stay these if you plan to appeal. ●

License Suspensions by the DMV

U nder certain circumstances, the Department of Motor Vehicles may suspend or revoke your license. This chapter deals with when and how this can happen, and what you can do about it.

Too Many Violations or Accidents

The most common type of license suspension occurs when a person gets too many "points" on his or her driving record by having too many moving-violation convictions and/or reported accidents within too short a time.

The "Point Count" System

The DMV can suspend or revoke your license if, at a hearing, it is determined that you're a negligent driver. In order to determine whether a driver is negligent, the DMV uses a point count system. Most moving violations and accidents reported by a police officer to be your fault count as one point. Violations that count as two points include reckless driving, hit-and-run, driving under the influence, driving the wrong way on a freeway or other divided highway, driving over 100 mph, participating in a speed exhibition or contest (VC § 12810), or driving with a suspended license. Seatbelt violations (VC §§ 27315 or 27360) are reported to the DMV but do not count for any points. Child-restraint violations (VC § 27360) count as one point. Reported accidents count for one point, unless the police officer investigating the accident advised the DMV that it wasn't your fault. (You can contest any decision at a license suspension hearing.)

You are considered negligent if you have four or more points in any 12-month period,

six or more in any 24-month period, or eight or more points in any 36-month period (VC § 12810.5). Truck or bus drivers with class A or class B licenses are allowed up to six, eight or ten points in 12-month, 24-month, or 36-month periods, respectively, as long as the violations occurred during the driving of a truck or bus for which a class A or B license is required. However, violations involving truck or bus driving count for one and a half or three points each, rather than the ordinary one or two points, respectively. This includes accidents or violations in any state or U.S. Territory and Canada, if they're reported to the DMV. (VC § 13363. See Chapter 3 on out-of-state tickets and Chapter 6 on federal tickets.)

If your license is suspended for this reason, you may be required to periodically post proof of insurance with the DMV for three years following the lifting of the suspension, in order to get your license back and keep it.

Other Criteria for Suspension

Even if your point count isn't high enough to classify you as "negligent," the DMV can still consider suspending or revoking your license for any of the following reasons (VC § 13800):

- You were involved in an accident that involved death, injury, or "serious damage to property"; or
- You were involved in three or more accidents in any 12-month period; or
- You were convicted of any of the following offenses (VC §13361):
  - a second offense of ordinary reckless driving (VC § 23103)
  - hit-and-run (VC § 20002), or
  - vehicular manslaughter (PC § 192(c));
- You violated restrictions imposed on your license (like driving for pleasure on a

temporary license that only allows you to drive to and from work (VC § 13360)) or allowed someone else to use your license.

Your Right to a Hearing Before Suspension

Whenever the DMV decides to suspend your license for having too many points on your record, you have the right to a hearing where you can present evidence and argue against the proposed suspension.

Requesting a Hearing

In most cases, the DMV will notify you that your license will be suspended or revoked unless you immediately call or write them a certified letter and request a hearing (VC §§ 13950, 14100, 14101). If you don't demand a hearing within ten days from the date the notice was mailed, you give up your right to have one, although the DMV may choose to grant you a hearing anyway (VC § 14103). Such a letter might look something like the following example.

If you call the DMV to request a hearing and have trouble connecting with the correct office, be patient. Most suspension notices fail to clearly list the phone number to call. Unfortunately, DMV "Driver Safety" offices have been moved and consolidated over the past years, concentrating in major cities like Los Angeles, San Diego, San Francisco, San Jose, Sacramento, and Fresno. If you can't find the number for a "Driver Safety" office under the DMV listing for a city near you, call information for one of the larger cities above by dialing 1 plus the area code plus 555-1212. Ask for the number for the "Driver Safety" office of the Department of Motor Vehicles, which will be listed in the government listings for the state of California.

Jason D. Wason
123 Parker Street
Sacramento, CA

June 25, 20xx

Department of Motor Vehicles
2415 First Avenue
Sacramento, CA 95818

Certified Mail Return Receipt Requested

Re: Proposed Driver's License Suspension,
Driver's License # A1234567

Dear Sir or Madam:

This is in response to your letter of March 3, 20xx in which your office proposed to suspend my driver's license on the ground that I am a negligent driver. Pursuant to § 14100 of the Vehicle Code, I request that an in-person hearing be held so that I may present evidence on my behalf in opposition to the proposed suspension.

Sincerely,

Jason D. Watson

Jason D. Watson

Note: Use the DMV address on the hearing notice, if it is different from this address.

Unfortunately, persons who attempt to request hearings over the phone face frustrating red tape. It often takes a few calls to locate the correct office. Callers are placed on hold for long periods of time. Clerks often don't have immediate access to records, and the earliest available in-person hearing is often months away, sometimes well into the suspension period. For this reason, your hearing request should be made within ten days of the date on the suspension notice in order to maximize your chances of getting the suspensions "stayed" (delayed) pending the outcome of the hearing.

The Hearing

In recent years, the closure of Driver Safety DMV offices and their centralization into major cities has resulted in fewer in-person DMV hearings, and more hearings by telephone. Telephone hearings are conducted in the same manner as in-person hearings (see below), but occur over the phone. For a telephone hearing, you will be notified in writing of the exact date and time, at which time the DMV hearing officer will call you at the number you give them when requesting a hearing. Be sure to have with you, at the phone, any witnesses whose testimony you wish to present.

For in-person hearings, the hearing will take place in a little room at the DMV Driver Safety Office. When you get there, you will probably see the hearing referee seated at a desk or the end of a long table. You and any witnesses you bring will be seated in front of the desk or at the table. A recording device will be there to make a record of the hearing.

The hearing officer will introduce herself. If you have witnesses, tell her. If any of your witnesses do not show, you can ask for the hearing to be held over to another day. The referee will consider how crucial your witness is and make a determination.

Note: Witnesses can be very important. If, for example, you have too many violation points in too short a time, a couple of reputable people who will testify that you are an excellent driver will be a great help. So will any favorable witnesses to reported accidents that you claim weren't your fault, if the proposed suspension is based on a point count that includes any points for such an accident. But choose your witnesses

well. Lenny Lowrider and Walter Wino aren't going to help you much, while Fred Firefighter probably will. If attending the hearing would be inconvenient, your witnesses can file written statements. You can also request the DMV to issue subpoenas to compel their attendance (VC §§ 13952, 14100). The referee will then summarize the case as it appears in the file. After you are sworn in (it is perjury to lie at the hearing), you will be asked to present your case.

A hearing is more informal than a traffic court trial. No one will be there to testify against you. You will probably be allowed to testify to any information that may be important, though in a court of law it might not be admissible. This means you can present your case entirely in writing if you want (VC § 14104). But don't do this unless you know you'll be too nervous to present a coherent case in person. It's better to present your evidence to the hearing officer face-to-face at an in-person hearing. You will need to convince the referee that there are sound reasons why your license shouldn't be suspended or revoked.

Here are some examples of the types of evidence you may want to present:

- Any circumstances in the violations counted against you that tend to cast you in a favorable light;
- Why an accident the DMV is counting against you wasn't your fault;
- Evidence that you drive a great many miles—personal and business—each year;
- How your livelihood depends on your ability to drive;
- Statements by employers or other "responsible" people as to how carefully, cautiously, and conservatively you drive;
- Evidence of a recently completed defensive driving, driver training, or other driving-related courses; or

- Physicians' reports of your physical condition and ability to drive.

Discuss your points clearly. The hearing officer may ask you questions to help you explain your case. If you have any evidence to present, such as a doctor's statement, a driver training certificate, a written statement from someone who couldn't appear, or anything else, present it.

Then, any witnesses you have will be given a chance to testify. You should have each witness testify in her own words, or in response to your questions. (A leading question is one that, in essence, includes the answer. "Was the car red?" is a leading question because it contains the answer to the question. "What color was the car?" is a proper nonleading question. Proper nonleading questions usually begin with the word "what," "who," "where," "when," "why," or "how.")

After each witness presents his testimony, the hearing officer might ask questions.

During the hearing, stick to the points you are trying to make. Don't get carried away in unnecessary detail. Don't feel you have to rush through. You'll have plenty of time to explain your position.

The hearing officer can either suspend your license or grant probation. The terms of the probation can include a suspension, the issuance of a probationary license that is subject to certain restrictions, or the requirement that you take a driver education course (VC §§ 14250, 14250.5). At the end of the hearing, the hearing officer may give a decision right there or inform you later by mail.

Further Review of the Decision

You may appeal the referee's decision by writing a letter to the hearing board within 15 days of the effective date of the decision. Instructions on how to go about this will be included on the notice you receive of the referee's decision (VC § 14105.5). The appeal is merely a process called an "administrative review," where DMV employees look at the referee's hearing report and any written evidence you presented. You do not have an opportunity to present further evidence or argument on your behalf, and it is likely that the referee's decision will be affirmed. But you have nothing to lose by requesting a review. Your only further avenue of appeal is through the court system.

Although you can have the Superior Court review the DMV's final decision, the courts seldom reverse the DMV. The procedure is extremely formal and complicated, is beyond the scope of this book, and should be handled by an attorney. Strictly speaking, this type of proceeding does not involve an appeal, but rather an original lawsuit against the DMV in which you seek a "writ of mandate" to prevent it from suspending your license. This type of lawsuit must be brought within 90 days of the DMV's decision. (VC § 14401(a). See also CCP § 1094.5. How to handle "writ" cases is thoroughly discussed in Witkin, *Criminal Procedure, and California Civil Writs*, by CEB (Continuing Education of the Bar), available in virtually all California public law libraries.)

Driving With a BAC of 0.08% or More

As we saw in Chapter 8, your license can be suspended by the DMV for four months or a year (if you had a previous conviction or suspension within the past ten years) for driving with a blood alcohol content (BAC) of 0.08% or above. The officer who arrests you serves you the suspension notice—effective in 30 days (VC §§ 13353.2–13353.7). To contest it, you must apply to the DMV for a hearing within ten days. If you wait longer, the DMV might still give you a hearing, but probably not before the suspension goes into effect (VC § 14103). At the hearing the issues are:

1. Whether the officer had "reasonable cause" to believe you were driving under the influence or with blood alcohol over 0.08%;

2. Whether you were placed under arrest (almost never in dispute); and

3. Whether you were in fact driving a motor vehicle while under the influence or with a blood alcohol level over 0.08%.

A person under 21 can also receive a one-year license suspension—regardless of whether he or she is convicted of any offense—for driving with an extremely low blood alcohol level of 0.01% or greater, as measured by a hand-held, roadside "preliminary alcohol screening" (PAS) device, or for driving under the influence with a BAC of 0.05% or more. As with the suspension applicable to a person 21 or older with a blood alcohol level of 0.08% or higher, the officer serves the suspension notice—effective in 30 days—and takes the driver's license. The procedure for requesting a hearing is the same, and the issues are:

1. whether your blood alcohol level was 0.01% or higher as measured by a PAS device, and

2. whether you were driving a vehicle.

A person under 21 whose license is suspended can get a restricted license by showing a "critical need to drive," even though a person over 21 whose license has been similarly suspended for 0.08% or more alcohol cannot (VC §§ 23136, 13353.2).

The procedure for these hearings is similar to that for other license-suspension hearings, except that the issues are limited to those discussed above.

If you are also charged criminally with driving under the influence, you should request a hearing in order to avoid a suspension. A later acquittal in court will entitle you to a lifting of the suspension.

It is *very* difficult to win such a hearing if your blood, breath, or urine showed a blood alcohol level of 0.08% or more (0.01% or more if under 21). Also, if you testify at such a hearing, your testimony there could later be used against you at trial. For that and other reasons, you should be represented by a lawyer at this stage.

Refusal to Take a Blood or Breath or Roadside "PAS" Test

As we discussed in detail in Chapter 8, California has an "implied consent" law. Driving a vehicle on the road implies that you consent to a blood or breath test for blood alcohol. Also, if you took a breath test and passed it, and the officer had "reasonable cause" to believe you were under the influence of drugs, you also have agreed to a test of your blood or urine. If you refuse to take a test, the DMV suspends your license for a year in addition to any suspension for driving under the influence or with a BAC of 0.08% or more. You could face a two- or three-year suspension if you have one or two prior convictions for:

- driving under the influence

- driving with a BAC of 0.08% or more

- having plea bargained for an alcohol-related reckless driving conviction (VC § 23103.5)

- having previous DMV suspensions for over-0.08% BAC, or

- refusing a blood or breath test.

If you suffered a previous suspension or were convicted of driving under the influence (or plea bargained reckless driving) within the previous ten years, the suspension is for an additional two years. If you suffered two such convictions or suspensions within the previous seven years, your license is revoked for an additional three years. This is true even if you're found not guilty of the current charge (VC § 13353). The officer who arrests you serves you the notice of suspension; to contest it, you must apply to the DMV within ten days for a hearing. Again, for this type of suspension, requesting a hearing does not automatically prevent the suspension from going into effect after 30 days, unless you request a hearing within ten days of your arrest.

At the hearing, the issues are whether all of the following occurred:

1. Whether the officer had "reasonable cause" to believe you were driving under the influence or with blood alcohol over 0.08%;

2. Whether you were lawfully placed under arrest (almost never in dispute);

3. Whether you refused to submit to and complete any of the three tests; and

4. Whether you were told that failure to complete at least one test would result in a license suspension.

The procedure for implied consent hearings is similar to that for other hearings, except that the issues in an implied consent hearing are limited to those discussed above (VC § 13353). A hearing must be requested by you within ten days in order for the suspension to be stayed before it goes into effect (30 days from the date of your arrest), if the DMV can't schedule a hearing before then (VC § 13358(e)).

In almost all implied consent hearings, the main issue is whether your refusal to take the test was reasonable. Did the police fail to give you a choice of properly administered tests, or fail to warn you of the consequences of refusing to submit to one of them?

Reasonable excuses for not taking the tests include:

- The police didn't really give you a choice of tests; perhaps they coerced you to take a certain one (usually a blood test).

- They failed to tell you your license would be suspended if you refused to take one of the tests.

Note: If you were taken to a hospital because you needed medical treatment, you can't use this excuse if the test you insisted on (such as a breath test) wasn't "feasible" there.

Excuses that definitely *won't* work include:

- Not being able to give blood or blow hard enough into the breathalyzer. If you cannot complete a particular test, you have to submit to the one you can complete. (Also, if you pass a breath test and the officer reasonably believes you were on drugs, you have to submit to a test of blood or urine if a blood test is available (VC § 23157.5).)

- Refusal to take the test until your attorney or physician shows up. You have the right to have an attorney present eventually, and to have a private physician give you an additional test later, but you cannot condition or delay the test based on either one having to show up.

- Insistence on taking two or three tests or none at all.

- Being too drunk to understand the police explanations.

"Implied consent" hearings are notoriously difficult to win, especially in cases where the officer says he read you your rights and saw you refuse all tests. The DMV hearing referee will almost always believe the officer, instead of you, on any point where your testimony differs from the officer's. Also, case law over the years has severely limited the types of technicalities you can raise at these hearings.

In any event, since a license suspension of one, two, or three years is very severe, and since you may want to have a formal hearing in order to better preserve your right to have a court review the DMV's decision, you may want to hire an attorney to represent you at the hearing. (See Chapter 9.) But be aware that your chance of winning this type of hearing is exceedingly slim, and you may be better off saving your money to cope with any fines or other economic hardships you are likely to face.

In addition, under similar procedures, a person under 21 faces a one-year suspension for refusing to take a roadside preliminary alcohol screening ("PAS") or other chemical test (see above) at the request of a police officer. Procedures for hearings are similar (VC §§ 13353.1, 23157).

Automatic Suspension or Revocation

Sometimes the law requires that the DMV suspend or revoke a driver's license regardless of the particular circumstances. (The only significant difference between a "suspension" and a "revocation" is that a "suspension" is for two years or less and a "revocation" is for three years or more.) In the following situations, since the suspension or revocation is automatic, there is no opportunity for a hearing.

Conviction of a Felony Where a Vehicle Was Used

The DMV is required to revoke or suspend your license for at least one year when you're convicted of any felony (other than felony driving under the influence, covered below) in which a motor vehicle was used, including manslaughter and hit-and-run where death or injury resulted.

Conviction of Driving Under the Influence—Injury or Death

As we saw in Chapter 8, a drunk driver who kills or injures someone in an accident can be convicted of either a felony or a misdemeanor. Either way, the DMV must impose the following license suspensions or revocations (VC § 13352(a)(2), (4), (6)):

Driving Under the Influence—Resulting in Injury or Death	
First Offense	Suspension for one year.
Second Offense (within 10 years) (including earlier noninjury DUI offenses as a prior conviction)	Revocation for three years—or for 18 months if, by then, you have completed a second-offender alcohol treatment program, followed by a license restriction for the rest of the three-year period where you can only drive to, from, and in your work.
Third Offense (within 10 years) (also including non-injury DUIs as priors)	Revocation for five years.

After the period of suspension or revocation, you'll have to show proof to the DMV that you completed the applicable alcohol-treatment program in order to get your license back.

Conviction of Misdemeanor Driving Under the Influence— No Death or Injury

For misdemeanor driving under the influence (or with over 0.08% blood alcohol) not involving death or injury, the DMV must suspend or revoke your driver's license as follows (VC § 13352(a)(1), (3), (5), (7)):

Driving Under the Influence— Not Resulting in Injury or Death	
First Offense	Six-month suspension only if ordered by the court or if probation is denied. Ten-month suspension if blood alcohol of 0.20% or more.
Second Offense (within 10 years) (including reckless driving plea bargained from DUI as a prior conviction)	Suspension for two years—or for one year if enrolled in an alcohol-treatment program followed by a two-year restriction—allowing driving only to, from, and at your work, and to and from the treatment program.
Third or Fourth Offense (within 10 years) (including plea bargained reckless driving as a prior conviction)	Revocation for three years (third offense) or four years (fourth offense).

Note: This chart refers only to DMV-imposed suspensions following conviction, and from which there is no right to a DMV hearing. In addition, the DMV imposes the four-month or one-year suspension (as to which a hearing is allowed) for driving with an over-0.08% blood alcohol level, regardless of conviction.

After the suspension or revocation period, you still cannot get your license back unless you have completed the applicable alcohol-treatment program.

Conviction of Other Offenses

If you're convicted of reckless driving or hit-and-run involving bodily injury, vehicular manslaughter, or any felony in which a motor vehicle is used, the DMV must revoke your license. Also, revocation is required if you're convicted of three reckless driving and/or hit-and-run offenses within any 12-month period. Finally, a six-month or one-year suspension (or restriction, to allow driving only to, from, and in your work) is required for respective second or third offenses, within three years, of driving over 100 mph.

Regarding misdemeanors, anyone convicted of any offense relating to possession of illegal drugs (even prescription drugs without a valid prescription) will lose his or her license for six months—or for up to three years if the court chooses to do so—even if the offense had nothing to do with driving or a vehicle. (See Chapter 5 and VC §§ 13202, 13202.3, 13202.5, 13350(a), 13351, 13355.)

Other non-driving-conduct convictions that can result in driver's license suspensions include truancy, if under 18 (one year), prostitution within 1,000 feet of a residence if a vehicle is "used in the solicitation" (30 days), vandalism by graffiti (six months), and nonpayment of child support (indefinite). For persons under age 21, any offense involving alcohol or illegal drugs will result in a one-year license suspension (VC §§13201.5, 13202.5, 13202.6, 13202.7, Welfare & Institutions Code § 11350.6).

Not Having Insurance at the Time of an Accident

In addition to the laws allowing you to be fined if you drive without insurance, a separate law allows the DMV to suspend your license for a year if you're involved in an accident without insurance—regardless of who was at fault.

Accidents

Whenever you're involved as a driver in an automobile accident where over $750 in property damages (to any one person) results, or if anyone (including yourself) is injured or killed, you are required to report the accident to the DMV within ten days. You are allowed to have your insurance company do this for you (VC § 16000). (Forms for this purpose are available from any DMV office or from your insurance company.) If you don't file the report, and the DMV finds out about the accident (if it's reported by the other driver or the police), your license will be suspended until you either file the report or provide proof that you were covered by auto insurance on the date of the accident (VC §§ 16004, 16070). One exception: If you were driving a vehicle owned by your employer, your employer must report the accident (VC § 16002).

Even if you were driving someone else's vehicle, you must still report the accident yourself, because you were the driver. That means you must also report the owner's insurance information if you weren't insured for the vehicle yourself. If the owner won't provide that information, you should remind him or her that to fail to provide you with it under those circumstances is a criminal offense (VC § 16050.5).

Even if you do file an accident report within the required ten days, you will still have your license suspended for one year if you weren't covered by insurance at the time of the accident—whether or not you were at fault. Even after the year is up, you still don't get your license back until you show the DMV proof that you've obtained auto insurance. Any lapse in your insurance for the next three years will be reported by your insurance company to the DMV, which will suspend your license again (VC §§ 16070, 16072).

However, you can get the one-year suspension reduced to a restriction under which you can drive only to, from, and in your work, or to and from a hospital or doctor for recurring medical treatments if a physician certifies that you have a "serious health problem." To do this, you must pay a $250 penalty to the DMV and get insurance right away. (You can also drive your minor children to and from school if the principal certifies that public transportation to and/or from school is not readily available.) This sort of restriction still lasts a year, and after that you must keep your insurance in force for three years during which your license will be suspended if your insurance lapses (VC §§ 16072, 16076–16078).

License Suspension Proceedings Resulting From Accidents

The DMV will mail you a notice of its intent to suspend your license for not reporting an over-$750 or injury accident, or for not being covered by insurance (VC § 16070). The suspension takes effect within 15 days unless you either:

- Send the DMV an SR-22 form (available from your insurance company) that you were covered by insurance at the time; or

- Make a written demand for a hearing.

If you weren't insured, you have nothing to lose by demanding a hearing, and the DMV can't suspend your license on the basis of the other driver's written statement of the accident. If no one shows up personally to testify about the accident, you can object to the DMV hearing officer's attempt to introduce the other driver's written statement into the record. You can also refuse to testify yourself (*Daniels v. DMV* (1983) 33 Cal.3d 532). The only issues on which you will be allowed to present evidence at such a hearing are:

- Whether you were a driver in an accident resulting in over $750 worth in damages to any one person (including yourself), or in injury (even just to yourself) or death; and

- Whether you were insured at the time (VC § 16075).

Unfortunately, the DMV considers it irrelevant whose fault the accident was, and will not let you present any evidence in that regard (*Annacker v. Sillas* (1977) 65 Cal.App.3d 416, 135 Cal. Rptr. 537). This means that if you can't afford auto insurance and have an accident that's entirely someone else's fault, you can still lose your license for a year—and for up to three years after that, if you can't find affordable insurance. Your mistaken belief that you had insurance—perhaps because you didn't know about a cancellation—is also irrelevant, unless it occurred because your insurance broker fraudulently absconded with the premiums you paid, without paying the insurer (VC §§ 12807(c), 40509(a), 16030(a)).

Holding a License in Abeyance

The DMV will hold your driver's license in limbo, either by refusing to renew it, or by suspending it, if you:

- fail to answer to a moving violation ticket you've signed

- fail to pay a fine a judge sentenced you to pay, or

- fail to pay a civil court judgment arising out of an auto accident.

Your license will be returned or renewed once you remedy these problems.

"Failure-to-Appear" on a Ticket You Signed

When you violate a written promise to appear by ignoring a ticket you signed, the court to which the ticket is sent will also charge you with the misdemeanor of failure to appear. It will then notify the DMV of this charge. The DMV will then suspend your license until you have all the original and failure-to-appear charges "adjudicated"—cleared with the court by either forfeiting bail, or by contesting the charge and then winning—or losing and paying the fine (VC § 13365).

Note: Some judges and commissioners will notify the DMV to rescind the suspension once you have pleaded not guilty and before the case goes to trial. It doesn't hurt to ask for this at arraignment.

Even if, for some reason, the court has neglected to notify the DMV of your failure to appear, or the DMV simply hasn't gotten around to suspending your license, you may still have a problem when it comes time to renew your driver's license. The DMV will refuse to issue you a renewal license until you have both the original and the failure-to-appear charges adjudicated (VC § 12808(b)). If you've waited until the last day to renew your license and you decide to contest the matter, you may find yourself out of luck. It may take one or two months before you have your trial on both the original violation and the failure-to-appear charge. If you want the court clerk to send the "clearance" certificate (which tells the DMV not to suspend or hold your license on account of the particular violation) to the DMV right away, you'll have to appear in court and maybe also plead guilty to both charges—including the misdemeanor of failure to appear—or pay the fine.

On the other hand, if you're in this situation, you may wish to insist on an arraignment. There, if you plead not guilty, you should ask the judge to direct the clerk to issue the DMV "clearance," because VC § 40509(a) allows issuance of one "if the case … is adjudicated or the person who has violated the court order *appears in court* or otherwise satisfies the order of the court …." Although this "appears in court" language seems to address the situation where the defendant disobeyed a judge who personally ordered a fine paid or proof of correction to be filed, "or appear in court" on a certain day, the law is unclear enough to give you some maneuvering room. Tell the judge you've appeared and offer to post bail prior to trial, and you might get a clearance.

Also, the DMV will hold up your vehicle registration if you have any unresolved failures to appear or unpaid fines for moving violations. You will not be able to renew your registration until you resolve the unpaid fines or failures to appear.

Unpaid Parking Tickets

Similarly, the DMV will refuse to renew your auto registration if you ignore a parking ticket. The DMV can also refuse to renew your driver's license based on unpaid parking tickets (VC § 12801.1). In order to get your registration renewed, you'll have to either fight the parking ticket and win, or pay the fine plus a hefty "administrative fee." (See Chapter 6.)

You can pay this directly to the DMV, which will then forward the money to the proper court. If someone else's tickets are holding up registration of a vehicle you recently purchased, you won't have to pay the tickets that person got if you sign a statement to that effect, under penalty of perjury.

Failure to Pay a Judge-Imposed Fine

If you were found or pleaded guilty on a ticket, and were fined by a judge or traffic commissioner, the court will report a failure to pay the fine to the DMV (VC § 40509(b)). This applies only to offenses that are normally entered on your driving record—including all moving violations. (See Chapter 3.) When you apply for a renewal license, the DMV will refuse to renew it until you pay the fine (VC § 12807(d)).

Not Paying Off an Accident-Related Court Judgment

Your license can be suspended (without a hearing) for failing to pay off all or a certain portion of a civil court judgment arising out of a lawsuit filed against you as the result of an auto accident. You can't get your license back until you pay off the required amount and provide the DMV with proof that you're insured (VC §§ 16250–16381, CCP §§ 116.870, 116.880 (Small Claims Court)). ●

Appealing a Conviction

After you've been found guilty of a misdemeanor or infraction, you have the right to appeal the decision to the Appellate Division. Doing your own appeal is very time-consuming and complicated, even more so than preparing and arguing a written pretrial motion. You will have to prepare quite a bit of paperwork and attend at least two hearings.

Your chances of getting your conviction reversed on appeal are low. Judges who hear appeals do not review the evidence of the case again. Even if the trial judge made a mistake in believing the police officer over your truthful testimony, the higher court will not reverse the decision. Appeals courts overturn a conviction only if the trial court improperly ruled on a point of law. For example, if the judge insisted on hearing the case after you properly filed a Peremptory Challenge, she committed a legal error and the appeals court will reverse. Errors of law commonly made by traffic court judges are listed in "Possible Grounds for Appeal," below.

Moreover, it's not enough to merely note in your appeal that the judge made a legal error. You usually have to show that your ability to present your case was "prejudiced" (for example, "compromised," or hurt) as a result of the judge's error. For example, if the judge erred in denying your motion to dismiss the case for excessive delay of the trial, you usually have to show that the delay actually hurt your case. (This might happen if a witness died, moved away, or simply forgot important details.)

Finally, you will have to become familiar with legal research and writing techniques and spend some time in a law library. To learn more about this, it is highly recommended that you read *Legal Research: How to Find & Understand the Law,* by Stephen Elias and the Editors of Nolo, available from Nolo. This book shows you how to look up cases and statutes, how to see if they are up-to-date, and how to use all sorts of secondary sources, such as law reviews, legal encyclopedias, and law texts. Chapter 9 also explains how to find cases (court decisions) or statutes. It is important that you read the cases cited in this chapter before relying on them, to be sure that they apply to your specific fact situation.

As we saw in Chapter 10, there are various types of motions that can be made in traffic court, and the text of the legal arguments for those motions appears mostly in that chapter.

You will notice that many of the grounds for appeal listed below stem from erroneous denials of the motions or requests you may have raised at or before trial. To save time and effort, you can include, in the brief you will file in the appellate court, the relevant text of the legal arguments from those motions, with relatively minor changes. However, do not just insert the text of any of these motions into your appellate briefs without reading the material and making any appropriate changes based on format and context. Otherwise, you will simply convince the judges that you really don't know what you are doing, and they will be less likely to rule in your favor.

When you do finally go to your hearing on the appeal, you will have to be able to argue the points that are raised in your appellate brief. In fact, it is likely that you will be asked questions regarding your legal arguments. This is why we strongly recommend that you read the cases that are cited in any motions whose denial you will be claiming was wrong, as well as the cases cited below, before you write your brief. That way, you will have a better understanding of the legal theories on which you rely, and will be more able to advocate your point of view.

Before you begin, remember that a successful appeal may only get you a new trial. However, successful appeals on some grounds, such as insufficiency of the evidence or violation of your right to a speedy trial, will terminate the case. A few cases suggest that a reversal of a traffic-infraction conviction should *always* terminate the case—on the basis that an appeal is punishment enough, given the minor nature of the offense. (See *People v. Kriss* (1979) 96 Cal. App.3d 913, 921, 158 Cal.Rptr. 420; *People v. Bighinatti* (1975) 55 Cal.App.3d Supp. 5, 7, 127 Cal.Rptr. 310; and *People v. Ruhl* (1976) 63 Cal.App.3d Supp. 6, 134 Cal. Rptr. 62.)

Below, we tell you which grounds on appeal will result in termination of the case, and which ones may result in a retrial. If your appeal is one that may only get you a new trial, you may not want to go to the trouble. On the other hand, if you request termination of your case in your brief, the appeals court might agree to do it in the interests of justice.

Possible Grounds for Appeal

Here is a list of the most likely bases for appealing traffic court decisions, with a few comments about each. It is not intended to be complete. Included with each appeal ground is the appropriate authority—statute or case(s). Use these legal references as a starting point in your legal research; they are not the exclusive authority on the subject. And remember, don't try to use one of these bases of appeal unless it applies to your particular fact situation.

Prearraignment Delay

You can appeal on this ground when there was a delay of several months before your arraignment, you weren't responsible for the delay, you made a timely motion to dismiss that was denied, and your presentation of the case suffered as a result of the delay. (See Chapter 10.) See the following cases: *In re Mugica* (1968) 69 Cal.2d 516, 72 Cal.Rptr. 645; *Burker*

v. Municipal Court (1966) 64 Cal.2d 806, 51 Cal.Rptr. 921; *People v. Valenzuela* (1978) 86 Cal.App.3d 427, 150 Cal.Rptr. 314; *People v. Guaracha* (1969) 272 Cal.App.2d 839, 77 Cal.Rptr. 695; *People v. Flores* (1968) 262 Cal. App.2d 313, 68 Cal.Rptr. 669; *Zimmerman v. Superior Court* (1967) 248 Cal.App.2d 56, 56 Cal.Rptr. 226. A reversal on this ground will terminate the case. It will not be sent back for retrial.

Prearrest Delay

If a misdemeanor complaint was filed against you in court (usually for failure-to-appear), but the police didn't arrest you until at least a year had passed, you might have made a motion to dismiss at your arraignment. (See Chapter 10.) If such a motion was denied, and your presentation of the case suffered as a result of the delay, you should appeal. See *Rost v. Municipal Court* (1960) 184 Cal.App.2d 507, 7 Cal.Rptr. 869; and *Rice v. Superior Court* (1975) 49 Cal.App.3d 200, 122 Cal.Rptr. 389 (felony case, but same rule applicable). In *Ibarra v. Municipal Court* (1984) 162 Cal.App.3d 853, 208 Cal.Rptr. 783, the appeals court held that a court must hold a full evidentiary hearing on whether the defendant's case was hurt as a result of prearrest/prearraignment delay. (See also *People v. Rogers* (1981) 120 Cal.App.3d Supp. 7, 174 Cal.Rptr. 313.) In *Serna v. Superior Court* (1985) 40 Cal.3d 239, the court said that a one-year delay preceding arrest is presumed to hurt the defendant's case. Also, the U.S. Supreme Court case of *Moore v. Arizona* (1973) 414 U.S. 25, 94 S.Ct. 188, 38 L.Ed. 2d 183, says that your ability to present your case doesn't have to have suffered in order for your conviction to be reversed on account of unconstitutional delay. (See Chapter 10.) Again, a successful appeal on this ground will terminate the case.

Your Peremptory Challenge to Disqualify the Judge Was Ignored

When you made a timely motion to disqualify a particular judge before she did anything on the case, the judge had "no jurisdiction" to continue. (See *Brown v. Swickard* (1985) 163 Cal.App.3d 820, 209 Cal.Rptr. 844.) You do not have to show your case was "prejudiced" by this. We refer you to CCP § 170.6 and the following cases: *Retes v. Superior Court* (1981) 122 Cal.App.3d 799, 176 Cal.Rptr. 160; *Bouchard v. Insona* (1980) 105 Cal.App.3d 768, 164 Cal.Rptr. 505. The California Supreme Court ruled in *People v. Hull* (1991) 1 Cal.4th 266, 2 Cal.Rptr.2d 526, that a person whose peremptory challenge is improperly denied must seek a "writ of mandate" from an appellate court, rather than wait to be convicted and then appeal. However, it is unclear whether this rule applies to cases in which the challenge is presented on the date of trial, or even to misdemeanor or infraction cases at all. This is because the court ruled on the language of CCP § 170.3, which refers to "court of appeal" cases where the appeal is to the Superior Court Appellate Division rather than to the Court of Appeal. If your conviction is reversed on this ground, the appeals court can send the case back for a new trial.

Your Informal Discovery Request Was Ignored

If you made an Informal Discovery Request to the prosecuting and police agencies, who didn't respond (Chapter 10), and despite your discovery motion you didn't receive a copy of the officer's notes, and/or any engineering and traffic survey in a radar speed case, in time to prepare for trial, you may be entitled to reversal. We refer you to Penal Code Sections 1054–1054.7, and *Hobbs v. Municipal Court* (1991) 233 Cal. App.3d 670, 284 Cal.Rptr. 655, which rule that these "discovery" laws apply to misdemeanors, and hence also to infractions under PC § 19.7.

Your Motion for Transfer to the County Seat Was Ignored

A non-county-seat judge who ignores a proper request for transfer of a case to the county seat has "no jurisdiction" to conduct the trial. You don't have to prove that your case was compromised by this (VC § 40502). (See Chapter 10.) We refer you also to *Smith v. Municipal Court* (1959) 167 Cal.App.2d 534, 344 P.2d 931. In *People v. Beltran* (1981) 124 Cal.App.3d 335, 177 Cal.Rptr. 262, and Government Code § 23600, "county seat" is defined. Again, if your conviction is reversed on this ground, the appeals court can order a retrial.

Delay After Arraignment

If you didn't go to trial until more than 45 days after your arraignment had passed, you didn't waive your right to a speedy trial, and you weren't responsible for causing the delay, you may get your conviction reversed. However, you must have objected to the delay before trial, and your presentation of the case must have suffered because of the delay. See PC § 1382 and the many cases in the annotations, including *Rhinehart v. Municipal Court* (1984) 35 Cal.3d 772, 200 Cal.Rptr. 916; *Arreola v. Municipal Court* (1983) 139 Cal.App.3d 108, 188 Cal. Rptr. 529; *Castaneda v. Municipal Court* (1972) 25 Cal.App.3d 588, 102 Cal.Rptr. 230; *Hankla v. Municipal Court* (1972) 26 Cal.App.3d 342, 102 Cal.Rptr. 896; and *Beasley v. Municipal Court* (1973) 32 Cal.App.3d 1020, 108 Cal. Rptr. 637. (See also Chapter 10.)

Improper Use of Speed Trap Evidence

In many cases, if the officer testified that he used radar to determine your speed, but failed to either: (1) properly introduce into evidence a traffic and engineering survey justifying the speed limit on the section of the street where he nabbed you, or (2) establish that the street was a statute-defined "local street (or) road," you should have objected to his testimony at trial. (See Chapter 11.) If you objected, but the judge convicted you after allowing this testimony, you can appeal on this ground. (See VC §§ 40801–40805, particularly § 40803(b).) Also, read the cases of *People v. Halopoff* (1976) 60 Cal.App.3d Supp.1, 131 Cal.Rptr. 531; *People v. Sterritt* (1976) 65 Cal.App.3d Supp. 1, 135 Cal.Rptr. 552; *People v. Flaxman* (1977) 74 Cal.App.3d Supp. 16, 151 Cal.Rptr. 799; *People v. Abelson* (1980) 104 Cal.App.3d Supp. 16, 164 Cal.Rptr. 369; *People v. Peterson* (1986) 181 Cal.App.3d Supp. 7, 226 Cal.Rptr. 544; *People v. DiFiore* (1987) 197 Cal.App.3d Supp. 26, 243 Cal.Rptr. 359; *People v. Ellis* (1995) 33 Cal.App.4th Supp. 25, 40 Cal.Rptr.2d 111; and *People v. Conzelman* (1995) 33 Cal.App.4th Supp. 6, 39 Cal.Rptr.2d 156. *Conzelman* holds that without the survey, even the officer's "visual" estimate of speed was inadmissible. For a case involving a survey that was produced but found lacking for not justifying the speed limit, see *People v. Goulet* (1993) 13 Cal.App.4th Supp. 1, 17 Cal.Rptr.2d 801. (Also see Chapter 4.) The failure of the officer to do one of the above is actually a failure to present evidence on all the essential elements required to be proved (under § 40803(b)) when radar is used. This will support an appeal for insufficient evidence. (See below.) In such cases, a new trial is barred under the "double jeopardy" clause of the Constitution (*Burks v. U.S.* (1977) 437 U.S. 1), because the prosecution has failed to prove an essential element of its case—as required by VC § 40803(b)—that the area is not a "speed trap" as defined in VC § 40802. Thus, if you win an appeal, your fight is over.

Verdict Not Supported by Evidence/Erroneous Denial of Motion for Acquittal

For some fairly complex Vehicle Code violations with lots of elements, it's possible that the officer failed to establish every element of the violation. If you can analyze the section you were charged with and find at least one element to which the officer didn't testify at all, then the evidence wasn't sufficient to convict you (unless you inadvertently supplied the missing element in your own testimony). (See Chapter 12.) If this is the case, no retrial is allowed and you win, period.

Note: Don't confuse this with trying to get the appeals court to "reweigh" the evidence. As long as there is *any* evidence in the record to support the conviction, the conviction will be upheld. For example, if you were charged with failing to yield the right of way at an intersection controlled by a stop sign (VC § 21802), and the officer testified that a stop sign was there, the appeals court won't reverse a guilty verdict, even if you and three other witnesses testified that there was no stop sign. However, if the officer never testified that a stop sign was there, one essential element would be completely unproved, and the verdict of guilty would not be supported by the evidence.

If you made a motion for acquittal (as described in Chapter 12), your appeal can be based on the ground that the trial judge erred in denying your motion. If, at the time you made your motion, you did not argue that the prosecution's evidence was insufficient and explain to the judge why (because the judge would not agree to prevent the prosecution from reopening its case against you), then you will need to address that issue on appeal. In doing so, you should refer to the cases of *People v. Belton* (1979) 23 Cal.3d 516 and *People v. Martinez* (1982) 132 Cal.App.3d 119, which ruled that you do not have to assist the prosecution in that regard.

Judge Acted as Prosecutor

In *People v. Carlucci* (1979) 23 Cal.3d 249, 152 Cal.Rptr. 439, the California Supreme Court suggested that trials conducted without a prosecutor were proper, but only "if the conduct of the court, including its questioning of the witnesses, is fair and properly limited in scope." See also *People v. Daggett* (1988) 206 Cal.App.3d Supp. 1, 253 Cal.Rptr. 195. (Read the excellent dissent, in any event.)

Another good case on this point is *People v. Municipal Court* (1990) 220 Cal.App.3d 602, 269 Cal.Rptr. 542. Although the Court of Appeal overruled a traffic judge's requirement that prosecutors attend traffic court, it emphasized that, in the absence of a prosecutor, the judge must not "help" the police present their case, writing: "...no court should be placed in the position of appearing to assist one side or the other. This principle should be most carefully and rigorously followed where the party being questioned appears for the prosecution, to avoid the inference that the court and law enforcement are "in cahoots" and the result of the trial a foregone conclusion." This means that if the judge acted as a prosecutor in cross-examining you, or in reminding the officer to supply testimony important to the prosecution, the judge went too far and the conviction might be reversed. See also *People v. Handcock* (1983) 145 Cal. App.3d Supp. 25, 30, 193 Cal.Rptr. 397, and *People v. Ferguson* (1981) 126 Cal.App.3d Supp. 22, 30–31, 179 Cal.Rptr. 437. If you win on this basis, the case may be ordered retried.

Judicial Bias

If the judge indicated from the beginning of the trial that she thought you were guilty, you were denied a fair trial and are entitled to a reversal. It is extremely hard to prove judicial bias, however. See CCP § 170.1 and cases interpreting it, including *Pacific and Southwest Conference of United Methodist Church v. Superior Court* (1978) 82 Cal.App.3d 72, 147 Cal.Rptr. 44, and *Taliaferro v. Taliaferro* (1962) 203 Cal.App.2d 642, 21 Cal.Rptr. 864. Winning on this ground may result in a retrial.

Refusal to Allow Relevant Testimony

You may have found that judges often refuse to allow testimony by "expert witnesses." Expert witnesses are people who, because of their education, training, or experience, can testify as to the reliability of certain types of evidence. In traffic cases, defendants will sometimes bring in engineers or scientists to testify as to the fallibility of radar speed-measuring devices. A judge who does not give the expert witness a chance to establish her qualifications to testify may be in error. See Evidence Code § 720; *People v. McDonald* (1984) 37 Cal.3d 351, 208 Cal.Rptr. 236. However, a judge's determination that the person is not qualified to testify as an expert will probably be affirmed by an appeals court. See *People v. Kelly* (1976) 17 Cal.3d 24, 130 Cal.Rptr. 144, and *Cooper v. Board of Medical Examiners* (1975) 49 Cal. App.3d 931, 123 Cal.Rptr. 563. Even if you win on this ground, the case may be retried.

Refusal to Allow Final Argument

In *People v. Douglas* (1973) 31 Cal.App.3d Supp. 26, 106 Cal.Rptr. 611, the Appellate Department of the Los Angeles County Superior Court reversed a traffic court conviction because the judge refused to allow the defendant to make a closing argument. In *Herring v. New York* (1975) 422 U.S. 853, 95 S.Ct. 2550, 45 L.Ed.2d 593, the U.S. Supreme Court reversed a felony conviction (after a nonjury trial) because the trial judge refused to allow a concluding statement by the defendant's lawyer. Closing statements are always allowed in misdemeanor trials, and the same provisions of law apply to infraction trials. See PC § 19.7 and *People v. Matthews* (1983) 139 Cal.App.3d 537, 188 Cal.Rptr. 796.

Refusal to State Guilty Verdict in Open Court

In *People v. Kriss* (1979) 96 Cal.App.3d 913, 158 Cal.Rptr. 420, the Court of Appeal ruled that a judge must state the decision (that is, guilty or not) in open court while you're there—unless you give the judge permission to take the case under advisement. If you didn't give the judge this permission, the appeals court will reverse your conviction. (See Chapter 12.) In the *Kriss* case, the court ordered the case terminated in light of the minor nature of the traffic infractions involved. An appeals court might just remand your case for resentencing or retrial, so you should emphasize the dismissal in the *Kriss* case during your appeal.

Sentenced Too Early

If you were sentenced right after the judge found you guilty (as usually occurs in traffic court), but the judge didn't ask you about giving up your right to be sentenced at least six hours later, you can make a motion to vacate the sentence. (See Chapter 14.) If your motion is denied, you can appeal the sentence—but the conviction will remain. (See PC § 1449 and *In re Elsholz* (1964) 228 Cal.App.2d 192, 39 Cal. Rptr. 356.) However, the appeals court will probably only vacate the sentence and send the case back for resentencing. You therefore gain very little from an appeal on this ground, unless the sentence imposed was unusually harsh.

Sentence Greater Than Maximum for First-Time Infraction

If the judge sentenced you to pay more than the basic first-offense infraction fine of $100 plus the appropriate penalty assessment, but the prior offenses on which he based this heavier fine were neither (1) alleged and proved at trial, nor (2) admitted by you, you should have moved to vacate the sentence. If you did, but the judge refused to change it, the appeals court should order the trial court to do so. See *People v. Ford* (1964) 60 Cal.2d 772, 794, 36 Cal. Rptr. 620, and VC § 42004. See also *In re Tahl (1969) 1 Cal.3d 127, 81 Cal.Rptr. 557, and People v. Matthews* (1983) 139 Cal.App.3d 537, 188 Cal.Rptr. 796. Your case will be sent back for resentencing.

If you were sentenced based on prior convictions about which the judge improperly questioned you (see Chapter 14), and, as we recommended, you objected to this procedure, your grounds of appeal would be that only a first-offense fine was proper and that the judge improperly acted as a prosecutor. As to this latter ground, we refer you to the cases discussed in the section, "Judge Acted as Prosecutor," above. If you read all the cases and apply their rulings to the facts of your case, you should be able to craft a very persuasive appellate brief showing that the sentence should be reversed. Moreover, you can argue that the trial judge's extreme behavior warrants reversal of this conviction as well, and *dismissal* of the entire case! In this regard, we suggest you modify the language in our "discovery" motion (see Chapter 10), where we argue that errors on the part of the trial court, in traffic cases, necessitate dismissal rather than retrial.

Excessive Delay in Appeal

If the trial court judge, the clerk, or the prosecutor delays for several months any step of the appeal (such as "settling" the statement of trial proceedings, or transmitting it and other papers (the "record") to the appeals court), you might be able to file a motion in the appeals court to have the conviction reversed and ordered dismissed. See *People v. Jenkins* (1976) 55 Cal. App.3d Supp. 55, 61, 127 Cal.Rptr. 870; *People v. Ruhl* (1976) 63 Cal.App.3d Supp. 6, 134 Cal. Rptr. 62; and *People v. Bighinatti* (1975) 55 Cal. App.3d Supp. 5, 127 Cal.Rptr. 310. The cases of *Ruhl* and *Bighinatti*, as well as *People v. Kriss* (1979) 96 Cal.App.3d Supp. 26, 106 Cal.Rptr. 611, have also held that an *infraction* case should not be sent back to the trial court for a new trial, but rather should be dismissed. See also *People v. Marcroft* (1992) 6 Cal.App.4th Supp. 1, 8 Cal.Rptr.2d 544. (For a contrary rule as to more serious misdemeanors, see *People v. Hernandez* (1985) 166 Cal.App.3d Supp. 1, 212 Cal.Rptr. 563.) The appellant, in having to appeal such a minor violation, has suffered enough.

The Steps in an Appeal

Prosecuting an appeal involves the filing of at least three written documents: a Notice of Appeal; a Proposed Statement on Appeal in the traffic court; and an opening brief in the appeals court once the case is transferred there.

The Notice of Appeal

The appeal is started by filing a Notice of Appeal with the clerk of the court in which you were found guilty. The Notice of Appeal is a one-page form simply stating that you are appealing the "judgment of conviction," the sentence, or both. It includes the date of conviction, the applicable county, and that you are appealing from the judgment. You must file it within 30 days of the date you were found guilty. This requirement can cause problems if you allow the judge to take your case under advisement and have the decision mailed to you. If you're not informed of the result in court, call the clerk every few days to find out whether you were found guilty.

If possible, you should file the appeal with the clerk of the court in which you were found guilty within a few days of the date of the conviction. The Vehicle Code requires court clerks to notify the DMV of convictions within ten days, whether they're appealed or not (VC § 1803). If the conviction is reversed on appeal, the traffic court clerk sends a corrected notice to the DMV (VC § 1803.3).

As noted in Chapter 14, the filing of an appeal does not automatically stay the sentence. So, even if you appeal, pay the fine when you're supposed to. If you don't, you could face a license suspension or be charged with the misdemeanor of failing to pay, even though an appeal is pending! A sample filled-in Notice of Appeal is shown on the following page.

Statement of Proceedings

Every appeal from a trial court is required to have some kind of written record of what happened at the trial. In serious criminal cases, the record is a written transcription of the testimony. In traffic cases, however, there is usually no court reporter present. The law thus allows the use of a "Settled Statement" (Rule 8.784, Calif. Rules of Court). A Settled Statement is a legal document that briefly lists your grounds for appeal and summarizes the proceedings, including testimony and other evidence relevant to those grounds. It is the result of a three-step process whereby:

TR-155

ATTORNEY OR PARTY WITHOUT ATTORNEY *(Name, state bar number, and address):*

DAVID W. BROWN
950 PARKER STREET
BERKELEY, CA 94710

TELEPHONE NO.: (510) 555-1212   FAX NO.:

ATTORNEY FOR *(Name):* Defendant in Pro Per

NAME OF COURT: SUPERIOR COURT OF CALIFORNIA, County of Alameda
STREET ADDRESS:
MAILING ADDRESS:
CITY AND ZIP CODE: Berkeley, CA 94710
BRANCH NAME: Berkeley-Albany BRANCH

PEOPLE OF THE STATE OF CALIFORNIA

vs.

DEFENDANT/APPELLANT *(Name):*   DAVID W. BROWN

NOTICE OF APPEAL (infraction)

CASE NUMBER:
B-123456-C

Defendant/Appellant *(Name):*   DAVID W. BROWN   in the above-entitled action hereby appeals to the

Appellate Division of the Superior Court in and for the County of *(name):*   ALAMEDA

State of California, from the [X] judgment and/or [ ] order entered in the above-named trial court on

(date): OCTOBER 10, 20xx

Date: OCTOBER 15, 20xx

DAVID W. BROWN
(TYPE OR PRINT NAME)

▶ _David W. Brown_____
(SIGNATURE OF DEFENDANT/APPELLANT OR ATTORNEY)

Form Approved for Optional Use
Judicial Council of California
TR-155 [Rev. January 1, 2007]

NOTICE OF APPEAL
(Infraction)

Cal. Rules of Court rule 8.782
www.courtinfo.ca.gov

1. The appealing defendant (appellant) prepares a "Proposed Statement" of what happened at trial, or if relevant, at arraignment or motion hearing;

2. The prosecution prepares its own version of what happened; and

3. The judge who presided at the trial "settles" the differences between the two versions, ruling as to what will be accepted as a final "Settled Statement" to be transferred to the appeals court.

Like the Notice of Appeal, your "Proposed Statement" must be filed with the court in which you were found guilty within 15 days after you file the Notice of Appeal. It must contain a brief statement of each legal ground for your appeal, and a summary of that part of the proceedings in which you claim the legal error occurred—whether at arraignment, a motion hearing, or trial.

For example, if the basis of your appeal is that the judge had no jurisdiction to hear the case, all you need is to list your basis for appeal, together with a statement as to when and how you made the request to disqualify the judge and what the judge said in denying it. Or, if your appeal is based only on the judge's refusal to let you make a closing argument, your statement need only indicate that you requested the opportunity to make a closing argument and that the judge refused to let you do so.

On the other hand, if one of the grounds for your appeal is insufficiency of the evidence, improper admission of radar evidence, refusal to allow relevant testimony, judicial bias, or any other ground relating to much or all of what happened throughout the trial, you will have to prepare a more extensive statement of the proceedings. For example, in appealing on the basis of a denial of a speedy trial, you will want to show how the judge's error compromised or "prejudiced" your ability to defend by referring in your statement to your complaint to the trial judge that one of your witnesses said she couldn't remember important details (that might have helped you had the trial been held earlier).

Your Proposed Statement on Appeal should not retell all your testimony in detail, nor should it include evidence you forgot to present at trial. You should only mention in detail the testimony relevant to your appeal. (If leaving out testimony that isn't relevant would seem to leave an awkward gap, you can briefly refer to it, however.)

In summarizing the testimony, you will often have to rely on your memory, since most traffic courts do not use court reporters or even tape recorders. In those courts that do electronically record the proceedings, you should be able to purchase a copy of the tape from the court clerk for $10 to $15. You can then listen to the tape and write down a brief summary of the proceedings, or even a verbatim record, attaching that to the Proposed Statement on Appeal.

However, if you do request a tape, don't wait too long for it to be mailed to you, lest you miss the Rule 8.784 15-day deadline that normally applies.

If the judge allowed you to record the trial proceedings yourself with a hand-held recorder (as permitted by Rule 1.150, California Rules of Court—see Chapter 12), you can use that recording in the same way, as an aid to drafting your Proposed Statement on Appeal.

Finally, you must have a friend serve a copy of the Proposed Statement on Appeal on the prosecution (either by mail or delivery to the district (or city) attorney's office) and fill out the Proof of Service on the last page of the form. This, too, is in the forms appendix in the back of this book. You can then file the whole set of papers with the court.

A sample Proposed Statement on Appeal follows:

TR-160

ATTORNEY OR PARTY WITHOUT ATTORNEY (Name, state bar number and address):

DAVID W. BROWN
950 PARKER ST.
BERKELEY, CA 94710

TELEPHONE NO.: 510-222-1234 FAX NO.:

ATTORNEY FOR (Name): DEFENDANT IN PRO PER

NAME OF COURT: SUPERIOR COURT OF CALIFORNIA, COUNTY OF ALAMEDA

STREET ADDRESS:
MAILING ADDRESS: 1225 FALLON STREET, ROOM 100
CITY AND ZIP CODE: OAKLAND, CA 94612
BRANCH NAME: RENE C. DAVIDSON COURTHOUSE

PEOPLE OF THE STATE OF CALIFORNIA
vs.

DEFENDANT/APPELLANT (Name): DAVID W. BROWN

PROPOSED STATEMENT ON APPEAL (Infraction)	CASE NUMBER: B-123456-C

Defendant/Appellant (name): DAVID W. BROWN   submits the following *Proposed Statement on Appeal*:

GROUNDS FOR APPEAL

1. *(Specify in detail your reasons for why you feel the judge committed "error" regarding the law or procedure. Note that credibility of witnesses is generally **not** a basis for appeal):*

   a. The Court was without jurisdiction to try defendant, following his request at arraignment that the action be transferred to the court at the county seat; and

   b. The Court was without jurisdiction to find defendant guilty after having admitted, over his objection, testimony based on the use of speed-detection radar, when no foundation

   c. engineering and traffic survey had been properly introduced into evidence.

   d.

   e.

   f.

STATEMENT OF EVIDENCE

2. ☐ The above-entitled matter was reported by an official court reporter or electronically recorded and appellant intends to file a reporter's transcript of the evidence and proceedings so reported and to make the transcript appellant's statement on appeal.

3. ☒ Instead of a transcript the appellant is submitting the following statement on appeal:

   a. Officer (name): Bill Bustem   testified that *(set forth accurately and in detail the testimony of the officer; do not comment on or give your opinion regarding the officer's testimony):*

ARRAIGNMENT

Arraignment of defendant in this action commenced in the within-entitled Court on September 5, 20xx at 9:00 a.m., in Department 3, the Hon. T.M. Handimafine presiding. Defendant entered a plea of not guilty to the charge of

continued on Attachment 3a

Page 1 of 4

Form Approved for Optional Use
Judicial Council of California
TR-160 [Rev. January 1, 2007]

PROPOSED STATEMENT ON APPEAL
(Infraction)

Cal. Rules of Court, rule 8.784
www.courtinfo.ca.gov

TR-160

PEOPLE OF THE STATE OF CALIFORNIA vs. DAVID W. BROWN DEFENDANT APPELLANT *(Name)*:	CASE NUMBER: B-123456-C

3. *(Continued)*

    b. Defendant testified that *(set forth defendant's testimony accurately and in detail)*:

Though not relevant for the purpose of this appeal, defendant took the stand to testify that he had been driving at a speed of 35 mph, as indicated by his speedometer, and that the specific road, weather, and traffic conditions in any event rendered even a substantially higher speed to be safe. No cross-examination of defendant was conducted.

    c. Witness *(name)*:   was called and testified that *(set forth witness's testimony accurately and in*
        detail)*:

        NOT APPLICABLE

(Continued on page three)

TR-160 [Rev. January 1, 2007]

PROPOSED STATEMENT ON APPEAL
(Infraction)

Page 2 of 4

TR-160

PEOPLE OF THE STATE OF CALIFORNIA vs. DAVID W. BROWN DEFENDANT/APPELLANT *(Name)*:	CASE NUMBER: B-123456-C

3. c. *(Witness testimony continued)*

   NOT APPLICABLE

> **Please attach separate page(s) labeled "Attachment 3d," "Attachment 3e," etc. for each other witness.**

FINDINGS OF THE COURT

4. The court determined I was guilty and assessed a fine of: $ 85.00

5. Number of pages attached: One

Date: October 15, 20xx

DAVID W. BROWN   ▶   *David W. Brown*
....
(TYPE OR PRINT NAME)   (SIGNATURE OF DEFENDANT/APPELLANT OR ATTORNEY)

(Proof of service on reverse)

TR-160 [Rev. January 1, 2007]	**PROPOSED STATEMENT ON APPEAL** **(Infraction)**	Page 3 of 4

TR-160

| PEOPLE OF THE STATE OF CALIFORNIA
vs.   DAVID W. BROWN
DEFENDANT/APPELLANT (Name): | CASE NUMBER:
B-123456-C |

DIRECTIONS: **A copy of this document must be mailed to the district attorney/city attorney at the address listed below. YOU MAY NOT PERFORM THE MAILING YOURSELF. You must have a party who is at least 18 years old complete the information below and mail the front and back of each page of this document by first class mail, postage prepaid. When the fronts and backs of this document have been completed and mailed, the original may then be filed with the court.**

PROOF OF SERVICE BY MAIL

1. I am over the age of 18 and NOT a party to this action. I am a resident of or employed in the county where the mailing took place.

2. My residence or business address is *(specify)*:

    123 Galvez Street
    Oakland, California 94611

3. I served a copy of the *Proposed Statement on Appeal* by enclosing it in an envelope AND

    a. ☐ **depositing** the sealed envelope with the United States Postal Service with the postage fully prepaid.

    b. ☒ **placing** the envelope for collection and mailing on the date and at the place shown in item 4 following our ordinary business practices. I am readily familiar with this business's practice for collecting and processing correspondence for mailing. On the same day that correspondence is placed for collection and mailing, it is deposited in the ordinary course of business with the United States Postal Service in a sealed envelope with postage fully prepaid.

4. The envelope was addressed and mailed as follows:

    a. *(Name of county)*:   Alameda   District Attorney/City Attorney

    b. Address: 1225 Fallon St., Oakland, CA 94612

    c. Date mailed: October 15, 20xx

    d. Place of mailing *(city and state)*:   Oakland, California

5. I declare under penalty of perjury under the laws of the State of California that the foregoing is true and correct.

Date: October 15, 20xx

RICHARD MILLER
. . . .
(TYPE OR PRINT NAME)

▶ *Richard Miller*
_____
(SIGNATURE OF DECLARANT)

TR-160 [Rev. January 1, 2007]

PROPOSED STATEMENT ON APPEAL
(Infraction)

Page 4 of 4

ATTACHMENT 3A

violating Vehicle Code § 22350, an infraction. Defendant then requested that the action be transferred to the court at the county seat, at 600 Washington Street, Oakland; defendant stated that he based this request on the ground that such court was the proper court for trial because of his demand to the citing officer that the Notice to Appear specify that court as the place to appear, pursuant to Vehicle Code § 40502(b). Defendant referred the court to his previously-filed Notice of Motion for Change of Venue to County Seat and supporting Declaration and Points and authorities, included in the record herein. Defendant's request for transfer to the county seat was denied, and trial was set for October 10, 20xx, at 2:00 p.m. in Department 3 of the within-entitled court.

TRIAL

Trial of this action commenced on October 10, 20xx at 2:00 p.m., in Department 3 of the within-entitled court before the Hon. T.M. Handimafine, without a jury. No counsel was present on plaintiff's behalf, defendant was present *in propria persona,* and neither party made an opening statement.

PROSECUTION'S CASE

As the prosecution's only witness, Officer Bill Bustem of the Berkeley Police Department testified that he was parked facing north on Milvia Street, where a posted sign indicated a speed limit of 35 mph. He further stated that he observed a vehicle driven by defendant traveling at what he thought was a speed in excess of 35 mph, and raised his hand-held radar unit to measure the vehicle's speed.

At this time, defendant objected to the introduction of officer Bustem's radar-based testimony on the ground that the foundation had not been laid for introduction of such evidence by proper introduction of an engineering and traffic survey justifying the speed limit, as required by Vehicle Code § 40803(b) and the case of *People v. Halopoff* (1976) 60 Cal.App.3d Supp. 1. The Court overruled the objection, stating it was up the defendant to show the nonexistence of an engineering and traffic survey, and that in any event, one had been made. The Court then allowed Officer Bustem to continue with his testimony.

Officer Bustem continued that his radar unit indicated defendant's vehicle's speed to be 46 mph, that he gave chase and stopped defendant in order to give him a citation.

On cross-examination, Officer Bustem, in addition to answering questions not relevant to this appeal, admitted that defendant had requested that he list the court at which the defendant be directed to appear as the county seat. Officer Bustem also admitted that he refused this request because the address of the Berkeley court was already printed on his citation forms.

TR-150

INSTRUCTIONS ON APPEAL PROCEDURES FOR INFRACTIONS

The following information will assist you with the general guidelines on appeal procedures. It is not intended to be comprehensive in nature, but to act as an overview. You are advised to thoroughly read California Rules of Court, rules 8.702–8.709 and rules 8.780–8.793. The court clerks cannot assist you. You should direct any questions you have to an attorney of your own choosing.

1. **NATURE OF AN APPEAL**

   A party may appeal an unfavorable decision made in the trial court to the appellate division of the superior court. The appeal must be directed towards errors of law only. An appeal is not a retrial, and you will not be permitted to introduce *new* evidence.

2. **PARTIES**

   The party filing the appeal is called the APPELLANT. The party against whom the appeal is brought (People of the State of California) is called the RESPONDENT.

3. **NOTICE OF APPEAL**

   If you wish to appeal, you must file your Notice of Appeal with the clerk of the trial court within 30 CALENDAR DAYS after the rendition of the judgment (usually the date of sentencing). (Cal. Rules of Court, rule 8.782.) No extension of this time limit is allowed. Form TR-155, *Notice of Appeal*, is recommended for use in filing the notice.

4. **PROPOSED STATEMENT**

   a. In most cases you must prepare a Proposed Statement to provide a complete record on appeal. To submit a Proposed Statement, you must file it within 15 days after filing the Notice of Appeal. Form TR-160, *Proposed Statement on Appeal,* is recommended. (Cal. Rules of Court, rule 8.784.) The Proposed Statement should contain all of the following:

      (1) Grounds of appeal—a statement of the legal errors you believe were committed by the trial court. (Cal. Rules of Court, rule 8.784.)

      (2) An official transcript or a statement of the evidence or trial procedures relevant to each of your grounds of appeal. (Cal. Rules of Court, rule 8.784.) If your trial was recorded, you may obtain a copy of the recording and produce your own summary or transcript. In some counties, a certified transcript of a recorded trial may be available. If an official court reporter's transcript is available, you may use a certified copy of the reporter's transcript.

   > **NOTICE: The filing of a Proposed Statement is required in order to prepare a Settled Statement. Although it is technically possible for an appeal to proceed in the absence of a Settled Statement, as a practical matter in almost all cases such a statement will be necessary for the appellate division to meaningfully review the appeal. The Proposed Statement must be filed with the clerk of the trial court.**

   b. If you proceed with your appeal by way of a Settled Statement, you may either complete form TR-160 or prepare your own Proposed Statement. The document should be TYPED if possible. If an official transcript is not available, your Proposed Statement must include a statement of the evidence or trial procedures. (See section 5 below.)

   c. In addition to filing the original Proposed Statement with the court, a copy of your Proposed Statement must be served in person or by mail to the district attorney or city attorney where the case was tried.

5. **SETTLING THE PROPOSED STATEMENT**

   a. The district attorney or city attorney has the right to file proposed amendments to your Proposed Statement within 15 days after it is filed. (Cal. Rules of Court, rule 8.785.) After the district attorney or city attorney has filed proposed amendments or the time for filing has passed, a hearing will be set by the clerk before the judge who decided your case for the purpose of settling the Proposed Statement. (Cal. Rules of Court, rule 8.788.)

   b. The trial judge may correct, alter, or rewrite the statement so that it fairly and truly sets forth the evidence and proceedings and may direct you to prepare a revised statement for his or her signature. However, your statement of grounds of appeal cannot be eliminated from the Settled Statement. (Cal. Rules of Court, rule 8.788.)

   c. After the revised statement is prepared, the judge will certify to its correctness.

6. **TRANSFER OF APPEAL**

   a. After a record of the trial court's proceedings has been prepared, it will be sent to the appellate division of the superior court. The superior court will then mail you a notice stating the date your opening brief is due. You must file an opening brief by the date set by the court. Failure to do so may result in the dismissal of your appeal. (Cal. Rules of Court, rule 8.792.)

   b. The preparation and filing of briefs is governed by California Rules of Court, rule 8.706. You should read this rule thoroughly and comply with it.

(Continued on reverse)

Form Approved for Optional Use
Judicial Council of California
TR-150 [Rev. January 1, 2007]

INSTRUCTIONS ON APPEAL PROCEDURES FOR INFRACTIONS

Cal. Rules of Court,
rules 8.702-8.709, 8.780-8.793
www.courtinfo.ca.gov

TR-150

6. c. If the district attorney files a respondent's brief, you may file a reply brief; however, one is not required. (Cal. Rules of Court, rule 8.706.)

7. **PAYMENT OF YOUR FINE**

The filing of an appeal does NOT postpone the payment of your fine or any other condition of the sentence. If the fine is not paid by the date specified or any condition ordered by the court is not met, a warrant may be issued for your arrest or a civil collections process may be instituted against you. (Pen. Code, § 1467.)

8. **ABANDONMENT OF APPEAL**

Should you decide not to proceed with your appeal, you must file an Abandonment of Appeal. Form TR-165, *Abandonment of Appeal*, is recommended for use in filing such a request with the court.

TIME CHART ON APPEALS OF INFRACTIONS

Document or Proceeding	Time Limitations
Notice of Appeal	Must be filed with the court clerk of the trial court within 30 days after rendition of judgment. (Cal. Rules of Court, rule 8.782.)
Appellant's Proposed Statement on Appeal	Must be served on respondent and filed with the clerk of the trial court within 15 days after Notice of Appeal is filed. (Cal. Rules of Court, rule 8.784.)
Transcript on appeal *(optional)*	If mentioned in the Proposed Statement on Appeal, *a* reporter's transcript must be filed within 15 days after filing of the Proposed Statement, or any lawful extension thereof. (Cal. Rules of Court, rule 8.784.)
Respondent's amendments to the Proposed Statement on Appeal or reporter's transcript	Must be served and filed within 15 days after service of a copy of the Proposed Statement on Appeal or Notice of Filing of Reporter's Transcript. (Cal. Rules of Court, rule 8.785.)
Hearing on settlement of Proposed Statement on Appeal or reporter's transcript	The trial judge shall set a hearing to settle the Proposed Statement on Appeal or reporter's transcript on the court's calendar that will allow at least 5 days' notice to all parties. (Cal. Rules of Court, rule 8.788.)
Engrossed Statement on Appeal	Must be presented to the judge for certification within 5 days after settlement, or any lawful extension thereof. (Cal. Rules of Court, rule 8.788.)
Certification by judge	No time limit. Ordinarily completed upon receipt of the Engrossed Statement on Appeal, or at the conclusion of the hearing on settlement, if engrossment not ordered. (Cal. Rules of Court, rule 8.788.)
Extension of time *(optional)*	By the trial court: up to 15 days for the doing of any act except the filing of the Notice of Appeal. (Cal. Rules of Court, rule 8.787.) By the appellate division of the superior court: same as above except no time limit. (Cal. Rules of Court, rule 8.787.)
Relief from default	The appellate division of the superior court may for good cause relieve a party from a default, except for failure to give timely Notice of Appeal. (Cal. Rules of Court, rule 8.783.)
Transmittal of the record on appeal	By the clerk immediately after the appeal record has been perfected. (Cal. Rules of Court, rule 8.783.)

**INSTRUCTIONS ON APPEAL PROCEDURES
FOR INFRACTIONS**

Prosecution's Proposed Statement

If the district or city attorney's office disagrees with your Proposed Statement, it must prepare, file, and serve on you, within ten days, its own Proposed Statement (Rule 8.784, California Rules of Court—15 days if your proposed statement was sent by mail. C.C.P. § 1013). This is very difficult for the prosecution to do in traffic cases where no prosecutor—just the officer—was present at trial. To find out what happened, the prosecution must interview the officer—who may have forgotten all sorts of details or may even be on vacation—or review any tape recording that was made at trial. The officer cannot prepare the Proposed Statement since he's not a lawyer.

If the prosecutor's office fails to file its version, that does not necessarily mean your version of events will be submitted to the appeals court. The judge is still required to conduct a hearing to "settle" the statement—that is, to determine whether your proposed statement accurately reflects what occurred at trial. The clerk is required to schedule this hearing upon receiving the prosecution's proposed statement, or on expiration of the 10 or 15 days they have to file it. (If the clerk fails to set a hearing date to settle the settlement, within two weeks after this period is up, you may wish to write the clerk a brief letter, stating, "Please schedule the hearing to settle the statement of appeal in the above-referred case.")

Hearing to Settle the Statement

After your Proposed Statement and that of the prosecution (if any) have been filed with the court, a hearing is set to reconcile the two versions.

Basic Procedure

This hearing takes place before the same judge who found you guilty. Sadly, we have heard of many judges trying to sabotage defendants' appeals by arbitrarily accepting the prosecution's version or preparing their own sanitized version—tailored to whitewash the judge's errors—when the prosecutor doesn't submit a response. (Some judges even go so far as to "strike" from the statement any ground of appeal that they disagree with. This, however, is prohibited by Rule 8.788 of California Rules of Court, and you should point this out to the judge.) If this happens, stick to your guns. Explain in detail the circumstances surrounding the disputed part of the trial, so as to refresh the judge's memory. After all, you're in a better position to remember than either the judge (who hears lots of cases and is likely to confuse or forget what happened) or the prosecutor (who also handles numerous cases and was probably not even there). It is improper for the judge to ask the officer, off the record, anywhere but in the courtroom, to restate his version (*People v. Marcroft* (1992) 6 Cal.App.4th Supp. 1, 8 Cal.Rptr.2d 544).

If the proceedings were tape-recorded or attended by a court reporter, you or the judge can go back and review any disputed issues that occurred at the trial. However, if the trial was not recorded, you may have no way to thwart a judge's attempt to sabotage your appeal by leaving out key testimony or inserting testimony that did not occur.

Problems With the Judge

Since this book was first published, in 1982, we have seen and heard of many cases in which traffic judges have tried to sabotage a traffic-court defendant's appeal (and often succeeded) by insisting on a final settled statement that covers up all the judge's errors. Indeed, where the proceedings are not recorded, this stage of the appeal process—wherein judges get a chance to cover up their own errors on which you're seeking a reversal—can render the whole process meaningless.

If you think that's an exaggeration, consider the sheer numbers of trials that are conducted before a single judge over a few hours, which almost guarantees that traffic-court judges will take shortcuts and commit legal errors. Some traffic-court judges, when given the opportunity at a hearing to settle the statement, will either knowingly cover up these errors or, at best, develop a selective memory about them.

EXAMPLE:

At Lenny Leadfoot's trial for doing 42 mph in a 25 mph zone, Lenny properly objected to the introduction of radar testimony, since the officer did not produce an engineering and traffic survey justifying the speed limit. A bored judge, more concerned with the speed of trials than the speed of cars, found Lenny guilty anyway. Lenny appealed, noting in his proposed statement on appeal that he made the objection. At the hearing to settle the statement on appeal, the judge "didn't recall" Lenny making the objection, and deleted that part in preparing a final settled statement. Since that kind of objection is essential to getting the appeals court to reverse Lenny's conviction, the trial judge has successfully sabotaged Lenny's appeal. Since the trial wasn't tape-recorded, Lenny has no way to prove the judge is mistaken.

As you can see from the above example, the chances of a judge sabotaging your appeal by developing a selective memory about what happened at trial are higher if the trial proceedings weren't recorded, either by the court or by you, as we suggest in Chapter 12. That is why, in Chapter 10, we showed you how to demand that the proceedings be recorded or reported. If that demand was refused *and* you and the judge cannot agree on a settled statement, you have another ground for appeal. In a 1976 case, the appeals court said that "if there was no court reporter at the trial and a Settled Statement cannot be drafted that will afford an adequate basis for appellate review, the defendant is entitled to a new trial as a matter of due process" (*People v. Jenkins* (1976) 55 Cal.App.3d Supp. 55, 61, 127 Cal.Rptr. 870). The court also said, "where there are conflicts as to what transpired at the trial, the court must resolve the dispute as to the facts and see to it that a single unified statement is prepared that sets forth the evidence and testimony received at the trial. To assist him in carrying out his responsibility to prepare an accurate statement of the evidence, the trial court may rely on the appellant's proposed statement, the respondent's proposed amendments, and his own notes or memory of the defendant. If a reporter was present, the trial judge may order the testimony read to him to refresh his memory. As a last resort, the trial judge may recall witnesses to give testimony anew." (See also Rule 187.5 (g)(3), California Rules of Court, on the judge using any sound recordings to refresh her memory.)

As we saw in Chapter 12, the case of *In re Armstrong* (1981) 126 Cal.App.3d 565 requires that a court reporter be present at a misdemeanor trial, and PC § 19.7 makes this rule applicable to infractions. (See *People v. Matthews* (1983) 139 Cal.App.3d 537.) This may irritate the judge, but the availability of a verbatim record will keep the judge from trying to wreck your appeal by refusing to certify an accurate Settled Statement. Be sure to note this in your opening brief and attach a copy of your proposed statement that the judge rejected as an exhibit.

If the trial proceedings were recorded, you might consider transcribing the tapes and incorporating the transcripts into your proposed statement at the outset, rather than preparing a narrative summary of what happened at trial. Or, at the hearing to settle the statement, you could bring transcripts of this kind *and* a tape recorder to play back the tapes in court, to refresh the judge's faulty or selective memory about what happened at trial. A hearing of this type, in which you assert your rights in this way, can be tense. However, the foremost thing to keep in mind is this: Do not let yourself be bullied by a traffic judge who tried to force you into accepting his or her version of what happened at trial, regardless of whether the trial proceedings were recorded or not. Be polite, but be firm, and object when appropriate. ("Your Honor, with all due respect, that is not what occurred at trial….")

If you have transcribed the tapes and have either incorporated them into your proposed statement or have them—and/or the tape plus a recorder—with you, you have a better chance to force the judge to accept more of your version over his or her own. To do so, you will want to explain to the judge that your transcript more accurately reflects the proceedings and explain why.

If the trial proceedings were recorded but using a transcript to augment your summary appears to be too much work, at least be prepared, when you go to the hearing, to play the tape recording of the trial proceedings. Playing the tape in court may force the judge to see the error of his ways, and to put the appropriate information in the final settled statement, or even to force him or her to accept your version. If you did not record the previous

hearings, then stick to your guns and rely on your best recollection.

If the judge has prepared his own version of the statement, you are likely to face a great deal of coercion. When you arrive at the hearing to settle this statement and the judge shows you his or her own version, simply ask the judge for time to review it while he hears other cases. Or, if you need more time, ask the judge to "continue" (postpone) the hearing, and also to allow you to take a copy of his version home to review. Then you can make notations on your copy of the judge's version, making appropriate additions, corrections, or deletions. When the judge recalls your case (or you return a second time for the hearing), politely state to the judge that you object to certain portions of his or her statement and wish to go paragraph-by-paragraph and line-by-line, utilizing the tape recording (or your own recollection) to demonstrate your objections.

You may wish to get the judge to allow you to bring a tape recorder to the hearing to settle the statement, to record those proceedings. If nothing else, this may keep the judge from going too far out of line. Further, if the judge refuses to accept any of your corrections, which are based upon your previous recordings or your own recollection, you will have ammunition to use in a motion to the appeals court, in the event you and the judge cannot reach an agreement.

Making a Motion in the Appellate Department

Finally, if the judge completely steamrolls you into accepting his version, or you are not satisfied with the version the judge insists that you accept, you still have an opportunity to correct the problem. You can make a motion in the Appellate Department. Doing this is fairly complex and very time-consuming, and there is no guarantee that you will be treated any better this time around. However, if you have strong grounds for your appeal, which will be thwarted if the trial judge's version is used or if the judge's actions were particularly egregious, it might be worth the effort to make this sort of attempt.

In your motion, you will ask the Appellate Department to either:

- Reverse your conviction and either grant a new trial because there is an inadequate record for review or order the case dismissed, given any egregious conduct on the part of the judge and in light of the minor nature of the offense; or

- Order the trial judge to settle your version of the proposed statement (if it's based on a tape recording); or

- Order the judge to incorporate your proposed corrections based on your recollection.

We cannot, in good conscience, provide you with a prepared motion on this issue because there are just too many factual and procedural variables that will be different for each case. However, we can give you general guidelines on how to draft, file, and argue your own motion of this sort, should the need arise. A rough outline for making this kind of motion follows.

What happens from here is impossible to predict. The Appellate Department may or may not schedule a hearing when you file it, or you may get notice of the hearing date in the mail. It is also possible that the court will rule on the motion without a hearing, after the prosecutor has had time to respond.

You may indeed receive a response from the prosecutor arguing against your motion. You can respond to their arguments by filing a "Reply to People's Response to Motion," if you are so inclined. If you do so, be sure to address only the points raised by the prosecution, and then serve and file it just as if it were a motion.

If you have to go to a hearing, be prepared to argue your motion. Here, unlike in traffic court, there are sometimes three judges, although counties are authorized to proceed with just one appeals judge in infraction cases. The judge (or judges) normally start by asking either side to begin with statements. Be brief, and do not repeat what is in your motion word for word. Your best strategy is to start with a brief description of the facts of your case. You then cite the authorities for your position, stating how they apply to the facts of your particular case.

More likely than not, you will be interrupted with questions by the judges. Be patient and answer them directly. If you are not sure of the answer, say so, and then tell the judges where to find the answer in your motion. Or, cite whatever case you think will best answer their question.

At this point, the prosecutor will have the opportunity to reply to your statements. You may be given a chance to respond to that. After all of this back and forth, the judges will either issue their ruling on the spot, or take the matter "under advisement," which means you will get their decision in the mail.

Note: If the trial judge writes you a letter claiming to reverse his own decision, you still need to keep your motion alive, if it is set for hearing. This is because once an appeal is filed, a trial court is not allowed to change its ruling—even if it now sees the error of its ways. So if your motion has not been set for hearing, call the prosecutor's office, locate the deputy who has been assigned to your case, and explain the situation. Here you want to talk the deputy into writing an agreement with you to the effect that you will "abandon" your appeal now, on the stated condition that the trial judge's order reversing his decision will be entered and provided to you, in writing, immediately after you file a Notice of Abandonment of Appeal.

Overview of Raising a Motion in the Appellate Department

A. Gather the legal authorities from the other portions of the book.

1. Use the cases and statutes cited in the section, "Excessive Delay in Appeal," above.

2. You can lift the paragraph and case citations (with slight modifications, of course) from the "discovery" motion (in Chapter 10), which argues that a large body of case law shows that where there is error on the part of the trial court or on appeal, minor traffic infractions should be reversed and dismissed rather than remanded for a new trial.

B. Go to the law library and read *all* the cases and statutes—do not write the motion without reading the cases. If you do not read the cases, you are likely to draft something that will only annoy the Appellate Department judges. Besides, you will need to understand the legal theories and case rulings that you will be arguing at the hearing, if you expect to prevail.

C. Draft the motion. (This is easier than you might expect.) On the first page, be sure that you list the proper court. Use the same type of caption shown below for the "opening brief." Title the motion, "Notice of Motion for Ordered Reversal," or, in the alternative, "Order to Settle or Augment the Statement on Appeal; Declaration; Points and Authorities," or something to that effect.

1. In the Notice of Motion, do not list the date, time, or place where the motion will be heard. The court will schedule a hearing on its own—if it's interested.

Instead, just state, "Defendant [your name] hereby moves the above-entitled Appellate Department for an order reversing his conviction and directing the trial court to dismiss," or, in the alternative, "to hold a new trial," or, in the alternative, "for an order directing the trial court to settle or augment the statement on appeal." Then state, "This motion is based on the within Declaration and Points and Authorities, and is made on the following grounds:" Then, state your grounds succinctly.

2. Follow the Notice of Motion with a "Declaration" that describes, in detail, your attempts to get the statement settled. Be sure to include a copy of the Notice of Appeal, a copy of your proposed statement, and any copy of the trial court's version, as exhibits to your Declaration. If you have tape-recorded the hearings to settle the statement, you should include a transcript of the tape as an exhibit and refer to it in your Declaration and the Motion. At the bottom, type, "I declare under penalty of perjury under the laws of the state of California that the foregoing is true and correct," and date and sign it.

3. Follow the Declaration with "Points and Authorities," a legal brief that explains your legal theory. For example, you may argue that since the case of *In re Armstrong* (1981) 126 Cal.App.3d 565 and PC § 19.7 requires the court to tape-record the trial, and since the trial court failed in that regard and you and the judge can't agree on a settled statement, the rule of *People v. Jenkins* (1976) 55 Cal.App.3d Supp. 55 entitles you to a new trial.

Overview of Raising a Motion in the Appellate Department (continued)	
D. Have a friend serve (mail) a copy of the Motion on the prosecutor and the trial judge and sign a Proof of Service (see the one for the "Opening Brief," below), and attach that as the last page.	E. File the motion in the Appellate Department. Make sure you have extra copies that you can have file-stamped for yourself. Ask whether or not a hearing will be scheduled at that time.

The "Settled Statement"

Eventually, if you don't take the above preappeal detour into the Appellate Department, or if you do and the matter is resolved short of reversal and an ordered dismissal, the traffic judge will eventually "settle" the matter, as far as the record is concerned, by signing an "Engrossed Settled Statement on Appeal." The facts of the case, as the Appellate Department sees them, will be fixed in this document. Normally, you can't turn around later and base your appeal on anything not contained in this final record.

After the final Settled Statement has been worked out, it will be up to you to prepare it and submit it to the judge. The Engrossed Settled Statement on Appeal must be filed with the clerk of the court in which you were found guilty within five days. It should be in the same format as the Proposed Statement, but at the end, a separate sentence should be added, saying: "The within Engrossed Settled Statement on Appeal is hereby certified as correct." This should be followed by a place for the judge to date and sign the statement. "Judge or Commissioner of the Court," should be printed directly beneath the line. Also, as with your Proposed Statement, a copy should be served on the prosecutor and a Proof of Service filled out.

Transfer to the Appeals Court

After the Settled Statement has been signed by the trial judge, and the record of documents is put together by the trial court clerk, the case file is transferred to the Appellate Department of the Superior Court for the county in which the trial court is located. The clerk will send you a notice of the transfer. The notice will also list your new appeals case number (entirely different from your traffic court case number, which should be used on everything you file in the appeals court, including your "Opening Brief"). You have 20 days from the time the notice says the record was transferred (not from the time the clerk sent out or you received the notice) to file your brief.

Your "Opening Brief"

Your opening brief will present your arguments as to why the trial judge committed one or more legal errors, which resulted in "prejudice" to your case.

The brief must have a cover, be typed (triple-spaced) on numbered 8½" by 11" legal paper, and cannot be more than 15 pages long. It must be accompanied by a Proof of Service. Although it's a matter of style, briefs should be broken down into the following four parts:

Statement of Facts

This is a two- or three-paragraph summary of the facts surrounding the conduct of the case, insofar as they're relevant to your ground(s) of appeal. You should not introduce any factual matters that aren't mentioned in the record or Settled Statement. Refer to pages and line numbers in the Settled Statement.

Questions or Issues Presented

These are one-sentence statements (usually in the form of questions) succinctly listing each separate legal issue you intend to argue. There should be at least one, and perhaps several, issues for each ground of appeal.

Summary of Argument

This is a several-paragraph summary of your detailed legal argument. It's optional, but useful, since it helps the appeals judge figure out what you're saying in the next part.

Argument

This is the "body" of the brief, and is written in the same way as the arguments in the Points and Authorities examples you saw in Chapter 10. Each distinct point must be listed under an appropriate heading, with subheadings as desired. A short sample brief follows.

The "Responding Brief"

If there is a hell to which deputy prosecutors are relegated, it is handling traffic appeals by pro per defendants. Doing an appeal may be interesting for you, but it's boring for them, and this often shows in the poor quality of their briefs. Also, they have many cases to work on, but you have just your own. If you do a good job of researching, writing, and preparing your brief, it will probably be a lot better than the prosecution's and you might even favorably

impress the appellate judges. The prosecution also has 20 days to file this brief, and must mail you a copy.

The Optional "Reply Brief"

You may file a "reply brief" in response to the prosecution's responding brief within ten days after the prosecution has filed its brief. (This may work out to only a few days after you receive a copy in the mail.) Although you are not required to file a reply brief, it is a very good idea. Some judges regard the failure to file a reply brief as an admission that everything said in the prosecution's responding brief is true. The scope of your reply brief should be limited to new questions or arguments raised by the prosecution. The format of the Reply Brief is the same as the Opening Brief, except without a Statement of Facts.

Three copies and the original of the Reply Brief and Proof of Service must be filed in the Appellate Department of the Superior Court, after respective service and "deposit" of copies on the prosecution and trial court clerk.

The Hearing

You will be notified of a hearing date, usually several months after the record has been transferred from the traffic court to the Superior Court Appellate Department. This hearing is where you and the prosecutor present your arguments and/or respond to questions from the judge or judges. There are sometimes three judges, but many counties now have the option of using one judge for traffic infraction appeals, just not the same judge who tried the case. Unlike the trial, this hearing is usually not the most important part of your appeal. The briefs are the most important, and most appeals judges will have tentatively decided whether to "affirm" or "reverse" after reading them. The judge(s) may question you about some points of

DAVID W. BROWN
950 Parker St.
Berkeley, CA 94710
(510) 555-1234

Defendant and Appellant in Pro Per

IN THE SUPERIOR COURT OF CALIFORNIA, COUNTY OF ALAMEDA
APPELLATE DEPARTMENT

THE PEOPLE OF THE STATE
OF CALIFORNIA

Plaintiff and Respondent,

vs.

DAVID W. BROWN,

Defendant and Appellant.

No. CR - 1234

APPELLANT'S OPENING BRIEF

SUMMARY OF FACTS

Appellant was cited on July 8, 20xx for an infraction violation of Vehicle Code § 22350, the "Basic Speed Law." At the time he was cited, he requested that the citing officer specify, on the Notice to Appear, the court at the county seat as the place for his appearance, pursuant to Vehicle Code § 40502(b). The officer refused to comply with this request, and directed him to appear instead at the court for the Berkeley-Albany area.

At his arraignment on September 5, 20xx appellant appeared in the court at Berkeley and moved for a change of venue to the court at the county seat, namely Oakland, a city that was also defendant's principal place of business. The motion was based on a previously filed Notice of Motion, Declaration, and Points and Authorities, a part of the record herein. The court, Hon. T.M. Handimafine presiding, denied the motion and set trial for October 10, 20xx in Department 3 of the Berkeley court.

At trial, the citing officer, Officer John Smith of the Berkeley Police Department, testified that, using a hand-held radar unit, he measured the speed of appellant's vehicle as 48 mph in a posted 35-mph speed zone on Milvia Street in Berkeley. Appellant objected to this testimony on the ground that the foundation

for introduction of such testimony had not been established. That foundation requires proof of an engineering and traffic survey justifying the speed limit on that portion of Milvia Street. The court, Hon. T.M. Handimafine presiding, overruled appellant's objection, satisfying himself with a statement by Officer Smith that such a study had been made.

On cross-examination, Officer Smith admitted that he had not participated in conducting the alleged traffic study, and also admitted that he had refused appellant's request to cite him to the municipal court at the county seat. At the conclusion of this cross-examination, appellant testified as to his own vehicle's speed, and to the road, weather, and traffic conditions at the time he had been driving.

The court then found appellant guilty as charged.

Questions Presented

I. **WHETHER THE TRIAL COURT WAS WITHOUT JURISDICTION TO TRY APPELLANT FOLLOWING HIS REQUEST AT ARRAIGNMENT THAT THE ACTION BE TRANSFERRED TO THE MUNICIPAL COURT AT THE COUNTY SEAT FOR TRIAL.**

II. **WHETHER THE COURT WAS WITHOUT JURISDICTION TO FIND APPELLANT GUILTY WHEN, OVER APPELLANT'S OBJECTION, THE COURT ADMITTED TESTIMONY BASED ON THE USE OF SPEED-DETECTION RADAR EVEN THOUGH NO ENGINEERING AND TRAFFIC STUDY HAD BEEN INTRODUCED INTO EVIDENCE.**

Summary of Argument

The trial court was without jurisdiction to try appellant, given appellant's timely request to be tried in the county seat of Oakland under Vehicle Code § 40502(b), and Penal Code § 1462.2, which, upon defendant's motion, require the court to transfer the case to such district.

In addition, even assuming the matter had been commenced in the proper court, the court nevertheless lacked jurisdiction to enter a judgment of conviction based upon a "speed trap" (Vehicle Code §§ 40801–40805), where accompanying evidence of a "traffic and engineering survey" justifying the posted speed limit was not also introduced, as required by Section 40803(b) (*People v. Halopoff* (1976) 60 Cal.App.3d Supp. 1). A certified copy of the original study must be introduced into evidence (*People v. Sterritt* (1976) 65 Cal.App.3d Supp. 1). If the prosecution fails to do this, and the court nevertheless allows radar-based testimony, it is without jurisdiction to convict the defendant.

The prosecution's failure to establish this essential element of the case bars retrial, since the constitutional bar against double jeopardy forbids a second criminal trial where the prosecution failed to present sufficient evidence the first time (*Burks v. United States* (1977) 437 U.S. 1).

In any event, case law indicates that convictions for minor traffic infractions, when reversed, should be, in the interests of justice, *ordered dismissed* by the appellate court, rather than be sent back to the trial court for retrial (*People v. Kriss* (1979) 96 Cal.App.3d 913; *People v. Bighinatti* (1975) Cal.App.3d Supp. 5).

ARGUMENT

I. THE TRIAL COURT WAS WITHOUT JURISDICTION TO TRY APPELLANT FOLLOWING HIS REQUEST AT ARRAIGNMENT THAT THE ACTION BE TRANSFERRED TO THE MUNICIPAL COURT AT THE COUNTY SEAT.

A. WHEN A PERSON CITED FOR A TRAFFIC VIOLATION SO REQUESTS, THE MATTER MUST BE COMMENCED IN THE MUNICIPAL OR JUSTICE COURT AT THE COUNTY SEAT.

[Note: Rather than repeat why this is so, we simply refer you back to "Demanding Transfer to the County Seat" in Chapter 10. The format and style of writing should be the same as in the motion papers for a motion requesting a transfer to the county seat.]

B. THE TRIAL COURT WAS WITHOUT JURISDICTION TO TRY THE MATTER FOLLOWING APPELLANT'S MOTION FOR TRANSFER TO THE COURT AT THE COUNTY SEAT.

Penal Code Section 1462.2 states that "except as provided by the Vehicle Code," the proper court for trial of a misdemeanor (also infraction—see Penal Code § 19d) is the court in the county in which the offense is alleged to have been committed. The explicit reference to the Vehicle Code indicates that venue for Vehicle Code offenses may be different. In the instant case, appellant invoked Vehicle Code § 40502(b) to make the court at the *county seat* the only proper court for trial.

Section 1462.2 goes on to state that when the action is commenced in a court other than the proper one, it may nevertheless be tried there, "*unless the defendant, at the time he pleads, requests an order transferring the action or proceeding to the proper court.*" The statute concludes:

"If after such request it appears that the action or proceeding was not commenced in the proper court, the court shall order the action or proceeding transferred to the proper court."

In *Smith v. Municipal Court* (1959) 167 Cal.App.2d 534, 334 P.2d 931, the court held that it was the duty of a non-county-seat court to transfer the action, on defendant's request, to the county-seat court in which it would have been commenced had the citing officer abided by the dictates of Penal Code § 1462.2, now § 40502(b) of the Vehicle Code, stating;

The Municipal Court for the Los Angeles Judicial District being the proper place for the trial of the action against petitioner, § 1462.2 of the Penal Code made it the duty of the respondent court [Glendale Judicial District] to transfer the case to the municipal court for the Los Angeles Judicial District (167 Cal.App.2d, at 541).

Accordingly, the trial court in the instant case was without jurisdiction to try appellant. While *Smith* was a mandamus action, language therein noted that even following trial, this type of error "might be reviewed upon an appeal from the final judgment" (167 Cal.App.2d, at 541).

II. THE COURT WAS WITHOUT JURISDICTION TO FIND APPELLANT GUILTY WHEN OVER APPELLANT'S OBJECTION THE COURT ADMITTED TESTIMONY BASED ON THE USE OF SPEED DETECTION RADAR, EVEN THOUGH NO TRAFFIC AND ENGINEERING STUDY HAD BEEN INTRODUCED INTO EVIDENCE.

Section 40802 of the Vehicle Code defines a "speed trap" as follows:

"A particular section of a highway with a prima facie speed limit...if that prima facie speed limit is not justified by an engineering and traffic survey conducted within five years prior to the date of the alleged violation, and where enforcement involves the use of radar..."

The ramifications of such a definition of a speed trap are listed in §§ 40803, 40804(a), and 40805. The latter section states that any court that admits evidence based on the use of a speed trap "shall be without jurisdiction to enter a judgment of conviction...for a violation of this code involving the speed of a vehicle." Section 40804 (a) states that no such evidence shall be admitted. Finally, subdivision (b) of that section states:

"(b) In any prosecution under this code of a charge involving the speed of a vehicle, where enforcement involves the use of radar...the prosecution shall establish, as part of its prima facie case, that the evidence or testimony presented is not based upon a speed trap as defined in subdivision (b) of § 40802. Evidence that an engineering and traffic survey has been conducted within five years of the date of the alleged violation or evidence that the offense was committed on a local street or road as defined in subdivision (b) of § 40802 shall constitute a prima facie case that the evidence or testimony is not based upon a speed trap...

In summary, the prosecution, in order to introduce radar-based testimony in a speed violation case, must introduce into evidence an engineering and traffic survey justifying the prima facie speed limit within the past five years. If it fails to do so, a "speed trap" involving radar must be presumed. In that event, the officer testifying as to his measurement of the defendant's vehicle's speed by radar is "incompetent as a witness" and the court may not receive such evidence. And in the event it does receive such evidence, it is "without jurisdiction" to convict the defendant of a speed violation (VC § 40805).

The "truth-in-evidence" provisions of the California Constitution Article I, Section 28(d), do not get rid of Sections 40802 through 40805, because in 1992, the Legislature by more than the required two-thirds vote enacted Section 40808, which states, "Subdivision (d) of Section 28 of Article I of the California Constitution shall not be construed as abrogating the evidentiary provisions of this article," thus overruling *People v Sullivan* (1992) 234 CalApp.3d 56. See *People v Munoz* (1992) 11 CalApp.4th 1190.

The provisions of subdivision (b) of Vehicle Code § 40803 are a codification of the law as set forth in *People v. Halopoff* (1976) 60 Cal.App.3d Supp. 1, 131 Cal.Rptr. 531, where §§ 40801 through 40805 were construed. In *Halopoff*, the court reversed a conviction of a defendant for violation of § 22350, where the trial court overruled defendant's objection to the introduction of radar-based testimony without direct evidence of the existence of an engineering and traffic survey. In speaking of the policy requiring the People to disclose material evidence favorable to the accused (*In re Ferguson* (1971) 5 Cal.3d 525, 532), the court held that the prosecution has the burden of proving the existence of such a survey as a prerequisite to the use of radar-based testimony, stating;

It is consonant with this policy to require the People to disclose without request that radar was used and to produce the engineering and traffic survey or declare their inability to do so. The prosecution will always know when radar has been used to apprehend a speeder. The defendant and the court may not be aware of that fact. Simple fairness, and ease of procedure, dictate that the prosecution make that fact known.

* * * * *

If the burden is placed on the defendant to establish the existence of a speed trap, he is required to prove a negative—the absence of the requisite survey. This is an onerous task which militates against the policy of the legislation. If is far more easy and realistic in this connection to place the burden on the People... (60 Cal.App.3d Supp., at 6-7).

In the instant case, no engineering and traffic survey was introduced into evidence by the prosecution. The officer merely testified that he knew of the existence of such a survey. This is not sufficient. When an officer who did not participate in conducting such a survey merely states that it exists, but does not produce it, any speed violation conviction based on the use of radar must be reversed (*People v. Sterritt* (1976) 65 Cal.App.3d Supp. 1, 135 Cal.Rptr. 522). The prosecution has failed to meet its burden of proving that the officer's use of radar did not constitute a speed trap. Therefore, the officer was incompetent as a witness, and his testimony should not have been admitted. In any event, the court was without jurisdiction to convict appellant after having admitted such evidence.

<u>CONCLUSION</u>

For the reasons set forth above, appellant's conviction should be reversed. In addition, the trial court should be ordered to dismiss the matter rather than retry appellant. The People's failure to introduce the survey into evidence constituted a failure of proof of an essential element expressly required by Vehicle Code Section 40803(b). In other words, the evidence was insufficient to support a conviction. Retrial is therefore barred by the Double Jeopardy clause (*Burks. v. United States* (1977) 437 U.S. 1). Reversal would also

advance the interests of justice. In *People v. Kriss, supra*, the court reversed traffic violation convictions for ten defendants in a consolidated appeal, and ordered them dismissed, stating;

Given the relatively minor nature of the infractions involved and the fines imposed, and the necessity for retrials that an unqualified reversal would require, we conclude that in these instances it would not be in the interest of justice to prolong these matters. Accordingly, the judgments are reversed with directions to dismiss the complaints (96 Cal.App.3d, at 921).

DATED: November 10, 20xx

Respectfully submitted,

David Brown
DAVID W. BROWN, Appellant in Pro Per

PROOF OF DEPOSIT WITH TRIAL COURT

I, RICHARD MILLER, declare:

On November 2, 20xx I caused a copy of the within Appellant's Opening Brief to be deposited with the trial court below by personally delivering a true copy thereof to a deputy clerk of the said court for delivery to the Hon. T.M. Handimafine, the judge who presided below at the trial in this action.

I declare under penalty of perjury under the laws of the State of California that the foregoing is true and correct.

DATED: November 2, 20xx

Richard Miller
RICHARD MILLER

PROOF OF SERVICE

I, RICHARD MILLER, declare:

I am over the age of eighteen and not a party to the within action.

My business address is 123 Galvez Street, Oakland, California, in the county within which the within-mentioned mailing occurred.

On November 2, 20xx I served the within Appellant's Opening Brief on Respondent by placing a true copy thereof in a separate sealed envelope, with the postage thereon fully prepaid, in the United States Postal Service mailbox at Oakland, County of Alameda, California, the envelope being addressed as follows:

Office of the District Attorney
County of Alameda
1225 Fallon Street
Oakland, CA 94612

I declare under penalty of perjury under the laws of the State of California that the foregoing is true and correct.

DATED: November 2, 20xx

Richard Miller
RICHARD MILLER

Checklist for Filing a Motion

(Follow *all* steps.)

☐ 1. Type a Notice of Appeal stating that you are appealing from a finding of guilty rendered on a certain date. This must be filed with the clerk of the traffic court in which you were found guilty within 30 days of the date you were found guilty. Keep a file-stamped photocopy for your records as proof that you filed it on time.

☐ 2. Type a Proposed Statement on Appeal listing your grounds on appeal and a statement of the proceedings relevant to those grounds. Make two copies of this and have a friend mail one copy to the prosecutor. Your friend should fill out a Proof of Service on the last page of the original. This can be filed with the Notice of Appeal, or up to 15 days later. Keep a stamped copy for your records.

☐ 3. You will be notified of a date for a hearing, before the judge who found you guilty, to "settle" your Statement on Appeal. If you received a Proposed Statement from the prosecution, read it carefully before you go to the hearing. Be prepared to counter anything the prosecution suggests that would hurt your case. Don't let the judge bully you. After the hearing, the judge will ask you to prepare an Engrossed Statement on Appeal. You must type this, make two copies, and have a friend mail a copy to the prosecutor and fill out the Proof of Service, present it to the judge to sign, and file it with the trial court within five days. Keep a file-stamped photocopy. Start researching and writing your brief.

☐ 4. The trial court clerks then send the Notice of Appeal, Engrossed Statement, and other papers to the appeals court. The appeals court will notify you when it has received them.

☐ 5. You have 20 days from the time the appeals court receives the case file (not from the time the clerk sent out or you received the notice) to submit your opening brief. You should make six photocopies of your brief. Have a friend mail one copy to the prosecutor's office and deliver another to a traffic court clerk (with instructions to give it to the trial judge). Your friend then fills out a Proof of Service on the last page of the original brief. Three copies and the one original are filed with the appeals court clerk. The remaining copy is yours. Have the clerk file-stamp it.

☐ 6. You will receive the prosecution's brief in the mail. Read it immediately and decide whether you should answer any of the points made in a Reply Brief. You have only a few days to file it.

☐ 7. If you wish to file a Reply Brief, do so within ten days of the date the prosecution filed its brief. The Reply Brief is prepared, served, and filed in the same manner as an Opening Brief.

☐ 8. Go to the appeals court hearing. Be prepared to argue your case and answer any questions you can anticipate.

your legal theory. You should not be defensive in answering such questions. The fact that you're being asked them is a good sign. Do not make the mistake of reiterating everything in your brief. If you must summarize the points raised in your brief, make that summary very short. The judge(s) will have already read your argument.

After you and the prosecutor have made your statements, the judge(s) may give their decision, usually by saying "affirmed" or "reversed." Sometimes the Appellate Department judge(s) will take it under advisement; unlike in traffic court, there's no requirement that they tell you their decision right away.

The "Remittitur"

Some time after the appeal has been decided, the court will mail you a copy of the written decision, usually just a one-sentence reversal or affirmance. It will also send a similar notice to the trial court (called a "Remittitur"). If it's affirmed, you will have to comply with whatever part of the original sentence that was postponed or "stayed" while the appeal was pending, unless the appeals court has ordered otherwise in its decision.

If the trial court's decision is reversed with nothing else said, a new trial will have to be held before a judge other than the one who presided at your first trial. If it's reversed with orders to dismiss, you've won. Any fine you may have paid is refunded to you by the trial court. In either case, if the trial court clerks notified the DMV of your conviction, they will send an amended note telling the DMV to remove it from your driving record. Of course, if you're convicted after a new trial, the court clerks will notify the DMV again, and the offense will go back on your record.

A Final Word

For further information on traffic court appeals, read Rules 181 through 190 of California Rules of Court and any cases citing those rules. The procedure for filing, settling, and arguing motions in the appeals court when something goes wrong with the appeal is covered in Rule 104. A good source of summary information on criminal procedure is found in Witkin, *Criminal Procedure.*

An appeal beyond the Superior Court Appellate Department is very complex and probably should be handled by an attorney. The right to go to a higher court isn't automatic; it depends upon whether that court wants to take the case. They will only grant a hearing if it is an exceptional situation.

Staying Out of Trouble

If you're like most readers of this book, you bought it to help you fight a ticket you have already received. Well, now that we've shown you how to fight your ticket, here are some tips on how you can avoid tickets in the future, and be better prepared if you are pulled over.

Avoiding the Traffic Officer

The best way, of course, to minimize your chance of receiving a ticket is not to drive. Short of that, though, the next best way is to scrupulously obey all traffic laws. Unfortunately, however, police officers do stop and cite innocent drivers. Also, it's quite easy for a conservative and safe driver to be cited for a technical violation that defies common sense and endangers no one.

The purpose of this section is not to suggest ways for you to break the law and drive unsafely with impunity. Rather, it is written with the recognition that even a conscientious and safe driver may be unjustly cited by a police officer whose primary interest is in meeting his quota rather than encouraging safety. We don't advise you to "fight back" by breaking the law. But knowing that you and many others will do just that—while driving perfectly safely—we note a few ways for you to keep your contacts with traffic officers to a minimum.

On the Freeway

Speeding is by far the most common traffic offense for which people are cited. And most of these involve exceeding the maximum 65 mph speed limit (70 mph on some freeways and 55 mph on two-lane undivided roads). Here are a few suggestions for avoiding a ticket in this situation.

Make Sure You Can Spot the Police

First, make sure your car's equipped with decent mirrors that give you an unobstructed view. To this end, periodically clean your mirrors and rear window, do not put stickers on your rear window unless you have to, and keep objects off the back ledge that may block your view.

If your rearview mirror vibrates at freeway speeds—as some do—try to correct the problem. A mirror that vibrates only a little will blur the subtle features that often give away a following patrol car or motorcycle. (You can notice the difference a nonvibrating mirror makes by temporarily damping the vibration—that is, by holding the mirror tightly between your right thumb and forefinger.) Try tightening or slightly loosening any screws on the mirror mounting; if that doesn't help, remove the screws to add fiber, hard rubber, or even homemade cardboard or paper washers or shims to the mounting. Sometimes, you can reduce mirror vibration by having your front wheels balanced—usually for no more than $20.

With a little practice, you can learn to recognize a CHP car's front in your side or rearview mirrors. Most CHP cars are manned by one driver and no passenger. They are either white, or black and white in color. The roof is always white (in order to reduce heat from the beating sun). The fronts of CHP cars usually don't have much chrome, and often have black bumpers. One telltale sign of a CHP car behind you is the shotgun mounted vertically on a rack in the front of the car. From your rearview mirror, the shotgun on its rack seems to divide the police car windshield in two.

The CHP is also moving toward increased use of smaller semicompact cars, which are much harder to distinguish as patrol vehicles. While many larger CHP cars have conspicuous red-

and-blue roof-rack lights, the smaller cars (and even some of the larger ones) use internally mounted red lights that become noticeable only when they're turned on and it's too late.

Black-and-white CHP vehicles can also be noticed by their all-white doors, which become visible in your rearview mirror as you enter a slight curve. (However, some CHP cars are painted all-white.) Another feature is that they have very large and powerful engines that allow them to accelerate very quickly. Adopting a regular habit of glancing at your rearview mirror every five or ten seconds will help you to distinguish any quickly accelerating cars whose distant image on your mirror seems to grow too fast.

Some Common Police Tricks

You may notice a CHP vehicle ahead of you, and slow down to the posted limit. If you then see the officer pull off onto an exit ramp, resist the temptation to speed up right away. CHP officers regularly do this, only to reenter the freeway from a nearby on-ramp a few seconds later. With your false sense of security at having seen the officer exit the freeway, the officer will be far enough behind so that you won't notice, but still close enough to begin "pacing" your car. Whenever you see the officer ahead of you get off the freeway, watch your mirrors to try and see what else she does. Even if you don't see the car re-enter the freeway, take a heightened interest in your rearview mirror for the next few miles.

Also, CHP officers will often park very near on-ramps, to allow them to quickly get onto the freeway to chase or pace a car they think is going too fast. It isn't a bad idea to glance about the area as you approach an on-ramp. After all, your heightened awareness will not only help you avoid a traffic officer, but will also help you be a better and safer driver!

Another trick CHP officers use is to "pace" you from a parallel frontage road. Watch out for this, too.

Keep in mind that another maneuver CHP officers can perform with amazing skill is a high-speed U-turn. You aren't safe from a CHP officer just because he's traveling in the opposite direction and thus can't "pace" your car. First, many CHP officers use radar units with a "moving radar" feature that allows a moving police vehicle to read the speed of an oncoming vehicle. Second, even without using radar this way, most police officers are very good at judging the speed of oncoming vehicles. If an officer thinks yours is too high, he may well execute a movie-grade high-speed U-turn to chase you. Even freeways have frequent spots where this can be done, and an officer who regularly patrols a particular section of road knows where such spots are. With the high-powered engines on CHP cars, he'll catch up with you in no time.

Motorcycles and Airplanes

In your search for CHP cars that might pull you over, don't forget that the CHP uses motorcycles as well. A CHP motorcycle can usually be recognized by its large size, radio antenna, emergency kit, red light in front, and uniformed, blue-and-gold-helmeted driver. There are times when the CHP rarely uses motorcycles—at night or when it rains.

Patrol cars and motorcycles aren't your only worry. As we discuss in Chapter 4, the CHP makes extensive use of aircraft to catch speeders. Not all roads are appropriate for aircraft patrols, however. Freeways that are not straight over long distances, that are near the flight paths of major airports, or that are simply too far from a local airport or airstrip, are less than ideal for the use of aircraft patrols. Straight highways in rural areas are preferred. In fact, highways patrolled by CHP aircraft usually have signs that warn "patrolled by aircraft," and have white mile-markers (several inches wide, by three or four feet long) painted on the side of the freeway every mile. Even so, this doesn't mean that aircraft are used every hour of the day. Such aircraft are never flown at night for this purpose, and are flown during the day only when weather conditions permit. Ideal weather for this type of flying is a clear day (or at least days with high clouds) with little or no wind, and no rain.

We don't suggest that you stick your head out the window to look for CHP aircraft, or point your side-view mirror upward. Still, if you can do so safely, there's nothing wrong with being alert for any small Cessna-type airplane flying parallel to the freeway, either ahead of you in your direction, or coming toward you from the other direction, especially on freeways with mile markers.

Don't Call Attention to Yourself

The best way to avoid speeding tickets on freeways is to remain as inconspicuous as possible. In earlier years, when the maximum speed limit was raised from 55 to 65 mph, most people who wanted to be careful about exceeding the speed limit tried to stay within ten miles of it—the speed at which most CHP officers began to write tickets. Indeed, on roads where the limit is still 55 mph, a CHP officer who sees you doing 62 mph in the center lane (of three lanes in your direction) is likely to be going too fast to slow down and bother with you anyway—he's chasing the other cars doing 70+ mph.

Now that freeway speed limits have gone back up, however, many CHP officers say they won't be giving that 10-mph-over leeway any longer. In other words, doing 75 mph on a 65 mph limit freeway is more likely to get you a ticket than was doing 65 on the same freeway when its limit was 55 mph. Also, on 70 mph freeways, many officers say they'll begin writing tickets at less than 75 mph.

Other ways of avoiding freeway tickets include staying out of the far-left lane if possible, since that's where officers usually look for the faster drivers. Also avoid using your headlights in the daytime while barreling down the fast lane—a sure sign of a speeder who wants slower traffic to get out of his way.

You might also want to avoid unusual car decorations or adornments. Anything out of the ordinary—such as racing stripes, stickers, or jacked-up front or rear wheels—will call unnecessary and possibly unwanted attention to your driving.

In *A Speeder's Guide to Avoiding Tickets* (Avon Books, 1991), the author, retired New York highway patrolman Sgt. James M. Eagan, says that the type and condition of your vehicle may make an officer more likely to pull you over. Among the factors officers might consider are the following:

- bumper stickers and unnecessary window decals. Most bumper stickers—even those favoring sports teams—are capable of offending someone. Conversely, the "Support Your Local Police" or "Police Benevolent Association" bumper stickers are such obvious attempts at getting favorable treatment that they sometimes have the opposite effect;

- personalized license plates. These are okay, but make sure your plate isn't likely to single you out by occupation or other category likely to offend. (One young man with a "NEC BRKR" personalized plate on his 4x4 truck kept wondering why he got so many tickets!);

- radar detectors. Police will often issue a ticket once they see a radar detector, even though they otherwise might have let you off with a warning;

- general good condition. An officer is going to be at least slightly more favorably disposed toward the driver of a neat, well-maintained vehicle than to the driver of a sloppy wreck. (Police seem to get more than their share of verbal abuse from drivers of the latter types of vehicles.) Repair large noticeable dents, replace cracked windows, keep your car presentably painted, and keep the interior neat and clean—including the glove compartment and ashtray in the event the officer looks in there (and many do);

- worn tires. Replace these. An officer inclined to give only a warning may think otherwise after noticing you were speeding on bald tires.

Although the CHP still primarily uses pacing to catch speeders, it is increasingly using radar on many four-lane highways, including freeways. So, although relying on a radar detector can give you a false sense of security (it won't guarantee freedom from being "paced"), we now recommend one as an added safeguard when driving on freeways as well as in town.

Off the Freeway

The two most common traffic violations for which people are cited while not driving on a freeway are speeding and rolling stops.

Speeding

After speeding on the freeway—in violation of the Maximum Speed Law—the next most common violation is—you guessed it—speeding off the freeway, usually in town, in violation of the Basic Speed Law.

Don't get us wrong. It's a lot more dangerous to exceed the speed limit in a city than it is to do 70 mph on a freeway built for safety at that speed and posted at 65. We do not suggest speeding in the city under any circumstances. However, there are times when a perfectly safe driver will exceed a posted speed limit and invite a ticket—from a city police officer whose job is partly to provide needed revenue for the city. Here are a few tips on how you can avoid tickets under these circumstances.

When you first drive through a city or town, take a close look at the police cars. (You may see one stopped at a red light and have time to look it over thoroughly.) You will see mostly large American cars painted white or black-and-white (with the top always white). Often a large number of the cars are the same make and/or model, since cities purchase them in quantity from dealers or manufacturers. Unlike the CHP, city police departments are not moving rapidly toward purchasing small cars with hidden lights. Most are large and have roof-rack (or "bar") lights.

All police vehicles (except undercover ones, which can't be used for routine traffic enforcement) have front and rear license plates which contain as their first character a small letter "E" inside a diamond or hexagon. Knowing this can come in handy at times, even though the "E" is often too small to notice at a distance. For example, when you're stopped at a stop light and suddenly notice the lower part of the front of a car in your rearview mirror, you may be able to identify the car right behind you as a police car.

City police rely much more on radar to catch speeders than do CHP officers, and much less on techniques like pacing that render patrol cars or motorcycles visible. We refer you to Chapter 4 for a discussion of where radar is most often used, and on the features and fallacies of radar detectors. Also, city police use motorcycles for radar enforcement more often than the CHP.

One thing that will lessen your chances of being pulled over by an officer using stationary radar (aimed in the same direction of travel) is to drive in the left lane. True, the "fast" lane is where more speeders can be found. However, driving in the left lane will increase the angle between your car and a radar beam directed backward from a patrol car parked on the road shoulder in your direction of travel. The higher this angle, the lower the apparent speed on the radar unit, since this "cosine angle factor" error works in your favor.

Rolling Stops

The second most commonly cited violation off the freeway is for running a stop sign in what's called a "rolling stop." Sadly, this is also one of the most harmless violations, at least where the driver is carefully looking out for cross traffic. If you must do this (it seems almost instinctual, actually), you should get in the habit of thinking about hidden police cars. Glance in your rearview mirror (as you should anyway, for safety reasons), just before coming to the stop sign. Then be prepared to come to a complete stop if you encounter any cross traffic or see any police cars parked on either side of the cross street or the other side of the intersection. If you see an officer, come to a complete stop even if you've already crossed the limit line. Under these circumstances, an officer is still less likely to ticket you than if you roll through. Then wait at least a full three seconds before proceeding.

Being Pulled Over

In this section and the next two, you'll learn what you should and shouldn't do in that initial encounter with a police officer who pulls you over. Being observant of weather and road conditions, asking the officer the right questions, and making specific requests of the officer at this early stage, can put you in a much better position to fight your ticket later on. Also, if you've been drinking, there are certain things you can do to minimize the problems that can result from your encounter with the authorities.

When You See the Police Car

Your battle to beat the ticket begins the instant you realize you're being pulled over by a police officer. If a police car is following you with its siren blaring or emergency lights flashing, pull over to the right quickly (but safely) and come to a complete stop in a safe place. Do not be one of those people who nonchalantly continues to drive and pretends to be amazed at having been pulled over. This tactic will just irritate an officer and give him ammunition to claim at trial that you were inattentive (and therefore likely to have violated a traffic law).

Pulling over right away is not an admission of guilt. It just means that you were very alert to everything that was happening around you. Also, by stopping as soon as you can, you'll have a better chance of figuring out exactly where the officer says you drove too fast, made an illegal U-turn, didn't signal, etc. This information can be useful in preparing your defense.

Pull over in a way that will be most likely to calm down an angry or annoyed traffic officer. Use your turn signal to indicate any lane changes from left to right, and slow down fairly quickly, but not so quickly that the officer will have to brake to avoid hitting you. Pull over as far to the right as possible, so that when the officer comes up to your widow, he won't have to worry about being clipped by vehicles in the right lane.

Avoid Giving the Officer an Excuse to Search

A police officer who stops you for a traffic violation is normally not allowed to search your vehicle. However, there are several exceptions to this. An officer who observes you trying to either hide something under the seat or throw something out the window may legally search your car. Once the cop is on your rear bumper with his spotlight silhouetting your every move, he's watching for any sort of "furtive movement." A sudden lowering of one or both shoulders will tip him off that you're attempting to hide something under the seat. This gives him legal cause to search a car, and he'll know exactly what to look for and where. Police have had more experience watching people try to hide things than you've had trying to hide them.

Also, once you are stopped, a police officer may seize any illegal objects in your car that are in "plain view" (like open beer or wine bottles, joints or roach clips). Once they see the object, they can open the car door to reach in and get it. Once they do, they may come across other objects that are in plain view and shouldn't be in your car, and they can seize these too. (If you are pulled over at night, there is somewhat less risk of plain-view observations if the car is not parked under a bright street lamp. However, an officer can still shine his flashlight into the car.)

Finally, your car and its occupants may be searched if any occupant in it—passenger or driver—is physically arrested. If you're arrested and your car is towed, the police may make a supposed "inventory search" afterward, even if they have no reason to suspect there is anything illegal inside.

Right After You've Stopped

After you've pulled over onto a safe spot, you might want to show the officer a few other token courtesies. At this point, you have little to lose and perhaps something to gain.

First off, roll down your window all the way. You may also want to place your hands on the steering wheel, and, if it's dark, turn on your interior light. This will tend to allay any fears the officer may have. (After all, police officers are killed every day in such "ordinary" traffic-stop situations, and the officer's approach to the vehicle is the potentially most dangerous.) It may offend your dignity a little, but remember that you're just doing a few simple things to put the officer in an optimal frame of mind.

Finally, don't start rummaging through your back pocket for your wallet and license, or in your glove compartment for your registration, until the officer asks you for them. For all he knows, you could be reaching for something else.

Should You Get Out of Your Car?

An officer who stops you for an alleged traffic violation has the right to insist that you and your passengers get out of your car. You should do so if asked. But what if the officer doesn't ask you to get out of your car?

Getting out of your car may make it easier for you to check road conditions, the weather, the place the violation supposedly occurred, and, in radar-detected speeding violations, perhaps even the read-out on the officer's radar detector.

On the other hand, you may wish to appear innocuous. After all, if the officer thinks that you are preparing yourself to contest the ticket, she will be sure to write copious notes on the back of her copy of the ticket, to refresh her memory if she has to testify later at a trial. If you want to look around and take notes, you can come back and do it a few minutes after the officer leaves.

To put an officer at ease—and hopefully to make him reluctant to cite you—there are a few things you can do when pulled over. First, put out any cigarettes, put away any chewing gum, and put both your hands on the steering wheel. At night, turn your inside dome light on before putting your hands on the wheel. Silly as all this sounds, it signals to the officer that you have a compliant attitude, and aren't going to reach for a weapon—a legitimate fear for traffic cops. The more cooperative you can be, the more possible it is that the officer will let you off with a warning.

Many police officers prefer that you stay in your car, and will tell you to stay there if you start to get out. If this happens, obviously you should cooperate. If you get out of the car against the officer's orders, don't be surprised to see a gun pointing at you. Cops are trained to expect the worst. When you get out of your car they may assume you're about to pull a weapon or attempt to flee. So, don't panic, and make it apparent to the officer that you intend no harm.

If an officer has any reason to believe that you might be dangerous, she has a right to conduct a quick "pat-down" search of your outer clothing while she is standing next to you, to make sure you don't have a concealed knife or gun that you could pull on her. If the officer feels any weapon-sized object during the pat-down search, she can reach in and get it. Also, the officer's good-faith belief that you may be dangerous justifies a search of the passenger compartment of your car for weapons.

For more on car searches, read the section, "Searches," below.

Talking to the Officer

Many people stopped by an officer make the mistake of saying the wrong thing, and failing to say the right things. As we see below, a case can be won or lost depending on what you say—or don't say—to the officer.

Don't Admit Anything

Many drivers who are pulled over destroy any chance they might have had to successfully contest a violation in court, because they mistakenly believe they can talk their way out of it. This is usually not true.

One of the first things traffic cops learn in the police academy is to decide, before leaving their vehicle, whether they're going to give a ticket or just a warning. They may act as though they still haven't made up their minds and are going to let you off only if you'll "cooperate." Don't fall for this. The hesitating officer is often just trying to appear open-minded in order to extract admissions out of you, to use them against you in court if necessary. (Your admissions can be used against you even though the officer doesn't give you a "Miranda" warning of your right to remain silent. See *Berkemer v. McCarty* (1984) 468 U.S. 420, 104 S.Ct. 3138. You still have the right to remain silent, but a traffic officer doesn't have to tell you.) The strategy is to try to get you to admit either that you committed a violation, or that you were so careless, inattentive, or negligent that you don't know whether you did or not. One way this is commonly done is for the officer to act friendly. If you learn nothing else from this book, learn that a police officer with a ticket book in his hand is not your friend.

On the other hand, you have nothing to lose by being polite, even charming. After all, this officer may be one of the few who has decided to give you only a warning. Would you like to change that by acting like a jerk?

Don't speak first. Especially don't start off with a defensive or hostile "What's the problem?" or similar words. Let the officer start talking. He will probably ask to see your license, vehicle registration, and proof of insurance. Many people make the mistake of insisting the officer tell them why he stopped them, before they'll comply. Don't make that mistake. Reply "Okay," or "Sure," then hand over the documents.

The officer then might ask you the sort of question whose lack of a definite answer would imply guilt, like "Do you know why I stopped you?" (Suppress the impulse to reply, "Gee, no, officer, I thought *you* would know why you stopped me!") Or, he might ask, "Do you know how fast you were going?" Your answers, if any, should be noncommittal and brief, like a simple "No" to the first question or a very confident, "Yes, I do," to the second. (Most officers are not impressed with a bootlicking "Sir" appended to every yes or no. Try to avoid saying "Yes, sir" more than once, if at all.) If he then tells you how fast he thinks you were going or what he thinks you did, don't argue. Either give a noncommittal answer, like "I see," or no answer at all. Silence is not an admission of guilt and cannot be used against you in court.

If the officer persists, you may want to try to change the subject with something like, "Is it possible to pay the fine by mail?" This statement changes the subject, avoids an actual admission, and lulls the officer into thinking you're one of those 19 out of 20 who'll pay your ticket without a fight—which will make it harder for him to remember you later on in court. If changing the subject doesn't work, and the officer still asks you pointed questions, you may simply have to say that you have nothing more to say or that you prefer not to answer

any questions. And don't fall for the inevitable, "Got something to hide?" If he says this, just tell him, "I have nothing more to say. Please just write the ticket and we can both be on our way." Or you can say, "Do I have the right to remain silent?"

Remain Quiet or Ask a Few Questions?

Traffic officers issue many citations each day. By the time your case goes to trial, the officer who stopped and cited you may have issued dozens or even hundreds of tickets since. That being so, chances are good that he won't recall the events pertaining to your ticket very well by the time he has to come to court to testify against you, unless you've either committed an unusually outrageous offense or done something to focus his attention. If you're cited for a routine moving violation, you may be better off saying very little in order to increase the chance that the officer won't recall the circumstances of the alleged violation later on, and won't be tempted to make copious notes in anticipation of testifying in court about the incident later. (Needless to say, an officer is more likely to remember you, and more likely to make notes, if you are rude or offensive, so you should always be polite.)

On the other hand, you may wish to ask the officer a few polite questions, even at the cost of fixing you better in his memory, in the hope that he will give you information which may prove helpful. You may especially want to ask questions if you've done something else that will stand out in the officer's mind—like demanding that your trial be held in the county seat. In this situation, you have nothing to lose—there's no use keeping quiet when you have already made clear that you intend to fight your ticket.

If you decide to ask questions, you should try to get the officer to commit himself to where he was when he saw you, how far he followed you, and to similar facts noted below. If you're able to write this information down while it's fresh in your memory, you may be able to use it in court later on, especially if he changes his story. One way to do this without tipping him off that you intend to fight the ticket and without making an actual admission is to smile and say, "Could you please tell me how you nailed me?" Most officers will be more than happy to brag a little about this to you, unless they're expecting you to contest the ticket. If you have a witness in your car, so much the better. While some officers will refuse to answer more than a few direct questions, others will very happily answer most questions, if only to convince you that you haven't got a chance if you take it to court.

You might consider asking some of the following questions:

- *"Where were you when you first saw me?"* (If he tells you, you can go back to that spot later to check what he was able to see. Any obstructions to the view might show that he may have missed an essential element of the alleged violation.) Never ask a question that also contains an admission, like *"Where were you hiding when I ran the red light?"*

- If the charge is speeding:

  "How did you determine my speed?" (He will probably tell you this without your having to ask, particularly if he used radar. He may even show you a speed reading. Most people mistakenly assume that radar is infallible and will give up all hope of fighting a ticket if they see a radar reading.)

- If he did not use radar:

  "How far did you follow me?" (If he followed you for just a short distance prior to charging

you with speeding, you can later argue in court that he rapidly closed the distance between his car and yours, but wrongly attributed that speed to you. (See Chapter 4 on speed violations to see how this calculation is done.)

- If he used radar to determine your speed:

  "May I see the speed reading on the radar unit?" (Although the officer is not required to do this, the chances are good that she will be happy to, in order to convince you that you don't stand a chance of successfully fighting the ticket. This is called "selling the ticket" to you, and is such standard practice that if the officer refuses to show you his radar reading of your speed, it suggests something is amiss.

If you have been stopped by a particularly talkative officer, you may also want to ask one or more of the following questions (some are pretty technical, but can be very useful, as we pointed out in Chapter 4):

> *"Where were you located when you took the reading?"*

> *"Where did you see my car when you took the reading?"*

> *"Do you know the angle of the spread of the beam (the beam width angle)? How many degrees?"*

Finally, always keep in mind that the more questions you ask, the more likely the officer is to realize that you intend to fight the ticket. This will tip him off to write detailed notes to himself. So don't ask questions just for the sake of doing so, or to annoy the officer. Also, *never* say, "See you in court," or words to that effect. You might as well say, "Be sure to take good notes about this, to refresh your memory about it when you have to go to court."

If You've Been Drinking

If you've had anything substantial to drink, it's best not to engage the officer in any conversation beyond brief, noncommittal answers. No use letting him hear your speech or giving him extra chances to study your eyes closely. Probably he'll ask the inevitable, "How much have you had to drink?" Many people will admit to "just a glass of wine" or "just two beers" in the hope that the officer will believe them and let them go. Rather, the officer will assume that you've had much more, and such an admission will do you no good. In addition, your statement that you have been drinking can be used against you in court.

The best answer to questions about whether or how much you've been drinking is, "I prefer to remain silent," unless, of course, you've had little or nothing to drink.

Which brings us to a minor point. Did you ever wonder why the cops always shine their flashlights right into your eyes at night? It's not necessarily because they're mildly sadistic (though some are). Rather, it's to see whether your eyes are watery or bloodshot, and also to see how fast the pupils of your eyes contract upon sudden exposure to the light. A slow contraction of the pupils, or none at all, suggests you're under the influence. Therefore, it's wise to avoid looking directly into the flashlight or the officer's eyes if you've had any alcohol, drugs, or even prescription medication (particularly tranquilizers). Try to look down at the ground or at your wallet or purse as you remove your driver's license. It's also helpful to look directly into a lighted street lamp for a moment to contract your pupils before the officer gets a chance to shine the light into your eyes.

Making the Place of Trial Inconvenient for the Officer

If your residence *or* workplace is located closer to the "county seat" than to the local court near where you're pulled over, then you have a right to insist that the officer send the ticket to the county seat. This little known provision of the Vehicle Code (§ 40502(b)) can often work to your advantage, as we discuss below. Of course, this will probably tip the officer off that you intend to fight the ticket, and may result in the officer taking detailed notes. However, it may be worth it.

The County Seat

Your right to request the county seat as the place of your trial requires some explanation. Every county has a "county seat," which is a sort of "capital" of the county and is usually the largest city in it. (Consult the chart later in this section for a list of the seats of all California counties.) Most California counties have several court locations including at the county seat.

At the bottom of a traffic ticket, there is a space to list the "place to appear." Normally it will be the courthouse closest to where the cop pulled you over, usually within ten miles. This court will most likely be close to the officer's home base. But if the court at the county seat is different, as it commonly is, it may be quite a distance from the officer's base.

EXAMPLE:

If you're stopped and cited in El Monte, in Los Angeles County, the officer would note on the ticket that you should appear at the local court there. But, since you work in Santa Monica, which is a lot closer to the county seat (Los Angeles city), you can insist that the court at which the ticket directs you to appear be the one at the county seat—Los Angeles.

Making such a demand will result in the following advantages:

- The officer is less likely to show up at a court miles away from his usual place of duty; if he doesn't show up for trial, your case will almost surely be dismissed. (See Chapter 10.)

- The police officer will most likely be a total stranger to the judge. This puts him on a more equal footing with you. In his hometown court, there is a good chance that the officer knows the judge, having often appeared before her. Going to the county seat evens your odds a little.

- The ticket might get lost. Sending a ticket to the county seat court goes against the usual procedure, and a confused clerk faced with the problem of properly routing your ticket may misplace it. Even if it turns up much later, you may be able to get the charge dismissed on the grounds that you have been denied the right to a speedy trial. (See Chapter 10.)

Note: You may have been stopped in a city that is a county seat, or in a nearby area. In this situation, requesting the county seat won't help. (You may wish to review the tables set out later in this section and make a mental note of the county seat locations for the counties in which you normally drive.)

Making the Demand

Note: In order to preserve your right to have the county-seat court hear your case, you *must* demand the county seat *when the officer starts writing the ticket.*

There are two ways to make your county seat demand. One is to simply say, *"I want this citation sent to the court at the county seat, because that's closer to where I work/live. Could you please specify that court as the place to appear?"* Be prepared to give the officer your residence address—if different from that on your driver's license—or your business address, to establish that one or the other is closer to the county seat than to the local court.

Be prepared—the officer may try to talk you out of your county seat request. If he does, be firm. If he asks you why you want the county seat, just say *"It's more convenient for me."* The officer may try to tell you that you have no right to demand the county seat, or that if you wish to do so, your request must be made to the clerk or judge of the local court. Many cops believe this, but they're wrong. In an appeals court case known as *Smith v. Municipal Court* (1959) 167 Cal.App.2d 534, 334 P.2d 931, an appeals court ruled that VC § 40502(b) says the choice of the county seat is entirely up to the person cited and that the officer must comply with the request. (Since the case was decided, the law was amended to require such compliance only if your business or residence address is closer to the county-seat court.) This applies to *all* Vehicle Code violations, even jaywalking and littering, for which you're issued a Notice to Appear ticket. (See Chapter 3.)

Note: Some judges (and police) in certain counties think the county-seat law doesn't apply now that judicial districts have been consolidated into one "unified" county-wide superior court district. This is based on a belief that the term "county seat" has no meaning when applied to such counties. We disagree. "County seat" refers to the city in which the county's Board of Supervisors meets. However, it includes all branch courts in the city limits of the city in which the Board of Supervisors meets. (Thus, for example, since the "city" of Van Nuys is actually part of the City of Los Angeles, the branch court in Van Nuys also qualifies as the county seat.)

County Seats of California Counties

County	County Seat	County	County Seat
Alameda	Oakland	Placer	Auburn
* Alpine	Markleeville	Plumas	Quincy
* Amador	Jackson	Riverside	Riverside
Butte	Oroville	Sacramento	Sacramento
* Calaveras	San Andreas	San Benito	Hollister
* Colusa	Williams	San Bernardino	San Bernardino
Contra Costa	Martinez	San Diego	San Diego
* Del Norte	Crescent City	* San Francisco	San Francisco
El Dorado	Placerville	San Joaquin	Stockton
Fresno	Fresno	San Luis Obispo	San Luis Obispo
Glenn	Willows	San Mateo	Redwood City
Humboldt	Eureka	Santa Barbara	Santa Barbara
Imperial	El Centro	Santa Clara	San Jose
Inyo	Independence	Santa Cruz	Santa Cruz
Kern	Bakersfield	Shasta	Redding
Kings	Hanford	Sierra	Downieville
Lake	Lakeport	Siskiyou	Yreka
* Lassen	Susanville	Solano	Fairfield
Los Angeles	Los Angeles	Sonoma	Santa Rosa
Marin	San Rafael	* Stanislaus	Modesto
* Mariposa	Mariposa	* Sutter	Yuba City
Mendocino	Ukiah	Tehama	Red Bluff
Merced	Merced	Trinity	Weaverville
* Modoc	Alturas	Tulare	Visalia
Mono	Bridgeport	Tuolumne	Sonora
Monterey	Salinas	Ventura	Ventura
Napa	Napa	Yolo	Woodland
Nevada	Nevada City	Yuba	Marysville
Orange	Santa Ana		

* In counties marked with an asterisk (*), the county seat has the only court in the county. All tickets will be tried there whether demanded or not.

Note: As you can see, the county seat is often the city with the same name as the county, yet the cities of Alameda, Marin, Monterey, San Mateo, Santa Clara, and Sonoma are not county seats of their respectively named counties.

District or Branch Court Locations of the Six Largest Counties

County	Superior Court Locations	County	Superior Court Locations
Los Angeles	Alhambra	Orange	* Central Orange County (Santa Ana)
	Antelope (Lancaster)		North Orange County (Fullerton)
	Baldwin Hills Branch of L.A. ("ticket office")		Orange County Harbor (Newport Beach)
	Beverly Hills		South Orange County (Laguna Niguel)
	Burbank		South Court Annex of S. Orange County (Laguna Hills)
	Calabasas Branch of Malibu		West Orange County (Westminster)
	Catalina Branch (Avalon)	San Diego	El Cajon
	Chatsworth Branch of L.A.		Escondido Branch of N. County
	Citrus (W. Covina)		North County (Vista)
	Compton		Ramona Branch of El Cajon
	Culver (Culver City)		* San Diego
	Downey		San Marcos Branch of N. County
	* E. Los Angeles		South Bay (Chula Vista)
	Glendale	Santa Clara	Gilroy Facility
	Inglewood		Los Gatos Facility
	Long Beach		Palo Alto Facility
	Los Angeles ("Metropolitan Branch" * 1945 S. Hill Street)		* San Jose Traffic Facility (Ruff Drive)
	Los Cerritos (Bellflower)		South County Facility (San Martin)
	Malibu		Sunnyvale/Facililty
	Newhall (Valencia)	Alameda	Alameda
	Pasadena		Berkeley/Albany
	Pomona		Fremont/Newark/Union City
	Robertson Branch of L.A.		Livermore/Pleasanton
	Rio Hondo (El Monte)		* Oakland/Piedmont/Emeryville
	* San Fernando Branch of L.A.		San Leandro/Hayward
	* San Pedro Branch of L.A.	Sacramento	Galt Branch of S. Sacramento
	Santa Anita (Monrovia)		* Sacramento (Carol Miller Justice Ctr.)
	Santa Monica		S. Sacramento (Elk Grove)
	South Bay (Torrance)		Walnut Grove/Isleton Branch of S. Sacramento
	Southeast (Huntington Park)		
	* "Valley Division" (Van Nuys) of L.A.		
	"West Valley Ticket Office" (Canoga Park)		
	Whittier		

* Indicates district containing county seat court.

Note: The location is underlined for courts with multiple jurisdiction.

If the Demand Is Refused

If the officer refuses to specify the court at the county seat as the place to appear, you should do one of the following:

- Sign the ticket, but protest in the presence of any passengers so they can be witnesses.

- Sign the ticket, but add the notation, "County seat requested and refused," in small capital letters next to your name. That way, you'll have indisputable proof on the citation that you made the demand. This will help you get the case transferred later. (See Chapter 10.)

- If it's not at night or a weekend (so you won't have to languish in jail) and you're willing to risk being physically arrested, you might want to consider refusing to sign the ticket until the officer gets the court right. This may cause the officer to arrest you for refusing to sign. Or, the officer might detain you while he calls in to headquarters for instructions.

Arrests, Searches, and Seizures

This section deals with arrests, searches, and seizures. We will discuss when and how an officer can arrest you, search your car, or have it towed away and impounded if you don't have your driver's license with you.

The laws governing arrest, search, and seizure are constantly changing. In this section we provide a general overview of the subject in the traffic stop context. But if you need a definitive opinion on a specific set of facts, see a criminal defense attorney.

Arrests

If you are stopped for one of the more serious traffic offenses (like driving under the influence or reckless driving), you may be arrested and taken to jail. The officer has some discretion, but he is required to arrest you in the following situations:

- He has "probable cause" to believe you committed a felony (see Chapter 3);

- You are charged with driving under the influence of alcohol or drugs (see Chapter 8);

- You don't have a driver's license or any other "satisfactory identification";

- You refuse to sign the ticket (thereby refusing to promise to appear in court); or

- He discovers there's a warrant out for your arrest (VC § 40302).

The officer might also arrest you in any of the following instances:

- You're charged with reckless driving, engaging in a "speed contest" (drag racing) or "exhibition of speed";

- You tried to outrun the patrol car;

- You refused to honor the officer's request to test whether your lights or brakes work;

- You're involved in a "hit-and-run" accident involving property damage (when there's personal injury, it's a felony and arrest is mandatory); or

- You're caught driving while your license is suspended or revoked.

To state the obvious, it's never wise to resist an arrest, even an illegal one. Whether an arrest is legal is beyond the scope of this book. We suggest you check with a lawyer.

Searches

It used to be the case that, if you had anything in the car you'd rather have the officer not see, you could protect your rights by getting out of your car and walking away from it. But the law about searching cars has changed a lot in the past decades, and your privacy rights have been whittled away by federal and state court rulings.

Whether or not you are in your car, it is always perfectly legal for the officer to walk around the car and peer through the windows and shine a flashlight inside. The officer may seize anything illegal that is in "plain view" (such as marijuana in an open ash tray, an open alcoholic beverage container on the floor, the butt of a weapon protruding from under the seat). They don't need any excuse to do this.

The police may open the door of your car and search it, regardless of whether you are in it, in a wide range of circumstances. The basic rules are that an officer may search your car if he has:

- your permission
- a reasonable belief that there may be weapons in your car
- probable cause to believe that there is something illegal in your car
- a reason to place you or a passenger under arrest, or
- a reason to have your car towed.

Interestingly, most automobile searches are conducted not because an officer has probable cause to search, or sees something in plain view, but rather because the driver gives the officer permission. Estimates are that permission is given for about 90% of all traffic stop searches! Why would anyone agree to a search of their car? Because the driver is at her unprepared worst, and the officer is at his prepared and experienced best. He is just as adept at conning and cajoling you (*"Got something to hide?"*) into agreeing to a search as he is in getting admissions from you.

If you're absolutely sure that you have nothing to hide, consenting to a search may make the officer more accommodating toward you. (When was the last time you cleaned the inside of your car? Are you sure there are no partially empty beer cans from a picnic several months ago, or no marijuana debris from the last five years still sitting in the ash tray, on the floor, or wedged in a crack in the seat cushions?) Consenting to a search might make the officer a little less likely to cite such a "cooperative" person—but don't count on it. At this point, the officer's purpose is to get evidence to convict you of a crime. Don't let his friendly smile disarm you.

If the officer has legal grounds to search your car, he doesn't need your consent. If he asks to do so (and you don't want him to), simply tell him, *"I do not consent to a search."* He'll probably go ahead and search anyway, even without your consent. If that happens, there's a chance that anything the officer finds won't be admissible evidence in court. But if you consent to the search, you'll never be able to "exclude" any evidence that he finds from use against you at trial. (Getting illegally seized evidence excluded from trial is usually a complicated procedure—you should confer with a lawyer about this. If you wish to do some legal research, a good place to start is the case annotations in West's Annotated California Codes—Penal Code, under § 1538.5.)

If you're with a friend, try to arrange things so that he can hear the conversation between you and the officer. If you are outside the car, stand just outside the rolled-down window on your friend's side or ask your friend to join you outside. If the officer tries to separate the two of you, inform her that you are exercising your right to have a witness present. Your friend should just listen and say as little as possible.

Note: Keep in mind that you don't have to —and shouldn't—appear hostile or menacing in order to protect your rights. An obnoxious attitude toward a cop won't help you a bit, and may irritate him enough to cite you for additional violations he'd otherwise overlook. He may even find sufficient cause to arrest you if you give him a hard enough time. Just be polite but firm when you refuse permission to search.

Currently, the police can conduct a search without your consent if they have any reason to think you are a threat to their safety. In this situation, the search must be limited to a search for weapons in the passenger compartment.

They can also search your car if they have probable cause to believe you have something illegal inside it (the odor of pot would give them cause to suspect that you have more inside). In this situation they can search the *entire* car—including in the trunk, under the seat, in the glove box, and in the ash tray—and they can open any containers found in the vehicle, such as purses, paper bags, suitcases, or crumpled cigarette packages (*United States v. Ross* (1982) 456 U.S. 798). The police can seize anything illegal they find (like an open beer can or liquor bottle, or marijuana) or anything dangerous (like a weapon), and use it as evidence against you.

If the police have legal cause to physically arrest you, they can search you, and every inch of your car, as well as its contents. (See *New York v. Belton* (1981) 453 U.S. 454.) The U.S. Supreme Court ruled in 1999 that a passenger may also be searched during a traffic stop. See *Wyoming v. Houghton* 526 US 295 (1999).

Finally, if your vehicle is towed away, the police can thoroughly search it in order to take an "inventory" of its contents—all for your "protection," of course.

If none of these circumstances are present, the officer does not have legal grounds to search your car.

Seizure of Your Vehicle

A police officer who stops you can have your car towed away if you're unable to produce a valid driver's license. Later, if it turns out you were unlicensed, owned the vehicle you were driving, and had previously been convicted of misdemeanor driving without a license (VC § 12500(a)) or with a suspended license (VC §§ 14601–14601.5), you will lose the vehicle. It will be "forfeited" to the state, whether or not you're charged with any new offense.

Vehicle Code § 14607.6 is fairly complicated and involves numerous provisions, exemptions, and procedures. As written, the law is supposed to work like this:

If an officer stops you for any valid reason, and you cannot produce a valid driver's license, he or she should check "by other means, to verify that the driver is properly licensed." This usually means radioing in to check any identifying information (name, address, date of birth, driver's license number) you give, to see if the DMV computer system shows you as being licensed. Unfortunately, the law does not *require* the officer to do this, and an officer might wrongfully seize your vehicle. On the other hand, since the officer's department can be liable for the towing and storage charges if it turns out that the driver is licensed, officers will probably be under orders to make thorough checks before towing away the cars of people who can't produce a license on the spot.

If the officer cannot verify that you have a valid driver's license, he will have the car "impounded"—towed away and stored. However, if you're unlicensed only because your license expired within the previous 30 days and you simply failed to renew it, your car won't be towed; but you can still be cited for unlicensed driving (VC § 12500(a)), which is a misdemeanor.

Once your car has been impounded, it can be retrieved in one of the following ways, if applicable:

- The registered owner—who is a person other than the driver—claims it;

- The driver has no previous convictions of being unlicensed (VC § 12500(a)) or driving with a suspended license (VC §§ 14601–14601.5);

- The driver shows a valid license and pays towing, storage, and unspecified "administrative" charges. If the license was valid at the time of "impoundment," these charges can be avoided by requesting a "post-seizure hearing" from the police agency, as to whether the impoundment was legal. A request for this type of hearing must be made within three working days of the impoundment, or ten working days if a co-owner or lienholder had to be notified by mail. The hearing must occur within two working days of the date it is requested and can be conducted by the same agency—though not the same individual—responsible for towing the vehicle. The agency "is responsible for the costs incurred for towing and storage if it is determined that the driver at the time of impoundment had a valid driver's license";

- A licensed spouse of the unlicensed owner/driver: (1) shows she has a "community property" interest in the vehicle (written proof is required), (2) shows her own valid driver's license, (3) pays towing, storage, and administrative charges, (4) signs a "vehicle release agreement" allowing automatic forfeiture over the next seven years if an unlicensed driver drives it again, and (5) no such document has previously been signed with respect to that vehicle.

If the police agency will not release the vehicle, the registered owner or lienholder can file a "claim" with the district attorney, in order to try to avoid forfeiture of the vehicle. Instructions for filing such a claim should be included with a notice that is supposed to be mailed by certified mail to any lienholder, and also to any registered owner who was not personally given such a notice when the vehicle was first impounded. The claim must be filed with the district attorney within five working days of the impoundment or 15 working days if any registered owner or lienholder had to be notified by mail.

The basis for such claim may be that: (1) the driver of the vehicle was not the owner, (2) the driver was properly licensed at the time of impoundment, (3) the driver/owner has no previous VC § 12500(a) or VC §§ 14601–14601.5 convictions, or (4) a spouse of the owner had a community property interest in the vehicle.

Be careful, because the time for filing the claim may run concurrently with the time for retrieving the vehicle. If you've spent a few days before trying to get the vehicle back, and failed, you may only have a few days to file a claim. If no claim is filed within the time allowed, the vehicle is automatically forfeited to the state. If a claim is filed in a timely manner, the district attorney must, within ten working days of receiving the claim, file a "petition of forfeiture" with the local court. At some point, the claimant must pay a filing fee of up to $60, but the law is unclear when, and whether, the fee is paid to the district attorney or to the court.

Within several weeks or months after the district attorney files the "petition for forfeiture," the court will set a hearing at which the district attorney will have the burden of proving that the forfeiture was proper. No conviction of a second offense of driving without a license or driving with a suspended license is necessary. The district attorney must prove only that: (1) the driver of the vehicle drove on a public road or highway; (2) the driver also owned the vehicle; (3) the driver was not licensed at the time (normal expiration for less than 30 days doesn't count); and (4) the driver had a prior misdemeanor conviction of VC § 12500(a) or § 14601–14601.5.

If the driver/owner prevails at the court hearing, the vehicle is released. However, it is unclear who, at that point, is liable for the towing and storage costs. If, on the other hand, no claim is filed, or the person filing the claim does not prevail at the court hearing on the district attorney's petition for forfeiture, the vehicle is forfeited to the state. It is then sold at auction, with the proceeds used first to pay costs of towing, storage, administration, and sale, then to pay off the lienholders, and finally, to anyone having a community property interest. Half of the balance goes to the general fund of the city or county whose police agency took the vehicle and half goes to the state. Meanwhile, the lienholder who's only partly paid off will go after the registered owner for the balance.

EXAMPLE:

Larry Licenseless bought his Mercedes for $25,000. He borrowed $20,000 from Lienholder Bank, which by financing the purchase became the lienholder. Larry's luck ran out when he was stopped a second time for driving without a license. His Mercedes was sold at auction for $16,000, $1,000 of which was applied to towing and storage, and $15,000 of which was paid to Lienholder Bank. Still, this was less than the $20,000 Lienholder Bank was owed. So the bank sued Larry for the deficiency of $5,000.

In short, the law now severely penalizes unlicensed driving of your own vehicle, especially if you've previously been convicted of unlicensed driving. In addition, unlicensed driving on a second occasion is punishable as indicated in Chapter 7 on misdemeanors.

Preparing for Your Trial—Notes and Pictures

As soon as you and the officer leave the scene, you may want to drive back to it, find a safe and legal parking place, and pull out that little note pad you've been keeping in your glove compartment. Write down what happened, what the officer said, and what you said in response. The facts surrounding the ticket will probably never be clearer in your mind than in those first few minutes after you were cited. For this reason, your immediate handwritten recollections of your version of the incident can be used as important evidence later on. There is nothing, of course, to prevent you from putting more emphasis on the evidence that would tend to help you while paying less attention to evidence that might convict you. But don't write down anything that is untrue—if you do, you'll be committing perjury when you use the notes as evidence.

EXAMPLE:

Many speeding tickets can be beaten if the driver shows that his speed, even though slightly over the speed limit, was nevertheless safe. If the speed limit was 30 and you know you were doing a pretty safe 35 on a clear, dry day while just keeping up with the flow of traffic, you will want to write down all the evidence indicating that such a speed was safe, without admitting you were doing 35. (See Chapter 4 for more information on this defense.)

Try to remember exactly what you did when the officer observed you. If you have a camera (including a cellular-phone camera), you may want to take pictures from several different angles. You can later pick out the one or two most favorable to your case. Judges are often very impressed by people who come to their courts properly prepared, with original notes and pictures, to credibly testify against an unprepared officer who has numerous other tickets to think about.

Accident Citations

An officer called to the scene of an accident will sometimes issue a citation to a person who the officer believes contributed to the accident by disobeying the law. For example, the driver whose car rammed into the other vehicle may be cited for a speed violation or failure to yield the right of way by an officer who never saw the violation take place. If you were involved in an accident and receive such a citation, you should never plead guilty or pay the fine to the clerk. Your doing so could be used against you in a lawsuit by other people involved in the accident. Also, since the officer didn't personally observe the violation, he can't testify against you (unless you admit things to him), and thus beating the ticket will be a lot easier. (See Chapter 2.) ●

Where Do We Go From Here?

Much of this book was written on the assumption that you will get a fair hearing in traffic court. To a person wrongly accused of a traffic violation she knows she didn't commit, a fair hearing is obviously very important. Unfortunately, rather than a fair process, many folks accused of traffic violations experience a sham and corrupt system that mocks justice.

Most judges presume that a person who has received a ticket is guilty. They will too often believe the word of a police officer over an individual accused of a violation and will turn off their minds when it's the defendant's turn to tell her side of the story.

Traffic court is designed primarily to find people guilty as efficiently as possible. But so what? With all the problems in the world, you may ask whether fairness in traffic court merits much attention. Just how important is a fair shake in traffic court? I believe it's very important. Traffic court is the place where the greatest number of Americans come into contact with the American justice system. Even serving on a jury is a distant second in terms of bringing ordinary folks to experience firsthand, and participate in, the court system.

What people see when they're called to court affects how they see the entire system. If they see an evenhanded system presided over by a neutral judge who seriously considers testimony and arguments, they are more likely to feel that our justice system is a good one—just as we were all told in our high school civics classes. Even where the judge (or commissioner, or referee) wrongly finds a person guilty, the trial may still have been fair, with the judge using the full force of his impartiality, fairness, and intelligence. Obviously no system of justice based on the perceptions of humans—on the road or in the courtroom—can ever be perfect. But if the basic system is perceived to be fair, everyone wins. In the foreword to *The Law on Speeding and Radar* by A. S. Manraj and P.D. Haines (Butterworths, 1985), R. Roy McMurtry, the former attorney general of the Canadian province of Ontario, states: "Most persons who come into contact with the justice system do so in response to the alleged infraction of the laws governing the use of motor vehicles. The fairness and justice they find in the courts dealing with these matters will color their perception of the entire justice system. It is accordingly very important that the courts that administer these laws demonstrate a rigorous respect for, and a deep commitment to, the even-handed administration of justice."

Of course, the reality is otherwise. All too often, what we see when we fight our tickets is an impersonal assembly-line court system presided over by a bored judge who assumes we're guilty and that police officers never lie or make mistakes. Not all traffic court judges are this way, but too many are. Fair and impartial judges seem to be vastly outnumbered by those who regard traffic infraction trials as an annoying obstacle to the raising of revenue. The result is often that people emerge from traffic court disillusioned with the whole system of justice.

Am I exaggerating the defects of traffic court? Ask anyone who's contested a ticket for a moving violation. One reader says this:

> "The officer's testimony is apparently accepted as the one/only/total truth and the defendant is listened to grudgingly, as only a show of compliance with the forms of the law. I watched several cases before mine. The verdict was invariably guilty, even when the defendant had witnesses and documentation, which the judge did not look at. In my case, the judge seemed to have prejudged me. He seemed to barely listen to me, preferring to listen to a conversation between the officer and the prosecuting attorney, and he seemed to be communicating with them by means of signals. The judge refused to accept or even look at documents I wished to present as evidence. I presented various motions for dismissal, but the judge summarily dismissed them, sometimes cutting me off before I had finished the first sentence."

Another reader, before deciding whether to fight her ticket, took the time to watch a few traffic-court trials conducted by the judge before whom she would have to appear if she chose that option. She also took the time to note her observations, as follows:

> "I attended traffic court to observe the judge's pattern in judging traffic cases. The room was packed with angry and demoralized people. We were sternly warned that Her Honor finds people guilty in 99% of the cases. I watched several people plead their case, and they were all found guilty. Even though some had pretty good cases, their fines were all dramatically increased. In light of my visit to the court, I decided to just pay the fine, as it was clear I stood no chance of winning or having the fine reduced below the original amount."

Many folks report similar experiences of feeling that the judge only grudgingly and half-heartedly gave the appearance of letting them say what they wanted before finding them guilty. Others have noted the smug and nonchalant attitudes of police officers in court, who seem to know they won't lose. One Los Angeles County judge admitted that he always believes the word of a police officer over that of someone defending himself in traffic court. This judge's "defense" was that only he had the courage to say openly what in fact almost all judges believe and practice in their own courtrooms every day.

Why is traffic court so poorly run? Surely being appointed a judge or commissioner doesn't instantly convert a lawyer into a rubber-stamp for police and prosecutors. But as a judge settles into office, he begins to realize just how dependent he is on police officers' groups for both financial and public support come reelection time. Police officers who appear before traffic-court judges all the time are generally part of an efficient political organization—you and the countless other ordinary folks brought into traffic court are not. A judge who frequently rules against police officers is likely to wake up next election to find police-organization support and money going to his opponent, probably an ambitious deputy prosecutor ready to accuse the judge of being "soft on crime." And although appointed traffic "commissioners" don't have to stand for election, many, if not most of them, hope some day to get promoted to the more prestigious and higher-paying office of judge, which is extremely difficult without police support.

Another part of the problem is the role that tickets play in generating revenue for all sorts of purposes unrelated to promoting traffic safety. Over the years, this factor has assumed a greater importance than the quite legitimate concept of ticketing—and hopefully deterring—people who drive dangerously. If you figure that, on the average, a $65 fine is collected for each of the six million traffic citations handed out in California each year, the total fines would generate approximately $400 million. This is a very big business indeed. This amounts to an average of approximately $20 for every licensed driver during the year, or $15 for every car on the road.

The money collected from moving-violation ticket fines initially goes to the county treasury. After the county takes its share, some of the remaining revenue is returned to the various cities that produced it. Cities sometimes receive an amount as high as 75% of the fines collected. The county's share goes into a "road fund," and the city's share goes to a "Traffic Safety Fund" to be used to purchase "equipment and supplies for traffic law enforcement"—more radar equipment, to catch more "speeders," to get more money. The fund cannot be used directly to pay police officers' salaries, but the effect is the same. If no money came in from traffic fines, the cities would have to look elsewhere for money to maintain and buy "traffic safety" equipment, and might be a little short of funds to pay police salaries.

In more recent years, the practice of adding onto each fine an ever-increasing "penalty assessment" (a sort of tax added to generate revenue for a specific stated purpose) has at least shown up the traffic-enforcement system for what it primarily is—a source of government revenue. As of this writing, the penalty assessments added to fines have sky-rocketed up to over 260% of the fine. Thus a "$100" fine actually is $360. Money generated from these penalty assessments goes to:

- a "peace officer's training fund"
- a "correction training fund"
- in some counties, a fund for "Institutionalization Prevention Services" (crazy, isn't it?)
- a jail construction fund in each county, and
- dearest to the hearts of judges, a courthouse construction fund in each county.

Funds for training police and constructing jails and courthouses used to be derived in large part from property taxes. But back in 1978, with the passage of Proposition 13, the voters' message of less government went unheeded. Over the next several years, our special-interest-ridden legislatures and politicians—Republicans and Democrats alike—secretly made up the difference by drastically jacking up the penalty assessments added onto traffic fines. Between 1982 and 2007, conservatives and liberals didn't raise "taxes," they increased penalty assessments from $2.50 for every $10 of fine to $26 for every $10 of fine—the equivalent of secretly doubling taxes every two years!

A judge who consistently applies the "reasonable-doubt" rule, and who too frequently fails to find people guilty and impose fines, is considered by the system to be short-changing the county of revenue needed to replace overcrowded and deteriorating courthouses and jails in the county. Is it any wonder that judges find traffic-court defendants guilty 90% of the time in cases where the officer does appear?

And then there are police-officer ticket quotas to make sure that enough tickets are issued to keep the flow of money coming in. If you've ever angrily asked an officer writing you a ticket something like, *"Got to make this month's quota, eh?"* you most likely got an emotionless, canned response like, *"No, quotas were abolished by the legislature in 1977."* Don't be fooled. Although public pressure has forced police departments to abandon formal numerical quotas, every police department in the state still uses an unwritten quota system. One way this works is the system of police officers' "performance evaluations." If a cop turns up short in the ticket race, her chances for promotion decline. In some cases, officers are suspended or even fired for "inefficiency" when they fail to produce enough tickets.

As a result of performance evaluations, each officer tries hard to write at least slightly more than the average number of department tickets per month. With everyone trying to beat the average, it doesn't take a mathematical genius to see that the average is likely to increase over time, and thus, average-beating becomes an important contributing factor to the rise in the number of tickets issued each year.

Ticket fighters are also faced with the systematic effort to remove from traffic court any constitutional protections that stand in the way of a more "efficient" production of revenue. Every important right mentioned in the Bill of Rights whose purpose is to protect the people from oppression by government adds a financial cost to the system. Jury trials cost money. So, starting in 1968, California politicians began a quiet campaign to gradually eliminate all procedural rights that interfered with the revenue-raising aspects of the traffic-enforcement system. The legislature did this by creating a new category of crime known as the "infraction." Before that, offenses were either felonies or misdemeanors. Anyone charged with either could, and often did, demand a trial by jury. The "infraction" was a new type

of category for which no jury trial was allowed, even if demanded by the accused. As a trade-off, the law provided that no one could be imprisoned for conviction of an infraction. In practice, only repeat offenders ever went to jail anyway when all traffic offenses were misdemeanors. Repeat offenders can still go to jail today, since VC § 40000.28 allows a person accused of a fourth infraction in a year to have a traffic offense charged as a misdemeanor. Thus, nothing has really changed, and the system's supposed trade-off of taking away the right to a jury trial, in exchange for a guarantee of not going to jail, is a pretense.

At first, only parking violations were classified as infractions. Then, when no one objected (or even noticed), running a stoplight was also defined as an infraction. No one objected to that either. Finally, the right to a jury trial was taken away from a whole list of common traffic offenses. Indeed, all but a few of the most serious traffic offenses (such as drunk or reckless driving and drag racing) were classified as infractions. Again, few people complained; apparently, most never realized that they had lost a valuable right. The right to a trial by an impartial jury is more important than you might think. Judges, prosecutors, and even many defense attorneys often assume that the accused person is really guilty. Their years of experience dealing with criminals often sours them into thinking that nearly everyone must be guilty, or else why would they have been arrested? Although some people selected as jurors also have this attitude, it tends to be more widespread among people in the legal profession. Furthermore, the possibility that an accused defendant may opt for a jury trial in the face of a known "hanging judge" may itself serve as a check on such judges.

The right of an indigent person to the free services of a court-appointed attorney to defend against an infraction was also taken away. Then, the legislature passed a law that allowed lower-paid nonjudges to hear traffic cases. Appeals courts quickly rubber-stamped it.

Even rights that don't cost the system very much have been ruled inapplicable to traffic matters. Appeals courts have ruled that the double-jeopardy clause of the Constitution, which protects individuals from being convicted twice for the same offense, and a state law prohibiting multiple prosecutions for the same act, don't apply to infractions (*In re Dennis B.* (1976) 18 Cal.3d 687; *People v. Battle* (1975) 50 Cal.App.3d Supp. 1). Neither does the right against self-incrimination. No police officer who stops you is required to tell you that you have a right to refuse to answer his questions, and that he can use any of your admissions against you. Hardened criminals get the benefit of "Miranda" warnings, but you, the law-abiding citizen, are undeserving of such niceties (*Berkemer v. McCarty* (1984) 468 U.S. 420, 104 S.Ct. 3138). This is true even though California law defines a traffic stop as an "arrest."

Finally, the California Supreme Court, picking up where the politicians left off, decreed that the state doesn't even have to pay prosecuting attorneys to appear in traffic cases (VC § 40500–40502, 40504, *People v. Superior Court* (1972) 7 Cal.3d 186, 200). Since facing a prosecutor in traffic court is certainly no fun, even fewer people objected, failing to realize that the mere presence of a prosecutor reminds the judge that he or she is the neutral party whose job is to evenhandedly apply justice. Without prosecutors, traffic judges—in what is often a misguided desire to be helpful to the police—frequently help officers who neglect to testify to all the necessary elements of the offense. For example, the judge will ask (remind) the officer to testify that he was

driving a marked patrol car and wearing his uniform, or that an engineering and traffic survey allowing the use of radar speed enforcement on a particular road has been conducted. In this way, the judge in a very real sense becomes prosecutor as well. With prosecuting attorneys gone from traffic court, many judges have indeed assumed the prosecutorial roles themselves—a concept completely foreign to the Anglo-American legal tradition.

The slow erosion of rights by the legislature continues. In 1993, it became impossible to contest parking tickets in court, except for appeals. Instead, you have the "right" to a hearing at which a city or county bureaucrat determines whether or not you should pay. All the information in the parking ticket is assumed to be true, without the officer who issued it ever having to appear and testify. In 2000, politicians passed a law allowing reducing the number of appeals court judges necessary to review an appeal from three to one.

Perhaps we should not get so excited about this, because only parking tickets are affected. However, that is how the politicians and bureaucrats work in this state. They gradually deprive us of our freedoms by starting slowly and innocuously, and by hoping we won't notice. The legislature may well expand this grossly unfair procedure to tickets for moving violations if few people protest.

Indeed, politicians and special interests are now attempting to allow tickets for moving violations to be handled this way, too. The legislature may indeed attempt to take away all of our rights with regard to moving violation tickets. The right to confront one's accuser and the right to a fair hearing before a neutral decision maker may, in the future, be reserved only for hardened criminals.

Most of us have been led to believe that any excesses of the system can be corrected by an appeal if you lose. Unfortunately, this is almost always a false hope. Appeals courts will only reverse cases on technicalities, and never on the basis that the judge should have believed you and your witnesses rather than an untruthful police officer. Appeals court judges will always rubber-stamp traffic-court judges' "findings of fact," on the basis that the trial judge, who observed the defendant, police officer, and other witnesses testify, was best able to tell who was telling the truth. (This will happen no matter how many believable witnesses supported your version of events, or how evasive and self-contradictory the officer was.) The rule that allows appeals courts to do this (called the "substantial evidence standard"), was originally adopted to prevent elitist English-trained judges from overturning common sense verdicts of juries. Today, though, where the right to trial by jury has been taken away, it makes little sense and simply shields dishonest judges from any meaningful scrutiny (*People v. Carlucci* (1979) 23 Cal. 3d 249 and *People v. Daggett* (1988) 206 Cal.App.3d Supp. 1).

What it boils down to is that appeals courts won't second-guess traffic court judges, who in turn don't want to think of themselves as second-guessing the police officer who writes you a ticket. Only you, the driver, get your driving conduct second-guessed—by the officer, the judge, and the appeals court.

The point is that, over the years, it's become too convenient for those in power to "economize" and "streamline" a system that generates a lot of money and deals with a lot of people. What started out as a legitimate offshoot from the criminal justice system, designed to correct the behavior of errant motorists and to deter dangerous drivers, has degenerated into an assembly line that grinds up your constitutional rights and spits out money into government coffers, at little overhead cost. Today, your rights consist mostly of hoping your case will be dismissed if the officer doesn't show up for trial or the prosecution or judge commits a serious legal error. If the officer doesn't show up for trial, you have the right to present your case to a judge who more than likely wants you to hurry up and speak your piece so he can find you guilty, have the clerk collect your fine, call the next case, and finish up in court.

In the case of *People v. Daggett* (1988) 206 Cal.App.3d Supp. 1, two out of three judges predictably ruled that in traffic cases, no prosecutor need be present, and that the judge can assist in presenting the government's case. The third judge stated this leads to "the inescapable conclusion that the court is, or at least appears to be, both the prosecutor and the court, rather than being impartial." He continued, "The people of this country have fought hard against a police state. Their success should not be erased by elimination of an adversary trial. Actually, traffic court is one of our most important venues. To a large part of our population, this will be their only contact with the justice system. They are certainly going to wonder what happened to the impartial, blind Miss Justice and the doctrine of separation of powers."

How would a fair traffic violation scheme work? A good start would be to instruct the police to hand out citations only where there was a clear violation of the law that either resulted in rudeness to another driver (or bicyclist or pedestrian) or caused a dangerous situation. Officers now hiding behind bushes with radar guns could be instructed to look for drunk drivers instead.

A traffic-enforcement system can serve a valid purpose. We all know of people who drive carelessly or dangerously, who legitimately deserve to be deterred before they injure or kill someone. Unfortunately, our current system utterly fails to distinguish between this sort of individual and one who innocently violates a rule in a book without creating any danger to himself or others.

To achieve a better system in this regard, we must start by having money collected from fines go some place other than to the government entities—cities and counties—that must raise the money to pay the police and maintain the courts. The unholy alliance of politicians, judges, and police officers going after your fine money will never abate as long as everyone knows that more fines mean more police cars and radar units and more luxurious courthouses.

Another measure of fairness would be to allow jury trials for at least those violations that are reported to the Department of Motor Vehicles and can be used as a basis for suspending your license (but not for parking or equipment violations). How would this work? Why not the same way it does with traffic cases in some eastern and New England states? A person accused of a moving traffic violation would first have a nonjury trial. If he lost and was dissatisfied with the way he was treated, he could "appeal" for a new trial, in Superior Court, where he could request a jury.

But wouldn't this hopelessly tie up the courts? I don't think so. Jury trials are time-consuming and difficult; it is for this very reason that even before 1968, when everyone accused of a traffic violation was allowed the option of a jury trial at the outset, few people actually opted for one. Even so, the possibility that a traffic defendant treated unfairly by a traffic judge may appeal for a new trial—by jury—may keep judges a little more honest. In fact, judges could be evaluated based on the number of appeals they generated; a consistently arbitrary judge whose unfair decisions provoke an unusually high

number of such appeals for trials by jury could be given a different assignment—or perhaps tossed out of office.

Finally, how about an appeals court system that honestly looks at whether the defendant was really guilty, and not one that blindly rubber-stamps convictions based on the weakest of evidence? How about a system that does more than wink at officers who fabricate evidence, lie, and conspire to protect their fellow officers—as noted on tape by former LAPD officer Mark Fuhrman? Let's have a system of appeals courts that thrives not just on technicalities. Appeals court judges should have the guts to decide cases on the real issues.

In other words, let's resolve to bring the fairness and justice envisioned in it back into the traffic court process. Let's work for the recall and election defeat of judges who think the Constitution is just for vicious criminals, but not for law-abiding folks who wind up in traffic court.

Sadly, there's no sign that even one of our legislators is on the right track. Many conservative legislators, while congratulating each other for voting to "get government off our backs," hypocritically voted for higher taxes (penalty assessments), pushed for increased punishments that bear no relation to the offense, agreed to "trial by bureaucrats" in parking cases, and voted for more $80,000-a-year prison guards. Liberals fare no better, trying to outdo their more authoritarian colleagues lest they appear "soft on crime." Indeed, as recently as 1996, liberal and conservative legislators teamed up to let police tow our cars away if we've forgotten our driver's license.

As time passes, the three branches of state government—legislative, executive, and judiciary—continue to erode our freedoms away, with no end in sight, at least where the enforcement of traffic laws and procedures are concerned. Our government chips away at our freedoms on many other fronts as well. If we don't stop it at some point, we'll wake up one day to a true totalitarian police state. Is this an exaggeration? The late Justice William Brennan of the U.S. Supreme Court, concerned over the approval, by the other members of the Court, of low-flying helicopter surveillance, said this of his colleagues' headlong rush toward this very danger:

"The Court today approved warrantless helicopter surveillance from an altitude of 400 feet… The Fourth Amendment demands that we temper our efforts to apprehend criminals with a concern for the impact on our fundamental liberties of the methods we use. I hope it will be a matter of concern to my colleagues that the police surveillance methods they would sanction were among those described 40 years ago in George Orwell's dread vision of life in the 1980s:

"The black-mustachio'd face gazed down from every commanding corner. There was one on the house front immediately opposite. BIG BROTHER IS WATCHING YOU, the caption said… In the far distance a helicopter skimmed down between the roofs, hovered for an instant like a bluebottle, and darted away again with a curving flight. It was the Police Patrol, snooping into people's windows." *Nineteen Eighty-Four* (1949)."

Who can read this passage without a shudder, and without the instinctive reaction that it depicts life in some country other than ours? I respectfully dissent.

Have I rambled for a long time? I guess I have. But now it's your turn. If you have any ideas and comments on how you would like to see traffic laws and court procedures changed, let me know. You can write down your thoughts and mail them to me at Nolo, 950 Parker Street, Berkeley, CA 94710. Or you can email me at DavidWayneBrown@aol.com.

Blank Forms

Informal Discovery Request

Proof of Service by Mail

Request for Trial by Written Declaration

Request for New Trial (Trial de Novo)

Demand for Court Reporter or Electronic Recording of Proceedings

Peremptory Challenge

Civil Subpoena

Civil Subpoena Duces Tecum

Notice of Appeal (Infraction)

Proposed Statement on Appeal (Infraction)

CAUTION

Tear out and photocopy these forms. Do not write on them. Court filing rules require the use of 8½ by 11 inch paper. Unfortunately, our book cannot be printed to precisely these measurements, but copy machines do use this size paper. When you come to the point where you want to fill out the forms, tear them out and copy them, making sure to make an extra copy to use as a "working" copy. If the form has a back side, either make a separate page for it or, if you choose to copy onto the back of the first page, be sure to copy the back "upside down," the way our form is printed.

Recycled paper requirement Rule 201(d) of the California Rules of Court requires that all original papers filed with the court, and all copies of papers, documents, and exhibits, whether filed with the court or served on the parties, be on recycled paper. The act of filing and serving constitutes a certification by you that you are complying with the Rule (in other words, it is presumed that you know and follow the law). To what extent this Rule is enforced by the clerks of many California courts is unknown.

Blank Forms

Informal Discovery Request

Proof of Service by Mail

Request for Trial by Written Declaration

Request for New Trial (Trial de Novo)

Demand for Court Reporter or Electronic Recording of Proceedings

Peremptory Challenge

Civil Subpoena

Civil Subpoena Duces Tecum

Notice of Appeal (Infraction)

Proposed Statement on Appeal (Infraction)

> ## ⚠ CAUTION
>
> **Tear out and photocopy these forms. Do not write on them.** Court filing rules require the use of 8½ by 11 inch paper. Unfortunately, our book cannot be printed to precisely these measurements, but copy machines do use this size paper. When you come to the point where you want to fill out the forms, tear them out and copy them, making sure to make an extra copy to use as a "working" copy. If the form has a back side, either make a separate page for it or, if you choose to copy onto the back of the first page, be sure to copy the back "upside down," the way our form is printed.
>
> **Recycled paper requirement Rule 201(d)** of the California Rules of Court requires that all original papers filed with the court, and all copies of papers, documents, and exhibits, whether filed with the court or served on the parties, be on recycled paper. The act of filing and serving constitutes a certification by you that you are complying with the Rule (in other words, it is presumed that you know and follow the law). To what extent this Rule is enforced by the clerks of many California courts is unknown.

INFORMAL DISCOVERY REQUEST

Name: Address: Defendant in Pro Per	
SUPERIOR COURT OF CALIFORNIA COUNTY OF	
THE PEOPLE OF THE STATE OF CALIFORNIA, Plaintiff vs.	CASE NUMBER

Citing Agency:	Citation No.:	Date Issued:

INFORMAL DISCOVERY REQUEST (Traffic Infraction) PC 1054– 1054.1, PC 19.7

TO THE DISTRICT ATTORNEY FOR THE ABOVE-REFERENCED COUNTY, AND TO THE ABOVE-REFERENCED POLICE AGENCY:

1. Pursuant to Penal Code §§ 1054 and 1054.5(b), the above-named defendant hereby requests that you provide disclosure of the following:

    a. Defendant's statements and any and all relevant written or recorded statements of witnesses, including any statements, diagrams, or drawings, made by the citing police officer on the reverse of the above-referenced Notice to Appear or on any piece of paper or other medium of information storage. YOU ARE SPECIFICALLY REQUESTED TO PROVIDE THE ABOVE-REFERENCED DEFENDANT OR ATTORNEY OF RECORD WITH A PHOTOSTATIC COPY OF THE REVERSE SIDE OF THE CITING OFFICER'S COPY OF THE ABOVE-REFERENCED NOTICE TO APPEAR, IF THE CITING OFFICER HAS MADE ANY NOTATIONS ON IT.

    b. The names and addresses of all prosecution witnesses who will testify at trial.

    c. ( ) [If checked] Any engineering and traffic survey within the meaning of VC § 627(a), conducted within the last five years, which justifies the prima facie speed limit relevant to the alleged violation charged in the above-referenced Notice to Appear. IF THIS ITEM IS CHECKED AT LEFT, YOU ARE SPECIFICALLY REQUESTED TO PROVIDE A COPY OF THE ENGINEERING AND TRAFFIC SURVEY, MEETING THE DESCRIPTION ABOVE, WHERE SUCH SURVEY WILL BE PRODUCED AT TRIAL.

    d. ( ) [If checked] Any observation logs kept or maintained by CHP officer in aircraft speed cases. IF THIS ITEM IS CHECKED AT LEFT, YOU ARE SPECIFICALLY REQUESTED TO PROVIDE A COPY OF AIRCRAFT OBSERVATION LOGS KEPT OR MADE BY OFFICER WHO ALLEGEDLY OBSERVED DEFENDANT'S VEHICLE EXCEED SPEED LIMIT.

2. The following is disclosed to you pursuant to Penal Code § 1054.3:

    a. NAMES AND ADDRESSES OF WITNESSES (OTHER THAN DEFENDANT) WHO WILL TESTIFY AT TRIAL:

    ( ) None.

    ( ) The Following:

    b. RELEVANT UNPRIVILEGED WRITTEN OR RECORDED STATEMENTS OF WITNESSES:

    ( ) None.

    ( ) See Attached

Dated _____   _____

Defendant in Pro Per

PROOF OF SERVICE BY MAIL

PARTY WITHOUT ATTORNEY (My Name and Address) MY TELEPHONE NO.:	
NAME OF COURT: STREET ADDRESS: MAILING ADDRESS: CITY AND ZIP CODE: BRANCH NAME:	
PLAINTIFF/JUDGMENT CREDITOR: DEFENDANT/JUDGMENT DEBTOR:	
PROOF OF SERVICE BY MAIL (CCP Sections 1013a, 2015.5)	CASE NUMBER

I declare that:

1. At the time of service I was at least 18 years of age and not a party to this legal action.

2. I am a resident of or employed in the county where the mailing occurred.

3. My business or residence address is:

4. I served copies of the following paper(s) in the manner shown:

   a. Papers served [list exact titles of paper(s)]:

   b. Manner of service: by placing true copies in a sealed envelope addressed to each person whose name and address is given below and:

      ☐ depositing the envelope in the United States Mail with the postage fully prepaid; or

      ☐ (If deposited at a business:) placing for collection and mailing following ordinary business practices. I am readily familiar with the business practice for collection and processing of correspondence for mailing with the United States Post Office. The correspondence will be deposited with the United States Post Office on the same date as the date of deposit (below) in the ordinary course of business.

      (1) Date of Deposit: _____

      (2) Place of Deposit (city & state; business address if deposited at a business):

      _____

5. I declare under penalty of perjury under the laws of the State of California that the foregoing is true and correct.

Executed on _____ at _____, California.

Print Name _____   _____
                                                 [Signature of Person Who Served Papers]

Name and Address of Each Person to Whom Documents Were Mailed:

☐ Additional names and addresses on reverse

NAME OF COURT: SUPERIOR COURT OF CALIFORNIA, COUNTY OF STREET ADDRESS: MAILING ADDRESS: CITY AND ZIP CODE: BRANCH NAME:	**FOR COURT USE ONLY**

PEOPLE OF THE STATE OF CALIFORNIA

vs.

DEFENDANT:

REQUEST FOR TRIAL BY WRITTEN DECLARATION (Vehicle Code, § 40902)

CITATION NUMBER:

CASE NUMBER:

TO BE FILLED OUT BY COURT CLERK

A. **DUE DATE** (for receipt of this form and any unpaid bail) (specify):

B. Bail amount required: $

C. Bail amount already deposited by defendant: $

D. Date mailed or delivered by clerk:

E. Mail or deliver completed form, evidence, and mail to the Clerk of the (specify):   Court at (mailing address):

REQUEST FOR TRIAL

1. I have reviewed the Instructions to Defendant (Trial by Written Declaration) (form TR-200).

2. I request to have a trial by written declaration

3. The facts contained in the Declaration of Facts on the reverse are personally known to me and are true and correct.

4. I know that I have the right not to be compelled to be a witness against myself. I understand and agree that by making any statement, I am giving up and waiving that right and privilege.

5. EVIDENCE   The following evidence supports my case and includes everything I want the court to consider in deciding my case:
   a. ☐ photographs (specify total number):   e. ☐ diagram
   b. ☐ medical record   f. ☐ car repair receipt
   c. ☐ registration documents   g. ☐ insurance documents
   d. ☐ inspection certificate   h. ☐ other (specify):

(Declaration continued on reverse)

Form Adopted by the Judicial Council of California TR-205 [New January 1, 1999] **Mandatory Form**	**REQUEST FOR TRIAL BY WRITTEN DECLARATION** (Trial by Written Declaration—Traffic)	Vehicle Code, § 40902

PEOPLE v. DEFENDANT (Name):

CASE NUMBER:

6. **DECLARATION OF FACTS** (Type or print only. State what happened and explain all the items of evidence you checked in item 5 on the reverse and tell how they support your case. You may add additional pages.)

(Name):

(Current mailing address):

STATEMENT OF FACTS (begin here):

7. **Number of pages attached:** _____

I declare under penalty of perjury under the laws of the State of California that the foregoing is true and correct.

Date:

....
(TYPE OR PRINT NAME)

_____
(SIGNATURE)

	FOR COURT USE ONLY
NAME OF COURT: SUPERIOR COURT OF CALIFORNIA, COUNTY OF STREET ADDRESS: MAILING ADDRESS: CITY AND ZIP CODE: BRANCH NAME:	

PEOPLE OF THE STATE OF CALIFORNIA

vs.

DEFENDANT:

REQUEST FOR NEW TRIAL (TRIAL DE NOVO)
(Trial by Written Declaration—Vehicle Code, § 40902)

CITATION NUMBER:
CASE NUMBER:

1. The clerk mailed the court's *Decision and Notice of Decision* (form TR-215) in my trial by written declaration to me on *(date)*:

2. I am submitting this request to the court within 20 days of the date in item 1. *(The court must receive this request within 20 days of the date in item 1.)*

3. I am dissatisfied with the court's decision. I request a new trial (trial de novo) for the following violations *(specify)*:

Date:

. . . . ▶ _____
(TYPE OR PRINT NAME)   (SIGNATURE)

**IF YOU WISH TO REQUEST A NEW TRIAL, YOU MUST SUBMIT A *REQUEST FOR NEW TRIAL (TRIAL DE NOVO)*
WITHIN 20 DAYS OF THE DATE STATED IN THE CLERK'S CERTIFICATE OF MAILING (see item 1 above).**

Form Adopted by the
Judicial Council of California
TR-220 [New January 1, 1999]
Mandatory Form

REQUEST FOR NEW TRIAL (TRIAL DE NOVO)
(Trial by Written Declaration—Traffic)

Vehicle Code, § 40902

Name:
Address:

SUPERIOR COURT OF CALIFORNIA, COUNTY OF _____

_____ BRANCH

THE PEOPLE OF THE)
STATE OF CALIFORNIA) Case No. _____
)
Plaintiff,) **DEMAND FOR COURT REPORTER**
vs.) **OR ELECTRONIC RECORDING**
) **OF PROCEEDINGS**
_____ ,)
)
Defendant.)
_____)

The above-named defendant in the above-entitled action hereby requests that the Court provide for attendance of

trial proceeding herein by a stenographic court reporter, or that the proceedings be electronically recorded.

DATED: _____   _____
                                    Defendant in Pro Per

POINTS AND AUTHORITIES

According to case law set forth in *In re Armstrong* (1981) 126 Cal.App.3d 568, all misdemeanor proceedings

must, on the defendant's request, be recorded electronically or by a stenographic court reporter. This requirement

is incorporated into infraction proceedings by Penal Code Section 19.7, which states, "Except as otherwise provided

by law, all provisions of law relating to misdemeanors shall apply to infractions ..." According to *People v. Matthews*

(1983) 139 Cal.App.3d 537, this statute incorporates into infraction procedure all constitutional procedural protections

applicable to misdemeanor procedure, even where not required by the Constitution for infraction procedure per se.

Thus, infraction trials must be recorded or reported at the defendant's request.

DATED: _____   _____
                                    Defendant in Pro Per

Name:
Address:

SUPERIOR COURT OF CALIFORNIA, COUNTY OF _____

_____ BRANCH

THE PEOPLE OF THE
STATE OF CALIFORNIA

                    Plaintiff,

vs.

_____ ,

                    Defendant.

_____

)
)
)
)
)
)
)
)
)
)
)

Case No. _____

PEREMPTORY CHALLENGE
[CCP § 170.6]

I, the above-named defendant, declare:

I believe the Hon. _____, the judge or commissioner

before whom the above-entitled matter is assigned to or pending before, is prejudiced against my interest, so that I

cannot have a fair trial before such judge or commissioner.

WHEREFORE Defendant requests, ex parte, per CCP Section 170.6, that the said judge or commissioner be

disqualified from hearing the above-entitled matter.

I declare under penalty of perjury under the laws of the State of California that the foregoing is true and correct.

DATED: _____   _____
                                        Defendant in Pro Per

ATTORNEY OR PARTY WITHOUT ATTORNEY *(Name, State Bar number, and address)*:	*FOR COURT USE ONLY*

TELEPHONE NO.:   FAX NO.:

ATTORNEY FOR *(Name)*:

NAME OF COURT:
STREET ADDRESS:
MAILING ADDRESS:
CITY AND ZIP CODE:
BRANCH NAME:

PLAINTIFF/ PETITIONER:

DEFENDANT/ RESPONDENT:

CIVIL SUBPOENA For Personal Appearance at Trial or Hearing	CASE NUMBER:

THE PEOPLE OF THE STATE OF CALIFORNIA, TO *(name, address, and telephone number of witness, if known)*:

1. **YOU ARE ORDERED TO APPEAR AS A WITNESS** in this action at the date, time, and place shown in the box below **UNLESS** you make an agreement with the person named in item 2:

    a. Date: Time: ☐ Dept.:   ☐ Div.:   ☐ Room:

    b. Address:

2. **IF YOU HAVE ANY QUESTIONS ABOUT THE TIME OR DATE FOR YOU TO APPEAR, OR IF YOU WANT TO BE CERTAIN THAT YOUR PRESENCE IS REQUIRED, CONTACT THE FOLLOWING PERSON BEFORE THE DATE ON WHICH YOU ARE TO APPEAR:**

    a. Name of subpoenaing party or attorney: b. Telephone number:

3. **Witness Fees:** You are entitled to witness fees and mileage actually traveled both ways, as provided by law, if you request them at the time of service. You may request them before your scheduled appearance from the person named in item 2.

DISOBEDIENCE OF THIS SUBPOENA MAY BE PUNISHED AS CONTEMPT BY THIS COURT. YOU WILL ALSO BE LIABLE FOR THE SUM OF FIVE HUNDRED DOLLARS AND ALL DAMAGES RESULTING FROM YOUR FAILURE TO OBEY.

Date issued:

▶

_____   _____
(TYPE OR PRINT NAME)   (SIGNATURE OF PERSON ISSUING SUBPOENA)

_____
(TITLE)

Requests for Accommodations

Assistive listening systems, computer-assisted real-time captioning, or sign language interpreter services are available if you ask at least 5 days before the date on which you are to appear. Contact the clerk's office or go to *www.courtinfo.ca.gov/forms* for *Request for Accommodations by Persons With Disabilities and Order* (form MC-410). (Civil Code, § 54.8.)

(Proof of service on reverse)

Form Adopted for Mandatory Use
Judicial Council of California
SUBP-001 [Rev. January 1, 2007]

**CIVIL SUBPOENA FOR PERSONAL
APPEARANCE AT TRIAL OR HEARING**

Code of Civil Procedure, §§ 1985,1986,1987
www.courtinfo.ca.gov

PLAINTIFF/PETITIONER:	CASE NUMBER:
DEFENDANT/RESPONDENT:	

PROOF OF SERVICE OF CIVIL SUBPOENA
FOR PERSONAL APPEARANCE AT TRIAL OR HEARING

1. I served this *Civil Subpoena for Personal Appearance at Trial or Hearing* by personally delivering a copy to the person served as follows:

   a. Person served *(name)*:

   b. Address where served:

   c. Date of delivery:

   d. Time of delivery:

   e. Witness fees *(check one)*:
   - (1) ☐ were offered or demanded and paid. Amount: ...... $ _____
   - (2) ☐ were not demanded or paid.

   f. Fee for service: .... $ _____

2. I received this subpoena for service on *(date)*:

3. Person serving:
   - a. ☐ Not a registered California process server.
   - b. ☐ California sheriff or marshal.
   - c. ☐ Registered California process server.
   - d. ☐ Employee or independent contractor of a registered California process server.
   - e. ☐ Exempt from registration under Business and Professions Code section 22350(b).
   - f. ☐ Registered professional photocopier.
   - g. ☐ Exempt from registration under Business and Professions Code section 22451.
   - h. Name, address, telephone number, and, if applicable, county of registration and number:

I declare under penalty of perjury under the laws of the State of California that the foregoing is true and correct.

Date:

▶ _____
(SIGNATURE)

(For California sheriff or marshal use only)
I certify that the foregoing is true and correct.

Date:

▶ _____
(SIGNATURE)

PROOF OF SERVICE OF CIVIL SUBPOENA FOR PERSONAL APPEARANCE AT TRIAL OR HEARING

ATTORNEY OR PARTY WITHOUT ATTORNEY *(Name, state bar number, and address):*	*FOR COURT USE ONLY*
TELEPHONE NO.:　　　　　　　FAX NO.:	
ATTORNEY FOR *(Name):*	
NAME OF COURT:	
STREET ADDRESS:	
MAILING ADDRESS:	
CITY AND ZIP CODE:	
BRANCH NAME:	
PLAINTIFF/ PETITIONER:	
DEFENDANT/ RESPONDENT:	

CIVIL SUBPOENA (DUCES TECUM) for Personal Appearance and Production of Documents and Things at Trial or Hearing AND DECLARATION	CASE NUMBER:

THE PEOPLE OF THE STATE OF CALIFORNIA, TO *(name, address, and telephone number of witness, if known):*

1. **YOU ARE ORDERED TO APPEAR AS A WITNESS** in this action at the date, time, and place shown in the box below **UNLESS** your appearance is excused as indicated in box 3b below or you make an agreement with the person named in **item 4 below.**

a. Date:　　　　　　　Time:　　　　　☐ Dept.:　　☐ Div.:　　☐ Room:
b. Address:

2. **IF YOU HAVE BEEN SERVED WITH THIS SUBPOENA AS A CUSTODIAN OF CONSUMER OR EMPLOYEE RECORDS UNDER CODE OF CIVIL PROCEDURE SECTION 1985.3 OR 1985.6 AND A MOTION TO QUASH OR AN OBJECTION HAS BEEN SERVED ON YOU, A COURT ORDER OR AGREEMENT OF THE PARTIES, WITNESSES, *AND* CONSUMER OR EMPLOYEE AFFECTED MUST BE OBTAINED BEFORE YOU ARE REQUIRED TO PRODUCE CONSUMER OR EMPLOYEE RECORDS.**

3. YOU ARE *(item a or b must be checked):*

   a. ☐ Ordered to appear in person and to produce the records described in the declaration on page two or the attached declaration or affidavit. The personal attendance of the custodian or other qualified witness and the production of the original records are required by this subpoena. The procedure authorized by Evidence Code sections 1560(b), 1561, and 1562 will not be deemed sufficient compliance with this subpoena.

   b. ☐ Not required to appear in person if you produce (i) the records described in the declaration on page two or the attached declaration or affidavit and (ii) a completed declaration of custodian of records in compliance with Evidence Code sections 1560, 1561, 1562, and 1271. (1) Place a copy of the records in an envelope (or other wrapper). Enclose the original declaration of the custodian with the records. Seal the envelope. (2) Attach a copy of this subpoena to the envelope or write on the envelope the case name and number; your name; and the date, time, and place from item 1 in the box above. (3) Place this first envelope in an outer envelope, sea] it, and mail it to the clerk of the court at the address in item 1. (4) Mail a copy of your declaration to the attorney or party listed at the top of this form.

4. **IF YOU HAVE ANY QUESTIONS ABOUT THE TIME OR DATE YOU ARE TO APPEAR, OR IF YOU WANT TO BE CERTAIN THAT YOUR PRESENCE IS REQUIRED, CONTACT THE FOLLOWING PERSON BEFORE THE DATE ON WHICH YOU ARE TO APPEAR:**

   a. Name of subpoenaing party or attorney:　　　　　　　b. Telephone number:

5. **Witness Fees:** You are entitled to witness fees and mileage actually traveled both ways, as provided by law, if you request them at the time of service. You may request them before your scheduled appearance from the person named in item 4.

DISOBEDIENCE OF THIS SUBPOENA MAY BE PUNISHED AS CONTEMPT BY THIS COURT. YOU WILL ALSO BE LIABLE FOR THE SUM OF FIVE HUNDRED DOLLARS AND ALL DAMAGES RESULTING FROM YOUR FAILURE TO OBEY.

Date issued:

_____　　▶　_____
(TYPE OR PRINT NAME)　　　　　　　　　　(SIGNATURE OF PERSON ISSUING SUBPOENA)

　　　　　　　　　　　　　　　　　　　　_____
(Declaration in support of subpoena on reverse)　　(TITLE)

Form Adopted for Mandatory Use
Judicial Council of California
SUBP-002 [Rev. January 1, 2007]

CIVIL SUBPOENA (DUCES TECUM) FOR PERSONAL APPEARANCE AND PRODUCTION OF DOCUMENTS AND THINGS AT TRIAL OR HEARING AND DECLARATION

Page 1 of 3

Code of Civil Procedure,
§ 1985 et seq.

PLAINTIFF/PETITIONER:	CASE NUMBER:
DEFENDANT/RESPONDENT:	

The production of the documents or the other things sought by the subpoena on page one is supported by *(check one)*:
☐ the attached affidavit or declaration   ☐ the following declaration:

**DECLARATION IN SUPPORT OF CIVIL SUBPOENA (DUCES TECUM) FOR PERSONAL
APPEARANCE AND PRODUCTION OF DOCUMENTS AND THINGS AT TRIAL OR HEARING**
(Code Civ. Proc., §§ 1985, 1987.5)

1. I, the undersigned, declare I am the   ☐ plaintiff   ☐ defendant   ☐ petitioner   ☐ respondent
   ☐ attorney for *(specify)*:   ☐ other *(specify)*:
   in the above-entitled action.

2. The witness has possession or control of the following documents or other things and shall produce them at the time and place
   specified in the *Civil Subpoena for Personal Appearance and Production of Documents and Things at Trial or Hearing* on page one
   of this form *(specify the exact documents or other things to be produced)*:

   ☐ Continued on Attachment 2.

3. Good cause exists for the production of the documents or other things described in paragraph 2 for the following reasons:

   ☐ Continued on Attachment 3.

4. These documents or other things described in paragraph 2 are material to the issues involved in this case for the following reasons:

   ☐ Continued on Attachment 4.

I declare under penalty of perjury under the laws of the State of California that the foregoing is true and correct.

Date:

....
(TYPE OR PRINT NAME)   ▶ _____
                                              (SIGNATURE OF   ☐ SUBPOENAING PARTY   ☐ ATTORNEY FOR
                                                                                        SUBPOENAING PARTY)

SUBP-002 [Rev. January 1, 2007]   **CIVIL SUBPOENA (DUCES TECUM) FOR PERSONAL APPEARANCE
AND PRODUCTION OF DOCUMENTS AND THINGS
AT TRIAL OR HEARING AND DECLARATION**

PLAINTIFF/PETITIONER:	CASE NUMBER:
DEFENDANT/RESPONDENT:	

PROOF OF SERVICE OF CIVIL SUBPOENA (DUCES TECUM)
FOR PERSONAL APPEARANCE AND PRODUCTION OF DOCUMENTS
AND THINGS AT TRIAL OR HEARING AND DECLARATION

1. I served this *Civil Subpoena (Duces Tecum) for Personal Appearance and Production of Documents and Things at Trial or Hearing and Declaration* by personally delivering a copy to the person served as follows:

   a. Person served *(name)*:

   b. Address where served:

   c. Date of delivery:

   d. Time of delivery:

   e. Witness fees *(check one)*:
      (1) ☐ were offered or demanded
         and paid. Amount: . . . . . . $ _____
      (2) ☐ were not demanded or paid.

   f. Fee for service: . . . . $ _____

2. I received this subpoena for service on *(date)*:

3. Person serving:
   a. ☐ Not a registered California process server.
   b. ☐ California sheriff or marshal.
   c. ☐ Registered California process server.
   d. ☐ Employee or independent contractor of a registered California process server.
   e. ☐ Exempt from registration under Business and Professions Code section 22350(b).
   f. ☐ Registered professional photocopier.
   g. ☐ Exempt from registration under Business and Professions Code section 22451.
   h. Name, address, telephone number, and, if applicable, county of registration and number:

I declare under penalty of perjury under the laws of the State of California that the foregoing is true and correct.

Date:

▶ _____
(SIGNATURE)

(For California sheriff or marshal use only)
I certify that the foregoing is true and correct.

Date:

▶ _____
(SIGNATURE)

**PROOF OF SERVICE OF CIVIL SUBPOENA (DUCES TECUM) FOR
PERSONAL APPEARANCE AND PRODUCTION OF DOCUMENTS
AND THINGS AT TRIAL OR HEARING AND DECLARATION**

ATTORNEY OR PARTY WITHOUT ATTORNEY *(Name, state bar number, and address)*:

TELEPHONE NO.:   FAX NO.:

ATTORNEY FOR *(Name)*:

NAME OF COURT:

STREET ADDRESS:

MAILING ADDRESS:

CITY AND ZIP CODE:

BRANCH NAME:

PEOPLE OF THE STATE OF CALIFORNIA
vs.

DEFENDANT/APPELLANT *(Name)*:

NOTICE OF APPEAL (infraction)

CASE NUMBER:

Defendant/Appellant *(Name)*:   in the above-entitled action hereby appeals to the

Appellate Division of the Superior Court in and for the County of *(name)*:

State of California, from the ☐ judgment and/or ☐ order entered in the above-named trial court on *(date)*:

Date:

. . . .
(TYPE OR PRINT NAME)

▶ _____
(SIGNATURE OF DEFENDANT/APPELLANT OR ATTORNEY)

Form Approved for Optional Use
Judicial Council of California
TR-155 [Rev. January 1, 2007]

NOTICE OF APPEAL
(Infraction)

Cal. Rules of Court rule 8.782
www.courtinfo.ca.gov

ATTORNEY OR PARTY WITHOUT ATTORNEY *(Name, state bar number and address)*:

TELEPHONE NO.:   FAX NO.:

ATTORNEY FOR *(Name)*:

NAME OF COURT:
STREET ADDRESS:
MAILING ADDRESS:
CITY AND ZIP CODE:
BRANCH NAME:

PEOPLE OF THE STATE OF CALIFORNIA
vs.

DEFENDANT/APPELLANT *(Name)*:

PROPOSED STATEMENT ON APPEAL (Infraction)	CASE NUMBER:

Defendant/Appellant *(name)*:   submits the following *Proposed Statement on Appeal*:

GROUNDS FOR APPEAL

1. *(Specify in detail your reasons for why you feel the judge committed "error" regarding the law or procedure. Note that credibility of witnesses is generally **not** a basis for appeal)*:

   a.

   b.

   c.

   d.

   e.

   f.

STATEMENT OF EVIDENCE

2. ☐ The above-entitled matter was reported by an official court reporter or electronically recorded and appellant intends to file a reporter's transcript of the evidence and proceedings so reported and to make the transcript appellant's statement on appeal.

3. ☐ Instead of a transcript the appellant is submitting the following statement on appeal:

   a. Officer *(name)*:   testified that *(set forth accurately and in detail the testimony of the officer; do not comment on or give your opinion regarding the officer's testimony)*:

Form Approved for Optional Use
Judicial Council of California
TR-160 [Rev. January 1, 2007]

PROPOSED STATEMENT ON APPEAL
(Infraction)

Cal. Rules of Court, rule 8.784
www.courtinfo.ca.gov

PEOPLE OF THE STATE OF CALIFORNIA	CASE NUMBER:
vs.	
DEFENDANT APPELLANT (Name):	

3. *(Continued)*

b. Defendant testified that *(set forth defendant's testimony accurately and in detail)*:

c. Witness *(name)*: _____ was called and testified that *(set forth witness's testimony accurately and in detail)*:

(Continued on page three)

TR-160 [Rev. January 1, 2007]

PROPOSED STATEMENT ON APPEAL
(Infraction)

PEOPLE OF THE STATE OF CALIFORNIA VS. DEFENDANT/APPELLANT *(Name)*:	CASE NUMBER:

3. c. *(Witness testimony continued)*

Please attach separate page(s) labeled "Attachment 3d," "Attachment 3e," etc. for each other witness.

FINDINGS OF THE COURT

4. The court determined I was guilty and assessed a fine of: $

5. Number of pages attached:

Date:

▶

. . . .
_____

(TYPE OR PRINT NAME)   (SIGNATURE OF DEFENDANT/APPELLANT OR ATTORNEY)

(Proof of service on reverse)

PROPOSED STATEMENT ON APPEAL
(Infraction)

PEOPLE OF THE STATE OF CALIFORNIA vs. DEFENDANT/APPELLANT *(Name)*:	CASE NUMBER:

DIRECTIONS:	**A copy of this document must be mailed to the district attorney/city attorney at the address listed below. YOU MAY NOT PERFORM THE MAILING YOURSELF. You must have a party who is at least 18 years old complete the information below and mail the front and back of each page of this document by first class mail, postage prepaid. When the fronts and backs of this document have been completed and mailed, the original may then be filed with the court.**

PROOF OF SERVICE BY MAIL

1. I am over the age of 18 and NOT a party to this action. I am a resident of or employed in the county where the mailing took place.

2. My residence or business address is *(specify)*:

3. I served a copy of the *Proposed Statement on Appeal* by enclosing it in an envelope AND
   a. ☐ **depositing** the sealed envelope with the United States Postal Service with the postage fully prepaid.
   b. ☐ **placing** the envelope for collection and mailing on the date and at the place shown in item 4 following our ordinary business practices. I am readily familiar with this business's practice for collecting and processing correspondence for mailing. On the same day that correspondence is placed for collection and mailing, it is deposited in the ordinary course of business with the United States Postal Service in a sealed envelope with postage fully prepaid.

4. The envelope was addressed and mailed as follows:
   a. *(Name of county)*: District Attorney/City Attorney
   b. Address:

   c. Date mailed:
   d. Place of mailing *(city and state)*:

5. I declare under penalty of perjury under the laws of the State of California that the foregoing is true and correct.

Date:

▶

. . . .	
(TYPE OR PRINT NAME)	(SIGNATURE OF DECLARANT)

PROPOSED STATEMENT ON APPEAL
(Infraction)

Index

Driver Safety offices, 309–310

license suspension hearings, 143, 309–312, 316–317

for Vehicle Code purchases, 11, 146

See also Driver's license suspension; Driver's licenses; Driving records; Point count system; Vehicle registration

Diamond (high-occupancy vehicle) lanes, 74

Direct examination techniques, 276

Dismissal of case

for failure of officer to appear, 4–5, 46–47, 139, 216, 223, 226, 270

for ignoring order, 191

for long delay before arraignment, 200–204

motions in Appellate Department, 338–341

motions to dismiss, 165, 167, 169, 212, 229, 268, 270

remittiturs, 348

See also Appeals *entries*

District or city attorneys, 184, 268–269

See also Prosecutors

Drag racing. *See* Exhibitions of speed and speed contests

Driver's License Compact, 28

Driver's licenses

DMV hold on renewals, 204, 302, 317–318

driving without, 363, 365–367

impounded, 104, 302

restricted, 308–309, 316

Driver's license suspension

accidents and, 315–317

administrative suspensions, 113

appealing, 306, 311

automatic suspension or revocation, 314–317

clearance certificates, 317–318

DMV hearings, 143, 309–311, 312, 316–317

for driving without insurance, 315–317

for drug possession or use, 79

for drunk driving, 27, 110, 116–117, 127–129, 311–314

excessive points and, 19

for failure to report accidents, 80

for ignoring tickets/failure to appear, 27, 102, 104, 168, 317–318

insurance rates and, 81

judge-imposed, 302–303

for misdemeanors, 97, 107

for people under 21, 129, 312, 314, 315

point count system and, 19, 107, 308–309, 310

postponing convictions to avoid, 167

for reckless driving, 98

for refusal to take blood/breath tests, 112, 312–314

for speed contests, 100

stay of sentence during appeals, 306

Driver's license violations

base fines, 26

consequences of ignoring, 14, 88

driving with expired/suspended license, 26, 363, 365–367

driving without insurance, 26, 315–317

forged licenses, 86, 89

noncorrectable, 89

Notice to Correct Violation, 14, 88

overview, 25–26, 86

procedures for correcting, 87

proof of correction, 14

Driving on wrong side of freeway, points for, 308

Driving records

bail forfeiture and, 155

Driver's License Compact, 28

driving with suspended license, 26

effect of appeal decisions on, 348

nolo contendere pleas and, 154

prior convictions shown on, 300–301

sealing, 97

ticket consequences and, 19–20

traffic school completion and, 155

who can look at, 19, 23

See also Point count system

Driving under the influence (DUI)

attempted DUI, 114–115

coordination test, 112

defense strategies, 110–113

description of offense, 111–113

DMV record of, 19

evaluating case, 130–132

federal government tickets, 92

legal representation, 27, 110, 113, 132–135, 143

overview, 27, 110–112

people under 21, 78, 113, 312, 314

plea bargaining, 132–133

pretrial court proceedings, 133–135

prior convictions, striking, 135

roadside advice, 359

See also Blood alcohol content; Blood tests for alcohol; Breath tests for alcohol; Urine tests for alcohol

NOLO

Keep Up to Date

 Go to **Nolo.com/newsletter** to sign up for free newsletters and discounts on Nolo products.

- **Nolo Briefs.** Our monthly email newsletter with great deals and free information.

- **Nolo's Special Offer.** A monthly newsletter with the biggest Nolo discounts around.

- **BizBriefs.** Tips and discounts on Nolo products for business owners and managers.

- **Landlord's Quarterly.** Deals and free tips just for landlords and property managers, too.

 And don't forget to check **Nolo.com/updates** to find free legal updates to this book.

Let Us Hear From You

 Comments on this book? We want to hear 'em. Email us at feedback@nolo.com.

FYT13

NOLO   *Online Legal Forms*

Nolo offers a large library of legal solutions and forms, created by Nolo's in-house legal staff. These reliable documents can be prepared in minutes.

Online Legal Solutions

- **Incorporation.** Incorporate your business in any state.
- **LLC Formations.** Gain asset protection and pass-through tax status in any state.
- **Wills.** Nolo has helped people make over 2 million wills. Is it time to make or revise yours?
- **Living Trust (avoid probate).** Plan now to save your family the cost, delays, and hassle of probate.
- **Trademark.** Protect the name of your business or product.
- **Provisional Patent.** Preserve your rights under patent law and claim "patent pending" status.

Online Legal Forms

Nolo.com has hundreds of top quality legal forms available for download—bills of sale, promissory notes, nondisclosure agreements, LLC operating agreements, corporate minutes, commercial lease and sublease, motor vehicle bill of sale, consignment agreements and many, many more.

Review Your Documents

Many lawyers in Nolo's consumer-friendly lawyer directory will review Nolo documents for a very reasonable fee. Check their detailed profiles at **lawyers.nolo.com.**

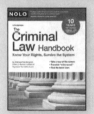

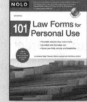